CORNERSTONE
BIBLICAL
COMMENTARY

1 Corinthians
William Baker

2 Corinthians
Ralph P. Martin
with Carl N. Toney

GENERAL EDITOR
Philip W. Comfort

featuring the text of the
NEW LIVING TRANSLATION

TYNDALE HOUSE PUBLISHERS, INC. CAROL STREAM, ILLINOIS

Cornerstone Biblical Commentary, Volume 15

Visit Tyndale's exciting Web site at www.tyndale.com

1 Corinthians copyright © 2009 by William Baker. All rights reserved.

2 Corinthians copyright © 2009 by Ralph P. Martin. All rights reserved.

Designed by Luke Daab and Timothy R. Botts.

Library of Congress Cataloging-in-Publication Data

Cornerstone biblical commentary.
    p. cm.
  Includes bibliographical references and index.
  ISBN-13: 978-0-8423-8343-1 (hc : alk. paper)
    1. Bible—Commentaries. I. William Baker. II. Ralph P. Martn.
BS491.3.C67 2006
220.7´7—dc22   2005026928

Printed in the United States of America

15 14 13 12 11 10 09
 7   6   5   4   3   2   1

CONTENTS

1 Corinthians: William Baker
BA, Lincoln Christian College;
MA, MDiv, Trinity Evangelical Divinity School;
PhD, University of Aberdeen;
Professor of New Testament at Cincinnati Bible Seminary.

2 Corinthians: Ralph P. Martin with Carl N. Toney
Ralph P. Martin
MA, University of Manchester;
PhD, King's College, University of London;
Distinguished Scholar in Residence at Fuller Theological Seminary;
Distinguished Scholar in Residence at the Graduate School of Theology of Azusa Pacific University;
Distinguished Scholar in Residence at Logos Evangelical Seminary.

Carl N. Toney
BA, Wheaton College;
MDiv, Fuller Theological Seminary;
PhD, Loyola University Chicago;
Adjunct Assistant Professor of New Testament at Fuller Theological Seminary.

GENERAL EDITOR'S PREFACE

The *Cornerstone Biblical Commentary* is based on the second edition of the New Living Translation (2007). Nearly 100 scholars from various church backgrounds and from several countries (United States, Canada, England, and Australia) participated in the creation of the NLT. Many of these same scholars are contributors to this commentary series. All the commentators, whether participants in the NLT or not, believe that the Bible is God's inspired word and have a desire to make God's word clear and accessible to his people.

This Bible commentary is the natural extension of our vision for the New Living Translation, which we believe is both exegetically accurate and idiomatically powerful. The NLT attempts to communicate God's inspired word in a lucid English translation of the original languages so that English readers can understand and appreciate the thought of the original writers. In the same way, the *Cornerstone Biblical Commentary* aims at helping teachers, pastors, students, and laypeople understand every thought contained in the Bible. As such, the commentary focuses first on the words of Scripture, then on the theological truths of Scripture—inasmuch as the words express the truths.

The commentary itself has been structured in such a way as to help readers get at the meaning of Scripture, passage by passage, through the entire Bible. Each Bible book is prefaced by a substantial book introduction that gives general historical background important for understanding. Then the reader is taken through the Bible text, passage by passage, starting with the New Living Translation text printed in full. This is followed by a section called "Notes," wherein the commentator helps the reader understand the Hebrew or Greek behind the English of the NLT, interacts with other scholars on important interpretive issues, and points the reader to significant textual and contextual matters. The "Notes" are followed by the "Commentary," wherein each scholar presents a lucid interpretation of the passage, giving special attention to context and major theological themes.

The commentators represent a wide spectrum of theological positions within the evangelical community. We believe this is good because it reflects the rich variety in Christ's church. All the commentators uphold the authority of God's word and believe it is essential to heed the old adage: "Wholly apply yourself to the Scriptures and apply them wholly to you." May this commentary help you know the truths of Scripture, and may this knowledge help you "grow in your knowledge of God and Jesus our Lord" (2 Pet 1:2, NLT).

PHILIP W. COMFORT
GENERAL EDITOR

ABBREVIATIONS

GENERAL ABBREVIATIONS

b.	Babylonian Gemara	Heb.	Hebrew	NT	New Testament
bar.	baraita	ibid.	*ibidem,* in the same place	OL	Old Latin
c.	*circa,* around, approximately	i.e.	*id est,* the same	OS	Old Syriac
		in loc.	*in loco,* in the place cited	OT	Old Testament
cf.	*confer,* compare			p., pp.	page, pages
ch, chs	chapter, chapters	lit.	literally	pl.	plural
contra	in contrast to	LXX	Septuagint	Q	Quelle ("Sayings" as Gospel source)
DSS	Dead Sea Scrolls	M	Majority Text		
ed.	edition, editor	*m.*	Mishnah	rev.	revision
e.g.	*exempli gratia,* for example	masc.	masculine	sg.	singular
		mg	margin	*t.*	Tosefta
et al.	*et alli,* and others	ms	manuscript	TR	Textus Receptus
fem.	feminine	mss	manuscripts	v., vv.	verse, verses
ff	following (verses, pages)	MT	Masoretic Text	vid.	*videtur,* it seems
		n.d.	no date	viz.	*videlicet,* namely
fl.	flourished	neut.	neuter	vol.	volume
Gr.	Greek	no.	number	*y.*	Jerusalem Gemara

ABBREVIATIONS FOR BIBLE TRANSLATIONS

ASV	American Standard Version	NCV	New Century Version	NKJV	New King James Version
CEV	Contemporary English Version	NEB	New English Bible	NRSV	New Revised Standard Version
		NET	The NET Bible		
ESV	English Standard Version	NIV	New International Version	NLT	New Living Translation
GW	God's Word	NIrV	New International Reader's Version	REB	Revised English Bible
HCSB	Holman Christian Standard Bible	NJB	New Jerusalem Bible	RSV	Revised Standard Version
JB	Jerusalem Bible				
KJV	King James Version	NJPS	The New Jewish Publication Society Translation (*Tanakh*)	TEV	Today's English Version
NAB	New American Bible			TLB	The Living Bible
NASB	New American Standard Bible				

ABBREVIATIONS FOR DICTIONARIES, LEXICONS, COLLECTIONS OF TEXTS, ORIGINAL LANGUAGE EDITIONS

ABD *Anchor Bible Dictionary* (6 vols., Freedman) [1992]

ANEP *The Ancient Near East in Pictures* (Pritchard) [1965]

ANET *Ancient Near Eastern Texts Relating to the Old Testament* (Pritchard) [1969]

BAGD *Greek-English Lexicon of the New Testament and Other Early Christian Literature,* 2nd ed. (Bauer, Arndt, Gingrich, Danker) [1979]

BDAG *Greek-English Lexicon of the New Testament and Other Early Christian Literature,* 3rd ed. (Bauer, Danker, Arndt, Gingrich) [2000]

BDB *A Hebrew and English Lexicon of the Old Testament* (Brown, Driver, Briggs) [1907]

BDF *A Greek Grammar of the New Testament and Other Early Christian Literature* (Blass, Debrunner, Funk) [1961]

BHS *Biblia Hebraica Stuttgartensia* (Elliger and Rudolph) [1983]

CAD *Assyrian Dictionary of the Oriental Institute of the University of Chicago* [1956]

COS *The Context of Scripture* (3 vols., Hallo and Younger) [1997–2002]

DBI *Dictionary of Biblical Imagery* (Ryken, Wilhoit, Longman) [1998]

DBT *Dictionary of Biblical Theology* (2nd ed., Leon-Dufour) [1972]

DCH *Dictionary of Classical Hebrew* (5 vols., D. Clines) [2000]

DLNTD *Dictionary of the Later New Testament and Its Development* (R. Martin, P. Davids) [1997]

DJD *Discoveries in the Judean Desert* [1955–]

DJG *Dictionary of Jesus and the Gospels* (Green, McKnight, Marshall) [1992]

DOTP *Dictionary of the Old Testament: Pentateuch* (T. Alexander, D.W. Baker) [2003]

DPL *Dictionary of Paul and His Letters* (Hawthorne, Martin, Reid) [1993]

DTIB *Dictionary of Theological Interpretation of the Bible* (Vanhoozer) [2005]

EDNT *Exegetical Dictionary of the New Testament* (3 vols., H. Balz, G. Schneider. ET) [1990–1993]

GKC *Gesenius' Hebrew Grammar* (Gesenius, Kautzsch, trans. Cowley) [1910]

HALOT *The Hebrew and Aramaic Lexicon of the Old Testament* (L. Koehler, W. Baumgartner, J. Stamm; trans. M. Richardson) [1994–1999]

IBD *Illustrated Bible Dictionary* (3 vols., Douglas, Wiseman) [1980]

IDB *The Interpreter's Dictionary of the Bible* (4 vols., Buttrick) [1962]

ISBE *International Standard Bible Encyclopedia* (4 vols., Bromiley) [1979–1988]

KBL *Lexicon in Veteris Testamenti libros* (Koehler, Baumgartner) [1958]

LCL Loeb Classical Library

L&N *Greek-English Lexicon of the New Testament: Based on Semantic Domains* (Louw and Nida) [1989]

LSJ *A Greek-English Lexicon* (9th ed., Liddell, Scott, Jones) [1996]

MM *The Vocabulary of the Greek New Testament* (Moulton and Milligan) [1930; 1997]

NA^{26} *Novum Testamentum Graece* (26th ed., Nestle-Aland) [1979]

NA^{27} *Novum Testamentum Graece* (27th ed., Nestle-Aland) [1993]

NBD *New Bible Dictionary* (2nd ed., Douglas, Hillyer) [1982]

NIDB *New International Dictionary of the Bible* (Douglas, Tenney) [1987]

NIDBA *New International Dictionary of Biblical Archaeology* (Blaiklock and Harrison) [1983]

NIDNTT *New International Dictionary of New Testament Theology* (4 vols., C. Brown) [1975–1985]

NIDOTTE *New International Dictionary of Old Testament Theology and Exegesis* (5 vols., W. A. VanGemeren) [1997]

PGM *Papyri graecae magicae: Die griechischen Zauberpapyri.* (Preisendanz) [1928]

PG *Patrologia Graecae* (J. P. Migne) [1857–1886]

TBD *Tyndale Bible Dictionary* (Elwell, Comfort) [2001]

TDNT *Theological Dictionary of the New Testament* (10 vols., Kittel, Friedrich; trans. Bromiley) [1964–1976]

TDOT *Theological Dictionary of the Old Testament* (8 vols., Botterweck, Ringgren; trans. Willis, Bromiley, Green) [1974–]

TLNT *Theological Lexicon of the New Testament* (3 vols., C. Spicq) [1994]

TLOT *Theological Lexicon of the Old Testament* (3 vols., E. Jenni) [1997]

TWOT *Theological Wordbook of the Old Testament* (2 vols., Harris, Archer) [1980]

UBS^3 *United Bible Societies' Greek New Testament* (3rd ed., Metzger et al.) [1975]

UBS^4 *United Bible Societies' Greek New Testament* (4th corrected ed., Metzger et al.) [1993]

WH *The New Testament in the Original Greek* (Westcott and Hort) [1882]

ABBREVIATIONS FOR BOOKS OF THE BIBLE

Old Testament

Gen	Genesis	Deut	Deuteronomy	1 Sam	1 Samuel
Exod	Exodus	Josh	Joshua	2 Sam	2 Samuel
Lev	Leviticus	Judg	Judges	1 Kgs	1 Kings
Num	Numbers	Ruth	Ruth	2 Kgs	2 Kings

1 Chr	1 Chronicles	Song	Song of Songs	Obad	Obadiah
2 Chr	2 Chronicles	Isa	Isaiah	Jonah	Jonah
Ezra	Ezra	Jer	Jeremiah	Mic	Micah
Neh	Nehemiah	Lam	Lamentations	Nah	Nahum
Esth	Esther	Ezek	Ezekiel	Hab	Habakkuk
Job	Job	Dan	Daniel	Zeph	Zephaniah
Ps, Pss	Psalm, Psalms	Hos	Hosea	Hag	Haggai
Prov	Proverbs	Joel	Joel	Zech	Zechariah
Eccl	Ecclesiastes	Amos	Amos	Mal	Malachi

New Testament

Matt	Matthew	Eph	Ephesians	Heb	Hebrews
Mark	Mark	Phil	Philippians	Jas	James
Luke	Luke	Col	Colossians	1 Pet	1 Peter
John	John	1 Thess	1 Thessalonians	2 Pet	2 Peter
Acts	Acts	2 Thess	2 Thessalonians	1 John	1 John
Rom	Romans	1 Tim	1 Timothy	2 John	2 John
1 Cor	1 Corinthians	2 Tim	2 Timothy	3 John	3 John
2 Cor	2 Corinthians	Titus	Titus	Jude	Jude
Gal	Galatians	Phlm	Philemon	Rev	Revelation

Deuterocanonical

Bar	Baruch	1–2 Esdr	1–2 Esdras	Ps 151	Psalm 151
Add Dan	Additions to Daniel	Add Esth	Additions to Esther	Sir	Sirach
Pr Azar	Prayer of Azariah	Ep Jer	Epistle of Jeremiah	Tob	Tobit
Bel	Bel and the Dragon	Jdt	Judith	Wis	Wisdom of Solomon
Sg Three	Song of the Three Children	1–2 Macc	1–2 Maccabees		
		3–4 Macc	3–4 Maccabees		
Sus	Susanna	Pr Man	Prayer of Manasseh		

MANUSCRIPTS AND LITERATURE FROM QUMRAN

Initial numerals followed by "Q" indicate particular caves at Qumran. For example, the notation 4Q267 indicates text 267 from cave 4 at Qumran. Further, 1QS 4:9-10 indicates column 4, lines 9-10 of the *Rule of the Community*; and 4Q166 1 ii 2 indicates fragment 1, column ii, line 2 of text 166 from cave 4. More examples of common abbreviations are listed below.

CD	Cairo Geniza copy of the *Damascus Document*	1QIsa[b]	Isaiah copy [b]	4QLam[a]	Lamentations
		1QM	*War Scroll*	11QPs[a]	Psalms
1QH	*Thanksgiving Hymns*	1QpHab	*Pesher Habakkuk*	11QTemple[a,b]	*Temple Scroll*
1QIsa[a]	Isaiah copy [a]	1QS	*Rule of the Community*	11QtgJob	*Targum of Job*

IMPORTANT NEW TESTAMENT MANUSCRIPTS

(all dates given are AD; ordinal numbers refer to centuries)

Significant Papyri (𝔓 = Papyrus)

𝔓1 Matt 1; early 3rd
𝔓4+𝔓64+𝔓67 Matt 3, 5, 26; Luke 1–6; late 2nd
𝔓5 John 1, 16, 20; early 3rd
𝔓13 Heb 2–5, 10–12; early 3rd
𝔓15+𝔓16 (probably part of same codex) 1 Cor 7–8, Phil 3–4; late 3rd
𝔓20 Jas 2–3; 3rd
𝔓22 John 15–16; mid 3rd
𝔓23 Jas 1; c. 200
𝔓27 Rom 8–9; 3rd
𝔓30 1 Thess 4–5; 2 Thess 1; early 3rd
𝔓32 Titus 1–2; late 2nd
𝔓37 Matt 26; late 3rd
𝔓39 John 8; first half of 3rd
𝔓40 Rom 1–4, 6, 9; 3rd

𝔓45 Gospels and Acts;
early 3rd
𝔓46 Paul's Major Epistles (less
Pastorals); late 2nd
𝔓47 Rev 9–17; 3rd
𝔓49+𝔓65 Eph 4–5; 1 Thess
1–2; 3rd
𝔓52 John 18; c. 125
𝔓53 Matt 26, Acts 9–10;
middle 3rd

𝔓66 John; late 2nd
𝔓70 Matt 2–3, 11–12, 24; 3rd
𝔓72 1–2 Peter, Jude; c. 300
𝔓74 Acts, General Epistles; 7th
𝔓75 Luke and John; c. 200
𝔓77+𝔓103 (probably part of
same codex) Matt 13–14,
23; late 2nd
𝔓87 Philemon; late 2nd

𝔓90 John 18–19; late 2nd
𝔓91 Acts 2–3; 3rd
𝔓92 Eph 1, 2 Thess 1; c. 300
𝔓98 Rev 1:13-20; late 2nd
𝔓100 Jas 3–5; c. 300
𝔓101 Matt 3–4; 3rd
𝔓104 Matt 21; 2nd
𝔓106 John 1; 3rd
𝔓115 Rev 2–3, 5–6, 8–15; 3rd

Significant Uncials

ℵ (Sinaiticus) most of NT; 4th
A (Alexandrinus) most of NT;
5th
B (Vaticanus) most of NT; 4th
C (Ephraemi Rescriptus) most
of NT with many lacunae;
5th
D (Bezae) Gospels, Acts; 5th
D (Claromontanus), Paul's
Epistles; 6th (different MS
than Bezae)
E (Laudianus 35) Acts; 6th
F (Augensis) Paul's
Epistles; 9th
G (Boernerianus) Paul's
Epistles; 9th

H (Coislinianus) Paul's
Epistles; 6th
I (Freerianus or Washington)
Paul's Epistles; 5th
L (Regius) Gospels; 8th
P (Porphyrianus) Acts—
Revelation; 9th
Q (Guelferbytanus B) Luke,
John; 5th
T (Borgianus) Luke, John; 5th
W (Washingtonianus or the
Freer Gospels) Gospels; 5th
Z (Dublinensis) Matthew; 6th
037 (Δ; Sangallensis) Gospels;
9th

038 (Θ; Koridethi) Gospels;
9th
040 (Ξ; Zacynthius) Luke; 6th
043 (Φ; Beratinus) Matthew,
Mark; 6th
044 (Ψ; Athous Laurae)
Gospels, Acts, Paul's
Epistles; 9th
048 Acts, Paul's Epistles,
General Epistles; 5th
0171 Matt 10, Luke 22;
c. 300
0189 Acts 5; c. 200

Significant Minuscules

1 Gospels, Acts, Paul's Epistles;
12th
33 All NT except Rev; 9th
81 Acts, Paul's Epistles,
General Epistles; 1044
565 Gospels; 9th
700 Gospels; 11th

1424 (or Family 1424—a
group of 29 manuscripts
sharing nearly the same
text) most of NT; 9th-10th
1739 Acts, Paul's Epistles; 10th
2053 Rev; 13th
2344 Rev; 11th

f¹ (a family of manuscripts
including 1, 118, 131, 209)
Gospels; 12th-14th
f¹³ (a family of manuscripts
including 13, 69, 124, 174,
230, 346, 543, 788, 826,
828, 983, 1689, 1709—
known as the Ferrar group)
Gospels; 11th-15th

Significant Ancient Versions

SYRIAC (SYR)	OLD LATIN (IT)	COPTIC (COP)
syr^c (Syriac Curetonian) Gospels; 5th	it^a (Vercellenis) Gospels; 4th	cop^{bo} (Boharic—north Egypt)
syr^s (Syriac Sinaiticus) Gospels; 4th	it^b (Veronensis) Gospels; 5th	cop^{fay} (Fayyumic—central Egypt)
syr^h (Syriac Harklensis) Entire NT; 616	it^d (Cantabrigiensis—the Latin text of Bezae) Gospels, Acts, 3 John; 5th	cop^{sa} (Sahidic—southern Egypt)
	it^e (Palantinus) Gospels; 5th	OTHER VERSIONS
	it^k (Bobiensis) Matthew, Mark; c. 400	arm (Armenian)
		eth (Ethiopic)
		geo (Georgian)

TRANSLITERATION AND NUMBERING SYSTEM

Note: For words and roots from nonbiblical languages (e.g., Arabic, Ugaritic), only approximate transliterations are given.

HEBREW/ARAMAIC

Consonants

א	aleph	= '	מ, ם	mem	= m	
בּ, ב	beth	= b	נ, ן	nun	= n	
גּ, ג	gimel	= g	ס	samekh	= s	
דּ, ד	daleth	= d	ע	ayin	= '	
ה	he	= h	פּ, פ, ף	pe	= p	
ו	waw	= w	צ, ץ	tsadhe	= ts	
ז	zayin	= z	ק	qoph	= q	
ח	heth	= kh	ר	resh	= r	
ט	teth	= t	שׁ	shin	= sh	
י	yodh	= y	שׂ	sin	= s	
כּ, כ, ך	kaph	= k	תּ, ת	taw	= t, th (spirant)	
ל	lamedh	= l				

Vowels

ַ	patakh	= a	ָ	qamets khatuf	= o	
ַה	furtive patakh	= a	ֹ	holem	= o	
ָ	qamets	= a	וֹ	full holem	= o	
ָה	final qamets he	= ah	ֻ	short qibbuts	= u	
ֶ	segol	= e	ֻ	long qibbuts	= u	
ֵ	tsere	= e	וּ	shureq	= u	
ֵי	tsere yod	= e	ֲ	khatef patakh	= a	
ִ	short hireq	= i	ֳ	khatef qamets	= o	
ִ	long hireq	= i	ְ	vocalic shewa	= e	
ִי	hireq yod	= i	ַי	patakh yodh	= a	

Greek

α	alpha	= a	ι	iota	= i	
β	beta	= b	κ	kappa	= k	
γ	gamma	= g, n (before γ, κ, ξ, χ)	λ	lamda	= l	
δ	delta	= d	μ	mu	= m	
ε	epsilon	= e	ν	nu	= n	
ζ	zeta	= z	ξ	ksi	= x	
η	eta	= ē	ο	omicron	= o	
θ	theta	= th	π	pi	= p	
			ρ	rho	= r (ῥ = rh)	

σ, ς	sigma	= s		ψ	psi	= ps
τ	tau	= t		ω	omega	= ō
υ	upsilon	= u		'	rough	= h (with
φ	phi	= ph			breathing	vowel or
χ	chi	= ch			mark	diphthong)

THE TYNDALE-STRONG'S NUMBERING SYSTEM

The Cornerstone Biblical Commentary series uses a word-study numbering system to give both newer and more advanced Bible students alike quicker, more convenient access to helpful original-language tools (e.g., concordances, lexicons, and theological dictionaries). Those who are unfamiliar with the ancient Hebrew, Aramaic, and Greek alphabets can quickly find information on a given word by looking up the appropriate index number. Advanced students will find the system helpful because it allows them to quickly find the lexical form of obscure conjugations and inflections.

There are two main numbering systems used for biblical words today. The one familiar to most people is the Strong's numbering system (made popular by the *Strong's Exhaustive Concordance to the Bible*). Although the original Strong's system is still quite useful, the most up-to-date research has shed new light on the biblical languages and allows for more precision than is found in the original Strong's system. The Cornerstone Biblical Commentary series, therefore, features a newly revised version of the Strong's system, the Tyndale-Strong's numbering system. The Tyndale-Strong's system brings together the familiarity of the Strong's system and the best of modern scholarship. In most cases, the original Strong's numbers are preserved. In places where new research dictates, new or related numbers have been added.[1]

The second major numbering system today is the Goodrick-Kohlenberger system used in a number of study tools published by Zondervan. In order to give students broad access to a number of helpful tools, the Commentary provides index numbers for the Zondervan system as well.

The different index systems are designated as follows:

TG	Tyndale-Strong's Greek number	ZH	Zondervan Hebrew number
ZG	Zondervan Greek number	TA/ZA	Tyndale/Zondervan Aramaic number
TH	Tyndale-Strong's Hebrew number	S	Strong's Aramaic number

So in the example, "love" *agapē* [^{TG}26, ^{ZG}27], the first number is the one to use with Greek tools keyed to the Tyndale-Strong's system, and the second applies to tools that use the Zondervan system.

The indexing of Aramaic terms differs slightly from that of Greek and Hebrew. Strong's original system mixed the Aramaic terms in with the Hebrew, but the Tyndale-Strong's system indexes Aramaic with a new set of numbers starting at 10,000. Since Tyndale's system for Aramaic diverges completely from original Strong's, the original Strong's number is listed separately so that those using tools keyed to Strong's can locate the information. This number is designated with an S, as in the example, "son" *bar* [$^{TA/ZA}$10120, ^{S}1247].

1. Generally, one may simply use the original four-digit Strong's number to identify words in tools using Strong's system. If a Tyndale-Strong's number is followed by a capital letter (e.g., TG1692A), it generally indicates an added subdivision of meaning for the given term. Whenever a Tyndale-Strong's number has a number following a decimal point (e.g., TG2013.1), it reflects an instance where new research has yielded a separate, new classification of use for a biblical word. Forthcoming tools from Tyndale House Publishers will include these entries, which were not part of the original Strong's system.

1 Corinthians

WILLIAM BAKER

INTRODUCTION TO
1 Corinthians

THE CORINTH OF PAUL'S DAY was a vibrant collection of socially and racially diverse people drawn to the city by the prospect of creating better lives for themselves and their families. Unique in its day, the continual influx of ambitious immigrants energized the Corinthian marketplace with an unparalleled, self-sustaining vitality that continued to lure others. Corinth was a perpetual boomtown, growing from 3,000 colonists to 100,000 inhabitants in less than 100 years. Picture New York or Chicago in the early nineteenth century or Los Angeles in the twentieth century, maybe Phoenix today. Those who live in urban America would have felt very much at home in Corinth—a potpourri of faces, foods, dress, goods, entertainment, get-rich-quick schemes, gods, ideas. It even had an open-air shopping mall.

At the time Paul wrote, the Corinthian church was no more than five years old and still only a collection of new believers meeting in a few scattered homes. We should think of it as similar to a modern church plant begun with only new, adult believers with no previous experience of Christianity, drawn from a cross section of this very diverse, driven population. With this in mind, we can begin to relate to the kinds of issues Paul addressed when he wrote to these people in 1 Corinthians. Their social and economic diversity created many problems when they met and did things together. Their individual ambition created rivalries about who was right and who was the best. They were not clear on what the key Christian principles are, and they certainly were not clear on how to implement these in their culture. They wondered who best represented Christian thought and practice—despite the fact that Paul first brought the gospel to them—and were confused about the role the Holy Spirit was supposed to play in their community.

The Corinthian community was young, confused, adrift in the sea of its own culture, embattled by its own immature members, with much to learn from its spiritual father. It is like us in many, many ways, so much so that the messages of Paul to these Christians—enclosed in 1 Corinthians—speak to us, too. These messages for the most part are not theological; this is not Romans or Galatians. They are eminently pragmatic, befitting its readers and us. Yet in solving these practical problems, Paul reveals crucial, universal Christian principles that equip us to deal with our own pragmatic situations born out of cultural diversity, personal ambition, and immature confusion. This is a good letter for us to read and understand.

AUTHOR
The opening words of 1:1 name Paul as author of 1 Corinthians, and his authorship has never been seriously questioned. In the annals of critical inquiry, 1 Corinthians

joins Romans, 2 Corinthians, Galatians, Philippians, and 1–2 Thessalonians as one of the major epistles that form the core of Paul's writings, and by which the vocabulary, style, and theology of the rest are measured with regard to authenticity. First Corinthians joins Galatians, Colossians, 2 Thessalonians, and Philemon in having a note of authentication near or at the end of the composition (16:21; Gal 6:11; Col 4:18; 2 Thess 3:17; Phlm 1:19). The statement "HERE IS MY GREETING IN MY OWN HANDWRITING—PAUL" indicates that it is like a signature. All the references except Galatians include his name, "Paul." Although many Hellenistic letters did not end with such a "signature," since the author's name is always stated at the outset (as it is in 1 Corinthians; Collins 1999:2), other writers in Hellenistic times chose to sign off with their own personal signature (a good example is P. Fayum 110; for a photograph, see Comfort 2005:145; see also P. London II, 308, P. Oxyrhynchus 246, 286, and 3057, the last of which is perhaps the earliest Christian letter). Although it is not displayed in all his writings, Paul appears to have had some concern about inauthentic letters circulating to churches under his apostolic care.

This "signature" is evidence that Paul did not pen 1 Corinthians personally but used an amanuensis. The use of a writing secretary like this was normal in the first century, and we can assume that Paul had help in this way for all his letters, even when the individual is not named. Paul does name Tertius as his amanuensis for Romans (Rom 16:22), as 1 Peter names Silvanus (or Silas) to be its amanuensis (1 Pet 5:12). But these are the only two mentioned by name in the New Testament. Thus, the fact that the amanuensis for 1 Corinthians is not named is not unusual.

The role of a first-century amanuensis could vary from simply taking dictation to composing the letter on behalf of the author. Given the consistency of style and vocabulary in Paul's letters, few doubt that Paul took a personal, active role in providing oral dictation to his writing secretaries. Letters were normally composed on papyrus sheets (about 8 inches by 10 inches) or scrolls (20 sheets pasted together). It is possible that one full scroll dictates the optimum length of the longest of Paul's letters, like 1 Corinthians, 2 Corinthians, and Romans. However, some suggest that Paul used the codex form (i.e., leaves bound together as a book), which would not limit the length of the writing.

Paul's letters were probably not edited after composition, either by him or by the amanuensis. If Paul did any amending, it was through the course of dictation. The prime example of this is in 1:14-16, where Paul begins in 1:14 by stating uncategorically that he personally baptized none in Corinth except the households of Crispus and Gaius. Yet he meekly admits in 1:16 that he also baptized Stephanas's household (as if someone, perhaps the amanuensis or Stephanas himself just reminded him), then finally acknowledges that he may have baptized others whom he no longer remembers. Given the confusion that undermines Paul's point, and the fact that he was only a few sentences into the letter, why not just crumple this one up and start over again as we might do? As far as we know, he just didn't. Perhaps it was due to the use of permanent ink and the cost of scrolls. It might just be the convention of the times. Regardless, we have to keep this in mind as we try to understand Paul in his letters. Sometimes he overstated his case and then amended his point on the fly in the comments that follow.

Paul intended his letters to be read aloud to the entire Christian community gathered together, or at least to the meetings of the various small groups that met in individual homes (Col 4:7; Horsley 1998:21). Thus, Paul wrote as if he were speaking to them. Indeed, he was speaking aloud on his end of the communicative process, just as the recipients would hear his words read aloud (and probably explained) by Paul's delegate at their end of the process. We could think of a letter from Paul as a sort of singing telegram. The letter is the medium to bring him into their presence when he cannot be there himself. Paul's letter carriers and readers are not always named, but Romans names Phoebe (Rom 16:1-2), and Ephesians and Colossians name Tychicus (Eph 6:21; Col 4:7). First Corinthians implies that Stephanas, Fortunatus, and Achaicus, who brought him a letter from the Corinthians (7:1), would return to Corinth with his letter (16:17). Stephanas, named as the head of the first household to become Christians in Corinth (16:15), baptized by Paul (1:16), and listed first among the three messengers, most likely functioned as the reader of the letter (Collins 1999:4).

DATE AND OCCASION OF WRITING

Paul wrote 1 Corinthians from Ephesus during AD 54 or 55, no more than five years after first entering Corinth alone. This entrance happened shortly after Paul fled for his life from Thessalonica and Berea and made his famous speech to the Areopagus in Athens. He remained in Corinth for 18 months (spring AD 50 to fall AD 51), by far his longest period of residence during his second evangelistic journey among the Gentiles. After this visit, he returned to Antioch of Syria, his home base. He quickly reorganized and set out on a third trip, which took him through his previously established churches in Asia Minor before arriving in Ephesus, on the western coast, where he remained for three years.

During his three-year period with the Ephesian church, approximately 250 miles straight across the Aegean Sea from Corinth, Paul carried on a very active pastoral relationship with the Corinthians via letters, messengers, and a personal trip. Eventually, he would leave Ephesus and make the 600-mile overland trip to Corinth, where he would remain for three months before heading back up the coast to Troas to sail to Jerusalem with the money collection he had gathered from the Greek and Asian churches.

First Corinthians is actually the second of four letters we know Paul wrote to the believers at Corinth. The first letter, normally designated the "previous letter," is referred to in 5:9-10 and contained a warning against associating with fellow believers whose lifestyles remain immoral and worldly. This previous letter may have been prompted by information Paul received from Apollos, who went to Corinth (Acts 18:27–19:1) but had by then probably returned to Ephesus (Murphy-O'Connor 1996:103-108; Thiselton 2000:31). Certainly, Apollos was back in Ephesus with Paul at the time he wrote 1 Corinthians (16:12).

Paul's third correspondence to the Corinthians occurred before he wrote the letter we know as 2 Corinthians. The backdrop of both this third letter and 2 Corinthians (described in 2 Cor 2:4-11 and 7:5-13) was an impromptu personal visit Paul made to Corinth by ship. What he thought would be a happy reunion was instead a disaster. Some individual, who seemed to represent the views of a lot of people, publicly insulted Paul, questioning his personal integrity, his apostolic authority, and the legitimacy of the collection of the funds in which he was urging the Corinthian believers to participate. Stunned and hurt by this incident, particularly because no one in the Corinthian church came to his defense, Paul skulked out of Corinth without a response. After arriving back at Ephesus, he sent a stinging letter of rebuke to all concerned, delivered personally to them by Titus. The backbone of 2 Corinthians narrates Paul's intense, personal worry about how this "severe letter" was received. Traveling up the Asia Minor coast to the prearranged rendezvous point in Troas, Paul expected to meet up with Titus to hear his report. Titus never showed up. So Paul went on into Macedonia, finding him there, probably in Philippi. Awash with relief from Titus's report that all was well, Paul sent 2 Corinthians, his fourth letter and a fifth contact with the Corinthian believers in the three and a half years since leaving them.

Acts 18 describes the key events of Paul's initial 18-month ministry in Corinth. Right away he met Aquila and Priscilla (probably in the marketplace), fellow tentmakers and also seasoned believers who had been expelled from Rome along with other Jews. These two became Paul's most trusted colleagues. They participated in evangelizing Corinth and then accompanied Paul to Syrian Antioch and on the third missionary journey through Ephesus. Eventually they made their way back to Rome before Paul wrote Romans. Paul preached in the Jewish synagogue every Sabbath and in the marketplace as he plied his trade (Hjort 1979:443). After Timothy and Silas arrived from Macedonia (Thessalonica and Philippi), he even more actively pursued Jewish Corinthians with the gospel. Eventually, the number of believers grew so significantly that they were expelled from the synagogue only to set up a rival "Christian" synagogue next door to the Jewish synagogue. From there, sparks flew to the point that those from the Jewish synagogue made an official protest to the Roman governor. Gallio, most likely only recently appointed, saw no just cause for convicting Christians as breakers of any Roman law; he dismissed the charge.

Historically, the overlap of Gallio and Paul in Corinth marks one of the most important intersections of New Testament and secular dating, providing a foothold for dating the rest of Paul's movements before and after his period in Corinth. Fragments of a stone inscription were discovered in the 1930s at Delphi, not far from Corinth. This inscription mentions the Roman Emperor Claudius, the proconsul of Achaia (the region surrounding Corinth), Gallio, date information, and words clarifying a boundary dispute (Murphy-O'Connor 2002:161-165). Since proconsuls were appointed for one-year terms (July–June), it allows us to date Gallio's term as most likely AD 51–52 (Conzelmann 1975:13; Horsley 1998:29; Murphy-O'Connor 2002:165; Thiselton 2000:29). The beginning of Gallio's term overlapped, then, with the end of Paul's time in Corinth.

Paul wrote 1 Corinthians midway between the period of Jewish hostility to the planting of the church and the period of internal hostility among some in the church toward Paul. The careful order that characterizes 1 Corinthians should not convey the false notion that Paul was writing to these believers during a tranquil lull in their brief history. These believers were still coping with division and hostility from their fellow Jews (which Acts 20:3 indicates never subsided) and were nurturing the seeds of division from one another and from Paul that would sprout during the painful visit only months ahead. We should not interpret 1 Corinthians in isolation from these well-established realities when we try to understand the events that gave rise to its composition.

At least two particular events prompted Paul to write 1 Corinthians. The first was the arrival in Ephesus of an official delegation (consisting of Stephanas, Fortunatus, and Achaicus) from Corinth with a letter asking Paul to answer specific questions. The second event was an unofficial visit from "Chloe's people," probably employees or slaves of hers who came to Ephesus principally for business purposes and who also shared some of Chloe's concerns about the situation in Corinth with Paul. A third possible event was the return of Apollos from his period of ministry with the Corinthian believers. Apollos shared his perspective with Paul on how the Corinthian believers were doing, which was probably not well, because Apollos expressed his reluctance to return to Corinth (16:12).

Paul began by responding to the information reported to him by Chloe's workers; he addressed the critical need for unity among those who serve Christ (1:10–4:17). He responded to the questions from the official letter beginning in 7:1, addressing in turn questions about marriage and celibacy (ch 7), eating and serving meat sacrificed to idols (chs 8–10), use of gifts from the Spirit (chs 12–14), and probably details about the relief collection for Jerusalem believers (16:1-4). Each of these four topics begins with the same expression ("Now regarding"). A few remaining topics are probably matters the three-person delegation bearing the letter reported to Paul: (1) the church failing to take disciplinary action against a man who was living in a sexual relationship with his stepmother (ch 5), (2) believers instigating lawsuits against one another (ch 6), and (3) how the Corinthian believers were conducting worship in their meetings (11:2-33). Perhaps Paul's compulsion to address the topic of the resurrection of Jesus in chapter 15 responds to the informed opinion of Apollos, but he could have had his own reasons for this extended apologetic.

Those who study 1 Corinthians contemplate whether a unified opposition group might have lurked behind Paul's variegated concerns as is the case in many of his letters (e.g., Galatians, Colossians). The first direction they look is toward 2 Corinthians, which identifies a group in Corinth who opposed Paul (2 Cor 1:5-11; 3:1-3; 11:1–12:12) and was probably influenced by outsiders whom Paul labels "false apostles" and, sarcastically, "super apostles" (2 Cor 11:13; 12:11). Some speculators consider whether this could be an ultraconservative band of Jewish Christians who did not accept the apostolic council's ruling recorded in Acts 15 (that Gentiles need not be circumcised to become Christians), who had now followed Paul from Jerusalem and Galatia (Baker 1999:27-31; Barrett 1971; Marshall 1987:260-265; R. Martin 1987). If so, a connection is often made to the Peter party of 1:12 as Paul's identification of this opposition group in 1 Corinthians (Baur 1831; Goulder 2001:22). Other speculators, not seeing any mention of circumcision or law in 2 Corinthians, think emphasis on their charismatic experiences and special knowledge (2 Cor 11:4; 12:12) makes these opponents representative of an early form of Gnosticism and thereby connect them to Paul's detailed argument against human wisdom and knowledge in chapters 1–4 (Conzelmann 1975:15; Schmithals 1971). The difficulty with either of these two speculations is that Paul did not identify an opposition group in 1 Corinthians; rather, he focused the entire epistle on all the Corinthian believers (Fee 1987:5-6). The most that can be said is that the nucleus of the opposition to Paul, identifiable by 2 Corinthians, was probably in an early stage at the time of his writing 1 Corinthians (Marshall 1987:264-265); it had not reached the point where Paul considered it a group he must attack (whether that group is identified as Gnostics or Judaizers).

Speculators also look for evidence of an opposition group behind 1 Corinthians in the letter itself, apart from 2 Corinthians. Those who do this find that despite the lack of evidence for Paul opposing a specifically identifiable group, Paul's hard-line posturing in places indicates that he felt under attack by at least some in Corinth (Fee 1987:6-10; Furnish 1999:10-12; Garland 2003:20; M. Mitchell 1997:48). A growing suggestion is that this group consisted of people who became so enamored with Apollos's intellect and oratory skills while he was there (out of no self-promotion of his own) that they began to question Paul's authority and leadership over them (Horsley 1998:34-35; Ker 2000:76-77; Smit 2002:234; Wenham 1997:138). This may be why Apollos was so reluctant to go back to Corinth (16:12).

The third direction speculators take is to abandon any hope of discovering a completely formulated opposition group at all. They simply take the evidence from 1 Corinthians that various factions had splintered the Corinthian church, perhaps into rival house groups. Thus, the vision of 1 Corinthians was to bring them into unity around the cross (Conzelmann 1975:16; M. Mitchell 1993:198-199; Thiselton 2000:34-35). Further, it is recognized that the Corinthians were not only splintered between themselves, and some with Paul, but that the root cause of these divisions was within the materialistic, high-achievement culture of Corinth from which they really did need to separate themselves (Garland 2003:5-6; M. Mitchell 1993:6-7; Soards 1999:6-7; Witherington 1995:46-47). It is pointed out that unlike the Thessalonians, for instance, who suffered persecution for their faith and thus were forced to separate themselves from their culture, neither Corinthian letter mentions a single word about persecution. Could this be because the Corinthians generally had not distinguished themselves and Christian teaching from that of their neighbors and culture?

A fourth position is that it is not possible to identify either a single opposition group or a unified theological purpose behind 1 Corinthians and that to do so only prejudices forthright exegesis of the epistle itself (Collins 1999:17; Garland 2003:7, 13).

Perhaps a position combining various aspects of these arguments is warranted. First, what became a full-scale, open opposition to Paul in 2 Corinthians probably did begin previous to the writing of 1 Corinthians, since it was written only a matter of months before Paul's disastrous surprise visit to the Corinthians that precipitated the severe letter and 2 Corinthians. Paul probably went there because he knew trouble was brewing. Second, questioning of Paul's authority does seem evident in 1 Corinthians, particularly in the sections in which Paul responds harshly to information he received orally from Chloe's people and the three-person delegation—in contrast to the sections where he answers their questions (Thiselton

2000:35). Third, the Corinthians' failure to recognize how Christian theology and values discredited their socially inherited behaviors of individualism and success fueled their rivalries as well as their lack of respect for Paul.

AUDIENCE

Paul addressed this letter to a small band of novice believers who met together in the homes of their wealthier colleagues, no more than 30 per home (Murphy-O'Connor 2002:178-284; 1984:157), perhaps in 8 to 10 homes. Despite the fact that the earliest converts were Jewish (according to Acts 18:4-8), none of the issues Paul addresses in the letter appear to stem from Jewish-Christian controversies. Rather, all the issues derive from the Corinthian culture and society in which they lived. This makes it paramount that we strive to understand this critical spot on the ancient map if we are to understand this letter and the people to whom it is addressed. Fortunately, we know a great deal about this city, both from ancient historians and modern archaeological excavation.

The Corinth of Paul's day had prospered enormously since being rebuilt as a Roman city in 44 BC. For a hundred years it had lain in ruins after the Roman army, incensed by its opposition to Rome, conquered it and burned it to the ground, killing the men and carting off the women and children into slavery. It was once again a very proud city by Paul's day, but the vast majority of its inhabitants were no longer native to the area. Rebuilt in the style of a Roman city, complete with public courtyards, an outdoor stadium (seating 20,000 people), a smaller theater, Roman baths, and Roman architecture throughout, it was forcibly repopulated by about 3,000 freedmen (former slaves who had originally been brought to Italy from all the lands Rome had conquered) and retired Roman soldiers. But by Paul's day its population had swelled to 100,000, far outstripping Athens, due to the fact that people were flocking to it voluntarily from all over because of the prosperity that could be gained from working there. It was a truly cosmopolitan ancient city with parallels to a modern, market-based economy (Engels 1990:19; O'Mahony 1997:117-118; Thiselton 2000:4).

Corinth flourished partly because of its unique location and its residents' ingenuity and industriousness in exploiting this advantage. It straddled the five-mile-wide isthmus (land bridge) that served as the major thoroughfare between the Greek mainland and the Peloponnese. Ancient sailing vessels often foundered because of high winds as they attempted to negotiate the extra 200 miles around Cape Malea at the tip of the Peloponnese (especially in the winter). Sailors were thus willing to pay a fee to cross at the isthmus controlled by Corinth. Back in the days of Old Corinth, in the sixth century BC, residents had constructed a grooved pavement, called the Diolkos, between the ports on either side of the isthmus. Wheeled carts actually transported smaller vessels intact, while for larger ships, goods were unloaded from a ship from one harbor and reloaded onto a waiting ship in the other harbor. By Paul's day, many industries had been built up alongside this lucrative situation: shipbuilding and repair; bronze, tile, and pottery factories; and warehousing transportable goods. Its own marketplace became a bazaar of goods and trinkets and skilled services from all over the empire. Typical of a seaport, it was known for its immorality.

Larger than Athens (located 46 miles east on the Greek mainland side of the isthmus), Corinth had become the capital of Achaia, hosting the biannual Isthmian Games. Similar to the Olympics in Athens, these games featured not only sports competitions but also oratory, music, and drama performances and included female contestants. The government, modeled after the early republican organization of Rome, consisted of a city council elected by the voting citizens, plus two city magistrates elected annually by the council. The council worked to enhance public space, roads, buildings, and facilities; the magistrates presided over civil suits. Most significant is that freedmen could be elected to the council and therefore also as magistrates (Hays 1997:3; Horsley 1998:25). Highlighting the distinctive Roman culture of Corinth, in contrast to the surrounding Greek regions, its language of choice was Latin (not Greek), its coinage was Roman (Thiselton 2000:6), its most revered temple honored the Roman mother goddess, Venus, not the Greek goddess Aphrodite (who had the most prestigious temple in Old Corinth), and its public buildings were filled with public inscriptions honoring various Roman emperors (Engels 1990:101-102). Like early Americans who looked to England and France for the finer things of life, Corinthians craved all things Roman.

Because the refounded city of Corinth started from scratch, it had no landed gentry or aristocracy. People from all over scrambled to the top rung of society primarily by earning a great deal of wealth, which was very possible to do in this wide-open commercial era. Corinthian architecture reveals an intense, competitive desire among wealthy freedmen and their descendants to receive public acclaim and recognition for providing the funds for public buildings and monuments. These structures often include a commemorative dedication to the benefactor (Garland 2003:4-5; Thiselton 2000:8-9). One such monument, built by a freedman, was inscribed *twice* for good measure (Murphy-O'Connor 1996:270; Thiselton 2000:8).

The Corinthian believers probably represented a cross-section of this society. Paul, referring to the time of their conversion in 1:26, says, "Not many were influential; not many were of noble birth" (NIV). Being sons and daughters of freedmen, the latter is certainly true, but Paul's statement does imply that at least some of the Corinthian believers were prominent in Corinth. We know of one such person, Erastus, whose name not only appears as a city council member and a benefactor on one of the city monuments (dedicating a portion of the paved road) but also appears in Romans 16:23 as Corinth's "director of public works" (NIV), who sends his greetings to people in Rome. Most agree that the rarity of this name and compatibility of time and place make it highly likely that both references are to the same person (Collins 1999:23; Murphy-O'Connor 1996:268-270; Thiselton 2000:9; Winter 1994:180-197). Wealthier believers like Erastus would likely be the ones hosting other believers of lower economic status weekly in their homes for worship and the Lord's Supper, which created some of the problems Paul addresses in 11:17-34. On the other end of the spectrum, 7:21-22 indicates that some of the Corinthian believers currently were slaves.

For the competitive, self-driven entrepreneur, regardless of social or economic status, Corinth was the place to be in the Roman Empire of the mid-first century— but it was not for everyone. The ancient proverb "Not for every man is the voyage to Corinth," rang true in Paul's day. But this is why he went there! He believed that if the gospel was to be successful in the "modern" era of his time, it would catch hold among these people, who were open to anything new. His success in Corinth stands in stark contrast to his tepid reception up the road in conservative, old-school Athens (Acts 17:16-34). However, along with this success in establishing house churches in Corinth came the problems associated with the kind of people who were drawn to the robust, challenging life of Corinth: immensely confident in themselves, craving honor for their achievements, and just as open to other philosophical or religious notions as they were to Christianity. We must keep this picture of these people in mind as we study 1 Corinthians.

CANONICITY AND TEXTUAL HISTORY

Authoritative quotations from 1 Corinthians appear in *1 Clement,* a document from the AD 90s, and in Ignatius's *Epistle to the Ephesians, Epistle to the Romans,* and *Epistle to the Philippians,* documents from about AD 110. It appears on Marcion's Pauline canonical list around AD 140, which declares its author to be "the apostle." It also appears in the Muratorian canonical list, dated about AD 170, listed first of the 13 Pauline epistles, and appears on every other canonical list, including the list from Athanasius in AD 367. It may have been among the collected letters of Paul referred to in 2 Peter 3:16. No dispute regarding its canonicity has ever occurred.

The earliest manuscript of 1 Corinthians is 𝔓46 from the Chester Beatty papyrus collection, dated about AD 175-200; it contains all but three verses of the entire letter. Major uncial witnesses in the Alexandrian group of texts include B (Vaticanus) and ℵ (Sinaiticus), as well as C. When the testimony of 𝔓46 supports the Alexandrian manuscripts, the witness is usually quite reliable. Another papyrus containing a small portion of 1 Corinthians is 𝔓15 (third century). Evidence from among Western texts includes manuscripts D, F, G, Old Latin, and the Western church fathers. Byzantine witnesses are plentiful and are normally considered authoritative when they agree with Alexandrian and Western readings (Conzelmann 1975:1; Robertson and Plummer 1911:lvi-lxvii).

Early speculation by Weiss (1910:xxxix-xliii; 1937:341) that distinguished three separate letters within 1 Corinthians, though fine-tuned by Schmithals (1973:263-288), has never gained wide acceptance (Barrett 1968:15; Conzelmann 1975:4; Kümmel 1975:278). Some scholars have proposed (1) that the previous letter mentioned in 5:9 is largely contained in 6:12-20, 10:1-23, and 11:2-34; (2) that Paul wrote 7:1–9:23, 10:24–11:1, 12–15, 16, in response to the questions in the letter brought by the Stephanas delegation; and (3) that 1:1–6:11 is a third letter responding to the information from Chloe's workers. But this characterization has no textual support. Whatever unevenness may be present in 1 Corinthians is better explained by more natural means.

De Boer's (1994:240) more recent suggestion that Paul had completed chapters 1-4 before the arrival of the Stephanas delegation with the letter from the Corinthians is possible but hardly a necessary conclusion. Mitchell, who most recently has put the epistle under the scrutiny of rhetorical criticism, believes the occasional abrupt turns in the letter provide no need to view 1 Corinthians as anything but one letter composed on one occasion (M. Mitchell 1993; cf. Thiselton 2000:39). Certainly the length of the letter requires more than one sitting to complete, whether or not new news arrived while it was being composed (Collins 1999:14).

Fee's novel speculation (1987:699-708) about 14:34-35 being a gloss mistakenly incorporated into the text by a scribe has convinced very few others (see Carson, Moo, and Morris 1992:283). (See note and commentary on these verses for further discussion.)

LITERARY STYLE AND STRUCTURE

Paul wrote 1 Corinthians in Koine Greek ranging from highly sophisticated to common style. He wrote in a style that is at times emotional but often didactic. He is not hot under the collar, as he appeared to be in Galatians, or emotionally wrung out as he will later seem to be in 2 Corinthians. This is reflected in the formally organized composition of the letter, even if Paul trailed off on the occasional digression, characteristic of all his writing.

Theological words often associated with Paul, like "law," "righteousness," and "faith," prevalent in Romans and Galatians, are rare in 1 Corinthians, reflecting that Paul's goals for 1 Corinthians were distinct from those epistles. He was not so much attempting to articulate the heart of his gospel. Instead, demonstrating that Paul is more concerned about living out the gospel in an inhospitable climate and with respect to specific issues, words like "spiritual," "subordinate," "faithless," "weak," "discern," "wise," "knowledge," "nullify," "prophecy," "marry," and "cup" dominate this epistle. Paul also used over 220 words in 1 Corinthians that he did not use in any of his other epistles. He quoted 30 times from the Old Testament, always from his knowledge of the Septuagint, the Greek translation created in the second century BC that functioned as the Old Testament resource for all New Testament writers (except Jude).

As in all of Paul's letters, 1 Corinthians demonstrates Paul's dependence on rhetorical techniques within his argumentation. The epistle is dotted with diatribe (asking and answering one's own questions, as in 7:21), flurries of rhetorical questions (4:7; 9:1), beginning sentences without conjunctions for effect (7:27), parallelism (1:25), antithesis (4:10), chiastic puzzles (5:2-6), catchwords (10:1-5), and more. Recalling the charred history of Old Corinth, burned down in 146 BC, Paul employs burning imagery in 3:9-17, and drawing upon the wild enthusiasm in Corinth for the Isthmian Games, Paul uses athletic imagery in 9:24-27.

In comparison with other ancient letters, 1 Corinthians has been classed as a letter of commendation because of the commendation of Stephanas in 16:15-18 (Kim 1972:119), as a letter of admonition (Collins 1999:10), and as a letter of exhortation and advice (Furnish 1999:15). The latter two fit well with the very common rhetorical designation of 1 Corinthians as predominantly employing the rhetoric of deliberation (Collins 1999:19; M. Mitchell 1993:20-64; Witherington 1995:46). In classic rhetoric, a deliberative framework was intended to persuade the audience to make decisions about their future, as opposed to judging past action (forensic) or celebrating the present (demonstrative).

Paul's argumentation in 1 Corinthians appeals to a variety of authoritative resources shared in common with his audience. The most dominant of these is Old Testament Scripture. Also common is appeal to known traditions about Jesus, whether these be sayings (7:10-11; 9:14; 11:23-25), statements about his life and death (11:23; 15:3), or confessional statements of his significance (6:11; 8:6; 16:22). Paul also appeals to his readers' own life experience (5:6; 10:15; 11:13). Finally, Paul appeals to their experience and recognition of his apostolic calling (3:5-9, 10-17; 4:1-7; 9:1-14; 15:9-11). Compared to most New Testament letters (especially 2 Corinthians), the foundational structure of 1 Corinthians is easily recognizable and agreed upon by nearly all who study it. Major sections are delineated by different information to which Paul responds: chapters 1–4 to information from Chloe's workers about division in the church; chapters 5 and 6 to information (perhaps from the Stephanas delegation) about undisciplined sexual sin and lawsuits in the community; chapters 7–16 (except for chs 11 and 15) to questions in the letter brought from the Stephanas delegation. The structure of chapters 7–14 is determined by Paul's use of the transitional phrase "now regarding" (*peri de* [TG4012/1161, ZG4309/1254]) that occurs at 7:1, 25; 8:1; 12:1; 16:1. This phrase does not occur at the introduction of Paul's advice about worship (11:2-34) nor at the beginning of the long chapter about the evidence for and significance of Jesus' resurrection (ch 15), yielding the common conclusion that these chapters do not respond to questions in the letter but from other oral sources.

MAJOR THEOLOGICAL THEMES

Those who study the New Testament often note that as important as it is to the development of theology for the church, the New Testament itself does not provide for us a systematic theology about anything, whether in reference to God or salvation. It provides the raw materials from which fully nuanced theology must be drawn. This can only be done by respecting the occasional nature of each biblical book. Each is first written within the context of a certain community existing at a certain time and a certain place, with certain issues that needed to be addressed, whether this was done by a prophet, a psalmist, or an apostle.

This perspective—so true of the discipline of theology as a whole—is showcased by 1 Corinthians. Point-by-point throughout the book, Paul deals with one issue, then another, applying his principled theological perspective to each. The theology rarely comes out directly. Rather, it is assumed within each separate discussion, surrounding each response without being voiced explicitly. In fact, some have described 1 Corinthians as one of the best New Testament examples of articulating "applied theology." In contrast, Romans is the best New Testament example of a developed theology, at least of salvation. Interestingly, though, certain places in 1 Corinthians appear to "apply" the theology articulated by Romans (cf. 1:18-31 with Rom 1:18-32; chs 8–10 with Rom 14:1–15:6; chs 12–13 with Rom 12:3-21; 15:22, 45-49 with Rom 5:12-19). Though Romans was written later than 1 Corinthians, it was written from Corinth only a couple of years later, during Paul's very last stay of three months.

Jesus Christ. Everything Paul teaches in 1 Corinthians is controlled by Christ's impact on him and on the Corinthians' community. Having initially brought the gospel to them, he not only was their apostle but also their spiritual father in Christ

(1:1; 4:15). Christ was the sole mediator of their newfound relationship with God (1:9; 3:23), which was accomplished on the cross (1:18). Despite how ridiculous this gruesome act of self-sacrifice may seem to most people, this is the focal point of God's wisdom, acceptance of which defines who is and who is not part of the saved Christian community (1:18-30). Being in Christ defines believers as fools from the standpoint of the world (4:10) but also establishes them as a corporate entity that is the body of Christ (12:27). This new identity is celebrated through participation in the Lord's Supper (10:16). It also impacts the way they are to relate to one another in a myriad of ways that involve loving each other in the tangible ways addressed throughout the letter. It also affects how they continue to interact with the pagan culture that surrounds them. Belief in the resurrection of Jesus Christ in particular sets them apart from their culture, which was skeptical about any substantive aspect of an afterlife (15:1-58). Their hope in Christ should cause them to anticipate his return (1:7) and to believe in their own bodily resurrection and eternal future in fellowship with God.

The Spirit of God. Paul's theology of the Spirit is a good example of how we must examine Paul's responses to specific concerns to discern his general theological views. His 23 references to the Spirit concentrate in just two sections of the letter, 2:4-14 (7 times) and 12:1-13 (11 times). Consistent with other New Testament writings, Paul did not consider the Spirit's activity or identity to be independent from that of God or Christ. Paul favored referring to the Spirit as "God's Spirit" (2:11, 12, 14; 3:16; 6:11; 7:40; 12:3) but also referred to the Spirit as the "Holy Spirit" (6:19; 12:3), once just after referring to him as the "Spirit of God." He associated the "power of the Holy Spirit" with the "power of God" (2:4-5), revelation of the Spirit as revelation from God (2:10, 11, 12, 13, 14), and the Spirit as received from God (6:19). He also associated the Spirit tightly with the lordship of Christ, particularly in enabling someone to believe and publicly confess this absolute truth (6:11, 17; 12:3). In three places Paul binds God, Christ, and the Spirit together in working on the same task: in the act of justification (6:17), utterance of confession to Jesus' lordship (12:3), and distribution of gifts of service, emphasizing the "same Spirit," "Lord," and "God" to be involved (12:4-6). The Spirit himself has the ultimate responsibility for empowering believers with spiritual gifts (12:11).

The movement of the Spirit in the lives of people progresses into the human population in an observable way. It begins with proclamation of the gospel by someone else in whom the Spirit is already living, and it continues on as others believe that gospel. Thus, Paul preached the word faithfully, and the Corinthians were enabled by the Spirit to receive it as true, making them also empowered by the Spirit to serve and ignite the Spirit in others who believe. Paul acknowledged that the Spirit was in him (7:40) and that both the content and the manner of his preaching were due to the influence of the Spirit in his life (2:4). The true message he preached about the crucified Lord and the significance of this for salvation came directly from God through the Spirit, who knows everything God knows (2:10-11; 13:2). Paul's ability to understand it well enough to explain it to others is particularly the activity of God's Spirit at work in him (2:12-13).

People whom the Spirit has enabled to accept the gospel as true are transformed by the Spirit from their old life to a new life, having been cleansed from the sins of their old life through baptism and made acceptable to God (2:14-15; 6:11; 12:13). People who have not been able to discern the truth of the gospel, despite the Spirit's work to help them, cannot be and are not transformed by the Spirit (2:14). The Spirit lives in those who have been transformed by the Spirit.

This indwelling of the Spirit has two consequences. First, the Spirit provides them with special abilities to enable them to serve the new social community—consisting of others who have also been transformed by the Spirit and in whom the Spirit lives—into which they have now been incorporated, regardless of their ethnic or civil status (12:7-13). The purpose of these special abilities is to help the church grow and develop (14:12). Second, the Spirit makes those in the new community the temple of God, both corporately (3:16) and individually (6:19). The fact that the Spirit lives in them as God's new community means that it is crucial that they display the most emphatic truth known about God, the truth first revealed to Abraham: that God is one. Thus the church is commissioned to display God's oneness in the unified manner in which believers conduct their Spirit-enabled activities (3:17). But the fact that the Spirit lives in every believer means that their very physical bodies are also temples of God (6:19), a thought at odds with most Greek thought, which viewed the soul as godlike but the corporeal body as evil.

This has major moral ramifications requiring individual believers to use their bodies only in ways that are acceptable to God and which reverence him (6:20). To go back to their old ways of sin before the Spirit began dwelling in them is totally unacceptable.

The Body. Though it was common for Greek philosophers to disparage the human body as the pristine spirit's corrupt prison, which one finally escapes at death, Paul's 46 statements pertaining to the "body" show that he did not concur. He certainly viewed people's bodies as the vehicle for much of their sinful behavior, thus requiring discipline (9:27; 13:3). However, he also believed that the bodies of believers are under new ownership and that this changes everything. God now owns their bodies, having willingly paid an exorbitant price for them, the dead body of his only Son, Jesus Christ (6:13, 20). Since the Spirit of God has taken up residence within the bodies of believers (6:19), they are obligated to honor God with their bodies (6:20). This means no sex outside of marriage (6:12-20), but it also requires tempering all lifestyle choices by this exacting standard of pleasing God with what they do. Within marriage, it means that their bodies belong to their spouses, who have rights of ownership, too (7:4). At the resurrection, the bodies of believers will be transformed into bodies appropriate for being with God for eternity (15:35-58).

Another aspect of the body the reader discovers in 1 Corinthians is the mystical body of Christ, the church. Paul viewed the church as an organism consisting of the members of the believing community. They are initiated into this living body through baptism into Christ (1:13-17), and they participate in this unity by sharing in the Lord's Supper, the body and blood of Christ, as a gathered community (10:17, 24). They are woven together as one body, each vital to the whole, through celebrating in worship and experiencing the work of the Spirit in each of their lives (chs 12–14).

The Church. The Corinthian believers were one local fellowship parallel to others that Paul had a part in establishing in municipalities across Greece and Asia (16:1, 9). Despite the fact that they met in various people's homes (11:22, 34; 16:19), they constituted one entity. Paul consistently addressed them as such. In fact, he worked hard in this letter to motivate them to demonstrate their unity by cooperating together as a cohesive group. Since they were one body in Christ (12:27), they should show this by the way they functioned together, with each person being valued for what they bring to the whole. Any competitive pride that arose among those who met together was unwarranted and disrespectful to Christ himself (1:10-17; 3:21-23). Any social disrespect to fellow believers—especially those who are poor or working class (11:22)—is reprehensible. Any flaunting of one's spiritual gift that marginalizes the exercise of others' gifts within the church body creates unwarranted cracks in the church's unity and must be curtailed (14:26-39).

The Corinthian church was a holy fellowship that required its members to respect its sanctity as God's new temple (1:2; 6:19). This means that behavior dishonoring God and his values disrespects the entire church body, and the church body has obligations to discipline individual members. This may require expelling individuals from fellowship with the church (5:1-5). It may mean pressuring others to refrain from the culturally accepted practice of suing one another (6:1-7). Still others needed to voluntarily curtail inappropriate personal conduct, either within the assembly of believers regarding what they wear (11:2-11), with unbelievers involving what they eat (10:27–11:1), or within the times of worship and teaching involving what they themselves do (chs 12–14).

Remarkably, despite Paul's apostolic stature and his role as the chief planter of the church in Corinth, he respected its corporate sanctity as God's church—his most common way of referring to it (1:2; 10:32; 11:16, 22; 12:28; 15:9). Even when he was telling the Corinthians in no uncertain terms that they needed to expel a certain member who was living with his stepmother, he would not violate their own due process when they met together to evaluate the situation (5:4). Paul believed that God would tell them clearly what to do; he was absolutely convinced God would confirm to them Paul's assessment and recommendation.

This respect for God to convict the church or individuals in the church to do the right thing shines through all of Paul's efforts to persuade through theological argument and scriptural interpretation throughout the letter. He was convinced that God speaks to the church and through the church by means of the Holy Spirit and the gifts he enables in believers. In all this, Paul also respects the freedom and autonomy God has given individual believers through his act of creation. They must be convicted to act or to change and cannot be forced, not even by an apostle.

Wisdom and Knowledge. Although wisdom and knowledge are usually treasured in biblical literature, in this letter Paul created an uncrossable chasm between human wisdom and knowledge and that of God. In chapters 1–3, Paul associates wisdom with the wit and rhetoric of Greek philosophers, who cunningly deceive people to believe things about the world and how it works that are not true. Wisdom is painted as a symbol for the limit of human understanding and thus the absence of true wisdom about what really matters: knowing God and having a true, eternal relationship with him. God's true wisdom, in contrast, cannot even be seen as such by the best and the brightest of the human race. This has to do with the fact that for Paul the essence of true wisdom is the cross upon which Jesus Christ died a horrible death in shame and misery—a substitute experiencing what every human being deserves.

This truth makes no sense from the perspective of any human philosophy of Paul's day or even today. It could not have come from any philosophy, either. It could only be revealed by God directly to those to whom he chose to tell this Good News, like Paul and others, who traveled the world to share it with others. Shame and weakness, abhorred by human philosophers, are power and strength in God's philosophy of wisdom. It is only by admitting their lostness and destiny for destruction that people can avoid destruction to find meaning and life filled with God's power and wisdom.

Knowledge in 1 Corinthians is not turned upside down like wisdom, but its value is severely downplayed. As Paul describes it, mostly in chapter 8, knowledge creates arrogance in people, including believers, which can cause them to disregard the sensibilities of others. It encourages seeking one's own happiness and fulfillment at the expense of others. The knowledge of this world is only partial; it does not compare with the full revelation that will occur in eternity with God (13:12).

The World and This Age. Due to modern notions of human progress, people today typically view the world and the present time in a positive light. This was not at all true for Paul, as is evident in 1 Corinthians. For him, the world encompassed the suffocating stranglehold that human civilization has had on people, typified by idol worship, which prevented them from knowing the true God of creation (1:10-31; 10:14). The world is dominated by human depravity and sin, seen not only in the personal immoral behavior of individuals but also in the atrocities of human society. The world brainwashes people with ideas and philosophies counter to God's, which make them resistant to the true ideas from God when confronted with them. The world despises the weak, whom God elevates via the weakness of the cross.

Though moderns usually think of the world and human society continuing on from age to age, Paul viewed the age in which he lived as the penultimate age, at the end of which God would come in judgment upon the world. This drove him not only to spread the gospel to all the civilizations of the world as quickly and efficiently as possible, but also to be sure that believers were safeguarded from destruction by living out the claims of the gospel in their lives with integrity (3:10-23). Thus, he wanted engaged Christian couples to consider not marrying so they could devote themselves to the urgency of the times to spread the gospel (ch 7); he was adamant that Christian people participate in their culture in a way that made the gospel and the church as attractive to them as possible. This can be seen especially in his advice about how women and men should adorn and conduct themselves in public worship settings (11:2-16; 14:22-25), as well as how shrewd believers must behave in dealing with various social settings that include eating meat offered to idols, both inside and outside the church (8:1–11:1).

Since the world will be destroyed as the age comes to an end (7:31; 13:10), the church is preparing for a life beyond this one. For this, new, transformed bodies will be provided after death, bodies designed for eternal life together with God in the company of Christ and all his followers (15:50-57).

Love and the Christian Life. Like other New Testament authors, Paul wrote in the wake of Jesus' radical teaching about love: One must love one's enemies and social inferiors, not only friends and relatives. So Paul and the other New Testament authors put love on the top of the agenda for believers. In his most famous passage on the subject, he pronounces that one of the very few human endeavors to breach the chasm between this age and the next is love (13:8, 13). Love is also one of the few human endeavors that can overcome the sinister evil of the world. It should replace human arrogance (8:1; 13:4). Without it miracles and even martyrdom are robbed of their value (13:2-3). Love should be the Christian way of life because it is always a positive force for human dignity and self-worth, both in society at large and in the fellowship of believers (8:1; 16:14).

Paul's admonitions to the Corinthians show how love should be implemented as the principle for sorting through a myriad of critical issues in the church. Whether it is forgoing lawsuits against one another (6:1-8) or choosing to limit one's speaking among the gathered believers (14:26-40), love leads to these decisions. Fundamentally, practicing love means voluntarily choosing to limit what one is completely free to do for the benefit of someone else. For example, Paul encouraged women and men to limit their choices of what to wear to what is deemed appropriate in Corinthian public settings when they gather together (11:2-16). And he urged the people of wealth and status to subsume their social privileges for the sake of those who come from the working-class poor when they gather together (11:17-34). These actions befit the gospel generally, as well as people individually. By choosing to limit their freedoms, Christians refuse to make self-interest the center of their moral life.

OUTLINE
   I. Introduction (1:1-9)
      A. Opening Greetings (1:1-3)
      B. Thanksgiving (1:4-9)
  II. Paul's Reaction to Alarming Reports of Division (1:10–4:21)
      A. Divisions in the Corinthian Church (1:10-17)
      B. Real Wisdom or True Foolishness? (1:18-31)
      C. Wisdom from the Spirit of God (2:1-16)
      D. Unity in Christ (3:1-23)
         1. Many laborers in God's field (3:1-17)
         2. The foolish trap of rivalry (3:18-23)
      E. Arrogance Condemned (4:1-21)
         1. God judges motives (4:1-5)
         2. Arrogance has no part in apostolic life (4:6-13)
         3. Paul will come to confront the arrogant (4:14-21)
 III. Paul's Response to Reports of Negligent Community Discipline (5:1–6:20)
      A. Demand for Expulsion of the Believer Guilty of Immoral Conduct (5:1-13)
      B. Demand for an End to Internal Lawsuits (6:1-11)
      C. Encouragement to Abandon Immoral Sexual Behavior (6:12-20)

IV. Paul's Reply to Specific Questions in the Corinthians' Letter (7:1–16:12)
   A. Matters Related to Marriage (7:1-40)
      1. Marriage should include sexual relations (7:1-7)
      2. Those currently unwed may marry (7:8-9)
      3. Believers should not divorce their marriage partners (7:10-16)
      4. Believers should generally maintain current personal conditions (7:17-24)
      5. Those currently unwed may choose to marry or remain unwed (7:25-40)
   B. Matters Related to Food Sacrificed to Idols (8:1–11:1)
      1. Eating without compromising fellow believers' scruples (8:1-13)
      2. Paul abandons his apostolic rights for the sake of others (9:1-27)
      3. Lessons from Israel's wilderness experiences (10:1-13)
      4. Lessons from the Lord's Supper (10:14-22)
      5. Exercising freedom with mature compassion (10:23–11:1)
   C. Paul's Response to Reports about the Gatherings (11:2-34)
      1. Women must cover their heads to speak in worship (11:2-16)
      2. The Lord's Supper must demonstrate community harmony (11:17-34)
   D. Matters concerning Spiritual Gifts (12:1–14:40)
      1. The Holy Spirit, the source of every believer's gifts (12:1-11)
      2. One body with many parts (12:12-26)
      3. Each member serves a vital role (12:27-31)
      4. Love is the foundation for every gift (13:1-13)
      5. Everything spoken in public worship must be understandable and edifying (14:1-25)
      6. Public worship must be conducted in an orderly manner (14:26-40)
   E. Paul's Defense of the Resurrection (15:1-58)
      1. Christ's resurrection witnessed by many (15:1-11)
      2. No resurrection poses dire ramifications (15:12-19)
      3. Christ's resurrection will make all things subject to him (15:20-28)
      4. Disbelief in the resurrection is an affront to God (15:29-34)
      5. The resurrection bodies of believers are spiritual (15:35-49)
      6. The resurrection of believers is natural because of Jesus' resurrection (15:50-58)
   F. Matters Related to the Collection and to Apollos (16:1-12)
      1. Completion of the collection before Paul's arrival (16:1-4)
      2. Travel plans (16:5-12)
V. Conclusion (16:13-24)
   A. Final Admonitions (16:13-18)
   B. Greetings, Invocations, and Benediction (16:19-24)

COMMENTARY ON
1 Corinthians

◆ ## I. Introduction (1:1–9)
A. Opening Greetings (1:1–3)

This letter is from Paul, chosen by the will of God to be an apostle of Christ Jesus, and from our brother Sosthenes.

²I am writing to God's church in Corinth,* to you who have been called by God to be his own holy people. He made you holy by means of Christ Jesus,* just as he did for all people everywhere who call on the name of our Lord Jesus Christ, their Lord and ours.

³May God our Father and the Lord Jesus Christ give you grace and peace.

1:2a *Corinth* was the capital city of Achaia, the southern region of the Greek peninsula.   1:2b Or *because you belong to Christ Jesus.*

NOTES

1:1 Paul. This lone first word opens the letter, the typical way Greek letters indicated their authors. This is the author's Greek name. Saul, his Jewish name, while probably still used by him personally, is not employed in his epistles or in Acts after he began his missionary journeys (Acts 13:9).

chosen. Gr., *klētos* [TG2822, ZG3105], used by Paul only in Romans (Rom 1:1, 6-7) and 1 Corinthians (1:1-2, 24), emphasizes his apostolic vocation by divine mandate, like that of an OT prophet.

apostle. Gr., *apostolos* [TG652, ZG693], used by Paul in 1 Corinthians more than in any other writing (10 times), refers to a messenger or ambassador sent out with a specific responsibility. Paul's apostolic call came not from the historic Jesus (as with the original Twelve) but from the risen Lord on the Damascus road (Acts 9:5; Gal 1:1-5, 11-16). The NT does not restrict the term to the Twelve Jesus chose to follow him in his ministry. Seventeen individuals are called apostles, adding Paul, James (Gal 1:19), Matthias (Acts 1:26), Barnabas (Acts 14:14), and Andronicus and Junia (Rom 16:7) to the original Twelve. Such people not only were eyewitnesses to the resurrection (Acts 1:22) but preached the gospel and founded Christian communities.

Christ Jesus. Some early mss, including ℵ, have "Jesus Christ." However, 𝔓46 and B are surely correct, since Paul rarely reverses the order of Jesus' names without "Lord" preceding them, as in 1:3.

brother. Gr., *adelphos* [TG80, ZG81]. In the plural, this word usually refers to both male and female believers. In the singular, as here, it is a way for Paul to convey his feelings of kinship for someone working with him as an associate (2 Cor 1:1; 2:13; 8:22).

1:2 church. Gr., *ekklēsia* [TG1577, ZG1711]. This word originally referred to assembled Greek citizens whom a crier had "called out" to attendance. This word was used in the LXX to refer to Israel gathered together as a community (e.g., Deut 4:10). In the NT, it came to be used mostly to designate the community of believers in a specific location, as it is here, and occasionally of the worldwide church (15:9; Eph 1:22).

made you holy. Paul uses the verb *hagiazō* [TG37, ZG39] more often in 1 Corinthians than in any of his other letters (four times). In Jewish contexts it refers to things or people who had been set apart for God's use, like the Temple, the priests, the altars, and the sacrifices.

the name. Gr., *onoma* [TG3686, ZG3950], which commonly designates the honor and integrity of an individual.

1:3 *grace and peace.* "Grace" (*charis* [TG5485, ZG5921]) derives from the standard Greek greeting, and "peace" (*eirēnē* [TG1515, ZG1645]) is the traditional Jewish greeting. Previously used together in intertestamental Jewish writings, the intercultural greeting is standard in the openings of nearly all Paul's letters, probably reflecting the multiracial composition of churches to whom he wrote. Theologically, grace constitutes the whole of God's activity in Christ, and peace the result of that activity on our behalf.

COMMENTARY

Paul's opening to this letter is structured like most ancient Greek letters: naming the author and the recipient and offering a blessing. This is a pattern he follows in all his letters. His openings stand out by expanding these common features, as he does here. Whether consciously intended or not, these extras often tip off primary concerns elaborated in the course of the letter.

Paul's mention of himself as the author of the letter is expanded in two distinct ways. First, he emphasizes his divine calling to be an apostle. This was not unusual for him. He mentions being an apostle at the opening of most of his letters (except Philippians, 1 and 2 Thessalonians, and Philemon). This often signals that his credibility as an apostle was under attack among the people to whom he wrote, as in Galatians or Colossians, but this is not always the case, as with Romans or 1 Timothy. However, since we do know that his apostolic status suffered a major attack by Corinthian believers within the context of 2 Corinthians and the "severe letter" and painful visit mentioned there, it is not overly presumptuous to think that preliminary problems along this line began to appear among the Corinthians previous to the writing of 1 Corinthians. Though not as obvious as in 2 Corinthians, a strong case can be made that subversion of Paul's apostleship was a major issue for 1 Corinthians, rising to the surface in 4:1-5 and 9:1-23.

Paul stresses the divine origin of his apostleship in a way comparable only to Galatians and Romans. In other letters he mentions both the "will of God" and "apostle of Christ" (Eph 1:1; Col 1:1; 1 Tim 1:1; 2 Tim 1:1), but only here does he insert the word "chosen" (also used in Rom 1:1) immediately after his name, making the first three words of the letter "Paul, chosen apostle." He desired his readers' first and lasting impression to be that his role as their apostle was not just a title for him or even something he sought. Rather, he was compelled by God himself to enter God's service (bringing to mind Acts 9:1-5 and Gal 1:13-17). In 2 Corinthians 11:16-12:10, he will recount for the Corinthians that his life as an apostle was not filled with glory and honor but with suffering and pain (as predicted in Acts 9:16) like the life of Christ himself, whose message he has doggedly brought to Gentiles like the Corinthians. It is not without design that Paul will emphasize in the very next verse that the Corinthians are also "chosen" themselves ("chosen, holy") not for an easy life but for one which must struggle against the forces of the world.

Paul was first and foremost an "apostle of Christ," a commissioned messenger of the gospel sent especially to the Gentiles. Simultaneously, he viewed his apostolic life as occurring within God's overarching providence. Thus, he says he is an apostle "by the will of God." God himself was not merely the agent but also the compelling cause of his vocation to serve Christ rather than to oppose Christ and persecute his followers, as Paul once thought God wanted.

Paul's second expansion of his name adds "our brother Sosthenes." Paul often added the names of working companions who were with him at the time of writing (e.g., 2 Cor 1:1). Though some maintain that this means Sosthenes had a role in writing the letter (Murphy-O'Connor 1993), this does not fit with Paul's normal intention of including names at the beginning of a letter (Garland 2003:26). The intriguing mention of Sosthenes as "our brother" could be because he is the same man who failed to make the case against Paul and Christianity to Gallio in the days when Paul originally brought the gospel to Corinth (Acts 18:14-18). Could he have become a Christian since then and afterward begun serving with Paul in Ephesus? Calvin (1960:17) thought the identity was certain, but most today assert no more than that this is probable (Garland 2003:26; Hays 1997:15).

Paul's expansion on the addressees of this letter in 1:2 is more elaborate than usual. It underscores God's expectation for the Corinthian believers to view their assembly as God's special, holy people, like Israel of old. This can be seen first in Paul's designating them "God's church," a term he normally uses to identify the worldwide church (10:32; 11:22; 15:9; Gal 1:13). The Corinthians were God's people "in Corinth," a vital part of God's new work to bring "all people everywhere" into relationship with him through Christ. Their commission mirrors Paul's own, and so they are "called" like Paul was.

Second, encouragement for the Corinthians to view themselves as God's holy people can also be seen in Paul's double emphasis on their holiness. They are both "called" holy and "made" holy, having been summoned and prepared to function as God's people. They are separate from other people yet are entrusted with a mission to enable others to join God's people by calling "on the name of our Lord Jesus Christ." Paul's desire for the Corinthian believers to live as a holy community encompasses this epistle, even if the precise words are not used in each context.

Paul intentionally invoked the words of Joel 2:32, "Everyone who calls on the name of the LORD will be saved." God was now assembling his new covenant people from city to city around the world, including Corinth. The rallying cry voiced the name "Jesus Christ," who is now "Lord." He shares the title "Lord" with God because he has completed God's mission to save all people through his death on the cross. Both the worldwide church and its local representation in the Corinthian believers as God's people serve "their Lord and ours" and swear their allegiance to him. Indeed, it is "by means of Christ" that each one then and now enters into God's people, uniting with Christ and the church in baptism (Conzelmann 1975:21-23) and confessing Christ as Lord (Rom 6:1-7; 10:9).

Paul's blessing in 1:3 is a standard part of his introductions, appearing word for word in Romans 1:7, 2 Corinthians 1:2, Galatians 1:3, Ephesians 1:2, and Philippians 1:2. This formula's coordinated appeal to both God and Christ exemplifies the Christian belief, well established by Paul's day, that the two govern with equal power. The risen Christ stands at the right hand of the Father administrating his rule (Acts 7:56; Eph 1:10; Phil 1:5-11; Col 1:15-20). Thus, to invoke both is fitting. Attributing fatherhood to God and lordship to Christ is a typical way of distinguishing their functions. Jesus himself encouraged his followers to address God as Father (Matt 6:9), not because he is either male or female, but because he is the Creator and Provider for humanity, as well as for each individual. Addressing Jesus as Lord honors his resurrection, our devotion to him, and his cause to redeem every person from the bondage of sin.

◆   ## B. Thanksgiving (1:4-9)

⁴I always thank my God for you and for the gracious gifts he has given you, now that you belong to Christ Jesus. ⁵Through him, God has enriched your church in every way—with all of your eloquent words and all of your knowledge. ⁶This confirms that what I told you about Christ is true. ⁷Now you have every spiritual gift you need as you eagerly wait for the return of our Lord Jesus Christ. ⁸He will keep you strong to the end so that you will be free from all blame on the day when our Lord Jesus Christ returns. ⁹God will do this, for he is faithful to do what he says, and he has invited you into partnership with his Son, Jesus Christ our Lord.

NOTES

1:4 *I always thank.* This follows the typical pattern of Greek letter writing by initiating a "thanksgiving" section following the opening of the letter. Paul did this in all of his letters except Galatians, where the thanksgiving section was replaced by a stern rebuke.

my God. Gr., *theos mou* [TG2316/1473, ZG2536/1609]. Though missing from the normally reliable B and ℵ*, the "my" (*mou*) should be retained due to the widespread manuscript evidence. The NIV and RSV leave it untranslated, while NASB, ESV, and TEV have "my God."

gracious gifts. Simply "grace" (*charis* [TG5485, ZG5921]) in Greek, this is a dominant word in Paul's theological vocabulary. Though not employed as much as in Romans (24 times) or even in 2 Corinthians (18 times), its use in 1 Corinthians (10 times) is still significant. Paul's use of the word is wide-ranging; he even employed it to refer to the collection of money (16:3; 2 Cor 8:4, 6, 19). However, it is at the heart of his gospel—often pitted against law—blending together both the undeserved kindness of God for humanity as well as the expression of God's love in the decisive saving act of Christ on the cross. Here, it is the fount from which the spiritual gifts flow.

you belong to Christ. This is a two-word prepositional phrase in Greek (*en Christō* [TG5547, ZG5986]); it is Paul's most common, shorthand term for distinguishing a believer's total identification with Christ from a person who is outside of Christ. The term "Christ" occurs a surprising five times in 1:4-9.

1:5 *God has enriched your church.* In Greek the verb is passive (*eploutisthēte* [TG4148, ZG4457], "you have been enriched"). The NLT interprets this as a divine passive, meaning that God is assumed as the active agent, and makes the agent explicit. The verb's tense (aorist) communicates that this action has already taken place. The word and its cognates normally denote the accumulation of material wealth (Luke 18:25; 1 Tim 6:17), though Paul uses it here and elsewhere (2 Cor 6:10) to refer to spiritual wealth. The verb communicates that the recipients are "you," plural; NLT clarifies the limits of who is included with "your church."

eloquent words. This is a singular, lit., "word" (*logos* [TG3056, ZG3364]), which can refer literally to an actual word but also to a collection of written words or to a collection of oral words. The NLT interprets it in the latter sense. Speech contests were part of the biannual Isthmian Games in Corinth (Keener 1993:454). The addition of "eloquent" by the NLT may add a hint of sarcasm (in view of Paul's later criticism of the Corinthians' overvaluing the finely spoken words of public speakers) that Paul does not intend this early in the letter since these words are stated as gifts of God.

knowledge. Gr., *gnōsis* [TG1108, ZG1194]. This word appears 10 times in 1 Corinthians, far more than in any other letter of Paul. The accumulation of knowledge was a valuable human ambition in the Greek world. The appearance of this word here and elsewhere in 1 Corinthians prompted earlier scholars to propose that Paul combated a form of Gnosticism in Corinthians. Since the idea of offering special, "secret" knowledge about the nature of Christ to initiates is not documented earlier than the second century, current scholarship does not connect formal Gnosticism with Corinth (Schmithals 1971; Thiselton 2000:92-93; R. Wilson 1972–1973), though some less sophisticated, early type of Gnosticism may be a factor.

1:6 *This.* A few scholars lobby for *kathōs* [TG2531, ZG2777] to be taken in its normal sense of comparison and translated "just as" (Orr and Walther 1976:40; Soards 1999:25). However, this seems forced in this context compared to taking it as an explanation of how the gifts function (Robertson and Plummer 1911:6; Thiselton 2000:94).

confirms . . . is true. Gr., *bebaioō* [TG950, ZG1011], which is an aorist passive. This word is often associated with verifying the truth of a person's word and is highly appropriate in conjunction with testimony.

what I told you about Christ. This accurately renders "the testimony of Christ" (*to marturion tou christou* [TG5547, ZG5986]) as an objective genitive. It spells out what is implied in Paul's statement—that he had in mind his own personal witness to the gospel of Jesus Christ delivered when he was in Corinth with them. The word *marturion* [TG3142, ZG3457], originally a legal term, is commonly used in reference to the gospel in the NT (Acts 4:33; 23:11) and in later centuries to honor Christians who chose to be executed rather than deny Christ.

1:7 *spiritual gift.* Gr., *charisma* [TG5486, ZG5922]. This is not the same word translated "gracious gifts" in 1:4. *Charisma* refers to a favor or a free gift. Nearly exclusive to Paul's writings in the NT, his use of it is concentrated in 1 Corinthians (seven times) and Romans (six times) and always refers to special abilities provided by the Holy Spirit to Christians as a blessing for the Christian community. He will have much to say about this in ch 12.

the return. Gr., *apokalupsis* [TG602, ZG637], usually translated "revelation." This word was used by Paul to refer to special revelation of knowledge from God as a spiritual gift (14:6, 26; 2 Cor 12:1, 7), revelation of the gospel in particular to him (Rom 16:25; Gal 1:12; Eph 3:3), revelation of action he should take (Gal 2:2), and the great revelation of judgment against sinners (Rom 2:5; 8:19). As in 2 Thess 1:7 (also 1 Pet 1:7, 13; 4:13), Paul uses it here in association with the idea of the return of Christ.

1:8 *will keep you strong.* From *bebaioō* [TG950, ZG1011], which is the same word translated "confirms" in 1:6. The NLT (also NIV) is consistent with the implications of the word.

end. Gr., *telos* [TG5056, ZG5465]. This refers to the accomplishment or completion of a goal.

free from all blame. Gr., *anenklētos* [TG410, ZG441], a legal term denoting blamelessness, having no hint of accusability.

when our Lord Jesus Christ returns. Lit., "in the day of the Lord Jesus Christ." The phrase "day of the Lord" was formulaic in the OT prophets for God coming in judgment (Isa 13:6, 9; Jer 25:33; Ezek 7:10; 13:5; Joel 2:1; 3:14; Amos 5:18, 20; Obad 1:15; Zeph 1:7, 14; Mal 4:1). So now in the NT, the return of Christ signals his appropriation of God's role as eschatological judge over humanity (2 Cor 1:14; Phil 1:6, 10; 2:16; 1 Thess 5:2).

Lord Jesus Christ. Like most versions, the NLT retains "Christ," following the vast majority of textual witnesses, including ℵ. It is notably missing in 𝔓46 and B. If the original excluded it, a scribe could have added it to conform to 1:7 (Comfort 2008:484).

1:9 he is faithful. The word *pistos* [TG4103, ZG4412] refers to a person who is trustworthy in character, who can be believed. God has demonstrated his trustworthiness throughout the pages of Scripture, in keeping his end of the covenant with Israel even when they did not and in bringing to fruition his plan to save humanity through Jesus Christ.

invited. This passive form of "call" (*kaleō* [TG2564, ZG2813]) can mean "invite" as the NLT translates it. However, it has a much broader, theological connotation in the NT and in Paul's writings than the English word "invite" allows. For Paul, all believers have been called, with the implication that God not only has invited each one with the Good News, but that they have accepted the invitation and have come into his family, his people, the church. In ch 7 (7:15, 17, 18 [twice], 20, 21, 22 [twice], 24) he uses this term to refer to the precise point of a believer's conversion.

partnership. Gr., *koinōnia* [TG2842, ZG3126], which refers to people holding things in common. For Greek philosophers this kind of brotherhood bonding was foundational to their utopian dreams. However, for Paul this was never rooted in mere human solidarity but through kinship created by the common dependence believers have on Christ for salvation. In fact, the only other uses of this word in 1 Corinthians are in the context of the Lord's Supper (10:16 [twice]). Demonstrating its lexical fluidity for Paul, it refers to the collecting of offering money in 2 Cor 8:4; 9:13.

COMMENTARY

Paul's thanksgiving sections typically offer a preview of key themes to arise later. In 1:4-9, Paul first employs words that will return in force, like "gracious gifts" (*charis* [TG5485, ZG5921]), "eloquent words" (*logos* [TG3056, ZG3364]), "knowledge" (*gnōsis* [TG1108, ZG1194]), "spiritual gift" (*charisma* [TG5486, ZG5922]), and "partnership" (*koinonia* [TG2842, ZG3126]). Though Paul announces these ideas in positive terms, he will harshly criticize the Corinthians for their incorrect perspective on these matters.

The expression "I always thank my God" (1:4) refers to Paul's custom in his personal prayer life to include prayer for the various churches in his orbit, churches he had a hand in planting and which continued to fall under his pastoral care. His prayers for the Corinthians focused on how God demonstrated his benevolence in their lives in ways they could see and experience since they became Christians. So, "grace" (NLT, "gracious gifts") here does not focus simply on God's mercy to accept sinners into a saving relationship with him through Christ. Rather, grace envelops the whole of believers' lives, manifesting itself in observable activities in the life of the church. The expression "he has given you" (1:4) underscores the truth that God is the great benefactor in believers' lives. The precondition for receiving the benefits of God's grace is "now that you belong to Christ Jesus," that is, by confessing Christ and entering into his corporate body, the church, through baptism (Rom 6:3; 10:6).

In 1:5, Paul provides evidence for the presence of God's grace that he is sure the Corinthians had observed. He reemphasizes that this has happened because they are "in him" (NLT, "through him"), meaning they are connected to Christ and, through him, to the Christian community and the pipeline of God's bountiful spiritual blessings. He chooses two blessings, speech and knowledge, to showcase. No doubt he is looking ahead to his criticisms of the Corinthians' less-than-acceptable approach to both of these. In chapter 2 he will chastise them for confusing rhetorically well-crafted speeches with knowledge, and in chapters 11–13 he will criticize their practice of elevating the spiritual gifts of speaking in tongues and special knowledge over the supreme gift of love. His mention of these two here, however, is not tongue-in-cheek, for he genuinely believes these two to be real gifts God provides the church, even if they are misunderstood or abused (Soards 1999:25). Paul's emphatic repetition of "all" three times in this short verse (NLT, "every," "all," "all") emphasizes the overabundance of God's riches, more than enough to supply the church's needs.

In 1:6, Paul explains how the Corinthians' demonstration of speech and knowledge relates to being recipients of God's gracious gifts (1:4). They function as tangible evidence that the gospel Paul preached to them is in fact the true gospel, fully sanctioned by God. (This is a bigger issue in Galatians and addressed more fully there, but it is never far from Paul's concern.) Why else would God pour out his gifts of speech and knowledge on them? This confirmation of God's grace occurred primarily within them as a group, meaning they could see that speech and knowledge from God was manifested when they were congregated.

In 1:7, Paul places the reality of the spiritual gifts in the context of eschatology. As a result of being "enriched" (1:5), the Corinthians had everything they needed to thrive until Christ returns in eschatological splendor and judgment. The NLT appropriately puts in the positive what Paul actually says in the negative (NET, "so that you do not lack in any spiritual gift"), gauging that this verse falls under the umbrella of the positive language of 1:5 (Fee 1987:42). Since "you" is plural, Paul's perspective continues to be corporate. It is the spiritual needs of the church that will be satisfied by the spiritual gifts God supplies its members, a principle he will elaborate in chapters 12–14. The spiritual gifts help the church wait for the Lord expectantly because they occur as an overture or foretaste of the things to come, just as the miracles of Jesus demonstrated that the messianic age had arrived with his presence.

Paul acknowledges in 1:8 that remaining true to the gospel to the end might seem difficult, but the Corinthians would receive divine aid. The source of this help is interpreted as either God or Christ. The immediate proximity of Jesus Christ to the relative pronoun (hos [TG3739, ZG4005], "he") favors him as the referent (Thiselton 2000:101). Although some make a strong case that "God" (from 1:4) remains the primary agent throughout this paragraph through the repeated divine passives (Fee 1987:44; Soards 1999:27), Paul's emphasis that they will be (lit.) "confirmed blameless" indicates that it is the testimony of Christ, the content of the gospel (1:6), that is foremost in mind. People cannot be made blameless apart from God's grace, but it is Christ's death on the cross for humanity's sins that makes them blameless when they believe in Christ and continue to do so until he returns. The repetition here and in 1:7 of the title "Lord" with "Jesus Christ" emphasizes both his resurrection and his role as sovereign judge in light of his eschatological return.

The ultimate confirmation of the reality of salvation at Christ's return, Paul affirms in 1:9, is the proven character of God himself. Paul can testify to God's faithfulness from his own experience. Knowledge of God's character is certainly obtainable from reading his interactions with Israel in Jewish Scripture, but it was also experienced by the Corinthians in the gifts of words and knowledge they had seen working in their midst. In fact, it was God who made possible what they already had, even before the return of Christ.

◆ **II. Paul's Reaction to Alarming Reports of Division (1:10–4:21)**
  A. Divisions in the Corinthian Church (1:10-17)

¹⁰I appeal to you, dear brothers and sisters,* by the authority of our Lord Jesus Christ, to live in harmony with each other. Let there be no divisions in the church. Rather, be of one mind, united in thought and purpose. ¹¹For some members of Chloe's household have told me about your quarrels, my dear brothers and sisters. ¹²Some of you are saying, "I am a follower of Paul." Others are saying, "I follow Apollos," or "I follow Peter,*" or "I follow only Christ."

¹³Has Christ been divided into factions? Was I, Paul, crucified for you? Were any of you baptized in the name of Paul? Of course not! ¹⁴I thank God that I did not baptize any of you except Crispus and Gaius, ¹⁵for now no one can say they were baptized in my name. ¹⁶(Oh yes, I also baptized the household of Stephanas, but I don't remember baptizing anyone else.) ¹⁷For Christ didn't send me to baptize, but to preach the Good News—and not with clever speech, for fear that the cross of Christ would lose its power.

1:10 Greek *brothers;* also in 1:11, 26.   1:12 Greek *Cephas.*

NOTES

1:10 *I appeal.* Gr., *parakaleō* [TG3870, ZG4151]. Standing as the very first word in the body of 1 Corinthians, it sets the tone for the whole of the letter. Used five more times in the epistle (4:13, 16; 14:31; 16:12, 15) but 18 times in 2 Corinthians and another 30 times scattered through his other letters, it can be translated "urge," "comfort," and "appeal," as the NLT does here. More than a request, less than a command, it signals that what follows originates in concerned friendship. (See extensive discussion of its rhetorical function in Thiselton 2000:111-115; Witherington 1995:96-98.)

the authority. Lit., "the name." This word was commonly used with the understanding that one was invoking the presence of the person named, appealing to the full authority of that person over those addressed. It assumes the person invoking that name has the official capacity to function as a representative.

to live in harmony. This translates an idiomatic phrase literally rendered "that you might say the same thing." The phrase was heavily used in politics to refer to people who were ideologically allied (M. Mitchell 1993:68). The NIV reads, "that all of you agree with one another."

divisions. Gr., *schismata* [TG4978, ZG5388]. Often used of political alliances that had separated, its three uses in Scripture outside the Gospels are here and in 11:18 and 12:25. Welborn (1997:3-13) demonstrates that the word was used in Hellenistic times to denote the struggle Roman political groups engaged in for political power wherein they principally aligned themselves with individual leaders rather than party designations.

be of one mind. Gr., *katartizō* [TG2675, ZG2936], which connotes the re-fusion of something that has been broken or separated and thus pairs with *schisma*.

1:11 *members of Chloe's household.* This phrase refers to people under her authority, possibly slaves, servants, or employees who conducted business on her behalf. If she held residence in Ephesus, they came into contact with the church of Corinth while visiting there, probably on business, and had returned to Ephesus and provided Paul the alarming report on which he based his comments in chs 1–4. On the other hand, she may have resided in Corinth and asked her people traveling to Ephesus on business to inform Paul about the problems in Corinth (perhaps being covered by the official letter they sent to Paul). Regardless, she and/or her people were loyal to Paul.

quarrels. Gr., *eris* [TG2054, ZG2251], another word from Greek politics. This one highlights the bitter contentiousness that can arise between individuals or political ideologies as they compete for influence. It often appears in Paul's lists of unacceptable behavior (Rom 1:29; 2 Cor 12:20; Gal 5:20; 1 Tim 6:4).

1:12 *Apollos.* Acts 18:24–19:1 describes this native of Alexandria as extremely erudite and knowledgeable in Jewish Scripture. He energetically embraced Jesus Christ and received instruction from Priscilla and Aquila, Paul's coworkers, when they came into contact with him in Ephesus. He went to Corinth with the blessings of the Ephesian church and was highly successful there, as noted in Acts and affirmed in ch 2. He returned to Ephesus, from where Paul was now writing 1 Corinthians, but he did not want to return to Corinth (16:12). Of four persons named in Paul's rhetorical flourish, the most likely to have an actual group of adherents was Apollos, though most likely it had developed without Apollos's sanction (Hyldahl 1991:20-21; Ker 2000:96; Smit 2002:231-251).

Peter. The actual name here is *Kēpha* [TG2786, ZG3064], a Greek transliteration of the Aramaic name Jesus gave to Peter, found also in John 1:42 (but not used in the more famous Matt 16:18, which uses the Gr., *Petros* [TG4074, ZG4377]). "Peter" is a translation of Cephas (NLT mg), which means "rock" or "stone," used interchangeably with Cephas in many translations, including the NLT, three more times in 1 Corinthians (3:22; 9:5; 15:5) and also four times in Galatians (Gal 1:18; 2:9, 11, 14).

1:13 *Has Christ been divided into factions?* A few manuscripts (including 𝔓46) add *mē* [TG3361, ZG3590] to provide a parallel with the rhetorical question that follows and also to clarify that the implied answer is no. However, the difficulty *mē* presents for translation and the solid textual evidence (ℵ, A, B, C, D, G, 33) for its absence suggests it is the result of scribal addition.

crucified. Crucifixion was a purposefully gruesome form of capital punishment in the Roman Empire especially reserved for despicable criminals who had committed acts of treason or sedition against the state. The victim was beaten, attached to a cross-piece by the arms, and hoisted to rest on top of a permanent post. He would remain there until he died and his body was devastated by nature. Usually done on a major road into a city, it was intended as a warning to all to submit to the absolute authority of the Roman government. (See Hengel 1977 for a comprehensive analysis.) Because Christ was crucified, NT writers (especially Paul) found in the cross an appropriate focus for contemplating why Christ came and the significance of what he accomplished, especially regarding his suffering, his sacrifice, and his resurrection.

baptized. In the NT, baptism is the normative rite that signals a person's conversion to Christ. In the first century this was only done by total immersion in water and usually as a public event witnessed by the Christian community. It appears to have been carried over from the practice of John the Baptist, who called for his generation to recognize their sinfulness and to be baptized as an act of repentance. For Christians baptism is connected to birth into a new life. In Romans 6, Paul particularly points to baptism as the act that identifies believers with Christ, both in his suffering and death and his resurrection and presence with God. (See Beasley-Murray 1962 for the fullest treatment of baptism.)

1:14 *I thank God.* This has the support of $\aleph^2$ C D F G Ψ 𝔐. Other manuscripts (A 33) read, "I thank my God." The two earliest manuscripts, $\aleph^*$ and B, read, "I am thankful." This is most likely original because "God" and "my God" appear to be scribal additions assimilating to 1:4 and other characteristically Pauline passages like 14:18 and Rom 1:8.

Crispus. This is almost certainly the same man in Acts 18:8 who was the leader of the Jewish synagogue in Corinth before becoming one of Paul's first converts to Christianity.

Gaius. This is probably the same man mentioned in Rom 16:23 who provided Paul accommodation and who at least occasionally hosted all the believers in Corinth. This suggests he had an exceptionally large house and that he was financially well-off.

1:16 *Oh yes, I also baptized the household of Stephanas.* This redacts his statement in 1:14 that he baptized only Crispus and Gaius. Paul's continuing redaction reveals that he did not edit this letter after he wrote it, nor did he erase or stop and start over. Paper was valuable, ink could not be erased, and letters were conceived as written speech, so Paul simply corrected "verbally" as he went along as one would in extemporaneous speech.

Stephanas. Stephanas and his household were Paul's first converts in Corinth and God's servants in the ministry of the gospel (16:15). As Barrett (1968:48) notes, this mention of the household of Stephanas serving the church leans toward the assumption that the baptism of his household probably did not include young children.

1:17 *preach the Good News.* In classical Greek, this word (*euangelizomai* [TG2097A, ZG2294]) was used of public reports of victorious battles, political achievements, and the birth of kings and emperors. This word is employed 54 times and its noun cognate another 76 times in the NT to refer to spreading the news of Jesus Christ and the salvation available to all in the gospel.

clever speech. Lit., "the wisdom of the word" (*sophia logou* [TG4678/3056, ZG5053/3364]). The NIV translates it as "words of human wisdom," and ESV as "words of eloquent wisdom." It is tough to render Paul's double sense that captures both human knowledge and rhetorical cleverness (Fee 1987:65; Litfin 1994:188-192; Thiselton 2000:144). The latter would include logic and persuasive argumentation, highly esteemed skills in Greek and Roman cultures (Dunn 1995:49; Pogoloff 1992:109; Smit 2002:245) that were thought to be endowed to individuals by the gods (Horsley 1977:234).

lose its power. This refers to something that is empty. Paul uses the word in 9:15 and 2 Cor 9:3 to speak of vain or senseless boasting and in Rom 4:14 (most similar to the context here) of faith being emptied of its value.

COMMENTARY

Paul's opening appeal targets the urgent need for the Corinthian believers to find unity based upon Christ. Various social circumstances, such as meeting in separate house churches and the conversion of people from various social strata, had led to differences and misunderstandings regarding many theological and practical issues, which will be addressed throughout the letter. This threatened to splinter the Corinthians into competing factions, which Paul identifies in this opening paragraph. He did not address the Corinthians with a mean spirit but with affection, calling them "brothers and sisters," his most common term for addressing fellow Christians. However, without specifically identifying himself as an "apostle," he invoked the apostolic authority he had as an officially designated representative of Christ (Welborn 1997:7). Since Paul was their apostle who first brought them the gospel and was called by Christ to do so, the Corinthians needed to respect his urgent appeal. The thrust of Paul's appeal was simply that they get along with each other and allow no rift to threaten their unity. The cracks that had occurred already had to be mended before they grew into irreparable breaks.

In 1:11, Paul reveals that his concern for unity did not arise simply from idealist Christian philosophy. Rather, it arose from reliable personal reports from people who had witnessed firsthand the nasty rivalries causing troubling rifts between people and groups in Corinth. He knew more than they thought; he knew the embarrassing truth. As the Corinthians first heard this read to them, they must have felt like children who had been caught with their hand in the cookie jar. Yet Paul also tried to calm their alarm at having been found out by referring to them yet again in familial terms, "dear brothers and sisters." That they likely expected him to begin by answering the questions sent to him in their official letter—which had probably deftly avoided mentioning these problems—would have charged this verse with high drama.

The dramatic flair continues in 1:12 as Paul portrays each and every believer (*hekastos* [TG1538A, ZG1667]) in Corinth shouting out their champion in a public rally. This exaggeration for effect has prompted many interpreters to conclude that the Corinthian believers had in fact splintered into four contentious parties—the Paul, Apollos, Peter, and Christ parties. But given the rhetorical hyperbole, likely nothing in Corinth strictly paralleled this depiction (Horsley 1998:45; Robertson and Plummer 1911:11). Rather, this is a dramatic sampling of some of the ways in which the Corinthians were splintering, or maybe even a way of portraying how ludicrous any splintering is (M. Mitchell 1993:83). Were there people who literally considered themselves a Paul party or a Christ party? Probably not. People generally had their favorites, who may have included more than these four, but it is doubtful they formed distinct alliances. Paul did not fault any of the favorites (Garland 2003:50); rather, he focused his criticism on such human tendencies to splinter into rival groups as not only dangerous but treacherous to the Christian cause.

Since Paul first brought the gospel to the Corinthians and Apollos also visited Corinth recently, it is natural to wonder if Peter had visited there also. A few interpreters lean in this direction (Barrett 1968:44; Vielhauer 1994:133), primarily based on a possible inference from 9:5 that the Corinthians knew Cephas traveled with his wife. However, his significance as a leader in the early church and some other personal information about him could have been discovered from many sources other than a personal visit from him. It is possible that Peter's name was the rallying point for a Judaizing element in Corinth that got much worse after Paul wrote 1 Corinthians (Goulder 2001). We would be overreaching the text, however, to assume that the appearance of Peter's name (when conjoined with "Christ") is evidence for a deep division throughout early Christianity between conservatives (Peter, James) and liberals (Paul, Apollos), as Baur (1876:268-320) contended so influentially over a hundred years ago (Munck 1959:135-167). In fact, few contemporary scholars see evidence for such a division.

Of all the names, the suggestion of "Christ" as a slogan is the most perplexing, since he is not on a par with the others (Garland 2003:46; Oster 1995:53). One can see how the three human leaders could have their special supporters as well as their detractors, but it would seem all Christians would consider Christ a favorite hero. Interpreters who believe the four names each represent an actual separatist group tend to consider the Christ group a super-spiritual, perhaps charismatic, Gnostic group (Conzelmann 1975:34; Fee 1987:59; Thiselton 2000:129-133). However, it is at this point that other scholars recognize Paul's rhetorical motive (Collins 1999:73; Horsley 1998:45; Vielhauer 1994:132). A "Christ group" is absurd and points to the absurdity of there being any divisive groups. It may then function aptly to lead into the argumentation that follows.

In 1:13, Paul formulates three rhetorical questions, the second and third clearly assuming a no answer. Certainly none of the Corinthians were baptized into "Paul." At this very early stage of the Christian church, every convert was baptized quite literally into the name of "Jesus," which is why he makes this part of his argument. The common Trinitarian formula reflected in Matthew 28:19 was yet to become universal. And, of course, Paul did not suffer and die for their sins on the cross. Only Christ paid the price for the Corinthians' deliverance from sin.

The first question ("Has Christ been divided into factions?") poses difficulties for interpreters. The easiest route is to assume the negative response here, too (which the textual emender attempted to formalize; see note on 1:13): Christ cannot be divided, anticipating Paul's discussion of the church as the body of Christ in chapters 12–14. However, a subtler point may be in mind: Had Christ been inappropriately seized by various competing ideologies in Corinth? The answer then is yes, or nearly so, even though this must not be allowed to happen (Barrett 1968:46; Conzelmann 1975:35; Thiselton 2000:147). Paul in this case was reprimanding all those who trivialize Christ by taking him away from everyone else as if they were the only ones who understood the full implications of the gospel. This kind of arrogant, overconfident elitism is proved to be ridiculous in light of the second and third questions. Problems of this nature persist in various historic expressions of the Christian church, each seeing themselves as superior to the others.

In 1:14-16, Paul attempts to prove his point historically. He wanted to say that he did not, in fact, baptize anyone in Corinth, so that there is no possibility that anyone was baptized in his name. He assumed, for the case of his argument, the common notion in Greek mystery religions that the act of baptism spiritually links the baptized with the baptizer (Keener 1993:455). However, his initial noting of two exceptions, Crispus and Gaius (and probably their entire households) gives way to the household of Stephanas and others unaccounted for (perhaps as Paul's amanuensis or those with him continued to add other names to the list he did not at first recall; see note on 1:16). Of course, even if he personally baptized someone, he would baptize them into the name of Christ and not his own name. This whole argument strongly suggests that leaders like Paul did not normally baptize people personally and that no "official" person was necessary for its effectuality.

In an attempt to put the baptism of Christian converts into perspective, Paul minimized its significance compared with his call to spread the gospel (1:17). His call came at his Damascus road encounter with Jesus Christ, when he was commissioned to reach Gentiles with the gospel (Acts 9:3-5). This dramatic moment set the course for the rest of his life. Of course, Paul was aware of the significance of baptism, but he seems to say that anyone can do that physical task; the convicting and converting of people with the truth of the gospel was Paul's most important spiritual responsibility—indeed, it had become the consuming passion of his life.

Paul made a second contrast in 1:17, essentially between wisdom and the cross. This is the heart of the subject matter he will elucidate through the end of chapter 3 (Litfin 1994:187). Normally, wisdom (*sophia* [TG4678, ZG5053]) is a positive notion associated with the instruction of the Lord and the wonderful collections of Wisdom Literature in Scripture itself, including Proverbs, Ecclesiastes, and Job. Wisdom teaches respect for God and presents the knowledge of experience for all ages. Yet Paul realized that what he taught concerning the cross of Christ runs so counter to human wisdom that it could only have a divine origin. The proclamation of Jesus' gospel is totally out of sync with human knowledge.

But Paul was not only thinking about content. He had "form" in mind, as well. The NLT's "clever speech" attempts to capture this aspect of his concern. People in Paul's times were enamored of spectacular speakers of philosophy who could entertain and persuade at the same time. These were the "stars" of the day, as they went on tour from town to town. Paul was concerned that neither he nor the gospel could in anyway be compared to such trivial nonsense. To wrap the gospel in human cleverness is to strip it of its raw power that can convict people at the core of their being.

◆   ## B. Real Wisdom or True Foolishness? (1:18-31)

[18]The message of the cross is foolish to those who are headed for destruction! But we who are being saved know it is the very power of God. [19]As the Scriptures say,

"I will destroy the wisdom of the wise
  and discard the intelligence of the
    intelligent."*

[20]So where does this leave the philosophers, the scholars, and the world's brilliant debaters? God has made the wisdom of this world look foolish. [21]Since God in his wisdom saw to it that the world would never know him through human wisdom, he has used our foolish preaching to save those who believe. [22]It is foolish to the Jews, who ask for signs from heaven. And it is foolish to the Greeks, who seek human wisdom. [23]So when we preach that Christ was crucified, the Jews are offended and the Gentiles say it's all nonsense.

[24]But to those called by God to salvation, both Jews and Gentiles,* Christ is the power of God and the wisdom of God. [25]This foolish plan of God is wiser than the wisest of human plans, and God's weakness is stronger than the greatest of human strength.

[26]Remember, dear brothers and sisters, that few of you were wise in the world's

eyes or powerful or wealthy* when God called you. ²⁷Instead, God chose things the world considers foolish in order to shame those who think they are wise. And he chose things that are powerless to shame those who are powerful. ²⁸God chose things despised by the world,* things counted as nothing at all, and used them to bring to nothing what the world considers important. ²⁹As a result, no one can ever boast in the presence of God.

³⁰God has united you with Christ Jesus. For our benefit God made him to be wisdom itself. Christ made us right with God; he made us pure and holy, and he freed us from sin. ³¹Therefore, as the Scriptures say, "If you want to boast, boast only about the LORD."*

1:19 Isa 29:14.   1:24 Greek *and Greeks*.   1:26 Or *high born*.   1:28 Or *God chose those who are low born*.   1:31 Jer 9:24.

NOTES

1:18 *message*. Gr., *logos* [TG3056, ZG3364]. The translation "word" (ESV and RSV) or "message" here (and in NIV and TEV) both attempt to retain the rhetorical activity and the content involved in speaking. Thiselton (2000:153) lobbies for "proclamation" in an attempt to coordinate the translation of *logos* here with "proclamation/proclaim" (*kērugma/kērussō* [TG2782/2784, ZG3060/3062]) in 1:21 and 1:23. "Preaching" (KJV) focuses on the activity while losing the content. "Doctrine" (NEB) focuses on the content and loses the activity. (See notes for 1:5 and 1:17).

***cross*.** Gr., *stauros* [TG4716, ZG5089]. Surprisingly, 6 of Paul's 18 uses of "cross" (1:17, 18) and its verbal cognate "crucified" (1:13, 17, 18, 23; 2:2, 8) are found in this immediate context of 1 Corinthians, plus another six in Galatians (Gal 3:1; 5:11, 24; 6:12, 14 [twice]). Both an event and a proclamation, the cross for Paul summarizes the redemptive activity of God (see notes for 1:13).

***foolish*.** Gr., *mōria* [TG3472, ZG3702]. This is the first of five uses of this adjective in this context (1:18, 21, 23; 2:14; 3:19), the only place it appears in the entire NT. The noun (*mōros* [TG3474A, ZG3704]) appears another four times in this context (1:25, 27; 3:18; 4:10), five times in Matthew (Matt 5:22; 7:26; 23:17; 25:2, 3, 8), and two times elsewhere (2 Tim 2:23; Titus 3:9), and the verb "make foolish" appears in 1:20. The English "moron" actually has about the right sense (Soards 1999:39). Such people are dumb in the sense that they are obtuse or dense to what is plain and obvious. Something "moronic" is simply dumb; it makes no sense.

***those who are headed for destruction*.** Gr., *tois apollumenois* [TG622A, ZG660]. The NLT phrase accurately renders a present participle in Greek that is not so much continuous as "'axiomatic,' of that which is certain, whether past, present, or future" (Robertson and Plummer 1911:18). The Greek word conveys the idea of complete destruction, as a person being killed (10:10; Acts 5:37) or something being utterly demolished (2 Pet 3:6). Smit (2002:243-244) suggests Paul uses this word here and in 1:19 intentionally to play on the name of Apollos as a warning signal to the Apollos party.

***we who are being saved*.** Gr., *tois sōzomenois* [TG4982, ZG5392]. Mirroring *apollumenois* (F. Watson 1992:139), the emphasis is probably not on the process or stages of salvation, as the NLT translation allows, as much as on the certainty of the outcome.

***power*.** Gr., *dunamis* [TG1411, ZG1539]. Anachronistically equated in popular contexts as equivalent to the English "dynamite," the Greek word has nothing to do with explosions or anything destructive. Primarily, like its verb cognate *dunamai* [TG1410, ZG1538], it refers to the ability or capability to accomplish something.

1:19 *will destroy.* This is the future tense of the same word used as a participle in 1:18 (see note).

discard. Gr., *athetēsō* [TG114, ZG119]. Paul purposefully substituted this word for "hide" (*krupsō* [TG2928, ZG3221]), the word in Isa 29:14 in the LXX. A more natural synonym to "destroy" in the first phrase, it has a similar thrust, while also emphasizing God's intentional rejection (Collins 1999:103).

intelligence. Gr., *sunesis* [TG4907, ZG5304]. This word or its cognate "the intelligent" (*sunetōn* [TG4908A, ZG5305]), which immediately follows, is paired as a synonym with "wisdom" and "wise" elsewhere (Matt 11:25; Luke 10:21; Col 1:9). It identifies people who demonstrate the ability to understand something quickly, almost intuitively. It is a person with "street smarts" (Thiselton 2000:162) without the formal education of one who is wise. This is what the people call the 12-year-old Jesus in the Temple in Luke 2:47.

1:20 *philosophers.* This is the same word "wise" (*sophos* [TG4680A, ZG5055]) in 1:19. The NLT correctly attempts to focus on the specific occupation in Greek culture also identified as the Greek questioner in 1:22.

scholars. This is the same word for Jewish "scribe" (*grammateus* [TG1122, ZG1208]) in the NT but is not used for comparable Greek men of letters in Greek culture (Fee 1987:71). Mention of this Jewish professional prepares the way for the Jewish questioner in 1:22 (Collins 1999:105).

world's brilliant debaters. Gr., *suzētētēs tou aiōnos* [TG4804/165, ZG5186/172] (debater of this age). "Debater" probably refers to a professionally trained rhetorician (Keener 1993:456; Pogoloff 1992:159-160), a person adept at winning public and private arguments, the closest contemporary equivalent being a lawyer. Paul's use of the word "age" (NLT, "world") is one of the tips that he was speaking in an apocalyptic mode. In Jewish rabbinic literature cosmic history is divided between "this age" and "the age to come," the second being after God comes in judgment upon the world.

1:21 *world.* Gr., *kosmos* [TG2889, ZG3180]. Used in 1:20 as well, it is used 21 times in 1 Corinthians alone. Generally speaking, it is not the material earth itself but the ordering forces that hold it together, including the involvement of humankind in culture and society. Often it has a negative force associated with human sinfulness and moral depravity and stands in opposition to God, but it will ultimately be destroyed. Thus, its association in this context with human foolishness is not surprising.

know. Heavily used in the NT and by Paul, this word (*ginōskō* [TG1097, ZG1182]) is not limited to intellectual understanding but includes the kind of knowing that comes from active engagement and experience. With humans, it is knowledge based on personal, even intimate, relations.

used our foolish preaching. Long ago the KJV mistranslated this as "by the foolishness of preaching," giving the wrong impression to English readers that Paul was talking about the ministerial vocation of preaching. The RSV's "through the folly of what we preach" and subsequent contemporary translations have put the focus on the content of the message, and rightfully so. But this is not to say that the gospel should be delivered without oratorical care and skill.

1:22 *It is foolish.* This phrase does not occur in the Greek either of the two times it occurs here. By adding it, the NLT clarifies the unstated connection between the statements about Jews and Greeks and the "foolish preaching" of 1:21.

Greeks. Gr., *Hellēnes* [TG1672, ZG1818]. Though strictly referring to the people from the Hellenes, or Greece, it is often paired with "Jews" as a way of encompassing the whole of humanity, as here (see also 10:32; 12:13; Rom 3:9; Gal 3:28). Although it is sometimes used similarly, it is not the same as the word "Gentile" (*ethnos* [TG1484, ZG1620]), which refers to people of any culture other than Jewish. Since *ethnos* is used in 1:23, Paul may have been using *Hellēnes* here to accent the role of specifically Greek philosophers in not fathoming the message of the cross.

1:23 *that Christ was crucified.* Lit., "Christ crucified" as in NIV, RSV, and ESV. While it is true that the historic crucifixion of Jesus is at the heart of the Christian evangelistic proclamation, the NLT's rendering loses something crucial to Paul's point: its enduring effect for all humanity across the ages (Mare 1976:195; Thiselton 2000:171).

offended. Gr., *skandalon* [TG4625, ZG4998]. An important word in the NT, this is its only use in 1 Corinthians. Commonly rendered "stumbling block" following the KJV, it seems to have originated as a hunting term indicating the device that snares the game or triggers a trap. The NT occurrences tend to focus, as here, on the intrinsic nature of the gospel of the cross that people found disgusting and dangerous and thus avoided to save themselves from capture and becoming victims of this "scandal." The scandal of the cross mentioned in Gal 5:11 surely connects to this passage.

nonsense. This is the same Greek word (*mōria* [TG3472, ZG3702]) the NLT translates as "foolish" throughout this section. "Nonsense" does a good job of grasping the sneering rejection present in this verse.

1:26 *in the world's eyes.* Lit., "according to the flesh," Paul commonly used this word to refer, as here, to the human standards of the world (Soards 1999:49).

powerful. Gr., *dunatoi* [TG1415, ZG1543]. Related to the word "power" in 1:18, the word here focuses on people with political or military stature.

wealthy. Gr., *eugenēs* [TG2104, ZG2302]. Its only use in the epistles, this word usually marks out those of noble pedigree and high standing socially; in the setting of Corinth, it probably also indicates Roman citizens (Orr and Walther 1976:161).

1:27 *shame.* Gr., *kataischunō* [TG2617, ZG2875]. Its five uses in 1 Corinthians (here twice and in 11:4, 5, 22) are the most of any NT book. Care must be taken not to read into it the private, psychological guilt emphasis of contemporary Western culture. Rather, the idea of public humiliation and losing face current in Asian (e.g., Japanese) culture is a closer fit.

powerless. Gr., *ta asthenē* [TG772B, ZG822]. Translated "weakness" in 1:25, this is the second of its 12 uses in 1 Corinthians. Often applied to the physical human body, it can mean sick or feeble. Socially, as the NLT shows well, it would refer to people at the opposite end of the spectrum from the "powerful."

powerful. Gr., *ta ischura* [TG2478A, ZG2708]. Not the same Greek word as in 1:26, this word focuses on a person's physical strength, which explains the NIV's "the strong" here. In a social sense as here, the NLT's "powerful" is a fitting antonym to "powerless."

1:28 *despised.* NLT seems to condense two Greek expressions into this English word: *ta agenē* [TG36, ZG38] and *ta exouthenēmena* [TG1848, ZG2024]. This is the only use of *agenēs* in the NT. In classical Greek, as here, it is the opposite of *eugenēs* [TG2104, ZG2302] (1:26) in the sense of being born into a lowly family rather than a noble family (see NLT mg). The NLT's translation considers the world's disgust and poor treatment of such people. A synonym of "despised," *exouthenēmena* emphasizes something's worthlessness.

things counted as nothing at all. Gr., *ta mē onta* [TG3361/1510, ZG3590/1639]. The *mē* implies that the nonexistence is not absolute but an evaluation. The NLT rendering emphasizes the cultural value of people rather than that they do not exist. There is an alternative reading that adds *kai* to the beginning of this phrase; despite being found in B, this word was most likely added by a scribe to harmonize the phrase as a third item in the series that begins the verse. In context the phrase stands best in apposition to "things despised by the world," without the *kai,* as ℵ* and 𝔓46 have it.

1:29 *no one.* Gr., *mē pasa sarx* [TG4561, ZG4922]. Lit., "not all flesh." "All flesh" is a Semitism, common in the LXX, referring to all humanity.

boast. An important word for Paul in 2 Corinthians (20 times), this is the first of six uses of it in 1 Corinthians (three times in this context and in 3:21; 4:7; 13:3). Often used negatively of words uttered from false prideful sinfulness, it can be positive (as in this context) when coming from the perspective of humble dependence on God's power in the lives of believers.

1:30 *united you with Christ.* Lit., "in Christ," one of the most crucial phrases for understanding Paul's Christology. When believers are baptized into Christ they are made one with him in death (to sin), in resurrection (to eternal life), but also in suffering. Thus Christians in being united with him are also united together as his body, the church (Thiselton 2000:189-190).

made us right with God. Simply the noun "righteousness" (*dikaiosunē* [TG1343, ZG1466]) in Greek. Paul adapts this key theological term from the realm of the law courts to convey the judicial idea of Christ taking the penalty for the sins people are actually guilty of and thus making possible God's acceptance of them into a personal and saving relationship.

made us pure. Simply the noun "sanctification" (*hagiasmos* [TG38, ZG40]). This word comes from the world of the Temple where the priests, the artifacts, and the sacrifices are all set aside for God's use alone and no one else's. In terms of Christology, it refers to the purity of Christ's sacrificial death and its effect of making believers, who are in Christ, set apart to God as well.

freed us from sin. Simply the noun "redemption" (*apolutrōsis* [TG629, ZG667]). This word comes from the world of first-century slavery in which slaves could be manumitted if the price of their value was paid. This could be done by the slaves themselves, since they could earn wages, or by a benefactor. (See Bartchy 1973 on first-century slavery.) In respect to Christ, his sacrifice is then the price paid to free all humanity from their slavery to sin.

COMMENTARY

Paul must have realized that his case for the indivisibility of Christianity based on the relatively small number of baptisms he performed in Corinth was not sufficient to carry his point (Barrett 1968:51). Thus, he chose to delve deeper into the contrast between the gospel proclamation and mere human articulations of wisdom announced in 1:17. Despite the fact that he will make no direct reference back to the divisive atmosphere in Corinth (Hays 1997:28), the intended message to the Corinthians becomes clear: The divine message of the cross is reduced to just another human philosophy if it is identified as originating with any of its messengers.

The opening verse of this salvo, 1:18, functions as a thesis statement Paul will attempt to explicate in the verses that follow, at least through the end of the chapter. "The message of the cross," a unique phrase in the New Testament, picks up on Paul's preaching of the Good News of the cross in 1:17. For Paul, though, the cross was no mere message; it was the cataclysmic event in human history by which God has now divided people into two groups, the only two groups that ultimately mean anything and that are utterly and purposefully divisive: the destroyed and the saved (Garland 2003:63).

Thus, when proclaimed faithfully, the message of the cross creates this division, similar to the way Jesus' parables and activities were calculated to divide people into disciples or enemies (Mark 4:10-12). Thus, the "foolish," or spiritually dense who think the gospel message dumb when they hear it, place themselves in the "destroyed" category. By contrast, "the saved" recognize and experience God's work through the cross.

Paul plowed the fertile field of Isaiah's prophecies in 1:19 for the first of 20 Old Testament citations he will employ in the course of 1 Corinthians, six more of which will appear in this immediate context (1:31; 2:9, 16; 3:19, 20; 5:13) with a total of six Isaiah quotations in the book (2:16; 14:21, 25; 15:32, 54). The heavy use of Isaiah in 1 Corinthians should not be surprising since it is, as Collins (1999:95) notes, far and away Paul's favorite Old Testament book to quote (28 times), followed by Psalms (20 times), Deuteronomy (15 times), and Genesis (15 times). The quotation, though relying on the authority of the Old Testament, is far more than a proof text (Soards 1999:52). As Paul employs it, it functions as prophetic prediction (note the future tense) that was poignantly fulfilled in the cross. For Paul this is no simple general truth about God and human wisdom. The cross itself is the divine moment in history when God shatters all human efforts to explain the world and its purposes, however noble and brilliant, that came before it and will come after it.

Ironically, Paul uses his own rhetorical flair in 1:20, a string of three simple questions that indict three models of professional human brilliance as condemned to idiocy by the prediction of Isaiah 29:14. Though each can be generalized to apply to the most brilliant human specimens of any culture (probably today we would have to add the scientist, computer genius, and movie director), they stand as a unit of failed human effort to make sense of the world as we know it. Paul addresses now in particular the "destroyed" class of people (1:18) who consider the gospel of the cross to be dumb. On the contrary, says Paul, the cross makes the work of their best representatives, the most brilliant of the brilliant, dumb or "foolish."

What Paul conveys rhetorically in 1:20 he states matter-of-factly in 1:21. The maze of the world does not include a map to find God, and God designed it that way on purpose. The wise of the world think they are getting somewhere, but they cannot see the "satellite" view that shows them circling around and around getting further and further from God. What Paul says here he will flesh out in detail when he writes Romans 1:18-32. And try as they might, humans cannot reason themselves to a full-orbed understanding of God, much less an intimate, personal relationship with him. Pascal (1966) and Kierkegaard (1958) had it right when they argued that truly knowing God goes beyond reason, and Hans Küng (1978) brilliantly documents the failed human quest to reason our way to God.

But even if God could be proved, this would not give us what only the gospel message provides: a path toward full acceptance into God's presence. Only the message of the cross accomplishes this, and even it makes no sense on a human level. Only this proclaimed message based on a divine act of justice and love on the cross creates a "saved" class of people. Thus, what he says here applies to both Jews and

Greeks, for although the Jews know God to a degree, and Greeks not at all, the full revelation did not come until the cross.

In 1:22, Paul characterizes Jews as seeking confirmatory signs of God's messages to them and Hellenic Greeks as craving learning and knowledge. The Greek penchant for learning was widely known. Herodotus, a fifth-century BC Greek historian, says, "All Greeks were zealous for every kind of learning" (*Histories* 4.77). For their part, Jews demanded confirmatory signs not only from Moses and others in the Old Testament but from Jesus as well (Matt 16:1; Mark 8:11; John 2:18).

In 1:23, Paul indicates that he does not conform the gospel to the Greeks' liking nor does he subject it to the Jews' inspection methods. The gospel is what it is, the story of a crucified man from Galilee whose submission to a humiliating and painful death occurred because it was essential to God's plan to make a way for all people to be saved from their rebellion against him. If this redemptive act splits humankind into believers and unbelievers rather than their normal, ethnic divisions, then that's part of God's plan. Jewish rejection of Jesus as Messiah seems to have hinged on their expectation that he would be a conquering hero over the Romans rather than a seemingly failed and crucified insurrectionist. Greek rejection of Jesus as the Son of God seems to have resided not only in the generally repulsive idea of Jesus being crucified but also in the concept of a perfect god taking on human flesh, since in their minds human flesh was corrupt. Only a very low god would subject himself to such a menial form of existence, even temporarily.

Paul spoke in 1:23 of Jews and Gentiles as representative classes of humanity who have rejected and will continue to reject Christ. In contrast to that truth, 1:24 reports that individuals have embraced the gospel of the cross from across the spectrum of human cultures, including Jews and Greeks (using *Hellēnes* again, corresponding to 1:22). These, then, are the exceptional minority who were spiritually open to God's call through the offensive message, just like the few in Jesus' crowds who understood and welcomed the odd truths of Jesus' parables. They accepted the gospel message of the cross and were transformed by its power that Paul introduced in 1:18. Not only that, instead of being divided as Jews and Greeks, they now are united in the class of people who are "saved." In order to do this, the special contingent of first-generation Christians must have seen the futility of their own cultures' efforts to find God and opened their eyes to the wonder of the cross as wisdom on a completely different plane, just as Christians still must do.

In 1:25, Paul sums up his point by constructing a set of clauses that compare the incomparable: God's wisdom and human wisdom. He drenches his comparisons with rhetorical irony so that it is obvious that God's "wise" plan to save humanity is really in a league of its own, untainted by any thought of comparison with any form of "human" wisdom. Thus, even God's so-called "foolishness" is wiser than the most brilliant of human wisdom. To the point of the discussion, God's plan to save humanity is in a totally superior category because it overcomes the evil of sin, which separates humanity from God. It's not just an idea, a philosophy, or a discovery; it is a completed plan of action that has created an entirely new world order of "the saved" and "the destroyed," which cuts across ethnic differences and national borders.

Though Paul will expand on his theme of God's wisdom and foolishness in ensuing verses, he begins by first calling on the Corinthians in 1:26 to recall their own social standing when they responded to God's call to the gospel. Of course, they knew that Paul was aware of their social condition, too, since he personally brought them the gospel. Paul picked out two broad categories of socially prestigious people: those who acquired prestige through politics and those who got it through inheritance.

Although Paul's point emphasizes the rarity of such types of people in the Corinthian church, contemporary investigation tends to note that his statement allows for "some" believers to have been in such socially strategic positions in Corinth (Wuellner 1973:672). People with large enough homes for other believers to meet in, like Gaius (Rom 16:23), Stephanas, perhaps Crispus, Chloe (the businesswoman whose "people" have informed Paul in Ephesus), and Erastus, Corinth's "city treasurer" (Rom 16:23), likely numbered among the influential "some." Whether Corinth should be considered typical or exceptional among the churches Paul planted in this regard is debated (Judge 1960:49-61; Theissen 1982:69-119). But the tendency is to view all of Paul's churches as socially and economically mixed. Paul could also be emphasizing that the initial respondents to the gospel were lower class, while more people of prestige have joined the community since then and are part of the problem now.

In 1:27-28, Paul explains that not being among the social elite in fact is an advantage when it comes to God's modus operandi. In contrast to human operations, the social elite are not at the top. A reversal of the social order should be expected because God has shown this pattern consistently in history, from leading the slave nation of Israel to the Promised Land to granting lowly Hannah and Mary children who were instrumental to God's plans. Then the Corinthians are themselves yet another exhibit of this pattern and should consider themselves blessed. In the end, God's upside-down pattern will not take place behind the scenes of human history. Rather, the humiliation of the wise and powerful will be on public display for all to see. In the Greek text of these verses, only the adjective "wise" refers to a person; the rest, "foolish," "powerful," and "powerless," technically refer to "things" (neuter). This suggests that Paul's lens had a wide scope on this as a principle of God that goes beyond human factors in God's purposes.

In 1:28, Paul accentuates this sense of principle by using the neuter form four more times. Things the world has no use for, things lowly and "despised," God puts to good use. Artfully, Paul gathers these two descriptions up as "the things that are not," and explains their lofty purpose in God's plans, to make "the things that are" (according to those other than God) empty and lowly themselves. Indeed, the Corinthian believers themselves were part of this paradoxical reversal, which continues to take place as the gospel is preached and accepted and will be finalized in the eschatological future.

Anticipating the Scripture citation in 1:31, Paul pronounces the underlying truth of this divine reversal of social position. At the end of the day, God is smarter, stronger, truer than all his creatures, even the human variety, who seem easily to forget this. Just as Job went speechless when he finally got his audience with God (Job 42:1-6), so on the eschatological day the most egotistical will go silent in God's holy presence.

Before he gets to the Scripture citation, Paul draws together in 1:30 themes he had touched on since 1:18. The Corinthian believers had been blessed by God to be in their position, safely tucked away into the saving work of Christ. This has not happened because they were persuaded by some brand of human brilliance or because they were social elites. It happened because of what Christ did, specifically on the cross. But this was not an action Christ took totally of his own accord; it was a crucial event in God's plan to provide salvation to all who would believe. In that act, Christ became the culmination of all God's wisdom—and the message of the cross encapsulates this. Thus, this new position of acceptance before God is not anything the Corinthian believers should feel like they deserve. It had been handed to them by the despicable act of suffering and death that Christ experienced on the cross.

This strange kind of "wisdom" Paul attempts to explain with three theological terms he uses very commonly, especially in Romans—namely, righteousness, sanctification, and redemption (see notes on 1:30). When accepted, this kind of "wisdom" transforms believers, totally transfiguring their relationship with God. Those once condemned to death as in a court of law because of sin, those too contaminated to take part in temple proceedings, and those consigned to a lifetime of slavery—now because of being in Christ are released from execution, cleansed for use in the temple, and freed from slavery. Each of these images is a way of saying that Christ puts believers into a radically new relationship with God that is not possible by any other means humans might devise.

Some speculate that the mention made in 1:30 of Christ as "wisdom" connects to Jewish development of wisdom into a personified, preexistent, divine figure, both involved in creation and functioning as a medium by which people can access God's truth (Prov 8:22-31; Wis 7:22–8:1; Barrett 1968:60). However, no clear indicators in this passage make this connection, despite its critical importance to christological development in the New Testament (Hays 1997:33; Thiselton 2000:192).

The citation of what is essentially Jeremiah 9:24 (with perhaps some influence from 1 Samuel 2:10) in the Septuagint (Hays 1997:34; Robertson and Plummer 1911:28) is a rhetorical capstone to what has preceded and a kind of bookend with the Isaiah 29:14 quotation in 1:19. Whereas Isaiah 29:14 states the negative, Jeremiah 9:24 states the positive: "Those who wish to boast should boast in this alone: that they truly know [the Lord]." For Paul, it represents what those in the class of "saved" will say on that eschatological day when standing before God. They rightfully can boast of what the Lord has done for them in Christ—in Christ crucified—and be warmly accepted by God. By contrast, those in the class of "destroyed"—however smart or important—can and will say nothing as God metes out their punishment of destruction.

◆   ## C. Wisdom from the Spirit of God (2:1-16)

When I first came to you, dear brothers and sisters,* I didn't use lofty words and impressive wisdom to tell you God's secret plan.* ²For I decided that while I was with you I would forget everything except Jesus Christ, the one who was crucified. ³I came to you in weakness—timid and trembling. ⁴And my message and my preaching were very plain. Rather than using clever and persuasive speeches, I relied only on the power of the Holy Spirit. ⁵I did this so you would trust not in human wisdom but in the power of God.

⁶Yet when I am among mature believers, I do speak with words of wisdom, but not the kind of wisdom that belongs to this world or to the rulers of this world, who are soon forgotten. ⁷No, the wisdom we speak of is the mystery of God*—his plan that was previously hidden, even though he made it for our ultimate glory before the world began. ⁸But the rulers of this world have not understood it; if they had, they would not have crucified our glorious Lord. ⁹That is what the Scriptures mean when they say,

"No eye has seen, no ear has heard,
    and no mind has imagined
what God has prepared
    for those who love him."*

¹⁰But* it was to us that God revealed these things by his Spirit. For his Spirit searches out everything and shows us God's deep secrets. ¹¹No one can know a person's thoughts except that person's own spirit, and no one can know God's thoughts except God's own Spirit. ¹²And we have received God's Spirit (not the world's spirit), so we can know the wonderful things God has freely given us.

¹³When we tell you these things, we do not use words that come from human wisdom. Instead, we speak words given to us by the Spirit, using the Spirit's words to explain spiritual truths.* ¹⁴But people who aren't spiritual* can't receive these truths from God's Spirit. It all sounds foolish to them and they can't understand it, for only those who are spiritual can understand what the Spirit means. ¹⁵Those who are spiritual can evaluate all things, but they themselves cannot be evaluated by others. ¹⁶For,

"Who can know the LORD's thoughts?
    Who knows enough to teach him?"*

But we understand these things, for we have the mind of Christ.

2:1a Greek brothers. 2:1b Greek God's mystery; other manuscripts read God's testimony. 2:7 Greek But we speak God's wisdom in a mystery. 2:9 Isa 64:4. 2:10 Some manuscripts read For. 2:13 Or explaining spiritual truths in spiritual language, or explaining spiritual truths to spiritual people. 2:14 Or who don't have the Spirit; or who have only physical life. 2:16 Isa 40:13 (Greek version).

NOTES

2:1 *lofty words*. Lit., "according to a lofty word"—the preposition indicating a standard of measurement to which Paul did not attempt to comply, the singular form accentuating normative behavior. The word "lofty" (Gr., *huperochēn* [TG5247, ZG5667]) can refer literally to a mountain summit and here implies not simply superiority but excessive sophistication.

***impressive wisdom*.** The Greek contains simply "wisdom" (*sophia* [TG4678, ZG5053]). However, the NLT rightly attempts to convey the grammatical indication that "lofty" modifies both "words" and "wisdom." Given that this is something of a taunt against others who invest heavily in wooing people with their wisdom, Paul probably used "wisdom" tongue-in-cheek (Thiselton 2000:208). Such wisdom covered with lavish rhetoric is not really wisdom.

***secret plan*.** Gr., *to mustērion* [TG3466, ZG3696]. Ancient manuscripts, contemporary translations, and commentators are divided over whether this or the alternative "testimony" (*to marturion* [TG3142, ZG3457]) is original. 𝔓46vid ℵ* A C contain the first, while ℵ² B D F G 33 1739 have the second. Though the reading of 𝔓46 is listed as "vid.," the reading is quite certain (see Comfort 2005:343). NLT is joined by TEV, NRSV, NJB, and NAB in choosing the first, while NIV, ESV, RSV, NEB, REB, and NET choose the second. Other than Fee (1987:88), who strongly advocates the second reading, most agree with Conzelmann (1975:53) that it is too close to call, but in the end agree with Metzger (1971:545) to support the first reading (Collins 1999:118; Garland 2003:83; Mare 1976:199; Thiselton 2000:207). It is difficult to determine whether it is more likely that a scribe attempted to conform the text to *mustērion* in 2:7, or brought *marturion* in from 1:6. The NA²⁷/UBS⁴ choice of *mustērion* fits the context of ch 2 better and is probably original. The Greek word does not necessarily imply something completely unknown but something not completely revealed (Mare 1976:199). Six of Paul's 21 uses of *mustērion* occur in 1 Corinthians, twice with reference to a spiritual gift (13:2; 14:2), once to the resurrection (15:51), but the other three, as here, to the plans of God primarily involving Christ (2:1, 7; 4:1), which is a prevalent focus for him (Eph 3:3-9; 5:32; 6:19; Col 1:26-27; 2:2; 4:3).

2:2 *I would forget everything.* Lit., "I determined not to know anything." This does not mean Paul obliterated all else from his mind, as Thiselton (2000:211) observes, but that he concentrated on not allowing the logic of worldly wisdom to interfere with the pure simplicity of the gospel as best as he was able.

the one who was crucified. Gr., *touton estaurōmenon* [TG4717, ZG5090]. The perfect passive participle is identical to 1:23 and with its repetition here emphasizes the results of the crucifixion as central to the gospel. The demonstrative pronoun "that one" (*touton* [TG3778A, ZG4047]) points to the historical figure of Jesus Christ.

2:3 *in weakness.* Gr., *en astheneia* [TG769, ZG819]. Often referring to physical illness or infirmity (Luke 5:15; John 11:4; Acts 28:9; 1 Tim 5:23), even for Paul (Gal 4:13), this word can also refer to mental or moral failings and to Jesus' condition of suffering in his crucifixion (2 Cor 13:4). Paul may have had in mind both his physical and his emotional condition as he came to Corinth, having recently escaped from hostilities directed at him from Thessalonica and Berea, as well as having come from his less-than-successful encounter with Greek philosophers at the Areopagus. Speculation includes the possibility that this weakness refers to Paul's "thorn in the flesh" (2 Cor 12:7; Gal 4:13).

timid and trembling. Gr., *en phobō kai en tromō* [TG5401/5156, ZG5832/5571]. In Greek, three nouns are parallel, the preposition repeating three times: "in weakness [see previous note] and in fear and in trembling." The NLT, recognizing that the last two often occur as a pair both in the NT (2 Cor 7:15; Eph 6:5; Phil 2:12) and in the OT (Exod 15:16; Isa 19:16), groups them separately from "in weakness."

2:4 *my message and my preaching.* Though efforts to distinguish the intent of these two words are bountiful (Robertson and Plummer 1911:32), they both are used throughout this context for both the content and the proclamation of the gospel. Thus, the two are brought together here to cover the whole (Thiselton 2000:217).

very plain. Gr., *ouk en peithois sophias logois* [TG3981, ZG4273]. Lit., "not in persuasive words of wisdom," supported by B ℵ* D. The great variety of textual readings produces a low-level confidence in this preferred reading in the UBS text, which receives only a C rating. However, the lack of correlation in extant Greek manuscripts for *peithois* should not be held against it as original, being coined (perhaps by Paul) from *peithō* [TG3981.1, ZG4274] ("persuasive power"; Robertson and Plummer 1911:32). The addition of *anthrōpinēs* [TG442, ZG474] to *sophias* [TG4678, ZG5053] in some manuscripts is superfluous. 𝔓46 F G read "not with persuasion of wisdom," a reading supported by Zuntz (1953:23-25) and followed by NEB and REB.

I relied only on. Lit., "in demonstration," intended as the contrast to "in persuasive words of wisdom." The noun *apodeixei* [TG585, ZG618] (demonstration) has a technical meaning in Greek formal logic to refer to a syllogism proved true by stating undisputed premises (Keener 1993:457; Robertson and Plummer 1911:33).

the power of the Holy Spirit. Gr., *pneumatos kai dunameōs* [TG4151/1411, ZG4460/1539] (Spirit and power). This is a hendiadys (an idiom which uses two words for a single idea), as the NLT recognizes, referring to power displayed by the Holy Spirit.

2:6 *mature.* This word (*teleiois* [TG5046B, ZG5455]) can be translated "perfect" in contexts referring to God (Matt 5:48), the law (Jas 1:25), and love (1 John 4:18). In Greek mystery religions, it referred to people who had completed the initiation phase of their training. The NLT properly reflects that Paul intended to differentiate between novice believers and those who demonstrated mature conviction.

world. Lit., "age," referring to a defined period of time, sometimes a generation. Usually it is doubled, "age of ages," to refer to eternity, or as in rabbinic literature, "the age to come." Appearing alone, as here, it can refer to the human age (Eph 1:21) or "world," as the NLT has rendered it.

rulers. Beginning with Marcion and continuing to Origen (Conzelmann 1975:61), many early writers thought this word (*archōn* [TG758, ZG807]) referred to demons, evil spirits who command the arena of human activity. This is related to the view that ancients believed the lights in the sky were super-spirits who orchestrated world affairs (still persisting in astrological charts today). Although Paul did use this word in the singular to refer to Satan, in line with other NT authors (Eph 2:2; cf. Matt 9:34; 12:24; John 14:30; 16:11), in this context the meaning is almost certainly human rulers since its repetition in 2:8 clearly refers to those governing bodies and individuals who presided over Jesus' crucifixion (Fee 1987:103; Garland 2003:93; Hays 1997:44; Robertson and Plummer 1911:36; Soards 1999:59).

who are soon forgotten. Lit., "who are passing away." The word often portrays things that are destroyed, as in 15:24, 26. The NIV has "who are coming to nothing." The NLT rendering draws out the implication of the gradual irrelevance of human rulers as generations succeed generations and certainly once this temporary age is over.

2:7 *mystery of God.* Lit., "in a mystery." This is the same word identified as "the mystery of God" in 2:1 (which explains the NLT translation here) and which will be mentioned again in 4:1. Paul's use of this word here should not be used to identify Pauline Christianity as a kind of mystery religion (Collins 1999:130). This is not the secret knowledge of an elitist cult. However, there is a mysterious aspect to the gospel because of its relationship to the unfolding plan of God.

that was previously hidden. The NLT properly adds "previously" to make it clear that however obscure before, this mystery of God is now fully available to know. Paul's discussion elaborates on incisive comments Jesus makes in Matt 11:25-26 and Luke 10:21-22 (Gaffin 1995:106-107).

made it . . . before. Translated "destined" by the NIV and "decreed before" by the ESV, the word (*proorizō* [TG4309, ZG4633]) refers to a predetermined plan. Paul used it elsewhere in only two other contexts (Rom 8:29-30 [twice]; Eph 1:5-11 [twice]) but in a similar sense as here.

our ultimate glory. Lit., "our glory." The NLT correctly attempts to transmit the eschatological intention of the phrase, as Robertson and Plummer (1911:38) put it, "the final state of the redeemed."

2:8 *glorious Lord.* Lit., "the Lord of glory." The word "glory" (*doxa* [TG1391, ZG1518]) is commonly employed in reference to God (Acts 7:2; Eph 1:17) but only occasionally to Christ (Jas 2:1). It depicts the splendor of God and the resurrection of Jesus into God's presence. This is the only use of the phrase "Lord of glory" in the NT. The term is used in the Jewish apocalyptic throne visions of *1 Enoch* 63:2, which demonstrates that the term arises from such Jewish contexts (Collins 1999:131; Newman 1992:235-240; Thiselton 2000:247).

2:9 *That is what the Scriptures mean when they say.* This is usually translated "as it is written" (NIV, ESV); it is the stock formula in the NT for introducing a quotation from the OT. The perfect passive, lit., "it has been written," is recognized to have present force because Scripture, though written in the past, still speaks with authority in the present. Paul cites words that in part can be found in Isa 64:4 and perhaps also in Isa 65:16 (Collins 1999:131; Hays 1997:44; Thiselton 2000:251). The principal connection is in the disclaimer to people hearing or seeing God's work. The LXX (Isa 64:3) also opens with the word for "ages," paralleling Paul's use of the same Greek word with "rulers" in 2:6 and 2:8, and closes with a reference to those who "wait for his mercy." Interestingly, the Gospel of Thomas (17), from the second century AD, contains what appears to be a version of Isa 64:4 with closer parallels to what Paul cites than either the Hebrew OT or LXX. From this, it is best to conclude that Paul probably knew a Greek version of this passage that is different from our sources and/or that he may have added his own flourishes, as he sometimes did, to fit better with his point.

2:10 But. The difference in this context is not significant, but the textual evidence for the alternative "for" (*gar* [TG1063, ZG1142]) in 𝔓46 and B should be seen as an attempt by copyists to correct the weak but not uncharacteristic "but" (*de* [TG1161, ZG1254]) supported by ℵ and a host of manuscripts.

to us. Despite the claim that the first-person plural occurrences here through 2:12 are editorial, referring to Paul alone (Kaiser 1981:311), it is contextually better to understand that Paul includes all true believers in his explanation of the Spirit's role in both communicating and receiving the gospel (Garland 2003:99; Lofthouse 1955:75).

revealed. Gr., *apokaluptō* [TG601, ZG636], which refers to something formerly hidden or covered that has been unveiled. For Paul, this word, used 13 times, almost always is connected to the gospel and Jesus Christ (Rom 1:17; Gal 1:16; 3:23; Eph 3:5) with God as the revealer (as here).

searches out. Gr., *eraunaō* [TG2045, ZG2236] assumes an exhaustive investigation. Paul's only other use of it, in Rom 8:27, is similar—with respect to God searching the hearts of believers in relation to the "mind of the Spirit."

deep secrets. Lit., the "depths" of something. Paul used this in reference to God also in Rom 8:39; 11:33 (see also Job 11:7). The NLT tries to get at the specific context of God's mysterious plan. Thiselton (2000:257) lobbies that Paul was trying to refer to the most private recesses of God's being.

2:13 the Spirit's words . . . spiritual truths. Gr., *pneumatikois pnematika* [TG4152A, ZG4461]. The NIV has "spiritual truths in spiritual words," and the ESV has "spiritual truths to those who are spiritual." The variations reflect differences in how *pneumatikois* is taken. First, is it neuter or masculine? Second, is the dative instrumental, or is it dative of personal benefit? Those who favor the masculine point out that spiritual people as receivers of spiritual things makes this an implicit contrast with the unspiritual people in 2:14 (Barrett 1968:76; Witherington 1995:128). However, the immediate grammar favors the neuter (hence, "spiritual words"; Bruce 1971:40; Collins 1999:135; Conzelmann 1975:67; Fee 1987:115; Garland 2003:100; Kaiser 1981:317; Robertson and Plummer 1911:77). This is partly due to the fact that the dative is most likely instrumental, intending to function the same as *en didaktois* [TG1318, ZG1435] *pneumatos* (in spiritual teaching), which it immediately follows.

to explain. The Greek verb *sunkrinō* [TG4793, ZG5173], used only here and in 2 Cor 10:12 (twice), normally refers to putting two things together in order to compare them, as it does there. Less specifically, it can mean "interpret" or "explain," which is the sense here. The NIV has "expressing" and the ESV "interpreting."

2:14 who aren't spiritual. Gr., *psuchikos* [TG5591, ZG6035]. The ESV has "natural." Though *psuchikos* is related to *psuchē* [TG5590, ZG6034], which can mean life, breath, soul, or even spirit, it is clearly intended to contrast with "spiritual." The only other use of the word by Paul occurs in 15:44-46 (three times), where it modifies "body" and is intended to refer to a person's physical or natural body versus their spiritual body. Thus, this word is not negative so much as limiting human beings to the natural plane.

foolish. See notes on 1:18 and 1:23.

for only those who are spiritual can understand what the Spirit means. Gr., *pneumatikōs anakrinetai.* The NLT attempts to paraphrase what literally reads, "it is discerned spiritually." The verb *anakrinō* [TG350, ZG373], the first of 10 uses of this word in 1 Corinthians (2:15 [twice]; 4:3 [twice], 4; 9:3; 10:25, 27; 14:24), refers to something that is investigated thoroughly and can connote a judicial setting in which individuals and evidence are examined, resulting in a judgment being rendered, the latter fitting better the context of 2:14-15. Some in Corinth may have believed that their own spiritual nature they received at birth was all they needed to understand the truths of God, but Paul teaches that the Holy Spirit is needed (Pearson 1973:39-41).

2:16 *thoughts.* Or, "mind" (*nous* [TG3563, ZG3808]). It is the same Greek word in the LXX quotation as in the application that follows. Employed by Paul four times later, all in chs 14–15, and once earlier in 1:10, this word refers to the capacity of individuals to think and make intelligent decisions based on a variety of data. Animals, who function instinctually, do not have this capacity.

Christ. This has the excellent support of ℵ A C D¹ Ψ 048 0289ᵛⁱᵈ 33 1739. The substitution of "Lord" by a few manuscripts (B D* F G) was likely an attempt by copyists to line this up with the reference to "Lord" in the quotation from Isa 40:13 that precedes it.

COMMENTARY

In 2:1, Paul reaches back to 1:17 to pick up his thread of thought based on the time five years ago when the Corinthians first responded to his gospel message. By appealing to his well-known history with them, Paul will demonstrate that he remained true in practice to the carefully considered principles about the gospel he elaborated in 1:18-31. Corresponding to the fact that the gospel is not "wisdom" by any normal human standards because of its seemingly contradictory message of a crucified Christ, Paul affirms that he did not package the gospel as some kind of human wisdom, as sophisticated Greek philosophers did with their ideas. God's mystery (a term Paul uses frequently to refer to the gospel plan in places such as Eph 3:3-9; Col 1:26-27; 2:2), created and carefully unfolded by him throughout human history until its full revelation in Christ, would only have been diminished by rhetorical frills and unnecessary efforts to exaggerate it.

In 2:2, Paul shares that he thought hard about how the gospel message should be presented to people living in a Greek environment. In fact, he seems to indicate that he had to fight with himself to keep it from being adulterated by worldly influences. The natural human thing to do would be to try to make a good thing better and to do anything to help people believe it because it is true. For the most part, he believed he resisted these temptations, and the Corinthians knew it. The Christian message was counterintuitive; it was un-wisdom; it was the bloodied and bruised body of Jesus, the Christ, expiring on a Roman cross, executed as a revolutionary— but actually paying for the sins of the world. That's the simple message they heard from him and believed.

Had Paul changed his approach with the Corinthians, whom he encountered immediately after his Areopagus speech at Athens (Acts 17:22-31)? Probably not (so Barrett 1968:63; Fee 1987:92; Garland 2003:84; Thiselton 2000:212). "Christ crucified" is solidified as Paul's message as early as Galatians 3:1. Paul's philosophical approach at Athens should be deemed an aberration from his normal presentation, stimulated by the unique occasion and context.

In describing himself foremost as "weak" when he first brought the gospel to the Corinthians (2:3), Paul adopted the term for himself that he used in 1:27 to describe the kind of person who is the ideal vehicle for God to confront the "powerful" with the gospel. Despite the fact that Paul already seemed to carry with him some kind of physical ailment or deformity that made him an easy target for scorn, tagged as his "thorn in the flesh" (2 Cor 12:7), he seems to be saying that he felt especially vulnerable or intimidated by the situation he encountered in Corinth. This had only gotten worse by the time he wrote 2 Corinthians, so that he responds by listing his weaknesses and defiantly declaring that he boasts in them (2 Cor 11:21–12:6). Acts 18:1-18 does record a very tumultuous situation, including Jews eventually rioting against Paul and pressing charges with Gallio, the Roman proconsul. Also, 2 Corinthians 10:1-10 and 11:6 suggest that Paul was unimpressive in his personal presence and perhaps also in his oratorical ability, compared to the strength and capabilities displayed in his letter writing. The addition of "timid and trembling," often associated with a person's reverent awe of God, suggests that Paul also felt a weighty responsibility to please God in fulfilling his commission specifically having to do with Corinth.

In any case, his appeal to remember the gospel that came to them unadorned by anything in his person is complemented in 2:4 by the simplicity of the message he presented. Despite the fact that sophisticated rhetoric and exaggerated confidence were viewed as the welcomed trappings of true philosophy in Greek culture and in Corinth (Lim 1987:146), Paul reminded the Corinthians that he used none of these ploys to entice them to believe in his message of the crucified Christ. It is likely, even though his writing does display rhetorical training even here, that he knew he was no match for the level of rhetorical sophistication he would run into in Corinth. So, perhaps determining not to play that game was part of what initially weighed him down. The payoff in not playing the rhetorical game was that the Holy Spirit, rather than his words, did the convicting. They were not converted to Paul or to Paul's version of the gospel, but to the gospel, period.

How exactly the Spirit displayed his power to convince the Corinthians was probably in the realm of inner, spiritual conviction (Fee 1987:95; Thiselton 2000:221; Witherington 1995:126) or perhaps in their changed lives (Horsley 1998:54), but probably not in charismatic display at the time of their conversion, as with Cornelius (Hays 1997:36; Keener 1993:457), since the latter would work against his argument of the simple gospel message penetrating their lives without added external performance.

The function of 2:5 is to summarize his point thus far. Distinguishing the gospel of the crucified Christ from the kind of wisdom that Greeks sought (noted in 1:22 and now labeled specifically as "human wisdom") was something he believed he achieved intentionally when he was with them. Thus, they would know—and still must know—that what they converted to came from the one and only God himself. They had experienced—and still experienced—the very power of God to convict them of truth and continually demonstrate his power in their lives. With this last phrase, "the power of God," Paul effectively bookends his initially stated affirmation in 1:18 that those being saved know this occurs only though "the power of God."

For those in Corinth who thought his gospel was too simplistic—so undeveloped to the point of being insulting—Paul responded forcefully, beginning in 2:6, that plenty of depth is available in Christianity to those who are ready for it. He had not spoken of this to the Corinthians thus far because, frankly, they had not shown themselves to have moved beyond the novice stage of Christian commitment. Their current attraction to those who desire Christianity to compete as just another philosophy in the world of ideas demonstrated their continued immaturity. Paul calls them "infants" in 3:1 and unspiritual in 2:14, in contrast to those who walk in their Christian life as "spiritual" (2:15) and as mature adults (2:6). However, even if they were mature enough to receive this instruction from him, he explained that the deep wisdom of Christianity is of a wholly other kind from whoever might dominate human thinking, whether wise philosophers or ruling civil authorities. This Christian un-wisdom is simply beyond the confines of human history and inquiry, where ideas and authorities come and go.

In 2:7, Paul identifies the deeper wisdom of the Christian life as something formerly mysterious because it involved God's premeditated plan created even before his creation. The Jewish patriarchs and prophets only caught occasional glimpses. But then the revelation of this plan became intrinsic to the gospel Paul consistently preached. Impenetrable by human wisdom, philosophy, or reason—even after being revealed—its central event, indicated in 2:8 to be the cross (though adequately explained by the simple gospel), contains a depth that is not fathomable by mere human inquiry.

To bolster his point that human intelligence and power is not privy to God's special "un-wisdom" of the cross, Paul offers the indisputable historical record of Jesus' crucifixion, presided over by leading representatives from the world of Jews and Gentiles—Pilate, the Roman governor, and Caiaphas, the head Jewish priest and leader of the Jewish Sanhedrin (2:8). Paul assumed it to be obvious that these representatives of human ignorance not only were unaware that Jesus was the embodied messenger of God's wisdom—even after looking him squarely in the face and conversing with him, they deemed him a menace to society and doomed him to torturous execution. The message of the cross as conveyed to all by these representatives of human wisdom is crystal clear: "This man is not from God! Forget his claims to be the ultimate spokesman God sent!" Despite their rejection, he was and is the "glorious Lord." In fact, he came from God, and this has been documented by his bodily resurrection and his elevation to God's right hand. Even now, this rejected messenger speaks God's "un-wisdom" through his own apostolic heralds, like Paul.

Climaxing his case that God's "un-wisdom" is outside the realm of human knowledge, Paul cites words primarily from Isaiah 64:4. More poetic and balanced than what appears in English versions of this passage based on the Hebrew Masoretic

Text, Paul appears to be reciting a version more closely related to the Septuagint, manicured somewhat to fit his own immediate context. The addition of "mind" (lit., "by the heart") corresponds with his discussion of humanity's lack of knowing God. The word "prepared," used nowhere else in the New Testament as a word associated with God's activity, is stronger than "does" (*poieō* [TG4160, ZG4472]) in the Septuagint and corresponds better with "made it . . . before" (*proorizō* [TG4309, ZG4633]) of 2:7.

Identifying himself as one of "those who love him," Paul suggests that a new age has dawned (2:10). Though not comprehended previously, the wisdom of God's plans are now known to people like Paul. Still not accessible by the brilliant or the powerful, it has become known in the only way it could, through God's own decision to reveal it to those whom he chooses. The vehicle for this revelation is the Holy Spirit, whom all believers receive upon their baptism (Acts 2:38; Rom 6:2; 7:6). The Spirit is the coordinator of communication between God and believers and between believers and God (cf. Rom 8:26-27). Despite the fact that Paul was talking about knowing God intimately through the Spirit, he was not referring to knowledge available only to an elite group of Christians, like the 12 apostles or Paul or a clique in Corinth. He was talking about an intimacy with God that goes beyond mere knowledge, an intimacy that links the core of our being to the core of God's being.

In 2:11, Paul draws an analogy to make what he has said about God more understandable. We all realize that no person—no matter how intimate they are to us, not even a spouse—penetrates to the core of our being. We all retain our secrets, our personal experience, history, hurts, and joys that even our very closest human friends know only partially. The only one who knows us completely and particularly is our own self, our individual spirit, or "that person's own spirit," as Paul puts it. God, Paul suggests, is like us in this respect: Only his own spirit knows him thoroughly, too.

The amazing thing, as Paul shares in 2:12, is that the same Spirit who knows God intimately indwells believers. Thus, the Holy Spirit that believers receive from God is in fact God's very own Spirit. With this divine connection to God made upon conversion, believers now share an intimacy with God unprecedented in the history of humankind. The spirit of the world (or humans) cannot accomplish this—ever. God himself has made it possible for believers not only to know but to appreciate fully what God "has freely given us." The Spirit of God conveys to us the "un-wisdom" of God, totally unavailable to even the most inquiring human minds. Believers don't just receive previously unknown knowledge; they come to know the previously unfathomable God, the God whom until now men and women could not look upon and live (Exod 33:20).

In 2:13, Paul explains how this unique knowledge of God communicated to believers via his Spirit can become known to others. If human intelligence can't penetrate it or convey it, how does anyone come to know and believe it? Again, Paul sees the Holy Spirit as the answer. The Spirit, he explains, teaches him what to speak in human language to convey this profound mystery of God. But how does this happen? His answer is that "spiritual interprets spiritual" (see note on 2:13). Since Paul and God were connected by the Holy Spirit, the Spirit was able to convey these spiritual truths in spiritual language. Thus, the human language Paul used to deliver the truth about God in his evangelistic activity was not derived from human ideas or wisdom but came though the Spirit from God himself.

When some people hear this message, they have trouble recognizing its truthfulness. The problem, not surprisingly, is at the spiritual level. People who operate only on the human level, with aspirations and conduct that never moves beyond this limitation, cannot be penetrated by truth conveyed in language originating in the Spirit of God. The "un-wisdom" of God sounds to them like foolishness. They simply cannot assess it in any other way. They are blocked by their own unspiritual orientation from accepting something that can only be discerned spiritually.

By contrast, Paul adds in 2:15 that people not limited to the natural but oriented to the spiritual are equipped to determine the truthfulness of the spiritually rooted Christian message. Not only that, but since the Spirit is also a pipeline to God, they have the capacity to draw conclusions concerning the world around them and all its ideas, including things considered "wisdom" by human standards. Thus, uniquely equipped compared to all other people, Christians and their beliefs cannot be fairly evaluated by others who are not similarly equipped. The fundamental aspects of a Christian's beliefs remain "an enigma," as Thiselton (2000:274) puts it, "unless others share the same insight of the Spirit of God." Paul was not trying to make the Christian faith elitist; rather, he was simply trying to explain why some people see the Christian claims as true while others see them as ridiculous. As Fee (1986:120) appropriately warns, this passage cannot be recited by super-spiritual movements within Christianity to justify their spiritual elitism or to quarantine them from criticism by orthodox believers.

In 2:16, Paul verifies his claims regarding the exclusion of the unspiritual person from discerning God's message by quoting from Isaiah 40:13, a passage similar in force to Isaiah 64:4, which he quoted in 2:9. Once again he followed the Septuagint version, which speaks of the Lord's "mind," rather than "spirit" (Heb., *ruakh* [TH7307, ZH8120]) as in the Hebrew version. Assuming Paul knew the Hebrew version as well, it seems odd that he did not use it since he had just focused on the Spirit and the spiritual to explain the difference between believers and nonbelievers. However, when it is recognized that his argument has moved toward the issue of drawing decisive conclusions (*anakrinō* [TG350, ZG373]; NLT, "understand") in 2:14-15, the scriptural comment on not knowing God's "mind" (NLT, "thoughts") makes sense.

Even more surprising in 2:16 is the conclusion Paul draws. We would expect him to say that despite God's exclusivity before, now believers have "the mind of God," since this is what the Scripture says, and it is what would seem to follow from his comments in 2:10-12. Paul has not mentioned Christ since 2:2. However, that seems to be precisely his reason for mentioning Christ in 2:16: to draw us back to 2:2. Remember, "Christ crucified" was Paul's plain message (2:2-3), a message that divides the saved from the doomed (1:18). To say those who are spiritual have the "mind of Christ" means that God through his Spirit has communicated the truth of the cross to their spirit so that they can be said to "understand" its wisdom, something the doomed do not have the capacity to do. Not only that, if those among the Corinthian "believers" cannot receive or apply the "un-wisdom" of the cross, they put themselves in the category of the world (Grindheim 2002:690; Willis 1989:121), as Paul will further emphasize in what follows.

◆   **D. Unity in Christ (3:1-23)**
     1. Many laborers in God's field (3:1-17)

Dear brothers and sisters,* when I was with you I couldn't talk to you as I would to spiritual people.* I had to talk as though you belonged to this world or as though you were infants in the Christian life.* ²I had to feed you with milk, not with solid food, because you weren't ready for anything stronger. And you still aren't ready, ³for you are still controlled by your sinful nature. You are jealous of one another and quarrel with each other. Doesn't that prove you are controlled by your sinful nature? Aren't you living like people of the world? ⁴When one of you says, "I am a follower of Paul," and another says, "I follow Apollos," aren't you acting just like people of the world?

⁵After all, who is Apollos? Who is Paul? We are only God's servants through whom you believed the Good News. Each of us did the work the Lord gave us. ⁶I planted the seed in your hearts, and Apollos watered it, but it was God who made it grow. ⁷It's not important who does the planting, or who does the watering. What's important is that God makes the seed grow. ⁸The one who plants and the one who waters work together with the same pur-pose. And both will be rewarded for their own hard work. ⁹For we are both God's workers. And you are God's field. You are God's building.

¹⁰Because of God's grace to me, I have laid the foundation like an expert builder. Now others are building on it. But whoever is building on this foundation must be very careful. ¹¹For no one can lay any foundation other than the one we already have—Jesus Christ.

¹²Anyone who builds on that foundation may use a variety of materials—gold, silver, jewels, wood, hay, or straw. ¹³But on the judgment day, fire will reveal what kind of work each builder has done. The fire will show if a person's work has any value. ¹⁴If the work survives, that builder will receive a reward. ¹⁵But if the work is burned up, the builder will suffer great loss. The builder will be saved, but like someone barely escaping through a wall of flames.

¹⁶Don't you realize that all of you together are the temple of God and that the Spirit of God lives in* you? ¹⁷God will destroy anyone who destroys this temple. For God's temple is holy, and you are that temple.

3:1a Greek *Brothers.*   3:1b Or *to people who have the Spirit.*   3:1c Greek *in Christ.*   3:16 Or *among.*

NOTES

3:1 *spiritual people.* Gr., *pneumatikois* [TG4152A, ZG4461]. This is the same word used three times above in 2:13-15.

belonged to this world. Gr., *sarkinois* [TG4560A, ZG4921]. Used only three other times in the NT (Rom 7:14; 2 Cor 3:3; Heb 7:16), this word, derived from the often theologically loaded word "flesh" (*sarx* [TG4561, ZG4922]), refers to something that has some kind of connection to the human body, or "of the flesh." The fact that Paul will use yet another word, *sarkikos* [TG4559, ZG4920], derived from *sarx*, in 3:3 (twice) has caused some (Garland 2003:109; Keener 1993:458; Robertson and Plummer 1911:52; Witherington 1995:131) to suggest the sense there is "of the flesh" in a more carnal or ethical sense, while *sarkinos* here is more material in the sense of sharing the many limitations of being human. Since Conzelmann (1975:72) declared that "there is no difference in meaning" between these two, others have followed suit, especially Thiselton (2000:288), who emphasizes that both words in this context encompass "human self-sufficiency" as opposed to those who are spiritually dependent on God, which undoubtedly has negative ethical and relational consequences, emphasized in 3:3. The NIV translates both words in 3:1 and 3:3 as "worldly" and the TEV as people who "belong to this world." The ESV distinguishes "people of the flesh" in 3:1 from "of the flesh" in 3:3. The NLT distinguishes the two by using "sinful nature" in 3:3 (translating *sarkikos* as the NIV translates *sarx* throughout Rom 7–9). Despite the fact that *sarkikos* can overlap with the "material" sense of *sarkinos* (9:11; Rom 15:27), Paul's use of the two words in this immediate context suggests that he was drawing upon the distinction between them.

infants. Gr., *nēpios* [TG3516A, ZG3758]. This refers to very young children, usually younger than age seven (the word *pais* [TG3816, ZG4090] being used approximately from age seven to twelve) with limited language development, completely dependent on parents for survival, perhaps even to a child who is still nursing.

3:2 milk . . . solid food. The reference to "milk" reinforces that the infant in mind is nursing (see previous note). "Solid food" suggests a stage when nursing is no longer being practiced. The spiritual contrast of milk and food is also made in Heb 5:12-13.

3:3 sinful nature. Gr., *sarkikos* [TG4559, ZG4920]. See notes on 3:1. This word is also used in 9:11; Rom 15:27; 2 Cor 1:12; 10:4; and 1 Pet 2:11. The NLT translates it in these other contexts as "physical," "human," "worldly."

jealous. Gr., *zēlos* [TG2205, ZG2419]. Used only here in 1 Corinthians but five times in 2 Corinthians (2 Cor 7:7, 11; 9:2; 11:2; 12:20), this word can refer to ardent enthusiasm for something in a positive sense but can also refer to overenthusiasm to the point of being offensive and disrespectful to others. In ethical lists, it is usually translated "jealousy" as in the NLT (2 Cor 12:20; Gal 5:20), and in Gal 5:20 it also appears next to *eris* (see next note).

quarrel. Gr., *eris* [TG2054, ZG2251]. Some mss (𝔓46 D F G) add the synonym "discords" (*dichostasiai* [TG1370, ZG1496]) to *eris*. Although it is found in 𝔓46, its absence in 𝔓11 ℵ A B C P Ψ 0289 1739 and its presence in Paul's vice list in Gal 5:20 following "jealous" (*zēlos*) and *eris* make it most likely that it was added by a copyist.

living. Literally, this word (*peripateō* [TG4043, ZG4344]) means "walk" but was commonly used to refer to a person's conduct or the way people live their lives. The Corinthians were failing to live out their Christian convictions like mature adults (Francis 1980:41).

3:4 people of the world. Gr., *anthropoi* [TG444, ZG476] (merely human). Using this term reinforces the basic point of calling the Corinthians *sarkinos* [TG4560, ZG4921] and *sarkikos* [TG4559, ZG4920] in 3:1, 3.

3:5 who is Apollos? Who is Paul? A few minor Greek manuscripts change the order of the names to make Paul first, but this is no doubt a scribal contrivance to reflect Paul's greater importance. The series of rhetorical questions is a common technique of Greek diatribe.

servants. Although this term (*diakonos* [TG1249, ZG1356]) can sometimes refer to the formal church appointment of "deacon" in the NT (Phil 1:1; 1 Tim 3:8, 12), Paul used it here and elsewhere to emphasize his personal allegiance to the work to which God had called him (Eph 3:7; Col 1:23-25).

believed the Good News. Lit., "believed," the past tense referring back to Paul's initial 18-month period in Corinth.

3:8 work together with the same purpose. Lit., "are one" (*hen eisin* [TG1520/1510, ZG1651/1639]). The attempt to clarify the point is accomplished in various ways. The NIV has "have one purpose," while the TEV reads "there is no difference between."

rewarded. This word (*misthos* [TG3408, ZG3635]) can refer to the wages workers earned and were paid at the end of each day or at the end of a job (Luke 10:7; Rom 4:4; Jas 5:4). However, it can also refer to the nonmaterial reward associated with heaven and God's ultimate judgment (Luke 6:23). Because Paul placed the work of God's servants within the metaphor of workers in a field, the sense of the word begins in common life within the metaphor but moves to the spiritual realm as application is made to God's workers.

hard work. The word *kopos* [TG2873, ZG3160] refers to manual labor (John 4:38) and has this sense within the metaphor. However, its primary sense is "trouble" or "difficulty" (2 Cor 6:5; Gal 6:17), which fits with Paul's application to God's workers.

3:9 both God's workers. Gr., *theou . . . sunergoi* [TG2316/4904, ZG2536/5301]. Translators struggle to get the right sense. The NLT is an improvement over "God's fellow workers" in the NIV and ESV, which incorrectly (but probably unintentionally) reads as though God, Paul, and Apollos are a trio working together, when Paul surely means that he and Apollos are coworkers allied under God's direction (Soards 1999:77). The TEV has "partners working together for God."

God's . . . God's . . . God's. Paul has carefully constructed the three sentences in parallel by beginning each with "God's" (*theou* [TG2316, ZG2536]), a genitive in Greek indicating God's ownership of each. The staccato effect leaves no doubt about who is in control.

field. Gr., *geōrgion* [TG1091, ZG1176]. This refers to a farmer's field cultivated for crops and is the only appearance of this word in the NT. The cognate noun, *geōrgos* [TG1092, ZG1177], is a "farmer" or, literally, "a tiller of the ground," and is used 19 times in the NT.

building. Gr., *oikodomē* [TG3619, ZG3869]. The word refers to any structure constructed by human workmanship, usually a house or building (Mark 13:2). It can also have a figurative sense of strengthening or building people up, as it does in 14:3, 5, 12, 26. It is not unusual to find architectural and agricultural imagery in close proximity to one another in a wide variety of ancient literature, as in Deut 20:5-6; 1QS 8:5; and Plato *Laws* 1.643b (Collins 1999:147).

3:10 foundation. Paul used this word (*themelios* [TG2310, ZG2529]) three times in this context (3:10, 11, 12), as well as in Rom 15:20; Eph 2:20; 1 Tim 6:19; and 2 Tim 2:19. Only here does he contemplate the initial stabilizing materials of a building. Elsewhere, he used the term figuratively.

expert builder. Lit., "wise architect." When building a structure, one highly skilled, heavily experienced worker was needed who supervised the other laborers and procured prices, materials, and designs for the project (Derrett 1997a:130). Such a person was more like a crew chief today than a general contractor because of the relatively small number of workers used and the fact that such people were not involved in paying the other workers (Shanor 1988:461; Thiselton 2000:308).

3:12 gold, silver, jewels. These three elements commonly adorned temples. This could be an allusion to Herod's temple in Jerusalem in Paul's day (Mare 1976:207). More commentators see it as a literary allusion to descriptions of Solomon's temple in places like 1 Chr 22:14-16; 29:2; 2 Chr 3:6 (Conzelmann 1975:76; Fee 1987:140-141; Kuck 1992a:177). Regarding "jewels" (lit., "precious stones"), some suggest that consistency demands that this refer to building materials, like marble (Collins 1999:157; Thiselton 2000:311). However, gold and silver are not strictly building materials either. Fee (1986:140) contends that the plural, as here, usually refers to jewels while the singular refers to construction material.

wood, hay, or straw. Common homes were framed with wood, with the walls made of hay and mud and the roofs thatched with straw (Collins 1999:157; Mare 1976:207).

3:13 judgment day. Lit., "the day," short for "the Day of the Lord." Reference to God's eschatological day of judgment in this abbreviated form also occurs in Rom 13:12; 1 Thess 5:4; Heb 10:25, but "that day" occurs in 2 Thess 1:10; 2 Tim 1:12, 18; 4:8. "The Day of the Lord" appears in 1 Thess 5:2, and "the day of judgment" appears in Matt 12:36. The full expression appears regularly in the prophets (Isa 2:12; Jer 46:10; Ezek 7:10; Mal 4:1-6).

fire. Fire is frequently associated with the day of the Lord in the OT (Dan 7:9; Joel 2:3, 30; Mal 4:1) and the NT (Matt 3:10-12; 13:40-50; 2 Thess 1:8; Heb 12:29; Jas 3:6; 2 Pet 3:10-12).

will show if [it] . . . has any value. Specifically, this word (*dokimazō* [TG1381, ZG1507]) described the process of assaying metallic ore to determine its level of purity and thus its value. This process involved melting the sample with very hot fire. Paul clearly drew on this special meaning, as did Peter (1 Pet 1:7). Generally, in the NT it refers to people being tested (2 Cor 8:8, 22) or examining themselves (11:28; 16:3; 2 Cor 13:5; Gal 6:4) to show proof of the quality of their lives. That this testing is to be done by fire as a step leading to rewards at judgment day is well-established in early Jewish literature in the OT (Dan 7:9; Joel 2:3; Mal 4:1) and other Jewish literature, such as *Psalms of Solomon* 15:4 and *Testament of Abraham* 13 (Hollander 1994:98-100).

3:14 reward. See comments on Paul's use of the word in 3:8. Here he refers to wages earned by the chief architect and his workers for a job well done.

3:15 burned up. Fairly common in the NT but dominant in Revelation (Rev 8:7 [three times]; 17:16; 18:8), this word (*katakaiomai* [TG2618A, ZG2876]) refers to something burned down to the ground until the fire goes out. The fiery destruction of Corinth by the Roman general Mummius in 146 BC was part of the cultural memory of all Corinthians.

will suffer great loss. This word (*zēmioomai* [TG2210A, ZG2423]) does not refer to punishment so much as being deprived of something one expects to have (Thiselton 2000:314). Shanor (1988:462, 469) examines an inscription from fourth-century BC Arcadian Tegea that specifically uses this word to refer to fines or lost payments for poor construction work. Paul was not threatening loss of salvation of the "builders" but loss of reward (Kuck 1992b:178).

3:16 Don't you realize? This is the first of ten times, six in ch 6 alone, where Paul will use this rhetorical formula in 1 Corinthians (5:6; 6:2, 3, 9, 15, 16, 19; 9:13, 24). This formula may mean that what follows is information the Corinthians had been instructed in previously (Collins 1999:160), or, more probably, it simply draws attention to Paul's emotional intensity at the time of writing (Thiselton 2000:316), as he tells them something crucial that should ring true to them based on what they do know.

temple. Gr., *naos* [TG3485, ZG3724]. This is one of two words used in the NT to refer to the Temple in Jerusalem. The broader term, *hieron* [TG2411, ZG2639], referred to all the courts and facilities in the Temple while the more narrow term used here usually focuses on the sanctuary, where God dwelt (Witherington 1995:134). However, this is not a strict division, since in the LXX *naos* can encompass a wider range of temple facilities (1 Kgs 6:17 [LXX, 3 Kingdoms 6:17]).

in you. The pronoun is plural in Greek. Thus, Paul had in mind a corporate identity, not the individual.

COMMENTARY

At 3:1, Paul begins to draw together the strands of thought he has developed since 1:10 into a junction that applies directly to the Corinthian situation. Despite his voiced recognition of the Corinthians as true believers, baptized into Christ and therefore receivers of the Holy Spirit, they functioned like the "unspiritual" nonbelievers he just described in 2:13-16. Like them, the Corinthians showed themselves incapable of discerning spiritual things from the Spirit. They remained his "dear brothers and sisters," as he addressed them at the outset of the verse. However, this relationship could not be any more tenuous, as he chastised them about their strong ties to "the world" in the sense of their discerning things on a human level—totally disconnected from the voice of the Spirit available to them.

They were full-grown adults on a human level, but spiritually they were new-borns, eyes closed, nursing from their mother's breast. This was no compliment, since it had now been at least five years since many of them embraced the gospel upon Paul's first visit there. He develops this imagery in 3:2, contrasting where they *are* spiritually with where they *should be*. They should be beyond the stage of being nourished by mother's milk to being sustained by adult food. The Corinthians should have grown enough to progress to adult food while he was with them for 18 months, but they didn't. Now, five years later, they were no more ready to be weaned than they were then!

In 3:3, Paul explains why he concluded this about them. Starkly, he says they demonstrate themselves to be living by the same human, debased principles they employed before they became Christians. They were no different from anyone else in Corinth. It is as if believing in the crucified Christ had made absolutely no impact on them—beyond their initial confession. This was obvious from the division among them fostered by bad attitudes and infighting.

This leads Paul in 3:4 full circle, back to where he began in 1:10: his knowledge of their bitter group rivalries born out of allegiance to a variety of *human* influences on them. This time he mentions only two group rivalries: those who view themselves as related to Paul and those related to Apollos. This may mean the mention of Cephas (Peter) and Christ in 1:12 was mere window dressing. In any event, Paul now gets down to what was the real Corinthian issue, two combative segments of the church, a Paul group and an Apollos group. Furthermore, Paul insinuated that this was why Apollos left Corinth and did not want to return. As explained earlier, multiple rival groups had emerged in Corinth, well beyond the suggestion of three or four earlier. Here, Paul and Apollos were the focus because they epitomized the correct relationship between God's missionaries, who were cooperative servants of one master. Both Paul and Apollos understood this, and the Corinthians had witnessed this cooperative spirit in operation. Indeed, Apollos and Paul were, in microcosm, an exact model of how the Corinthian church itself should function: cooperative agents of God working together to complete his goals.

In 3:5, as in 3:4, only the names of Paul and Apollos appear, though reversed. This is no mistake. Rather, this reversal ensures readers that Paul did not view himself as superior to Apollos, regardless of the fact that he came to the Corinthians with the gospel first. In the playing field of God's mission to humanity, he and Apollos were teammates. They were both "God's servants," as he puts it, each doing his best to complete his assignment. The fact of the matter is that Apollos may very well have been the pioneer missionary in other fields that others later followed. Paul, for his part, despite viewing himself as called to plant the gospel in virgin soil, as he explains in Romans 15:20, did minister to Roman believers well after the gospel was firmly established among them.

In 3:6-8, Paul develops the agricultural metaphor as a way of explaining to the Corinthians how God's work is accomplished. He pictured the Corinthians themselves as a fertile field, never tilled until Paul came along five years earlier and planted the gospel, broadcasting it throughout the city. It germinated among those who believed, as he says, "in your hearts." His work was just phase one. As in cultivating a field, a second phase is critical to seeds sprouting: watering. This he pictured as having been done by Apollos after he (Paul) had left the area. He could easily have extended the metaphor to other phases, like weeding, protecting from weather or insects, thinning, harvesting, etc. He seemed content to stop at two phases because his chief subject was the role he and Apollos played in the fruition of the gospel among the Corinthian believers. They were both mere laborers working under God's direction. Not only did God supervise their phases of work among the Corinthians, he is also the true source of any growth and development that occurred among them, since he is the source of all spiritual life.

In 3:7, Paul reemphasizes God's vital role in the growth of gospel seeds. However, Paul also emphasizes the relative insignificance of any phases of the work done by God's human agents. Literally, he says that the planter and the waterer are nothing compared to the grower. The agent of growth is the only absolutely vital component, both in the growth of tomatoes and in the growth of the gospel. Paul aimed this comment directly at those who were exaggerating the role of mere workers like him and Apollos at the expense of all the devotion and thanksgiving that should be directed at God, the one truly responsible for their new life in Christ. They fixed their gaze way too low, at mere humans, and not high at the one who deserves their devotion. This had needlessly created divisions among them.

At 3:8, Paul considers God's workers and their relationship. He says that the planter and waterer, literally, "are one." By this he means that they have a single purpose toward which they work together. Despite those who might use them as tokens in bitter rivalry, Paul and Apollos held each other in mutual respect, as all God's workers should. As they focused on a singular goal set by God to spread the gospel, their allegiance to God made them loyal also to one another. However, they were also aware that each of them was accountable to God for the quality and success of their own, individual work.

Paul brings his metaphor of the farmer's field to a succinct, closing point when he says in 3:9, "We are both God's workers." God is in charge of both Apollos and Paul—and all kinds of workers—in working the fertile field of the world for the gospel's advance. But he offers two other summary statements. The first, "You are God's field," cultivates the metaphor he just developed in 3:5-8. The second, "You are God's building," looks ahead to the metaphor he will construct in 3:10-15.

Paul shifts to the building metaphor beginning in 3:10 to enhance the potential for the eschatological imagery he wants to develop and apply to the Corinthian situation. Fire will simply decimate crops no matter how well they are planted and tended. Paul also liked the implications of the role he saw for himself in the construction of the gospel building. As the senior builder or crew chief, he was principally involved in laying out a secure foundation in Corinth, while others had come along to put up the walls, rooms, and roof. Paul believed God had called him and prepared him for this role. It is not insignificant that foundations in the ancient world were made of big, solid stones expertly placed. There was no other material available for constructing a good foundation (even modern construction uses stones in the form of cement), just as there is only one appropriate material no matter who lays it for the gospel foundation, this being Jesus Christ (3:11). He knew that the foundation laid among them by him was done right.

In the Corinthian gospel building, Paul was aware that construction had moved past the laying of the foundation to other phases, and more notable yet, the construction was not complete. He said, "Others are building on it." Though probably he vaguely included Apollos in this group in a positive sense, it is notable that he did not mention him by name as he did in the agricultural metaphor. Anyway, Apollos was now with him in Ephesus (16:12), his phase of work being over. So, Paul primarily had in mind "others," who were in Corinth. These others would bring to the job a mixed bag of skill and materials. Some were highly qualified; others were inept. Precisely here is where the work site gets dangerous. Every poorly done feature of the building makes the whole that much more vulnerable to collapse. The very problems of rivalry he was attempting to counter were evidence of some bad workmanship in Corinth.

Paul seems to conceive of the construction of the Corinthian gospel building as ongoing, once again using the present tense "builds" in 3:12. As the church at Corinth developed, many workers would come and go, adding, improving, decorating. One can conceive of ancient public buildings that took centuries and multiple generations of workers to construct and were constantly improved and expanded. By introducing a variety of construction materials, Paul had the ingredients to express eschatological realities. The six materials listed basically amount to three that are combustible and three that are not. The three that are—wood, hay, straw—were materials for common homes but would never be used in massive, public building projects. The three noncombustible materials—gold, silver, jewels—would not be used for building structures but would provide the decorative splendor of a palace or a temple. That these were and continue to be highly valuable, in contrast to wood, hay, and straw, feeds right into Paul's eschatological application that follows.

In 3:13, Paul arrives where he has been headed with his construction metaphor—namely, the testing that occurs on judgment day. Like most Jews, Paul believed that God would one day come in judgment upon humanity, and, like most Christians, Paul incorporated into this belief the return of Christ in judgment upon all humanity. This judgment would amount to condemnation for those who rejected Christ but salvation and reward for those who trusted in him. Though salvation was understood to be secure in Christ because of God's grace, reward would vary according to the way a person served. Paul brought these assumptions to bear on the Corinthian situation by introducing fire as the testing agent of a building's quality of construction. Most public buildings are tested by weather or by invading armies or by fire, as were the buildings in Corinth itself only 100 years before, when it was sacked and burned by the Roman general Lucius Mummius. Most buildings will perish, but some or parts of some will stand (Shanor 1988:471). Paul believed this would be the case with the gospel building among the Corinthians. One day, judgment will come, and only the best workmanship will survive. This should come as a warning to the builders!

Paul did not conceive of the builders as everyone in the church (although he moves in that direction in chs 12–14). Rather, the builders are the leaders, the teachers, those responsible for developing, maturing, and strengthening the people, and thus erecting the gospel building. Are their materials and craftsmanship top quality or poor? This will be found out for certain on the eschatological day, and this will affect the "reward" of these leaders, just as ancient construction workers received fines and bonuses for their work (see note on 3:15). The idea that teachers are more responsible for their work than others is also found in James 3:1.

The fact that Paul envisaged both "reward" and "great loss" in 3:14-15 suggests that he did not consider all the Corinthian leaders to be doing shoddy work. It does mean, however, that some were doing such a lousy job that all their work would be "burned up." Paul will detail in 3:18-22 the warning this implies for the Corinthian church. For now, he was warning the builders, the leaders themselves. Though barely comforting, Paul did assure even the worst of them that their failure as leaders would not necessarily doom their personal, eternal destiny. Though their work may come crashing down around them, they could escape in the nick of time but with nothing left to show for their service to Christ.

The introduction of the temple metaphor in 3:16-17 develops from the building metaphor. If this building were a temple, or in fact "the temple of God," then other specific consequences must be entertained. This enabled Paul to become yet more harsh in his denunciation of a small minority of the current leaders in Corinth. He drew special attention to the importance of this metaphor with his opening words, "don't you realize." Saying that the Corinthian believers as a corporate unit are *the* temple of God is an incredibly bold assertion. Nearly all gods in the ancient world were enshrined in elaborate buildings, including the God of the Jews, who dwelt in the Most Holy Place. Paul's statement was a radically new paradigm that would not be easy for the Corinthians or any other ancient people to get their mind around. If it were true, though, it would be axiomatic to them that some representation of God would reside within their walls (Thiselton 2000:317). Thus, declaring that "the Spirit of God lives in you" will follow. Paul wrote earlier in chapter 2 about the Spirit's role in enabling people to embrace the un-wise truth of the crucified Christ. The focus in 3:16-17 is different. It is on the permanent indwelling of the Spirit, not in individual believers, but in the corporate entity of the people of God. And the emphasis is not universal but local. Believers in one locale, like Corinth, are a temple building where a true representation of God dwells. This makes this Corinthian building "holy," a sacred shrine, and desecrating it in any way a sacrilege. Thus, "anyone" who harmed the local church would be dealt with severely by God himself. If anyone "destroys" the church, God will "destroy" that person on that eschatological day anticipated in 3:12-15. With this severe warning, Paul was aiming at the worst of the Corinthian "builders," current leaders whose work was not just unintentionally shoddy but premeditated to destroy the church by, among other things, creating bitter divisions among the Corinthian believers. This becomes very clear in 3:21.

◆   ## 2. The foolish trap of rivalry (3:18-23)

¹⁸Stop deceiving yourselves. If you think you are wise by this world's standards, you need to become a fool to be truly wise. ¹⁹For the wisdom of this world is foolishness to God. As the Scriptures say,

"He traps the wise
    in the snare of their own
        cleverness."*

²⁰And again,

"The LORD knows the thoughts
    of the wise;
he knows they are worthless."*

²¹So don't boast about following a particular human leader. For everything belongs to you—²²whether Paul or Apollos or Peter,* or the world, or life and death, or the present and the future. Everything belongs to you, ²³and you belong to Christ, and Christ belongs to God.

3:19 Job 5:13.   3:20 Ps 94:11.   3:22 Greek *Cephas.*

NOTES

3:18 *Stop deceiving yourselves.* This is a rebuke formula Paul also uses later in 6:9 and 15:33, and also in Gal 6:7. The NLT correctly renders the negated present imperative to be calling the current readers to cease a current practice or thought. Twice Paul employs this verb to describe what the serpent did to Eve in Genesis 3 (2 Cor 11:3; 1 Tim 2:14).

If you think. Lit., "If anyone thinks." Paul used this phrase routinely to introduce rival views he opposed, as in 8:2; 11:16; 14:37; Gal 6:3; and Phil 3:4 (Soards 1999:83). The KJV's "seemeth" has been recognized universally to perpetuate a misleading notion, and therefore, the NLT corrects it to "think." The focus is on the perception individuals have of themselves, not on how others might mistakenly view them.

this world's standards. Lit., "this age." Paul uses the word "age" here, as he does in 1:20 and 2:6-8, to refer to the human limitations that are incumbent with the temporariness of this period until "the age to come," the period of eternity after this age. This, however, is not the same word as "world" (*kosmos* [TG2889, ZG3180]) in 3:19, which focuses more strictly on human activity and perspective. (See note on 1:21.)

fool. See note on 1:18.

3:19 *He traps . . . in the snare.* The verb *drassomai* [TG1405, ZG1533] from which this participle derives, only used here in the NT, means "catch." The cognate noun (*dragma*) describes "as much as one can grasp in a handful." There is no association with hunting as implied by the NLT. The NIV and ESV have "catches." In Job 5:13, it seems intended to play off the "hands" of the crafty. God's hand catches their hands to thwart their misdeeds. This is the only quotation of Job in the NT, although a likely allusion to Job 41:11 appears in Rom 11:35.

cleverness. Gr., *panourgia* [TG3834, ZG4111]. As in 2 Cor 4:2; 11:3; and Eph 4:14, this word refers to the trickery of people with sinister motives. Although it appears in Job 5:12 and not 5:13, it is an allowable translation of the Hebrew of Job 5:13. Paul probably transposed it from 5:12 into his translation of 5:13 (Soards 1999:84).

3:20 *the wise.* This is the only major substitution to Ps 94:11 [93:11, LXX] Paul made in this quotation, replacing "man" in order to align it to his subject matter.

worthless. Gr., *mataioi* [TG3152, ZG3469]. Only used two other times by Paul (15:17; Titus 3:9), the cognate verb of this adjective (*mateō*) refers to someone who is standing idle or loitering. Thus, it can mean empty, fruitless, or "worthless," as the NLT has. It is what we would expect to say of a "fool" rather than of a wise man.

3:21 So. This Greek word (*hōste* [TG5620, ZG6063]) usually introduces a result. Here and in 4:5; 10:12; 11:33; 14:39; 15:58 it introduces an imperative, a rarity in the NT (Robertson and Plummer 1911:71). In each case the "result" is that necessary behavior was demanded of the Corinthians, and in most cases this closes out Paul's discussion of an issue.

a particular human leader. Gr., *anthrōpois* [TG444, ZG476]. This is actually plural, so, more literally, "people." The NIV and ESV read "men." Though losing the plural, the NLT nicely tailors the sense to the context and eliminates the exclusive male language.

COMMENTARY

Beginning with 3:18, Paul abruptly moves to the pragmatic application of his carefully crafted effort to convict the Corinthians of the dangerous path they had taken in exalting human leaders. He openly demands reform. A stinging imperative occurs in 3:18 ("Stop deceiving yourselves!"), and another appears in 3:21 ("Don't boast!"). Paul also signals he is wrapping up his argument by reintroducing terms like "world," "fool," and "wise," which dominated 1:18–2:16. He rebuked their current behavior of rallying around different leaders as self-deceiving, because it was guided by sinful human principles rather than by Christian ideals. This absolutely must end.

In order for it to end, the Corinthians must invert their approach. In a reprise of 1:18-31, Paul called on those among them who considered themselves wise to renounce the normal human perspective on this and fully embrace the principles of the cross, principles of humility and self-sacrifice, which the world ridicules as folly (3:18; Witherington 1995:135). In calling for this reversal Paul may have also been mimicking a popular maxim of Socrates that extols ignorance as the necessary beginning of wisdom (Thiselton 2000:321). Even so, Paul kept it in the world of Jewish-Christian thought by solidifying its truth from God's perspective (3:19-20).

In these verses, Paul begins by restating the point of 1:25: What people normally consider wise and what God considers wise are in no way compatible; his wisdom confounds the wisdom of the world so much that it appears foolish. Paul then goes on to quote two passages of Scripture that establish God's superiority over human wisdom and God's utter disregard for those humans who consider themselves wise. The first, a fairly free version of Job 5:13, typical of the entire chapter of Job 5, pictures the so-called wise as deceitful thieves whose hands are grabbed by God's powerful hands. They might seem clever to other people, but God sees right through them. The second, identical to the Septuagint for Psalm 94:11 except replacing "people" with "the wise," describes the wise as though they are really fools. They might think they know the deep secrets of the world, but God knows they really know next to nothing.

With 3:21, Paul focuses his words on exactly what he wants from the Corinthians. Indicating this with the opening "so" followed by a four-word imperative clause, he demands that the Corinthians halt their rampant, divisive, unchristian attachment to mere human Christian leaders right now! Having spent nearly three chapters providing various arguments that led to this demand, he ventures down a new path of argumentation that is thoroughly theological. It opens with his audacious assertion that the Corinthians already possess everything. If this is true, it means that seeking to build up one's own self-esteem by declaring allegiance to different charismatic leaders of the church was aiming way too low. God had already made all those leaders plus many other things for the purpose of serving the Corinthians' needs. Each church leader "must be your servant," as Jesus taught (Mark 10:43).

Paul repeats the exact phrase "everything belongs to you" again at the end of 3:22 and then continues with his theological logic in 3:23. In between the repeated phrase he encloses eight words, each preceded by the word "and," or more literally, "or." This is a rhetorical device to make the audience consider the items one at a time. The eight are intended to be representative of "everything." He begins with "Paul or Apollos or Peter," three names that came up at the very beginning of the letter as having their own overzealous followers in Corinth. Surprisingly (and not necessary to his point), Paul extends the list to include five more items, none of them people but all of them progressively bold. The "world" comes first, perhaps because in Greek it alliterates with Peter (*Kēphas* [TG2876, ZG3064], *kosmos* [TG2889, ZG3180]) but also because it had been employed so negatively in the letter so far. Even human forces, both positive and negative, were subordinate to the Corinthians. If this is so, it follows that the most positive and negative forces that affect humanity, that is, life and death, are also now under their rulership and thus subordinate to them. For that matter, so too is whatever occurs currently in their lives as well as whatever remains to occur (Robertson and Plummer 1911:73). The thrust of the list is that everything that matters to their existence is already under subjection to them because these are under subjection to Christ, who is under subjection to God. It makes no sense to subject themselves blindly to someone or something that is already in subjection to Christ, even human leaders of the church like Paul or Apollos, who are mere "servants" of Christ (3:5) as are they.

In 3:23, Paul adds two necessary steps to establish his theological assertion that all these things are subordinate to the Corinthians. First, he reasons that this follows from the truth that as baptized believers in Christ, they are one with Christ in his victory over sin and death through the cross (Rom 6) and because of the resurrection that followed. As all things are in subjection to him (Phil 2:10; Col 2:10) so are all things in subjection to them. Note that Paul remains true to his corporate image of Christians, so important to the metaphors throughout this chapter. The pronouns "you" in 3:21-23 are all plural. As one people, as "the bride" (Eph 5), they belong to Christ, and only as one people, united around Christ and his cross, can they function unchained from subjection to the world, its people, and life's forces on them. The moment they divide into factions and allegiances, they sever their tie to Christ's lordship over all things.

Second, Paul reasons that Christ's lordship over all things follows from Christ's subordination to God as his servant. Often expressed in terms of sonship in the New Testament, with God as "father" and Christ as "son," this language attempts to grasp that God and Christ share the same divine nature, yet Christ performs a subordinate function when he voluntarily entered humanity as a man in the saving role as Messiah. In this sense he is God's willing agent just as the church is Christ's willing agent, and likewise the church's "servants are willing agents" (Barrett 1968:98).

Some consider this subordinate relationship between God and Christ to be only temporary, or soteriological, until his mission is fully completed (Fee 1987:155; Garland 2003:125; Witherington 1995:135). Others consider it permanent, or "ontological" (Barrett 1968:97; Oster 1995:104; Thiselton 2000:329). Paul's argument here in 3:23 does not answer this challenging theological matter. Later in 8:6, when discussing food offered to idols, he describes both in the exact same way as over "all things," and in 11:3, when discussing conduct in worship, he stair-steps as he does here to God as the head over Christ. Most importantly, in 15:20-28, he describes the final subordination of everything under Christ as seemingly the final "soteriological" act, yet he still says that after all this the Son will subject himself to God, so that God is "all in all." It would appear from this passage that Christ's subordination to God is not temporary but in some sense eternal.

It is not insignificant that the very last word in 3:23 is *theou* [TG2316, ZG2536], meaning "of God." To Paul's way of thinking God's sovereignty over all things trumps every thought, every relationship, every sociological order, every aspect of salvation, every aspect of Christ's mission. It must certainly trump the divisive rivalries that were occurring in the Corinthian church. His theological order of agents involved in this situation flows like this: God, to Christ, to the church, to the leaders of the church. The Corinthians erred by elevating mere human leaders of the church over the church itself. This is a grievous error that must be corrected.

We don't know how seriously the Corinthian church took Paul's warning. However, this divisive error of rallying around leaders over the church has played itself out over and over in the course of church history. The church has continued to divide itself into smaller and smaller segments over the centuries, many times over allegiance to personalities, both on the national and international scale, as well as on the small-town, local scale. Can we even conceive of the church as one and its leaders as *servants* of the church, which is the *servant* of Christ, who is the perfect example of a *servant* of God? We must.

◆   E. Arrogance Condemned (4:1-21)
      1. God judges motives (4:1-5)

So look at Apollos and me as mere servants of Christ who have been put in charge of explaining God's mysteries. ²Now, a person who is put in charge as a manager must be faithful. ³As for me, it matters very little how I might be evaluated by you or by any human authority. I don't even trust my own judgment on this point. ⁴My conscience is clear, but that doesn't prove I'm right. It is the Lord himself who will examine me and decide.

⁵So don't make judgments about anyone ahead of time—before the Lord returns. For he will bring our darkest secrets to light and will reveal our private motives. Then God will give to each one whatever praise is due.

NOTES

4:1 *Apollos and me.* In Greek this is the plural pronoun "us." The NLT has incorporated into the translation the common interpretation that it refers to Paul and Apollos, named in 3:4-6, 22, and again later in 4:6. Although very possible, this interpretation needlessly narrows the principles articulated, not only in 4:1-5 but also 4:6-13, to exclude Cephas (Peter), also named in the most immediate reference (3:22) and the wide network of apostolic workers in God's field.

servants . . . who have been put in charge. In order to simplify a redundancy in the Greek text (Barrett 1968:99; Horsley 1998:67), the NLT has incorporated two synonymous nouns for "servants" into one phrase. This occurs also in the NIV but not in the ESV. The first word (*hupēretas* [TG5257, ZG5677]) in classical Greek referred to a lower class of ship-rower, literally "under-rower," stationed at the lowest deck of a ship. It came to designate a servant (slave) who took orders from others, an assistant. Given that Paul has paired the two as synonyms in this context, it is best to avoid overemphasizing the difference between this type of servant and the second type, as was done in the past (Carson 1984:27-28; Robertson and Plummer 1911:74). This is a general term for a servant, perhaps even one with some managerial duties (Fee 1987:159; Thiselton 2000:335-336). The second word (*oikonomos* [TG3623, ZG3874]), more central to the image Paul wanted to cast for his comments to follow, is usually translated "steward" (ESV, RSV, NASB). It is the title for the servant, usually a slave, who has been placed in authority by the master over all his other servants (slaves) for making the household run productively. It is also used of individuals chosen to perform religious duties on behalf of societal and tradesmen associations, and even of city managers, like Erastus, named in Rom 16:23 (Collins 1999:168). In Titus 1:7, overseers of the church are called stewards. Many English-speaking churches have used the term "steward" in the modern era to designate the facilities manager of the church building.

God's mysteries. Gr., *mustēriōn theou* [TG3466/2316, ZG3696/2536]. The NLT renders the singular form of this phrase as "God's secret plan" in 2:1 and "the mystery of God" in 2:7, referring in both cases to the gospel (see notes on 2:1 and 2:7). The plural here surely includes the gospel (Barrett 1968:100; Fee 1987:160; Hays 1997:65) but may include wider aspects of God's revelation taught by apostolic workers. The plural may be intended to complete the image of apostles as "stewards of the mysteries," parallel but superior to positions held in the popular mystery cults, like Isis and others (Barrett 1968:99; Fee 1987:160).

4:3 *evaluated.* Translated "understand" in 2:14, "evaluate" in 2:15, "judgment" in 4:3, and "examine [me] and decide" in 4:4, this word (*anakrinō* [TG350, ZG373]) is used ten times in 1 Corinthians and only six more times in the rest of the NT. It emphasizes the very thorough scrutiny sometimes necessary to reach a good decision. In some contexts, as in 4:4, it includes the decision. In a court setting, it would include interrogation and cross-examination of witnesses (W. Schneider 1979:362).

human authority. Lit., "human day." Its use here seems to play off the common Hebrew practice of calling the final judgment day "the Day of the Lord" or even just "the Day" (see note on 3:13). Thus, the NLT rendering "human authority" correctly attempts to convey Paul's idea of some kind of lesser, human alternative setting in which people attempt to cast judgment on others.

4:4 *conscience.* Gr., *sunoida* [TG4894, ZG5323], only found elsewhere in Acts 5:2. The cognate noun (*suneidēsis* [TG4893, ZG5287]) is much more common, found 30 times in the NT, 8 times in 1 Corinthians (8:7-12 [three times]; 10:25-29 [five times]). Both are usually translated "conscience" in the sense of personal moral scruples people use to evaluate their own character. It is important not to impose on this NT word modern psychological assumptions of a guilty conscience or complex emotional struggle (see note on 8:7), as does Theissen (1987:59-66).

4:5 *make judgments.* Used 17 times in 1 Corinthians (*krinō* [TG2919, ZG3212]), this is not the same word used in 4:3 and 4:4 (*anakrinō* [TG350, ZG373]). This word focuses on the decision rendered rather than the considerations leading up to it, as in an athletic contest, judicial case, or in personal situations. In the court setting, it can refer to a negative verdict or condemnation. In the NT and in Paul's writings, when God's final verdict on people is intended, this is usually the word used (5:13; 11:32; Heb 13:4; 1 Pet 1:17; Rev 11:18).

bring . . . to light. This word (*phōtizō* [TG5461, ZG5894]) refers literally to shining a light on something and then metaphorically to enlighten or even instruct. It is used only here in 1 Corinthians and three times elsewhere by Paul (Eph 1:18; 3:9; 2 Tim 1:10).

darkest secrets. Lit., "the secrets of the dark." The aim is to complement the metaphor of "light" as an examiner of the darkest corners of people's lives.

reveal. Though frequent in 2 Corinthians (nine times) and in the rest of the NT, this is the only use of this word (*phaneroō* [TG5319, ZG5746]) in 1 Corinthians. A synonym of "bring to light" (*phōtizō* [TG5461, ZG5894]), it refers to making something clearly seen.

private motives. Lit., "the desires of the heart." In Hebrew idiom, the heart is the center of personhood and decision-making, not the mind as in Western thought. The NIV has "the motives of men's hearts," and the TEV reads "the hidden purposes of people's minds."

COMMENTARY

Paul opens chapter 4 by focusing on the role of the apostles as servants. Having initiated this connection in 3:5 when he called himself and Apollos "servants," he picks it up again in 4:1 when he urged people to consider "us" to be "servants." He even introduced two new words for servant (see note on 4:1). One is fairly generic, but the second is a specific type of servant—i.e., a steward handpicked by the owner to manage the estate and supervise the other servants in his stead. Rather than being in charge of a farm, business, or household, Paul named the responsibility he had been given to be the revealer of "God's mysteries," which focuses on the gospel message of the cross (2:1, 7). Paul's identification with this type of leader-servant will work well as he moves forward to consider his own personal accountability for his work and how out of place arrogant boasting is in serving the Lord.

Paul wasted no time honing in on the aspect of the leader-servant that he wanted to connect to his own apostolic work: faithfulness. The managing slave has a relationship of accountability only to the owner/master, no one else, and certainly not to other slaves managed on behalf of the master. For the master's part in this relationship, the master would not have chosen this servant to administer such immense responsibility unless the servant had demonstrated trustworthiness and the ability to make good decisions in the master's stead. Paul believed this fit perfectly his relationship to God—and to the Corinthians.

In 4:3, Paul shows that he adopted the leader-servant image as a setup to respond to the personal criticism he had received from some of the Corinthians. This may hearken back to his choice not to employ fancy rhetoric to enhance the gospel, as others had done (2:4-5; Witherington 1995:137). It may involve unknown criticisms of his apostleship related to the divisive rivalries Paul was concerned about (Barrett 1968:101; Fee 1987:156; Hays 1997:66; Horsley 1998:67; Soards 1999:86). However, Collins's (1999:167) contention is that Paul's language was mere "rhetorical strategy" unrelated to any kind of attack on him from the Corinthians. But this seems to ignore the personal language Paul uses and the criticism he mentions in 9:3, as well as the indisputable evidence from 2 Corinthians that Paul suffered humiliating criticism from people in Corinth.

What Paul says in 4:3 is that he is not at all concerned about what others think of him, including those in Corinth. They did not have jurisdiction over him, nor did any one person. As a leader-servant, his only concern was that he pleased the owner/master who selected him to run his operation. Neither did he put any stock in his own self-evaluation. He knew full well that, as any human, he more than likely would overestimate his accomplishments. This subtle point was a jab at leaders in Corinth, not directly noted until 4:18, who were arrogantly plugging their own accomplishments and contributing to the whole problem of divisive rivalries in the church.

In 4:4, Paul notes that his own self-evaluation shows nothing that he had done wrong in his dealings with them or with anyone else. The very fact that he mentions this, however, reveals that he had thought about it. Perhaps wondering whether criticism aimed at him from some people in Corinth was true, he conducted his own soul search and came up empty. However, he was not so vain as to offer his own self-test as proof of his innocence, only proof of his self-awareness of innocence. He fully acknowledged he may have messed up in ways only the "Lord himself" knew and would reveal upon his own extensive evaluation of Paul's life and ministry. However, since this cannot be known until the future day of judgment, Paul was content to wait.

Paul's reference to the time when "the Lord returns" in 4:5 makes most commentators feel confident that Paul had Christ in mind as his final evaluator in 4:4 (Barrett 1968:102; Fee 1987:162; Robertson and Plummer 1911:77). This makes sense because he calls himself a servant "of Christ" in 4:1, his call to apostleship was from Jesus Christ himself on the Damascus road (Acts 9:5; Gal 1:11-17), and final judgment in the New Testament usually depicts Christ acting on God's behalf (2 Tim 4:1). However, 4:5 also names God as the one who will be the arbiter of "praise" upon his army of workers. God is also clearly the controlling figure of chapter 3 and the one from whom the mysteries are revealed in 4:1. Paul was probably more interested in maintaining the imagery of the servant than uniformly assigning God or Christ exclusively to the role of Master (Collins 1999:173).

In 4:5, Paul again picks up the theme of final judgment from 3:12-15, beginning with his stated assumption that Christ's second coming will be its necessary prelude, a basic teaching throughout the New Testament. The notion that no one can hide even their thoughts and motives from God's searching eye (assumed about fools in 3:19-20) is stated plainly here regarding God's assessment of everyone. Highly unusual is Paul's assumption of a positive evaluation encased in the word "praise." This perhaps reveals that he was thinking about the judgment of Christian believers rather than the general judgment of all humanity, including those outside of Christ. His startling use of the word "praise" also intentionally contrasts with his castigation of the Corinthians (or others) who were completely out of place and inadequate in prematurely pronouncing "judgments" on God's servants (like himself) or anyone else. The present tense of the imperative "don't make judgments" suggests this activity was occurring in Corinth at the time of writing. Paul wanted to stop it.

2. Arrogance has no part in apostolic life (4:6-13)

⁶Dear brothers and sisters,* I have used Apollos and myself to illustrate what I've been saying. If you pay attention to what I have quoted from the Scriptures,* you won't be proud of one of your leaders at the expense of another. ⁷For what gives you the right to make such a judgment? What do you have that God hasn't given you? And if everything you have is from God, why boast as though it were not a gift?

⁸You think you already have everything you need. You think you are already rich. You have begun to reign in God's kingdom without us! I wish you really were reigning already, for then we would be reigning with you. ⁹Instead, I sometimes think God has put us apostles on display, like prisoners of war at the end of a victor's parade, condemned to die. We have become a spectacle to the entire world—to people and angels alike.

¹⁰Our dedication to Christ makes us look like fools, but you claim to be so wise in Christ! We are weak, but you are so powerful! You are honored, but we are ridiculed. ¹¹Even now we go hungry and thirsty, and we don't have enough clothes to keep warm. We are often beaten and have no home. ¹²We work wearily with our own hands to earn our living. We bless those who curse us. We are patient with those who abuse us. ¹³We appeal gently when evil things are said about us. Yet we are treated like the world's garbage, like everybody's trash—right up to the present moment.

4:6a Greek *Brothers.*   4:6b Or *If you learn not to go beyond "what is written."*

NOTES

4:6 *illustrate what I've been saying.* The verb *metaschēmatizō* [TG3345, ZG3571] means to change the form of something in the sense of disguising the true form. In Greek literature, as here, it refers to the use of allegory and figures of speech as a technique for conveying the truth about something else. Many recommend translating it "covert allusion" here (Collins 1999:176; Hall 1994:143-144; Thiselton 2000:349). Thiselton explains this as a "device to maintain the anonymity of the accused parties." While Paul spoke overtly of himself and Apollos, he was aiming covertly at other anonymous teachers in Corinth who were filled with self-importance.

If you pay attention to. Lit., "in order that you might learn from us." The clause is a part of the previous sentence. The final article (*to* [TG3588, ZG3836]) is intended as an introduction to a quotation. The NIV has "so that you may learn from us the meaning of the saying."

what I have quoted from the Scriptures. Although the NLT does a nice job of smoothing this together with the previous clause, it loses the fact that this is a quotation of a compacted teaching or saying. The saying goes, "Not beyond what is written" (cf. NLT mg). It is difficult to be sure what this means (Conzelmann 1975:86 says it is "unintelligible"), though many (Fee 1987:169; Hays 1997:69; Oster 1995:110; Robertson and Plummer 1911:81) take its intention to be what the NLT states: that the Corinthians are not free to ignore or reinterpret the points Paul has made so far based on the Scripture he has cited (1:19, 31; 2:9, 16; 3:19, 20). Since "what is written" is a formulaic expression for introducing a quotation from Scripture, it was probably a Jewish maxim of interpretation warning people not to interpret OT Scripture too loosely or twist it to say what they want it to say. It could possibly be a warning not to ignore the behavior requirements of the law (Garland 2003:135) or more likely the warning of Jer 9:24 against boasting, which Paul quotes in 1:31 (Hooker 1963-1964:129; Wagner 1998:282-283). Less likely is that it refers to a foundational congregational document (Hanges 1998:289) or that it alludes to young children tracing out letters as they learn to write (Fitzgerald 1988:124; Tyler 2001:252) applied in a moral sense to not going beyond a scriptural model in one's conduct (Ebner 1991:336). See Thiselton 2000:351-356 for a thorough discussion.

won't be proud. Only used one time outside 1 Corinthians (4:6, 18, 19; 5:2; 8:1; 13:4; Col 2:18), this verb (*phusioomai* [TG5448A, ZG5881]) focuses on the physical aspect—the swelling of the chest—that accompanies boastful pride. The ESV has "puffed up."

4:7 *make such a judgment.* The verb *diakrinō* [TG1252, ZG1359] is not the same word as in 4:5, referring to the final judgment reserved for God (*krinō* [TG2919, ZG3212]). Used five times in 1 Corinthians (4:7; 6:5; 11:29, 31; 14:29), this word literally refers to separating people who are in a fight. Paul uses it here in the not uncommon sense of making a distinction between people in terms of preferring one over another. The NIV reads "makes you different."

4:8 *already . . . already.* Gr., *ēdē . . . ēdē* [TG2235, ZG2453]. This word appears at the beginning of each clause, signaling emphasis.

have everything you need. Gr., *kekoresmenoi este.* Grammatically, this is a periphrastic perfect. The verb *korennumi* [TG2880, ZG3170], only used here and in Acts 27:38, can describe a person's stomach being full to the point of having no more appetite, then generally to describe anything that has been filled to absolute capacity.

rich. Only used here in 1 Corinthians, this word (*plouteō* [TG4147, ZG4456]) primarily refers to material wealth but can mean to be rich in other things.

begun to reign in God's kingdom. The emphasis here, as Fee (1986:173) notes, is not on the Corinthians' status as kings but on their acting—quite inappropriately—as though they were royalty. Paul wryly drew upon the well-known sayings of Stoics and Cynics that true wealth and true royalty lie with those who are truly wise. See Epictetus (*Dissertationes* 3.22, 49), Plutarch (*De tranquillitate animi* 427a), Seneca (*Benefits* 7.2.5), Cicero (*Pro Murena* 29.61), and Philo (*Abraham* 261).

4:9 *prisoners of war.* Strictly, this refers to people who are "condemned to die" (*epithanatios* [TG1935, ZG2119]) such as criminals and other prisoners. The NLT rendering, coupled with translating *eschatos* [TG2078, ZG2274] as "the end of a victor's parade," reflects a decision to interpret all of these to allude to the regular occurrence of victory parades of conquering generals with their prisoners captured in battle to the city arena where they were often slaughtered (Oster 1995:112). Paul clearly depicts apostles in such a parade in 2 Cor 2:14, but the language is different here. The NIV reflects the same decision, and many interpreters agree (Fee 1987:175; Hays 1997:71; Witherington 1995:143). However, more recent interpreters (Blomberg 1994:90; Collins 1999:188; Thiselton 2000:360) favor an allusion to the gladiatorial arena where the last contestants were required to fight to the death. The more generic ESV translation ("God has exhibited us apostles as last of all, like men sentenced to death") allows for either allusion.

spectacle. Gr., *theatron* [TG2302, ZG2519]. This word refers literally to a theater, as it does in its only other appearances in the NT (Acts 19:29-31). It can also refer to the spectators or, as here, to the actual show. The word choice indicates that Paul was playing off the gruesome type of display shown in the gladiatorial arena of victims mauled to death by animals or slaughtered at the end of a victory parade.

4:10 *Our dedication to Christ makes us look like fools.* Lit., "We are fools because of Christ." The NLT attempts to explain a sarcastic figure of speech that Paul imported from the Corinthians' criticisms of him. "Fools" may play off the Greek theatrical stereotype of the buffoon, commonly used as the butt of jokes for their stupidity (Welborn 2002:424).

honored. Related to the word "glory," this word (*endoxos* [TG1741, ZG1902]) includes the benefits of being honored. As 4:11 lists the visible attributes of being dishonored, the visible conditions of being honored are included.

ridiculed. This word (*atimos* [TG820, ZG872]) negates the widely used word for "honor" (*timē* [TG5092, ZG5507]) in the sense of the lack of respect a person receives from others.

4:11 *we don't have enough clothes to keep warm.* Used only here in the NT, this word (*gumniteuō* [TG1130, ZG1217]) literally means "to be naked" not only in the literal sense but often, as conveyed by the NLT, in the sense of having less clothing than necessary for the weather conditions or perhaps simply of a person who has only the clothes on their back. The NIV translates it as "in rags"; the ESV reads "poorly dressed."

have no home. This is another word (*astateō* [TG790, ZG841]) used only here in the NT. It refers to something that is unstable or to a person who is a wanderer, with no permanent home. Paul's use of it connects to Jesus' words about himself (Luke 9:58) and to his disciples (Mark 6:8-11). Overcoming hardship, such as homelessness, was the mark of a truly wise man in the ancient Greco-Roman world (Fitzgerald 1988:203).

4:12 *work . . . with our own hands.* One of the core values of Jewish culture was that every male should learn a skill, including rabbis (*Avot* 2:2; 4:5; t. *Qiddushin* 1:11; b. *Qiddushin* 29a). Greek philosophers, except for a few Cynics and Stoics, frowned on performing manual labor, preferring to live by fees collected from students (Collins 1999:185). Paul had a habit of emphasizing his manual labor (Still 2004:25).

4:13 *appeal gently.* Used six times in 1 Corinthians (1:10; 4:16; 14:31; 16:12, 15) and 18 times in 2 Corinthians, this word (*parakaleō* [TG3870, ZG4151]) normally adds urgency and sincerity to the idea of calling someone. Thus, "exhort" or "implore" are common meanings of the word. However, it can move toward the overtly positive side of communication in the sense of "comfort," "encourage," and here of "speaking in a friendly manner."

when evil things are said about us. This is the only use of this word (*dusphēmeō* [TG1425.1, ZG1555]) in the NT; it specifically refers to speaking an evil omen against someone. It generally refers to "slander," or publicly defaming the character of another person.

garbage. Gr., *perikatharmata.* The only use of this word in the NT, it refers to the scum that comes off when one thoroughly scours a pan or utensil. Since the removal of such material makes the utensil clean or pure, this word can have a cultic or theological meaning of "scapegoat" as in Prov 21:18. Based on this some would press that Paul means the apostles, in their suffering that comes from their identity with Christ, are a kind of scapegoat (Barrett 1968:112-113; Soards 1999:98) or even "expiation" (Hanson 1987:32), but this demands too much from this context. The normal sense fits best here as a complementary synonym to the word that follows (Fee 1987:180; Collins 1999:191; Conzelmann 1975:90; Robertson and Plummer 1911:88; Thiselton 2000:364-365). The NIV and ESV translate it "scum."

trash. Gr., *peripsēma* [TG4067, ZG4370]. The only use of this word in the NT, it refers to what has been rubbed off, the dirt from people's bodies, perhaps from people's shoes (Thiselton 2000:365). Both this word and its synonym above (*perikatharma* [TG4027, ZG4326]) were used as derogatory terms for criminals or the worst people in society, the sense Paul most likely means here. The NLT's "garbage . . . trash" is a good functional-equivalence translation.

right up to the present moment. Gr., *heōs arti* [TG2193/737, ZG2401/785]. As the final words of 4:13, this intentionally bookends with "even now" (*achri tēs arti hōras* [TG5610, ZG6052], "hour") in 4:11, sectioning off the hardships in between. Both phrases contrast with the repeated "already" of 4:8 (Collins 1999:191), marking out the opposite condition of the apostles (like Paul) and the Corinthians, who believed they had already arrived at the pinnacle of Christian success.

COMMENTARY

Arrogant boasting has no place in the life of the church or in the relationships between those who serve God together in spreading the gospel. Beginning with 4:6, Paul seeks to explain to the Corinthians that this is what he has been trying to drive home to them both in his analogies and in his exposition of Scripture. The metaphors he used with respect to himself and Apollos, especially the field imagery (3:5-9) but probably also the building (3:10-15), were presented as teaching tools and nothing else. He didn't want anyone to think that he had a real problem with the way Apollos conducted himself in Corinth or that he thought Apollos had done any arrogant boasting. That there was no rift between them is clear, since Apollos had returned to Paul in Ephesus (16:12).

The Scripture Paul most likely had his eye on is Jeremiah 9:24, which he quoted in 1:31: "If you want to boast, boast only about the LORD." He saw arrogant boasting to be the fundamental sin in the Corinthian problem. Division in the church was perpetuated by people who attached personal pride to their favorite leader and then became competitive with those who attached themselves to another. Some unnamed, local Corinthian leaders probably encouraged this behavior and thereby are the real targets of Paul's harshest warnings, as seen in the metaphor of the temple in 3:16-18. Boasting, a natural human trait, must focus on God and what he has done and is doing. Paul's "boasting" in 2 Corinthians 11–12 is a good example. For people to elevate themselves above the power of God's handiwork goes "beyond Scripture" and distorts this trait into personal sin that can destroy the very thing God is trying to build: unity of the church through the cross of Christ.

In 4:7, Paul supports his pronouncements in the previous verse with a series of rhetorical questions. Despite the "What" in the NLT, the first question literally asks "Who": Who really has the authority to differentiate between people? The clear implication is that it is "not you," the Corinthians, who were making unwarranted distinctions by selecting their favorite leaders and lifting them up over others. The only one who can make such distinctions fairly and will do so ultimately is God (3:13).

The second rhetorical question in 4:7 makes it apparent that Paul had in mind not only God's eschatological discerning of believers' rewards but also the advance on those awards they had already received. In terms of their salvation, they had received nothing that is not from God. Recall that God is the one who brings the gospel to full flower in a person's life (3:6). Even those who plant the gospel in peoples' lives plant with seed they have been given by God. Besides all that, as Paul emphasized, no human being is wise enough to accept the gospel apart from the work of God's Spirit (2:10-16). Paul may also be anticipating what he wrote in 1 Corinthians 12–14 concerning the gifts of the Spirit (Collins 1999:181), visible manifestations of God's discernment of people's individual spiritual capacities to dispense the gospel and contribute to the well-being of the believing community.

The third rhetorical question in 4:7, framed as part of a conditional clause, accuses the Corinthians of doing the exact opposite of what they should be doing.

Knowing they have received their salvation as a gift from God, they were absolutely out of place in giving the ultimate praise to one of his many agents who had played a part in their fortunate position. Regardless of the fact that very capable human agents have worked on God's behalf, it is God and God alone who got them where they are. Any boasting in one of his agents or exalting one of his agents insults God. They must not do this. To use a strange contemporary phrase, they are "looking the gift-horse in the mouth" regarding their salvation and spiritual growth. They were not showing proper appreciation for God and were improperly stepping in territory that is his alone in sizing up his workers and calling one out for praise.

In 4:8, Paul comes closest to revealing the theological error that may have fueled the Corinthians' unacceptable arrogance and boasting. Despite the fact that it is dripping with sarcasm, Paul's mocking depiction of them as reigning kings and his accent on "already" strongly suggests that they, or at least those most at fault, had accepted what we would call today an "overrealized eschatology" (Fee 1987:173; Hays 1997:70; Thiselton 1977–1978:511; Thiselton 2000:358). This means that they had appropriated future promises of the kingdom of God to themselves in the present. Paul's fierce skepticism of their position comes in the last clause of the verse when he wonders how the promised kingdom could have come without him knowing about it. He seems to be missing out on the party; yet the Corinthians—who had only been believers for just a few years and who first heard the gospel from him—were now insiders about the realized kingdom and were already celebrating!

When Paul described the way the Corinthians were behaving—as being rich and reigning as royalty—he could have been spouting back in their faces slogans he knew they used to describe themselves. He heard this from his informants, Chloe's people. The slogans themselves mirror Stoic thought that would have been very familiar in Corinth. This suggests, at least, that the Corinthians were being influenced indirectly by non-Christian philosophy in their popular culture—a common problem for Christianity in all ages. It may suggest that some of their own, unnamed, homegrown leaders had mingled popular secular teachings with Christian notions of the future.

In 4:9, Paul wishes to paint a picture that is antithetical to the one the Corinthians had painted. Quite the opposite from the reign of God dominating, the Christian church, its leaders and those who believe, are on a death march. They have been subject to ridicule, scorn, persecution, and death, like the last subjects for slaughter in the arena or the last in a parade of captured people. At least this was Paul's experience and probably that of most believers at that time (e.g., the Thessalonians), especially apostles and other leaders who were naturally more visible. Oddly, the Corinthians did not seem to have experienced this negative response from those around them, despite the problems when Paul was there initially (Acts 18:12-17). To their disgrace, Paul wondered how the Corinthians could possibly view themselves as regal spectators, sitting beside the cultural enemies of Christianity, watching apostles and other believers getting slaughtered. If so, theirs was an entirely different version of the Christian life than what he taught them—one that was completely unacceptable and at odds with reality.

The world of spectators Paul envisaged includes "angels," God's own messengers, because he viewed the clash of the Christian church with human culture to be a cosmic spectacle. God's angels provide moral encouragement and comfort, as apostles and others suffer in the struggle to spread the gospel. In contrast, the general populace at the arena thrills at the demise of Christian adherents, as if it were entertaining sport. The spectacle of struggling apostles alluded to in 4:9 will lead Paul into a longer discussion of the life of an apostle like himself in 4:10-13.

Further dramatizing the Corinthians as being above the fray while everyone else—including Paul—was being rejected by the dominant culture, Paul constructed a series of three antithetical statements in 4:10. The first pits against each other the two broadest categories Paul used in the epistle (1:18-25; 3:18-19): the wise and the foolish. In the eyes of the world, those like Paul who are committed to the gospel of the cross are fools. Paul embraced this label as a badge of honor, but the Corinthians resisted it. They wanted the world to view them as wise, something Paul considered impossible if they were committed to the true gospel.

The second antithesis sets in contrast two categories also introduced in 1:18-25 and then reemphasized in 2:3-5: power and weakness. Paul identified with weakness, while the Corinthians showed by their actions that they wanted to identify with power. In this, once again, they were on the wrong side. Power-seeking is worldly, all too human, like arrogant boasting. The gospel requires that believers renounce such an outlook and submit to one another in love (Rom 12:10) and, equally important, submit to the undeserved abuse from the world (1 Pet 2:17-25).

The third antithesis attacks the Corinthians at their most vulnerable point. Like Japanese culture today, the lives of people in Greco-Roman culture and no doubt in Corinth were largely driven by the quest to receive cultural honor and to avoid shame. Paul's mocking challenged them to renounce this prime directive. Accepting the Christian faith means embracing shame, the shame of the cross. Paul had done so, but would the Corinthians, who still clung to honor in the world's eyes?

In 4:11, Paul lists five hardships that characterized his life and would be paralleled in the lives of other true apostles and Christian leaders. He would list many more in 2 Corinthians (2 Cor 4:7-12; 6:4-5; 11:23-29; 12:10), where the credibility of his apostolic ministry was challenged much more fiercely than it was at this point in 1 Corinthians. In both cases, his purpose was to describe how his life and ministry embodied the suffering and rejection of Christ. Here, in particular, the list of hardships illustrates his acceptance of cultural rejection that sees him as foolish, weak, and ridiculed. Lack of sufficient water, food, clothing, and housing put him in the ranks of the poor and slaves. These stand in stark contrast to the Corinthians, whom Paul depicted as wealthy (4:8). The notion that Paul had no home parallels Jesus' statement that he had "no place even to lay his head" (Matt 8:20; Luke 9:58).

A sixth characteristic of Paul's ministry is introduced in 4:12. Although performing manual labor was a characteristic of the poor and slaves, and probably made some of the Corinthians think less of him, it was a hardship that Paul imposed on himself. Supporting himself by his skill as a tentmaker was a matter of principle with him, deeply ingrained from his training as a rabbi and reinforced by his conviction that people needed to see that the gospel was totally free (Acts 18:3; 20:34;

1 Thess 2:9; 2 Thess 3:8). This principle seems to have been a bone of contention between Paul and some in Corinth who desired to be his benefactors (9:4-18; 2 Cor 11:7-9; 12:13-17).

As a further way of characterizing his apostolic ministry, beginning in 4:12 and continuing into 4:13, Paul lists three types of abuse he endured, followed by the way he responded to each. Each couplet is grammatically parallel, the abuse listed as a particle first, followed by a verb stating the response. The first two, blessing those who curse and enduring those who abuse, echoes Jesus' teaching in the Sermon on the Mount (Matt 5:44; Luke 6:27). The third is similar to the teaching in 1 Peter 2:23 and 3:16-17 in that it calls upon believers to respond in a friendly manner to those who verbally abuse. To summarize his mistreatment by Christianity's cultural opponents, Paul came up with two words used nowhere else in the New Testament. He says people treat apostles (like himself) as they do the scum scraped from a used pot or the muck from their shoes (see notes on 4:13).

Thus, the lot of apostles and true Christian leaders is far from the life of privilege and rule some Corinthians and their leaders seemed to think. Rather, the Corinthians needed to look at Paul and his life as a model of what to expect and how to behave. They should expect rejection and abuse from those in their world rather than a welcome reception. Most likely, they would have to choose Christ or social acceptance. This leaves no room for arrogant boasting in their own attainments but only in what Christ has accomplished through them.

◆   ### 3. Paul will come to confront the arrogant (4:14-21)

¹⁴I am not writing these things to shame you, but to warn you as my beloved children. ¹⁵For even if you had ten thousand others to teach you about Christ, you have only one spiritual father. For I became your father in Christ Jesus when I preached the Good News to you. ¹⁶So I urge you to imitate me.

¹⁷That's why I have sent Timothy, my beloved and faithful child in the Lord. He will remind you of how I follow Christ Jesus, just as I teach in all the churches wherever I go.

¹⁸Some of you have become arrogant, thinking I will not visit you again. ¹⁹But I will come—and soon—if the Lord lets me, and then I'll find out whether these arrogant people just give pretentious speeches or whether they really have God's power. ²⁰For the Kingdom of God is not just a lot of talk; it is living by God's power. ²¹Which do you choose? Should I come with a rod to punish you, or should I come with love and a gentle spirit?

NOTES

4:14 *to shame.* Formed from the verb *trepō* ("turn," not found in the NT in the base form) and *en* [TG1722, ZG1877] (in), this word (*entrepō* [TG1788, ZG1956]) can refer to turning in on oneself from a sense of shame (as here and in 2 Thess 3:14 and Titus 2:8) or to one person turning toward another in respect or honor (as in Luke 20:13 and Heb 12:9). Shame (and honor) were powerful moral forces in ancient Greek culture in ways not present in Western culture but more akin to their role in Eastern culture still today (Thiselton 2000:369).

4:15 *ten thousand.* Gr., *murious* [TG3463A, ZG3692]. Only used here and in 14:19 in the NT, in the singular form, it means "numberless" or "countless"; in the plural, as here, it refers specifically to 10,000.

others to teach. The Greek behind this is *paidagōgos* [TG3807, ZG4080], who was not merely a teacher but a highly valued guardian, companion, and tutor. In wealthy homes, the master's sons would each be assigned a highly educated slave to raise them from childhood to adulthood, accompany them to school, drill them on assignments, discipline them, and protect them.

spiritual father. The word here is simply "father," but Paul certainly intended it in the sense of the NLT. It was common in the Greco-Roman world for students to call their teachers "father" and likewise for teachers to call their students "sons" (Keener 1993:461). More importantly, the parental relationship gave teachers responsibilities in moral and social guidance and not simply knowledge. The Corinthians idealized the Roman emperor as a father figure, and Paul may have drawn on this image both in benevolence and discipline toward the Corinthians in this context (Lassen 1991:134-135). It is possible that Paul appealed to his fatherhood so as to be able to demand that they imitate him (Castelli 1991:98-101).

4:17 *Timothy.* He was one of the most faithful of Paul's lieutenants on his missionary team. A young man of mixed race (Jewish mother, Greek father), he joined up with Paul when he revisited Lystra and Derbe at the early stage of the second missionary journey (Acts 16:1-3). He was with Paul during the writing of seven of his epistles (Rom 16:21; Phil 1:1; Col 1:1; 1 Thess 1:1; Phlm 1:1), including both 1 and 2 Corinthians (16:10-11; 2 Cor 1:1). Timothy was sent out to Corinth and perhaps some other cities along the way before Paul wrote 1 Corinthians (Barrett 1968:116; Fee 1987:188; Thiselton 2000:374).

Christ Jesus. Gr., *Christō Iēsou* [TG5547/2424, ZG5986/2652]. This reading has the excellent support of 𝔓46 ℵ C D¹ 33 1739. The alternative reading in some Western manuscripts (D* F G) of "the Lord Christ" (*kuriō Iēsou*) was influenced by "the Lord" (*kuriō* [TG2962, ZG3261]) in the previous line. The alternative of "Christ" (*Christō*) alone, though shorter and found in manuscripts A and B, was probably influenced by the dominance of the single name in 1 Corinthians. Yet the double name does occur in the immediately preceding usage in 4:15 and is most likely correct.

4:20 *the Kingdom of God.* This is key terminology in the synoptic Gospels. This instance is one of only nine uses of the term in Paul's letters, three more times in 1 Corinthians (6:9-10; 15:50) and five more times elsewhere (Rom 14:17; Gal 5:21; Eph 5:5; Col 4:11; 2 Thess 1:5). The phrase nearly always carries with it the eschatological expectations established in Jesus' teaching (Barrett 1968:118) without excluding some sense of its present inauguration.

4:21 *rod.* This word (*rhabdos* [TG4464, ZG4811]) refers to a stick or walking staff (Matt 10:10), even a fishing stick/rod. As a tool of corporal punishment of children by fathers, it is advocated in the OT (2 Sam 7:14; Prov 10:13; 22:15; cf. Exod 21:20; Isa 10:24; Lam 3:1) and also in Greek literature (Plato *Laws* 3.700c; Plutarch *Moralia* 268d; 693f). The NIV's "whip" is inappropriately misleading (Thiselton 2000:378).

COMMENTARY

With 4:14, Paul begins to explain why he was harsh in what he had previously written, especially the severe rebuke in 3:18-21 and the mockery of the Corinthians in 4:8. His denial that he had spoken like this to shame them (4:14) to conform to his teaching seems at first to be empty. Who wouldn't feel shame upon hearing their unacceptable attitudes and behavior exposed as forcefully as Paul had done? However, it is best to take him at his word, especially since he does in fact admit to desiring to shame them twice later in the epistle, with regard to their lawsuits (6:5) and their questioning Christ's resurrection (15:34). What he was doing was giving them a stern warning as a father would give his children. He was not disgusted or appalled by their party spirit and arrogant boasting, just terribly disappointed. He was also fearful that if they did not correct their behavior, serious consequences could follow. He wrote to warn them, as he says—an approach common in his writings to other communities of believers (Rom 15:14; Col 1:28–3:16; 1 Thess 5:12, 14).

In 4:15, Paul states his right to admonish the Corinthians in their wrong thinking and misdeeds. He had the right to discipline them as a father because in the spiritual sense he was their father, having preached the gospel to them first, birthed them into the faith, and nurtured them for the first 18 months of their new life in Christ. Other teachers may have come along, and that is all well and good. But only he was their father with the special responsibility toward children that comes with parenthood. Although he exaggerated the number of teachers they had as "10,000," he did speak of these teachers positively. He used the special term that refers to the tutor-companions who were functional guardians of boys from wealthy homes in the Greco-Roman world. This is somewhat surprising given the metaphorical images that implicated some of their leaders (3:12-23). Perhaps, in the interests of tapping their good will, he was being conciliatory as he explained his own actions in the letter.

Paul's appeal to imitate him (a closing appeal in 4:16) may seem vain to us, but it was not meant so, nor would it have been received so by the Corinthians. He did so elsewhere (Gal 4:12; 1 Thess 1:6; 2:14; 2 Thess 3:7-9), as well as later in this epistle (11:1). Teachers in the ancient world were not simply information givers. They worked to model their own teaching in their person, to become a living example of their teaching to their students and others. To observe and imitate was the best way for their students to appropriate their teaching. Paul was doing nothing different. As he had explained at length in the preceding paragraph in particular, he had attempted to embody the gospel of the cross in his own person (Still 2004:27; H. Williams 2003:124-125). Since it is this that they had not yet grasped properly, Paul was not at all reticent to encourage them to model their behavior after his. Maybe this was the best way for them to get it. It also makes clear that Paul was not "all talk" about taking "Christ crucified" into their lives. He was doing it, too.

With his argument concluded by 4:17, Paul transitions into travel details, something more typical near the end of a letter. Using the same tender, fatherly language he used with the Corinthians in 4:14-16, he notes that Timothy was on his way to them. His description of Timothy as his "beloved and faithful child" suggests that Paul was not only involved in Timothy's conversion but that Timothy, now after traveling with Paul for a while, had gained his complete trust. He went in Paul's stead with a commission to reinforce the teaching Paul had just provided in the opening chapters of this epistle, including testimony about how Paul lived his life in conformity to Christ. Paul did not need to explain to the Corinthians who Timothy was because he was with Paul in Corinth for at least a portion of the 18 months when Paul founded the church (Acts 18:5).

With the same Greek word (*phusioomai* [TG5448A, ZG5881]) used in 4:6 (NLT, "proud"), in 4:18 Paul names the problem he has been aiming to correct: arrogance. Arrogance led to the boasting about leaders that led to the strain on the unity of the Corinthian church. Whether "some" refers to leaders or their followers or both, at least it was a minority. They must have had enough power, however, that they didn't believe anyone but Paul could stand up to them. They thought they were safely insulated by distance. Perhaps they had already run Apollos out of town (16:12). Regardless, Paul now confronted them with what he said in the letter. He sent Timothy to reinforce the message of the letter. Most importantly, as he explains in 4:19, Paul was planning his own trip from Ephesus to deal with them. He warned them to alter their outlook and behavior or face the consequences.

Paul's plan, as he continues to discuss it in 4:19, was to come as quickly as possible, and 16:5-7 says he has scheduled his trip. However, Paul knew that if he had somehow run ahead of God's will on this, it might be delayed. Sometimes God had other emergency plans for him, as when he was called in a vision to abort his plans in order to go to Macedonia (Acts 16:7-10). In typical Jewish form, "if the Lord wills" (see Jas 4:15), Paul will restate his deference to God's will regarding this trip again in 16:7, using an expression he uses elsewhere (Rom 15:23; 1 Thess 3:11; Phlm 1:22).

Paul's specific mention of the "talk" of these arrogant people and whether it had any "power" indicates that these people were leaders or teachers and that they were the same people who were criticizing Paul for the poor quality and lack of force in his rhetoric (2:1-5). He was confident that should he be required to go toe to toe with them in person, they would back down. This would not be because of any persuasive rhetoric of Paul's but strictly because of the power of God in his teaching. Paul did not believe that their teaching—which was antithetical to his, as he had demonstrated—contained God's power and authority. Inevitably, they would wilt, and God's true teaching would reign supreme. Rarely mentioned in his writing, Paul introduces the Kingdom of God in 4:20 because of the language of reigning used in their teaching (4:8). The future reign of God does manifest itself in the present but not in arrogance and boasting. Rather, its power should be manifested in the humble lives of those who identify with the crucified Christ.

The power of God's present reign is also evidenced in stern discipline against people like these who arrogantly transpose the power of the gospel into privilege. Paul offered them a choice: Give up their current position, which inverts the true implications of the gospel, or be prepared for him to come carrying God's rod. Remaining true to his father-child disposition, he spoke to them like children caught red-handed in their sin. He would wield a rod of punishment if necessary, but he would rather greet them with a warm embrace of forgiveness and love, like a patient father deepens his relationship with his repentant children.

What happened? Paul actually ended up scrapping his original travel plans and taking a boat across the Aegean Sea from Ephesus in order to see them quickly (as 2 Cor 1:15–2:4 describes). As he describes it there and in 2 Cor 7:5-13, this trip was an embarrassing disaster. Paul apparently did confront these people he wrote against here in chapters 1–4; he was not triumphant as he predicted. Rather, it appears they heaped personal abuse on him. No one in Corinth came to his defense, and he left humiliated, returning to Ephesus furious and fearful the Corinthian church might be a lost cause. Reconciliation did not come until after he wrote the so-called "severe" letter (see Introduction). God's power does indeed overcome counterfeit teaching in the church, but even so, not always in the timing and manner we expect.

◆ III. Paul's Response to Reports of Negligent Community Discipline (5:1–6:20)

A. Demand for Expulsion of the Believer Guilty of Immoral Conduct (5:1-13)

I can hardly believe the report about the sexual immorality going on among you— something that even pagans don't do. I am told that a man in your church is living in sin with his stepmother.* ²You are so proud of yourselves, but you should be mourning in sorrow and shame. And you should remove this man from your fellowship.

³Even though I am not with you in person, I am with you in the Spirit.* And as though I were there, I have already passed judgment on this man ⁴in the name of the Lord Jesus. You must call a meeting of the church.* I will be present with you in spirit, and so will the power of our Lord Jesus. ⁵Then you must throw this man out and hand him over to Satan so that his sinful nature will be destroyed* and he himself* will be saved on the day the Lord* returns.

⁶Your boasting about this is terrible. Don't you realize that this sin is like a little yeast that spreads through the whole batch of dough? ⁷Get rid of the old "yeast" by removing this wicked person from among you. Then you will be like a fresh batch of dough made without yeast, which is what you really are. Christ, our Passover Lamb, has been sacrificed for us.* ⁸So let us celebrate the festival, not with the old bread* of wickedness and evil, but with the new bread* of sincerity and truth.

⁹When I wrote to you before, I told you not to associate with people who indulge in sexual sin. ¹⁰But I wasn't talking about unbelievers who indulge in sexual sin, or are greedy, or cheat people, or worship idols. You would have to leave this world to avoid people like that. ¹¹I meant that you are not to associate with anyone who claims to be a believer* yet indulges in sexual sin, or is greedy, or worships idols, or is abusive, or is a drunkard, or cheats people. Don't even eat with such people.

¹²It isn't my responsibility to judge outsiders, but it certainly is your responsibility to judge those inside the church who are sinning. ¹³God will judge those on the outside; but as the Scriptures say, "You must remove the evil person from among you."*

5:1 Greek *his father's wife.*   5:3 Or *in spirit.*   5:4 Or *In the name of the Lord Jesus, you must call a meeting of the church.*   5:5a Or *so that his body will be destroyed;* Greek reads *for the destruction of the flesh.*   5:5b Greek *and the spirit.*   5:5c Other manuscripts read *the Lord Jesus;* still others read *our Lord Jesus Christ.*   5:7 Greek *has been sacrificed.*   5:8a Greek *not with old leaven.*   5:8b Greek *but with unleavened [bread].*   5:11 Greek *a brother.*   5:13 Deut 17:7.

NOTES

5:1 sexual immorality. Gr., *porneia* [TG4202, ZG4518]. Used five times in 1 Corinthians (5:1 [twice]; 6:13, 18; 7:2), more than in any of Paul's other letters, this is the technical word for prostitution and the general word for any sexual activity outside of marriage. It comes into English in words related to pornography.

is living. This is the very common word "have" (*echō* [TG2192, ZG2400]) applied to the cohabitation and sexual activity of these two people. The present tense indicates this was ongoing.

stepmother. Lit., "the wife of his father," referring not to his mother, but a young step-mother, or possibly a concubine of his father (De Vos 1998:106). The father may have no longer been living or may have divorced her. The language is borrowed from Lev 18:7-8 (LXX), where this sin is banned among the Hebrews (Fee 1987:200). In the OT incest is banned (Lev 18:18; 20:11; Deut 27:20, 22-23). In the Mishnah (*Sanhedrin* 7:4) this sin is punishable by stoning. Roman authors expressed disgust at incest, including marriage to a mother-in-law or stepmother (Gaius *Institutes* 1:63; Cicero *Pro Cluentio* 5.27).

5:2 *mourning in sorrow and shame.* Its only use in 1 Corinthians, this word (*pentheō* [TG3996, ZG4291]) simply means "mourn" (ESV) or "filled with grief" (cf. NIV). The NLT has attempted to convey the purpose of this attitude among the Corinthians, principally the shame they should feel for the way they accepted the sinful man in their midst rather than disciplining him.

remove. This is the aorist passive subjunctive of a very common word (*airō* [TG142, ZG149]), meaning "lift" or "carry." Here, it has the sense of expulsion from the group, by force if nec-essary. It can mean "kill" in very special contexts, an important consideration in light of the controversies in interpreting "handing over to Satan" in 5:5.

5:3 *Spirit.* Gr., *pneuma* [TG4151, ZG4460]. The NIV, ESV, TEV, and alternative NLT translation is "spirit." There is some hesitation in taking this to indicate Paul's metaphysical pres-ence with them apart from his body. While Barrett (1968:123) and Collins (1999:211) lean toward this view by favoring the translation "spirit," Thiselton (2000:390), Fee (1986:204-205), and Witherington (1995:158) lobby for the primary sense to be the Holy Spirit, as the NLT has. Rightly, they emphasize that Paul was drawing upon Matt 18:15-20, where Jesus promised to be present with the church as it exercises just discipline over its members. Having imparted his Spirit to the church and to its individual members upon their baptism into it, Paul's theological conviction is that the Spirit's presence among them, when they met to deal with this matter, would link them to Paul's apostolic authority.

5:4 *in the name of the Lord.* Translations are equally divided over whether this phrase goes with what precedes it in 5:3 or what follows it in 5:4. RSV and TEV put it with 5:3, as does the NLT. NIV, ESV, and the NLT mg put it with 5:4. It is probably best to take it with 5:4, providing the authority not for Paul to make his pronouncement but for the church to call an authorized, judicial meeting to deal with this man where Christ's own judgment on the matter will be heard and carried out. This also probably means that the invocation of Christ's name also governs the judgment described in 5:5 (Barrett 1968:125; Thiselton 2000:393-394).

our Lord Jesus. Despite the fact that ℵ, 𝔓46, and other manuscripts add "Christ," the shorter reading of B is more likely original. It makes more sense that a copyist would have expanded the text to provide a greater sense of authority than that the original included "Christ" and a copyist inadvertently dropped it off.

5:5 *hand him over to Satan.* The verb (*paradidōmi* [TG3860, ZG4140]) can suggest physical suffering and death as when Jesus was "betrayed" into human hands (Matt 17:22; 20:18-19; 24:9). That this man's body, Gr., *sarx* (flesh), would be destroyed coincides well with the Lord's striking Ananias and Sapphira dead (Acts 5:1-11)—with the difference in this case that the spirit of the man might be saved (Barrett 1968:126; Conzelmann 1975:97; G. Harris 1991:16; Kistemaker 1992:43). However, since the stated purpose of handing him over to Satan was for his salvation, the other interpretation is that he was put outside the Christian community into the power of their archenemy in an effort to drive him to sincere repentance and destruction of his "sinful nature," at which point he would reenter the Christian community (so Blomberg 1994:105; Fee 1987:209; Garland 2003:168-177;

Gundry-Volf 1990:115-120; Hays 1997:85-86; South 1993:561; Thiselton 1973:225-226; Thiselton 2000:395).

the Lord. Though ℵ and other manuscripts add "Jesus," this appears to be an attempt to mimic the formula of 5:4. The shorter reading found in B and 𝔓46 (as translated in NLT) is more likely.

5:6 yeast. Gr., *zumē* [TG2219, ZG2434]. Used four times in this passage (5:6-8) and again when the proverb is repeated in Gal 5:9 and not elsewhere outside the synoptic Gospels, this word technically refers to "leaven," as the ESV has it. Although both yeast and leaven spread through dough to lighten bread, people in the first century did not add new yeast to each new batch. Rather, they held back a portion of the leavened dough to mix with the next batch and ferment it. "Leaven" refers to this portion of the dough that was set aside. This process continued week to week until, at least for Jews, all the old leaven was discarded from the house once a year for the Feast of Unleavened Bread, as stipulated in Exod 12:14-20 (Mitton 1973:342; Thiselton 2000:401; Witherington 1995:159).

5:7 Get rid of. Used only here and in 2 Tim 2:21, this word (*ekkathairō* [TG1571, ZG1705]) adds "out of" (*ek* [TG1537, ZG1666]) to the word for "cleanse" or "purify" (*kathairō* [TG2508, ZG2748]), giving the sense that the removal of the guilty person from the group was urgent and necessary for them to retain their corporate purity in Christ.

Passover Lamb. Gr., *pascha* [TG3957, ZG4247]. This usually refers to the Passover Feast generally but can also, as here, refer to the sacrificial lamb itself, as in Mark 14:12 and Luke 22:7. For Jews the Feast of Unleavened Bread and Passover coincided in commemorating the crucial events of the Exodus—namely, placing a lamb's blood on the doorpost to protect their firstborn sons and the flight from Pharaoh's armies in haste with unleavened bread. Jews celebrated Passover by eating ritually slain lambs in the evening, then consuming only unleavened bread for seven days thereafter (Exod 12:15-20; 13:3-7).

5:8 sincerity. Gr., *eilikrineia* [TG1505, ZG1636]. Used only three times in the NT, here and in 2 Cor 1:12 and 2:17, this word refers to something that has been examined under clear sunlight and found clear or clean. In the moral sense, it would refer to pure or sincere motives. NIV and ESV likewise have "sincerity."

truth. Gr., *alētheia* [TG225, ZG237]. Only used here and in 13:6 in 1 Corinthians, this word can mean not only to speak the truth as opposed to falsehood but, as here, to live with integrity, conducting oneself in accordance with moral principles (Thiselton 2000:407).

5:9 I wrote. The past tense refers to a letter Paul wrote to the Corinthian believers previous to 1 Corinthians that has never been discovered. Some commentaries in the past have identified 2 Cor 6:14–7:1 as being this letter or a portion of it (Hurd 1965:235-237; Weiss 1959:357). However, the 2 Corinthians passage specifically warns against close association with unbelievers, not believers who are sinning.

associate. Paul is the only one who uses this word (*sunanamignumi* [TG4874, ZG5264]) in the NT, and he does so only in the context of breaking social contact with one who has been cast out of the Christian community, as here and in 5:11 (also 2 Thess 3:14).

5:10 who . . . cheat people. Used in 1 Corinthians three times (5:11; 6:10) and only twice elsewhere (Matt 7:15; Luke 18:11), this word (*harpax* [TG727A, ZG774]) can refer to a more subtle kind of robbery (a "swindler"), or to one who literally steals items from others. It is joined to "greedy" (*pleonektēs* [TG4123, ZG4431]), suggesting that they are intended to be taken together as one idea: "greedy swindlers."

worship idols. Corinth was the home of many Greek temples, the most prominent of which was the imposing temple to Aphrodite, Greek goddess of love, beauty, and fertility, on a mountain overlooking the city. Also significant in the life of Corinth were the temples of Apollo (god of prophecy), Asclepius (god of healing), Hera Argaea (goddess of marriage), Tyche (goddess of fate), and many others. Sexual activity was an aspect of most Greek religions (Witherington 1995:12-19).

5:11 abusive. Gr., *loidoros* [TG3060, ZG3368]. Only used here and in 6:10 in the NT, this word refers to a person who is verbally abusive or who rails against the gods.

drunkard. Gr., *methusos* [TG3183, ZG3500]. The only NT use is here and in 6:10. This word refers to someone who has become intoxicated with wine; in this context it implies this is a regular condition.

5:13 *You must remove the evil person from among you.* Paul's citation of this formula comes from Deut 17:7, where it calls for the stoning of Israelites who worship idols. The formula occurs also in Deut 22:24 following the stipulation that a man not have sexual intercourse with another man's wife. Though the formula is absent, specific condemnation of a man having intercourse with his father's wife occurs in Deut 27:20. The exclusion formula follows commands in Deuteronomy directed at those who give malicious false testimony (Deut 19:16-19), rebellious drunken sons (Deut 21:18-21), and kidnappers/slave traders (Deut 24:7). Rosner (1994:61-93) views these in turn as overlapping with "abusive," "drunkard," and "swindler," all items on Paul's vice list. Thus, he makes the case that the six items on Paul's vice list (with greedy wrapped into swindler) all come from community covenant violations associated with the exclusion formula in Deuteronomy. (See also Collins 1999:223; Hays 1997:87-88; and Thiselton 2000:412, 417.)

COMMENTARY

Paul not only heard about the arrogance creating division and negating the true gospel among the Corinthian believers, he indicates (in 5:1) that he also was told about shameful conduct occurring among them: incestuous sexual activity (ch 5) and frivolous lawsuits (ch 6). His informants about these matters were probably not people from Chloe, whom he relied on for his censure in 1 Corinthians 1–4, but the three men (Stephanas, Fortunatus, and Achaicus) who brought the official letter with specific questions from the church that Paul would answer beginning in chapter 7.

In the first-century world, Christian communities (who adopted many traditionally Jewish biblical values) were unusually restrictive compared to their pagan neighbors about sexual activity outside of marriage (Fee 1987:200; Witherington 1995:153). So it was no easy task to convince relatively new Christians like the Corinthians (many of whom had come from completely pagan backgrounds) to change their promiscuous habits. Paul, however, believed making this break from the social and ethical practices of their former pagan lifestyles was crucial. What stunned him about the news he had just heard about the believer sexually cohabiting with his father's former wife (not his mother) is that it defies not just biblical restrictions but the social mores of idol worshipers and even Roman law. As he does in 1 Thessalonians 4:5 and elsewhere, Paul accentuated the sinfulness of this man's action by measuring it from the standpoint of his non-Christian neighbors (Collins 1999:209; Conzelmann 1975:96; Garland 2003:157).

This man's relationship with his father's former wife was no secret. What galled Paul, as he makes clear in 5:2, is that the church in Corinth was openly condoning this illicit sexual relationship as though it were an excellent advertising campaign for freedom in Christ to draw their neighbors to the Christian faith. However, it was the exact opposite. Instead of expressing joy, they should have been weeping tears of shame. This was a black mark on the church in their community and an insult to God. Paul compels the believers to cleanse their corporate body by the age-old practice of expelling the sinner from among them (Lev 18:24-30; 20:22-24; Josh 7). That this expulsion was directed only at the man suggests that the woman involved was not part of the Christian community, putting her out of Paul's jurisdiction (5:12).

Beginning with 5:3, Paul inserts himself into the situation, despite his distance and lack of personal knowledge about the individual guilty of this shameful sexual conduct. The rhetorical effect of this put him in direct opposition to the Corinthian church, which was doing nothing to expose this man for his despicable activity. It also signals that this situation was so serious that it could not be tolerated even another day. We wonder how he could have possibly "already passed judgment" based on this third-party accusation. It must be because the facts of the case were irrefutable, and if so, the judgment demanded is crystal clear from Scripture. What Paul wanted was for the church to meet and take action immediately (as 5:4-5 directs).

Twice in 5:4 Paul invoked the name of Jesus upon this judicial meeting of the Corinthian believers. He did this in conformance to Jesus' own directives found in Matthew 18:15-20 calling for a formal, public meeting to discipline community members. Paul was positive that if they met in Jesus' name, justice would prevail and Paul's judgment upon this man would be confirmed through them. Although Paul was not reticent in giving churches under his care directives based on his own apostolic authority, in this case he had no intention of bypassing the authority of the church guided by the will of Christ. This was Paul's pragmatic acknowledgment that these churches, including the one in Corinth, were not *his* churches but were under the authority of the Lord Jesus, just as he himself was. To be sure, he believed the Corinthian church would learn a great lesson about their need to discipline their members when they recognized the Lord's swift agreement with Paul's recommended course of action. The power of Jesus was also invoked because of the impending role of his evil opponent, Satan, in this judgment scenario.

Since Jesus defeated the forces of evil through his death and resurrection, Paul believed that those who put their trust in him are protected from the wiles of Satan. Thus, the worst punishment for an errant believer is to be removed from the wall of safety provided by the church body and thrust back into the cold, harsh world spiritually naked, completely vulnerable to the evil rampant in Satan's realm. The point is not simply to get rid of the person but to retain the sanctity of the church. As expressed in 3:16-17, they are the temple of God (Garland 2003:175; Rosner 1991b:144; Rosner 1992a:470; Vander Broek 1994:7). As in this instance in Corinth, it was an effort to bring a defiantly unrepentant member back into the fold. Perhaps experiencing the world as he once knew it before coming to Christ would awaken his need to recommit and return to spiritual protection in the church. Satan thus functioned as Christ's instrument of punishment—with the goal of bringing the errant one back to the church. The worst-case scenario is that he would revel in Satan's environment and get the eternal punishment he deserved. At least he would not defile the believing community any longer.

Paul's directive about how this man should be treated by the Corinthian church is bewildering to many today. This is partly because many are not inclined to take sin very seriously anymore; we would probably only send this man to counseling. It is also partly because we no longer draw a deep line between the church and the world outside the church; Satan is not very real to us. Also, we are not inclined to meddle in anyone's personal life in the church, much less know what they are doing in their bedroom. But perhaps the purpose of this passage for us is to shake us up no less than Paul intended to do with the Corinthians. Historically, the church has been quick to expel people over doctrinal matters, but despite all kinds of big theological issues in this epistle, over unity (chs 1-4), spiritual gifts (chs 11-14), and even the resurrection (ch 15), it is worth noting that Paul only called for this ultimate treatment of a believer on a moral issue that was bringing public disgrace to the church.

Beginning with 5:6, Paul reveals clearly that his main concern was with maintaining the integrity of the Christian community in Corinth and that he had deep-rooted theological convictions about this. As far as he was concerned, the church's inattention to disciplining the man living openly with his father's wife had fueled what was already a big problem with them: arrogant boasting. In chapters 1-4 he exposed the root problem of their disunity to be arrogance. Now, their ignorant boasting in this kind of twisted freedom in Christ must be cast out of the community along with the man whose actions symbolized it. His reference to "this sin" is a double entendre. Both the man's illicit sexual activity and the boasting of the Christian community about it are infectious to a whole, healthy, unified body of believers fostering the true gospel of Jesus Christ. Both individual and corporate sin were active.

The proverb Paul cites in 5:6 about the capacity of yeast (or leaven) to expand to permeate an entire loaf of bread is not found in Scripture. Interestingly, he uses the same proverb in Galatians 5:7-15 to warn the Galatians of a specific but unnamed agitator whom he feared was infecting them with the false gospel of legalism (probably the opposite of the problem here). In Galatians he does not specify how to deal with this individual, but, as here, Paul assumes an identification of the Christian communities theologically as the corporate people of God. Like the oft-repeated call to Israel in the Old Testament, they were to be holy because God is holy. In addition, now that Christ has come, they were to live in the new life Christ had bought for them, both individually and corporately. So, sin cannot remain unchecked, opening the way for it to grow. If so, it will negate what Christ died for, threatening the viability of his body, the church, and individuals who are part of it.

Thus, just as all Israelite families were required to cleanse every bit of leaven from their home in preparation for celebrating the Feast of Unleavened Bread (which immediately followed Passover for the next seven days), the new people of God in Corinth, the church, were to eliminate this moral sinner, and thereby their boastful sin, from among them. Like an Israelite home the day after the Feast of Unleavened

Bread and like their ancestors fleeing from Egypt with only the shirts on their backs, new life and new possibilities are opened up for the church when it deals with its sin and returns to Christ.

Paul quickly moves from speaking about unleavened bread to the Passover; this is not surprising given their virtual identity in Jewish custom (Mark 14:12; Luke 22:7). By introducing Christ as the Passover Lamb (5:7), Paul picks up a powerful symbol of what Christ accomplished for people by his death, an idea probably already deeply embedded in Christian thought. Like the unblemished lambs slaughtered annually as the sacrifice for the sins of the people, the sinless Jesus bore the sins of all humanity in his suffering and death. According to John 19:14, 31, Jesus' death occurred on the same day as the Passover. The images of his broken body and shed blood were incorporated by Jesus himself into the powerful sacrament of Eucharist, or the Lord's Supper, celebrated by Christians everywhere since the beginning of the church.

In 5:8, Paul works out his metaphor in an unexpected way but one that is very fitting for his point. Instead of talking about eating unleavened bread, cleansed of the fermenting germ of sin, he moves to the first day of eating newly leavened bread after the seven days of eating unleavened bread. Rather than leavening with traditional products, symbolic of "evil," he recommends consuming an entirely different kind of bread—i.e., bread leavened with moral goodness. This disjunction of the new from the old comes as the direct result of Christ being the perfect and eternal sacrifice, ending the need for any further sacrifices and ushering in the new covenant (Heb 9:12-15). In the Gospels, Jesus himself talks of the need to throw out old wineskins and start filling brand-new ones to contain his message (Matt 9:17; Mark 2:22; Luke 5:37-39). Elsewhere, Paul often speaks of believers leaving behind their old life and acting out their new life in Christ (11:25; 2 Cor 3:6; 5:17; Gal 6:15; Eph 2:15; 4:24). Eating bread filled with Christ's goodness on a daily basis will make believers the moral opposites of the incestuous man. Corporately, as the church consumes the bread of moral goodness, rather than growing in arrogant boasting, they will grow in humility and harmonious unity.

Paul's reference to an earlier letter he wrote to the Corinthians in 5:9-11 may come as a surprise to us (see note on 5:9). Nonetheless, he assumes they knew the letter and remembered its contents. He introduces it here because he believed they had either ignored it in their handling of the incestuous believer in their midst or they had misunderstood what he meant. Its mention also explains why he felt justified in being so curt in his comment about the situation. He admits he told them to be very careful about whom they socialize with. Apparently, they took the warning to pertain to unbelievers. He clarifies now that he was more concerned about believers associating blithely with confessing Christians cavalierly living unholy lifestyles— including sexual promiscuity—exactly the situation with the incestuous man.

Most likely Paul did not explain his theological reasoning in the earlier letter as he does in 5:6-8, and he probably made a very general pronouncement. Amazingly, Christians have continued to confuse this issue of disassociating with openly sinful believers, just as the Corinthians did. However, it is patently obvious to Paul, as he explains in 5:9-10, that Christians can't help but live among non-Christian people in their neighborhoods and social institutions. Remember, Christians were a small portion of the population of Corinth or of any ancient city or village in which they existed. Regardless, evangelism, the prime directive of Christianity, is impossible if Christians aren't mingling with non-Christian families, friends, and acquaintances. Christians, however, can decide as a matter of community discipline to sever social contact with those in their number who embrace unholy lifestyles and refuse to renounce them. Such concerted efforts to be communities that honor God and serve Christ with reverent lives can become powerful evangelistic witnesses in and of themselves.

In common with Greek moral literature, Paul provides a catalogue of vices to be shunned. His list in 5:10 has four items, which expands to six in 5:11 and to ten in 6:9-10. Fitting for the specific concern of incest that prompted Paul's reaction, sexual immorality (*porneia* [TG4202, ZG4518]) heads each list. This may mean that this was the most difficult area of change for Greeks converting to Christ. In the first list, "greedy" and "[who] cheat people" are depicted grammatically as overlapping vices in the same person, the first being the attitude and the second the action (see note on 5:10). This results in three basic vices: sexual promiscuity, theft, and idolatry. Paul probably considered the first two to be natural results of the last (Collins 1999:221). Paul also considers greed itself to be idolatry (Eph 5:5; Col 3:5). And since worship of idols saturated every ancient culture other than Judaism (and now Christianity), Paul probably assumed all Greeks to be sexually promiscuous and out to swindle everyone they could. Note that all three are condemned in the Ten Commandments (Deut 5:6-21).

Paul's second list, in 5:11, separates "greedy" and "[who] cheat people" and adds two other intolerable vices: those who are verbally abusive in their speech and those who are drunks. As in the previous list, believers should not be characterized as conducting themselves in these ways. The Christian community as a corporate unit must serve notice that certain behavioral boundaries must be maintained for the church to be the church. All believers require disciplining to embrace this holy lifestyle. The consequence of brandishing unholy lifestyles is being disenfranchised from the corporate body.

As Paul specifically advises in 5:11, at minimum this punishment meant no table fellowship with other believers. Since Christians met only in the homes of other believers, and mostly in shared communal meals, this effectively barred such people from the community. To exclude those who were disgracing Christ from table fellowship was also to exclude them from sharing in the Lord's Supper, which clearly was practiced as the concluding element in these shared fellowship meals (11:17-22).

In 5:12-13, Paul sums up his argument and dramatically directs the Corinthians to the action they must take. In explaining further why the warnings in his earlier letter could only apply to believers in the Christian community, he elaborated that his jurisdiction and that of the church only extends to those in the church. Only those who have committed themselves to Christ in public confession and baptism could ever be expected to devote themselves to holy lives honoring Christ's sacrificial death. Only they are liable for community discipline when they disavow their commitment in effect by their blatantly sinful lifestyles. As such, the community must take this responsibility seriously, for the good of the community, the individual, and to honor Christ fittingly. Those outside the church are under God's jurisdiction. As such, they are under God's sure condemnation should they continue to behave rebelliously against him (Rom 1). This is the world into which those being disciplined by the church are thrust. It is also the realm in which Satan is allowed to work (5:5).

Finally, Paul quotes Deuteronomy 17:7. This is the clincher, both to stipulate once again the required action the community must take against the incestuous man and to expose the theological basis that demands this. The call to remove the evil among them applies this command (originally spoken by God to Israel) directly to the Corinthian community, once again reminding us that Paul identified the church as the new Israel, as the new covenant people of God (10:1-13). The command in its original context in Deuteronomy is repeated regarding the covenant violations that match the items in Paul's list in 5:11 (Deut 17:2-7; 19:16-19; 21:18-21; 22:21-22; 24:7). They also each presume execution by stoning the offender. Paul was calling on the church to expunge the violator from the church and thereby give him the death penalty—his eternal condemnation by God—if he stayed in the realm of Satan's dominion. The hope of the punishment was that it would drive him back to the grace of Christ and the welcoming arms of the believing community.

◆   ## B. Demand for an End to Internal Lawsuits (6:1-11)

When one of you has a dispute with another believer, how dare you file a lawsuit and ask a secular court to decide the matter instead of taking it to other believers*! ²Don't you realize that someday we believers will judge the world? And since you are going to judge the world, can't you decide even these little things among yourselves? ³Don't you realize that we will judge angels? So you should surely be able to resolve ordinary disputes in this life. ⁴If you have legal disputes about such matters, why go to outside judges who are not respected by the church? ⁵I am saying this to shame you. Isn't there anyone in all the church who is wise enough to decide these issues? ⁶But instead, one believer* sues another—right in front of unbelievers!

⁷Even to have such lawsuits with one another is a defeat for you. Why not just accept the injustice and leave it at that? Why not let yourselves be cheated? ⁸Instead, you yourselves are the ones who do wrong and cheat even your fellow believers.*

⁹Don't you realize that those who do wrong will not inherit the Kingdom of God? Don't fool yourselves. Those who indulge in sexual sin, or who worship idols, or commit adultery, or are male prostitutes, or practice homosexuality, ¹⁰or are thieves, or greedy people, or drunkards, or are abusive, or cheat people—none of these will inherit the Kingdom of God. ¹¹Some of you were once like that. But you were cleansed; you were made holy; you were made right with God by calling on the name of the Lord Jesus Christ and by the Spirit of our God.

6:1 Greek *God's holy people;* also in 6:2.   6:6 Greek *one brother.*   6:8 Greek *even the brothers.*

NOTES

6:1 *dare.* The only use of this word (*tolmaō* [TG5111, ZG5528]) in 1 Corinthians, it can refer to bold, even courageous action in a positive sense; but as here, in a negative sense, it denotes rash, even insulting action.

file a lawsuit. Lit., "have a matter," though the phrase in a legal sense means to bring a case or, as in the NLT, a lawsuit, against someone. The language makes it clear that this is not a criminal case but one involving property or perhaps business matters. In civil cases, such as these in Corinth, two citizens would have been appointed by the court to adjudicate the matter (Collins 1999:226; Thiselton 2000:420).

ask a secular court to decide the matter. Lit., "to be judged by the unjust one." The NLT captures the intent of the phrase for contemporary readers. However, it loses Paul's moral denunciation of "ungodly" (NIV) or "unrighteous" (ESV) conveyed by the word *adikos* [TG94A, ZG96]. Paul visualized a wide chasm between the world of believers and nonbelievers. He probably also considered the courts corrupt (Winter 1991:561). Another possible concern is that Roman courts as found in Corinth favored the wealthy and privileged over the poor (Collins 1999:226; A. Mitchell 1993:563; Thiselton 2000:419; Witherington 1995:163).

6:2 *will judge the world.* The idea for this is found in Dan 7:22, Wis 3:7-8, and also in the Qumran text of 1QpHab 5:4. The suggestion of Matt 19:28 and Luke 22:30 is that followers of Christ will sit on thrones as judges over the 12 tribes of Israel.

6:3 *we will judge angels.* Second Peter 2:4; Jude 1:6; and *1 Enoch* 1:10-12; 10:11-14; 19:1; 21:1-10 refer to the judgment of fallen angels but not necessarily by believers. Thiselton (2000:426-427) makes a strong case that Paul's idea stems from his assumption that the resurrection of believers with Christ identifies them with him in such a way that they share corporately with his lordship over all—i.e., over all people who reject or embrace him, all angels, those who serve his kingdom well, and those who have worked against it. Others suggest that Paul was thinking of believers judging only condemned fallen angels—namely, Satan and his cohorts (Collins 1999:232; Fee 1987:234; Hoskins 2001:296).

ordinary disputes in this life. Gr., *biōtika* [TG982, ZG1053]. Two of its three NT uses are in this passage (6:4); the other is Luke 21:34. It refers to everyday matters of daily life. The implication here is that these are so common that lawsuits generating from such matters are frivolous. The NIV has "things of this life," and ESV "matters pertaining to this life."

6:4 *why go.* The word (*kathizō* [TG2523, ZG2767]) refers to "appointing" judges. Part of the dispute over whether to take the judges as those inside the church or those outside relates to the question of how to render the verb: as an imperative (NIV) or as a question (NLT). Rendering it as a question is consistent with the view that Paul meant to refer to the judges as those outside the church. A minor view argues for the imperative (Kinman 1997:353). Precedent for the appointment of competent folks in the community was set by Moses's following Jethro's counsel in Exod 18:13-26; Deut 1:9-17 (Rosner 1991a:276).

outside judges who are not respected. Gr., *exouthenēmenous* [TG1848, ZG2024]. This is a participle from a verb that refers to something or someone who is despised and rejected. It is used of Jesus this way in Luke 23:11 and Acts 4:11. Paul used it to refer to Christians in 1:28. Because of this, some are convinced that the word is a sarcastic reference to the least respected believers in the church (Bruce 1971:60; Collins 1999:232), and this is reflected in the NIV rendering "men of little account in the church." However, in this context, it most likely refers to asking the regular courts to hear their cases; therefore, these are nonbelievers who have no standing in God's realm of the church but who hand down rulings in disputes between believers (Barrett 1968:127; Blomberg 1994:117; Fee 1987:235; Thiselton 2000:433).

6:6 *one believer sues another.* The word "sues" (*krinō* [TG2919, ZG3212]) is the same used in 6:1 and 6:2, translated respectively as "file a lawsuit" and "judge." Literally, the text speaks of "brother against brother," invoking a familial relationship between believers in the church.

6:7 *cheated*. Used three times in 1 Corinthians (6:8; 7:5), this word (*apostereō* [TG650, ZG691]) refers to someone who defrauds another. It alliterates with the previous verb "accept the injustice" (*adikeō* [TG91, ZG92]).

6:9 *those who do wrong*. Gr., *adikoi* [TG94A, ZG96]. This word is only used here and in 6:1 in 1 Corinthians. Translated "secular" there, it is the negated form of "righteous" or "just" (*dikaios* [TG1342, ZG1465]). A related verb form of the word is used in 6:7 and 6:8.

***Kingdom of God*.** Gr., *theou basileian* [TG2316/932, ZG2536/993], the most prevalent subject of Jesus in the synoptic Gospels. Paul used a "short" version of the phrase here and in 6:10, 15:50, and Gal 5:21 and the more usual form (*basileia tou theou*) elsewhere (4:20; Rom 14:17; Eph 5:5; 2 Thess 1:5). Given the prevalence of this phrase in the teaching of Jesus as found in the synoptic Gospels, Paul's few references are notable. Despite the fact that Paul had no personal contact with Jesus, these references do show that Paul had contact with the teaching tradition of Jesus after his conversion.

***commit adultery*.** Gr., *moichoi* [TG3432, ZG3659]. Used only here and in Luke 18:11 and Heb 13:4, this word consistently refers to married people having sexual relations with someone other than their marriage partner.

***male prostitutes*.** Gr., *malakoi* [TG3120A, ZG3434]. Used in Matt 11:8 and Luke 7:25 to refer to soft or fine clothes, this word is used in Greek literature to describe men or boys who are "soft" or effeminate. It developed a technical sense to refer to boys involved in pederasty (D. Martin 1996:124-126; Scroggs 1983:65, 106-108), young men functioning effectively as prostitutes to older men, the "most common form of homosexuality in antiquity" (Witherington 1995:166). The teaming of this word with the one that follows (*arsenokoitai*) suggests to some interpreters that this word refers to the passive partner in a homosexual relationship (Barrett 1968:140-141; Bruce 1971:61; Collins 1999:237; A. F. Johnson 2004:97; L&N 772). Both words receive careful study in Elliott 2004:18-31.

***practice homosexuality*.** Gr., *arsenokoitai* [TG733, ZG780]. No known use of this word occurs in Greek literature previous to its occurrence here by Paul, and it is little used later. This is not to argue that Paul coined it as some suggest (De Young 1995:61; Malick 1993:482) but that its functional meaning is difficult to determine, especially since its appearance only as an item in this list (also in a list in 1 Tim 1:10) provides no syntactical context to help. It is a compound of two Greek words, *arsenikos* [TG730, ZG781], which means "masculine" or "male," and *koitos* [TG2845, ZG3130] (bed), a euphemism for "sexual intercourse." Though some contend that neither this word nor the one previous in themselves refer to a homosexual relationship comparable to some contemporary commitments (Boswell 1980:112-114; Horsley 1998:87, 89), strong linguistic similarities link this second word to the LXX of Lev 18:22 and Lev 20:13, which name a man lying with a man as a violation of the holiness code (Hays 1997:97; Soards 1999:126). Also, the two words side-by-side in this list of unrighteous acts strongly suggests that together they are intended to cover various types of homosexual activity between males (De Young 1995:62; Garland 2003:213-215; Malick 1993:479; Oster 1995:138-139; Thiselton 2000:440-452).

6:11 *you were cleansed*. The only other use of this word (*apolouō* [TG628, ZG666]) in the NT is in Acts 22:16, where it is used in association with baptism. The connection to baptism is implied here, as well, in that when people submit to Christian baptism, this focal point of their conversion enacts the complete spiritual cleansing from sin in their life made possible through Christ's sacrifice. Joined with the next two verbs, a picture of someone starting to live all over again with a clean slate is presented (Thiselton 2000:454).

***made holy*.** See note on this word's first appearance in 1:2.

made right. Used only one other time in 1 Corinthians (4:4), this word (*dikaioō* [TG1344, ZG1467]) dominates Paul's discussion of salvation in Romans (15 times) and Galatians (8 times). It assumes that the disjuncture in the relationship between a person and God (because of sin and rebellion) has been mended, making possible a life activated by God's power.

Lord Jesus Christ. Although the shortest reading, "Lord Jesus," occurs in A D² 𝔐, the reading adopted by the NLT occurs in 𝔓11^vid, 𝔓46, 𝔵, and D*; it is slightly preferred because it has better textual support and because it is the more common formula following "in the name of." A longer reading "our Lord Jesus Christ" occurs in B C 33 and 1739, but the "our" was probably added by a scribe to balance the "our" in the next reference, "in the Spirit of our God."

COMMENTARY

Stephanas, Fortunatus, and Achaicus carried the official letter from the Corinthians containing the questions that Paul would respond to in chapters 7–16. In addition to telling Paul about the incestuous relationship being condoned by the church, these men must also have told him about civil lawsuits that were pending between people in the church. Fortunately, the Corinthians were not boasting about this situation, but Paul's ire was raised nonetheless because of how this again exposed the very poor understanding the Corinthian Christians had of their relationship with the world around them. No doubt the lawsuits exacerbated division in a church already splintered by the group alignments that Paul chastised in chapters 1–4.

Paul seemed shocked to hear about this situation of lawsuits (6:1). This does not seem to be about one notorious instance, as was the case with the incestuous relationship in 5:1. It was a matter of routine procedure the believers were following, one totally in sync with the Corinthian culture and their life prior to becoming Christians, especially people of power and means against people of low status. The problem is that their conversion to Christ was supposed to change the orientation of their lives on many matters. Paul couldn't believe that it had not dawned on anyone that a Christian taking a fellow believer to a pagan court, especially over a relatively minor matter, flies in the face of their new life in Christ.

The Corinthians were one body. How can one part litigate against another part without damaging the whole? Jewish synagogue communities who lived and worked outside Palestine had been dealing with such matters internally for centuries (Barrett 1968:135), having no desire to put Jewish issues of morality and legality into the hands of Roman courts that had little understanding or sympathy for them (Keener 1993:463-464). Many of the first believers in Corinth came from the synagogue, including Crispus, the synagogue leader (Acts 18:8). The synagogue had its own judicial system as indicated by Gallio's referral of the case brought to him about Paul (Acts 18:15). Surely they should have seen the need to set up their own system for dealing with strident relationships in the church by then. The lopsided advantage people of means had over others in the civil court system (Collins 1999:226; Hays 1997:93; Keener 1993:464; Witherington 1993:163; Winter 2001:60-64) should also now be recognized as an obvious affront to God's concern for fairness toward the poor. Likely the wealthier believers among the Corinthians were using the Roman judicial system to their advantage against the poor like others of their social class did routinely in Roman society (A. F. Johnson 2004:93-94).

In 6:2, Paul delivers the first of a two-pronged eschatological argument for why the Corinthians should resolve their own disputes among themselves. Employing lesser-to-greater logic, he believed they needed the practice of making judgments, since they will one day judge matters of eternal consequence. Based on Daniel 7:21-22, Jewish teaching held that God's community of believers would be involved in the judgment of the nations. For Paul, the transfer of that promise to the new people of God was obvious. He even signals his contact with the Daniel passage specifically in 6:1 and 6:2 by using *hagioi* [TG40A, ZG41], the Greek word for "holy ones" or "saints" (NLT, "believer," "believers"), found in the Septuagint version of Daniel 7:22. Given the crucial identification he later makes between Christ's resurrection body and that of believers in 15:49, Paul probably understood this judgment aspect for believers christologically; that is, their corporate identity with Christ put them within the scope of his own eschatological lordship and absolute judgment upon the world, specifically against those who refuse to confess him as Lord (Thiselton 2000:426-427).

The second prong of Paul's eschatological argument assumes another element of eschatological judgment for God's people, though it essentially duplicates the argument of 6:2. He ups the ante, though, by placing "angels" where he had "the world" in 6:2. Paul goes for dramatic effect with this idea, since even Jews considered angels more powerful than humans. However, Paul's thinking runs parallel to that of the author of Hebrews, who places Jesus Christ, the "Son of Man," higher than the angels in God's created order (Heb 1:1-13) and says God's people have a share in his heavenly calling (Heb 3:1). Although Paul may only have had in mind the condemnation of fallen angels, Satan and his demonic helpers (2 Pet 2:4), it is more likely that he viewed all angels, good and bad, to be a part of "the world." Since Christ will judge the world, and since believers are one with Christ in resurrection, angels are under the jurisdiction of the corporate body of believers, too. Judgment on a higher plane again is intended as motivation for the community of believers to settle their own daily and ordinary disputes.

In 6:4, Paul asks a question that gets at the heart of the matter: Why were they taking their petty, interpersonal squabbles to the regular Corinthian court system? Those who administrate this system Paul pointedly labels as "not respected" by the church. However, his language is much stronger than this. He calls them "despised," ironically the same language used about Jesus when he was mistreated by the courts in his trial and crucifixion (Luke 23:11). Paul did not mean that believers should retain a vendetta against all judicial systems. Rather, he was employing rhetorical language to impress upon the Corinthians what they had not seemed to have grasped: Their acceptance of Christ had opened up a wide gulf separating them from nonbelievers who rejected Christ. Why seek advice and resolution from people with whom they have so little in common when they can take such matters to fellow Christians?

In notable contrast to his desire not to shame them (4:14) for their tendency to think too highly of themselves, in 6:5 Paul squarely states that he most certainly intended to shame them. This would have been a very serious action in a culture that treated honor and shame as seriously as did the Corinthians (A. Mitchell 1993:574). This shows just how concerned Paul was to get the Corinthian believers to abandon the Corinthian court system to resolve the personal squabbles between believers in the church. Instead, they should find trusted individuals in the church to help in these matters. Sarcastically, he told them to identify "wise" people among them since many of the Corinthians thought of themselves as so wise anyway (which was what he chastised them for in 1:18-31 and 3:18-23).

Employing the familial language of "brother against brother" to open 6:6 (see NLT mg), Paul compares the horror of suing one's own family member with bringing a grievance against a Christian brother or sister in public court. To Paul's mind, believers are family. He uses the language of family regularly in this letter, constantly addressing them as "brothers and sisters" and even referring to himself as their spiritual father (4:15). Families work things out within the family. They do not ask those outside the family, who don't know anything about them, to fix their problems. Noting that the Corinthians were doing exactly this "right in front of unbelievers" suggests that another aspect of Paul's alarm about all this was that it gave a very poor witness of the gospel to the non-Christian public. Those who have received such overwhelming grace from God through the suffering and sacrifice of Christ ought to be able to find ways to settle matters and offer forgiveness within the church. How were they demonstrating their spiritually transformed lives if they sued one another just like everyone else in Corinth did?

Since the Corinthian lawsuits involved minor matters, Paul issued an even greater spiritual challenge to them (6:7). Why not just drop the grievances altogether? Surely as those who have been recipients of God's grace, they should be prepared to suffer injustice as Christ did, a major New Testament theme (especially in 1 Pet 2-3). Even if they were to win their personal lawsuits, spiritually they had already lost. They had disgraced the name of Christ before pagans, they had sullied the reputation of a brother in Christ, and they had lost an opportunity to deepen their own spiritual lives.

Despite the fact that someone may feel wronged by a fellow Christian, Paul turned the tables on those who continued to proceed with these kinds of lawsuits (6:8). From a Christian perspective, they would be seen as the wrongdoers. They would be the ones cheating their own Christian family members of the respect they deserved as fellow believers. They should drop these things for the benefit of everyone!

Continuing to play on the word "wrong" in 6:9, Paul reminded the Corinthians that behavioral standards are in place for those who will participate in the eternal community God is creating through Christ. Even though they have become Christians, if they behave as those outside God's community, the security of their position cannot be maintained. Being among those "who do wrong and cheat even your fellow believers" by suing them in court puts them outside God's community standards and provides due cause for God to reconsider the salvation that has been extended to them. In fact, it puts them in league with a host of wrongdoers that Paul lists in 6:9-10. If they thought it didn't matter what kind of life they led after becoming a Christian, they were deceiving themselves.

The list includes ten items or types of people who indulge flagrantly and routinely in sinful behaviors. Four of them were named in Paul's earlier lists in 5:10 and 5:11 (sexual sin, idol worshipers, greedy, and those who cheat people), two repeat from 5:11 (drunkards, abusers/slanderers), and three are new. The three new items identify specific forms of sexual sin (*pornoi* [ᵀᴳ4202, ᶻᴳ4518]). The first, "adulterers," refers to those who are unfaithful to their marriage partner. The second and third, "male prostitutes" and those who "practice homosexuality," refer to the variety of homosexual relationships practiced in the ancient Greco-Roman world (see notes on 6:9). Specifically why Paul added these three sexual misbehaviors is difficult to say. Probably he desired the rhetorical effect of shock. He wanted to get the Corinthians' attention so they would fully realize that their behavior of suing fellow believers—which he already labeled as "cheating," one of the misbehaviors on the list—sits right alongside homosexuality and adultery in terms of its possible result of placing a person outside the present and future messianic community. If they continued in this behavior, they would not "inherit" what had already been reserved for them—namely, God's Kingdom.

To Paul's mind, this was no idle threat. As he explains in 6:11, he truly believed that when the Corinthian Christians confessed Christ and were baptized before the church, they began a wholly new life. Christ's sacrifice for their sins made them "whiter than snow," as the hymn by James Nicholson says. Spiritually cleansed as instruments for the implementation of God's will and given an interpersonal relationship with God, they were ready to start their life over—and Paul acknowledged that the Corinthians had done so. They turned their backs on their sinful lives filled with behaviors like the nine listed. His warning here is that they cannot turn back to those behaviors—or incorporate new ones like them into their new life—without disastrous present and eternal consequences.

Notably, Paul mentions all three persons of the triune God in 6:11. God is the one with whom people ultimately must have a good relationship. Paul named Christ as the one who washes away the sins of believers, makes them holy, and justifies them before God. The Spirit makes God's power available for believers to transform their lives into those that offer acceptable service to God. The role of all three makes it entirely possible for believers to overcome habitual, sinful behaviors in their lives.

◆ ## C. Encouragement to Abandon Immoral Sexual Behavior (6:12-20)

¹²You say, "I am allowed to do anything"—but not everything is good for you. And even though "I am allowed to do anything," I must not become a slave to anything. ¹³You say, "Food was made for the stomach, and the stomach for food." (This is true, though someday God will do away with both of them.) But you can't say that our bodies were made for sexual immorality. They were made for the Lord, and the Lord cares about our bodies. ¹⁴And God will raise us from the dead by his power, just as he raised our Lord from the dead.

¹⁵Don't you realize that your bodies are actually parts of Christ? Should a man take his body, which is part of Christ, and join it to a prostitute? Never! ¹⁶And don't you realize that if a man joins himself to a prostitute, he becomes one body with her? For the Scriptures say, "The two are united into one."* ¹⁷But the person who is joined to the Lord is one spirit with him.

¹⁸Run from sexual sin! No other sin so clearly affects the body as this one does. For sexual immorality is a sin against your own body. ¹⁹Don't you realize that your body is the temple of the Holy Spirit, who lives in you and was given to you by God? You do not belong to yourself, ²⁰for God bought you with a high price. So you must honor God with your body.

6:16 Gen 2:24.

NOTES

6:12 *You say, "I am allowed to do anything."* This is the first of three Corinthian slogans that Paul counters (Omanson 1992:204), though some dispute that this is a Corinthian slogan (Dodd 1995:57; Garland 2003:228). It coordinates with the thoughts of a variety of Greek philosophies, including Stoicism (Deming 1996:309). Some suggest that it was a Corinthian version of what Paul says in 9:1-2 (Barrett 1968:145; Hays 1997:101). The second slogan parallels this one.

6:13 *Food was made for the stomach, and the stomach for food.* Despite the fact that all major versions, including the NLT, end the quotation of the slogan here, the unanimous view of major current interpreters is that the quotation should extend through the following clause (Collins 1999:244; Fee 1987:252; Hays 1997:102; Thiselton 2000:462): "though someday God will do away with both of them." The NLT's phrase "this is true" is not present in the Greek. Paul was not countering the idea that food and stomach are cooperative partners in man's existence but that the logic of their destruction runs parallel to how people use and will eventually lose all parts of their human body, including their sexual organs. The relationship between food and sexual promiscuity may have connected in Corinth where the availability of prostitutes was part of the gluttony of cultic banquets and festivals (Rosner 1998:337; Winter 1997:79).

bodies. This word is used 46 times in 1 Corinthians, mostly in chs 6, 12, and 15; it refers to the physical, human body. In most Greek philosophies, this aspect of human existence is considerably secondary to a person's essence, the spirit or soul, which is imprisoned in the body and freed upon death.

6:14 *will raise.* Gr., *exegerei* [^{TG}1825, ^{ZG}1995]. The confusion in the manuscript tradition over the tense of this verb is characterized by the fact that the respected papyrus 𝔓46 first had it in the present, which was changed to the future, and then finally changed to the aorist (Collins 1999:247). The verb in the future, as the NLT has it, seems required by the context to stand in parallel to "will do away with" in 6:13 and is heavily supported by ℵ, C, and many others. The aorist, supported by normally influential B, parallels the immediately preceding aorist of "raised" regarding Christ and, if accepted, would convey that Paul was referring to baptism. The present tense supported (in addition to a corrected version of 𝔓46) by 𝔓11, D, and P appears to be accidental, adding the iota to the future tense of the word.

6:15 *parts.* This word refers to the arms, legs, and organs of the body, the separate physical elements that make the whole. Used three times in this verse, all in the plural, the word is a major component of Paul's monologue in 12:12-27 (13 times) on the value of every part of the corporate body of the church. (See also Rom 6:13, 19; Eph 4:25; 5:30; Col 3:5.)

Never! Gr., *mē genoito* [^{TG}3361/1096, ^{ZG}3590/1181]. The most repeated optative phrase in the NT, this is the verb "become" or "be" constructed as only a mere possibility. Preceded by a negative particle, it becomes the strongest possible way in Greek to deny that something can or should ever happen. Sometimes it is translated "May it never be!" or "God forbid!"

6:16 *a man joins himself.* This is a participle form of a verb (*kollaomai* [TG2853, ZG3140]) that includes various ways of sticking two items together in a bond that will be more or less permanent, including gluing, cementing, or welding. It can refer, as here, to the sexual and relational union of a man and woman. Notably, a word related to this (*proskallaomai* [TG4347, ZG4681]) is used in Gen 2:24, a portion of which is quoted in this verse, regarding the bonding of a man and a woman in a marriage relationship. The use of this word may entertain an ironic twist of a man selling himself in bondage to a prostitute whom he has solicited (Porter 1991:105).

6:18 *Run from sexual sin!* Paul may have had in mind the story of Joseph in Gen 39 and probably also *Testament of Reuben* 5:5 (Rosner 1992b:125).

No other sin so clearly affects the body as this one does. Lit., "every sin a person might commit is outside the body" (cf. NIV, ESV). This sets up the vital contrast to the next clause, when Paul says, "for sexual immorality is a sin against your own body." The first clause is probably another slogan, highly compatible with Greek stoicism, which the Corinthian believers used to justify their behavior (Barrett 1968:150; Collins 1999:248; Thiselton 2000:471-472). Sexual promiscuity is linked to idol worship and apostasy in the OT (Derrett 1997b:98; Rosner 1998:345). Sexual sin not only violates the intimacy of the marriage bed, but it also defiles an intimacy that is reserved for believers to share with God alone through the implanted Holy Spirit (Byrne 1983:615).

6:19 *temple.* Gr., *naos* [TG3485, ZG3724]. See note on 3:16.

6:20 *bought.* The Greek verb is *agorazō* [TG59, ZG60]. An *agora* [TG58, ZG59] was the marketplace where goods were bought and sold. This verb indicates that the purchase price has been paid. Though not specifically mentioned here, the fact that it speaks of the Corinthians themselves being bought, plus the clearer use in 7:23, suggests that Paul specifically had in mind the slave market and that Christ had manumitted them from their former lives as slaves to sin (Collins 1999:249; Fee 1987:264).

your body. This shortest reading, supported by 𝔓46, א, and B, is surely correct. The longer version, which adds "and in your spirit, which is from God" is not strongly supported, adds unnecessary elements to Paul's conclusion that effectively weakens his emphasis on the body, and would not likely have been dropped if it was original.

COMMENTARY

What Paul deals with in this section provides a further explanation of why he added three additional sinful sexual activities to his vice list of 6:9-10. He wanted to expand on his objections to the unacceptable sexual conduct of Corinthian believers. Recognizing that the Corinthians would likely object to his clampdown on their sexual behavior, Paul opens in 6:12 by employing the common Greek rhetorical technique of diatribe, citing the opponents' objections to his argument, and then overcoming their persuasive force with counterarguments. He does this twice in 6:12, and then 6:13 takes up a third argument and counterargument.

The first projected Corinthian argument must have been a controlling principle for them because it comes up again almost identically in 10:23 and then in similar language elsewhere in Paul's correspondence with them (7:35; 10:33; 12:7; 2 Cor 8:10). The idea that one has freedom in Christ (Gal 5:1) would certainly resonate with many influential Greek philosophies, as it does with contemporary democratic freedoms. However, freedom is not anarchy. Restrictions of behavior are necessary for people to get along. Exercise of my freedom can trespass on yours. Likewise, in Paul's understanding of Christianity, the freedom that Christ acquired for believers is from slavery to sin's power over them. His agonizing death does not buy them a free pass to do whatever they want. They are free from the eternal death that sin causes, but that freedom is for service to Christ and the cause of furthering his Kingdom, which includes high moral expectations. Paul no doubt was misunderstood on this score, as Romans 3:8 and James 2:24 reveal. Paul's counterargument is unassailable. Indeed, what good is freedom if people use it to harm themselves or others? Voluntary restrictions must apply to freedom of any kind, including Christian freedom.

The second projected Corinthian argument is stated exactly as the first (even in the Greek), but Paul counters it in a slightly different way. Here, he takes the fairly profound position that freedom to do anything without restraint can in itself lead to slavery to any number of destructive habitual behaviors. Today we would talk about addictions to things like alcohol, drugs, food, computer games, or gambling, as well as sexual promiscuity. Paul understood that a believer's attachment to Jesus Christ as Lord (as he will explain further in 7:22) trumps all other commitments and behaviors.

In 6:13, Paul utters the third projected Corinthian argument, which speaks of the symbiotic relationship between a person's stomach and food. It forcefully states a point that is emphasized in Jesus' teaching (Matt 15:17; Mark 7:19) and that Paul would agree with: Under Christ's new covenant the dietary restrictions of Jews need not be forced upon new Gentile converts. Since God created the stomach to consume food, supplying it with the food needed is only natural, regardless of its source. This is an argument Paul himself will make in chapters 8–11. He would also agree that the ultimate destiny of material items like food and stomachs is destruction. However, Paul strenuously disagreed that the same principle applies to the human body in general and especially every organ.

The physical bodies of Christians—specifically their sexual organs—were not designed for illicit sexual activity. Being committed to Christ adds a moral element to the picture that must be taken into account. Paul states this very starkly: The body of a Christian is "for the Lord," and the Lord is "for the body." What he means is that the symbiotic relationship principle in sexual matters is not between the body (its organ) and the outside activity of physical contact with another person that includes sexual intimacy; rather, the symbiotic relationship of Christians is between their bodies and Christ. This new relationship supersedes all others, particularly the moral behavior of Christians, including their sexual relationships. Paul will go into more detail about why this is so in 6:15-17.

In order to counter the Corinthian argument with their new relationship to Christ, Paul relied on what he said in 6:11 about now being clean, holy, and right before God. This transition from their old life to this new one occurred when they were baptized into Christ. As he explains in Romans 6, their baptism united them with Christ with powerful results. One of these results, as he explains in 6:14, is that believers have the promise of resurrection when their human bodies have expired. This is exemplified in God's act of raising the human body of Jesus from the dead, the cornerstone event of Christian belief. Another result of being united with Christ has to do with the morality of the human body.

Paul explains his thinking beginning in 6:15. He wanted to convey something of a mystery to the Corinthians. Their new relationship was beyond just the symbiotic relationship of one body being attached to another. Rather, upon entrance into Christ in baptism, a believer is integrated into Christ's own body as one of its working parts (M. Mitchell 1993:121). This mystery will emerge yet again, but he will apply it in a slightly different way to the controversies Paul deals with in chapters 12–14. His concern was that Corinthian believers would realize that when they engage in sexual activity outside of marriage, they are causing Christ to participate in that sinful life as well. They are hooking Christ up to a prostitute. The very thought of a Christian who loves Christ linking the sinless Lamb of God into any promiscuous sexual activity is completely unimaginable. And thus Paul shouts, "Never!"

In 6:16, he quotes a portion of Genesis 2:24 as the authority for his thinking. God says that in marriage, husband and wife become one person, and this truth is conceptualized and enacted in their sexual activity. Paul believed that this truth extends to all sexual activity. Thus, when a person engages in sexual relations with another person, even outside a marriage covenant, the two have become united in this profound way. If one of them has been united with Christ in baptism, Christ has also become an illicit lover. Paul realized this is not simply a matter of a physical connection that occurs between the two promiscuous lovers and Christ. Thus, in 6:17 he notes that the union between Christ and the believer is a spiritual one. Nonetheless, the juncture between Christ, the believer, and the illicit lover has occurred in their sexual activity. This makes such activity completely unacceptable within a Christian framework.

Beginning in 6:18, Paul sums up his will for the Corinthians in all this with a straightforward command: "Run from sexual sin!" This should be enough to say, after the reasoning he had provided in 6:13-16, especially the disturbing image of Christ being united to a whore. However, he added another line of reasoning. This approach appears to take the familiar form of countering a popular slogan the Corinthians may have been repeating to justify retaining the sexual lifestyles of their popular culture. A common belief among the Greeks was that human sin and evil is located merely in the physical part of a person. The human spirit is pure and is forced to participate in sinful activity by the afflicted body. Thus, to say sin is merely outside the body is to say it is strictly physical. If humans sin against others, this is against the bodies of others. We still tend to focus on sin as physical action (like murder or theft) in Western culture.

So, for the Corinthians, even sexual sin was simply physical. However, Paul disagreed fiercely, and singled out sexual sin from the vice list in 6:9-10. Sexual sin affects a person inside (*eis* [TG1519, ZG1650] in Greek). It is sin against one's own inner person, one's spirit, and for that matter, against the inner person of the other participant. This is because, as Paul already explained, a union takes place in sexual intimacy that goes well beyond the physical. Today, we would talk about the emotional and psychological attachment that takes place. The union Paul chiefly had in mind is the one between believers and Christ, which he explained in 6:15-17.

Paul adds another line of reasoning in 6:19. Here he expounds on yet another mystery of Christian anthropology, and he does this via the corporate unity of the church. He teaches that the Holy Spirit resides now in the corporate dwelling of the church as God once dwelt in the temple of Israel. Though he will expound on the significance of this in terms of the gifts of the Spirit in chapters 12–14, at this point he means to get at the idea that the Spirit of God also dwells in individual believers. If he resides in the believers as a whole, then in some sense he resides in believers individually. God gave his Spirit to the church by giving it to the individual believers who compose the church.

The last sentence of 6:19, regarding who has ownership of believers, leads into 6:20, which develops the idea that believers as a corporate entity, and thus as individuals, are owned by God. Paul believed they had been bought and paid for by God's handing over his Son, Jesus Christ, to be tortured and executed on a Roman cross. This ultimate sacrifice paid the ransom price for slaves (with sin as their former master) to be freed. No longer slaves to sin, they belong to God and should pay him the respect he is due for the grace and love he has shown them by his sacrifice. Their allegiance is now to God and him alone through Christ. This allegiance is shown in many ways, but one crucial way is by honoring God with their individual bodies. This means honoring God with sexual purity and not dishonoring him with sexual immorality.

◆ IV. Paul's Reply to Specific Questions in the Corinthians' Letter (7:1–16:12)
A. Matters Related to Marriage (7:1–40)
1. Marriage should include sexual relations (7:1-7)

Now regarding the questions you asked in your letter. Yes, it is good to abstain from sexual relations.* ²But because there is so much sexual immorality, each man should have his own wife, and each woman should have her own husband.

³The husband should fulfill his wife's sexual needs, and the wife should fulfill her husband's needs. ⁴The wife gives authority over her body to her husband, and the husband gives authority over his body to his wife.

⁵Do not deprive each other of sexual relations, unless you both agree to refrain from sexual intimacy for a limited time so you can give yourselves more completely to prayer. Afterward, you should come together again so that Satan won't be able to tempt you because of your lack of self-control. ⁶I say this as a concession, not as a command. ⁷But I wish everyone were single, just as I am. Yet each person has a special gift from God, of one kind or another.

7:1 Or *to live a celibate life;* Greek reads *It is good for a man not to touch a woman.*

NOTES

7:1 *Now regarding the questions.* Lit., "Now concerning what." This formula, repeated in 7:25; 8:1; 12:1; 16:1, 12 serves as Paul's indicator that he was responding to questions raised specifically in the letter the Corinthians sent him (see Introduction). Though Paul was responding to their questions, there is no conclusive reason for assuming he orders chs 7–16 according to the sequence of their questions (M. Mitchell 1989:229-256; M. Mitchell 1993:190).

it is good to abstain from sexual relations. Lit., "it is good for a man not to touch a woman" (so NLT mg). The first rendering in NLT mg, "to live a celibate life," is not viable because the context indicates that this issue is about sexual intimacy within marriage (Fee 1980:307-314; Fee 1987:275; Soards 1999:141; Thiselton 2000:499). Paul's use of the statement itself most likely mimics the position of some of the Corinthians for rhetorical effect (Barrett 1968:155; Collins 1999:253; Thiselton 2000:499), though some commentaries take the phrase to be Paul's (Conzelmann 1975:115). Paul's pattern was to quote the slogans of those he opposed, as he did earlier in 6:12-13. In the third century, Origen speculated that the slogan was from the Corinthians (Thiselton 2000:498). The value of refraining from sexual intimacy for spiritual benefit was extolled by Cynic and Stoic philosophers, as well as by the cult of Isis, known to be vibrant in Corinth, and the Therapeutae, whom Philo describes approvingly as encouraging both men and women who are married to become "elderly virgins" (Cha 1998:105; Collins 1999:253; Gundry-Volf 1994:110; Hays 1997:114; Horsley 1998:96; Oster 1992:61; Wire 1990:83-85; Yarborough 1985:32-46).

7:2 *so much sexual immorality.* Gr., *porneia* [TG4202, ZG4518]. This is the same word used in 5:1; 6:13; and 6:18 to refer to sexual activity outside of marriage. The plural here, nicely conveyed by "so much" in the NLT, directs readers back to those instances.

have his own wife. Gr., *tēn heautou gunaika echetō* [TG1135, ZG1222]. In this context, this phrasing refers to sexual union (cf. Mark 6:18). Note its earlier use in 5:1 in reference to the man and his father's wife.

each woman should have her own husband. The reciprocity to include the wife's conjugal expectations is noteworthy when compared to how these were ignored in both Greek and Jewish cultural thought.

7:3 *should fulfill his wife's sexual needs.* Literally, this refers to paying back the obligation of a binding debt. The wife and the husband each owe the other this service based upon their mutual commitment. Again, emphasis on the husband's obligation to the wife becomes highlighted as a peculiarly Christian emphasis.

7:4 *gives authority.* Gr., *ouk exousiazei* [TG1850, ZG2027]. Although the noun form of this word abounds in the NT (over 100 times), this verbal form occurs only four times—twice in this verse, earlier in 6:12, and in Luke 22:25. It refers to someone in authority who exercises it in a given situation. The statement regarding the wife and the husband is literally that they do not have authority over their own bodies. The NLT appropriately states this as a positive, while the NIV is also correct to infer that they do not have exclusive authority over their own bodies (Thiselton 2000:505).

7:5 *Do not deprive.* Gr., *mē apostereite* [TG3361/650, ZG3590/691]. Translated "cheat" earlier in 6:7 and 6:8, this verb, used elsewhere only in Mark 10:19; 1 Tim 6:5; and Jas 5:4, primarily refers to robbing someone of their valuables. The sense of "deprive" here is most similar to Jas 5:4, which talks of landowners not paying their laborers.

both agree. Lit., "by agreement" (*sumphōnou* [TG4859, ZG5247]). This noun form is used only here in the NT. Cognates refer to people coming to agreement, as in terms for hire (Matt 18:19; 20:2, 13), or even the musical harmony of voices or instruments in music (Luke 15:25). The English word "symphony" derives from this word.

limited time. Gr., *kairon* [TG2540, ZG2789]. Though this word is sometimes synonymous with *chronos* [TG5550, ZG5989], which refers to a quantity or length of time, it often refers to an appropriate or appointed time, as here.

give yourselves more completely. Gr., *scholasēte* [TG4980, ZG5390]. Only used here and in Matt 12:44, this word refers to having leisure time, which thus enables people to devote themselves fully to something without distraction.

prayer. The late addition of "and fasting" to a few medieval manuscripts is explained by the pairing of the two words in Luke 2:37; Acts 14:23; and in some manuscripts of Mark 9:29. But the words "and fasting" are not original. The Jewish pseudepigraphic document *Testament of Naphtali* 8:8 parallels Paul's principle when it says, "There is a time for one to have intercourse with one's wife and a time to abstain for the purpose of prayer."

lack of self-control. Gr., *akrasian* [TG192, ZG202]. Only used here and in Matt 23:25, this word is the negation of a word frequently used to refer to power (*kratos* [TG2904, ZG3197]; see Col 1:11). Thus, it describes a person without the personal fortitude to overcome the impending challenge. Its opposite, "self-control" (*enkrateia* [TG1466, ZG1602]), appears in the virtue catalogs of Gal 5:23 and 2 Pet 1:6.

7:6 concession. Gr., *sungnōmēn* [TG4774, ZG5152]. Only used here in the NT, this word refers to the sympathy one person has for the actions another person takes under difficult circumstances, which leads to pardoning or excusing them for what the person has done.

7:7 But. Gr., *de* [TG1161, ZG1254]. The appearance of "for" (*gar* [TG1063, ZG1142]) in a number of manuscripts, including ℵ² and B, derives from interpreting the entire paragraph (7:1b-7) incorrectly as a call for asceticism (Collins 1999:260), with Paul supplying further evidence from his own life as support.

I wish everyone were single, just as I am. Lit., "I wish everyone to be as I am." The idea that Paul was without a wife is inferred from this passage. Though disputed (Roetzel 1999:151), many agree that since Paul was both a Pharisee and a rabbi, it would have been highly unusual for him not to have been married at least earlier in his life (Murphy-O'Connor 1996:64; Collins 1999:260; Jeremias 1926:310-312), as prescribed by *b. Yevamot* 62b-64a. That he had become a widower previous to his call to be an apostle is fueled by the fact that he seems to rank himself among the widowers in 7:8. Celibacy was thought to promote one's communication with God within the prophetic context of Judaism (Poirier and Frankovic 1996:13-14) and was advocated by some rabbis (Yarborough 1985:21-22).

everyone. Gr., *pantas anthrōpous* [TG3956/444, ZG4246/476]. This can refer to males but usually refers to people in general, male and female. Since Paul had carefully balanced his comments about husbands and wives up to this point, it is notable that in this principled statement he has combined them together in his reference. Up to now Paul has carefully used the normal word for male or husband (*anēr* [TG435, ZG467]) to refer to the male spouse (7:2, 3, 4).

COMMENTARY

With 7:1, Paul begins responding to questions the Corinthians posed in the letter sent via Stephanas, Fortunatus, and Achaicus, first about marriage, next about food sacrificed to idols, then about spiritual gifts, and finally about the collection for the Christians in Jerusalem. In all his New Testament correspondence, this is the only known letter that Paul answers. Although his responses constitute the remainder, indeed the bulk of 1 Corinthians, it is significant that Paul did not begin the letter by addressing their concerns. Rather, he had left this for last, providing his thorough, theologically grounded perspectives only after he had confronted the splintering of their community with the unifying theology of the cross, a grounding he will draw upon in his responses (Hays 1997:111).

Despite the fact that Paul shifted into a new mode at this point in his letter, he built a bridge from chapters 5–6 into chapter 7 on the topic of sexual conduct for believers. Christians must turn their back on sexual immorality and discipline those who do not. Sexual promiscuity is a sacrilege against the Christian's body, now joined to Christ and indwelt by the Holy Spirit. Assuming this principle, which was presented at the end of chapter 6, the natural follow-up question Paul sought to answer is, What is the role of sexual relations within marriage for transformed believers? This will lead him into other questions about marriage that extend from there.

Paul starts off by quoting a slogan that was most likely part of the Corinthians' question in their letter (namely, "it is good to abstain from sexual relations"; 7:1). Their question was not about whether new Christians should be single (despite the fact that he does address this later in the chapter). The concern was about sexual relations within marriage. The question could be raised because of the theology of the Christian's body Paul discussed at the end of chapter 6. However, the Corinthians were likely wondering, in light of this, if Christianity was another cult that required sexual asceticism—complete abstinence from sexual relations even for the married—since this would not be all that unusual in the first century. The effect of this prevalent approach to spirituality on young Christian congregations like Corinth can be seen in Paul's efforts to confront such notions in other letters (Col 2:20-23; 1 Tim 4:3).

It may sound at first like Paul agrees with this position that men should not touch women, in or outside marriage, especially since he prefaces this with the favorable comment that "it is good." However, this is to misunderstand his rhetorical approach. He wanted to agree with what the Corinthians had said as much as he could, out of respect, and he will reveal in his discussion that he believed there is value in being celibate. But he will clarify that this is only for some people and that it is certainly not a principle that applies in marriage. There, other principles control the expected Christian behavior. Anyway, for him to agree with this slogan would place him at direct odds with Genesis 2:18: "It is not good for the man to be alone. I will make a helper who is just right for him."

In contrast to any notions about sexual celibacy in marriage, in 7:2 Paul advocates marriage (J. Ellis 2001:91; Laughery 1997:110), verifying its value probably from his own Jewish culture, as well as its value for populating the earth (Gen 1:28; 2:24). Though his opening statement names only his concern about sexual immorality as influencing his support for marriage, later comments will reveal that he was probably more influenced by biblical support for the mutual commitment involved in marriage. The prominence he gives up front to sexual immorality was motivated by his desire to link his comments to those of chapters 5 and 6, where the expression "sexual immorality" (*porneia* [TG4202, ZG4518]) figures so prominently (5:1; 6:13, 18).

One of the most striking aspects of Paul's promotion of marriage is how deliberate he was to balance his comments with regard to both husbands and wives throughout this chapter. Relative to the patriarchal views of marriage prevalent in his day, Paul's comments mark him as fairly radical in elevating the status of wives (Horsley 1998:95; Witherington 1995:170). He does this right away in 7:2 when he speaks generally of Christian marriage. Each should "have" the other, which refers to their sexual relationship but probably includes their mutual commitment in all aspects of their marriage relationship. In 7:3, he also spells out the mutual giving involved specifically in their physical intimacy.

For the sake of his argument, Paul depicts marriage as a binding business contract. His language in 7:3-4 was more normally used for payment of a debt. He viewed the marriage bed as the location where the debts of husband and wife are exchanged. Because both have given their bodies to the other in the bonds of marriage, each has an obligation to attempt to repay the debt this creates. Of course, this debt can never be paid in full. Is there a limit to the value of a human life? Thus, both are continually and forever in debt to the other; each giving to the other of sexual intimacy is a major area of their relationship in which payment can be applied to this debt.

Again, the surprising aspect of Paul's argument is the mutuality described and especially the husband's obligation to the wife, which he names first. This reinforces the idea that Paul was cutting against the grain of the views of marriage that were prominent in both Greek and Jewish cultures, namely, that the husband was in charge of his wife in all ways, including sexually, but that he had few if any obligations to his wife, unless it was to give her children (Keener 2005:62).

In 7:4, Paul expands on why he views the husband and wife as being mutually in debt. Both have already freely given their lives away to the other when they married. Their very bodies belong to the other. They cannot any longer think of themselves only as an "I." They have to think of themselves as a "you." They give themselves away to the other, purposefully limiting their own personal rights and privileges to create a joyful "us." To draw back from this self-giving in a marriage is to take a step that could eventually unravel the entire relationship.

In 7:5, Paul puts his stamp of approval on one legitimate exception to the mutual engagement of married couples in regular sexual intimacy. Any other reason he associates with robbery, based on his view of mutual ownership and mutual debt. To take what the other offers without a reciprocal offering of oneself cheats the other party. Any decision that involves refraining from sexual relations within marriage must be mutually agreed upon. The only reason Paul names as a bona fide reason is their mutual spiritual benefit that comes from concentrating on prayer for a period of time. However, the prayer time must have a clear purpose that is achievable within a number of days that can be estimated from the outset.

Paul apparently adapted this concession from Jewish tradition, which allowed men one week (so Hillel) or two weeks (so Shammai) of sexual abstinence for prayer that involves consent from the wife. Rabbis were allowed to make vows of sexual abstinence from their wives for up to 30 days without consent (*m. Ketubbot* 5:6; *t. Nedarim* 5:6). Also demonstrating the link between prayer and sexual activity, Jewish men were encouraged to refrain from saying the Shema (the Jewish daily prayer that begins "Hear, O Israel, the Lord our God is one") for a few days after being wedded (Barrett 1968:156). The Old Testament also demonstrates the importance of sexual abstinence for some holy days and generally for occasions of spiritual consecration (Exod 19:15; Lev 15:18; 1 Sam 21:4-6; 2 Sam 11:11-13; Joel 2:16).

What stands out as new, from Paul's perspective, is that he views both the husband and the wife agreeing to replace their sexual activity with prayer for a time and that either could initiate the agreement. From the Jewish perspective, the husband alone is viewed as abstaining for the purpose of prayer. This spiritual mutuality corresponds with the mutual nature of the Christian marriage that Paul paints throughout the chapter. It even continues over into his concern about temptation from Satan, which he phrases in the plural *you*. Sexual temptation for a married couple in Paul's understanding was not simply a problem for the husband; it can also be a problem for the wife, if the abstinence is prolonged. Above all, Paul was adamant that no sexual promiscuity should occur in the lives of believers, both those married and unmarried. The difficulty for humans to control their sex drive is not restricted to one gender. Because of this, couples need to rekindle their intimacy within a reasonable time frame. The last thing Paul wants is for sexual abstinence to provide an opportunity for Satan to fan the flame of sexual sin and adultery. (Satan's role as the ultimate tempter is described most clearly in Matthew 4:1-11.)

In 7:6, Paul admits that the priority in marriage is to fulfill the commitment to sexual intimacy. Such times of marital sexual abstinence are not at all required for either the husband or the wife to achieve spiritual depth and maturity in their Christian lives. It is, however, an option they may choose to exercise as far as Paul was concerned. Of all the verses in this chapter, this most clearly demonstrates that Paul did not embrace ascetic values as the necessary means to lofty spiritual attainment, as some later in the church have done and which Roman Catholicism perpetuates by requiring celibacy of its priests and nuns.

In 7:7, Paul shares his personal desire that people exercise their gift of singleness, if they have this gift. However, marriage is a gift, too. He had likely experienced both in the course of his life. Probably having had a wife earlier, he was now single, a widower; he found this to be an advantage for serving the Lord and completing his call (see note on 7:7). He will expand on this perspective later in the chapter (7:32-35). But he certainly also extols the blessing of marriage in this verse, a gift equal in promise. He couldn't make it clearer that such personal matters are entirely up to each individual and that God has a hand in whatever a believer embraces.

◆   ## 2. Those currently unwed may marry (7:8-9)

⁸So I say to those who aren't married and to widows—it's better to stay unmarried, just as I am. ⁹But if they can't control themselves, they should go ahead and marry. It's better to marry than to burn with lust.

NOTES

7:8 *those who aren't married.* Gr., *agamois* [ᵀᴳ22A, ᶻᴳ23]. Only used in this chapter in the NT (7:8, 11, 32, 34), the word simply negates the word for marriage (*gamos* [ᵀᴳ1062, ᶻᴳ1141]) and thus means "unmarried." Usually a general term, the question is whether it is intended to be all-inclusive here, including those of both genders who are divorced, whose spouses have died, as well as those who never married. A strong case is made by some (Collins 1999:268; Fee 1987:287-288) for the context expecting a narrow function of the word in terms of a widower, pairing nicely with widow. However, the stronger position (Garland 2003:276-277; Thiselton 2000:516), based on its later uses in the chapter, is that its reference is broad, since the word refers to women in 7:11 and 7:34 and men in 7:32, and the advice given in 7:9 fits with Paul's general advice to all, even those never married in 7:25-29.

7:9 *control themselves.* Gr., *enkrateuontai* [TG1467, ZG1603]. In 9:25, the only other use of this word in the NT, it refers to the kind of bodily discipline required to prepare for rigorous athletic contests. The same kind of personal physical strength required for that is now applied to controlling sexual urges.

burn with lust. Gr., *purousthai* [TG4448A, ZG4792], the verbal cognate of "fire" (*pur* [TG4442, ZG4786]). Paul's other two uses of this word (2 Cor 11:29; Eph 6:16) connect it to sin, though not sexual craving as here. The suggestion by Bruce (1971:68) that this "might possibly mean 'to burn in Gehenna' because of falling into fornication" in this passage (Barré 1974:193-202) has rightly been rejected as interesting but not supportable by anything in the context (Soards 1999:145; Thiselton 2000:517).

COMMENTARY

Paul moves on from commenting on the importance of sexual relations between married couples who are believers to other possible situations people may be facing with regard to marriage. First, in 7:8-9, he makes general comments about those who are currently single, for any reason, before following up later with particular circumstances (7:17-28). Next, he will make general comments about those who are married in whatever type of relationship (7:10-11), following up with later comments (7:12-16).

Paul's advice in 7:8 is that those whose personal status currently finds them unmarried should seriously consider remaining in that state. His only reasoning at this point is that this is what he had done, and therefore he recommended it. He did not provide any further reasoning until 7:17-24, in which he develops his reasoning theologically. The word he uses for "unmarried" most likely refers to people of both genders and people who are now single for any reason, whether through death of a spouse, divorce, or age. His naming of "widows" specifically remaining unmarried is emphasized because this cut against the grain of both Jewish and Greek cultures, which put great social and economic pressure on widows to remarry quickly (Rousselle 1992:316; Thiselton 2000:516). Though the pressure was also there for widowers, it was not as great, since men normally had the means to provide for themselves and protect themselves from danger. Women normally moved from the protection and provision of their fathers to that of their husband or succession of husbands (Witherington 1995:170).

Paul's bridge to 7:5 involves the difficulty people have in controlling their God-given urges for sexual fulfillment. There he applied this reality to married couples carefully limiting their time-out from sexual intimacy. Here he applies the same reality to people who are not currently married. The idea of maintaining a perennial celibate state for spiritual reasons might sound very appealing to both men and women who want to serve God with every ounce of their life, but the biological needs of their bodies could very well make this far more difficult at points than they ever realized. In this case, perhaps they didn't have the gift of singleness Paul spoke of in 7:7 (a gift he had). It was better for them to recognize this and pursue marriage before they were drawn into sexual promiscuity, activity completely banned for a Christian. Thus, their noble commitment to serve God as a single person could lead them to spiritual ruin. From Paul's perspective there was absolutely no need for this to happen. Marriage is a perfectly legitimate state in which to serve God, and it is probably better overall for most people.

◆   ### 3.   Believers should not divorce their marriage partners (7:10-16)

¹⁰But for those who are married, I have a command that comes not from me, but from the Lord.* A wife must not leave her husband. ¹¹But if she does leave him, let her remain single or else be reconciled to him. And the husband must not leave his wife.

¹²Now, I will speak to the rest of you, though I do not have a direct command from the Lord. If a Christian man* has a wife who is not a believer and she is willing to continue living with him, he must not leave her. ¹³And if a Christian woman has a husband who is not a believer and he is willing to continue living with her, she must not leave him. ¹⁴For the Christian wife brings holiness to her marriage, and the Christian husband* brings holiness to his marriage. Otherwise, your children would not be holy, but now they are holy. ¹⁵(But if the husband or wife who isn't a believer insists on leaving, let them go. In such cases the Christian husband or wife* is no longer bound to the other, for God has called you* to live in peace.) ¹⁶Don't you wives realize that your husbands might be saved because of you? And don't you husbands realize that your wives might be saved because of you?

7:10 See Matt 5:32; 19:9; Mark 10:11-12; Luke 16:18.   7:12 Greek *a brother.*   7:14 Greek *the brother.*   7:15a Greek *the brother or sister.*   7:15b Some manuscripts read *us.*

NOTES

7:10 *a command . . . from the Lord.* The phrase contrasts with how Paul introduces his views in 7:12 as not being from the Lord. This is only one of four times in the NT (9:14; 11:23; 1 Tim 5:18) that Paul refers directly to a logion (saying) of Jesus to support his teaching. That Paul can distinguish between his own interpretive teaching and the commands of Christ provides evidence that Paul was well versed in Jesus' teaching via the oral transmission of the Twelve (Garland 2003:282). Evidence for this command of Jesus about divorce appears in Matt 5:32, Mark 10:11-12, and Luke 16:18, though none of these would have been written prior to 1 Corinthians. Paul's dependence on Jesus' teaching may be wider than this verse, and it may encompass multiple parallels between 6:12–7:11, Matt 19:3-12, and Mark 10:2-12 (Olender 2001:70).

leave. Gr., *chōristhēnai* [TG5563, ZG6004]. Used four times in this context alone (7:11, 15 [twice]), this word refers to two things that are severed or divided. The NIV has "separate." Paul favors using this word to refer to the ending of a marriage by women and uses the more common word for divorce (*aphiēmi* [TG863, ZG918]) for the ending of a marriage initiated by husbands. The NIV and ESV maintain this distinction by translating that word as "divorce" in 7:11c-13. However, the NLT translates both words "leave" to show that in Roman law there was no distinction in process with regard to a husband or a wife getting a divorce. The legal process in both cases simply involved separating by leaving the home and making a declaration (Thiselton 2000:520; Witherington 1995:171). That Paul used the passive voice for women divorcing their husbands (lit., "a wife must not be separated from her husband") but the active voice for husbands divorcing their wives may reflect a patriarchal understanding of marriage resident in Paul's language (Collins 1999:269).

7:11 *single.* Gr., *agamos* [TG22A, ZG23]. See note on 7:8.

reconciled. Used five other times in the NT (Rom 5:10 [twice]; 2 Cor 5:18, 19, 20). All the uses of this word (*katallassō* [TG2644, ZG2904]) outside 1 Corinthians are theological, regarding Christ's reconciliation of the world to God. It refers to the transformation of a situation of hostility to a situation of peace and trust, here applied to the reconstitution of a faltering marriage.

7:14 brings holiness. Gr., *hēgiastai* [TG37, ZG39]. Used two other times in 1 Corinthians (1:2; 6:11), this is a verbal cognate of "holy," which refers to things that are sacred—i.e., separated out from the mundane to serve God. The NIV renders this "has been sanctified" and the ESV "is made holy." The NLT helps make clear that holiness comes into a marriage between Christian spouses and nonbelieving spouses, having a positive effect on their relationship to God that may lead to their salvation without implying that salvation is in any way automatically implied (Martens 1996a:34). Extensive discussion of this issue from Jewish and Greek perspectives is found in Gillihan 2002:711-744.

Christian husband. The actual Greek word here is *adelphō* [TG80, ZG81] (brother), providing special emphasis on the believing husband's added Christian relationship with his wife upon her conversion. Just like the NLT has switched the translation to "husband," so also some scribes did the same, substituting "husband" (*andri* [TG435, ZG467]) or "believing husband" (*andri tō pistō* [TG4103, ZG4412]) for "brother" (*adelphō*). However, the reading "brother" (*adelphō*) has ample manuscript support (𝔓46 ℵ A B C) to be considered original.

7:15 peace. Gr., *eirēnē* [TG1515, ZG1645]. This word, the Greek equivalent of the common Jewish greeting *shalom* [TH7965, ZH8934], is often used by Paul in combination with "grace" (*charis* [TG5485, ZG5921]) to form the opening greetings of his letters, as in 1:3. On its own it constitutes a crucial theological truth about the expected impact of the gospel: It brings reconciliation with God and man. Paul emphasizes this especially in Ephesians 2:14-18, when he speaks of Christ in his very person uniting Jews and Gentiles. Later in 1 Corinthians, Paul will call God a God of peace (14:33). So, using peace as a byword for the Christian life here is not surprising.

7:16 be saved. Gr., *sōseis* [TG4982, ZG5392]. Outside the NT, this word describes someone who is rescued from danger. Used over 100 times in the NT, it nearly always refers to being saved from eternal destruction to experience everlasting life with God.

COMMENTARY

Paul's general comment about marriage in 7:10 is that it should remain intact. This is the case whether it involves two Christians or one. His position came from the value placed on marriage in Jewish culture and, no doubt, from Genesis 2:24, but he also drew upon a teaching of Jesus well documented in the Gospels. That teaching bans divorce outright (Mark 10:11-12; Luke 16:18), though Matthew 5:32 admits that a spouse's adultery provides a permissible cause to initiate divorce.

True to his pattern, Paul balanced applications of this teaching for husbands and wives in 7:10 and 11. However, this is the only circumstance in the whole chapter in which he reversed the order. Instead of enjoining men not to divorce their wives (7:2-3, 4, 12-13, 14-15, 27-28, 32-34), he first instructs the women not to divorce their husbands and then follows up with the men. This causes many interpreters to suggest that Paul was aware of Christian women in Corinth who were considering divorcing their husbands, something rare in Jewish society but commonplace in Greek and Roman society (Garland 2003:281; Hays 1997:120; Thiselton 2000:522). Given his more focused comments in 7:12-16, it may also be that a contingent of Christian women had already divorced their non-Christian husbands.

Paul immediately moved from the ideal to the practical. What if a wife had divorced her husband, whether before she became a Christian and was aware of this command, or sometime in the future for any number of personal reasons? What then? Paul says she has two choices, either remain single (as he himself was) and then use this status to serve the Lord fully, or seek to reestablish her original marriage. If she pursued a divorce from her husband, she must have serious grievances against him, but Paul enjoined her to take the initiative with her former husband in order to reunite with him. The concern, probably based on Jewish practice, was that once the man married someone else, she would not be permitted to marry him again (Deut 24:4); thus, from Paul's perspective the door had been shut for her to ever remarry. Although this injunction is not repeated for the man who divorces his wife, it can be assumed that Paul meant to apply this also to men. Underlying all this is God's ordinance that marriage between one man and one woman is binding.

Having dealt with the unmarried generally in 7:8-9 and those married generally in 7:10-11, Paul in 7:12-16 addresses a special circumstance in marriage created by the infusion of the gospel into Corinthian culture: husbands or wives who converted to Christianity without their spouses. That this was a common enough occurrence for Paul to address suggests that Christianity's claims on the individual superseded normal social mores. In Greek homes, wives were expected to worship the gods of their husbands (Collins 1999:265), though in emerging mystery religions of the first century (especially the cult of Isis, which was very strong in Corinth) they were beginning to shirk this expectation. In Judaism, marriage to a non-Jew was not considered a valid marriage (*b. Qiddushin* 68b; *b. Yevamot* 45a).

Without a specific command for this circumstance, Paul reasoned from the command of Christ regarding the binding nature of marriage in 7:10 that the only proper course of action is for believers, whether husbands or wives, to continue in their religiously mixed marriages and make the best of it. The spiritual transformation involved in conversion to Christianity should not be complicit in the spread of divorce. Rather, it should result in a deepening resolve to advance marriage. Paul did not want to see the ranks of the unmarried, who *could* devote themselves to the advance of the gospel, swelled by Christians who had divorced their unbelieving spouses.

In 7:14, Paul shows that he viewed the marriage union inversely from the ways pagans or Jews viewed it. One rotten apple does not automatically spoil the one next to it. Rather than believing that the purity of the marriage is contaminated by the unbelieving partner, Paul believed the purity of the marriage was enhanced by the believing partner. Robertson and Plummer (1911:142) explain this well: "The purity of the believing partner overpowers the impurity of the unbelieving one." For Paul this is proved by what he considered an established premise: The children of mixed marriages are "holy."

Such children are allowed to participate fully in the life of the Christian community without taint or compromise. This follows for Paul from Jewish practice that the children of mixed marriages are Jewish through their maternal lineage and that the children of proselytes were treated as legitimate members of the Jewish community (Collins 1999:267). It is consistent with the principle of Exodus 29:37 that "whatever touches [the altar] will become holy." For Paul, this may follow further from Jesus' blessing of the children (Matt 19:13-15) but not from any assumption that children were baptized (Barrett 1968:165; Robertson and Plummer 1911:142). This acceptance of children into the Christian community does not imply that they are saved before confessing faith in Christ and receiving baptism, any more than the holiness the believing spouse brings to marriage automatically saves them. In short, they must become converted.

In 7:15, Paul considers the flip side of the mixed-marriage scenario. What if the nonbelieving spouse is not at all happy that their mate has defected to a strange, new religion like Christianity and desires to initiate a divorce with the believing spouse? Maybe he or she was not neutral on the subject but held severe animosity toward the believing spouse. What then? Paul saw no advantage for a Christian to remain in such a hostile environment, as long as it was the spouse who initiated the divorce action. In actual fact, very little could be done by the divorced party since divorces could not really be contested (Garland 2003:292-293). The one initiating the divorce simply moved out. The other could not do anything legally to prevent this.

Paul invites believing Christians to accept being divorced by their antagonistic spouses if they wish. The binding rule about marriage can be dissolved in this situation. Presumably, Paul's advice to other divorced believers about seeking remarriage with their ex-wives and husbands does not apply here because the situation foments hostility (personally and toward Christ) that is superseded by the overriding principle that Christianity brings peace into the world. Accepting divorce from an unbelieving spouse in the long run may be more conducive for the impact of the gospel in his or her life than staying in the marriage.

By contrast, 7:16 seems to encourage believing spouses to stay in their relationship with an unbelieving spouse. If they can get past a period of hostility, maybe they can persuade their spouse with the gospel and thereby make peace. In the end, though, this is a personal decision. The believer has to balance the negative effect of the hostile partner on their own spiritual growth and development with, no doubt, their intense desire to see their partner accept the gospel.

The remaining question is whether this scenario leaves a divorced believer free to remarry, presumably to a believer this time rather than an unbeliever. Being no longer "bound" or "enslaved," is the first marriage annulled? In this context Paul's silence can be taken either as permission or as restriction. Interpreters are divided. Fee (1986:294-295) says no (also Olender 1998:94); Conzelmann (1975:121) says yes (also Borchert 1999:127; Keener 2005:65). Thiselton (2000:534-536) chews over the issue most thoroughly and concludes maybe. It is probably best that remarriage in such situations not be excluded as a viable personal choice. Despite Paul's stance against remarrying anyone other than one's former spouse, he does not advocate embracing singleness as the only alternative here either, as he did earlier. The key for application is recognizing that Paul had not taken a clear position on this question but that, as on every matter involving marriage in the chapter, he did not dictate but allowed for the variableness of real, individual choices in light of personal situations (Horsley 1998:95).

◆   ## 4. Believers should generally maintain current personal conditions (7:17-24)

[17] Each of you should continue to live in whatever situation the Lord has placed you, and remain as you were when God first called you. This is my rule for all the

churches. ¹⁸For instance, a man who was circumcised before he became a believer should not try to reverse it. And the man who was uncircumcised when he became a believer should not be circumcised now. ¹⁹For it makes no difference whether or not a man has been circumcised. The important thing is to keep God's commandments.

²⁰Yes, each of you should remain as you were when God called you. ²¹Are you a slave? Don't let that worry you—but if you get a chance to be free, take it. ²²And remember, if you were a slave when the Lord called you, you are now free in the Lord. And if you were free when the Lord called you, you are now a slave of Christ. ²³God paid a high price for you, so don't be enslaved by the world.* ²⁴Each of you, dear brothers and sisters,* should remain as you were when God first called you.

7:23 Greek *don't become slaves of people.*   7:24 Greek *brothers;* also in 7:29.

NOTES

7:17 *in whatever situation the Lord has placed you.* Lit., "as the Lord has divided." The verb *merizō* [TG3307, ZG3532] refers to dividing something into portions and sometimes also, as here, to distributing them. In Mark 6:41 Jesus divided the two fish among the people. This word was used in 1:13 to refer to Christ being divided among the Corinthians and comes up again to describe the divided interests of a husband between his wife and larger matters.

called. Gr., *keklēken* [TG2564, ZG2813]. Nine of the twelve uses of this word in 1 Corinthians occur in this specific context (7:15, 17, 18 [twice], 20, 21, 22 [twice], 24). Outside the NT, it refers to someone summoning someone else to come. Paul used it in two specifically Christian senses: (1) the spiritual moment of a believer's acceptance of God's invitation to a restored relationship by means of the gospel (1:9; Rom 9:11; Gal 5:8; 2 Thess 2:13); (2) God's commissioning someone to a special role within his overall mission, as to apostleship (1:1; Gal 1:15). The first is meant throughout this context. The idea that it might refer to a person's vocation or social circumstance here or later in this context is a forced understanding from the church fathers and Luther (Bartchy 1973:132-159; Bruce 1971:71; Garland 2003:303; Talbert 1987:40-41; Thiselton 2000:550). The perfect tense of the verb emphasizes the settled closure of the call and leans toward the NLT's rendering of "when God first called you."

This is my rule. Gr., *diatassomai* [TG1299, ZG1411]. This verb was used as a military term for arranging troops for battle and providing them their orders. Paul's use of the middle voice softens the impact of this instruction (Soards 1999:158). It is the precedent he was setting; it was not an absolute rule, since it was not directly from Christ.

7:18 *circumcised.* This is its only use in 1 Corinthians (used twice in this verse). It refers to the ancient Jewish custom of cutting off the foreskin of male infants on their eighth day to initiate them into the nation and into the promises of God. Paul's use of the perfect tense of the participle intentionally parallels his use of the perfect for "called" in 7:17 since both mark a person's entry into God's community.

try to reverse it. The only use of this word (*epispaomai* [TG1986, ZG2177]) in the NT, it is a technical term to refer to a fairly common surgery in the ancient world, called an epispasm, to restore foreskin to the penis. As early as the second century BC, social stigma brought on by the encroachment of Hellenism upon Jewish society motivated Jewish men to obtain this surgery (1 Macc 1:15; Collins 1999:284).

7:20 *as you were when God called you.* Lit., "in the calling to which he was called." The redundancy in Greek emphasizes the enormous significance of the time of a believer's call to salvation in Paul's discussion.

7:21 *slave.* Gr., *doulos* [TG1401, ZG1528], used over 100 times in the NT. Four of its five uses in 1 Corinthians are in this context (7:21, 22 [twice], 23). Slaves were common in the ancient world, with as many as two-thirds of the population experiencing this condition at some point in their lives (Bartchy 1973:58). People became slaves from being captured in war or because of debt, but usually managed to free themselves within 10 years or so. They were not kept from one generation to the next as in America. Former slaves populated a segment of society called "freedmen." The prospects for a slave were sometimes advantageous over free peasants since they were protected from economic uncertainties by the provision of their masters. Slaves could own property and earn money. Many of those in Paul's churches, such as Corinth, no doubt were slaves. (See Bartchy 1973:60-62; Collins 1999:278; Keener 2005:66.)

take it. Gr., *mallon chrēsai* [TG3123/5530, ZG3437/5968]. This means "make the most of," with an assumption that the expected object (dative) will be filled in by the context. The question pondered by interpreters is what that should be: freedom or slavery? Does one make the most of the opportunity for freedom or make the most of the opportunity slavery provides for the gospel? Advantage falls to freedom, as the NLT correctly clarifies (Bartchy 1973:159; Deming 1995:137; Garland 2003:308; Glancy 1998; Harrill 1994:5; Talbert 1987:42; Thiselton 2000:557).

7:23 *paid a high price.* Gr., *timēs ēgorasthēte* [TG59, ZG60]. The verb is the common word for purchasing goods in the marketplace (*agora* [TG58, ZG59]). The noun (*timē* [TG5092, ZG5507]) normally means "honor" in the NT and for Paul, but it can occasionally, as here, refer to the purchase price (Matt 27:9) or to money paid (Acts 5:3). The exact phrase was used in 6:20 in the context of Christians preserving their bodies from sexual sin. In both contexts the NLT's "high price" comes from a theological understanding that the cost was the priceless life of Christ on the cross.

COMMENTARY

In this section, Paul offers a general principle that applies to marital status, as well as to the cultural and social context of new believers' lives, a principle that should be helpful for individual Corinthians to apply to their many and varied personal situations. The principle is this: Don't make any sudden changes in your life unless it is absolutely necessary. This applies to those who are married, single, or contemplating divorce, as discussed in the previous verses (7:1-16), or to situations like those who are betrothed (7:25-38) or widowed (7:39-40), which he discusses next. Christianity's impact on society should not disrupt basic institutions but live within them for the overall spread of the gospel. Paul's principle bridges from his notion, expressed in 7:15, that God has called believers "to live in peace." He will repeat his general principle twice more in this passage (7:20, 24).

Paul's first statement of his principle in 7:17 makes clear that it begins from the point of a person's acceptance of the gospel. Because of the noticeable demarcation this should make in the personal lives of believers between their former lives and their new lives, it would be natural for the Corinthian believers to think they should reconsider everything, even such embedded social institutions as marriage and social order. Paul's principle vocalizes that the radical impact Christianity makes on a person's life has limits. Thus, the principle is that new believers should stay put as much as possible in the social locations of their lives.

The principle is really stated twice in 7:17: once from the perspective of Christ

("Lord") and again from the perspective of God. With regard to Christ, Paul thought of a person's social location as a gift, not unlike the gift of singleness he mentions in 7:7 or some aspect of the table of Christ's gifts that he will develop extensively in chapter 12. With regard to God, the fact that God offered them salvation via the gospel at their social location amounts to God's blessing on it. They should accept their social location along with the gospel. The second version of Paul's principle is what he repeats in 7:20 and 7:24.

Paul also wanted the Corinthians to understand that in offering his principle, he was not singling them out or saying anything different from what he had said in all the Christian communities he had established. When the NLT calls what he teaches a "rule," it should not be read as if this is a legal rule that can be violated and prosecuted. Rather, it is a principle he worked out and believed offers the best guidance for believers to apply to the varied situations and social locations of their lives. His discussion reveals that he understood there to be exceptions, both generally and individually.

In 7:18-19, Paul offers the first of two illustrations for his general principle of maintaining one's current status upon conversion. Both of them are examples in which the Corinthians had already seen this principle in operation as a result of Paul's teaching among them. So, his key plan for demonstrating its legitimacy is consistency. Not only did he apply this principle to marriage consistently in all the churches, but he also applied it to circumcision and slavery.

The Corinthians knew full well that no one among them, whether Jewish or Greek, was required or asked to reverse their circumcision status when they became believers, even though a certain logic in both instances might have made this seem valid. Despite being the legitimate sign from the Old Testament for men to enter into covenant status with God, circumcision was not a prerequisite for becoming a Christian. In fact, Paul fought fiercely for this liberty in the churches, which is most evident in his letter to the Galatians. Furthermore, under the new covenant in Christ, which opens its arms to all people whether Jewish or not, it might be possible to argue that Judaism and its sign of circumcision was a needless hindrance to embracing a diverse Christian community. Since a common surgery was available to reverse circumcision, Christian men could easily undergo this procedure.

Paul's general principle denies both arguments and validates either status, Jewish or Gentile, as legitimate points of entrance and acceptance into the Christian community. Thus, even today, none of the diverse people of the world need to deny their ethnic status in the process of entering into the Christian church. One of the truest marks of the Christian church is that it has the capacity to embrace all ethnic groups, including most of their central cultural traditions, and contextualize them in a manner consistent with Christian ideals. Yet this is a *general* principle. With some Gentile individuals, as with Timothy (Acts 16:3), circumcision was best. With other individuals, perhaps even epispasm, a surgical procedure to reverse circumcision, seemed necessary. Thus, room for some individual diversity in how people adapt their ethnic and cultural practices into Christian life must be allowed as part of Paul's general principle of maintaining one's ethnic status in light of becoming a believer.

Those reading Paul's comments in 7:19 from a strictly Jewish perspective would have been offended (Fee 1987:313; Hays 1997:124). To make circumcision simply a matter of personal opinion would be, in fact, to break God's covenant law with the Jews found in the Old Testament (Gen 17:9-14). Since it occurs on the eighth day of life for Jewish males, no individual opinion enters into the matter. It is a matter within the covenant community. However, the New Testament era inaugurated a new covenant community that outstrips the old rules, particularly the rules of membership. To obey God's laws in the new covenant means to accept people of all ethnic backgrounds into the covenant community, with or without Jewish circumcision and with a new initiation procedure for all, Jew or non-Jew, male or female: baptism (Rom 2:25-29; 6:1-4).

After repeating in 7:20 his general principle of retaining one's status upon conversion, Paul provides a second illustration in 7:21-22. Slavery in the ancient world was every bit as much of a social institution as marriage and ethnic customs. It was an intricate part of the economic and social fabric of life, with most people of any economic means owning slaves and most people of lower economic status being slaves at some time in their lives (see notes on 7:21-22). However, since it was normally a temporary condition, people did expect to be released from it within certain understood parameters of economics and duration. So, the question slaves had about their freedom was not "if" but "when." Thus, Paul's application of his principle to slavery incorporates this eventuality. During the course of their status as slaves, believers should not apply Paul's principle to mean that they should turn their backs on the opportunities for freedom that would normally present themselves. This would apply the principle too literally. Freedom from slavery was part of the foundational social fabric of first-century life and thus part of the principle.

In 7:22, Paul reminds the Corinthians of an important theological truth: Even if they are slaves currently (and had been when they became Christians) and their prospects for release were distant or questionable, they should take heart because they were already free in the most important sense of the word. That is, they are free from slavery to sin and the world because God paid the ransom price with the life of his Son, Jesus Christ. They have become slaves of Christ now, as are all believers, a status that supersedes their economic slavery. As 1 Peter 2:18-22 elaborates, they now serve their spiritual Lord by means of serving their earthly lord—and this they now do freely. So, regardless of their slave status, they are free in Christ, and that should provide encouragement to endure their current status as slaves, if that is their situation.

Paul closes his comments with yet a third repetition of his general principle of believers maintaining the social location they were at when they first responded to the gospel. He demonstrates that although he was currently applying it to various marital situations, it has wide and enduring application to other strategic aspects of their lives, including both their ethnic status and their economic or social status. As a general principle, Christians today should understand that it can still be applied to situations similar to these and to a great many more. The key is to recognize that Paul knew he was generalizing and that individual settings may require variation from it.

Today, some believers may be convicted to live a simple life, to turn down promotions, and to give their money to missions. Others may see accepting promotions as part of fulfilling God's call to have greater opportunity to enact Christian principles in the company. Some turn their back on the celebration of secular Christmas, while others transform it into valuable Christian traditions for themselves. The key for believers is to recognize the necessary latitude Paul allows while noting the principle as a help in living their Christian lives.

◆   ### 5. Those currently unwed may choose to marry or remain unwed (7:25-40)

25Now regarding your question about the young women who are not yet married. I do not have a command from the Lord for them. But the Lord in his mercy has given me wisdom that can be trusted, and I will share it with you. 26Because of the present crisis,* I think it is best to remain as you are. 27If you have a wife, do not seek to end the marriage. If you do not have a wife, do not seek to get married. 28But if you do get married, it is not a sin. And if a young woman gets married, it is not a sin. However, those who get married at this time will have troubles, and I am trying to spare you those problems.

29But let me say this, dear brothers and sisters: The time that remains is very short. So from now on, those with wives should not focus only on their marriage. 30Those who weep or who rejoice or who buy things should not be absorbed by their weeping or their joy or their possessions. 31Those who use the things of the world should not become attached to them. For this world as we know it will soon pass away.

32I want you to be free from the concerns of this life. An unmarried man can spend his time doing the Lord's work and thinking how to please him. 33But a married man has to think about his earthly responsibilities and how to please his wife. 34His interests are divided. In the same way, a woman who is no longer married or has never been married can be devoted to the Lord and holy in body and in spirit. But a married woman has to think about her earthly responsibilities and how to please her husband. 35I am saying this for your benefit, not to place restrictions on you. I want you to do whatever will help you serve the Lord best, with as few distractions as possible.

36But if a man thinks that he's treating his fiancée improperly and will inevitably give in to his passion, let him marry her as he wishes. It is not a sin. 37But if he has decided firmly not to marry and there is no urgency and he can control his passion, he does well not to marry. 38So the person who marries his fiancée does well, and the person who doesn't marry does even better.

39A wife is bound to her husband as long as he lives. If her husband dies, she is free to marry anyone she wishes, but only if he loves the Lord.* 40But in my opinion it would be better for her to stay single, and I think I am giving you counsel from God's Spirit when I say this.

7:26 Or the pressures of life.   7:39 Greek but only in the Lord.

NOTES

7:25 *Now regarding.* Gr., *peri de* [TG4012/1161, ZG4309/1254]. Since this duplicates the opening of 7:1, this again signals that Paul is picking up on a direct question in the Corinthians' official letter to him.

young women who are not yet married. Interpreters remain sharply divided over whether the noun (*parthenōn* [TG3933, ZG4221]) is generic, including males and females who have yet to marry, or refers to females only. Although this word usually refers to females and most certainly does in later verses (7:28, 34, 36, 37, 38), this does not require that meaning here. The word can refer to unmarried men as well (Rev 14:4; *Joseph and Aseneth* 4:9; 8:1; Collins 1999:293; Ford 1966:299). The significant difference is that the word is plural instead of singular, and it heads a section. Also, the passage (7:25-28) discusses the whole idea of marriage, from both the male and female perspective rather than simply from a female perspective. Interpreters tend to agree that most likely Paul was referring to a situation of formal engagement for marriage (Fee 1987:327; Garland 2003:320; Hays 1997:126; Horsley 1998:104) or to an engaged couple (Collins 1999:293; Thiselton 2000:568).

command. The seven uses of this word (*epitagē* [TG2003, ZG2198]) in the NT are all from Paul, two of them in this context. Both here and in 7:6 Paul wants to be forthright about the fact that he had no authoritative instruction from Christ on the matter at hand, in contrast to his teaching to the married in 7:10. Paul made the same contrast between this word and his "advice" (*gnōmē* [TG1106, ZG1191]) on a matter in 2 Cor 8:8, 10. Paul's "advice" may indicate that what follows in 7:26 is a "maxim" in Greek rhetorical circles (Ramsaran 1995:540).

7:26 *crisis.* Gr., *anankēn* [TG318, ZG340]. Used three times in 1 Corinthians, this word can refer to a disaster, as here, or to the actions people are compelled to take because of such situations, as in 7:37 and 9:16. Because in Luke 21:23 Jesus uses this word in an apocalyptic context and because of the mention of a "short time" in 7:29, interpreters are inclined to conclude that Paul had the impending eschatological crisis of Christ's return in mind here (Barrett 1968:175; Bruce 1971:74; Conzelmann 1975:132; Robertson and Plummer 1911:152; Schweitzer 1931:311). More current interpreters are influenced by the work of Blue (1991:221-239) and Winter (1989:86-106) to consider that Paul may have had in mind a famine that the city of Corinth was facing or some other local, non-eschatological crisis that induced suffering. Incorporation of something local and real to the Corinthians without eliminating the general eschatological climate created by the impact of the gospel probably best represents Paul's concern expressed in using this word (Fee 1987:329; Garland 2003:324; Thiselton 2000:573).

7:28 *troubles.* Used heavily by Paul (24 times), especially in Romans (5 times) and 2 Corinthians (9 times), this is the only use of the word (*thlipsis* [TG2347, ZG2568]) in 1 Corinthians. Outside the NT, it refers to an object pressing upon another object to create stress upon it. Paul used the word frequently to refer to his own physical hardships experienced in the course of conducting his apostolic mission. It is used in Matt 24:21 and Mark 13:19, 24 in the same kind of apocalyptic context that Luke 21:23 uses "crisis" (*anankē* [TG318, ZG340]; see previous note). Paul's use here seems to assume the same general eschatological climate as in 7:26 but applies the hardship to the emotional stress that such times place on a married couple.

I am trying to spare. Gr., *pheidomai* [TG5339, ZG5767]. The only use of this word in 1 Corinthians, it literally refers to rationing supplies to make them last longer. Figuratively, as here, it refers to protecting or saving someone from harm.

7:29 *time.* Gr., *kairos* [TG2540, ZG2789]. As in 7:5, the distinction between this word and *chronos* [TG5550, ZG5989] ("season" or "period of time," 7:39) should be observed (Garland 2003:328; Soards 1999:167). It refers here to a distinctive moment in time, perhaps with an emphasis on opportunity for the gospel (Thiselton 2000:579) and/or on the fact that the eschatological period has already begun (Garland 2003:328; Talbert 1987:49).

should not focus only on their marriage. Lit., "being as those who do not have." The NIV has "should live as if they had none." The NLT attempts to observe that Paul was not advocating that believers abandon their marriages but that they align their marriages within the gospel priorities appropriate to this special period in history.

7:31 world. See note on 1:21. The *kosmos* [TG2889, ZG3180] is not the earth itself, but the things on the earth, particularly as developed by human culture.

as we know it. Gr., *schēma* [TG4976, ZG5386]. This word refers to the external appearance or form of something. In its only other use in the NT (Phil 2:7), it refers to the look of a person. Here, it refers to the look of the world.

7:32 free from the concerns. Gr., *amerimnous* [TG275, ZG291]. Only used here and in Matt 28:14, this is the negative form of the word that refers to feeling troubled or anxious about matters. The verbal form of this word appears four times in this immediate context, later in this verse, and in 7:33, 34 (twice). The NLT renders it as "spend his time" first but later as "has to think about." The NIV renders it "is concerned about," and the ESV has "is anxious about." The presence of this word enforces the view that the asceticism Paul had in view may transcend eschatology and involve a concern about the negative impact of the world on believers (Wimbush 1987:49-71).

7:34 His interests are divided. In the same way, a woman who is no longer married or has never been married. Readings from some church fathers, like Tertullian and Jerome, punctuate "his interests are divided" (*kai memeristai* [TG3307, ZG3532]) to integrate with what follows to yield "married women and unmarried women, including virgins, are different." Connecting this phrase to what precedes, as the NLT and most modern versions have done, makes far more sense in the context. Other manuscripts, including 𝔓46 and ℵ, add "unmarried" (*agamos* [TG22A, ZG23]) with "virgin" (*parthenos* [TG3933, ZG4221]), resulting in "unmarried women and unmarried virgins." Despite the many variations of readings that suggest a corrupted text, the NLT is supported by 𝔓15 and B. Furthermore, its sense in the context makes this reading preferred. The rendering of the language by the NLT correctly distinguishes women who are currently unmarried for different reasons: either divorced or widowed (*agamos*) and a maid (i.e., virgin) who has yet to marry.

7:35 restrictions. Used only here in the NT, this word (*brochos* [TG1029, ZG1105]) refers to a noose for hanging something or a snare for catching a bird. Paul used it in the figurative sense of people not entangling themselves so as to make their lives more encumbered than they already are.

7:36 fiancée. Gr., *parthenos* [TG3933, ZG4221]. In contrast to 7:25, the word here clearly refers to women who have never been wed. The NLT's understanding that this refers to a woman who is engaged to a man is probably correct. Early in the interpretation of this passage, it was thought the relationship being described was a "spiritual marriage," an unconsummated bond between a man and a woman (Peters 2002:211-224). This idea dates back to Hermas (*Similitudes* 9:10-11). Another view, prevalent from the patristic era right up to recently (even reflected in many NT translations), was that the relationship in view was between a father and an unmarried daughter. Evidence has mounted to the point that nearly all interpreters agree that the relationship is between a betrothed man and woman (Collins 1999:302; Fee 1987:352; Garland 2003:337; Thiselton 2000:593-598) based on the compatibility of this issue with the context and on reconsidering the understanding of *gamizōn* [TG1061.1, ZG1139] in 7:38 (see note). Paul was covering various possible situations related to the marriage of men and women in light of the Corinthians' questions and the times they lived in.

passion. Used only here in the NT, this word (*huperakmos* [TG5230, ZG5644]) has been thought wrongly to refer to people who are losing their youthfulness and had been translated as such by the NIV. The NLT, like the ESV, has made the correction that reflects current research pointing to the word's referring to sexual passion (Collins 1999:302; Garland 2003:338; Winter 1998:87). The old meaning was influenced by the now overturned view that the man in this context was this woman's father and that she was aging beyond marriageability.

7:37 he can control his passion. The NLT has combined two clauses to arrive at this rendering. Lit., "he has authority over his own will and has decided this in his own heart." The reference to passions here is inferred from the occurrence of the word *huperakmos* in 7:36 (see previous note).

7:38 person who marries his fiancée. The Greek behind "marries" comes from the verb *gamizō* [TG1061.1, ZG1139]. The five uses of *gamizō* in the Gospels (Matt 22:30; 24:38; Mark 12:25; Luke 17:27; 20:35) all refer to a woman being "given in marriage" by her father—in contrast to a man and woman marrying (*gameō* [TG1060, ZG1138]). Thus, the use of this word has been the strongest piece of exegetical evidence influencing the view that this whole context, beginning with 7:36, is about a man and his daughter rather than a man and his betrothed (Garland 2003:337). However, the distinction between these two words regarding marriage was no longer maintained consistently in the NT period and thus should not be maintained here (Fee 1987:354; BDAG 188). The NLT's translation of this word as synonymous with *gameō* is justified.

7:39 is bound. This common word (*deō* [TG1210, ZG1313]) can literally refer to something or someone being tied up (Mark 3:27; John 18:24); it can also refer to someone being imprisoned (Acts 22:29). Paul used it here, almost identically to Rom 7:2, to refer to the union of wife to husband in marriage. This accords with Jesus' teaching, referred to in 7:10, and with Jewish and Hellenistic cultural understanding of the time. The perfect tense reinforces the finality of the marriage event.

as long as he lives. Lit., "for the whole time he lives." In contrast to the use of time (*kairos* [TG2540, ZG2789]) in 7:5 and 7:29, Paul uses *chronos* [TG5550, ZG5989] in the sense of duration of time. Adding "whole" (*hosos* [TG3745, ZG4012]) emphasizes the entire duration of the husband's life.

7:40 God's. The replacement of this word with "Christ" by a couple of manuscripts (𝔓15 33) was influenced by the reference to "Lord" in 7:39.

COMMENTARY

Having laid out his general principle in 7:17-24, Paul begins to apply it to the very delicate situation of engaged couples. In light of their newfound faith, should they break it off and each devote themselves individually to serving Christ, or should they forge ahead together? Should newfound faith in Christ annul the culturally and legally binding matter of engagement? The Corinthians were troubled by these questions, since Paul's opening language of "now regarding" reflects that the question was laid out as one of the matters in their letter to him. Interestingly, Paul seemed to assume both the man and the woman had become believers and did not contemplate the even more complex matter of only one of the two embracing Christ, which would then also include the tangle of issues he addressed in 7:12-16. The Corinthians' raising this matter was probably tied in with their larger question, addressed in 7:1-7, involving the spiritual value of asceticism and the application of this to married couples giving up sexual relations. If sexual relations in marriage is bad, then marriage itself might as well be abandoned.

Paul's comment on this situation parallels what he said in 7:8-9 about those who are unmarried, whether never married, divorced, or widowed, and matches his general principle of believers maintaining their current status. Like there and everywhere in this chapter except regarding marriage being binding (7:10-11, 39), Paul has no command from Christ. However, he underscored the weight of his words by appealing to his special relationship with Christ. Though he did not use the word "apostolic," the impact amounts to as much. The Corinthians should view his words as sagacious advice from one who knew Christ well.

What Paul actually says on this matter amounts to an application of his general principle of believers maintaining their status, as can be seen by his pronouncement in 7:26 to "remain as you are." However, he appealed to more than just his principle, noting the impetus of a compelling crisis that should impact the behavior of believers. Whether this was a local famine or the social impact of sexual immorality on the church, or whether these or other local issues were somehow tied in, Paul perceived the eschatological crisis of the Lord's near return as underscoring his point. The times were too urgent for engaged couples to accept the added challenges of marriage. He wanted them to break off their engagements if they could handle it.

In 7:27-28, Paul moves toward this recommendation by rehearsing conclusions he had already presented from the perspective of his general principle. He spoke to the men first, telling them to hold steady in their marriages if they are married, which is what he said in 7:10-11. However, if they were unmarried or had never been married, his encouragement is to hold off. These are not suitable times to pursue marriage. But marriage is still a viable option. It does not violate any command, nor could it be sinful to God, given its foundational status in his creation of man and woman. As has been his pattern, Paul balanced his address to men with one to women, focusing on young unmarried women. Assuming that what he said about men holding off on marriage also applies to women, he reiterated that they should not take from what he was saying about not marrying that there is anything wrong with doing so.

In 7:28, Paul foresees problems associated with marriage that can be avoided by remaining single. These problems relate in some way to the crisis the church was experiencing. The word "troubles" may relate to suffering because of the gospel or because of some other hardship, but it focuses on physical burdens. He seemed to see things getting worse, not better, for the Corinthian believers; as such, he viewed marriage and family as multiplying the hardship on all concerned.

In 7:29-31, Paul reveals most clearly that his perspective on eschatology is at the heart of his concerns. After drawing in his readers to pay special attention to what he is about to say, he succinctly states that not much time is left. As he elaborates, investing one's life in marriage, if one doesn't have to do so, is not the best use of the time remaining. His language about those who are married functioning as if they are not may connect to what Jesus says in Mark 12:25 about marriage being a human social institution that will be abandoned after the resurrection (Bruce 1971:75). So, Paul may have had in mind that, if they have the opportunity, Christians should begin living as they will live forever in the future with God. This new age will be ushered in by the Lord's return, which Mark 13:32-37 signals could happen at any time and which Paul believed to be soon, or at least in some ways already begun (Collins 1999:291).

In 7:30, Paul reinforces the point that not only will the human institution of marriage not carry over to the future age, neither will other normal aspects of human activity, such as our emotional reactions to life that manifest themselves as laughing, crying, and joy, as well as our constant concern to have material possessions. In all of these aspects our everyday world will be substantively altered in the future age. With so little time left before this new age appears, it is best to begin detaching ourselves from such orientations now.

In 7:32-35, Paul picks up on and expands his recommendation (in 7:25-28) for engaged couples to forgo marriage because of the special hardships affecting everyone in these intense days moving toward Christ's return. For the most part Paul phrases the issues as being the same for the husband or the wife and, as he has been doing, mentions each separately. He speaks of both men (7:32) and women (7:34) who remain unmarried being able to focus on doing what Christ wants them to do without also having to factor in how this would affect their spouse and family. Presumably, this would enable them to make bolder choices and take greater risks to achieve Christ's plan in such dangerous times. Surely, it would enable them to travel swiftly and to far-off places as needed.

Paul recognized the inherent responsibilities of marriage that prioritize the needs of the spouse and the family over other needs, even those of serving Christ. Such a commitment trumps a host of opportunities to which Christ might otherwise call a person. Paul emphasizes in 7:34 that a married person cannot help but struggle with divided loyalties between Christ and family. The value of singleness is simply that it eliminates this unavoidable difficulty that comes with marriage. So Paul's problem with marriage is not the result of a low opinion of it. Rather, it is because he had such a high opinion of it. A person's choice is really between two different burdens, as seen in 7:35: either serving the Lord with the burden of marriage or doing so with the burden of singleness (remembering that both are termed a gift in 7:7). Those who can handle the burden of singleness have more freedom to serve Christ. This is still true in many contemporary situations.

Paul makes two departures in what he says to women compared to men. First, he refers to two kinds of women who are not currently married, both those who were once married (now widowed or divorced) and those never married (maids), whereas for the men (7:34) he simply refers to those currently unmarried for any reason (7:32). Not much should be made of this other than its possible relationship to the second departure. The second departure is Paul's speaking of unmarried women as being "holy in body and spirit" (7:34). Many interpret this phrase as coming from an emphasis in the Corinthian community on the value of women giving themselves up to the service of Christ (Horsley 1998:107; Soards 1999:163; Thiselton 2000:591). Paul's specifying young maids indicates that this was especially valued with respect to virgins who had decided never to marry (Cha 1998:103; Collins 1999:296). As when Paul notes his opposition's perspective in 7:1, he may have agreed with the essential notion even though he would not elevate it to the spiritually prestigious thing for young female believers to do, as some may have been advocating in Corinth.

For the only time in this chapter (7:36-38), Paul addresses men without also addressing women on a matter (Horsley 1998:107). Regarding the issue of engaged couples completing their pledges to marry, it should be noted that he addressed men first (7:27, 32) before making a balancing statement to women. His directions to men likely reflect the cultural reality that men were the dominant partner in a marriage relationship, as well as in an engagement, having more say in breaking it off. There may be an assumption that men are likely to have more difficulty controlling their desire for sexual intimacy than women. Given that Paul had assumed these engaged couples were Christians from the beginning, he considered the decision *not* to consummate their engagement a decision they would both agree to.

The man's ability to control his need for sexual fulfillment in 7:37 should be seen as an indicator that he has the gift of singleness spoken of in 7:7 and as a key element in his decision not to continue the engagement. This would put him in the most advantageous position for serving Christ, as Paul reemphasizes in 7:38 when he says it is "better."

In 7:39-40, Paul addresses women again but singles out those who may become widows. He begins in 7:39 by enunciating the position that also drove his directions in 7:10-14 regarding women who divorce. The divine intention of marriage is that it should be permanent. Couples who marry should remain together till death. Thus, divorce was discouraged by Paul even if the spouse was not a believer. Here, though, with the death of the husband, the cultural mandate would be that she remarry for the economic survival of herself and her children. Moreover, since women who were wives were often 10–15 years younger than their husbands, they were more likely to survive their husbands. Perhaps Paul considered them older, with only adult children. Regardless, he maintained his position of discouraging marriage, even the divinely permitted remarriage of a widow, presumably for the same reasons he stated with regard to engaged couples—namely, the crucial times in which they were living. In these times, she could serve the Lord better if she was single. However, as with all of his directions in this chapter, he supplied no absolute mandate. She could remarry if she chose. Nonetheless, Paul was very firm that remarriage had to be to a Christian so that her service to the Lord would not be unnecessarily curtailed. Even though he only addressed Christian widows, there is no reason to think his directions don't apply equally to Christian widowers.

It is important to put Paul's advice in this chapter into a contemporary perspective. First, it must be noted that throughout all his comments, whether weighted by a command of the Lord or his own apostolic connection to the Lord, Paul empowers individual believers to make their own choices without fear of condemnation on all the matters he talked about related to marriage. Second, his comments are all contingent on the crisis he saw looming (Hays 1997:133-134). If no comparable crisis currently exists for Christians today, it is only fair to read Paul's advice in that light, thus removing his general principle of Christians keeping their current status on hold. This is not to say that Christians should not expect Christ's return, but it may not be the case that a comparable current or local crisis requires putting marriage on hold.

◆   B. Matters Related to Food Sacrificed to Idols (8:1–11:1)
        1. Eating without compromising fellow believers' scruples
           (8:1-13)

Now regarding your question about food that has been offered to idols. Yes, we know that "we all have knowledge" about this issue. But while knowledge makes us feel important, it is love that strengthens the church. ²Anyone who claims to know all the answers doesn't really know very much. ³But the person who loves God is the one whom God recognizes.*

⁴So, what about eating meat that has been offered to idols? Well, we all know that an idol is not really a god and that there is only one God. ⁵There may be so-called gods both in heaven and on earth, and some people actually worship many gods and many lords. ⁶But we know that there is only one God, the Father, who created everything, and we live for him. And there is only one Lord, Jesus Christ, through whom God made everything and through whom we have been given life.

⁷However, not all believers know this. Some are accustomed to thinking of idols as being real, so when they eat food that has been offered to idols, they think of it as the worship of real gods, and their weak consciences are violated. ⁸It's true that we can't win God's approval by what we eat. We don't lose anything if we don't eat it, and we don't gain anything if we do.

⁹But you must be careful so that your freedom does not cause others with a weaker conscience to stumble. ¹⁰For if others see you—with your "superior knowledge"—eating in the temple of an idol, won't they be encouraged to violate their conscience by eating food that has been offered to an idol? ¹¹So because of your superior knowledge, a weak believer* for whom Christ died will be destroyed. ¹²And when you sin against other believers* by encouraging them to do something they believe is wrong, you are sinning against Christ. ¹³So if what I eat causes another believer to sin, I will never eat meat again as long as I live—for I don't want to cause another believer to stumble.

8:3 Some manuscripts read *the person who loves has full knowledge.*   8:11 Greek *brother;* also in 8:13.
8:12 Greek *brothers.*

NOTES

8:1 *Now regarding.* Gr., *peri de* [TG4012/1161, ZG4309/1254] (now concerning). This formula, repeated exactly in 7:1, 25; 12:1; and 16:1, serves as Paul's indicator that he was responding to another question raised specifically in the letter the Corinthians sent him. See Introduction.

food that has been offered to idols. Gr., *eidōlothutōn* [TG1494, ZG1628]. Used four times in this immediate context (8:1, 4, 7, 10) and again in 10:19, this word usually refers to all food items offered up in pagan worship practices, including grains (Collins 1999:311). The restrictions on Gentile eating practices brokered at the apostolic council (Acts 15:29; 21:25) could be interpreted to limit the eating restriction placed on Gentiles to the meat that resulted from animal sacrifices. Paul's use of the actual word "meat" in 8:13 would support that this is the focus of his concern in this context. Pagan worship usually involved the slaughter of the animal but mostly involved the offering of the blood and internal organs in ritual (Garland 2003:365). The meat from the carcass would be cooked and offered in banquets held at the temple, as well as offered in the marketplace for private purchase (Keener 2005:75). The banquet halls could also be rented out for private parties, birthdays, and family events, or for other social events where the food (including meat) would be catered by the temple (Oster 1992:66; Thiselton 2000:618; Willis 1985:17-21). Those who availed themselves of meat would have been among the elite who could afford it (Horsley 1998:117; Hays 1997:137; Murphy-O'Connor 2002:161-162; Theissen 1982:121-127; 2003:371), though it may be that the nonelite could only avail themselves of very poor-quality meat in their regular food consumption (Meggitt 1994:138). Some argue that Paul was mostly concerned about location (temple restaurant versus home) for determining what is acceptable behavior or not in chs 8 and 10 (Fee 1987:363; Wither-ington 1993:242). Others argue that the situation was more socially subtle, involving the matter of a person's outlook, and that one could eat in a temple facility on a social occa-sion without honoring the temple's god (Fisk 1989:56-59; Horrell 1997b:99-101; Oropeza 1998:65; Still 2002:335; Willis 1985:62-64).

we all have knowledge. Though not used since 1:5, the word "knowledge" (*gnōsis* [TG1108, ZG1194]) will be used five times in this context (8:1 [twice], 7, 10, 11) and another four times in chs 12–14 (12:8; 13:2, 8; 14:6). The NLT has put the clause in quotes to indicate this is a slogan in their letter to Paul on this matter. Both the ESV and TNIV agree, though the NIV has this only in a footnote. Some consider "all" to be part of the Corinthian slogan (Willis 1985:67-70). However, Garland (2003:366) is probably correct to observe that Paul most likely added "all" to their phrase to emphasize that the knowledge the Corinthians were talking about was not exclusive to them but includes Paul and other believers. To call these two groups the strong and the weak, as is commonly done, is to import the language and setting from Rom 14–15, which is not equivalent to the situation here in 1 Corinthians (Cheung 1999:21; Dawes 1996:86-91; Garland 2001:181-183). Paul never refers to "the strong" or "the weak," but only calls one of the groups those having "weak consciences." For this reason, "majority" will be used here to refer those who claim to have knowledge and "minority" for those who are described as those who "do not know this" (8:7), and chs 8–10 will be interpreted without reference to Rom 14–15.

love. Gr., *agapē* [TG26, ZG27]. Not used since 4:21, the use of this word for sacrificial love anticipates its thematic role in ch 13, where it is used nine times and is lauded over knowledge (13:2, 8, 12).

strengthens the church. Gr., *oikodomei* [TG3618, ZG3868]. The first of six uses in 1 Corinthians (8:10; 10:23; 14:4 [twice], 17), this word literally refers to the building of a house. Paul regularly used it and its noun cognate metaphorically to refer to the bolstering and matur-ing of those in the church (14:4; Rom 15:2; 2 Cor 10:8; Eph 2:21; 1 Thess 5:11). The NLT adds "the church" to clarify this contextual assumption.

8:2 *all the answers.* Gr., *ti* [TG5100, ZG5516]. The word is a neuter indefinite pronoun, nor-mally translated as "something," which is what the NIV and ESV have. The NLT attempts to provide an understandable contrast with the latter part of the verse, which reads, "doesn't really know very much."

8:3 *God recognizes.* Lit., "is known by him," the verb being a divine passive and God being referred to by the pronoun in the prepositional phrase. Construing salvation this way, as being initiated by God, is typical for Paul (13:12; Gal 4:9). Two noteworthy manuscripts (𝔓46 and the corrector of א) omit "God" from the previous clause, yielding the NLT alter-native translation "the person who loves has full knowledge." In this rendition the word-play between love and knowledge is heightened effectively without the insertion of God and is thus championed by Thiselton (2000:625). This must be maintained as a genuine possibility. However, this shorter reading requires treating the verb in an active sense, which goes against Paul's normal perspective and is not attested by a diversity of textual witnesses.

8:4 *meat.* Gr., *brōseōs* [TG1035, ZG1111]. The only use of this word in 1 Corinthians, it nor-mally refers to food in general, including vegetables, fruit, and poultry, and not just red meat. In fact, all these kinds of food were part of most cultic, sacrificial systems, Jewish and pagan. The indication that Paul specifically has meat in mind comes from 8:13, where he uses a word that clearly means "meat" (*kreas* [TG2907, ZG3200]).

idol. Gr., *eidōlon* [TG1497, ZG1631]. The first of four uses of this word not compounded with another word in 1 Corinthians (8:7; 10:19; 12:2), it refers to the basic shape or image of something. This could be remembered in a person's mind or be formed into something solid. For Jews and Christians, it is the word that denotes statues of pagan gods, which God considers revolting. This word is used in the second of the Ten Commandments (Exod 20:4, LXX).

not really a god. Lit., "nothing in this world," Paul's phrasing is more absolute than the NLT rendition, which attempts to keep the referent clear. The NIV has "an idol is nothing at all in the world," and the ESV has "an idol has no real existence." Jews believed idols are not real (Isa 41:29; Jer 2:11), and yet they thought some sort of demonic powers lay behind their aura (Deut 32:17; Ps 106:37), as noted by Garland (2003:372).

there is only one God. Lit., "not one god exists, except One." The exclusivity of God results in Jewish and then Christian monotheism and is the most foundational truth of the OT. This statement parallels the Shema, the confessional prayer based on Deut 6:4, voiced three times a day by devout Jews for centuries, since before the NT period.

8:5 *gods both in heaven and on earth.* In the Greek pantheon of gods, some were in heaven, others on earth, and still more were somewhere in between in different phases of their mythologies (Fee 1987:372). The reference to earthly gods could also refer to deified emperors or to the worship of aspects of nature (Collins 1999:319). The phrasing could be intended to coordinate with the next phrase of "many gods and many lords" or to contrast with it, as Collins suggests (1999:314).

many gods and many lords. The addition of "lords" probably refers to the gods of the Greek mystery cults, who are regularly referred to by this word (Fee 1987:373), though this term could be a reference to deified emperors (Collins 1999:314).

8:6 *one God . . . one Lord.* The clear intention of this phrasing is to contrast with "many gods and many lords" in the immediately preceding statement.

8:7 *not all believers know this.* Lit., "this knowledge is not in everyone." The phrase deliberately modifies the phrasing of 8:1 ("we all have knowledge") to introduce a subgroup of people who have intellectual knowledge about the nonexistence of idols but who have not fully applied what this means in their lives (Collins 1999:324).

accustomed to thinking. Gr., *sunētheia* [TG4914, ZG5311]. Used only twice elsewhere (11:16; John 18:39), this word refers to a well-established custom or habit. Some later Greek manuscripts read this as "conscience" (*suneidēsei*), but this seems to be a straightforward case of transposing the later word to earlier in the verse (see next note).

consciences. Gr., *suneidēsis* [TG4893, ZG5287]. There are three uses of this word in this immediate context (8:7, 10, 12) and then five more two chapters later (10:25, 27, 28, 29 [twice]); it refers to personal self-awareness of knowledge or information. The temptation to equate this word with moral conscience that warns one of wrong action, though common in older commentaries and a few current ones (Garland 2003:383), has been fairly well documented to be a later Western development of the word not current in the NT period. See Thiselton 2000:642-644 for full discussion, but also Collins 1999:324; Fee 1987:381; and Soards 1999:180. Key persuasive research on this includes: Eckstein 1983:35-135; Gardner 1994:40-64; Gooch 1987:254; Horsley 1978:574; Pierce 1955:13-20; Thrall 1967:124.

violated. Only used here and twice in Revelation, this word (*molunō* [TG3435, ZG3662]) refers to defilement of sacred or pure domains, such as bringing unacceptable items into a temple, soiling a spotless garment (Rev 3:4), or virgins having sexual relations (Rev 14:4).

8:8 win God's approval. The only use in 1 Corinthians, this word (*paristēmi* [TG3936, ZG4225]) means to "stand near," as in Acts 23:4. It can, as the NLT demonstrates, refer to one person persuading another or winning the person over. The idea of drawing near to God visualizes his full acceptance of someone. The NIV has "bring us near," and the ESV has "commend."

lose anything. Used previously in 1:7 and later in 12:24, this word (*hustereō* [TG5302, ZG5728]) literally means to "come behind," or, in the context of time, to "arrive too late." Metaphorically, it can mean to be inferior, lack something, or as here, to be robbed of something.

gain anything. A very common word (*perisseuō* [TG4052, ZG4355]) for Paul, especially in 2 Corinthians (10 times) and Philippians (5 times), it refers to a surplus or abundance of something. This is the first of three uses in 1 Corinthians (14:12; 15:58).

8:9 freedom. Gr., *exousia* [TG1849, ZG2026]. The first of seven uses of this word in this context (9:4, 5, 6, 12 [twice], 18), this word is usually translated "authority," referring to the rights people have to exercise certain functions, such as those of a judge. The NLT's translation adapts this word to the immediate context but will translate it "right" or "rights" in later contexts.

8:10 temple of an idol. The only use of this word (*eidōleion* [TG1493, ZG1627]) in the NT, it refers to the building erected to display an idol in honor of a god.

8:11 will be destroyed. Gr., *apollutai* [TG622, ZG660]. Although this common word can refer to someone being killed in the sense of losing their life (even by Paul, e.g., 10:9), usually, as here and in 10:10 and 15:18, it refers to loss of eternal life and punishment by God.

8:12 believe is wrong. This is a verbalized form of "weak conscience" from 8:7, so literally, "feel weak in conscience." Though 𝔓46 omits the word "feel weak," its appearance in all other manuscripts suggests that this was a scribal accident.

8:13 causes . . . to sin . . . cause . . . to stumble. Both expressions translate Gr., *skandalizō* [TG4624, ZG4997]. The two uses of the word in this verse plus one use in 2 Cor 11:29 are the only ones in its verbal form in Paul's writings. See the note in 1:23 on the one use of the noun in 1 Corinthians. The term literally refers to falling into a fatal trap that has been dug, but the specific Christian use of the word refers to something that prevents someone from embracing Christian faith. Here, the sense would be to give up faith and thus lose salvation. The NIV has "causes . . . to fall into sin," and the ESV has "makes . . . stumble."

COMMENTARY

With 8:1, Paul begins to respond to questions contained in the Corinthians' letter to him about how to consider the eating of meat from the idol temples. Were Christians to consume this meat, which was readily available in their culture, in the market, in local dining venues, and at pagan festivals? This was an important matter, not just regarding meat but regarding the social involvement of new believers with their non-Christian neighbors, as well as with those in the Christian community who have varied opinions about what to do. Therefore, Paul will spend the next three chapters measuring out his carefully nuanced recommendation to them.

Paul may have been surprised that this matter came up, since it is almost certain that he would have instructed the Corinthians about food and idols when he was with them for 18 months (Garland 2003:354). He had agreed to the concord at the apostolic meeting recorded in Acts 15, which ends by stipulating that Gentile converts were to be instructed not to eat meat that had been offered to idols (Acts 15:20). He also routinely denounced association with idols in his teaching to Gentiles (Gal 4:8-9; 1 Thess 1:9-10). Paul seems to have been responding to people in Corinth who had some new ideas on the matter that they were already putting into practice and who expected Paul's blessing to continue. They would be surprised at his response (Hays 1997:137).

Paul begins by citing language from the letter that is part of their argument, "We all have knowledge." His agreement in principle is part of his rhetorical tactic. Typically, he lays out a base of agreement, as he did in 6:12, so that his correction does not become confrontational (Thiselton 2000:621). The knowledge necessary to make a determination about this issue is possessed by all believers, because fundamental to believing in Christ is believing that there is only one God, as Paul will stipulate in 8:4-6. Thus, "idol" meat is just meat. Yet, as Paul's discussion unfolds, it is clear that not all the Corinthian believers have fully grasped the "knowledge" necessary to agree with this determination. Thus, this minority group has been misrepresented in the quotation, and Paul was going to push for their opinion to be respected by the rest. From Paul's perspective, the expression "all have knowledge" means to respect diversity of opinion, while the Corinthian majority used the lingo to mean that everyone who had any knowledge would agree with them.

This is why, with language that anticipates his famous exposition on love versus knowledge in chapter 13 (Horrell 1997b:86), Paul immediately pounces on knowledge as all too easily leading to arrogance. The majority, even if they are right in terms of the evidence, have already lost the argument by their haughty demeanor. Such attitudes tear down the church rather than edify it because they weaken believers whose confidence in Christianity is being diminished by the unloving character of the majority, who espouse greater "knowledge." A loving attitude, even in someone with errors in knowledge, holds sway over an arrogant attitude in someone with correct knowledge. By definition, the person with a loving attitude is open to correction, whereas the arrogant one is not. An arrogant person with incorrect knowledge can be doubly damaging to a church.

Thus, in 8:2-3, Paul promotes the paradox that too much knowledge can become ignorance when it is teamed with arrogance, picking up on his considerable effort to debunk "human" wisdom in 1 Corinthians 1-4. To be truly knowledgeable, if nothing else, means to understand the limitations of knowledge. What people should seek is not knowledge but wisdom, because wisdom combines knowledge with humility, patience, and love. It is just such people who form close relationships with God because he himself is wise in just the same way, though of course on a much grander scale (1 Kgs 4:29; Job 12:13, 16; Pss 111:10; 136:5; Prov 15:33; also Barrett 1968:193; Horsley 1998:120).

Despite their arrogance, Paul takes up the point of the majority (8:4), probably repeating some of their own slogans (Blomberg 1994:161; Collins 1999:313). He certainly agreed with the knowledge they were promoting that asserted that gods other than the one true God do not really exist and therefore that solid images representing them are really nothing more than metal and stone (Dawes 1996:88; Horrell 1997b:88; Willis 1985:94). Such thoughts were embedded in the Jewish culture from which Christianity emerged, which also shaped Paul's thinking. The Corinthians' slogans may well have even come from his own teaching to them. It is almost impossible today to convey how sharply this knowledge collided with the cultures throughout the known world at that time, especially in a metropolitan city like Corinth.

The people of Corinth worshiped such gods as Poseidon, Aphrodite, Artemis, Isis, Dionysius, Apollo, Hermes, Zeus, and Asclepius, as well as nature gods like the sun, stars, fire, the sea, holy trees, mountains, and caves, and even divinized emperors such as Julius Caesar and Augustus. These varying types of gods are represented in 8:5 when Paul talks about gods located in heaven and on earth and lords. Everyone chose multiple gods to worship based on their own ethnic heritage, their craft, and other personal reasons. The only exceptions to this would have been the Jews in Corinth and the few Christians there.

Representations of gods would surround them everywhere, on buildings, in the marketplace, in homes, in business transactions, at schools, at civil ceremonies, in government policies, at social functions, and in any situation involving food, especially meat. It would be impossible for Jews or Christians to function in this Hellenistic society without making some accommodations. The matter of food is just one of the situations for them to deal with. But just how crucial was it to be concerned about this on a relative scale to everything else? When do Christians (and Jews) elect not to fit in with their culture, and when do they elect to fit in? Is the matter of food really an area to put in the "no compromise" pile?

In 8:6, Paul repeats the monotheistic ideal but with the purpose of extending the notion of divinity to include Jesus Christ. He underscored God's role as the source of all that exists but emphasized Christ's role in extending the life of believers into eternity. Both have a role in guiding the current life of believers. Paul purposely juxtaposed the "many gods and many lords" of Corinthian polytheists with the "one God" and "one Lord" of the Christian faith. The unified God of the Christian faith allows for a unified world, including creation, nature, a plan of salvation to rescue all people from their rebellion against God, and the possibility of an eternal future for all people who accept Christ. Here as elsewhere, Paul articulates a role for Christ in creation as well, underscoring God's unified personhood and laying the foundation for the Trinitarian concept that will later be developed in the second century from biblical evidence like this.

In 8:7, Paul describes his understanding of the minority in Corinth, who were not only in disagreement with the majority about idol food but who were harmed by the practices of the majority. They were sincere Christian believers who were experiencing genuine conflict between their faith and their culture. In theory, they knew idols do not represent real gods, but in practice they found it impossible to enter back into their former pagan lifestyles that included ritualistic and social consumption of idol meat. Their consciences were weak in the sense that what they knew to be true had not penetrated deeply into their personhood. The reality could not overcome their misgivings about eating this food. To them, it seemed like worshiping a god other than *the* one true God and serving a lord other than *the* Lord Christ. Perhaps they believed, as many Jews did (Isa 8:19; Bar 4:7; *Jubilees* 11:4-6; *1 Enoch*

99:6-10), that the power that lies behind these idols was exerted by demons working against Christ. Thus, for them to eat this meat in any cultural situation or even at home would taint their new Christian life in a way that could never be reversed. For them, this was a line that could not be crossed without doing irreparable damage to their spiritual condition. For them, it was a grievous sin.

In 8:8, Paul defines the position he held on this matter of eating idol meat. He voiced the position of the majority that idol meat is nothing, but he observed that this assertion actually undercuts their insistence that every believer agree with their lifestyle choice to eat idol meat. "Nothing" means nothing. If the meat is nothing, then not eating it poses no more of a problem than eating it does. Whether believers eat it or not makes absolutely no difference to their spiritual nearness to God (Witherington 1995:186). Eating does not make people super Christians, better Christians, or more godly—nor does not eating it. "Nothing" makes it neutral and thus either position is a defensible choice for a conscientious believer.

So, in 8:9 Paul begins to dash the hopes of the majority that he would side with them. Rather than support them, he starts to mount considerable arguments why they are wrong in the way they are handling this situation. Rather than insisting that the minority participate in their choice to eat idol meat, he will encourage the majority to be willing to abandon their choice to eat it. He pins the problem on their insistence that this is a right earned for them by the once-and-for-all sacrifice of Christ. Their personal, self-serving arrogance, noted in 8:1-2, surfaces again. Paul insists that this right does not support their freedom to exercise it at all costs and at every opportunity. Nor does it give them the freedom to look down their noses at those who in good conscience cannot embrace the majority's exercise of freedom nor embrace it for themselves.

In 8:10, Paul pictures a public scene in which someone of the majority was enjoying a meal at one of the pagan temples in Corinth. To participate in this would be a very common practice for people living in Corinth as part of the many festivals for the general populace or for those who could afford it at marriages, birthdays, or even celebrations of restored health (noteworthy for the temple of Asclepius). Paul believed that many of the minority position would be unduly influenced to let down their guard, to allow the social situation to override their religious scruples against eating the idol meat, and to ultimately join fully in the festivities. The resulting violation of their own beliefs about what is involved in being committed to Christ could cause them to question other aspects of their commitment. Perhaps, they would begin to think, "If it doesn't matter whether I segregate myself from my non-Christian neighbors in the matter of food, maybe other ways I have been instructed to separate myself from my culture don't matter, either. Maybe my Christian faith isn't as uniquely true as I was led to think it was." Paul was concerned that such scenarios could cause believers ultimately to lose their faith and thus their salvation. His concern continues to speak to all manner of situations contemporary Christians continue to face involving parties, movies, and social Web sites.

In 8:11-12, Paul pits the "knowledge" of the majority and their insistence on exercising their rights against sacrificing their rights for people they love. For Paul, Christ is the model in all things, and it is so here. It is not just "what would Jesus do?" but "what has he already done?" He let go of his rights. He relinquished his freedom and became human, even submitting himself to scorn and death on a cross (Phil 2:6-8). There was absolutely no question in Paul's mind about what Jesus would have them (or us) do in such situations—abandon the freedom for Christ's sake. To not do so with regard to a fellow believer is unconscionable.

The sin, then, is not about eating idol meat; it is about Christians not loving their brothers and sisters, and thus not loving Christ either. Given this spiritual reality, eating idol meat, Paul observes in 8:13, simply is not worth it. The clear implication is that the Corinthian majority should not find it difficult to draw the same conclusion. However, the conditional clause Paul constructs does not mean that Paul has taken up a vow to never again eat idol meat, nor that he was insisting the majority do the same. His condition does allow for other scenarios that would allow for eating idol meat. Among those could be perhaps in evangelistic situations when refusing to eat meat served would unnecessarily put people off from hearing the gospel message, or when one is eating with other believers privately who also consider eating idol meat a freedom that should be practiced (10:23–11:1). This gospel imperative or matter of church unity would, then, supersede the normal ban on eating pagan idol meat for those who could in conscience do so, even if doing so overstepped the deal made at the Apostolic Council described in Acts 15:1-29.

◆   ## 2. Paul abandons his apostolic rights for the sake of others (9:1-27)

Am I not as free as anyone else? Am I not an apostle? Haven't I seen Jesus our Lord with my own eyes? Isn't it because of my work that you belong to the Lord? ²Even if others think I am not an apostle, I certainly am to you. You yourselves are proof that I am the Lord's apostle.

³This is my answer to those who question my authority.* ⁴Don't we have the right to live in your homes and share your meals? ⁵Don't we have the right to bring a Christian wife with us as the other apostles and the Lord's brothers do, and as Peter* does? ⁶Or is it only Barnabas and I who have to work to support ourselves?

⁷What soldier has to pay his own expenses? What farmer plants a vineyard and doesn't have the right to eat some of its fruit? What shepherd cares for a flock of sheep and isn't allowed to drink some of the milk? ⁸Am I expressing merely a human opinion, or does the law say the same thing? ⁹For the law of Moses says, "You must not muzzle an ox to keep it from eating as it treads out the grain."* Was God thinking only about oxen when he said this? ¹⁰Wasn't he actually speaking to us? Yes, it was written for us, so that the one who plows and the one who threshes the grain might both expect a share of the harvest.

¹¹Since we have planted spiritual seed among you, aren't we entitled to a harvest of physical food and drink? ¹²If you support others who preach to you, shouldn't we have an even greater right to be supported? But we have never used this right. We would rather put up with anything than be an obstacle to the Good News about Christ.

¹³Don't you realize that those who work in the temple get their meals from the offerings brought to the temple? And those who serve at the altar get a share of the sacrificial offerings. ¹⁴In the same way, the Lord ordered that those who preach the Good News should be supported by those who benefit from it. ¹⁵Yet I have

never used any of these rights. And I am not writing this to suggest that I want to start now. In fact, I would rather die than lose my right to boast about preaching without charge. ¹⁶Yet preaching the Good News is not something I can boast about. I am compelled by God to do it. How terrible for me if I didn't preach the Good News!

¹⁷If I were doing this on my own initiative, I would deserve payment. But I have no choice, for God has given me this sacred trust. ¹⁸What then is my pay? It is the opportunity to preach the Good News without charging anyone. That's why I never demand my rights when I preach the Good News.

¹⁹Even though I am a free man with no master, I have become a slave to all people to bring many to Christ. ²⁰When I was with the Jews, I lived like a Jew to bring the Jews to Christ. When I was with those who follow the Jewish law, I too lived under that law. Even though I am not subject to the law, I did this so I could bring to Christ those who are under the law. ²¹When I am with the Gentiles who do not follow the Jewish law,* I too live apart from that law so I can bring them to Christ. But I do not ignore the law of God; I obey the law of Christ.

²²When I am with those who are weak, I share their weakness, for I want to bring the weak to Christ. Yes, I try to find common ground with everyone, doing everything I can to save some. ²³I do everything to spread the Good News and share in its blessings.

²⁴Don't you realize that in a race everyone runs, but only one person gets the prize? So run to win! ²⁵All athletes are disciplined in their training. They do it to win a prize that will fade away, but we do it for an eternal prize. ²⁶So I run with purpose in every step. I am not just shadowboxing. ²⁷I discipline my body like an athlete, training it to do what it should. Otherwise, I fear that after preaching to others I myself might be disqualified.

9:3 Greek *those who examine me.* 9:5 Greek *Cephas.* 9:9 Deut 25:4. 9:21 Greek *those without the law.*

NOTES

9:1 *free.* Gr., *eleutheros* [TG1658, ZG1801]. One of six uses of this word in 1 Corinthians (7:21, 22, 39; 9:1, 19; 12:13), this word is the antithesis to being in slavery. As a male Roman citizen (Acts 25:10-25; 26:32), Paul was about as free as someone could be in the first century (Marshall 1987:292-295). This is the normal word for this concept and is not related to the word translated "freedom" (*exousia* [TG1849, ZG2026]) by the NLT in 8:9.

apostle. Gr., *apostolos* [TG652, ZG693]. See note on 1:1.

9:2 *proof.* Gr., *sphragis* [TG4973, ZG5382]. Outside of Revelation (13 times), this word only appears here and in Rom 4:11 and 2 Tim 2:19. Usually translated "seal" (NIV, ESV), it refers to the impression from a signet ring or a stamp that marks something as legitimate, as on a permit or certificate.

9:3 *answer.* Gr., *apologia* [TG627, ZG665]. The only use of this word in 1 Corinthians. The word technically refers to the speech a defendant would deliver to the jury in response to charges. It is used this way in Acts 22:1 and 25:16 regarding Paul's defense after being arrested in Jerusalem; the verbal form is employed four times in the same context (Acts 25:8; 26:1, 2, 24). In 2 Tim 4:16 it is used of Paul's defense during his first Roman imprisonment. To some this word signals that Paul was responding to accusations against the legitimacy of his apostleship that surfaced in Corinth (Barrett 1968:200; Fee 1987:401; Hays 1997:147; Horsley 1998:124; Thiselton 2000:669), much like what occurs in Galatians or later in 2 Corinthians (though Paul does not use the word this way in either book). Others believe the function here is strictly rhetorical (Collins 1999:335; Garland 2003:406; Witherington 1995:203) such that any adversaries in Paul's mind were people in locations other than

Corinth. The fact that issues surrounding Paul's apostleship are so pronounced in 2 Corinthians leans toward the likelihood that some questioning had already begun before 1 Corinthians was written, just a few years earlier (Keener 2005:77).

my authority. Lit., "me," as noted in NLT mg. The NLT text, based on 9:2 and 9:4, clarifies that Paul was defending his right to *not* accept financial support (as argued in what follows).

9:4 *share your meals.* Lit., "to eat and to drink." The word "eat" is intended by Paul to make a surface connection to the major issue at hand: eating idol meat (Collins 1999:335).

9:5 *Christian wife.* Lit., "sister wife"; the term is not found elsewhere in the NT. The practice of calling female believers "sisters," however, is firmly established not only in 7:15 but elsewhere, including in references to Phoebe (Rom 16:1) and Apphia (Phlm 1:2). Tertullian argued that this referred to a female assistant who traveled with apostles (*Monogamy* 8), and Clement of Alexandria thought that it referred to wives of apostles who traveled with them under vows of sexual abstinence (*Stromata* 3.53.3). These ideas have given way to the understanding, true to the surrounding context as well as ch 7, that the term refers to the wives of the apostles, underscoring that they were also committed believers. Teams like Priscilla and Aquila may be how many of the apostles were viewed.

the Lord's brothers. Despite Catholic tradition that Mary and Joseph had no children after Mary bore Jesus, the widespread mention of both Jesus' brothers and sisters does not support this theory (Matt 12:46-49; 13:55; Mark 3:31-34; Luke 8:19-21; John 2:12; 7:3-10), with Matt 13:55 even providing the names of his brothers, probably in the order of their ages, as James, Joseph, Simon, and Judas. His brothers show skepticism about Jesus in John 7:3-10, but this changes after the resurrection, because Acts 1:14 says they were with Mary and the apostles in Jerusalem immediately thereafter. Some contemporary studies put Jesus' brothers in a more positive light during his period of ministry (Bauckham 2001:106-109; Painter 1997:13-44). James not only became one of the primary leaders of the early church (Acts 15:13; 21:18; Gal 1:19), but both James and Judas (Jude) both wrote epistles incorporated into the NT.

9:6 *Barnabas.* Actually named Joseph, this man was dubbed "Barnabas" (meaning "son of encouragement") by the apostolic leaders during the earliest days of the church in Jerusalem for selling all his land and offering the proceeds to the church (Acts 4:36-37). He took the initiative to bring Paul to the new church in Antioch (Acts 11:22-26) and afterward teamed with Paul to take the gospel west into Asia Minor on what is usually called Paul's first missionary journey (Acts 13–14). He spoke decisively at the apostolic council (Acts 15) but split with Paul over their disagreement about his nephew, John Mark, accompanying them on the next missionary journey (Acts 15:36-39). This positive reference to Barnabas as sharing Paul's philosophy of work (and perhaps marriage) and also the greetings Paul sends in Col 4:10 during his Roman imprisonment are indications that whatever rift occurred earlier was healed by this point in time.

9:7 *pay his own expenses.* The three other uses of this noun (*opsōnion* [TG3800, ZG4072]) in the NT (Luke 3:14; Rom 6:23; 2 Cor 11:8) support the NLT's expression that it refers to the payment of money. Paul used the word in its more technical sense here to refer to the provisions or supplies needed to support an army, primarily food. As Collins states (1999:338), the origin of the word blends the word "fish" (*opson*) with the word "buy" (*ōneomai*).

9:9 *You must not muzzle an ox to keep it from eating as it treads out the grain.* The quotation in the NLT Greek text is from Deut 25:4, exactly like the LXX, which has *ou phimōseis* [TG5392, ZG5821] (you must not muzzle). This follows the reading of 𝔓46 ℵ A B², etc., and it is also found in 1 Tim 5:18. An alternate text with some evidence, yet still considered less suitable, is a synonym for "muzzle" (*kēmōseis* [TG2777.2, ZG3055]). The NLT gives no note in the English, since the meaning is quite similar and could not be rendered sufficiently different to demand a note.

9:10 threshes. Gr., *aloōn* [TG248, ZG262]. Only used in these two verses (9:9, 10) and in 1 Tim 5:18 in the NT, this word describes an aspect of the process in harvesting grain. A sledge of heavy wood, studded with sharp stones, broken pottery, or iron spikes, was dragged around the threshing floor (25–40 feet in diameter) by oxen, donkeys, or horses to separate the grain from the sheaves.

share of the harvest. This is simply the infinitive "to share" in Greek. It is the first of five uses in this context (9:10, 12; 10:17, 21, 30), and it appears three times in Hebrews (Heb 2:14; 5:13; 7:13). It often refers to people consuming portions of food, but it can also refer to participants receiving fair portions of anything.

9:13 those who work in the temple. This probably refers to Levites who cared for the temple grounds in the Jerusalem temple, to be distinguished from the priests "who serve at the altar" and actually offer the sacrifices (Collins 1999:342). Their share of the grain and animals is attested in Lev 2:10; 5:13; 6:9-23; 7:6-34; 10:12-13.

9:15 lose my right to boast about preaching without charge. Lit., "no one will nullify my boasting." This has excellent manuscript support: 𝔓46 א* B D* 33 1739. The attempt by some scribes (א² C D² Ψ) to correct this reading to "in order that someone might nullify" fails to understand that Paul, in an emotional state, interrupted the grammatical flow of his previous thought, which literally is "it would be better for me to die than . . . my boast no one will make void." The phrase "lose my right" translates the Greek word normally rendered "empty" or "make void" (see note on 1:17). The NIV has "deprive me" and the ESV has "deprive me of my ground."

9:17 my own initiative . . . no choice. In Greek these are single words (*hekōn* [TG1635A, ZG1776] . . . *akōn* [TG210, ZG220]), the second being the antonym of the first. They refer to people doing things by their own free will or by being coerced. They can also convey an underlying sense of doing something purposefully or without purpose. The NIV has "voluntarily . . . not voluntarily."

payment. Gr., *misthon* [TG3408, ZG3635]. Normally rendered "reward," as in the NIV and ESV, the NLT specifies that the form of reward for Paul's work in this context is money from the Corinthians or from individual benefactors.

9:20 Jewish law. Though the word *nomos* [TG3551, ZG3795] can refer to law generically, it almost always in the NT, as here, refers to the religious law from God to the Jews found in the Pentateuch. Given that Paul calls it "the law of Moses" in 9:9, the NLT's clarification is warranted. Paul probably intended "those who follow Jewish law" to include Jews as well as "Godfearers"—i.e., Gentiles who practiced Judaism without being circumcised (Blomberg 1994:184), even though he did not develop this in his discussion.

Even though I am not subject to the law. This parenthetical phrase does not appear in the Textus Receptus but is heavily supported by major manuscripts (א A B C).

bring to Christ. Lit., "win" (NIV, ESV) or "gain." All of Paul's uses of this word (*kerdainō* [TG2770, ZG3045]) are in this context (9:19, 20 [twice], 21, 22) and in Phil 3:8. It comes from the world of commerce in which businesses make a profit or gain on the selling of their products, well-illustrated by the use of the word in Jas 4:13. Paul thought of a convert as a gain to the overall growth of the church and its goal to win all people to Christ. It is also used in first-century Jewish literature to refer to a proselyte converting to Judaism (Daube 1949:109-120).

9:21 Gentiles who do not follow the Jewish law. Gr., *anomois* [TG459A, ZG491], which means "those who are without the law." The four uses of this word in this verse are unusual. It normally refers to transgressors of law or criminals (Luke 22:37; 1 Tim 1:9; 2 Pet 2:8).

9:22 I try to find common ground with everyone. Lit., "I have become all things to all people" as in NIV and ESV. The NLT seeks to simplify the point of the phrase in light of the context.

9:23 share in its blessings. Used only here and in Rom 11:17; Phil 1:7; and Rev 1:9, the noun *sunkoinōnos* [TG4791, ZG5171] refers to someone who participates with another in a shared experience. Literally, the phrase is "its co-participant." In this context, the question is who does Paul believe he is partnering with, the gospel or the fellow believers? The NLT, like the NIV and ESV and many other translations, makes Paul a co-participant in the benefits of the gospel, looking ahead to the "prize" in the athletic analogy that follows (Barrett 1968:216; Fee 1987:432; Robertson and Plummer 1911:193). Most current commentators side with the view that Paul's participation in the gospel fits with the immediately preceding context, as his adaptation to various social contexts enables the gospel to be successful (Collins 1999:356; Garland 2003:437; Oster 1995:214; Soards 1999:194). However, Paul's other two uses of the word, particularly Phil 1:7, refer to converts sharing in the benefits of the gospel, "God's grace," with him.

9:24 race. Originally a standard distance measuring about 600 feet or one-eighth of a mile, the word *stadion* [TG4712, ZG5084] came to refer to a stadium in which athletes ran that distance on a circular track, and thus, as here, to the race itself. Though not uncommon, this is the only use of the word in this way in the NT; all others involve measured distances (cf. *stadios* [TG4712A, ZG5084]; Matt 14:24; Luke 24:13; John 6:19; 11:18; Rev 14:20; 21:16). Corinth had a public stadium, seating 20,000 spectators, which was the site for the Isthmian Games it hosted every two years, second in prestige only to the Olympics at Athens. The games included only individual contests like footracing and boxing. There were also oratory competitions.

prize. Gr., *brabeion* [TG1017, ZG1092]. Used only here and in Phil 3:14 in the NT, the prizes for winning competitions at the Isthmian Games were monetary or sometimes a reduction in taxes (Collins 1999:360).

win. Gr., *katalabēte* [TG2638, ZG2898]. Only used here in 1 Corinthians but 15 times in the NT, this is the only use of it in an athletic context. More generically, it refers to seizing or taking possession of something and holding on to it.

9:25 athletes. Lit., "the one competing" (*agōnizomenos* [TG75, ZG76]). Used only here in 1 Corinthians, this word is associated with competition against other athletes in the various events held in such places as the Isthmian Games—events such as running, boxing, and wrestling. Used also as an athletic metaphor in Col 4:12; 1 Tim 6:12; and 2 Tim 4:7, it represents the competitive drive to win the contest. The English word "agonize" comes from this Greek word.

are disciplined in their training. Gr., *enkrateuetai* [TG1467, ZG1603]. Used only here and in 7:9 in the NT, this word refers to exercising personal self-control. For athletes intending to compete at the Olympic or Isthmian games, training took place throughout the year and included the development of strength, endurance, skill, and careful regulation of diet and even sexual activity (Garland 2003:441).

prize. Gr., *stephanon* [TG4735, ZG5109]. Used only here in 1 Corinthians, this word refers to the victory trophy of a wreath made of pine; it is distinct from the monetary prize. At the Olympic games, winners received a crown wreath made from olive leaves (Garrison 1993:211).

9:26 *I run with purpose in every step.* Lit., "I run thus as someone not without a clear goal." The NLT has wisely removed the double negative as well as articulated the daily discipline expressed in 9:25. The NIV has, "I do not run like a man running aimlessly."

shadowboxing. Lit., "I do not box as someone thrashing at the air." Most likely Paul viewed this as the action of an undisciplined and unprepared boxer who was overmatched in a contest, rather than a boxer who has only practiced but never competed (Collins 1999:362; Garland 2003:442).

9:27 *discipline . . . like an athlete.* Gr., *hupōpiazō* [TG5299, ZG5724]. Used only here and in Luke 18:5 in the NT, this word comes directly from the world of boxing. It refers literally to being struck "under the eye," obviously a common occurrence in boxing, making the area black and blue. The Greek root *op* found in the English words "optician" and "optical" is part of the word. Paul was thinking of very serious training that prepares a boxer for the grueling reality of the ring.

disqualified. Gr., *adokimos* [TG96, ZG99]. Used only here in 1 Corinthians but three times in 2 Corinthians (2 Cor 13:5, 6, 7) and three times elsewhere in Paul's writings (Rom 1:28; 2 Tim 3:8; Titus 1:16), this word refers to athletes who are unable to make the cut even before the competition begins because they are simply not up to the standards of the other top athletes. They are unprepared because of poor training. The antonym of this word, "qualified" (*dokimos* [TG1384, ZG1511]), refers to items that are tested and found genuine. Paul used it frequently to refer to people who are faithful in their ministry (Rom 14:18; 16:10; 2 Cor 10:18; 13:7; 2 Tim 2:15).

COMMENTARY

Readers who open their Bible to 1 Corinthians 9:1 would think that Paul had begun addressing a new topic that pertains only to the legitimacy of his apostolic office and his novel way of doing it. Yet he was not finished with the issue of eating meat sacrificed to idols, a topic he began in chapter 8. He wanted to move indirectly to his practical conclusions on the matter by first expounding on two examples before finishing in 10:14–11:1. First, in all of chapter 9 he presents his own approach to functioning as an apostle in their midst, something that will be well-known to the Corinthians. This also allows him to explain some things they may have been wondering about or questioning. From Paul's perspective, some of the choices he himself had made should provide a good example of what he was asking from the Corinthians on the matter of eating meat sacrificed to idols. Second, in 10:1-13, he offers a powerful example of Israel's testing in the wilderness as a warning to the Corinthians of the danger in not keeping clearly separate from idols.

Paul opens with a volley of rhetorical questions in 9:1. This approach will characterize his methodology for the entire chapter, which includes a total of 18 rhetorical questions. He was fired up over the issues surrounding his apostleship; he was intent on answering his critics (Horrell 1997a:592). He also assumed that the Corinthians hearing this letter would know the answers to his questions (Witherington 1995:206). He was prompting them to see the pattern that applied to them, calming any concerns about his conduct along the way (Hays 1997:146).

With his first question in 9:1 ("Am I not as free as anyone else?"), Paul seeks to establish that he was just as free as those who acted on the knowledge that idols are nothing. He had no belief whatsoever in the reality of idol gods. However, his second question ("Am I not an apostle?") implies that as an apostle he was even freer than they were. Having personally seen the resurrected Jesus, as the third question mentions ("Haven't I seen Jesus our Lord with my own eyes?"), he had even deeper conviction about the reality of the Christian perspective on the world than they did. Paul was most likely alluding to his Damascus road experience, when he received his apostolic commission from Jesus (Acts 9:1-6; Gal 1:15-16). Seeing the risen Christ shows that Paul met one of the key qualifications for apostleship (Acts 1:22). Following on the heels of this third question, his fourth question ("Isn't it because of my work that you belong to the Lord?") reminds the Corinthians that their own knowledge of the Christian perspective in fact derives from his. They are Christians because they have believed and acted on his testimony that Christ is risen and that this event should change everything about how they view the world around them.

In 9:2, Paul picks up on the matter of his apostleship, leaving the matter of freedom to rest during the remainder of the discussion. Here he pits the Corinthians against others who question the legitimacy of his apostleship. Paul's detractors were conservative Jewish believers who attempted to undermine him in Galatia (Gal 1:6-9) and probably continued to spread their ideas that Paul was a second-rate apostle whose gospel to the Gentiles did not represent the views of the first-tier apostles. Did this rumor make it to Corinth? Paul's intense discussion suggests that it had. Further, 2 Corinthians proves that the issues Paul discusses here about apostles and financial support only got worse with time. Correspondingly, Paul would use a similar rhetorical tactic: In 2 Corinthians he calls the Corinthians his official letter of recommendation as a legitimate apostle (2 Cor 3:1-3); in 1 Corinthians he calls them his stamp of proof.

Having established his apostolic credentials in 9:1-2, beginning in 9:3 Paul moves on to his primary topic that constitutes the personal illustration from which he wanted to draw: his refusal to accept compensation as an apostle from the Corinthians. For this, he had been criticized by them, and what follows is his defense for his adamant stance on this question. Though some insist his defense lies in what precedes (Robertson and Plummer 1911:179), what follows lays out an argument that is more like a defense than those simple assertions. Furthermore, the word "this" as the final word in the sentence of 9:3 indicates that what follows is Paul's argument (Garland 2003:405).

As a traveling missionary, Paul had limited options for covering his expenses. As Hays (1997:147) notes, he could (1) charge fees to people to hear his teaching, as many philosophers, like the Sophists, did; (2) receive support from wealthy patrons; (3) beg for money as the Cynic philosophers did; (4) work for himself at a trade, as most Jewish rabbis did (*Avot* 2:2; 4:5; *t. Qiddushin* 1:11; *b. Qiddushin* 29a). He definitively denounces option one in 2 Corinthians 2:17 as unfitting because it would lower the gospel to just another philosophy. Option three would besmirch the gospel. Option two is what the Corinthians seem to have expected Paul to do and were insulted that he did not allow it. Option four is what Paul had opted to do and sought to defend here. This is confirmed by the description in Acts 18:3 that he practiced his trade of tentmaking, which probably involved crafting leather for many other purposes, and by his assertion that he worked hard at his craft when he was in Thessalonica (1 Thess 2:9; 2 Thess 3:7-8). While he clearly accepted occasional support from the Philippian church, this occurred while he was no longer in Philippi but afterward while imprisoned in Rome (Phil 4:18). Paul wanted the gospel to be as free as the promise inherent in it and to be independent of all human constraints so that only God himself could be seen as its benefactor/author.

Paul's own principle about receiving financial support, however, is not what he was attempting to prove in his argument here—quite the opposite. Beginning in 9:4, employing another volley of three questions, he wanted to establish the opposite of his own practice to be universal. He believed apostles had the right to expect believers to provide them hospitality as they traveled from place to place. A roof over their heads and food are minimal expectations considering the value of the gospel and Christian teaching that Christian communities received from the apostles.

Not only that, but Paul lobbies in 9:5 for the value of supporting the wives of apostles to travel with them. This is consistent with his teaching in chapter 7 that married couples view their marital condition at the time of their calling to the gospel as a gift to be used in the service of Christ. Not even an apostolic calling should cause the unnecessary separation of a wife from her husband. The New Testament evidences that husband-and-wife teams were important to the spread of the gospel. Priscilla and Aquila dominate this category (Acts 18:2; Rom 16:3) but Andronicus and Junia are probably another named husband-and-wife evangelistic team (Rom 16:7). Unnamed in this category are the husband-and-wife teams of the apostles and their wives (though Peter and his unnamed wife are acknowledged here), which Paul assumes were reasonably well-known in those days.

Paul specifically points to Peter and his wife, probably because he was well-known to the Corinthians, at least by reputation, since his name figures into the party slogans Paul derides (1:12). Peter's inclusion need not be because he and his wife visited Corinth (see Introduction), since the mention of "the Lord's brothers" certainly does not arise from this reason (Fee 1987:404). Like Peter, they were well known, especially James, who is paired with Peter as a key apostle very early on, as evidenced by Galatians 2:9. The New Testament does not indicate that James, who was the apostolic leader of the Jerusalem church, ever traveled. So, the principle of support would seem to be for all apostles and their wives who had devoted themselves to their call to be ministers of the gospel.

In 9:6, Paul names Barnabas as another apostle who, like Paul, worked to support himself. Barnabas did not have to come to Corinth for the Corinthians to be familiar with his name and his circumstances. He only traveled with Paul on his first missionary journey, which did not include Corinth. Nevertheless, Barnabas seems to have remained a traveling emissary of the gospel after separating from Paul to go on with Mark.

Squeezing in three more rapid-fire questions in 9:7, Paul forced his readers to admit that his point about apostles receiving support has precedent from other vocations. Speaking like the sages of Proverbs, Paul drew attention to the lifestyle practices of soldiers, farmers, and shepherds. All of them under normal circumstances draw benefits from their livelihoods. In each instance, Paul astutely emphasizes that what they get is food: for the soldier, food in general as the main part of his provision; for the farmer, grain that constitutes the most basic human food group and normally becomes bread; for the shepherd, milk. Soldiers probably comprise the closest analogy, since, like apostolic missionaries, they are usually on the move. It should be observed, however, that Paul does not proclaim that all soldiers, farmers, and shepherds do this, only that they have the right to. Under some extreme circumstances, armies run out of food and soldiers have to forage on their own. Other situations may influence farmers and shepherds not to consume what their work produces, perhaps the need to sell it all off.

In 9:8, with yet another rhetorical question ("Am I expressing merely a human opinion, or does the law say the same thing?"), Paul transitions from analogies to the bedrock of his position: scriptural authority. His analogies from human life strongly support his point, but in reality their truth only derives from Scripture, too, just like his own point that apostles have the right to receive support. He observes that the law as found in Scripture is the true anchor to his contemporary application of it.

In 9:9-10, Paul cites Deuteronomy 25:4, which guarantees the right for oxen to obtain nourishment from the grain they are producing as they push the threshing sledge round and round for the benefit of their masters. Though it sounds like just another analogy like those in 9:7, because it is found in the Pentateuch, it carries weight in Paul's argument that surpasses mere human analogy. Most striking, though, is his proclamation that God was speaking "to us" in this law, meaning to the very situation under discussion with the Corinthians about apostles receiving support.

Some are convinced that Paul used the Deuteronomy text for his own purposes in a way that is disingenuous (Conzelmann 1975:155). The law as written is not about people but about oxen. It was written for Jewish farmers, not new Christians in Corinth. However, others point out that the law about oxen occurs in a thicket of laws in Deuteronomy 24-25 aimed at humans and intended for their benefit (Thiselton 2000:686). Indirectly, people benefit from healthy, happy oxen, too. Still more commentators point out that Paul was employing traditional rabbinic interpretive arguments to reach his results (Collins 1999:340; Garland 2003:411; Horsley 1998:1260; Smit 2000:254-261; Soards 1999:185). Arguing from "light to heavy" (Heb., *qal wahomer*), he concludes that a law justifying oxen to eat while they work is so much more true when applied to humans. Arguing from "Scripture to tradition" (Heb., *gezera shawah*), he moves to the notion that the law can and must be applied beyond its original, narrow application (Brewer 1992:55; Kaiser 1978:16). Scripture speaks to new situations that it could not possibly speak to in its original context. Paul recognized, as we must, that the very quality of Scripture that makes it inspired is that it continues to speak with wisdom and truth to fresh, originally unimagined problems and situations, whether it be those encountered by first-century Christians in Corinth or by business tycoons in Tokyo or London or on Wall Street. So Paul confidently asserts that Deuteronomy 25:4 "speaks to us."

The last part of 9:10 ("the one who plows and the one who threshes the grain might both expect a share of the harvest") sounds like a traditional rabbinic interpretation of Deuteronomy 25:4 that was already well-circulated by Paul's time

(Kaiser 1978:15; Smit 2000:240). Something similar can be found in Sirach 6:19-20 (Collins 1999:340-341). The teaching enables Paul to make a smooth transition from not muzzling an ox to feeding apostles who work in different ways to advance the gospel.

With 9:11, Paul begins making his own application to the current question of supporting the ministry of apostles. Alluding back to his metaphor of 3:5-8 in which he pictured himself to be a farmer sowing seed, he connects the spiritual value of sowing the gospel among the Corinthians to the material benefit he deserves from this work. How much more deserving of physical sustenance is he than an oxen, since he was sowing the seeds that yield spiritual bounty?

It is in 9:12 that Paul reveals why he needed the references to both plowing and threshing provided by the word from tradition at the end of 9:10. He wanted to allow that apostolic work can be subdivided into a variety of valuable ministries. "Others who preach" surely includes Apollos, who is named in 3:6 as "watering" the seed planted among the Corinthians by Paul (Horsley 1998:126). But Paul had in mind more laborers than Apollos. The Corinthians themselves demonstrated that they agreed with Paul's point because they already supported Apollos. All who labor for the growth of the church as a vocation deserve support from the church.

However, in the second half of 9:12 Paul throws up his personal red flag. He had never accepted support from the Corinthians for his work among them. As he convincingly demonstrated, he believed this to be an unassailable right for those devoted to apostolic ministry and has nothing but respect for others like Apollos who had accepted the much-deserved support from the Corinthians. However, as he also now explains, he believes accepting money could be a barrier for some to accept the gospel. He was able and willing to work his trade (as had Barnabas) and had no pressures to support a wife and family, which is not everyone's position.

Though he could have concluded his argument for the right of apostolic work-ers to be supported by believing communities, he adds two more arguments in 9:13-14 as a kind of epilogue to prepare for a second round of concluding remarks in 9:16-18. With yet another rhetorical question in 9:13 ("Don't you realize that those who work in the temple get their meals from the offerings brought to the temple?"), he asks his readers to observe a more religious example of his point. Priests and Levites who work at the temple in Jerusalem have biblical warrant to eat and drink from the sacrifices they slaughter in the temple. This is by far his strongest parallel to apostolic workers serving the church.

Yet in 9:14 Paul has one more telling argument: a word from Christ appealed to with the same authority as Scripture. What Paul presents as a command was origi-nally more of a proverb that Jesus uttered as part of his advice to his disciples when he sent the Twelve (Matt 10:10) and the Seventy-two (Luke 10:7) out and about Galilee to spread the news about the coming of the Kingdom (Horrell 1997a:594). Part of his lengthy instructions included accepting hospitality in homes when it was offered, followed by the saying "those who work deserve their pay." Early tradition reinforces that the church leaned on these instructions from Jesus as a guide for not just the work of the Twelve but the many missionaries who would come after. The saying in fact is found again in *Didache* 13:1-2. It is used again (along with Deut

25:4) in 1 Timothy 5:18. It certainly provides the crowning precedent in support of Paul's argument that apostolic workers should receive support for their service.

Having laid out an incontrovertible argument for the support of apostolic workers in 9:2-14, Paul begins in 9:15 to set the parallel between this situation and that of eating meat sacrificed to idols. He did this by introducing his own personal response to this apostolic right. He refused this support and had no plans to assert his right to it. His point in arguing for this right has had nothing to do with his personal interest in the support. However, to establish so convincingly the right to accept the support heightens the drama of his declining to accept it, even to the point of death, a phrase he was so emotionally charged about that he added it without completing the clause (see note on 9:15). For him it meant everything to be able to give the gospel out as a free gift to people who would hear and accept it as God's offering of love for all the world. The fact that he was able to do this without receiving money from converts was a matter of personal pride.

In 9:16, Paul edits his previous remark so as not to be misunderstood, especially given his mandate against boasting in 1:31. He doesn't boast about preaching the gospel itself or the fact that he was called to be an apostle. This was his mandate from Jesus Christ that occurred on the Damascus road (Gal 1:15-16), regarding which he had no freedom to do otherwise. To refuse this charge would bring great calamity to his life. He could, however, boast in providing the gospel to people free of charge, as he explains in 9:17, because this was his personal gift, something he can offer freely.

In fact, it qualifies as "boasting in the Lord" because he was ministering under the conditions he was in when he was called to the gospel, free from obligation to family and having a perfectly marketable skill as a tentmaker. Thus, this situation was personal and not necessarily duplicated in others. For them, it was perfectly honorable to accept support from converts, but not for him. His "pay," he explains in 9:18, is his freedom to refuse pay, the freedom to annul his rights. He would never give up *this* right.

In 9:19, Paul explains why he views his apostolic calling as conscription. Though once a free man (and that meant something in his world), he lost that freedom by selling himself into slavery to Christ with a mandate to serve the world with the gospel. Thus, there is no pay for his work, and refusal to do it is punishable. Viewing himself as a slave in this way, Paul is consistent with many other places in his writing (Rom 1:1; Gal 1:10; Titus 1:1), but viewing himself as initiating this enslavement is unique to this passage (Collins 1999:342). He qualifies his enslavement with the single purpose that Christ had set over his life: to add people to the Christian community.

Beginning in 9:20 Paul divides his single-purposed life into two platforms: Jews and Gentiles. For each, his single purpose morphs into different strategies. Because he was raised as a Jew, he was fully able to participate in the rigid social customs of the Jews involving a restrictive diet (Lev 11:1-27; Deut 14:3-21). He was also comfortable worshiping in Jewish synagogues, which Acts notes he did frequently when he first entered a city, including Corinth (Acts 18:4), and taking part in Jewish festivals. However, his purpose in doing so was no longer because he was Jewish by nationality. In fact, with incredible clarity he asserts point-blank that he is under no obligation to Jewish law anymore, a stance that coincides with his carefully argued theology in Galatians and Romans. Christ nullified the law and released him from his obligation to it. He now practiced Judaism with people to make them more comfortable with hearing the gospel message. He wanted to remove any barriers (such as his own break from Judaism) that might blind Jews from the truth of the gospel. His single purpose to help them accept Christ drove this pragmatic choice.

In 9:21, Paul explains his second platform. Parallel with the way he chose to relate socially to Jews, he was also fully comfortable with setting aside Jewish customs when relating to Gentiles. He certainly felt no compunction to force Jewish customs on them, as evidenced from his arguments in Galatians. Since Christ freed him from obligation to these Jewish laws, he was able to eat and socialize with Gentiles according to their customs, which involved eating pork and other things banned for Jews. This would also mean working and living under the canopy of idols and pagan gods in their cities that influence their legal and social behavior. He could do this because his single purpose was to bring them to Christ.

There is only one law he obeys, Paul says in 9:21, "the law of Christ." This may be the gospel mandate to go into all the world and evangelize (Matt 28:19-20; Mark 16:15-16), a fitting consideration in this context. More likely, however, Paul had in mind Christ's law of loving one's neighbor, extolled by Jesus as part of the greatest commandment (Matt 5:43; 19:19; 22:39; Mark 12:31, 33; Luke 10:27) and repeated as the most basic principle of Christian behavior by Paul (Rom 13:9; Gal 5:14), as well as promoted by James as the "royal" law (Jas 2:8) and the "perfect" law that gives freedom (Jas 1:25; 2:12). In Galatians 6:2, the only other place Paul refers to "the law of Christ," he stipulates that Christ's model of self-sacrifice in bearing the burdens of another person fulfills this law (Collins 1999:355; Hays 1997:154). He had already appealed to love (8:1) and Christ's sacrifice (8:11) as key principles in resolving this tension regarding idol meat. In this immediate context, loving non-believers, whether Jewish or Gentile, not only leads to the desire to bring them the gospel but underlies strategies for how to do this, including the removal of unnecessary distractions that would hinder them from accepting the gospel's invitation to believe in Christ. Regardless of exactly what he meant by "law of Christ," Paul was most certainly intending his readers to understand that all other laws and customs, whether from a Greek or Jewish environment, have been replaced by this law.

By using the term "weak" in 9:22, not used since 8:11 in reference to the minority of believers in Corinth who have scruples against eating meat offered to idols, Paul nearly brings his long argument back to its starting point. However, in simplifying his philosophy of evangelism down to the matter of becoming weak to the weak, his intersection with 8:11 is tantalizing but not complete. Here in 9:22 the weak are those who have not been "won" to Christ (Garland 2003:433). They overlap with the Christians mentioned in 8:11 who prompted Paul's discussion, only in that they had a serious roadblock to accepting something that others already believed and acted upon. Paul uses the term "weak" to create this fleeting link because he believed his missionary principle applied to the controversy in Corinth over idol meat. However, he was not yet ready to move to that issue. He continued to talk about evangelism through the end of chapter 9, then used another illustration in 10:1-13 before addressing this controversy directly.

The weaknesses of the weak in 9:22 summarize, then, the very issues Paul described in 9:19-21. The weaknesses of the Jews involve their observance of Jewish law, and the weaknesses of Gentiles involve their observance of pagan customs. Paul's chameleon behavior adapted to all social environments, which for his world included Jews and Gentiles. The socioreligious commitments people have are matters he considered insignificant compared to their accepting the gospel. So, he could and did eat the food, stay in the homes, and generally fraternize with anyone. This strategy quite rightly continues to be successfully employed today by missionaries, from the post-Christian cities of Europe to the most isolated villages in Asia, from suburban America to suburban Africa. However, it could also be employed as a strategy for strengthening bonds within the church, both in terms of unity among denominations and unity within local congregations.

The goal above all others, as Paul repeats in 9:23, is to take the gospel across the map to all people. One of the glorious results of Paul's successful strategy is that he gained co-servants who served Christ with him and shared the rich rewards of God's grace. These rewards are eschatological in terms of salvation, looking ahead to 9:24-27, but they are also current in terms of the blessings and suffering God brings into the lives of believers (Rev 1:9).

In 9:24-27, Paul tops off the discussion of the purpose and strategy of his missionary activity by focusing on his goal, noted in 9:23, to do everything he possibly can to save those who might respond positively to the gospel message. Drawing on the Corinthians' familiarity with the Isthmian Games sponsored every two years by the city, complete with a year-round city official for the games, Paul conjured up images of sweat and struggle to achieve success in footracing, boxing, and maybe wrestling.

Though it might be easy to think that Paul's imagery is about winning at all cost and glory for the individual winner, this is not accurate. First, Paul's focus on himself as an individual competitor comes from the focus he had on his personal philosophy in this discussion from the beginning and from the fact that there were no team sports in the Isthmian or Olympic games, just individual competition. (Although in 9:24 he invites the Corinthians to run with him when he says, "Run to win!")

Second, Paul's major focus that parallels his missionary activity involves the training athletes engage in throughout the year in preparation for the competition of the games. Great athletes endure great personal hardship to get their bodies and their minds in top form. They embrace self-denial of personal pleasures in order to achieve victory. Here is the connection to Paul: His missionary philosophy also embraces self-denial and personal sacrifice—and suffering physically. These are the keys to his success, not only with the Corinthians when he first came to their city but everywhere he traveled.

The winning motivation for Paul, he makes clear, is not at all like the monetary prizes and pine crowns received by those who placed first in the Isthmian Games. It is not at all about achieving the adulation of the crowd or the admiration of his co-competitors. It is only about pleasing God, who alone can bestow the unfading reward of his good pleasure and eternal life in his company. Disqualification for this prize would come only from Paul's *not* doing his Christ-ordained job as an apostle in the rigorous, self-denying way he chose to do it—and ultimately failing to win converts to Christ. So, everything must be thrown off that hinders this evangelistic success. Preaching the gospel with personal sacrifice offers the optimum opportunity for success in helping people accept the gospel.

Though he still has not tipped his hat on the matter of eating meat offered to idols, the tone of this chapter and its closing paragraph point strongly to the conclusion he will eventually articulate: Self-sacrifice is the mantra of apostolic ministry and the path toward reconciliation with fellow believers in many matters, including whether to eat meat that has been offered to idols.

◆   ## 3. Lessons from Israel's wilderness experiences (10:1-13)

I don't want you to forget, dear brothers and sisters,* about our ancestors in the wilderness long ago. All of them were guided by a cloud that moved ahead of them, and all of them walked through the sea on dry ground. ²In the cloud and in the sea, all of them were baptized as followers of Moses. ³All of them ate the same spiritual food, ⁴and all of them drank the same spiritual water. For they drank from the spiritual rock that traveled with them, and that rock was Christ. ⁵Yet God was not pleased with most of them, and their bodies were scattered in the wilderness.

⁶These things happened as a warning to us, so that we would not crave evil things as they did, ⁷or worship idols as some of them did. As the Scriptures say, "The people celebrated with feasting and drinking, and they indulged in pagan revelry."* ⁸And we must not engage in sexual immorality as some of them did, causing 23,000 of them to die in one day.

⁹Nor should we put Christ* to the test, as some of them did and then died from snakebites. ¹⁰And don't grumble as some of them did, and then were destroyed by the angel of death. ¹¹ These things happened to them as examples for us. They were written down to warn us who live at the end of the age.

¹²If you think you are standing strong, be careful not to fall. ¹³The temptations in your life are no different from what others experience. And God is faithful. He will not allow the temptation to be more than you can stand. When you are tempted, he will show you a way out so that you can endure.

10:1 Greek *brothers*.   10:7 Exod 32:6.   10:9 Some manuscripts read *the Lord*.

NOTES

10:1 *I don't want you to forget.* The verb *agnoein* [ᵀᴳ50, ᶻᴳ51] (NLT, "forget") is part of a common introductory formula Paul uses to draw special attention to what he is about to explain (12:1; Rom 11:25; 2 Cor 1:8; 1 Thess 4:13). It means "not to know" or "not to perceive" and comes into English as "ignorant," the translation used for the NIV. The ESV makes the double negative, "I don't want you not to know," into a positive, "I want you to know." The NLT translation indicates that Paul believed the Corinthians already were familiar with the Exodus narratives that he explains, although the phrase itself does not convey that perspective specifically. Nonetheless, Paul had probably related the story of the Exodus to the Gentiles in Corinth during the time he had been with them a few years earlier.

in the wilderness. This is added by the NLT to assure that readers recognize the time period Paul plans to draw upon in the context that follows.

All. Gr., *pantes* [TG3956A, ZG4246]. This is the first of five uses of this word in this immediate context (10:1 [twice], 2, 3, 4), emphasizing that the Israelites received the blessings of God as a covenant community, not based on any individual advantage or disadvantage. This contrasts with "some of them" used in 10:7, 8, 9, 10.

cloud. Used only here and in 10:2 in 1 Corinthians. A cloud very often accompanies the presence of deity in the Bible. In the NT, God's voice speaks out of the cloud at the transfiguration of Jesus (Matt 17:5; Mark 9:7; Luke 9:35), Jesus promises to return on a cloud (Matt 24:30; 26:64; Mark 13:26; 14:62; Luke 12:54; 21:27; Rev 1:7), and Jesus sits on a cloud (Rev 14:14-16). In the OT, a cloud accompanies manifestations of God (Exod 14:19; 33:7-9; Num 9:15, 19-22; 11:25; 12:5; Deut 31:15) as in the Exodus narrative Paul relates in this verse.

on dry ground. The NLT adds this phrase to heighten the contrast with the wall of water and to harmonize with Exod 14:22, which emphasizes this. To Paul's point, however, emphasizing their passing through on "dry" ground detracts from the point that Paul was pointing to this as a baptismal experience.

10:2 *were baptized.* Gr., *ebaptisthēsan* [TG907, ZG966]. While the passive form of "baptize" has strong manuscript support (א A C D), the support of 𝔓46 B 1739 for a middle form (*ebaptisanto*) gives translators pause. This, combined with the fact that no adequate explanation can be given for how the middle could have come into the text if the passive were original, gives the middle the edge in being more likely original (Barrett 1968:220; Fee 1987:441; Conzelmann 1975:165; Robertson and Plummer 1911:200; Thiselton 2000:722). A strong "minority" report on the UBS committee that includes Metzger and Wikgren disputed the passive reading that appears in the UBS text upon which the NLT is based (Metzger 1971:559). The claim that Paul only uses the passive for Christian baptism is true (Garland 2003:470). However, the word here is not referring to the baptism of Christian believers but to the "baptism" of the Israelites when they crossed the Red Sea. They were not passively dipped into water by the one baptizing them but walked under their own power through the walls of water, though submitting to God's will. Thus, a middle sense fits well in the sense that "they baptized themselves," "they themselves were baptized," or "they offered themselves for baptism." Supporting this is that conventionally the baptism completing the initiation of a proselyte into Judaism in the first century was self-administered (Barrett 1968:221).

as followers of Moses. Lit., "into Moses."

10:3 *spiritual.* Gr., *pneumatikon* [TG4152, ZG4461]. Used 15 times in 1 Corinthians, this word refers to something that belongs to the realm of the spirit. For Paul, the connection often is the Holy Spirit, as in 12:1; 14:1, 37. However, it can also simply refer to the mysterious aspect of life that is not strictly material, the opposite of what is natural (15:44, 46). Here the emphasis is most likely on the latter (Fee 1987:447; Garland 2003:453), though there are those who lobby for the former (Barrett 1968:222; Conzelmann 1975:166). Others suggest that the word here conveys the more hermeneutical sense of "allegorical" or "typological" (Collins 1999:369; NIDNTT 3.706). Paul may have a figurative sense in mind, as his phrase "that rock was Christ" conveys, but even so a sense of unexplainable theological mystery beyond the natural world must be included.

10:4 *that rock was Christ.* Garland (2003:456) and Fee (1986:449) are probably correct to oppose those who contend that Paul's intention is to introduce Wisdom into this context (Barrett 1968:223; Dunn 1998:729; Horsley 1998:137; Thiselton 2000:729). However, it is probably the case that Wisdom as the personification of God, which was developed in Jewish thought, provided the conduit for Paul to associate Christ with God concerning this water-providing rock. Sources such as Wis 11:4 and Philo believe "the flinty rock is the wisdom of God" (*Allegorical Interpretation* 2.86). Early Christian authors, such as Paul, quickly seized on passages that personified the Wisdom of God as revealing the activity of the preexistent Christ (Bauckham 1998:16-20; Kreitzer 1993:109-126; Thiselton 2000:728) in such activities as the creation and sustaining of the world (as seen in Eph 1 and Col 1). This is the key path for the earliest Christians to recognize the divinity of Christ and his shared attributes with God, a fundamental building block for Trinitarian development in the second century.

10:5 *scattered*. Gr., *katestrōthēsan* [TG2693, ZG2954]. This word, used only here in the NT, means to strew material widely over a parcel of ground—here referring to the gruesome picture of Israelite bodies (all but Joshua and Caleb) left in the wilderness during the 40 years of wandering (Num 14:13-25).

10:6 *a warning*. Gr., *tupoi* [TG5179, ZG5596] (types, examples). Used only here in 1 Corinthians but 7 times elsewhere by Paul (Rom 5:14; 6:17; Phil 3:17; 1 Thess 1:7; 2 Thess 3:9; 1 Tim 4:12; Titus 2:7), it usually has the sense of someone being a positive example to others. The word originated in the world of coin-making, printing, and sealing letters, where a mold was made and then impressed on another material, leaving an exact image that could be duplicated over and over. In this case, the Israelites provided an anti-model not to be duplicated in the lives of the Corinthians (Robertson and Plummer 1911:203), which explains the NLT translation. The NIV and ESV have "examples." Together with the adverbial form of the word in 10:11, the two words form bookends around the teaching material in between. There, the negative sense of the word in this context is clarified with the addition of the word "warn" (see note on 10:11).

***crave*.** The verb *epithumeō* [TG1937, ZG2121] is used in many contexts where intense emotional desire is involved. This is usually negative, as expressed in one of the sins of the Ten Commandments, "You must not covet" (Rom 7:7; 13:9), but occasionally it is positive, as in Jesus being "very eager" to eat the Passover with his disciples again (Luke 22:15).

10:7 *worship idols*. Lit., "become idol-worshipers," a word used earlier in 5:10-11 and 6:9 (see note on 5:10). See notes on 8:4 regarding "idol."

***pagan revelry*.** Gr., *paizein* [TG3815, ZG4089]. Used only here in the NT, this word normally refers to playing games like children do, joking around, and even dancing. The insinuation of the word in Exod 32:6 is that sexual play, or an orgy, was involved (Thiselton 2000:734).

10:8 *engage in sexual immorality*. This is the same verb (*porneuō* [TG4203, ZG4519]) used in 6:18. Noun forms of this word are used in 5:1, 9, 10, 11; 6:9, 13, 15, 16, 18; 7:2. (See note on 5:1.)

***23,000*.** The number connects to the incident described in Num 25:1-9, when, while camping at Acacia Grove (Heb., *shittim*), Israelite men began cohabiting with Moabite women and participating in their sacrificial meals. God sent a plague that killed 24,000 Israelites. There are various theories about why the numbers do not match; these are best summarized in Garland 2003:462. The strongest suggestion is that Paul, working from memory, had inadvertently picked up the number 23,000 from the next chapter, where in Num 26:62 a census after the plague numbers 23,000 Israelite males (Collins 1999:371; Conzelmann 1975:168). An alternative explanation, favored by Garland (2003:462-463), is that the quotation of v. 7 is from Exod 32:6 (see NLT footnote) and relates to the judgment involving the gold calf. The Levites killed 3,000 (Exod 32:28), and (presumably) the Lord struck down with a plague (Exod 32:35) 20,000 (a myriad times two, as a huge inordinate number) for a total of 23,000.

10:9 Christ. Gr., *Christon* [TG5547, ZG5986]. This reading is supported by 𝔓46 D F G Ψ 1739 𝔐 Syriac Coptic Irenaeus Origen. An alternative reading, "Lord," is found in ℵ B C P 33, and "God" in A 81. The reading of 𝔓46 et al. adopted by the NLT and ESV is most likely correct, though the NIV adopts "Lord" as the reading. The prospect of a scribe amending the harder reading of "Christ" by substituting "Lord" (*kurion* [TG2962, ZG3261]) seems probable given the seeming historical incongruity of Israel tempting Christ. Scribes may have been reluctant to accept "Christ" as an acceptable reading because they questioned the idea of Christ being active in the OT era or that he would have destroyed so many Jews in judgment (Comfort 2008:506-507).

test. Gr., *ekpeirazō* [TG1598, ZG1733]. Only used elsewhere in the NT when Jesus retorts to Satan quoting Deut 6:16 ("You must not test the LORD your God"; Matt 4:7; Luke 4:12) and when a law expert tested Jesus (Luke 10:25), this word intensifies the standard word for "test" (*peirazō* [TG3985, ZG4279]) used later in this verse (though this is not reflected in the NLT). Psalm 78:18 [77:18, LXX] uses this exact verb to describe the rebellious Israelites in the desert.

snakebites. This refers to the incident in Num 21:4-9. When the Israelites complained to God and Moses about the lack of water and the monotony of the manna, God sent a plague of snakes into their camp. Moses made a pole and put a bronze snake on top of it to heal the snakebitten people who would look at it.

10:10 grumble. Gr., *gonguzete* [TG1111, ZG1197]. This word is formed by the sound of "gu-gu-gu," which is what the low sounds of people complaining to one another in murmurs might sound like. Paul's comment probably does not intend to relate to a specific event but to characterize the behavior of the Israelites during their desert experience in general (see Exod 16:2-3; Num 14:2, 36; 16:41, 49; 17:5, 10).

angel of death. Lit., "the destroyer." This designation relates to the destroying angel who was responsible for the 10th plague against the Egyptians and the slaying of the firstborn and who comes up again in association with the plague against David (2 Sam 24:16; 1 Chr 21:12) and the destruction of the Assyrians (2 Chr 32:21). This singular death agent of God is not associated specifically with any of the desert punishment incidents to which Paul alluded (Hays 1997:165; but cf. Wis 18:25).

10:11 These things. Gr., *tauta de* [TG3778A/1161, ZG4047/1254]. This shorter reading, supported by 𝔓46 A B 33 1739, is most likely correct. Some manuscripts (including ℵ C D F G Ψ) have the addition of "all" (*panta* [TG3956, ZG4246]), but this was almost certainly added by scribes seeking to further dramatize the results of these illustrations cited from Israel's history. These scribes were likely also encouraged by the frequency of "all" in 10:1-4.

as examples. Gr., *tupikōs* [TG5178.1, ZG5595]. This is the adverbial form of the word translated "warnings" in 10:6. Together they form bookends around the teaching material in 10:6-11.

the end of the age. Lit., "the ends of the ages," rendered "the fulfillment of the ages" by the NIV and "the end of the ages" by the ESV. Weiss (1910:245) makes the novel suggestion that the unusual phrase depicts the juncture of the OT age and the NT age. If this is *not* what Paul intended, the plural "ends" could simply be a Hebraism like "heavens," which in English is normally rendered as "heaven" (Bruce 1971:93). In this case, it would refer to the successive periods of human history that culminated in the age in which Paul lived, meaning the age of Christ (Garland 2003:465; Robertson and Plummer 1911:207).

10:12 standing strong. Gr., *hestanai* [TG2476, ZG2705]. The perfect tense of this infinitive accentuates the permanence conveyed by the word. The NLT conveys this by adding the word "strong." The NIV has "standing firm."

10:13 *temptation.* This is a verb in Greek (*peirazō* [TG3985, ZG4279]), the same word trans-lated "put to the test" in 10:9. Both the NIV and ESV also switch between rendering this word and its noun cognate as "test" and "tempt" in different contexts. Tempting is some-thing Satan does that afflicts people (7:5), but God does not tempt and is not tempted (Jas 1:13). His patience can be tested, and occasionally he can test individuals (Heb 11:17) and nations (Exod 15:25).

COMMENTARY
After mentioning in 9:27 that he himself was in danger of being disqualified from the prize if he failed to discipline his life (toward the goal of winning converts to Christ), Paul noted the potential for the Corinthians to expose themselves to God's judgment if they ate idol meat in utter disregard for their fellow believers (Sumney 2000:333). "Sinning against Christ," as he called this behavior in 8:12, could be much more serious than they supposed, even spiritually fatal. In chapter 10, he warned them of this hazard.

Paul begins in 10:1-13 with a lesson from the wilderness wanderings of the Israel-ites, which offer intriguing parallels to the Corinthian situation. Following conven-tional rabbinic midrashic procedure for interpreting Scripture (Collins 1999:364; Thiselton 2000:723), Paul offers a narrative in 10:1-5 (possibly one he previously constructed), which he follows up by the moral imperative that applies to the Corinthians in 10:6-10. Although he only quotes from the Old Testament once, in 10:7 (Exod 32:6), texts from Exodus and Numbers underlie his narrative and application. The fivefold "all" regarding the Israelites in 10:1-5 intentionally con-trasts with the "some" of 10:6-13 (Meeks 1982:65-66). All the Israelites shared in the covenant blessings of being God's people, yet some rebelled and were destroyed by God. Not incidentally, their rebellion involved eating food, which occurred in conjunction with reprehensible behavior toward God.

Paul indicates at the opening of 10:1 that he was initiating a new phase of his over-all argument by employing the direct address, "brothers and sisters," something he does commonly in Corinthians (1:10; 2:1; 3:1; 12:1; 15:1), and by imploring them to take notice of his instruction. The ease with which he includes the Corinthians as members of the Israelite ancestral clan is somewhat surprising but immediately makes the narrative of the momentous wilderness events relevant to them. Paul has no hesitation in thinking of Gentile believers like the Corinthians as true heirs of the rich Jewish heritage. This is in line with his teaching in Romans 11:17-24 that the Gentiles were grafted into the trunk of the olive tree and in Galatians 3:26–4:7 that if they are believers in Christ, they are "the true children of Abraham" (Gal 3:29).

After leaving their initial encampment in Succoth, the fleeing Israelites were led on their way by a pillar of cloud each day and a pillar of fire each night (Exod 13:20-21). Upon reaching the Red Sea, the cloud moved to their rear as a buffer against the advancing Egyptian army (Exod 14:19-22). After Israel crossed, God "looked down" from the pillar of fire and cloud at the Egyptian army and allowed the returning water to crush them (Exod 14:24). Paul drew on this narrative of the cloud in 10:1 as a picture of God's guidance and care for the Israelites as his covenant people. Psalm 105:39 describes the cloud as "a covering" provided by God. Thus, they walked through the path across the Red Sea through a tunnel of water, the sea on the right and left, and the mist of the cloud above (Fee 1987:445; Schnackenburg 1962:21-29).

With this picture in mind, it is not much of a stretch for Paul to depict this event as an initiation rite for Israel akin to the baptism of believers into Christ, as he does in 10:2. In this case, he literally says they were baptized "into Moses," copying the language he employs regularly for Christian baptism (1:13-16; Rom 6:3; Gal 3:27). No Jewish literature employs this phrase, so it is best understood in relationship to being baptized into Christ or into the name of Christ (Garland 2003:450; Thiselton 2000:725). Moses led them through water and eventually to the Promised Land. In that sense, as they followed him and trusted in him, they were saved (Robertson and Plummer 1911:200), both from the walls of water when they crossed the Red Sea and from the Egyptians, but also saved as a covenant people through the trials of the desert into a new land.

Having drawn the parallel between the baptism of the Corinthians with that of their Jewish ancestors, in 10:3-4 Paul moves to establish a parallel with the Lord's Supper. His analogy focuses on the manna and the water God provided for Israel during their 40 years of wandering. The manna, as explained in Exodus 16, appeared each morning but would spoil by the next day. The exception was the Sabbath, on which no manna appeared; but a double portion could be gathered the day before and it would not spoil the second day. The water, as told in Exodus 17:1-7 and Numbers 20:1-13, came from Moses' striking a rock at Horeb with his rod. Because of the repetition of this scene in Numbers 21:16-18 and the fact that Numbers 20:11 says that he struck the rock twice, a strongly held rabbinic interpretation (Pseudo-Philo *Biblical Antiquities* 10.7) asserted that this rock traveled with the Israelites in the form of a well. This is a view that Paul clearly held in some form (Barrett 1968:222; E. Ellis 1957:67; Enns 1996:30; Fee 1987:447; Thiselton 2000:447).

Paul called this regular sustenance in the desert "spiritual" in part because it was miraculous and was supplied from God. However, more importantly he was firming up the comparability of this covenant activity of the Israelites with the similar covenant activity of the Corinthians when they participated regularly in consuming the wine and bread of the Lord's Supper. They had "the same" spiritual significance in signaling the utter dependence of God's people on him for survival. In partaking together of the food of God's provision they communed with God. Looking at this from a New Testament perspective, this "food" is the body and blood of Christ, evoking his death for the sins of all humanity and his resurrection to the right hand of God.

Paul jolted his readers with this christological intrusion into the Old Testament event. He had replaced "God," who is identified as the rock in Deuteronomy 32:4, 15, 18, 30, 31, with "Christ" (see notes on 10:4, 9). Whether or not he believed Christ was actually present in the life-giving events of the Exodus, he certainly believed in the salvific significance of Christ for all humanity, reaching back to these formative days of Israel. All God's actions in the Old Testament were, from Paul's perspective, blanketed over by the Christ event. The "rock" easily caught his attention, since passages using this word were appropriated for christological purposes widely by the earliest Christian readers of the Old Testament, evidenced in such places as Romans 9:33 (quoting Isa 8:14; 28:16) and 1 Peter 2:4-8 (quoting Isa 8:14; 28:16; Ps 118:22).

Having brought the Corinthians and the Israelites under the same umbrella of God's people, both experiencing baptism and the Lord's Supper in theologically indisputable ways (Smit 1997a:43), Paul proceeds in 10:5 to drop the other shoe. Though the Israelites experienced God's covenant grace and its trappings, Numbers 14:29-30 and 26:65 describe the awful truth: None of the people over 20, except Joshua and Caleb, survived in the desert. Using the language of Numbers 14:16 (Fee 1987:450; Thiselton 2000:730), the gruesome picture of bodies deposited throughout the desert is intended to terrify the Corinthians. God did not hesitate to strike down those who grumbled against him and failed to recognize his daily provision of water and food as signs of the faithfulness of his promises. They failed their tests, and only a handful of people old enough to be culpable trusted God enough to survive. What about the Corinthians? Paul's poignant observation to come in 11:30 that "many of you are weak and sick and some have even died" suggests some of them in comparable straits.

In 10:6, Paul answers this question with his instruction that the Corinthians should not follow in the footsteps of their spiritual ancestors in the desert. If they did, God, whose character remains consistent, would surely bring a similar destruction upon them in terms of not reaching the goal of their salvation: eternal communion with God. He identified as their general downfall their uncontrollable desire for things they should not desire. The Corinthians who desired to eat meat offered to idols needed to check their motivations. Was this a desire born of rebellion against God and fuelled by the craving to accommodate the social practices of their pagan, nonbelieving family and friends?

In 10:7, Paul begins to pinpoint incidents in the desert to which the Corinthians should pay very close attention. The first involves the construction of the golden calf, narrated in Exodus 32, and all of the offensive behavior attendant to it. Paul quoted Exodus 32:6 exactly from the Septuagint because it describes their sinful activity in detail throughout the chapter, and it also stipulates activities that parallel concerns he had about the Corinthians, especially as the passage connected to Numbers 11 (Collier 1994:71-72). The Israelites ate the meat from sacrificed animals offered up to the calf idol. They drank to celebrate it. They partied in the pagan manner that included sexual frenzy. All of these things, including the illicit sexual activity, were also associated with the pagan temples of Corinth. Eating idol food and immoral sexual activity are linked directly in Acts 15:29 and Revelation 2:14, 20 (Witherington 1995:222), while pagan idol worship and abominable sexual practices are linked implicitly in Romans 1:18-31 (Thiselton 2000:735).

Although the Levites rallied to Moses and slew 3,000 men to quell the revelry associated with the calf idol (Exod 32:27-29), this punishment is not where Paul looked for the effect he wanted. Rather, in 10:8 his mind attaches to the much bigger number of 23,000 slain in a later incident, described in Numbers 25, when the men of Israel engaged in illicit sexual activity with the women of Moab while encamped at Acacia Grove (Heb., *shittim*), though possibly he construes this number from Exodus 32 (see note on 10:8). This occasion also fits Paul's scenario because the sexual activity was connected to participating fully in worship of Baal of Peor by joining the Moabites in eating sacrifices offered up to him. The eye-popping number of people slain (23,000) should have given the Corinthians pause. There were probably fewer than 100 Corinthian Christians.

Yet Paul was not through. In 10:9, with a single word, "snakebites," he conjured up an incident previous to the Acacia Grove affair, recounted in Numbers 21:4-9. As the Israelites took the long route around the land of the Edomites, it says they complained bitterly against God and Moses about the manna (and about the lack of water). They wanted *real* bread. The passage does not say how many died from the venomous snakes God sent among them. It just says "many," but many others infected were healed by looking at the bronze serpent Moses mounted on a pole. Paul must have been drawn to this passage because their sin caused grievous punishment. This is clear, since he will accentuate the matter of their griping in 10:10. Note that this passage also relates to food and the "Lord's Supper" elements in the Israelites' diet that echo the Lord's Supper.

With the second surprising reference to Christ in this context (10:9; see note), Paul grabs the Corinthians and pulls them into the picture he was painting of the Israelites. Were the Corinthians complaining to God about anything? Except for its emphasis in 10:9 and 10:10, we would not know that they were. It is possible that Paul had in mind the majority who were being very vocal in their complaints against the minority who wouldn't eat the meat offered to idols. Whether or not they were actually complaining like the Israelites, whatever they were doing, as far as Paul was concerned, comprised a testing of Christ every bit as audacious and insubordinate as what the Israelites did with respect to God in the desert. That Paul could associate the rock with Christ in 10:4 makes it much less difficult to accept that he believed Christ could be associated with God in the desert with Israel on this occasion, too. However, his primary reason for introducing Christ at this point was aimed at the Corinthians: They were drawing Christ into a confrontation that he did not want to have, but like God in the desert he would not hesitate to deal harshly with the situation.

To make matters worse, as 10:11 emphasizes, the Corinthians were standing in the final stage of God's master plan to save the people of the world. The stakes were high with the Israelites in the desert, but they were even higher now. The message of Christ had gained a foothold in the non-Jewish world in places like Corinth. Would it prosper and grow, or would it wither and fade? Paul believed a critical part of the answer lay in how the Corinthians handled the crisis over eating idol meat. Though the pressure was on them, one advantage the Corinthians had over their desert-roaming forefathers is that they could look back and learn from them. The Israelites present a negative lesson—what not to do: Don't test God by questioning his trustworthiness and by associating with pagan worship.

Yet there is also a positive lesson. Paul purposefully juxtaposed "all of them" (10:1 [twice], 2, 3, 4) and "some of them" (10:7, 8, 9, 10) in this passage. All the Israelites enjoyed God's blessings as his covenant people, but only some tested God's patience and received the death penalty. Paul was challenging the Corinthians to avoid being in that tragic minority. Instead, they should come to terms with the idol-meat controversy and move on happily as a crucial contingent of God's new covenant people in the spiritual frontier of Corinth.

In 10:12, Paul issues a chilling warning directed at the majority, who were so sure that eating idol meat and socializing at the pagan temples were completely accept- able Christian activities. He addressed them as people who were overconfident of their position, even arrogant, reminiscent of his depiction of them in 8:1-2. They saw themselves like a giant tree with deep roots, unfazed by a mighty wind, or like a great warrior holding his ground against all comers. Yet this was not their real situation. They were like a fragile, young tree just planted, completely vulnerable to threatening weather conditions, or like a new trainee surrounded by danger in his very first battle. They didn't know as much as they thought they did. They were going to have to back down.

Lest they think their predicament was unique, in 10:12-13 Paul reminds them that it was not, in both a negative and a positive way. All Christian believers face the challenge of tests and temptations to the integrity of their faith (Oropeza 1999:85). These may vary from person to person and from occasion to occasion, but the pressure is ever present to understand what Christ would have us do. It could be whether to eat meat offered to idols (still very real in some contexts today) or whether to participate in certain kinds of social gatherings—and Chris- tians may disagree about these matters. No believer is unique in the burden of the potential sin they bear.

However, on the positive side, every believer, the Corinthians as well as believers today, can find reassurance in the promise Paul issues here. Since God does not want his people to sin, he shields them from insurmountable pressure to succumb to its allure. He is aware of whether a person is a sapling or a weathered oak, a nov- ice recruit or a seasoned veteran. God also will clarify the thinking of the humble inquirer about what to do and provide the means to do it.

◆　　　4.　Lessons from the Lord's Supper (10:14-22)

[14]So, my dear friends, flee from the wor- ship of idols. [15]You are reasonable people. Decide for yourselves if what I am saying is true. [16]When we bless the cup at the Lord's Table, aren't we sharing in the blood of Christ? And when we break the bread, aren't we sharing in the body of Christ? [17]And though we are many, we all eat from one loaf of bread, showing that we are one body. [18]Think about the people of Israel. Weren't they united by eating the sacrifices at the altar?

[19]What am I trying to say? Am I saying that food offered to idols has some sig- nificance, or that idols are real gods? [20]No, not at all. I am saying that these sacrifices are offered to demons, not to God. And I don't want you to participate with demons. [21]You cannot drink from the cup of the Lord and from the cup of demons, too. You cannot eat at the Lord's Table and at the table of demons, too. [22]What? Do we dare to rouse the Lord's jealousy? Do you think we are stronger than he is?

NOTES

10:14 *flee*. Gr., *pheugete* [TG5343, ZG5771]. Used previously in 6:18 with regard to fleeing sexual immorality, this word is also used in 2 Tim 2:22 regarding the temptations to young believers. Outside the NT, it can refer to criminals fleeing prosecution or people exiling themselves for various reasons from their country.

10:15 *reasonable.* Gr., *phronimois* [TG5429, ZG5861]. Used only here and in 4:10 in 1 Corinthians, this word is very often translated "wise," as in describing the five more prepared maidens in Jesus' parable (Matt 25:2-9) or the man who built his house on a rock (Matt 7:24). The emphasis is not so much on reasoning but on common sense.

10:16 *bless the cup at the Lord's Table.* Lit., "the cup of blessing which we bless." The phrase originates in Jewish ritual and would have been used at either the third or fourth cup of the Passover meal, most likely the point at which Jesus initiated the commemorative and anticipatory meal with his disciples. It continued in church practice in the Lord's Supper. The blessing also occurred as a giving of "grace" at the end of every Jewish meal for the wine and could also be offered as thanksgiving to God for the bread (*m. Berakoth* 6:1). See Thiselton 2000:756-760 for an extended discussion.

sharing. Gr., *koinōnia* [TG2842, ZG3126]. Only used here (twice) and in 1:9 (in relationship to Jesus) in 1 Corinthians, this word and its word group are a staple of Paul's vocabulary (Rom 12:13; 2 Cor 9:13; Gal 2:9; Phil 3:10; Phlm 1:6). This word is also of critical importance in Petrine literature (1 Pet 4:13; 5:1; 2 Pet 1:4) and the Johannine epistles (1 John 1:3, 6, 7; 2 John 1:11). Paul will use another form of the word in 10:18, 20, which the NLT translates "united" and "participate." The NIV and ESV translate it "participation" here as well as "participate/participants" in 10:18. See notes on 1:9. The sharing calls them to unity and partnership (M. Mitchell 1993:141).

10:17 *one loaf.* In ancient oriental tradition, each person at the meal usually had their own loaf, though served from a common dish (Robertson and Plummer 1911:213). Paul evidences here that Christians shared one loaf in their early communion practices.

10:18 *the people of Israel.* Lit., "Israel according to the flesh." The literal reading is critical toward recognizing the very real possibility that Paul's addition of "according to the flesh" (*kata sarka* [TG2596/4561, ZG2848/4922]) had the purpose of referring to "sinful" Israel, who ate pagan sacrifices in the wilderness (Garland 2003:478; Thiselton 2000:771). See following note.

Weren't they united by eating the sacrifices at the altar? Lit., "Are not those who eat the sacrifices participating in the altar?" The NLT assumes that unification of the people takes place upon eating the sacrifices. This may be true in light of 10:17, but the point of the statement is that the people who eat sacrificial meals participate with the god being worshiped at the altar. Another question concerns just what Paul was referring to here. Established interpretation points to the consumption of the sacrificial food by Jewish priests (Lev 7:6-15) as representative of the people (Barrett 1968:235; Bruce 1971:95; Conzelmann 1975:174) or perhaps to the consumption of a tithe of the grain, wine, oil, and even animals they produced, noted in Deut 12:15; 14:22-27 (Conzelmann 1975; Fee 1987:470; Hays 1997:168). However, the determination that the mention of Israel in 10:18 is pejorative (see previous note) leads to the better interpretation that Paul was still thinking about the examples of the Israelites in the desert eating the sacrifices to pagan gods (Gardner 1994:165; Garland 2003:478; Hays 1989:93; Horsley 1998:141).

10:20 *No, not at all. I am saying that these sacrifices are offered to demons, not to God.* Lit., "but that these things are sacrificed to demons and not to God." The NLT has repeated the "I am saying" from 10:19 and added the exclamatory "No, not at all" for clarification. In some manuscripts (including 𝔓46 ℵ A C), the word "Gentiles" is added for the sake of clarity—that it was not "Israel" that Paul was speaking about (10:18), but that he had shifted to a new subject, the Gentiles.

demons. Demons are prevalent in the Gospels as evil forces that invade the bodies of individuals, causing all kinds of illnesses and personality disorders (Luke 8:27-38; 11:14). Satan is the chief one (Mark 3:22), and a significant aspect of Jesus' ministry was to assert his power over them even as they attempted to disrupt the advance of his ministry. Reference to demons falls off significantly outside the Gospels and is found only here (10:20-21, four times) and in 1 Tim 4:1 in Paul's writings, and only in Jas 2:19 in any other epistles. Paul's connecting demons to idols is probably based on similar comments in Deut 32:16-21; Ps 106:37; Isa 65:11.

COMMENTARY

Having used the tragedies of Israel's wilderness experience as a blaring horn to warn the Corinthians of the danger they were in if they remained belligerent against God regarding their intentions to keep eating meat offered to idols (10:1-13), Paul begins to share with them the theological problems of their position (10:14-22). To Paul, their position was indefensible.

He begins in 10:14 by speaking to the Corinthians with simple directness. Like someone about to be captured, their only recourse was to run as quickly as possible from advancing pursuers. They had been naive in thinking they could brush so close to the evil of idols without making themselves vulnerable to the sinister forces that lurk within them. Eating the food of idols in the temples of the idols is tantamount to worshiping idols, regardless of their protestations. Rather than "standing," as they thought they were (10:12), they needed to "flee." This was their only way out.

In 10:15, Paul appeals to their own vanity in a rhetorical ploy to get them to listen seriously to the case he was about to make (Barrett 1968:231; Garland 2003:475; Witherington 1995:224). Their own position had been that since idols don't represent anything real, there is no practical reason not to eat in their halls. Paul believed he could persuade them to cancel their current practice. He was totally convinced that the theological truth he was about to unfold would cause them to come over to his position of their own free will. He knew he couldn't *make* them do it, any more than Scripture can make Christians today stop doing things they shouldn't be doing. We, as they, need to be convicted to make the change in our behavior of our own accord or it is nothing more than hollow legalism.

Paul pushed the Corinthians to think matters through on their own by a series of rhetorical questions, six in all through 10:22, beginning with two in 10:16. These two questions draw attention to what exactly happens when Christians share together in eating the elements of the Lord's Supper, the wine and the bread, respectively. The order in which he deals with them is not related to their ceremonial order. Although two cups are mentioned in the Luke account of the institution, on either side of the loaf (Luke 22:17-23; *Didache* 9:1-4), Paul relays the order of institution as the bread and then the wine later in 11:17-34. The order reversal is more convenient for the expanded comments he wanted to make about the bread in 10:17 (Hays 1997:167; Thiselton 2000:764).

This order also allows him to emphasize up front that his greater concern is that the Corinthians understand the theological dimension of their communal Lord's Supper celebration (Thiselton 2000:762). Just as their baptism connected them to the death, burial, and resurrection of Christ when they were initiated as Christians

(Rom 6:1-14), so also does their regular participation in communion. In communion, they celebrate their lives as God's new covenant people, and the focal point of this is the blood, as in all sacrifices. Jesus says in Luke 22:20, "This cup is the new covenant . . . confirmed with my blood, which is poured out as a sacrifice for you." Christ's sacrifice was a *real* sacrifice. Communion *really* unites believers with him in his sacrifice, as well as in the new life it has provided them. This is not accomplished by his magical infusion into the cup or the bread as Christians partake of them (Fee 1987:467). Rather, it is in sharing together in eating and drinking the bread and the wine.

With the vertical dimension of the Lord's Supper, given its due attention in the cup, Paul looks to the bread to emphasize the horizontal dimension of what occurs when the cup and the bread are shared in the life of the church. In the second half of 10:16, he provides evidence that bread was broken as part of the communion ceremony, in keeping with Christ's own breaking of the bread when he instituted it as the host of the Passover meal (11:24; Matt 26:26; Mark 14:22). In parallel with his phrasing regarding the cup, Paul indicates that believers are uniting with the body of Christ by partaking of the bread. In Romans 7:4 Paul writes of believers dying to the law when they "died with Christ" in order to be united with "the one who was raised from the dead."

Paul, however, quickly moves on in 10:17 to develop the unity of fellowship that happens when believers partake of the bread together. Further revealing early church practice of one loaf being broken into pieces as part of the ceremony, Paul seized on the opportunity to see in this not only the broken body of Christ but also the oneness of the body of Christ now reborn in the solidarity of the church. The church, united by their bonds of faith in Christ, through communion regularly expresses and evokes their oneness that Christ bought by the sacrifice of his body. Paul will later draw richly from the idea of the church as the body of Christ at critical points—in regard to the Lord's Supper (11:27-34) and in regard to the gifts of the Spirit (chs 12-14).

In 10:18, Paul presents another point: Those who eat at the sacrificial altar of a deity commune with that deity. It is true of the Lord's Supper that they participate in every week. It is also true of Israel. Commentators have a problem, though, determining in what sense Paul refers to Israel here and thereby to what practices he had in mind. Was he still looking back at sinful Israel, who consumed sacrifices at the altars of pagan gods, or was he thinking of Jewish practices in his own day involving the priests' consumption of offerings at the Temple, or was he thinking of the people who consumed the meat offerings in their home towns? Present Israel makes sense because it moves to a universal truth that eating altar food connects a person to the god being worshiped at the altar, whether Christian, Jewish, or pagan, regardless of whether each individual fully understands this. Historical Israel also makes sense because Paul had specifically noted Israel's fraternizing with pagan gods in the wilderness as a warning to the Corinthians.

Regardless of Paul's meaning in 10:18, with 10:19 he culminates his reasoning with the Corinthians on this matter. In doing so, he offers both a carrot and a stick. He agreed with them entirely in their theological conclusion that the idols do not represent actual gods. He himself preached likewise (Acts 17:22-28). Idols are merely the images for fictitious gods conjured up from human myth and legend, however strongly most people still believe in them. The Corinthian cosmology, however, was only partially correct. They had not accounted for the fact that the hollowness of the idols is completely filled with the evil work of demons. Perhaps here is where the minority who refused to eat idol meat had a valid point. Since demons are all around, working against God in the world and in people, idol worship misdirects people away from God and incorporates the rebellion of people against him (Rom 1).

With demons behind idols, this makes doing anything to support the institutions surrounding their worship totally abhorrent for those devoted to the one true God and Jesus Christ. Thus, Paul, based on Deuteronomy 32:16-17 (Conzelmann 1975:173; Hays 1997:169; Horsley 1998:141), makes a final edict in 10:20: The Corinthians should not participate in food rituals that honor idols because in doing so they would be honoring the work of demons. To do so is to violate their commitment to God. He seals this point by coming back to Christian communion in 10:21. Despite that fact that pagans worship multiple gods and can split their devotion between various gods at the same time, this is not possible for Christians. Once one sits to commune with God at Christ's table, no other option is possible without insulting God. As with Israel, God requires exclusive rights to a person's devotion (Hays 1999:170). Thus, in 10:22, depending again on Deuteronomy 32:16-17, Paul speaks of God's "jealousy," so often mentioned in the Old Testament as his reaction to Israel's sin of associating with the idols of "other gods" (Rosner 1994:201) and his predisposition to punish this transgression (Josh 24:19-20; 1 Kgs 14:2-23; Ps 78:58; Ezek 8:3; Nah 1:2; Zeph 1:18). The mention of God's strength also conjures up images from the Old Testament and human beings' complete inability to deter his punishment (Rosner 1992c:179). Was there ever anyone who opposed him successfully, whether individuals, kings, Israel, or other nations? All human power is dwarfed by his presence (Job 9:23; 37:23; Eccl 6:10).

Thus, the Corinthians could not oppose Christ successfully on their point, even if they wanted to. And if they continued to try after hearing Paul's argument, they would be in deep trouble. The bottom line is that Christians cannot eat idol meat in temple eating rooms (Cheung 1999:36-38; Garland 2001:185). This is much too close to the dangerous designs of demons and much too supportive of institutions harmful to the need for people to discover the true God through hearing the gospel of Jesus Christ. Paul did not exactly stipulate this restaurant restriction, but it becomes clear that this is where he intended to draw the line as he proceeds through 10:27.

On the practical side today, Christians should learn a lesson here. Are there institutions and practices embraced by our cultures that we should not frequent or support because of their ability to draw people away from the truth of Christianity? Should Christians frequent Las Vegas or local casinos? What about certain restaurants or bars that feature a lewd or sexually provocative environment? These are serious issues Paul's teaching still addresses today.

♦   5. Exercising freedom with mature compassion (10:23–11:1)

²³You say, "I am allowed to do anything"*— but not everything is good for you. You say, "I am allowed to do anything"—but not everything is beneficial. ²⁴Don't be concerned for your own good but for the good of others.

²⁵So you may eat any meat that is sold in the marketplace without raising questions of conscience. ²⁶For "the earth is the LORD's, and everything in it."*

²⁷If someone who isn't a believer asks you home for dinner, accept the invitation if you want to. Eat whatever is offered to you without raising questions of conscience. ²⁸(But suppose someone tells you, "This meat was offered to an idol." Don't eat it, out of consideration for the conscience of the one who told you. ²⁹It might not be a matter of conscience for you, but it is for the other person.) For why should my freedom be limited by what someone else thinks? ³⁰If I can thank God for the food and enjoy it, why should I be condemned for eating it?

³¹So whether you eat or drink, or whatever you do, do it all for the glory of God. ³²Don't give offense to Jews or Gentiles* or the church of God. ³³I, too, try to please everyone in everything I do. I don't just do what is best for me; I do what is best for others so that many may be saved. ¹¹:¹And you should imitate me, just as I imitate Christ.

10:23 Greek *All things are lawful;* also in 10:23b.   10:26 Ps 24:1.   10:32 Greek *or Greeks.*

NOTES

10:23 *beneficial.* See note on 8:1, where the same Greek word (*oikodomeō* [TG3618, ZG3868]), meaning "build up," is used. Paul's clear intention to connect back to that opening verse by reintroducing this word is lost by the NLT's overly contextual translations of "strengthen" there and "beneficial" here.

10:25 *marketplace.* Only used here in the NT, this word (*makellō* [TG3111, ZG3425]) refers to a general food market that sold such things as meat and fish. In Corinth, the market was built as a gift from those of means to the common people (Collins 1999:383; Murphy-O'Connor 2002:32) and was probably located along the Lecheum Road, which traveled north just off the city center (Bruce 1971:98; Gill 1992:389-393; Thiselton 2000:783). Murphy-O'Connor (2002:33) argues that temple meat and non-temple meat would have not have been easily distinguishable, but Isenburg (1975:271-273) says the higher price of idol meat would have made it noticeable. Collins (1999:383) suggests that following major civic events (all sponsored by gods) a flood of available meat into the market would have lowered prices, making it more affordable than normal for common people.

10:28 *conscience.* Gr., *suneidēsin* [TG4893, ZG5287]. The shorter reading of "conscience" is supported by all the earliest manuscripts (א A B). Many Byzantine manuscripts add a long gloss based on Ps 24:1 and quoted in 10:26, "the earth is the LORD's and everything in it." This is probably the result of the eye of the scribe skipping from the first occurrence of "conscience" in 10:25 to its occurrence here (Collins 1999:388). See note on 8:7.

10:28-29 The parentheses, not used by other translations, is helpful for readers to see the connection of the puzzling rhetorical question of 10:29b with 10:27b. The parentheses are supported by Hays (1997:111-178) and Bruce (1971:100-101). Most of those who do not support the parentheses also interpret the rhetorical questions differently than those who do. They see the rhetorical questions as supporting the voluntary abstention from eating idol meat once this information is known, the sense being more readily apparent by adding a negative (not in the Greek): "Why *shouldn't* my freedom be limited by what someone else thinks?" This has plenty of supporters (Barrett 1968:241; Soards 1999:217; Thiselton

2000:788-792; D. Watson 1989:302-303). However, this unnecessarily undercuts Paul's intention at this point in his argument to be supportive of the majority who wish to eat idol meat.

10:32 *offense.* Gr., *aproskopoi* [TG677, ZG718]. Only used here and two other times in the NT (Acts 24:16; Phil 1:10), this adds the negative prefix to a military word (*proskopos*) that refers to scouting out the enemy before preparing an attack. Thus, the idea is not to fail to do this because one will then come up against impediments to success that could have been foreseen.

church of God. Paul designates the communities of believers by this term also in the opening (1:2) and in 11:16 (plural) and 11:22. See note on 1:2.

11:1 *imitate.* Gr., *mimētai* [TG3402, ZG3629], only used by Paul and in Heb 6:12. Its use for encouraging believers is only found here, in 4:16, and in 1 Thess 1:6. Ephesians 5:1 advocates imitating God and 1 Thess 2:14 of imitating God's churches. Imitation should not be seen as reproducing an exact copy but as using another as a model or pattern by which to enact one's own behavior (Thiselton 2000:796).

COMMENTARY

Having come down hard on the Corinthians who had lobbied for their right to eat meat sacrificed to idols and to do so in the banquet rooms of pagan temples, Paul now offers a concession to them (10:23–11:1). However, he also challenged them to think beyond themselves and their rights when trying to determine proper Christian behavior on this matter and regarding matters that will come up in the future.

In 10:23-24, Paul begins with a challenge. He picks up the libertarian slogan that he already disputed in 6:12 during his discussion on sexual immorality. Just as he did there, he repeats the slogan "I am allowed to do anything" twice, following the first instance with the rejoinder, "not everything is good." At the second rejoinder in 6:12, he cautions about the potential for an individual to be enslaved to liberty in a fashion that is in the end harmful. The second rejoinder here goes in a different direction entirely—that a higher priority should override a person's individual freedom. The rights of a Christian should be superseded by what "builds up" or what brings benefit to the believing community as a whole. This is made clear by Paul's follow-up adage in 10:24 (Conzelmann 1975:176), which literally says, "Let no one seek something for himself but rather for others." When seen like this, the correlation of this to Jesus' teaching to love one's neighbor can be seen. Thus, Paul had brought his readers back to where he began this discussion about idol meat in 8:1 (Smit 1997b:379), where he said, literally, "love builds up" (NLT, "it is love that strengthens").

In 10:25-26, Paul offers his concession to the Corinthians. It was a practical solution that should appeal to them, completely unexpected given the tenor of his lengthy argumentation to this point: They can eat all the meat (the first specific mention of this word in the discussion) they want that is sold in the marketplace no matter its source, whether it comes directly from a supplier or indirectly from a pagan temple. The presumption is that they were buying this meat and eating it in the privacy of their own homes. Brought out from the shadow of the temple and its demonic connections into the open market, the meat was to be deemed as part of the bounty of the Lord's provision (Garland 2003:492; Thiselton 2000:787; Wright

1992:134). Paul validated his direction by quoting Psalm 24:1, the sentiment of which was foundational to Jewish prayer given before meals (Garland 2003:492), perhaps reflecting a practice that was taken over into Christian meal blessings. The lack of an introductory formula may indicate that Paul viewed this quotation as a wise truism generally recognized even by those unfamiliar with Jewish Scripture.

In 10:27, Paul preempts a potential problem with what he just stated: Since meat was more often a luxury brought out on festive social occasions and shared with guests, rather than a centerpiece of daily, family meals, what is a Christian to do about meat offered to him in another person's home as a guest? To make it more ponderous: What if the host is not a Christian and therefore most likely unconcerned about the source of the meat being served? Should the Christian (1) refuse to accept the invitation so as to avoid the more-than-likely chance that idol meat would be served, (2) join in the festivities but not eat the meat, or (3) join in the festivities and apply Paul's concession to eat the meat without any concern?

Paul did not even consider the first option, probably on the grounds of offending the neighbor and giving him an unfavorable impression of the Christian faith. Rather, he assumed the Christian would attend the event. Paul candidly rejected the second option and embraced the third in 10:27b, urging such people to eat all the food that is presented without any concern whatsoever. The situation falls under the rubric of buying meat in the market. So, enjoy.

So far, so good. But Paul envisaged yet a thinner slice of the problem. What if, while in the very act of enjoying the festivities—and the food, including the meat—someone tells the Christian that the meat is from one of the temples. Paul says in 10:28 that this flips the scenario entirely. Don't eat the meat! Now the second option is in play. The situation has become too much like eating at the pagan banquet hall where the Christian "knows" the meat is from their supply of slaughtered sacrifices. Yet it is not so much that the Christian must flee the house for fear of being tainted or of supporting demonic activity, as with eating in the temple. The Christian can remain at the party but must spit out the meat.

It would be nice to know for certain who reveals this information in the hypothetical situation, but Paul did not provide a clear indication. Is this the host who, knowing the scruples of many Christians (the minority who totally abstain from idol meat altogether), warns his Christian guests about what's on the table that they might want to avoid (Garland 2003:496-497; Witherington 1995:227)? Is it one of the other non-Christian partygoers who inadvertently lets it slip out (Barrett 1968:241; Fee 1987:484; Garland 2003:496-497; Horsley 1998:143; Oster 1995:237)? Or is it another Christian who has also been invited and who is one of the minority who have vowed total abstinence against eating all idol meat (Blomberg 1994:203; Bruce 1971:100; Hays 1997:177; Robertson and Plummer 1911:221; Thiselton 2000:787)?

Most likely it is the Christian abstainer. Who else could Paul justifiably identify as a person of "conscience" about this, as he does in 10:29? Perhaps it could be a Jew who is not a Christian, but Paul's case for the majority limiting their freedom on this matter has been about the unity and edification of the church, which means putting the scruples of fellow believers above their own. It is possible that it did not matter much to Paul who would reveal the information about the source of the meat. His main point seems to focus on the matter of its becoming known to the Christian believer at the social event, even though he offered the further explanation that the problem about the meat belongs to the other person at the party. In any case, the second half of 10:29, following the parenthesis in the NLT, really picks up on the scenario of 10:27 that embraced the third option (eating the meat at the party) and the purchase of meat in the open market that began his discussion of a practical concession to the majority.

With his two rhetorical questions in 10:29a and 10:30, Paul affirmed the validity of these Christians living out the freedom Christ obtained for them in ways that do not impinge on the unity and integrity of the church body as a whole and particularly of the minority who object (Bruce 1971:101; Garland 2003:499; Hays 1999:178). One's freedom need not always be subsumed under the "conscience" of the most conservative church member. Paul does say and illustrates that there are ways that Christians can exercise behavioral freedom in good conscience without sinning. However, they must be on the alert. What may be thought to be a situation where the majority can exercise their personal, carefully considered prerogative could quickly change to one where they must curtail their behavior immediately for the sake of unity with other Christians.

In 10:30, Paul's encouragement to enjoy God's food in thanksgiving clearly comments on the quotation of Psalm 24:1 cited in 10:26. It assumes a routine blessing of food within Christian homes (Fee 1987:487; Thiselton 2000:792) that purifies the meat offered to idols (if this is what they bought at the market) from its demonic environment in the service of a temple altar.

Paul closes his long exposition on the matter of eating idol meat with a final challenge to all believers about how to conduct the affairs of their daily lives in 10:31–11:1. He recognized that a myriad of decisions confront serious Christians who truly desire to uphold the principles of Christian teaching in their lives. However, he also knew he could not personally dole out decisions on all these matters—nor did he want to—and he certainly could not anticipate future issues that put Christians at odds with each other. The idol-meat controversy, though, offered a good case study for other scenarios. His first bit of advice to the Corinthians, offered in 10:31, is to make esteeming the honor of God the chief aim of their lives. This is not just a subjective measure based on what they say their own purposes are. By that standard they could easily validate everything they do.

However, they should be able to gauge their achievement of this in their particular actions by the way God is perceived by *others* with whom they come into contact. This is clearly the point of 10:32-33. In 10:32, he targets at least three categories of people that should be kept in mind: Jews, Gentiles, and other Christians, but this should not be seen as a limit. Many cultures have social expectations that Christians may need to adapt to in order to participate in good conscience. Paul draws on the principles he elaborated back in 9:19-23. He realizes achieving this requires flexibility, tact, anticipation, and humility. One cannot please everyone all the time, but one can adapt to the expectations of one person at a time. Simply on the matter of eating food offered to idols, a Christian may determine not to eat it in the company of kosher Jews, to consume it freely with Gentiles, and to do either with Christians, depending on sensibilities to the issue. On any issue, though, understanding the other culture, as well as being thoroughly grounded in the principles of the Christian faith, is required to be able to make these adaptations with integrity.

In 10:33, Paul draws on what he said in 10:23-24 and the fact that Christians must be willing to subsume their freedom (duly achieved in Christ) under the pressing needs of other people in their lives, particularly the urgency of accepting Jesus Christ as their Savior. To Paul's mind, evangelism trumps everything. If pleasing God is our purpose, then saving people by bringing them to Christ is our objective. With regard to fellow Christians, the objective must be to advance them in their relationship with Christ but to never do anything that might threaten them to lose their faith and discard the only way of salvation. Fellow Christians who simply have a different opinion about a matter but are quite secure in their faith have a right to their view and practices but not the right to require all believers to conform to their view.

With 11:1 (a verse that should never have been severed from chapter 10 when Stephen Langton made the New Testament chapter divisions in the thirteenth century), Paul offers his final bit of advice to help the Corinthians guide their own decisions in the future. They can gauge their lives by how Paul has conducted himself. This they could understand, not only by having observed him when he lived among them for 18 months but by hearing his teaching both while he was there and in this letter. Paul was not so egotistical, however, to think that even though he was a chosen apostle of Christ, that somehow his life was not without flaws. Thus, he accents that his life is but an imitation of the one in whom Christians invest their hope. Paul is not so much thinking of modeling Jesus' life and ministry. Rather, drawing on what he said in 4:8-13, he sees his own suffering and endurance of physical hardship for the sake of others as parallel to Christ's torturous and humiliating death on a Roman cross for the sake of the world (Garland 2003:503; Thiselton 2000:796). This kind of self-sacrifice is precisely what Paul had been presenting as the behavioral paradigm for the Corinthians since he took up the issue of meat offered to idols in 8:1.

◆   C. Paul's Response to Reports about the Gatherings (11:2-34)
      1. Women must cover their heads to speak in worship (11:2-16)

²I am so glad that you always keep me in your thoughts, and that you are following the teachings I passed on to you. ³But there is one thing I want you to know: The head of every man is Christ, the head of woman is man, and the head of Christ is God.* ⁴A man dishonors his head* if he covers his head while praying or prophesying. ⁵But a woman dishonors her head* if she prays or prophesies without a covering on her head, for this is the same as shaving her head. ⁶Yes, if she refuses to wear a head covering, she should cut off all her hair! But since it is shameful for a woman to have her hair cut or her head shaved, she should wear a covering.*

⁷A man should not wear anything on his head when worshiping, for man is made in God's image and reflects God's glory. And woman reflects man's glory. ⁸For the first man didn't come from woman, but the first woman came from man. ⁹And man was not made for woman, but woman was made for man. ¹⁰For

this reason, and because the angels are watching, a woman should wear a covering on her head to show she is under authority.*

¹¹But among the Lord's people, women are not independent of men, and men are not independent of women. ¹²For although the first woman came from man, every other man was born from a woman, and everything comes from God.

¹³Judge for yourselves. Is it right for a woman to pray to God in public without covering her head? ¹⁴Isn't it obvious that it's disgraceful for a man to have long hair? ¹⁵And isn't long hair a woman's pride and joy? For it has been given to her as a covering. ¹⁶But if anyone wants to argue about this, I simply say that we have no other custom than this, and neither do God's other churches.

11:3 Or *to know: The source of every man is Christ, the source of woman is man, and the source of Christ is God.* Or *to know: Every man is responsible to Christ, a woman is responsible to her husband, and Christ is responsible to God.*   11:4 Or *dishonors Christ.*   11:5 Or *dishonors her husband.*   11:6 Or *should have long hair.*   11:10 Greek *should have an authority on her head.*

NOTES

11:2 *the teachings.* Gr., *paradoseis* [TG3862, ZG4142]. The only use in 1 Corinthians, this word normally refers to stories and critical information handed down from one generation to the next. Traditional teaching in the NT usually refers to Jewish or rabbinic teaching (Matt 15:2-6), and Paul's use of the word in Gal 1:14 also points in this direction. It can also refer to Christian tradition, as here, and even more narrowly to Christian tradition associated with Paul (2 Thess 2:15; 3:6). Paul's use of the cognate verb, "I passed on to you" (*paradidōmi* [TG3860, ZG4140]), in this verse increases the impact of his action to connect the Corinthians to established Christian teaching. The verbal form also reappears in connection to the Lord's Supper (11:23) and the resurrection reports (15:3).

11:3 *head.* Gr., *kephalē* [TG2776, ZG3051]. This word commonly denotes the physical head of a person's body in the NT and elsewhere. However, beginning in this verse Paul offers a wordplay between this meaning and a metaphorical sense in this context, employing the word nine times in 11:3-10. A consensus on the metaphorical sense has so far proven impossible to achieve. Various scholars support one of three interpretations: (1) "authority" (Fitzmyer 1993:57; Grudem 1985:38-65; 1990:3-72; 2001:25-65), (2) "source" (Barrett 1968:248; Bruce 1971:103; DPL 376; Fee 1987:503; Jervis 1993:240; Kroeger 1987; Mauser 1996:10; Murphy-O'Connor 2002:293), and (3) "preeminence" or "top," focusing on the head's position atop the body (Garland 2003:515; Gundry-Volf 1996:159; Perriman 1994:617; Thiselton 2000:816-817). "Authority" seems to derive much of its force from looking at other Pauline passages, like Eph 1:22; 5:23; Col 2:10, which speak of Christ's headship over the church and other entities, but this is not demanded in this context (Collins 1999:405). "Source" looks more to 11:8, though it has some lexical support. The stronger understanding is "preeminence." This satisfies the cosmological order of God, Christ, man, woman, without falling into subordination or subjection of any to the other. Individuals can be superior to others in some sense and not necessarily hold authority over them. They can be the head of the class, but they cannot be the teacher who has authority over the class, or they can win top prize in a contest or race and not be the judge. This metaphorical sense of the word has strong lexical support outside the NT.

man. Gr., *andros* [TG435, ZG467]. The word can refer specifically to a husband or generically to males. Although the ESV has translated the first use of the word in this verse as "man" and the second as "husband," the NLT's decision (supported by the NIV) to translate both as "man" is probably to be preferred (Garland 2003:514; Thiselton 2000:811). Despite the fact that Paul's specific concern in the passage involves husbands and wives, his argument draws on the wider relationship between God, Christ, man, and woman.

11:4 *dishonors.* Gr., *kataischunei* [TG2617, ZG2875]. Used earlier in 1:27 (twice), the double use of the word here (11:4-5) signals a critical underlying cultural concern hovering in the background of Paul's discussion. Honor and shame, particularly from the perspective of what others in society think about someone, was a powerful force in Corinth as elsewhere in the Mediterranean world (Gundry-Volf 1996:154; Malina 1993:28-62; R. Williams 1997:56-57). See note on 1:27.

covers his head. Evidence is still being marshaled to determine if this refers to long hair or to a physical item of clothing, like a hood, over the man's head, but the reference to a hood seems most likely. The use of the yarmulke or kippah does not go back to the NT period.

prophesying. This is the first of 11 uses of the verb (*prophēteuō* [TG4395, ZG4736]) in 1 Corinthians (11:4, 5; 13:9; 14:1, 3, 4, 5 [twice], 24, 31, 39), complemented by an additional six uses (12:28, 29; 14:29, 32 [twice], 37) of the noun "prophet" (*prophētēs* [TG4396, ZG4737]) and five uses (12:10; 13:2, 8; 14:6, 22) of the noun "prophecy" (*prophēteia* [TG4394, ZG4735]). This activity with the gathered Christian community involves certain believers imparting an interpretation of the will of God that has been conveyed to them by the Holy Spirit (Collins 1999:402). Paul will position it in his later discussions in 1 Corinthians as the most necessary and beneficial of all the spiritual gifts. Though in the OT it is restricted to those especially called to be prophets to their times, in the NT this ability appears to be available to anyone in the church regardless of gender, race, knowledge, or status, based on the fulfillment of the promise of Joel 2:28-30 at the beginning of the church on Pentecost as observed in Acts 2:17-18. Though some suggest that the practice of this gift must be spontaneous (Fee 1987:595), it is better to think of prophecy primarily as Spirit-inspired content that ministers to the present or future needs of the community, whether this occurs impromptu or as the result of thoughtful, prolonged biblical study and reflection (Garland 2003:583-584; A. F. Johnson 2004:224-226; Thiselton 2000:963-964). What were originally perceived by hearers and the speaker as prophetic messages could be mistaken and thus were subject to the scrutiny of those hearing them (Thiselton 2000:963; Grudem 1982:110-111), especially by those with the gift of discernment (1 Cor 12:10).

11:5 *without a covering.* Only used here and in 11:13 in the NT, this word's meaning is the opposite of the verbal form found three times in 11:6-7 referring to women. In most settings, what is in mind is an article of clothing that covers the head. Some tie this in with the fact that in Greek mystery cults like those of Dionysus, Cybele, and Isis, all very popular among women in the first century and in Corinth, women were encouraged to let their hair flow free, which was counter to the expected custom that women should keep their hair bound on top of their heads (Collins 1999:408; Fiorenza 1992:227-228; Hjort 2001:72-74; Khiok-khng 1998:10-13; Kroeger 1987; Murphy-O'Connor 1980:488). However, in Greek culture, free-flowing hair in men signified an effeminate tendency leaning toward homosexual practices (Murphy-O'Connor 1980:485-486). Despite Paul's harangue against long hair for men in 11:14, such an interpretation here in 11:5 seems to take the interpretation very far afield from the context. Plus, if long hair is analogous to the head covering, as it is there, it cannot also be the head covering there or here (F. Watson 2000:534). Though confusion about the distinct customs of Jews, Greeks, and Romans regarding head coverings and worship swirls around this passage, fairly convincing numismatic and archaeological evidence, explained convincingly by Oster (1988:493-497) and Gill (1990:246-248), indicate that in Roman culture (which predominated first-century Corinth) both men and women normally covered their heads with the hood from their cloaks when they entered pagan temples and performed sacred rites. Roman women also wore their hoods over heads as legal protection against inappropriate advances from men (D. Martin 1995:242-243; Rousselle 1992:315; R. Williams 1997:58) whenever they went outside of their home. Thus, the conventional practice of women wearing their hoods when they spoke in Christian worship settings in Corinth is what Paul is attempting to reinforce in his discussion (Collins 1999:400; Corrington 1991:27-28; Fee 1987:510; Garland 2003:519; Padgett 2003:18-19; Thiselton 2000:824, 831; Witherington 1995:831).

shaving her head. Gr., *exurēmenē* [TG3587, ZG3834]. Used only here, in the next verse, and in Acts 21:24, it refers to someone whose head is shaved bald. In this context, the feminine marker on the word suggests a certain type of woman whose head has been shaved, possibly a prostitute who had been publicly exposed (Garland 2003:520; Thiselton 2000:829; Winter 2001:128-129) or an adulterous woman. Tacitus (*Germania* 19) speaks of a husband cutting the hair of his adulterous wife and throwing her out of the house.

11:6 *refuses to wear a head covering.* Covering the head with a hood or veil outside the home was standard practice for women in Roman, Greek, and Jewish culture (3 Macc 4:6; *b. Nedarim* 30b; *m. Bava Qamma* 8:6; *m. Ketubbot* 7:6; Plutarch *Moralia* 232C, 267A). This covering was a signal of a woman's unavailability and provided her protection under the law from the unwarranted affections of men and of rape (Garland 2003:521; D. Martin 1995:229-249; Rousselle 1992:315; Thiselton 2000:801). It was a sign also of respect and loyalty to her husband if she was married.

11:7 *image.* Gr., *eikōn* [TG1504, ZG1635]. Used here and in 15:49 in 1 Corinthians, this word denotes the likeness of an emperor or of a god stamped on a coin (Mark 12:16). Here, Paul uses it to depict the imprint of God the Creator on humanity (2 Cor 3:18; 4:4; Col 1:15; 3:10), probably drawing from Gen 1:26.

glory. Gr., *doxa* [TG1391, ZG1518]. See note on 2:8.

11:10 *angels.* Generally a messenger or envoy from someone, in the NT the word *angelos* [TG32, ZG34] is used almost exclusively (over 150 times) to refer to special beings who work for God's purposes and occasionally bring messages from him to individuals. Older interpreters beginning as early as Tertullian, and more recently D. Martin (1995:244-245), tend to think that Paul was referring to rebellious angels here, of whom Satan is understood to be the leader. However, the presence of the article with the word suggests God's loyal angels are in mind here (Garland 2003:527). They are viewed as beings who worship God along with the church and who are offended by a lack of proper decorum from those in the church (see note on 6:3).

wear a covering on her head to show she is under authority. Lit., "have an authority on her head" (see NLT mg). The rendition of the NLT chooses one of numerous suggested interpretations for its main translation. This translation wrongly assumes that the term "authority" in Greek can be used in the passive sense of someone being in submission to someone else (Collins 1999:410; Fee 1987:519; Garland 2003:524). The NIV's translation, "sign of authority," understands a woman's covering of her head as the symbol that either shows she is under subjection to her husband or provides her the authority required to pray and prophesy in worship, the latter view developed by Hooker (1963–1964:415) and followed by others (Barrett 1968:255; Bruce 1971:106). The NLT's secondary translation, "should have an authority on her head," is more neutral in a similar way. However, predominant among interpreters is the view that Paul believed a head covering exhibits a Christian woman's exercise of authority over her physical head, which demonstrates her choosing to honor her head (her husband) and thus qualifies her as a participant with men in worship activities (BeDuhn 1999:302; Collins 1999:411; Fee 1987:521; Garland 2003:525; Thiselton 2000:839). She is doubly covered, by her hair and by her hood (Corrington 1991:27). Thus, perhaps the best conception of the word here might be "authorization." A woman should "wear a covering on her head to show she has authorization."

11:14 obvious. Gr., *phusis* [TG5449, ZG5882]. Usually translated "nature" (NIV, ESV), it refers to what is the natural, created order of things based on how God determined them, or it refers to things so ingrained they are not subject to human ability to change them. Thus, the Jews are God's people by nature (Rom 11:24), but every person by nature is an object of God's wrath (Eph 2:3). The NLT rightly tries to convey that in this context Paul has in mind the customary convention of his day regarding the grooming of men's and women's hair rather than a way of grooming hair that God has designed based on gender. This is preferred because in this case Paul is using an argument based on his own perception of cultural convention from his position in dominant Greek and Roman culture. See further explanation in commentary.

have long hair. Used only here and in 11:15 in the NT (with the noun cognate *komē* [TG2864, ZG3151] found in 11:15), this word (*komaō* [TG2863, ZG3150]) simply refers to having hair (and the noun cognate simply denotes "hair"). The NLT (as also the NIV and ESV) rightly conveys the contextual implication that Paul was thinking of long hair, since from its first use it would be strange to argue that it is shameful for a male to "have hair." Free-flowing hair on men was considered effeminate in Roman culture (see note on 11:5). In Paul's day, Stoics and other moral philosophers (Epictetus, Plutarch) argued against long hair for men (Collins 1999:413; Garland 2003:530; Hays 1997:189).

11:15 covering. Only used here and in Heb 1:12, this word (*peribolaion* [TG4018, ZG4316]) refers to something that is "put around" something else. For a person, this would be a garment or cloak, and specifically in this context, the hood of a woman's cloak over her head or another means of covering her head. Some wish to employ this passage in support of their view that hair literally is the head covering throughout this passage (Padgett 1994:186), but this is unlikely. See note on 11:5.

11:16 wants to argue. Lit., "wants to be a *philoneikos* [TG5380, ZG5809]." Only used here in the NT, this word describes someone who relishes verbal battles with others.

custom. Gr., *sunētheian* [TG4914, ZG5311]. This word is used only here, in 8:7, and in John 18:39; it refers to accepted habits that people develop from living together as a family or community. In this case, Paul was thinking of accepted practice in believing communities throughout Asia Minor and Greece associated with his apostolic ministry. The NIV and ESV translate it "practice."

COMMENTARY

With chapter 11, Paul interrupts his plan to address questions in the official letter the church has sent him by responding to disquieting reports (from Chloe's people or from the letter bearers) about their home gatherings. Two distinct practices troubled him: that men and women were coming to these gatherings with their heads improperly attired and that late-arrivers, probably laborers and slaves, were not being offered equal access to food. Seemingly simple pragmatic matters, both were fraught with social and economic issues and bumped up against cultural issues of honor and shame. Paul's placement of his response to these issues after addressing the issue of food being offered idols in chapters 8–10 makes sense, because his solution of Christians practicing freedom without giving offense to various cultural factions would also apply well regarding the two problems here. It also provides an understandable bridge to the next matter he will address (from the Corinthians' official letter) in chapters 12–14, which involves the use of spiritual gifts in the gathered community.

Paul begins in 11:2 on friendly terms, voicing two commendations about their church life about which he had heard positive reports. First, they were continuing to remember him personally as a vital influence on their community. This may mean simply that they had not forgotten his role in planting their church in Corinth and his continued importance as their apostolic mentor. However, in the context of community worship, it probably also means that they offered thanks to God for his work among them and interceded to God because of his continuing hardships in spreading the gospel. Paul often used the language of remembering in association with prayer, usually noting that he remembered to pray for the churches to whom he was writing (see, for example, Eph 1:16; Phil 1:3-4; 1 Thess 1:2-3).

Second, Paul commended the Corinthians for living by what he had taught them. This was the best way for them to honor his role in the formation and development of their new community of believers, and he appreciated their respect for him. What Paul taught them would have included what was still (at this time) oral tradition about the life and teachings of Christ that would later become published in written form in the four gospels. Regarding this material, he would have "passed on" what he also received. The same is true, as he acknowledges, regarding the teaching he repeats about the Lord's Supper (11:23) and the resurrection accounts (15:3) later on in 1 Corinthians. However, Paul also had his own peculiar teachings, especially regarding the universal rebellion of all people, including Jews, and the singular solution of faith in Christ (Romans and Galatians) unencumbered by any Jewish legalisms (Galatians).

In 11:3, Paul uses a formula ("I want you to know"; also in Col 2:1) to introduce a fresh perspective into their thinking (Conzelmann 1975:183). This is Paul's theological prolegomenon from which he will launch his corrective (Fee 1987:501). This is followed by a series of four patterned statements that suggest a stair-step understanding of the relationship between God, Christ, man, and woman, using the word "head" as the connector between each. Strikingly, Paul begins with Christ and ends with God. His orientation is Christocentric. The salvation of all believers is through Christ, who continues to mediate their relationship to God, whether in prayer, worship, or the life of the Christian community.

Paul leans on the creation story of Genesis 2:18-25 that puts the creation of man before that of woman. His statement that God is the head of Christ suggests that men and women are not alone in needing to restrict their freedoms. If Christ limits his freedom for the sake of God's purposes (to save humanity from judgment), or to bring glory to him, surely it is not too much to expect men to do this for Christ, and women to do this for men (husbands). In this order, everyone (except God) has someone above them whom they want to glorify, not shame (BeDuhn 1999:299; Gundry-Volf 1997:157; Stuckenbruck 2001:217-218).

Despite the fact that Paul speaks of men and women generically in their relationship with God and Christ in his stair-step paradigm, the mention of Christ rules out any application beyond a context where people confess him as "Lord." Thus, this does not legislate the perennial subordination of all women to all men any more than it subordinates Christ to God outside of his human incarnation, as indicated by Philippians 2:5-11, Ephesians 1:22, and Colossians 2:10 (Giles 2002:22-137).

Paul provides nothing for interpreting these relationships other than his specific application of it to how some of the Corinthians are attired when they gather for prayer and worship. Likewise, the fact that a nonliteral use of "head" in 11:3 is followed by multiple literal uses of a man or woman's head in the following verses suggests that Paul's choice to use "head" here in 11:3 is driven from the beginning by the desire to play off of the literal use of head that follows.

Thus, it is a mistake to make too much out of the meaning and purpose of this passage by itself without taking into account Paul's specific concern about how the heads of men and women are attired when they meet together for public worship (Gundry-Volf 1997:158). Trying to determine whether "head" in 11:3 means "authority" or "source" or "top" (see note on 11:3) simply from the repeated formula itself is futile, and elevating the conclusion to a universal biblical principle is reckless. The numerous, exhaustive lexical searches on the metaphorical uses of "head" in the ancient Greek literature demonstrate that interpreters are trying to wring more out of the word in this verse than it can possibly give (Ince 2000:64). The advantage in terms of a nonliteral sense goes to the most generic idea, "top," because this is the least intrusive (see note on 11:3). Simply, one is above the other. But what does that signify? Paul wanted readers to recognize that he was purposely outlining an order that has theological significance, but he would not color that in until he got to the specific matter at hand.

In 11:4, Paul makes his first connection between the literal and nonliteral use of "head." Keeping to the order of his stair-step phrases, he declares that for a man to have his head covered in the context of Christian worship is shameful. Not only is this a symbol of disrespect to Christ, it dishonors him in the eyes of those who are also in this public gathering of believers. His mention of praying and prophesying, mentioned also in 11:5, most likely was intended to represent the various ways people participate in community worship, perhaps those which in particular involve people speaking aloud, addressing either God or the group. All such speech activities in a Christian setting would be in the name of Christ. Thus, he would be the one dishonored if this was not done appropriately, whether this involves the matter of attire, attitude, or anything else. In this case, Paul was very concerned about attire.

With regard to having their head properly attired, Paul believed women and men should be adorned in opposite ways. For women, this means something on top of the head, but for men this means nothing on top of it. The big question to which interpreters are not at all agreed is whether Paul had in mind a head covering or actual hair. For women, this is about whether Paul was asking them to wear their hair on top of their head rather than loose and down the back (assuming all women had long hair in those times) or to wear an article of clothing on their heads. For men, this is about whether Paul was asking them not to wear their hair long or to not wear a material covering over their heads, both of which would be things women should do. Beyond this fundamental area of interpretation, regarding which a scholar as superbly qualified as Thiselton (2000:825) is resigned to throw up his hands, another question is why the Corinthian men or women were not coming to public worship in proper attire. Another question is whether the problem in

Corinth was just with women or with both men and women. Finally, why was this such a big issue?

The important initial question, involving whether Paul had in mind hair or a material covering, is difficult to resolve because Paul never actually uses a word for veil or head covering, only saying that the head is to be covered or uncovered. The first phrase he uses to describe this in 11:4 literally means something down from the head (see note on 11:4). Although interpreting this as flowing hair makes sense when Paul gets down to criticizing long hair in men in 11:14 (Hurley 1981:257), by the time he gets there, it seems he is developing an illustration in support of his earlier discussion (Garland 2003:519). If hair is an illustration of the point, it can't also literally be the point. Here, the stronger lexical support connects Paul's words to a covering. Furthermore, both men and women in Corinth, following Roman custom, probably wore hoods over their heads for pagan worship.

That both Corinthian men and women most likely covered their heads in worship before they became Christians suggests that both would have expected to continue this practice after they became Christians. While he was there in Corinth for 18 months, however, Paul probably taught the men who became believers to remove their hoods in Christian worship. In the couple of years that he had been away, perhaps new male converts had bucked his teaching on this point as a matter of opinion. In the interval also some of the Corinthian women, experiencing other social freedoms in the Christian community, seem to have begun removing their hoods for worship. Perhaps this was because of the social norm in mystery religions commonly frequented by women in Corinth (Collins 1999:408), but more probably because Christians met not in public temples but in private homes, where custom normally allowed women to leave their heads uncovered (Garland 2003:521; Keener 2005:92). The family atmosphere of Christian meetings, sharing food together and treating each other as brothers and sisters, also may have been a factor. In any case, the passage gives no indication that Corinthian men or women considered themselves to be rebelling against hard-and-fast rules when they chose what to wear or not wear on their heads. This is the very thing, though, that Paul wanted to make indisputable.

Historically, interpreters of this passage have focused only on the issue of women in Corinth, but this probably has been because of the prevalent social concerns of their own times regarding women's role in society. In fact, the passage, all the way down to 11:17, balances comments about men and women on the subject, not unlike Paul does in chapter 7 (Collins 1999:402). Current studies are correct to observe that beneath Paul's mandate about what men and women are to wear in worship is his understanding that despite the egalitarian nature of the Christian gospel, maintaining respect for the distinctions between genders, particularly in worship, is essential (Gundry-Volf 1997:152; Theissen 1987:161-162). God created men and women different but equal—equal in offering public words toward God and others, equal in community life, but different in their look and adornment.

Now, 2,000 years after Paul's letter to the Corinthians, it can readily be observed that the social conventions that distinguish men and women differ from culture to culture and change over time within every culture. Christians, both men and women, attempting to share together in Christian communities all over the world, need to be sensitive to social conventions where they live, especially those involving clothing. They should also be aware when those conventions have shifted and warrant change in Christian attire. Freedom must be allowed to be exercised but in a manner that honors the one who comes previous in Paul's ordering, men to Christ, women to men.

Part 2

Paul's mention of shaving the woman's head in both 11:5 and 11:6, though possibly a rhetorical exaggeration (BeDuhn 1999:300), makes clear that the determination of what to wear or not to wear for a Christian woman is determined by how this honors or dishonors or might indeed shame her husband. The performative function of such a public act in the ancient world was to shame a woman because she had shamed her husband in adultery or her family because she was a prostitute. Thus, for a Christian woman today, the barometer of what to wear, whether in public or in church, should be her own husband or family in accordance with the clothing decorum of the day.

Paul indicates in 11:7, that for a Christian man, not wearing anything on his head in worship is equally about honor and shame with respect to God. Baffling all interpreters, Paul never explains or even hints at what the connection is, and his words never reveal whether there were any social factors to provide clues as to why a man covering his head in worship dishonors God. Perhaps, if this is what Corinthian men normally did when they worshiped idols in their temples, Paul simply did not want Christian men to follow that social custom. In that case, though, his prescription for men and women are opposite: Women should follow the custom to cover their heads; men should break with culture not to do so. But even so, his foundation for banning covered heads for men focuses on Genesis 1:26-27 and 2:18-25. His point may only be that they both show respect for God by adorning themselves in ways that glory in the gender differentiation that is the triumph of his creation.

Even though Genesis 1:26-27 specifically states that both men and women bear the image of God (and Paul also makes this point in Rom 1:23), the relevance for Paul's point here is only that the male is created in God's image. From this, he moves quickly to invest his thoughts in the word "glory," particularly the distinction of glory between men and women. Genesis never mentions glory at all, but Paul attaches the concept to the fact that Genesis 2:18-25 specifies that woman came after man and from man and that man was thrilled when he saw her. Making this point is clearly the purpose of expanding his comments in 11:8-9 (Fee 1987:517). In using the word "glory" to capture this situation as prototypical of women and their husbands, Paul was probably influenced by Jewish thought (*y. Ketubbot* 11:3; Prov 11:16, LXX—"a gracious woman brings glory to her husband"), which is reflected in the inscription on a Jewish wife's tombstone discovered in Rome: "Lucilla, the blessed glory of Sophronius" (Collins 1999:410; from Vogelstein and Rieger 1895–1896:1.65, 466).

By emphasizing the word "glory," Paul accentuates the positive—that a man glories in his wife and God glories in man. These strong feelings of attachment and pride to the one on the stair-step below are equivalent and call for an appropriate, equivalent response. Thus, men should respond with actions that display honor and respect toward God, and women should respond with actions that display honor and respect toward their husbands. For Paul, for the sake of the issue in Corinth, this is completely entangled in whether or not they cover their heads in worship. In terms of contemporary application, wearing a hat or not is not really the point (K. Wilson 1991:461). Men honoring God with their lives, bodies, and clothing in a way that respects the difference between themselves and women is the barometer for them. For married women it is the same with respect to their husbands.

The significance of worship to Paul's thinking should not be overlooked. It is here where men and women and God come into spiritual contact in a special way different from everyday life. This heightened spiritual connection accentuates the need to honor the created order—men to God and women to men. But it must be clear that this is not about a differentiation of what men and women do in worship; it is about how they present themselves socially within the activities of worshiping together.

The fact that it is in the worship setting that Paul was most concerned about how men and women present themselves is suggested by Paul's enigmatic reference to angels who observe them (11:10). Interpreters have offered numerous approaches to explain this reference, but for the most part they have settled on one, suggested as long ago as Augustine: Paul must have thought of angels as being fellow participants in worship. In Qumran angels were said to be "among the congregation" (1QSa 2:8-9; 1QM 7:4-6). In Revelation 7:11-12 thousands of angels gather around the throne and worship the slain Lamb. In Hebrews 1:1-14 angels worship God and Christ their Lord and are said to be servants "sent to care for people who will inherit salvation." If such notions were in Paul's thinking here, then the issue for Paul may be that the special place of angels in God's created order, created chronologically before men and women but who are now ranked after Christian women, makes them concerned that the parameters created by God between men, women, and themselves are observed in worship (Hays 1997:188; Thiselton 2000:841).

The other statement in 11:10 (NLT mg, "[a woman] should have an authority on her head") is a slightly different attempt on Paul's part to explain the purpose for a woman to cover her head in worship. While the NLT includes a largely discredited interpretive translation ("under authority"—see note on 11:10), a credible consensus of interpreters give credence to an interpretive translation more along the lines of "should exercise authority over," referring to a Christian woman responsibly manifesting her freedom in Christ to honor her husband by pulling the hood of her cloak over her head while she prays and prophesies along with the other men gathered for worship. Because she demonstrates control over her physical head, this shows her to be qualified to use the organ of her mouth to speak responsibly in public prayer, prophecy, and in other ways. Her words should not be discounted simply because she is a woman, with little to no authoritative status, as they would be regarded outside the restricted confines of the gathered Christian community. Rather, her words, whether to God or to others gathered, have equal status to those of men, who must also be honoring their head, Christ, for their words to have status.

Though some find Paul's further reasoning in 11:11-12 to be counter to his point in the passage, this is only true if one views his point to be that, since women are subordinate to men by their order in creation, they must demonstrate this in Christian worship by covering their heads. However, 11:11-12 flows quite nicely from 11:10 under the interpretation of 11:10 above. The status of men and women within the Christian community is the same. Both are saved by faith in Christ and baptism into his name. Both speak in prayer and prophecy when gathered for worship. Although certain social conventions that distinguish their genders—inevitably set by the larger social world *outside* the church—should be maintained in respect for God's created order, the expression "in the Lord" (11:11, lit.; NLT, "among the Lord's people") creates a self-sustaining biosphere that allows the mutuality of genders to flourish. Thus, Paul at this point in his argument emphasizes the God-created aspect of man and woman's interdependence that everyone knows to be true. The first woman may have come from the first man, but every man since has come from woman.

Soteriology, sociology, and creation theology are intertwined in Paul's position. By noting God's hand embracing all of this (11:12), he draws the reader's attention back to 11:3, where he laid out his preliminary principle of order: God, Christ, man, woman. God's plan with the gospel is to bring men and women back to a mutual relationship with himself; at least one aspect of this quest is to bring them back into a mutual relationship with each other, a relationship that was lost in the garden. Both have been accomplished by the sacrifice of Christ. In him, functional mutuality can be observed in the church (Hays 1997:189); this anticipates a completely integrated mutuality when all Christians will be gathered together with him in the eternal future.

By virtue of being nearly the last of his arguments in support of men worshiping with heads uncovered and women with heads covered, the statements in 11:13-14 are Paul's weakest support. Although he calls it natural or "obvious" (NLT; see note on 11:14), Paul employs the social conventions of Greek and Roman society in his own times to support his position (Garland 2003:530). However, it really becomes an occasional illustration of his point, certainly nothing we can rest his argument on today, when we know the conventions of hair length alone are not gender restrictive in all societies and at all times. Paul assumed that the Corinthian Christians could observe that most men in their society had shorter hair than most women and that for this to be reversed for a particular man or woman would be considered odd and unnatural, even shameful from a social perspective (Fee 1987:527). Long, carefully groomed hair on a man would be effeminate; short, ungroomed hair on a woman would strike people as being masculine. Yet, outside the mainstream, some men, such as philosophers, peasants, and "barbarians" outside the borders of the Roman Empire, were known to wear their hair long (Horsley 1998:156) even in Paul's day.

So, Paul may appeal to Greek and Roman social convention in a way that does not ring true universally today or even then, but to those who held the conventional views, his illustration would have at least been a verification of his main point. Though wide ranges of hairstyles in contemporary Western culture for men and women largely have nullified the value of this last argument for Christians today, a general case could still be made that certain kinds of styles, cuts, curls, and perms would be considered more appropriate for people based on up-to-the-moment social convention for men, women, boys, or girls. In this sense Paul's last supportive argument holds true and helps his case. There remains a social convention for men's and women's hairstyles in every culture that more or less reinforces the natural differences that God created in women and men.

In 11:15, Paul extends his argument about hair length for men and women by adding a few more comments about long hair for women. He had observed that women as a general trait tend to care a great deal about their hair and spend much more time grooming it than men do theirs. Even though he speaks of this in terms of a woman's long hair, his point is true even if the social convention of long hair is not retained in a culture, whether a Western one or some other. In any event, he calls her long hair a "covering." Although this is the only place in this discussion of any word that unmistakably refers to a garment over the head, it is purposely ironic on Paul's part that here it actually refers to her hair and not to a hood covering her head. His point is intended to illustrate that since a woman has been provided a natural head covering, this should be viewed as a sign that she should wear a material covering over her head when she worships with men in the gathering of the Christian community (Fee 1987:529; Garland 2003:531).

Paul's final argument in 11:16 is more a statement of fact than anything else. He informs the Corinthians that the convention of women covering their heads and men not doing so when they worship together is the pattern in all of the Christian communities he knew about. The custom he was reinforcing by his teaching was universal. He was not singling out the Corinthians to do anything others had not been asked to do. Perhaps the Corinthian situation was a unique environment that had cultivated some of the new believers to be mavericks with regard to this assumed but perhaps not clearly explained dress code. Nevertheless, he put together substantial arguments to encourage them to conform voluntarily to the conventional head attire that reflected the social expectations of men and women in a public setting—with a view to providing women the culturally unique opportunity to express their thoughts freely both to God and to men in prayer and prophecy.

◆   2. The Lord's Supper must demonstrate community harmony (11:17-34)

[17]But in the following instructions, I cannot praise you. For it sounds as if more harm than good is done when you meet together. [18]First, I hear that there are divisions among you when you meet as a church, and to some extent I believe it. [19]But, of course, there must be divisions among you so that you who have God's approval will be recognized! [20]When you meet together, you are not really interested in the Lord's Supper. [21]For some of you hurry to eat your own meal without sharing with others. As a result, some go hungry while others get drunk. [22]What? Don't you have your own homes for eating and drinking? Or do you really want to disgrace God's church and shame the poor? What am I supposed to say? Do you want me to praise you? Well, I certainly will not praise you for this!

²³For I pass on to you what I received from the Lord himself. On the night when he was betrayed, the Lord Jesus took some bread ²⁴and gave thanks to God for it. Then he broke it in pieces and said, "This is my body, which is given for you.* Do this to remember me." ²⁵In the same way, he took the cup of wine after supper, saying, "This cup is the new covenant between God and his people—an agreement confirmed with my blood. Do this to remember me as often as you drink it." ²⁶For every time you eat this bread and drink this cup, you are announcing the Lord's death until he comes again.

²⁷So anyone who eats this bread or drinks this cup of the Lord unworthily is guilty of sinning against* the body and blood of the Lord. ²⁸That is why you should examine yourself before eating the bread and drinking the cup. ²⁹For if you eat the bread or drink the cup without honoring the body of Christ,* you are eating and drinking God's judgment upon yourself. ³⁰That is why many of you are weak and sick and some have even died.

³¹But if we would examine ourselves, we would not be judged by God in this way. ³²Yet when we are judged by the Lord, we are being disciplined so that we will not be condemned along with the world.

³³So, my dear brothers and sisters,* when you gather for the Lord's Supper, wait for each other. ³⁴If you are really hungry, eat at home so you won't bring judgment upon yourselves when you meet together. I'll give you instructions about the other matters after I arrive.

11:24 Greek *which is for you;* other manuscripts read *which is broken for you.*   11:27 Or *is responsible for.*
11:29 Greek *the body;* other manuscripts read *the Lord's body.*   11:33 Greek *brothers.*

NOTES

11:17 *meet together.* This is the first of five uses of this word (*sunerchomai* [TG4905, ZG5302]) in this immediate context (11:17, 18, 20, 33, 34), with two later (14:23, 26). These uses in 1 Corinthians are the only ones by Paul. In Greek, this is a compound word formed by the joining of the preposition "together with" (*sun* [TG4862, ZG5250]) and "come" (*erchomai* [TG2064, ZG2262]). It is used of people coming from different places together in one place, for battle in a military sense or more usually to interchange on a friendly basis. It is generally recognized that the Corinthian believers would have gathered in the homes of their three or four wealthiest members, whose homes could have accommodated approximately 30 people on a regular basis, whether daily or weekly (Garland 2003:536).

11:18 *divisions.* Gr., *schismata* [TG4978, ZG5388]. See note on 1:10.

11:19 *divisions.* Gr., *haireseis* [TG139, ZG146] (cf. English "heresies"). This is a different Greek word than in 11:18. In Acts it refers to religious sects, such as the Sadducees (Acts 5:17), the Pharisees (Acts 15:5), and Christians (Acts 24:5, 14; 28:22). Here and in the rest of the NT the word refers to people who have formally united together around a set of beliefs and practices in opposition to other sects. Second Peter 2:1 anticipates the prevalent use of the word by the church fathers to refer to the beliefs of groups who do not hold to orthodox Christian doctrine, or heresies, a simple transliteration of this word into English.

11:20 *the Lord's Supper.* The word "supper" in Greek normally refers to the evening meal in a home. This is the only place in the NT where the word is prefaced by the adjective "Lord's," suggesting a ceremonial meal that Christians shared together, probably following an evening meal, as this context suggests.

11:21 *drunk.* Only used here and in Matt 24:49; Acts 2:15; 1 Thess 5:7; and Rev 17:6, this word (*methuō* [TG3184, ZG3501]) refers to people whose bodies are figuratively "saturated" or "drenched" from the inside out by an intoxicating beverage.

11:24 *This is my body.* Before these words, the Textus Receptus (followed by KJV) and other late manuscripts add "take, eat" (*labete phagete* [TG2983/2068B, ZG3284/2266]). These words were borrowed from Matt 26:26 in an attempt to harmonize Jesus' wording. The appearance of the short reading (followed by NLT) in early manuscripts like 𝔓46 ℵ B makes it certainly the original.

for you. This earlier, shorter reading, supported by 𝔓46 ℵ B, appears to have drawn various attempts to fill it out with verbal expressions, like "broken," "broken in pieces," and "is given" (corresponding to Luke 22:19). The NLT incorporated "is given" not based on a textual decision (see NLT mg) but in the interest of clarifying the intention of the clause, just like early copyists must have done.

11:25 *cup of wine.* Lit., "cup." The NLT specifies the content to prepare for Paul's association of the cup's content with Christ's blood. In its original context when uttered by Jesus, this was most likely the third cup of blessing during the Passover meal he shared with his disciples in the upper room the night of his arrest.

new covenant. Gr., *hē kainē diathēkē* [TG2537/1242, ZG2785/1347]. The phrase is only used to refer to the cup in the Lord's Supper here and in Luke 22:20. Paul uses the phrase in 2 Cor 3:6 to explain what his ministry seeks to make known. Other than these two references, the phrase is found only in Heb 8:8; 9:15; 12:24, and these specifically connect the "new covenant" to Christ and his blood. The idea of a new covenant to replace God's old covenant with Israel is found in Jer 31:31-33.

11:27 *unworthily.* Gr., *anaxiōs* [TG371, ZG397]. The adverb presumes that the manner in which something is being done is so careless that it does not measure up to standard expectations.

11:28 *examine yourself.* See note on 3:13.

11:29 *drink . . . body.* Some manuscripts have transported "unworthily" (*anaxiōs* [TG371, ZG397]) from 11:27 to stand next to "drink" and "of the Lord" to stand next to "body." The manuscript evidence for the unencumbered readings is solid (𝔓46 ℵ A B C*).

honoring. Gr., *diakrinōn* [TG1252, ZG1359]. Lit., "separate," "distinguish," "judge"; this word is used again in 11:31. The NIV translates it "recognizing," and the ESV "discerning." See note on 4:7.

11:30 *weak and sick.* Gr., *astheneis kai arrōstoi* [TG772/732, ZG822/779]. These two can both mean either "weak" or "sick" and are used as overlapping synonyms here for emphasis and rhetorical effect, given that they create alliteration together as well. Commonly, the second word is used more narrowly for physical ailments, as in the Gospels (Matt 14:14; Mark 6:5, 13; 16:18). The first word has a wider scope, referring to anyone lacking power, perhaps socially or morally, as used by Paul earlier in 1 Corinthians (1:27; 4:10; 8:7; 9:22, for example). However, in the Gospels it always refers to those who are physically sick (Matt 25:44; Luke 9:2).

have even died. Lit., "are asleep." In the NT, it is almost always used as a euphemism for someone who has died (Matt 27:52; Acts 13:36; 1 Thess 4:13), as the NLT's translation properly indicates.

COMMENTARY

In 11:17-34, Paul takes up the second matter related to their assembling together. This has to do with the manner in which they went about celebrating the Lord's Supper. In 11:17, his statement "I cannot praise you" is in direct contrast to his saying "I praise you" (11:2, lit.; NLT, "I am so glad"). The second matter appears to have upset him a great deal more than the previous one (viz., attire for the head), for he reemphasizes his distinct displeasure with the Corinthians in 11:22. The problem was greater because what they were doing undercut the core meaning of the gospel and amounted to trivializing the cross.

His general estimate of the situation, conveyed in 11:17, is that the Corinthians' practices during church gatherings are damaging the faith and the development of believers rather than being uplifting. Of course, it should be the opposite. Their regular gatherings in the larger homes of believers, probably occurring at least weekly, ought to nourish the faith of all present. All should leave feeling better about their commitment to Christ and closer to others with whom they share this common bond of faith in Christ.

In 11:18, Paul indicates that his knowledge of their practices at the Lord's Supper came from sources who had reported these matters to him. Though he hated to think their observations were true, he was forced to confront the Corinthians with what he had heard. Hopefully, their intention had not been to be cruel to some in the fellowship or to be insulting to Christ. Blinded by their normal social conventions, they had just not realized the theological ramifications of what they were doing. Their very meeting together—the very few in Corinth with common loyalty to Christ—was dividing rather than uniting them.

Paul used the very same word (schism) to describe the divisions in 1:10, when he denounced the factional groups rallying around different iconic leaders. To some extent, it will be seen that his theological concern runs along the same lines: Divisions in the body of Christ (the church) divide Christ himself. Now, however, the divisions were not between the house groups but within house groups.

Archaeological work in the Corinthian area in the 1970s by Wiseman (1979:528), which was authoritatively explained by Murphy-O'Connor (2002:155), has revealed the design of the houses in which the Corinthian believers likely gathered for worship during this period. Larger homes, owned by wealthier believers, including perhaps Gaius, Crispus, Stephanas, and Chloe, were built in a villa style, having two areas where guests could gather to eat a meal. One area, called the triclinium, with a floor space measuring 18 x 24 feet, had couches and a table at which nine people could eat comfortably. About 30–40 people (standing or sitting with no table) could be accommodated in the atrium, measuring 16 x 20 feet, which would also have had a water-collection pool in the middle. The significance of this is that it reveals how the Christians gathering as the church in one of these homes could have become divided physically by their structural environment.

Surprisingly, in 11:19 Paul admits that division has its purposes in God's plans. Using a different word than in 11:18, he speaks primarily in terms of God dividing humanity between those who are his people and those who are not. As Israel was necessarily separated out from the Philistines, Amorites, and others, so also the Corinthians were among those who had been separated out from idol-worshiping pagans in Corinth. This separation is never more real than when the Christians gather together for worship, leaving the pagan world outside. At the very center of this separation is the Lord's Supper, which Paul already emphasized as a separating event for Christians (comparable to Israel) when he said in 10:14-22 that when they share in it, they no longer associate with the worship of demons as their pagan neighbors do. Yet, even among those inside the Christian assembly, there were phonies to be discovered and removed—as a necessary means to reveal the true people of God who remained. Paul seemed to believe it was possible that various people's responses to his teaching on the Lord's Supper would expose their true colors. Were they truly members, or were they really outsiders who happened to be inside for the time being, only awaiting a crucial event to make this plain? Paul reveals in 11:20 that this event is the Lord's Supper. For the Corinthians, at least, it was their test. According to Paul, they may have called what they were doing the Lord's Supper, but it really wasn't. They may have been eating the bread and drinking the wine, but the way they were doing it was voiding any true, spiritual effect connected with Christ. What they were doing was too much like any other pagan social gathering. As 11:21 elaborates, their gatherings had turned into segregated social clubs, with the wealthy on the inner circle and everyone else outside.

Most likely social elites were gathering in the spacious triclinium with the host; everyone else, like day laborers, slaves, and such, were out in the atrium (Blue 1991:233). Furthermore, in accordance with the social norm (Corry 1999:188-189), the elite eating in the triclinium were consuming much finer food and drink than those in the atrium (Thiselton 2000:861; Witherington 1995:249). It is possible that the wealthy, having more control over their schedule, were arriving early, while working people could not arrive until later (Collins 1999:422-423; Fee 1987:542; Theissen 1982:151-153). However, other commentators caution against this interpretation (Garland 2003:541; Hofius 1993:88-96; Thiselton 2000:863; Winter 1978:81-82). The dinner may have been conducted in a potluck style in which everyone shared their food (Collins 1999:417-418), or a basket style, in which each family brought and consumed their own food (Garland 2003:539-541; Hofius 1993:92; Lampe 1994:38-39), or some combination of the two. Regardless, Paul's criticism was against the wealthy for drinking themselves into a stupor even while others had nothing to eat. Such conduct might be normal at a Greek symposium (followed by a lecture and discussion), but that is not appropriate at the Lord's Supper (Corry 1999:191; Keener 2005:97; Witherington 1995:244). Paul was criticizing their conduct at what was supposed to be a full evening meal, which would be followed by a ritual sharing of the bread and cup of Christ, with perhaps other worship activities (Blue 1991:230; Klauck 1993:65-66; Lampe 1994:37).

Paul's sarcastic question in 11:22 about the worst abusers remaining at home to eat makes it very clear that a full meal was involved at the Christian gathering. That the problem at Corinth was an issue of class and money is evident when Paul stipulates that the poor were being shamed by the conduct of the social elite (Henderson 2002:203). Paul's pragmatic suggestion is that those who intended to continue to conduct themselves in this segregated way should remain at home. The humiliation of those in the lower class could thereby be avoided. Perhaps, after the wealthy had eaten their sumptuous meal, they could bring some to share when they came at the later hour. But there is an ironic twist here. Since they were already separating themselves from the others by their thoughtless, elitist actions, maybe it was best just to separate themselves completely and eat at home. It was not the poor, late-arrivers who were ruining this holy gathering of believers; the elite were spoiling the unity of Christ's body.

One of the most unique aspects of the Christian faith to those in Corinth was its appeal to all people, regardless of class, race, or gender. Yet the Corinthian believers would not at all be accustomed to being mixed together in regular social gatherings. The poor surely would never have been in the palatial homes of the wealthy believers under any other circumstances and would have felt immensely intimidated. Those of higher class would have felt right at home but would not have felt at all comfortable mingling with the others as peers.

Given this, the environmental separation and distinction by class may have seemed perfect to make these church gatherings work. However, Paul calls this a disgrace. They were to regard one another as brothers and sisters in Christ. As family, the care, nurture, and support of one another in their common faith must be real, and it must overcome the normal social barriers erected by culture. The best place to begin is eating together in an equitable way, mixing together socially. What better way to set the proper atmosphere for sharing in the holy meal together after supper, and then sharing together in prophecy and prayer after that?

The Corinthians needed a reminder about the seriousness of what they were doing when they shared in the Lord's Supper. In 11:23-26, Paul rehearses its institution by Jesus Christ himself, to be followed by stern warnings against abusing its practice. Despite the wording that emphasizes Paul's direct knowledge of its origins, his wording need not mean that the Lord told him this personally (Fee 1987:548). It could just as well mean, and probably does, that those who were present when Jesus instituted this commemorative ritual had passed his words directly to Paul, who then passed them on in writing to the Corinthians (Farmer 1993:54). There is no doubt, though, that he initiated the practice of sharing in the Lord's Supper among the Corinthians when he was first there with them, as he must have done with other churches he established in his ministry. Paul used the same formula of "pass on" and "received" regarding his narration of resurrection accounts later in 15:3.

With the synoptic Gospels' not being written until at least a decade later (i.e., in the 60s, whereas 1 Corinthians was written in AD 55), this makes Paul's rendition of the Lord's Supper institution in 1 Corinthians the first written account. The remarkable agreement between Paul's account and those in Matthew 26:26-28, Mark 14:22-24, and Luke 22:19-20 speaks to the solid oral transmission of this singular event through the first generation of believers until it found its way into Paul's account here and into the synoptic Gospels. Comparison between the four accounts puts Paul's and Luke's in closest proximity to each other (Collins 1999:426). Distinct from Matthew and Mark, both Paul and Luke include the wording (1) "which is given for you"; (2) "do this to remember me" (Luke only for the bread); (3) "the new covenant . . . with my blood"; (4) mention of the cup "after supper." Common to all four accounts are (1) taking bread; (2) giving thanks; (3) breaking the bread; (4) saying, "this is my body"; and (5) the cup.

Paul connected the ritual the Corinthians were celebrating at the end of their fellowship meal with its origin as a commemorative rite Jesus began at the end of a traditional Passover meal (Thiselton 2000:872-874), though a few insist the full meal would have occurred between the bread and the cup, as in Passover (Hofius 1993:80-88). At any rate, this was Jesus' last meal with the disciples only hours before his arrest, trial, and crucifixion. Paul's depiction attempts to capture the drama of those moments in which Jesus anticipated his death—the climax of his mission—and infused it with meaning for his disciples at the table with him and for later followers like the Corinthians. As the host of the meal, Jesus had already initiated each course of the meal with expected words from Jewish tradition, but as he took up the unleavened bread, his words took an unexpected turn. The very act of breaking the bread was connected in his mind to his own body, which would soon be broken (tortured with pain and the agony of a cruel death), and thus he spoke words that identify this ultimate act of self-giving with the bread. The expression "given for you" recognizes the exchange that occurred on behalf of others—his life, the ultimate sacrifice, given to redeem people estranged from God.

No other rendition of the Lord's Supper emphasizes the remembrance command like Paul's does. Although Luke includes it after the bread, only in 1 Corinthians does Jesus state this twice, following both the bread and cup. Paul wanted the Corinthians to understand without question that their own practice of sharing in the Lord's Supper should be done to honor Christ and his wishes. It was not an optional aspect of their community gathering. Although sharing in the bread and the cup would certainly help believers recall the events of Christ's crucifixion, reenacting these institutional moments in word and action constitute the remembrance (Fee 1987:553). Thus, the sacrament is not inherent in the bread or the wine (Fee 1987:550; Thiselton 2000:876) but within the believing community's participating together in the Lord's Supper (Engberg-Pedersen 1993:117; Schottroff 2000:601; Surburg 2000:206). Thus, when 11:26 describes the community's announcement of Christ's death and his return (which also assumes his resurrection), the public celebration of the Lord's Supper itself accomplishes this (Gaventa 1983:382-383; Soards 1999:242).

Also notable in Paul's rendition of the Lord's Supper is his emphasis, like Luke, on the new covenant and Christ's blood. The "new covenant" connects to Jeremiah 31:31 and its anticipation of a climactic phase of God's plan to save all people. Jeremiah 31:31 itself connects the new covenant to the institution of the old covenant (Exod 24:8), when Moses sprinkled the blood of sacrificial bulls upon the gathered people to seal their agreement to live as God's people under his laws given to Moses. The wine in the cup connects the gathered Corinthian believers to the sacrificial blood of Christ, which Luke says was, literally, "poured out for many." Thus, Paul saw the regular participation, probably weekly (Horsley 1998:165), in the Lord's Supper as the pronouncement of God's new plan that now includes Gentiles as his covenant people. All believers in Christ constitute God's new people, who through this new ritual of the Lord's Supper identify with him and his death. They also identify with each other as bonded together because of Christ (Hays 1997:199).

Beginning with 11:27, Paul demonstrates why he had gone over Christ's institution of the Lord's Supper with them. He wanted to reestablish with the Corinthians that any misconduct in connection with the presentation of the Lord's Supper in their gatherings shows contempt for Christ himself, who is the host who originated it and invites all believers to participate in it together ever after. Thus, what might appear simply to be a social slight against those who were segregated to the atrium of the home in actuality is a sin against Christ himself, a sacrilege against his very body and blood, for he was given over to suffer and die for the benefit of all. How a church practices the Lord's Supper is serious business.

With 11:28, in a somewhat unusual move, Paul focuses on individuals within the community (Soards 1999:245) rather than the community as a collective whole. Perhaps he was speaking of the same individuals he encouraged to stay home rather than come only to get drunk and insult the poor (11:21-22). He believed that if individuals would take an honest look at how they were conducting themselves, they would either be convicted to effect a change in their behavior or leave. In either case he wanted believers to prepare themselves properly before they consumed the bread and wine along with the others. If they did not, their presence contaminated themselves as well as the body of believers (D. Martin 1995:164-167).

Paul explains further what he meant by this self-testing in 11:29, where he speaks of not "honoring the body" as reaping dire consequences. This sin against Christ brings a person into judgment by Christ. This probably does not refer to an eternal condemnation as with those outside Christ, but nevertheless it is a harsh censure from Christ himself. What constitutes a violation of not "honoring the body" or not "discerning the body" (ESV) is understood in at least three possible ways. First, traditionally, going back to Justin and Augustine, commentators have thought that proper discerning is to recognize the true presence of Christ in distinction from the elements of the bread and wine. To fail to do so for any reason would be a sacrilege against the holiness of Christ, who has come into the presence of the assembled believers. This would encourage Christians to refrain from partaking in communion rather than to risk divine punishment.

Second, and more likely, Paul wanted each individual to consider honestly the way he or she was treating others in the church as a spiritual precursor to sharing in the Lord's Supper. This interpretation has the support of many commentators (Bruce 1971:115; Fee 1987:564; Gentry 1999:243; Hays 1997:200; Horrell 1995:199; Horsley 1998:162; Koester 1997:51; Soards 1999:247; Witherington 1995:252). Since the word Paul used in verse 29 (diakrinōn [TG1252, ZG1359]) literally means "separate," he may have been playing off the theme of separation that colored his comments in 11:20-22. Rather than believers separating themselves by social class and holding fellow believers in disdain, as some were doing with the Lord's Supper, Paul was admonishing them to separate fellow believers out for esteem and honor, to judge them favorably rather than unfavorably.

The second interpretation has the strongest support: (1) Paul mentions only the "body," not the cup or the blood. (2) He already made the theological connection that the church is the body of Christ in 10:17. (3) His entire discussion of the topic was initialized by the misconduct of certain Corinthian Christians against their fellow Christians not only in celebrating the Lord's Supper but also in the whole social context of their gathering. (4) Paul's follow-up in 11:30 focuses on the physical ailments of people in the church as an indication that some had already violated this instruction. (5) Paul's use of "honor" (diakrinō [TG1252, ZG1359]) is the same word as "examine" in 11:31, and this is juxtaposed by God's judging or disciplining people in the community with sickness.

A third approach to honoring (or discerning) the body suggests that Paul wanted the Corinthian believers to contemplate the cross and become convicted by Christ's self-sacrifice, which would motivate them to quit dishonoring others in their community (Barrett 1968:273; Blomberg 1994:209; Das 1998:205; Garland 2003:553; Koester 1997:50; Marshall 1987:114; Thiselton 2000:893). This certainly makes sense theologically and may in reality be what happens to effect the kind of change Paul wanted to happen in these believers. However, to see this as Paul's main point runs against the tenor of the context. Paul was most concerned at the practical level here, that those in the believing community honor Christ best by honoring one another. This creates the one body sharing together in the bread and the cup of Christ.

In 11:30, Paul cites as evidence that the Corinthians were not properly "honoring the body" the fact that significant numbers of Corinthian believers had fallen ill. To contemporary believers, who live in an era of modern medicine in which all diseases and illnesses are assumed to have purely natural causes related to germs, viruses, and defective genes, it is almost impossible to contemplate what Paul and most people in the ancient world assumed, that despite all appearances, some illnesses come from supernatural causes (D. Martin 1995:164-165). Sometimes, they are from evil, demonic forces, as when Jesus cast out demons to heal people of diseases (Mark 5:15-18). Sometimes they are from God for purposes of his own, as with Paul's "thorn in the flesh" (2 Cor 12:7-10). Sometimes, they are related to sin, when confession of sin is seen as the route to physical healing (Jas 5:15-16).

Truthfully, for all the medical advances that have occurred, none of them rule out the possibility of such supernatural causes of disease today, no more than the amazing discoveries of modern astronomy eliminate God's hand in the universe we live in. It should be noted that the diseases Paul has in mind are serious, especially when he notes that for some people their ailments resulted in death. Paul did not say or mean that there is a direct equation between an ailing believer and that person's mistreatment of others in the Christian community, and Jesus explicitly denied that sin was the cause of a certain person's being born blind (John 9:1-3). What Paul saw was that the Corinthian community had made itself vulnerable to disease as a part of God's discipline for the unwholesome spiritual climate in their midst as demonstrated by their mistreatment of the Lord's Supper (Fee 1987:565). That some had even died demonstrates the seriousness with which Christians should have observed the Lord's Supper, and this holds for Christians today, too.

In 11:31-32, Paul condenses and reiterates his point from 11:27-30. In 11:31 he uses a conditional statement to stipulate that the Corinthians need to correct their practice of the Lord's Supper. By showing respect to their co-worshipers, they could contribute to the good health of those in their community. Thus, they had a measuring rod of the spiritual health of their church body by noting their improved physical health. In 11:32, Paul makes unequivocally clear that this form of discipline from God is not in itself any kind of permanent condemnation, the kind that awaits pagans. The intention from God's standpoint is entirely preventative. God provides a physical warning so that the spiritual conditions related to it will not be allowed to spiral down to the point that someone turns away from the Christian faith.

In 11:33-34, Paul offers some practical solutions that could possibly accommodate all parties. In this case, he tells those who were arriving early or who were consuming the best food too quickly simply to consider the situations of others and patiently await their arrival. If that was not a good option for some, he once again suggests that these people go ahead and consume their luxurious food in the privacy of their own homes, with the assumption that they would still get there for the common gathering when most everyone else did.

Paul finishes out this section of instruction with a note anticipating his next visit to the Corinthian church, knowing that his instruction on this matter and others may need more smoothing out. Despite his cheery outlook about this visit from the vantage point of 1 Corinthians, 2 Corinthians 2:1-4 reveals that this would turn out to be the so-called painful visit, which was an utter disaster. Paul's note here also indicates that despite the length of his letter, he has more concerns about their church. But for the present, he seems pressed to get back to the Corinthians' concerns expressed in their letter to him. He will do this in chapters 12–14.

◆   **D. Matters concerning Spiritual Gifts (12:1–14:40)**
     1. The Holy Spirit, the source of every believer's gifts (12:1-11)

Now, dear brothers and sisters,* regarding your question about the special abilities the Spirit gives us. I don't want you to misunderstand this. ²You know that when you were still pagans, you were led astray and swept along in worshiping speechless idols. ³So I want you to know that no one speaking by the Spirit of God will curse Jesus, and no one can say Jesus is Lord, except by the Holy Spirit.

⁴There are different kinds of spiritual gifts, but the same Spirit is the source of them all. ⁵There are different kinds of service, but we serve the same Lord. ⁶God works in different ways, but it is the same God who does the work in all of us.

⁷A spiritual gift is given to each of us so we can help each other. ⁸To one person the Spirit gives the ability to give wise advice*; to another the same Spirit gives a message of special knowledge.* ⁹The same Spirit gives great faith to another, and to someone else the one Spirit gives the gift of healing. ¹⁰He gives one person the power to perform miracles, and another the ability to prophesy. He gives someone else the ability to discern whether a message is from the Spirit of God or from another spirit. Still another person is given the ability to speak in unknown languages,* while another is given the ability to interpret what is being said. ¹¹It is the one and only Spirit who distributes all these gifts. He alone decides which gift each person should have.

12:1 Greek brothers.   12:8a Or gives a word of wisdom.   12:8b Or gives a word of knowledge.   12:10 Or in various tongues; also in 12:28, 30.

NOTES

12:1 Now . . . regarding. Lit., "Now concerning what." This formula, repeated exactly in 7:1, 25, 8:1, here, and 16:1, shows that Paul is once again responding to the Corinthians' questions from their letter. (See notes on 7:1; 8:1; and Introduction.)

the special abilities the Spirit gives us. Gr., *pneumatikōn* [TG4152B, ZG4461]. The grammatical form of the word used here could be neuter (i.e., "spiritual things") or masculine plural (i.e., "spiritual people"). The neuter plural form (*pneumatika*) used in 14:1 makes it far more likely that the meaning here is also neuter: "spiritual things." Plus, the reference in the immediate context to "spiritual gifts" (*charismatōn* [TG5486, ZG5922]; 12:4) and "the manifestation of the Spirit" (12:7, lit.) support this conclusion. The NLT correctly tries to maintain the neuter plural sense while also showing that Paul's emphasis is on the Holy Spirit as the source of these spiritual gifts throughout this discourse (Thiselton 2000:910).

12:2 *you were led astray and swept along.* Paul employs the verb "lead" or "bring" (*agō* [TG71, ZG72]) followed by a cognate participle (*apagomenoi* [TG520, ZG552]), meaning "lead astray," to draw dramatic attention to how Gentiles can't help but get drawn in by pagan gods in their cultures. The NLT's "swept along" fits with the suggestion that Paul may be trying to get readers to picture the very common festival parades that drew in the crowds on their way to offer worship to pagan gods at their temples (Collins 1999:447; Paige 1991:59; Thiselton 2000:912).

12:6 *works in different ways.* Lit., "different kinds of works," mirroring "different kinds of spiritual gifts" and "different kinds of service" in 12:4-5.

12:7 *spiritual gift.* Lit., "the manifestation of the Spirit." It is not the same word used in 12:4, "gifts" (*charismatōn* [TG5486, ZG5922]). Although both words surely refer to the same phenomena in believers, the word used this second time emphasizes their singular source as the Spirit, whereas the word used earlier emphasizes their variety (12:4).

so we can help each other. Gr., *sumpheron* [TG4851B, ZG5237]. The word is formed by combining the very common verb that means "bring" or "carry" (*pherō* [TG5342, ZG5770]) with the preposition that means "together with" (*sun* [TG4862, ZG5250]). While the meaning of the word is not determined by separating and recombining the parts, it creates a helpful illustration referring to "bringing people together," implying that this will create a good, helpful, advantageous result.

12:8 *wise advice.* Gr., *logos sophias* [TG3056/4678, ZG3364/5053]. Lit., "word of wisdom," mirroring in formation the phrase that follows, "word of knowledge" (NLT, "message of special knowledge"; *logos gnōseōs* [TG3056/1108, ZG3364/1194]).

12:9 *the one Spirit.* Lit., "in one Spirit," supported by A B 33 1739. This is replaced in some manuscripts, including ℵ C D F G 0201, by "in the same Spirit," an effort to conform this third phrase with the previous two references to "the same Spirit" immediately preceding.

healing. Gr., *iamatōn* [TG2386, ZG2611]. Out of the list of Spirit manifestations, only this one and "miracles" are in the plural. In both cases the plural is probably trying to account for the huge variety of individual circumstances that may be remedied by the exercise of these gifts (Collins 1999:454; Thiselton 2000:946). Healings refer to aiding people to recover from physical illnesses. Corinth is the site of an extensive archaeological excavation of an Asclepius shrine, a place where people went for cures of all sorts. Terra-cotta objects of feet, hands, eyes, and ears have been found there; they were used as some part of the healing remedy or as an offering of thanks for healing (Collins 1999:462; Thiselton 2000:736).

12:10 *miracles.* Gr., *dunameōn* [TG1411, ZG1539]. This is simply the word "powers," though it can, as here, focus on the manifestation of miraculous powers of God that his agents can draw on to overcome otherwise immovable, and sometimes evil, forces. Thus, it is usually thought to be a broader term than "healings," covering a wider field of activity, including the casting out of demons or perhaps miracles of nature (Thiselton 2000:953-954).

ability to prophesy. See note on 11:4.

discern whether a message is from the Spirit of God or from another spirit. Lit., "separating of spirits." The NIV and ESV both have "distinguish(ing) between spirits." The NLT's expansion presumes that this gift is somehow related to the concern of 12:3 and that it is exercised in a worship setting.

unknown languages. Lit., "tongues" (*glōssōn* [TG1100, ZG1185]). This word is used 21 times in chs 12–14 in a way that clearly does not refer to the human tongue but to some kind of language. In Revelation it is used seven times to refer to the variety of languages and dialects associated with various cultures and "tribes" (Rev 5:9; 7:9; 10:11; 11:9; 13:7; 14:6; 17:15), as it does in Acts 2:4 and 2:11, when the early believers explained the gospel in the native dialects of thousands of people gathered in Jerusalem on that day. Though the idea that the word in 1 Corinthians refers to known languages seems likely to some interpreters (Forbes 1995:51-65; Gundry 1966; Hodge 1958:248), the extensive use of it in a seemingly more technical way points to some other kind of phenomenon. The oldest suggestion, dating back to Tertullian (*De Anima* 9) and still receiving some interest (Barrett 1968:300; Fee 1987:598; Witherington 1995:258), calls the Corinthians' phenomenon "angelic speech." This interpretation gets support from 13:1 and also references to angelic dialect in *Testament of Job* 48:2; 50:1. Yet 13:1 never states that humans speak angelic language, only that angels do. Some call this "ecstatic speech," relating it to the uncontrolled babble that occurred in the many religions of the Hellenistic world (Dunn 1975:234-242; ABD 6.597-598; TDNT 1.722-726), but there is no indication that this phenomenon was uncontrollable in the Corinthian church (cf. 14:26-30). Furthermore, the evidence that has formed the basis for connecting ancient cults to such frenzied activity has been seriously challenged (Forbes 1995:168-181). More recently, commentators have explained this phenomenon in connection with the "groanings" of Rom 8:26; these utterances come from thoughts and sensibilities tucked deeply into the recesses of the inner being and are expressed in language that is more primitive than any developed language but is a language nonetheless (Fee 1995:598; Macchia 1998:73; Stendahl 1977:109-124; Theissen 1987:276-307; Thiselton 2000:985-988). Tongues here and groanings in Rom 8:26 are not exactly the same thing, but the basis for tongues "transcends cognitive consciousness" akin to modern psychological notions of the subconscious (Thiselton 2000:985). Romans 8:26 refers to unworded or inarticulate noises, with groans being the noise that expresses without human language. All believers have their private, deep concerns that can be communicated to God for them by the Holy Spirit. Some believers, drawing on this same reality, utter these deep thoughts in tongues to the entire congregation in primitive, precognitive language aided by the Holy Spirit.

COMMENTARY

For the third time in the letter Paul employs his formula "Now . . . regarding" (*peri de* [TG4012/1161, ZG4309/1254]) to introduce a new subject queried in the official letter he received from the Corinthian church. His response to the first two questions, regarding marriage (ch 7) and meat offered to idols (chs 8–10), was interrupted by the attention he gave to head attire and the Lord's Supper (ch 11), both matters pertaining to their church gatherings. He now turns to the matter they actually asked about, the proper function of spiritual gifts. After putting spiritual gifts in theological perspective in chapters 12–13, in chapter 14 he will tackle not only their specific questions about prophecy and tongues, but then will add other concerns based on additional insider information (Bruce 1971:117) about the dysfunction of their congregational life.

In the second half of 12:1, Paul introduces his preliminary comments with an attention-getting introductory formula. This formula, by using what amounts to a double negative (lit., "I do not want you not to understand"), rhetorically blares out to the Corinthians that what is coming is immensely important and that this is new information essential for their sorting through issues relating to spiritual gifts (Collins 1999:445).

In 12:2, Paul replays for the Gentile Corinthian believers their former religious life. He pictures them caught up—as they often probably were only a few years prior—in the pagan revelry that was integral to life in Corinth. But this is only a picture of a bigger reality. Unless they had grown up in a Jewish environment, the cultural influences that led them to worship the idols of pagan gods were insurmountable. They worshiped idols because they learned to do so through their family and friends, and they really had no other choice. Having grown up in a Jewish household, Paul took a dig at the pagan gods by adding the description "speechless." They are dumb; their carved stones are lifeless and speak not a word, while God, who is real and living, speaks to his people throughout Old Testament history. Psalm 50:3 exclaims that God *cannot* be silenced.

It is evident that Paul emphasizes the silence of the idols in 12:2 as a point of contrast with the great deal of speaking that God does through the Holy Spirit in the church, the predominant subject of the next three chapters. However, Paul's more pressing concern is the validation of such speech as legitimately coming from God. So he laid out a basic rule that can easily be applied and must be applied first. Does the person who claims to be speaking on behalf of the Spirit of God to the church confess Christ as Lord, or does that person curse Christ? The big question for interpreters (and which is by no means settled) is the context in which Paul assumes these statements might be made. Although there are many specific suggestions (with Thiselton 2000:917-925 exploring 12!), they basically fall into two possible contexts. One is a conversion context and the other a worship context of gathered believers.

A worship context presumes that Paul brought up these antithetical confessions because they both actually occur within Christian worship activities. Words from those who curse Christ should not be heeded; words from those who confess Christ should be heeded. Normally, it is also assumed that what Christians were hearing in their communal worship practices (the subject of ch 14) are virtually the same as what they formerly experienced in pagan worship (Barrett 1968:280; Dunn 1975:234-235; Moffatt 1938:179; Soards 1999:253-254). So, backtracking to 12:2, the assumption is that the ecstatic utterances they heard or participated in as pagans were certainly false because idols (and pagan gods) do not really speak.

The biggest difficulty with this view—other than its questionable interpretation of data that pagan prophetic utterances were ecstatic (Forbes 1995:168-181)—is trying to conceive of a situation in which anyone in a Christian worship setting could possibly have uttered the anti-confession of Jesus Christ. Some suggest that perhaps nonbelieving Gentiles or Jews were occasionally joining in Christian assemblies and shouted out the curse under demonic influence or as a protest (Robertson and Plummer 1911:261). In fact, it is well documented in rabbinic literature that Jesus is called the son of Satan (*t. Hullin* 2:22-24).

However, Paul's picture of the believers assembling for teaching and the Lord's Supper (ch 11) is certainly exclusive to believers. Thus, many who hold this view suggest the cursing Jesus formula is only hypothetical to emphasize the positive (Fee 1987:577-581; Horsley 1998:168).

A conversion context suggests that Paul had in mind the fundamental entry point to becoming a Christian, confession that "Jesus is Lord" followed by baptism (5:4; 6:11; 8:6; 9:1; 11:23; 15:31, 57; 16:23; Acts 2:38; 16:31; Rom 6:2-3; 10:9; Phil 2:11). Those who hold this view note that Paul had said nothing about worship yet or anything that hints of Spirit-guided utterances (Garland 2003:567-572). They add that this simple, confessional formula is documented as evidence for conversion elsewhere in the New Testament (Rom 10:9) and that the mention in 12:13 of baptism complements this view (Collins 1999:445-446). They backtrack to 12:2 to say that all Paul is doing here is helping Corinthian believers demarcate their new life in Christ as inhabited by the Holy Spirit who speaks through them—in contrast to their old lives of devotion to stupid, speechless stones. Now, their initial confession of Christ evidences that the Holy Spirit influences them, and this makes them full and equal participants in the life of the church, especially in worship, but not just in worship. Their gifts should not be viewed as exclusively exercised in a worship setting. Rather, they are vital to everyday community life and interaction of believers. So, too, their confession is not just relevant to joining the community; their continual devotion to Christ enlivens their entire relationship with the community (Hays 1997:209; Thiselton 2000:925-927; Wire 1990:137). On balance, this better represents the overall context in 1 Corinthians.

Having established that all believers in Christ have the Holy Spirit in 12:2-3, in 12:4-6 Paul wants to show that the gifts the Spirit distributes come from God himself. He does this by devising a series of three statements in parallel that leads the reader from the Spirit, to Christ (Lord), to God (Robertson and Plummer 1911:262). Although Paul did not have a fully developed Trinitarian scheme—this will not come about until the second and third centuries—he anticipated and fueled the inevitable drive to develop this (see also Rom 8:11; 15:15-16, 30; 2 Cor 1:21-22; 13:14; Gal 4:6).

The parallelism suggests the equality of Spirit, Lord, and God, yet the order suggests an ascendancy of roles. The thrice-repeated contrast between innumerable gifts but the same Spirit, Lord, and God suggests the overlap in their roles. The diversity of words used to refer to the Spirit's gifts—spiritual gifts, kinds of service, and workings—are for the purpose of the parallel structure, and their distinctions should not be emphasized. They are all making the same point: The variety of abilities the Spirit gives believers enhances the community. These abilities, though emanating from the Spirit, are available only because of each believer's commitment to Christ, who was sent to complete God's mission to save humanity from condemnation because of their sin.

Before providing in 12:8-11 a sample of the variety of gifts the Spirit distributes, in 12:7 Paul creates a headline that curtly announces his principal position about spiritual gifts: Their only purpose is to provide an avenue for each believer to serve a vital need of the whole community. This principle will underline his teaching through the end of chapter 14. Each believer has a gift so that other believers might be strengthened and receive needed ministry. These gifts are not for self-aggrandizement.

In 12:8-11, Paul presents nine spiritual gifts as samples of what the Spirit provides. This is one of four such lists in Paul's writings (12:27-28; Rom 12:6-8; Eph 4:11). This list is distinctive in repeating four times the role of the Holy Spirit as the single source of each gift, no doubt intending to reinforce the point made in 12:4. It also creates three groups of gifts by shifting to a different word, "someone else" (*heteros* [TG2087, ZG2283]), to refer to those receiving the gifts before the third item (faith) and the eighth item (tongues; NLT, "unknown languages"). The first group includes two kinds of "words" or "messages." The third group includes two gifts involving "tongues." The group of five items in the middle appears to be miscellaneous (Hays 1997:211).

The first group, containing two types of messages, heads the list because they are both immediate examples of God's speaking to the believing community—in contrast to speechless idols (12:2). The expressions "wise advice" and "message of special knowledge" are intended to be viewed as overlapping since they are phrased in parallel, literally "word of wisdom" and "word of knowledge." Wisdom best relates to matters of practical living, or commonsense advice like that found in proverbial Wisdom Literature (Bruce 1971:119; Talbert 1987:82), while knowledge may refer to explaining a particularly Christian perspective on the world and God. Both words may refer to Christian wisdom and knowledge in contradistinction to the empty wisdom and knowledge of the world, which Paul debates in 1:18–2:16. However, assumptions that wisdom here is particularly oriented around the cruci- fied Christ (Dunn 1975:221; Fee 1987:592; Garland 2003:581; Soards 1999:258) unnecessarily confuses Paul's exposition there, which is geared against pagan, worldly wisdom, with the exclusively Christian setting of wisdom or knowledge being described here.

In the second, miscellaneous group of five, Paul first lists "faith" in 12:9. This cannot mean the basic, saving faith in Christ that all believers possess; more likely it means special confidence in pursuing God's will when others in the Christian community are unsure, questioning, or perhaps contemplating quitting a course of action. Perhaps this gift of extraordinary faith overlaps with the next two gifts, noted in 12:9b and 12:10a: the ability to bring about healings and miracles. These two themselves overlap but are distinguished by eliciting God's power to intervene in personal illnesses that befall believers and his power to intervene in a variety of life's circumstances that threaten to overpower believers, ranging from civil authori- ties to demonic forces.

Prophecy (12:10b), the fourth item in the miscellaneous list, has already been noted by Paul as an integral aspect of the public assembly of Corinthian believers in 11:2-10 and involves people who provide insight into God's will that is consis- tent with his goals and purposes for individuals and the church. The gift of proph- ecy may relate to the fifth item, distinguishing spirits, in that apparent prophetic insights may be incongruent with one another, implying that one is right and one is wrong; or one prophecy on its own may be so outlandish that it is question- able. Both instances would require another gifted person to discern the genuine message from God and recognize an inauthentic one. This may or may not mean that someone with a wrong message is a false prophet, only that he or she made a mistake in that instance.

The final group lists, literally, the gift of "tongues" and the "interpretation of tongues," as noted in the NLT text note for 12:10. The tongues group is last probably because it will emerge later in his discussion as gifts being unduly elevated among the Corinthian believers. The debate over what type of phenomenon this refers to is wide-ranging. Before the rise of Pentecostalism under Charles Parham and William Seymour and the Azuza Street revival at the turn of the twentieth century, it was considered an open-and-shut case that this was a phenomenon restricted to the early generations of the church that did not extend much beyond the second century. By way of demonstration of this point, the commentary by Robertson and Plummer, published in 1911 (257), but no doubt in process long before then, does not even contemplate any modern phenomenon of a Pentecostal/charismatic sort in light of this passage.

The main issue is what the nature of the language is that Corinthians and other early Christians were articulating as a gift from the Spirit. Those who oppose the reality of this gift today tend to conclude that any true form of this gift must be a repetition of what they believe occurred at Pentecost in Acts 2:1-13: that the Holy Spirit enabled people to speak in real languages and dialects they did not know. In 12:10, then, people in the Corinthian church must have been continuing this phenomenon of speaking human languages that were not native to them or learned by them. Other gifted individuals then translated the foreign languages to those gathered. If what is being spoken is not a real human language, then or now, the conclusion is that the phenomenon cannot be a genuine work of the Spirit.

One serious difficulty with this view is its inability to explain how a repetition of the phenomenon in Acts 2 (with its obvious purpose of converting nonbelievers) has any function in a Christian assembly or within the Christian community, even if there are a few unbelieving visitors present. Surely, being from the same community of believers, they will speak languages represented by the believers. Second, what is the purpose of labeling interpreting as a gift when a known language could be understood by a person of that nationality as it was in Acts 2? Third, in 14:23, Paul says that unbelievers do not recognize the phenomenon as human language, which is what was troubling them. Fourth, a closer reading of Acts 2:6 makes possible that the miracle there was in the hearer (Fitzmeyer 1998:240), while in Corinth the miracle was in the speaker and thus required an interpreter.

Most likely, the phenomenon is some kind of unintelligible language-like verbal demonstration that is not a known human language and would require an interpreter for any other believers or anyone else to know what was said. A current suggestion, best conveyed by Thiselton (2000:285-288), looks to the expression "groanings that cannot be expressed in words" (Rom 8:26) as the most productive window to explain the tongues phenomenon here (see note on 12:10). The Holy Spirit taps into generic human language capability that underlies all human language in order to enable the believers to express their deepest, personal thoughts and concerns. How this interpretation might relate to the modern charismatic/Pentecostal phenomenon is not entirely certain but would probably suggest that some have this genuine gift and some do not.

The really intriguing question is what kind of information is thought to be communicated by this means. Is this mysteriously cloaked words of wisdom, or knowledge, or prophecy, or some other kind of teaching for the believing community, or is this less-than-essential or even simply personal to the individual? Later, Paul will act as though it doesn't matter whether the church receives all these tongue messages or not when he tells people to be silent if there is no interpreter (14:28). This suggests that information is nonessential and usually personal, directed to God (14:2). Thus, those who today say that this gift is essential for all believers to exhibit their reception of the Holy Spirit are going against the grain of Paul's overall argument.

With 12:11, Paul summarizes 12:4-10 before embarking on his lengthy body metaphor in 12:12-26. He does so by repeating key words: "one," "the same" (NLT, "only"), "gift," "distributes," and "Spirit." The spiritual gifts come to believers from just one source, the Holy Spirit. This guarantees they are genuinely from God to unify and enliven the church. The expression "He [God] alone decides" emphasizes that believers have no control over what the Spirit might produce in them to minister to the others in the Christian community. Notably absent is any encouragement to pray for a certain gift and any guarantee that a certain gift to a particular individual is permanent. Indeed, believers can lose a gift due to neglect or spiritual malaise (1 Thess 5:19; 1 Tim 4:14; 2 Tim 1:6). The gifts are for the whole church, and the Spirit decides when and where they are manifested in individual members.

◆   2. One body with many parts (12:12-26)

[12] The human body has many parts, but the many parts make up one whole body. So it is with the body of Christ. [13] Some of us are Jews, some are Gentiles,* some are slaves, and some are free. But we have all been baptized into one body by one Spirit, and we all share the same Spirit.*

[14] Yes, the body has many different parts, not just one part. [15] If the foot says, "I am not a part of the body because I am not a hand," that does not make it any less a part of the body. [16] And if the ear says, "I am not part of the body because I am not an eye," would that make it any less a part of the body? [17] If the whole body were an eye, how would you hear? Or if your whole body were an ear, how would you smell anything?

[18] But our bodies have many parts, and God has put each part just where he wants it. [19] How strange a body would be if it had only one part! [20] Yes, there are many parts, but only one body. [21] The eye can never say to the hand, "I don't need you." The head can't say to the feet, "I don't need you."

[22] In fact, some parts of the body that seem weakest and least important are actually the most necessary. [23] And the parts we regard as less honorable are those we clothe with the greatest care. So we carefully protect those parts that should not be seen, [24] while the more honorable parts do not require this special care. So God has put the body together such that extra honor and care are given to those parts that have less dignity. [25] This makes for harmony among the members, so that all the members care for each other. [26] If one part suffers, all the parts suffer with it, and if one part is honored, all the parts are glad.

12:13a Greek *some are Greeks.*   12:13b Greek *we were all given one Spirit to drink.*

NOTES

12:13 *share.* This word (*potizō* [TG4222, ZG4540]) refers to people, animals, or plants being provided water for nourishment and sustenance (see NLT mg). Paul used it earlier for watering crops in reference to Apollos (3:6-8). Its most prevalent meaning in the Gospels is "drink" (Matt 25:35-46; Mark 9:41).

12:23 *we clothe.* Gr., *peritethemen* [TG4060, ZG4363]. Only used here outside the Gospels, it refers generically to putting something around something else, like a wall around property (Matt 21:33) or a crown of thorns on Jesus' head (Mark 15:17). In Matt 27:28, it refers to putting on an item of clothing (robe), but here it refers to the extra care men (and women) take to cover their private, sexual organs (Garland 2003:506; D. Martin 1991:567).

parts that should not be seen. Gr., *aschēmona* [TG809, ZG860]. Only used here in the NT, this refers to what is shameful or should not be exposed to the public. Since uses of cognate words in the NT suggest improper sexual activity—a man with his fiancée (7:36) and men with other men (Rom 1:27), or nakedness (Rev 16:15)—the word should be seen as a euphemism for male or female sexual organs. The word "honorable" that follows is this word's opposite.

COMMENTARY

Paul's emphasis on the Holy Spirit's endowing every believer with a special, community-enriching ability led him to develop an extended metaphor of the human body, beginning in 12:12 and continuing through 12:26. Choosing the human body as a point of comparison for social and civic dynamics was by no means novel in the ancient Greek world (M. Mitchell 1993:157-164). Examples go back to Aesop (Dio Chrysostom *Discourses* 33.16), Plato (*Republic*), Cicero (*On Duties* 3.5.22-23; 3.6.26-27), Seneca (*Anger* 2.31.7), Dio Chrysostom (*Discourses* 9.2; 33.44; 34.32; 40.21; 41.9; 50.3), and a famous speech by Roman senator Menenius Agrippa (Livy *History of Rome* 2.32.7-33.1).

Paul set up his development of the metaphor in 12:13 by first establishing theologically that the church is in fact one body. He did this by reminding the Corinthians of their baptism. Not unlike his comments in Galatians 3:26-29 in which he wanted to show that all believers in Christ are truly children of Abraham because of being clothed with Christ at their baptism, he specifically notes that people from different races or cultures (Jew or Gentile) and at polar ends of society and economics (slave and free) become one person when they are baptized into Christ. Notably missing in 1 Corinthians from his triad of covered distinctions is gender (male or female). Perhaps this is because the role of women in the assembly was already addressed as a touchy issue in 11:2-16, in which Paul emphasized that gender distinctions in terms of head covering should be maintained despite equal participation in assemblies, a topic treated again in 14:33b-35. Although some interpreters focus on the infusion of the Holy Spirit as Paul's primary point (Dunn 1970:129; Fee 1987:603-606), the fact that he relied on the commonality of the public immersion of believers into the Christian community does not exclude this (Garland 2003:591; Thiselton 2000:997-999).

Paul emphasizes the Spirit as the source who enlivens and enriches the body of Christ by isolating the role of the Spirit for the believer in the second part of 12:13. He uses a specific word that refers to liquid nourishment. This word can refer to the irrigation of crops or to someone drinking a cup of water (see note on 12:13). A few interpreters have become distracted by the picture of the church drinking from one cup as a reference to the sharing of the Lord's Supper (Calvin 1960:265; Collins 1999:463). Given the prior discussion of this in 10:14-21 and 11:17-34 and the temptation to see this as a balancing sacrament to baptism, this is understandable. However, any association of the Holy Spirit with the Lord's Supper or of the Lord's Supper as "drinking the Spirit," which is what this passage literally says, does not exist in the New Testament (Thiselton 2000:1001).

Other interpreters may be right to suggest that Paul was playing off his picture of baptism and wanted readers to visualize the body of Christ drenched or soaked in the Spirit (Garland 2003:591; Thiselton 2000:1001). However, the consistent image of the Greek word (*potizō* [TG4222, ZG4540]) is that of the water or some other liquid nourishing rather than cleansing. It is an internal image rather than external. Thus, the visual picture is of the Holy Spirit flowing into a person when they are baptized (Barrett 1968:289; Bruce 1971:121) and of the church, the body of Christ continually and regularly being filled with the Holy Spirit. In this way it nourishes every cubic inch of the body, both individually and corporately, and all its constituent parts, a point Paul will depend on in what follows.

In 12:14-21, Paul describes the relationship between the human body's parts nearly as an allegory or fable, animating the feet, the ear, the eye, and the head with speech. No matter what the foot and the ear *say* to bemoan their situations as seemingly less important than the hand or the eye, they are chastised to note that they are nonetheless essential to the body. Neither the hand nor the eye is so important that they can survive independently, and what a comical or grotesque sight it would be for the body only to be one giant hand or eye! All the parts are essential.

Interestingly, Paul does not maintain this as a conversation regarding the foot's grudge against the hand or the ear's frustration with the eye's arrogance. In 12:21, he has the eye speak to the hand of its value and the head speak to the feet. The result is to see that all the many parts of the body have an interest in seeing that all the rest of the parts are valued.

In 12:22-26, Paul transitions from the body metaphor to application for the church in Corinth. To do this he will contrast the parts of the body that people are most careful to keep covered with those that are readily and proudly displayed in public without clothing. Notably, the parts usually not clothed are the head (for men), eyes, ears, noses, feet, and hands. Those parts of the human body that people take greatest care to cover are those closest to their sexual organs. To be careless about exposing these in public would be shameful. From this generally agreed understanding, Paul employed reverse logic. The very fact that it is shameful to leave certain parts unclothed in public and that people take extra measures to keep them covered suggests, in fact, that those parts should not feel shamed but rather honored for all the attention they get (Garland 2003:596; D. Martin 1991:567). Paul may be speaking from the more modest, Jewish perspective, since nakedness for Greeks in their gymnasiums was not considered shameful.

Paul begins to unfold the implication of this for the church in 12:24. The church should receive the lesson from the way people treat their bodies. Those who appear to be weak and lowly esteemed by normal social estimates should receive all the more attention for how vital they are to the church. This lesson is not unlike his message to the Corinthians regarding their despicable Lord's Supper practices that dishonored the poor and others among their number. An approach to one another that functions in this way will help every member of Christ's body feel cared for and should spill over into helping provide for the needs of the "weaker" members who are struggling with many more life pressures than others. In fact, as Paul emphasizes in 12:26, the pain of any member, "weak" or "strong," should be felt by every other member. So, too, the joys of life—just as it is in the human body, where every aspect of it is integrated and connected by the whole.

◆   ## 3. Each member serves a vital role (12:27-31)

²⁷All of you together are Christ's body, and each of you is a part of it. ²⁸Here are some of the parts God has appointed for the church:

first are apostles,
second are prophets,
third are teachers,
then those who do miracles,
those who have the gift of healing,
those who can help others,
those who have the gift of
leadership,
those who speak in unknown
languages.

²⁹Are we all apostles? Are we all prophets? Are we all teachers? Do we all have the power to do miracles? ³⁰Do we all have the gift of healing? Do we all have the ability to speak in unknown languages? Do we all have the ability to interpret unknown languages? Of course not! ³¹So you should earnestly desire the most helpful gifts.

But now let me show you a way of life that is best of all.

NOTES

12:28 *gift of leadership.* Only used here in the NT, this word (*kubernēsis* [TG2941, ZG3236]) describes someone who steers or guides something, including government. Though translated as administration by the NIV and ESV, it involves the direction a wise person can give not only to organizations but also to individuals (Roberts 1997:304).

12:30 *speak in unknown languages.* Gr., *glōssais lalousin* [TG1100/2980, ZG1185/3281], lit., "speak in tongues." Here Paul begins to use a slightly different phrase to refer to the tongues phenomenon than earlier; he will use the term "speaks," *laleō* [TG2980, ZG3281], along with "in tongues" consistently 27 times from this point on through the end of ch 14. Earlier, in 12:10 and even just above in 12:28, the phrase literally is "other languages" (*genē glōssōn* [TG1085/1100, ZG1169/1185]), but as the NLT evidences, Paul does seem to equate the two phrases. Paul did not coin the new phrase, since it is also found in the LXX and in the Dead Sea Scrolls. As with all of chs 12–14, there is some debate over whether even in those sources it refers to ecstatic speech (Harrisville 1976:45) or simply to a foreign language or dialect (Engelbrecht 1996:302).

12:31 *But now let me show you a way of life that is best of all.* The NLT has not followed most versions, including the ESV and NIV, that separate out the second clause in the verse from the first in order to use it as an introduction to ch 13. Arguments for keeping the clauses together, although they take slightly different approaches, are convincing (Smit 1993:263; Thiselton 2000:1024; van Unnik 1993:159). At issue in all of ch 12 is not just the greater gifts but the zeal to seek after them. Paul wanted them to harness their energies on the truly greater gifts for the church, which can be accomplished by a new approach, a new way, based on love.

COMMENTARY

Having relayed the metaphor in 12:14-21 and provided a transition to its application to the church (12:22-26), beginning in 12:27, Paul speaks directly to the Corinthians the lesson he wants them to hear: They are the body of Christ. Since this is true, each one of them, regardless of where they came from in Corinthian society, deserves honor and respect from everyone else. Each one is vital for the health of the body. For this reason the Holy Spirit has provided vital functions for everyone to fill in service to the whole. He also goes on to list a sampling of the various roles people play in the Christian community. Before doing that, however, paralleling his emphasis in 12:18 on God's role in designing the human body, he declares in 12:28 that the varied parts of the church body have been fashioned by God as well.

Five of the gifts are identical to descriptions on the earlier list (12:8-10): people who do miracles, healings, relay prophecy, speak in "tongues," and translate "tongues." As before, those associated with tongues are listed last, and those associated with healings and miracles are in the middle. Prophets have jumped up from sixth to second. Given the discussion that will come up in chapter 14—pitting teaching and prophecy against tongues—it is nearly certain that Paul's list amounts to a ranking, at least with regard to the first three and the last two. This explains moving prophets to the first tier with teachers and apostles. It also explains the discontinuing of numbering after designating apostles, prophets, and teachers as first, second, and third. This probably relates to their perceived value in the church or perhaps to their chronology of appearance in the church (Hays 1997:217). The order also suggests that the first two items in Paul's earlier list (word of wisdom and word of knowledge) may be thought to be incorporated in the role of apostles, prophets, and teachers, though they are probably not exclusive to them.

Apostles and teachers are new to the list, as are those who help others and those who lead. Apostles are listed together with prophets in Ephesians 2:20 and also with teachers in 2 Timothy 1:11, and prophets follow immediately after apostles in the Ephesians 4:11 list, while teachers come fifth. Paul's understanding of apostles in terms of serving in the body of Christ is not limited to the original 12 apostles, or even to those called slightly later (like himself). Paul's understanding extended more widely to those who traveled as pioneer missionaries to establish and develop fledgling groups of believers in the first generation of the church. Teachers likely are those who pass on the essential instruction to new believers in Gentile societies. These teachings would include those of Jesus, as well as an understanding of the Jewish Scriptures (Barrett 1968:295; Bruce 1971:123).

Those who help others are probably related to the variety of gifts Paul relates in Romans 12:7-8 ("serving," "encouraging," "showing kindness"), just as the gift of leadership probably overlaps with "leadership ability" in Romans 12:8. Paul's inclusion of these two gifts illustrates that Paul's concept of gifts in the church is not restricted to specific terms nor to any restricted list of items. The gifts vary as widely as the individuals who are part of each local body of believers. We do not serve this understanding of the gifts well if we pigeonhole the gifts too rigidly.

In 12:29-31, Paul draws his extended metaphor to a conclusion, beginning with seven rhetorical questions that enumerate gifted people in the believing community.

All of the gifts have appeared in at least one of his two earlier lists (12:8-10, 28): apostles (second), prophets (both), teachers (second), doing miracles (both), healing (both), speaking in unintelligible language (both), and interpreting that language (first). All the questions expect negative responses, as the NLT depicts with "Of course not!" at the end of the list. Contemplating the whole church body being filled with only one type of gifted member recalls the ludicrous image conjured up in 12:17 of the human body as just one part.

It is not helpful, or even part of God's design, that everyone in the church be gifted in the same way. This destroys the diversity and interdependence inherent to what God has in mind. It also disables the Holy Spirit's prerogative to distribute gifts as he sees fit. Besides, Paul's encouragement to desire the greater gifts is addressed corporately (plural imperative) to the whole church. The entire congregation, not individuals, are told here to seek the more helpful gifts to benefit them all. It is apparent from Paul's determined effort to put the gift of tongues last on each of his three lists in this chapter that this gift had been exalted too highly and treasured too widely by believers in the Corinthian community as a status symbol (D. Martin 1991:547; 1995:88-92). Perhaps it was even prompted by some of the Corinthian leaders, but it was not seen by Paul to be as widely beneficial to all as were the other gifts. This will become much clearer when he speaks to pragmatic issues related to the gifts in chapter 14. His first clause in 12:31, encouraging Corinthians to seek better gifts, sets this up.

However, before he gets to that, his second clause in 12:31 provides the necessary entrée into the principled exposition on love that comprises chapter 13. Apparently, well aware that Jesus placed love at the heart of his teaching (Matt 5:43-46; 19:19; 22:39; Mark 12:30-31; Luke 6:27-36), Paul extolled love as the best way to live. In phrasing it like this, he stipulates that love is not one of the spiritual gifts but is foundational to every gift and its exercise in the body of Christ.

◆   ## 4. Love is the foundation for every gift (13:1-13)

If I could speak all the languages of earth and of angels, but didn't love others, I would only be a noisy gong or a clanging cymbal. [2]If I had the gift of prophecy, and if I understood all of God's secret plans and possessed all knowledge, and if I had such faith that I could move mountains, but didn't love others, I would be nothing. [3]If I gave everything I have to the poor and even sacrificed my body, I could boast about it;* but if I didn't love others, I would have gained nothing.

[4]Love is patient and kind. Love is not jealous or boastful or proud [5]or rude. It does not demand its own way. It is not irritable, and it keeps no record of being wronged. [6]It does not rejoice about injustice but rejoices whenever the truth wins out. [7]Love never gives up, never loses faith, is always hopeful, and endures through every circumstance.

[8]Prophecy and speaking in unknown languages* and special knowledge will become useless. But love will last forever! [9]Now our knowledge is partial and incomplete, and even the gift of prophecy reveals only part of the whole picture! [10]But when the time of perfection comes, these partial things will become useless.

[11]When I was a child, I spoke and thought and reasoned as a child. But when I grew

up, I put away childish things. ¹²Now we see things imperfectly, like puzzling reflections in a mirror, but then we will see everything with perfect clarity.* All that I know now is partial and incomplete, but then I will know everything completely, just as God now knows me completely.

¹³Three things will last forever—faith, hope, and love—and the greatest of these is love.

13:3 Some manuscripts read *sacrificed my body to be burned.*   13:8 Or *in tongues.*   13:12 Greek *see face to face.*

NOTES

13:1 *language of . . . angels.* See note on 12:10. An important parallel to this phrase occurs in the *Testament of Job* 48–50, a first-century BC document, recounting the legend that Job's three daughters were given the ability to speak and sing in angelic language. Although Paul may have had something like this in mind when he penned this verse, this does not necessitate that he equates the gift of tongues with angelic language. So, too, hyperbolic language regarding angelic language does not suggest that such language does not exist.

noisy gong. Gr., *chalkos ēchōn* [ᵀᴳ5475/2278, ᶻᴳ5910/2490]. Used only five times in the NT, this is the word for copper, the first metal employed by human industry. Thus, it could also refer to metal generally, and especially later on to bronze, which mixes copper with tin. In the NT, outside of its use here, it is used for coins made of copper (Matt 10:9; Mark 6:8; 12:41-42) and bronze in a list of cargo (Rev 18:12). Corinth manufactured and traded in copper and bronze products. W. Harris (1982:38-41) has argued persuasively that Paul is most likely referring to hollow, resonating chambers or cylinders made of brass placed strategically around ancient amphitheaters to amplify sound. Such devices would have been used and probably manufactured in Corinth. Thus, the word does not refer to a musical instrument of any type, including a "gong," much less a "noisy" one. Rather, the modifying adjective (*ēchōn*) suggests that this is a reverberating sound that could in fact be a pleasant one emanating from an empty vessel (Collins 1999:473; Garland 2003:612; Klein 1986:289; Thiselton 2000:1037). A better translation might be "hollow brass cylinder."

clanging cymbal. Gr., *kumbalon alalazon* [ᵀᴳ2950/214, ᶻᴳ3247/226]. The only use of "cymbal" in the NT, it probably refers to a musical instrument that creates a reverberating sound when two concave metal dishes are struck together, similar to the instrument used today. The modifying word, "clanging" (*alalazon*), only used here and in Mark 5:38, refers to crying out verbally in a wail during mourning or in a war cry. Here, it probably refers to the sustained sound of a cymbal as a musical instrument but may not be necessarily an irritating sound (Klein 1986:287; Thiselton 2000:1037). If there are negative implications to Paul's use here, it may be because this instrument was also used in street worship of pagan gods, like Cybele and Dionysus (Garland 2003:613), but cymbals were also central to Jewish temple worship (1 Sam 18:6; 2 Sam 6:5; 1 Chr 13:8; 15:16, 19, 28; 16:5; 2 Chr 5:12-13; Ps 150:5). That the word is in the singular here suggests that what Paul may have in mind is an ancient instrument that predates the modern orchestra cymbal called a "crotal," a thick metal plate that resounds when it is struck by a mallet (A. F. Johnson 2004:244; Thiselton 2000:1037).

13:2 *prophecy.* See note on 11:4.

13:3 *sacrificed my body.* Lit., "hand over my body." The NIV reads "surrender my body." The idea is voluntarily succumbing to physical hardship or perhaps even death.

boast. Gr., *kauchēsōmai* [ᵀᴳ2744, ᶻᴳ3016]. This word has excellent manuscript support, including 𝔓46 א A B 048 33. The NLT is rightly persuaded by the mounting scholarly consensus

that the long-standing reading of "burn" (*kauthēsomai* from *kaiō* [TG2545, ZG2794]) contained in the Textus Receptus, which made its way into the KJV and most modern translations, including the NIV, RSV, and ESV, does not have merit given its inferior manuscript
evidence—namely, C D F G L 𝔐 (Fee 1987:634; Garland 2003:627; Petzer 1989:229-253;
Thiselton 2000:1043). In light of Christian martyrdom by burning in later centuries, it
seems far more likely that a copyist would have viewed the chi as a mistake and replaced it
with a theta. Those still contending for "burn" include Collins (1999:476), who relies on
Caragounis (1995).

13:4 *Love.* Gr., *hē agapē* [TG26, ZG27]. In both occurrences in this verse, the word "love"
includes the article, referring to the love that is essential to undergird the spiritual gifts
described in the previous paragraph. Some manuscripts (א A C D F G) include a third
occurrence of "love" as a subject, before "proud," though others do not (including B 33).
It is more likely that it was originally included rather than added by a scribe, plus it has
significant manuscript support. Regardless, as with the NLT, neither the NIV nor the ESV
translate it.

13:5 *rude.* Gr., *aschēmonei* [TG807, ZG858]. The scribe of one major manuscript (𝔓46) made
an error by replacing "rude" with its antonym, "polite" (*euschēmonei* [TG2155.1, ZG2360]).
This probably came by making a mental mistake of switching the initial letters.

13:8 *unknown languages.* Gr., *glōssai* [TG1100, ZG1185]. See note on 12:10.

13:10 *when the time of perfection comes.* The Greek behind "the time of perfection" is
to teleion [TG5046C, ZG5455], meaning "the perfect" or "the complete." This unusual neuter
adjective, though in agreement with the following noun "partial" (*merous* [TG3313, ZG3538]),
does not appear like this elsewhere in the NT. The idea of perfection or completion (lit.,
"when the completion comes") is interpreted by most to refer to the period after Christ's
return when believers are in the presence of God (Oster 1995:308-309; Robertson and
Plummer 1911:299-300). The once-fairly-prominent interpretation that understood this
as referring to the Bible or the completion of the NT canon turns up only rarely in commentaries anymore, and then only as a brief dismissive footnote (Hays 1997:229), even
by evangelical commentators (Fee 1987:644; Garland 2003:622). Nonetheless, it still
has a few advocates (Gaffin 1979; Houghton 1996:344; R. White 1992:174). Thiselton
(2000:1062-1064) helpfully interacts with the history of the text through the eyes first
of early reformers wishing to discount claims of miracles by Roman Catholicism, then
through the Enlightenment philosophers who reduced the world to scientific explanation,
and then finally to modern dispensationalists who disdained the practices of the Pentecostal movement and later charismatic denominational reformers. (See also Ruthven 1993.)
Interpreting this verse as predicting the demise of tongues or any other spiritual gift flies
in the face of Paul's entire discussion in chs 12–14 and would have been impossible for
the original Corinthian audience to fathom. Virtually all the church fathers maintain that
the *eschaton* (the end of the age) is in view despite their awareness of the closed Canon
(Shogren 1999:121). An alternative interpretation referring to the maturity of the church
(rather than to the completion of the Canon) has also been suggested (Thomas 1993:188),
but even this view has been folded into the idea of the mature state of believers after
Christ's coming (Martens 1996b:40). One novel suggestion is that, rather than discouraging speaking in tongues, Paul was encouraging it in the face of some who thought that such
phenomena were dying out even in pagan contexts (Green 2001:121).

13:12 *imperfectly, like puzzling reflections in a mirror.* Lit., "through a mirror in an
enigma." Only mentioned here and in Jas 1:23, mirrors in the ancient world were made
of polished bronze and would have been manufactured in Corinth itself. Although such

mirrors did not reflect back so precise an image as do modern mirrors (which are made of glass covered with a thin layer of metal), it is probably not accurate to think that ancients thought of their mirrors as offering a fuzzy, poor reflection (as Garland 2003:624; Thiselton 2000:168). The mirror is more likely used by Paul, similarly in Plutarch (*Moralia* 382A-C) and other Greek philosophers, to convey the idea that humans can contemplate the meaning of life (or God) only indirectly based on what is reflected in human reality (Collins 1999:487; Thiselton 2000:1069).

COMMENTARY

Probably more than any other chapter of the Bible, chapter 13 is routinely torn from its context (an appeal to Christians to live out their intramural relations with respect and self-sacrifice) for use in a variety of cultural contexts, like weddings, funerals, and graduation ceremonies. In some ways, this is a tribute to the chapter's stylistic construction, soothing lyrical quality, powerful vocabulary, and ideological balance that places it at the top of poetry in the Western world, comparable to anything in the Greek and Roman classics or anything written since.

The star status of this encomium (a praise or hymn in form but an exhortation in function; Garland 2003:607) on love's virtues (Sigountos 1994:260) creates a pitfall every Christian reader must be careful to avoid. As eloquent as Paul is in developing this prose, probably in the course of his teaching ministry (Bruce 1971:125), Paul intended its insertion here to be a principled remedy to a real problem in Corinth involving the use of gifts, and so it should be seen as such when read today. Readers must not think he was singing praises to some personified abstraction of love (Holladay 1990:80-98). He was talking about a manner of conduct that must show itself in the lives of believers, foremost in the way they minister to one another in the body of Christ, though certainly also in their behavior to those outside the body and to God. It is to be the Christian's basic code of conduct.

The stylistic rhythm of Paul's tribute to loving behavior reveals three basic divisions to his ideas. First, employing a series of conditional clauses, he laments the emptiness of any personal action, however magnificent or self-sacrificing, without love as its root (13:1-3). Second, he rhapsodizes on the true attributes of love in 15 direct statements, alternating between what it is and what it is not, what those who love do not do and what they do (13:4-7). Third, using a string of contrasting statements, he extols the permanent value of loving behavior (13:8-13).

Most striking in the first division (13:1-3) is that Paul states all the conditional clauses in the first person. In so doing, he positions himself as a hypothetical "everyman," but he also seems to play on his position as an apostle. Thus, even if *he* had the gifts he mentions that would enable him to serve the church in amazing ways, without their being done in love, they would have no value. He also orders the seven activities from least to greatest in the sense of difficulty and ministry value to the church. Once again (12:10, 28, 30), this puts tongue speaking at the bottom. The seven gifts listed are taken from his three previous lists in 12:7-10, 27-28, 29-30, except the last one (sacrifice of body). For most of them he tries to add some description as to how a person might maximize its usage for the purpose of presenting the widest possible contrast between the most positive use of the gifts imaginable, which is then undercut by the absence of love as the foundation.

In 13:1, Paul begins with the gift of tongues. Hypothetically, he ponders, as the NLT makes clear, the amazing feat of mastering all known human languages. On top of that, he imagines conversing in the language angels use. Both of these go beyond whatever type of phenomenon tongue speaking refers to: This is knowing all the languages of the universe. Such a phenomenal gift would be a beautiful thing because of the beauty of language, but without being founded on love, it would convey no valuable meaning. He strives to make this point by introducing two "sound" images that in themselves are positive rather than negative (as conveyed by the NLT). The first is a hollow brass cylinder (not a "gong") that amplifies sound in a theater. This draws attention to a person's functioning as an empty piece of sound equipment adding no meaning to the communication. The second is a cymbal burst that creates a loud reverberating musical note. This adds a vital element to the song, but cannot vary its pitch nor sustain itself indefinitely, again highlighting limited communication.

In 13:2, Paul adds having the gifts of prophecy, fathoming mysteries (NLT, "[understanding] all of God's secret plans") and knowledge, and having faith. He phrases fathoming mysteries and possessing knowledge together after one "if," suggesting that these two may overlap at times. Both involve access to information about God's unfolding plan (4:1; Rom 11:25; 2 Thess 2:7), to which others are not privy. In addition, knowing mysteries probably relates to the "word of wisdom" (Thiselton 2000:1039) since "word of wisdom" precedes "word of knowledge" and "faith" in Paul's original list in 12:8-9, although it may extend beyond this. Paul also emphatically tags mysteries, knowledge, and faith with "all" (the NLT replacing the "all" modifying faith with "such"), implying that although he was hesitant to suggest that anyone could know all prophecy, he was not at all reluctant to extend his hyperbolic language to the other three. Mountain-moving faith, connecting Paul to Jesus' saying in Matthew 17:20 and Mark 11:23-24, solidifies the outlandish extravagance Paul places on these empowering gifts (Horsley 1998:176).

In 13:3, Paul adds two last gifts to this list. With these two, giving to the poor and bodily sacrifice, he moves into the arena of self-sacrifice for others. The language he uses to describe the first pictures someone cutting up food into little pieces to distribute and thus suggests a person dividing out all material possessions, item by item, to give away one by one until they are all gone. Once again, the inclusion of "everything" accents the extension of this gift of giving to its furthest borders, accentuating the waste if this is done without love. Though the word used is not in any of Paul's lists in chapter 12, he probably considers it a specification of "help[ing] others" from 12:28. This idea of giving away everything to the poor matches Jesus' spiritually incisive challenge to the rich young ruler (Mark 10:17-22). Caring for the poor is central to Jesus' self-understanding of his ministry (Luke 4:18), is announced as the essence of true religion in James 1:27, and is a judgment theme of the Old Testament prophets concerning Israel's failure to do so (Isa 3:14; Jer 2:34-35; Ezek 16:49-52).

The final gift pictures the ultimate sacrifice and is not mentioned or hinted at in any previous list. Extending from giving away all one's material possessions, it contemplates the only thing left, a person's physical body. The verb used, literally "handing over" (*paradidōmi* [TG3860, ZG4140]), conjures up many possible images from the ancient world, ranging from people selling themselves into slavery so as to keep their families from starving (Thiselton 2000:1045) to dying in battle, fighting so as to defend home and country. Paul saw his own body as wasting away in sacrificial service to the gospel (2 Cor 4:7-12; 11:21-33). As in the other instances, he added something to recognize the ultimate nature of the person's embodiment of this gift. In this case, he notes that self-sacrifice is so great that one might justifiably boast of its being accomplished. For Paul, boasting is normally a leading characteristic of worldly, self-promoting sinfulness, even noted as such in the very next verse, but like boasting in the cross, that tag does not apply here. Yet even exercising this ultimate gift in the ultimate way has no meaning if it is not founded on love for others.

The second major division in Paul's praise of loving behavior, 13:4-7, resounds like a drum pounding out what love is and what love is not. Adjectives and descriptions pile up to create an undeniable sense that love is the supreme virtue, a personified superhero fighting for truth and justice against all comers (vices or other virtues) who desire to supplant it. It describes the perfect person adored by all. If believers incorporated even a portion of the attributes described, their ministry and relationships would be overwhelmingly positive and successful.

Paul begins in 13:4 by describing two attributes of love followed by four anti-attributes. Being first and stated in the positive, Paul must consider patience and kindness to be elemental to love. These two, in fact, often appear together in Paul's catalogs of virtues (2 Cor 6:6; Gal 5:22; Col 3:12). The four anti-attributes are stated negatively as a point of comparison with behavior exhibited among the Corinthians that Paul had already openly criticized (Hays 1997:227; Horsley 1998:177). Using exactly the same Greek words, he accused them earlier of being jealous (3:3), boastful (1:29-31; 3:21; 4:7; 5:6), and proud (4:6; 4:18-19; 5:2).

The word "rude" (aschēmonō [TG807, ZG858]) literally refers to a shameful, often sexually shameful, act and is used to refer to the potential sexual activity of an engaged man towards his betrothed (7:36). But Paul probably also has in mind deplorable sexual activity among the Corinthians, like the man living with his stepmother (5:1-2) and the sexual immorality described in 6:12-20.

Four actions that love does not do are stated in 13:5-6. The first is: Love does not demand its own way. This repeats a word used earlier in the letter in the context of Paul's warnings against eating meat offered to idols (10:24), and also mentioned as an activity Paul disavows in his own behavior (10:33). The next three negative behaviors, becoming angered, keeping a record of being wronged, and rejoicing about injustice, are not mentioned specifically elsewhere in 1 Corinthians. However, all three could underlie the lawsuits Paul condemns in 6:1-8, the contentiousness involved in the idol-meat controversy (chs 8–10), the matter of head attire (11:1-16), and the hurt feelings surrounding the Lord's Supper practices (11:17-34). Regardless of their relationship to the Corinthians specifically, each one of the four negative behaviors pictures someone directly opposite from one whose behaviors are founded on love. This is someone who lives in hate rather than in love.

Love cannot be limited to a feeling, emotion, or even attitude or motivation. Rather, love must be lived out in real life in relationship to real people who may well be hard to get along with in the church. For love to be love, it must be shown in relationship to others within the life of the church.

Once Paul offers the positive contrast of rejoicing in the truth rather than in injustice at the end of 13:6, he remains upbeat, adding four more beneficial behaviors that love practices. This fills out his description of a loving person in 13:7. These four are constructed to create a pulsing rhetorical effect, four verbs all preceded by the word "all": literally, "bears all things, believes all things, hopes all things, endures all things." The fourfold "all" solidifies that Paul is describing an ideal person, but this is nonetheless the goal for all Christians to emulate in their lives. However, his rhetoric invokes encouragement rather than mere description at this point.

The verbs in 13:7 create a chiasmus (Fee 1987:640; Horsley 1998:177). When the passage is rendered literally, it becomes evident that the two outer words (first and last), "bears" and "endures," are nearly synonymous in depicting love as rising out of the real-life struggles that people face. The two inner words, "believes" and "hopes," overlap in describing the character quality that emerges out of the present struggles wherein one trusts that these struggles move toward a meaningful future. The relationship of the two inner words ("believes" and "hopes") to love will be magnified when they are transformed into nouns standing at the side of love in the climax of this chapter (13:13).

Paul's third major division on love (13:8-13) advocates the universal persistence of love as the lone human quality of behavior that stretches beyond current human conditions. Everything else is transitory, including the spiritual gifts, the point he develops in 13:8-10. In 13:8, he specifically notes three gifts from his list in 13:1-3: prophecy, tongues (reversing their order from there), and knowledge as representative. Notably, he does not mention faith from earlier, since it will be listed with love as ever enduring in 13:13, nor giving to the poor nor bodily sacrifice, which are, in fact, acts of love.

After first stating with forceful simplicity in 13:8 that love does not and cannot be stopped (lit., "never fails"), he emphatically declares that prophecy, tongues, and special knowledge will not continue. Leaving off tongues, he stipulates in 13:9 that both prophecy and knowledge only provide partial and imprecise revelation. God's purposes and plans are simply too vast for any human to utter or comprehend, even by the Holy Spirit among believers. But on the very day when that limitation will end, the need for prophetic words and special knowledge will also cease. Then, the community of believers will enter into a state of perfection in the presence of God, and understanding that is screened through human instruments will no longer have any purpose. Though he does not say so explicitly (see note on 13:10), Paul must have been thinking of the day of the Lord's coming as the end point of God's plan, when earth will be destroyed (Garland 2003:623; Thiselton 2000:1065) and the disrupted universe reunited with God.

In 13:11-12, Paul introduces two analogies to help convey his point about partial knowledge being replaced by complete knowledge. In 13:11, he first compares what he is talking about to the vast change in knowledge that occurs between childhood and adulthood. The world of children is confined to what their parents and immediate surroundings convey to them, enough for them to get by but not at all adequate to function in the world of adults. Paul emphasized that childhood knowledge, like outgrown toys, must one day be permanently put away.

In 13:12, Paul's second analogy involves a mirror. No matter how finely polished, a mirror can never provide more than an indirect image of a person's face. It is not even a remotely adequate substitute for seeing someone close-up in real life, or being seen by someone else in real life, face-to-face (NLT, "with perfect clarity"). Each person's face is unique and is the physical representation of individual personality. Even so, a person's face is only a window into the soul, a caricature of true personhood. True personhood can never be fully fathomed by our friends or family, or even our spouse—and certainly not in a mirror! Only our Creator knows us to our depths, and on the day of perfection, God himself will gaze beyond our eyes to the boundaries of our personhood. We will be known like we longingly seek to be known now. The quest for self-understanding will be over.

With 13:13, Paul reaches both the climax and the conclusion of his eloquent speech, extolling the eternal virtue of loving behavior over all other human actions. The artful construction of his monologue comes to a fitting end by placing the word "love" (agapē [TG26, ZG27]) as the very last word in the declaration that love is the greatest. Yet he introduces possible confusion by both complementing and comparing love with two other virtues, faith and hope, which he links in a triad, as lasting forever with love. The triad also appears (when rendered literally) in 1 Thessalonians 1:3 and 5:8 in the order of faith, love, and hope, with hope being emphasized in an epistle that focuses on eschatology. The triad appears (in literal translations) in a variety of orders elsewhere in Paul's writing (Rom 5:1-5; Gal 5:5-6; Eph 4:2-5) and in the New Testament (Heb 6:10-12; 10:22-24; 1 Pet 1:3-8).

The question is whether Paul intended to link the other two virtues with love as eternal (so phrased by the NLT) or whether he viewed them as essential to Christian life now, like love, but nevertheless earthbound in terms of their value once we reach perfection. It makes sense for both faith and hope to be limited to the current state of human life, especially for Christians, since their faith in Jesus Christ and hope in eternal life both would seem to be vindicated at his return and not needed thereafter (Bruce 1971:179; Fee 1987:650; Hays 1997:231; Horsley 1998:179; Witherington 1995:271-272). In this sense, the literal rendering of the word "remains" (menō [TG3306, ZG3531]), which the NLT translates as "last forever," is taken very seriously. All three—faith, hope, and love—remain as vital to the current state, but only love endures as vital into the next.

However, this may be forcing a strict reading and dichotomy Paul did not wish to make between his big three virtues, which he never subdivides like this elsewhere. Perhaps, in fact, he saw the three as so intertwined that his point should be taken straightforwardly. In this sense, faith and hope are vital aspects of loving behavior even in the hereafter (Garland 2003:626; Thiselton 2000:1071-1074). Trust and confidence in God and in one another would not seem to be irrelevant to loving behavior even then, though admittedly they would be on a different plane than they are now in the struggles Christians presently face.

◆ ## 5. Everything spoken in public worship must be understandable and edifying (14:1-25)

Let love be your highest goal! But you should also desire the special abilities the Spirit gives—especially the ability to prophesy. [2]For if you have the ability to speak in tongues,* you will be talking only to God, since people won't be able to understand you. You will be speaking by the power of the Spirit,* but it will all be mysterious. [3]But one who prophesies strengthens others, encourages them, and comforts them. [4]A person who speaks in tongues is strengthened personally, but one who speaks a word of prophecy strengthens the entire church.

[5]I wish you could all speak in tongues, but even more I wish you could all prophesy. For prophecy is greater than speaking in tongues, unless someone interprets what you are saying so that the whole church will be strengthened.

[6]Dear brothers and sisters,* if I should come to you speaking in an unknown language,* how would that help you? But if I bring you a revelation or some special knowledge or prophecy or teaching, that will be helpful. [7]Even lifeless instruments like the flute or the harp must play the notes clearly, or no one will recognize the melody. [8]And if the bugler doesn't sound a clear call, how will the soldiers know they are being called to battle?

[9]It's the same for you. If you speak to people in words they don't understand, how will they know what you are saying? You might as well be talking into empty space.

[10]There are many different languages in the world, and every language has meaning. [11]But if I don't understand a language, I will be a foreigner to someone who speaks it, and the one who speaks it will be a foreigner to me. [12]And the same is true for you. Since you are so eager to have the special abilities the Spirit gives, seek those that will strengthen the whole church.

[13]So anyone who speaks in tongues should pray also for the ability to interpret what has been said. [14]For if I pray in tongues, my spirit is praying, but I don't understand what I am saying.

[15]Well then, what shall I do? I will pray in the spirit,* and I will also pray in words I understand. I will sing in the spirit, and I will also sing in words I understand. [16]For if you praise God only in the spirit, how can those who don't understand you praise God along with you? How can they join you in giving thanks when they don't understand what you are saying? [17]You will be giving thanks very well, but it won't strengthen the people who hear you.

[18]I thank God that I speak in tongues more than any of you. [19]But in a church meeting I would rather speak five understandable words to help others than ten thousand words in an unknown language.

[20]Dear brothers and sisters, don't be childish in your understanding of these things. Be innocent as babies when it comes to evil, but be mature in understanding matters of this kind. [21]It is written in the Scriptures*:

"I will speak to my own people
  through strange languages
  and through the lips of foreigners.
But even then, they will not listen
  to me,"*
  says the LORD.

[22]So you see that speaking in tongues is a sign, not for believers, but for unbelievers. Prophecy, however, is for the benefit of believers, not unbelievers. [23]Even so, if unbelievers or people who don't understand these things come into your church meeting and hear everyone speaking in an unknown language, they will think you are crazy. [24]But if all of you are prophesying, and unbelievers or people who don't understand these things come

into your meeting, they will be convicted of sin and judged by what you say. ²⁵As they listen, their secret thoughts will be exposed, and they will fall to their knees and worship God, declaring, "God is truly here among you."

14:2a Or *in unknown languages;* also in 14:4, 5, 13, 14, 18, 22, 26, 27, 28, 39.   14:2b Or *speaking in your spirit.*   14:6a Greek *brothers;* also in 14:20, 26, 39.   14:6b Or *in tongues;* also in 14:19, 23.   14:15 Or *in the Spirit;* also in 14:15b, 16.   14:21a Greek *in the law.*   14:21b Isa 28:11-12.

NOTES

14:1 *special abilities the Spirit gives.* Gr., *pneumatika* [TG4152B, ZG4461]. See note on the same word in 12:1.

14:3 *strengthens.* This is a noun (*oikodomēn* [TG3619, ZG3869]) that refers to the process of constructing a building and sometimes to the completed product, as earlier in 3:9 of God's "building." The first of four uses of the word in this chapter (14:5, 12, 26), it functions metaphorically to mean build up, edify, or fortify people in the church.

14:7 *lifeless instruments.* Gr., *apsucha phōnēn didonta.* The only use of this word in the NT, *apsucha* [TG895, ZG953] is a neuter plural adjective that is the antonym of the word "life" or "soul." The NLT has adapted the word nicely to the musical context of the verse, but in so doing has used "instruments" as a surrogate for "sound" (*phōnēn* [TG5456, ZG5889]), which is important to this context, being found four times (14:7, 8, 10, 11), the only uses in 1 Corinthians. This word can be "sound" or "voice" or can refer to any articulate sound, the human faculty of speech, or language. Paul plays on the variable meanings of this word in this chapter.

flute. Gr., *aulos* [TG836, ZG888]. The only use in the NT, it refers to any wind instrument, which in the ancient world might be constructed out of a reed, a bone, ivory, wood, or brass.

harp. Gr., *kithara* [TG2788, ZG3067]. Used here and in Revelation (Rev 5:8; 14:2; 15:2) in the NT, this refers to stringed instruments, which includes lyres and lutes. This word comes into English as "guitar."

clearly. Gr., *diastolēn* [TG1293, ZG1405]. Only used here and in Rom 3:22 and 10:12 in the NT, the word refers to a "distinction" or "difference."

14:8 *bugler.* Lit., "trumpet." This word is used mostly in eschatological passages (15:52; Matt 24:31; 1 Thess 4:16; Rev 1:10; 4:1; 8:2, 6, 13; 9:14). It represents horn instruments in this passage, but such that are used for military purposes.

14:9 *empty space.* Gr., *aera* [TG109, ZG113]. See note on earlier use in 9:26.

14:11 *foreigner.* Gr., *barbaros* [TG915A, ZG975]. This is used consistently in the NT from the perspective of Greeks, who viewed their culture to be superior over other peoples'. As here, it often refers to those outside the Greco-Roman borders, particularly in middle and northern Europe, who were thought to speak in woefully unsophisticated languages that sounded like gibberish (bar-bar-bar) compared to Greek. The word comes into English as "barbarian."

14:14 *if I pray in tongues, my spirit is praying, but I don't understand what I am saying.* The last clause of this verse is literally "my mind is unfruitful." In Hellenistic anthropology, the spirit is far superior to the mind. It is the place in one's being from which the person communicates with the gods, while the mind is merely the physical capacity for creating human speech to communicate to mere humans (Collins 1999:502). This explains in part why the Corinthians considered the gift of tongues superior to the gift of prophecy. Paul, however, considered the mind and human language crucial because they edify and vivify the community of believers. The distinction between "spirit" and "mind" is maintained in 14:15, where "mind" is translated twice as "words I understand."

14:15 *sing.* Gr., *psalō* [TG5567, ZG6010]. Used here (twice) and in Rom 15:9, Eph 5:19, and Jas 5:13, this word, originally referring to the plucking of a harp, by the NT period came to refer to singing along with the harp or just to singing, as here.

14:16 *join you in giving thanks.* Lit., "say amen to your thanksgiving." The NLT gives the sense rather than the literal word "amen."

14:20 *Be innocent as babies.* Gr., *nēpiazete* [TG3515, ZG3757], the only use of the verb in the NT. The noun cognate of this verb is used five times in 13:11 to refer to a child. Technically, it refers to an infant who has not yet developed the ability to communicate in a learned language.

mature. Gr., *teleioi* [TG5046, ZG5455]. Used also in 2:6 and 13:10, this word means the opposite of being a child.

14:22 *sign.* Gr., *sēmeion* [TG4592, ZG4956]. In the NT, this word is commonly associated with miraculous signs of Jesus (Matt 12:38; John 2:11) or others (Acts 5:12); this is how Paul uses it in 1:22, the only other use in 1 Corinthians. Here, however, the mark of God's activity takes a negative turn, more like its use in apocalyptic texts (Matt 24:30; Luke 21:11, 25). The sign may be that people do not listen (Soards 1999:292) and thus are condemned (Barrett 1968:323; Bruce 1971:133; Hays 1997:240). Most likely a sign of judgment here (Lanier 1991:278), it may constitute a "double sign"—one for insiders, which is positive, and another for outsiders, which is negative (Forbes 1995:181; Sandnes 1996:10).

unbelievers. Gr., *apistois* [TG571A, ZG603]. Used eleven times in 1 Corinthians, four times alone in this sequence of verses (14:22-24), this word marks out those who have not made public confession of Jesus as Lord and submitted to baptism from those who have done so. Though not part of the official Christian community, such people were likely household members (spouses, slaves) of people already believers (Collins 1999:506) or friends. Though it is somewhat surprising to contemplate their presence in the Christian assemblies that included the Lord's Supper, it is probably helpful to think of them as inquirers who have interest in acquainting themselves further with the Christian faith before converting.

14:23 *are crazy.* Gr., *mainesthe* [TG3105, ZG3419]. One of five uses in the NT, this word generally refers to someone who demonstrates signs of insanity. Elsewhere, it is used to refer to Jesus (John 10:20), Rhoda (Acts 12:15), and Paul (Acts 26:24). It can refer simply to the temporary, disconnected state caused by drunkenness, perhaps related to Bacchic celebrations. It is particularly tempting to think that Paul intentionally used the word with reference to Corinth because the word was used to denigrate the frenzied state of female adherents of Dionysus. This cult was extremely popular in Corinth (Collins 1999:509; Theissen 1987:277-280; Witherington 1995:284). Yet caution must be exercised in this regard due to the exacting study of Forbes (1995:282), who calls this common interpretation of the data into question.

COMMENTARY

Having established in principle that each person's gift is needed for the benefit of the whole community (ch 12) and that loving behavior in a believer's life is primary (ch 13), Paul has ably prepared the way for dealing with practical issues involving gifts in the Corinthian community. The uncontrolled exercise of many of the gifts in these gatherings created a chaotic atmosphere that was not healthy or beneficial to anyone, whether believer or nonbeliever. Extending from his previously expressed concerns about improper head attire and inconsiderate eating practices at their gatherings (ch 11), Paul's instruction was intended to restore order.

Paul's first words in 14:1 ("Let love be your highest goal") helpfully reduces to a motto the point of chapter 13 and reaffirms its conclusion in 13:13 about love's singular, enduring value. The simple grammatical connection of this priority to the matter of spiritual gifts effectively connects the reader back to 12:1 to recall the true point of discussion. Given prophecy's high position in all of Paul's lists in chapter 12, it is not surprising that Paul would single it out as the one gift every believer should seek to receive from the Spirit. What is surprising is that he was making any kind of statement about all believers having the same gift—given his long exposé in 12:14-26 on how absurd and unhelpful this would be. The reason he was doing so must be that the Corinthians had already been setting their sights on one specific, less beneficial gift—the gift of tongues.

That tongues is the gift that the Corinthians deemed as the one they all wanted to have becomes apparent when Paul names it as the antagonist to prophecy, beginning in 14:2, and then proclaims the superiority of prophecy over it through 14:25. He also has prepared the way for this juxtaposition between tongues and prophecy by always placing tongues last in his earlier lists. Thus, the opening encouragement to desire prophecy should be read as a countermeasure for the sake of argument to the overenthusiasm for the gift of tongues being encouraged in Corinth: If a believer hopes to have any one gift, prophecy should be the goal, not tongues. He was not really urging everyone to prophesy.

Two of Paul's previous mentions of tongues carefully team it with the gift of interpreting tongues (12:10, 30). However, here in 14:2 he isolates tongues from interpretation and in doing so reveals its fatal flaw as a gift on its own: Without interpretation, it does not minister to others in the community, whether gathered together or separate. On its own, at best, it functions as an intimate kind of communication to God, perhaps a vocalization of the deep groanings aided by the Holy Spirit (Rom 8:26). Oddly enough, given Paul's description, people uttering in tongues to God would not understand the meaning of their own communication (14:13-14). This is not to say there is no spiritual value involved or that this gift should not be exercised. However, its value is strictly confined to the individual. Also, this value is not about communicating knowledge or meaning but more involved in confirming deeply the reality of one's relationship to God. Without being interpreted, whatever is spoken remains a mysterious, unfathomable puzzle.

In 14:3-4, Paul shines the spotlight on prophecy. Its greater value compared to tongues lies in its ability to minister to the whole community when they are gathered together. It is really the only gift that accomplishes this. He lists three separate benefits it gives: strength, encouragement, and comfort. However, the three are grouped more for rhetorical effect than individual distinction. All are subsumed under strengthening, or fortifying, as Paul proceeds, not only in 14:4 but also later in 14:5, 12, and 26. Paul assumes that prophecy communicates in normal human language that all can access and that it can accomplish a wide variety of purposes to help people grow in their faith. It helps the community coalesce around their deepening confidence in God's goodwill among them.

Prophecy here would seem to involve words of wisdom and knowledge (12:8), to include the function of teachers (12:28-29), and not to be limited to either instantaneous insights (Dunn 1975:228; Fee 1987:660; Forbes 1995:229) or studied pronouncements (Garland 2003:633; Thiselton 2000:1077, 1087-1094). The primary audience is the gathered community. However, the gift itself is certainly also exercised from individual to individual in the form of discipleship, deep conversation, and counseling.

The stark contrast Paul has delineated between prophecy and tongues might well make those who speak in tongues feel their gift in effect has no real value and to discard it. Of course, Paul did not think this, since it is a gift from the Spirit with valid purposes. Thus, 14:5 opens by encouraging people to speak in tongues. However, "all" should be taken for rhetorical effect. He no more means that everyone should speak in tongues than that he meant previously that everyone should prophesy. The Spirit will distribute the gifts as he wills for the building up of the community; based on 12:14-26, it is a given that not all will have the same gift, not even prophecy. Paul's rhetoric pits prophecy against tongues because of the proclivity the Corinthian community had shown to seek the gift of tongues. If Paul were to wish them all to have the same gift, it would be prophecy, because of its wider value, as he has already explained. However, the situation is completely altered if tongues are interpreted. This in essence converts tongues into prophecy (Barrett 1968:319).

In 14:6-8, Paul draws out the contrast between prophecy and tongues. In doing so, he associates with prophecy three other gifts. Two of them, knowledge (12:8) and teaching (12:28-29), have been mentioned in previous lists, while the one mentioned first, revelation, receives its first mention now. Revelation could pair with prophecy as its divine spark, while knowledge functions this way for teaching (Conzelmann 1975:235), or, being first, revelation could even be the necessary starting point for the other three gifts. However, Paul seems to view all four as distinct gifts that manifest themselves in verbal communication to the believing community. Thus, it seems more likely that revelation is an indiscriminate replacement for "word of wisdom," that preceded "word of knowledge" in 12:8 (see NLT mg). Spiritual gifts like these, which, like prophecy, involve speaking to the community in their shared language, have the capacity to benefit everyone gathered. Tongues, in contrast, even if shared in the assembly by Paul himself (note the first person singular, "I"), benefit no one but the speaker when no interpretation occurs.

Paul used the image of musical instruments to illustrate his point in 14:7-8. Interestingly, he selected three out of the four basic instrument groups, wind (flute), string (harp), and horn (trumpet), notably leaving out percussion (drums). He pictured the first two in their function of producing music for people to enjoy. What he observed is that if a flute or harp never varies from playing one note, this could not be called music; it would just make a sound or noise. Music communicates a clear message to a group of people because the performer employs a range of notes in a musical system that people recognize like they do shared language. The trumpet adds another layer to Paul's point. Not only is a tune created with the varying notes, but certain agreed-upon tunes communicate commands to distant troops.

It is not fair to deduce from the musical illustrations that those who speak in tongues make shrill, unpleasant noises or that the gift of tongues is in any way related to musical sounds. However, in 14:9, Paul makes very clear that whatever sounds come out of people in the exercise of this gift, even if they draw on some sort of deeply imbedded language function, sound like meaningless noise even to believers who are present. This is so true that Paul believed the audience could be removed altogether and it would make no difference to what is going on. One might as well speak alone into the void of space on a dark night.

Paul adds a third illustration in 14:10-12. This time he sees a way of making his point from the great varieties of human languages of which the Corinthians will be well aware. Living in a bustling seaport with people coming from the edges of the Roman Empire and beyond, the Corinthians would have been aware of certain language groups related to Greek being much more familiar to their ears than the talk they heard coming from the mouths of the Celtic, Germanic, sub-Saharan, or East Indian people of their day. Such people—really, all peoples other than themselves— were labeled by Greeks and Romans as uncivilized barbarians and their languages viewed as gibberish. This ethnocentric view of the world beyond the Mediterranean coastlines helped Paul make his point even better than musical instruments, since it involves how one person hears another person's native language. Yet, once again, the analogy should not be extended to imply that Paul considered the gift of tongues to be actual human languages, as some have concluded from these verses (Gundry 1966:303; Zerhusen 1997:144-148). The point he emphasized once again has to do with ready communication that edifies every person listening when the community has gathered for worship, instruction, and the Lord's Supper.

Before continuing his exposition on the superiority of gifts that involve clear communication (14:13-17), Paul once again in 14:13, as he did in 14:5, interjects that all his criticisms against tongues break down once the unlearned language is interpreted to the assembled believers. Paul's concerns on this point imply that interpreters were in short supply in Corinth and that people were often speaking in tongues without interpretation taking place. Thus, with no interpreters regularly present in the assembly, Paul put the burden of interpretation on the shoulders of those with the gift of tongues. Maybe the Holy Spirit would grant some individuals both gifts so what they were saying may be of more use to the community.

In 14:14, Paul clarifies why he has brought up interpretation again. It is because not even the person who speaks in tongues knows what he is saying when he is speaking. To explain this, Paul pictures human communication faculties divided into two completely separate parts that usually do not intermingle; at least they do not intermingle when a person speaks in tongues. The mind, which controls human speech to other people, Paul pictures as shut off or lying dormant when a person's spirit speaks to God in special language. Though releasing oneself totally to spiritual communication was viewed as superior by those in the surrounding culture and by the Corinthian believers who spoke in tongues (D. Martin 1995:90), Paul did not agree at all. His understanding of religion, speaking for Christianity in particular, is that it is not simply individualistic but rather essentially communal. Believers are the body of Christ serving one another with the gifts enabled by the Spirit. This makes engaging the mind and communicating meaningful words always essential when the community is gathered together.

In 14:15-19, Paul forcefully argues that tongue-speakers are working from a false dichotomy. A person can engage the faculties of both spirit and mind simultaneously, and this they must do when worshiping together. Thus, he says in 14:15 that a person can and should pray and sing, for example, with both spirit and mind actively engaged in whatever is being done. By this he must mean that people are speaking audible words in a language shared by their community while also truly engaging in deep, personal communication to God that goes beyond words. To not do this when gathered for public worship and teaching with the rest of the believing community is to inhibit the "spirituality" of the experience.

As Paul says in 14:16, engaging in worship with one's mind inhibited shuts out the rest of the believers from enriching the spiritual experience even further by sharing in it. To retreat inside oneself in the midst of a celebration of God's goodness is selfish, arrogant, and in the end self-defeating. A person who is one of God's people must participate with God's people. Remember, no tongue or any other body part can survive outside the body (12:14-20), and the rest of the body needs each part. As 14:17 emphasizes again, vocalizing one's praises enriches the lives of everyone else present.

In 14:18-19, Paul puts the matter of tongues and meaningful, shared communication into perspective but with an autobiographical thrust. Paul himself spoke in tongues, and apparently quite a lot—he says "more than any of you." The way he put this, it sounds like this would be surprising news to the Corinthians. It suggests that even though he worshiped and lived among them for 18 months while he worked to establish the church there, for the most part he must have engaged in his tongue speaking privately and not publicly, a practice he will recommend to the active tongue-speakers in Corinth as the practical solution to their dilemma of having this gift without interpretation.

That Paul was fully experienced in the gift of tongues yet argued forcefully for the necessity and superiority of understandable speech in the community is an enormously powerful argument that opponents cannot counter. He nailed the point by dramatically pronouncing that only five understandable words from the mind (and spirit) outweigh 10,000 unintelligible words. It might as well be a million or a trillion. Five will always outweigh zero.

Paul's thoughts turn pastoral in 14:20 as he contemplates what the posturing for tongues-speaking without interpretation says about the spiritual development of those in Corinth who were doing this. He warned them that they were acting like immature children who wanted their way regardless of the impact on others. If the gift of tongues was some sign of spiritual advancement, then they certainly were not demonstrating this in their understanding of the situation. Thoughts of their childishness prompted comparison to children at play or babies before they learn language. It is a pun on their false sense of superiority in light of the noncommunicative speech of tongues-speaking. Their indiscriminate use of this gift without concern for the welfare of the entire church exposed them as being infants in their Christian life. And since being immature made them open to evil, they should grow up.

Expanding on the word "evil" in 14:20, Paul then quotes in 14:21 a selection from Isaiah (Isa 28:11-12) to warn any tongue-speaking Corinthians of the tragic consequence for them and others if they continue to speak in tongues that are not interpreted. Paul considered their situation comparable to that of Israel in the days of Isaiah: Israel had mocked Isaiah's prophecies of doom as baby chatter (Isa 28:10). For their retribution, Isaiah pronounced that they would have to hear the message from the lips of foreign invaders—whose speech ironically would sound like babble, too—when they were in their streets destroying their cities and hauling them into slavery. Though they would not understand the words, God's message of doom will have been delivered.

In 14:22-25, Paul draws out the intent of highlighting this tragic scene in the history of Israel. In effect, he believed that speaking in tongues could be a negative sign (like the foreigners uttering prophetic doom by their invasion). These Corinthians, though, would find that their condemnation would be uttered by outsiders visiting their assemblies, as they pronounced Christians to be out of their minds and then left, never to return. While tongue-speakers may think their gift is a demonstration of God's power to unbelievers and an encouraging sign to believers, neither is true. Incessant tongue speaking looks like nothing more than immature grandstanding to believers and like uninhibited craziness to unbelievers. It is a sign to drive them away from God to their own condemnation apart from Christ.

By contrast, gifts related to prophecy are a positive sign, helpful all around. They encourage and develop fellow believers while also conveying the message of the gospel to nonbelievers. Paul reveals in 14:24 that hearing the gospel first leads to an overwhelming awareness in people of their sinful rebellion against God and their need to repent and find acceptance from him. In 14:25, Paul draws upon eschatological images from Isaiah 45:14 and Zechariah 8:23 (Hays 1999:393) to picture this conversion experience as the people falling to their knees and then joining the believers in worship and praise of God, acknowledging his presence in the assembly of the believers (Thiselton 2000:1130). In Paul's scenario this positive outcome occurs (rather than the negative outcome of them leaving unconverted) precisely because the believers conducted their public worship and instruction in language that everyone present could understand.

◆   ## 6. Public worship must be conducted in an orderly manner (14:26-40)

26Well, my brothers and sisters, let's summarize. When you meet together, one will sing, another will teach, another will tell some special revelation God has given, one will speak in tongues, and another will interpret what is said. But everything that is done must strengthen all of you.

27No more than two or three should speak in tongues. They must speak one at a time, and someone must interpret what they say. 28But if no one is present who can interpret, they must be silent in your church meeting and speak in tongues to God privately.

29Let two or three people prophesy, and let the others evaluate what is said. 30But if someone is prophesying and another person receives a revelation from the Lord, the one who is speaking must stop. 31In this way, all who prophesy will have a turn to speak, one after the other, so that everyone will learn and be encouraged. [32]Remember that people who prophesy are in control of their spirit and can take turns. [33]For God is not a God of disorder but of peace, as in all the meetings of God's holy people.*

[34]Women should be silent during the church meetings. It is not proper for them to speak. They should be submissive, just as the law says. [35]If they have any questions, they should ask their husbands at home, for it is improper for women to speak in church meetings.*

[36]Or do you think God's word originated with you Corinthians? Are you the only ones to whom it was given? [37]If you claim to be a prophet or think you are spiritual, you should recognize that what I am saying is a command from the Lord himself. [38]But if you do not recognize this, you yourself will not be recognized.*

[39]So, my dear brothers and sisters, be eager to prophesy, and don't forbid speaking in tongues. [40]But be sure that everything is done properly and in order.

14:33 The phrase *as in all the meetings of God's holy people* could instead be joined to the beginning of 14:34.   14:35 Some manuscripts place verses 34-35 after 14:40.   14:38 Some manuscripts read *If you are ignorant of this, stay in your ignorance.*

NOTES

14:28 *be silent.* Gr., *sigatō* [TG4601, ZG4967]. Used only here, in 14:30, and in 14:34 in 1 Corinthians, the word generally occurs where people who have been talking have become quiet or are asked to stop talking. In Luke 20:26, Jesus' answers quiet the crowd, and in Acts 12:17, Peter motions to the crowd to stop talking so that he can speak. The emphasis in 14:34 on women learning also appears in 1 Tim 2:11 using a different but comparable word, "quiet" (*hēsuchia* [TG2271, ZG2484]).

privately. Gr., *heautō* [TG1438, ZG1571]. This is a reflexive pronoun meaning "to himself."

14:29 *evaluate.* Gr., *diakrinetōsan* [TG1252, ZG1359]. This is the last of five important uses of this word in 1 Corinthians (4:7; 6:5; 11:29, 31; 14:29). See note on 4:7.

14:32 *in control.* Gr., *hupotassetai* [TG5293A, ZG5718]. The first of nine times this word will be used in 1 Corinthians (14:34; 15:27 [three times], 28 [three times]; 16:16), the word comes from the world of distinct social categories, where certain people are required by their social position to submit themselves to the will of others. It is used of wives to husbands (14:34; Col 3:18; 1 Pet 3:1, 5), slaves to masters (Titus 2:9), people to rulers (Rom 13:1, 5; Titus 3:1; 1 Pet 2:13), and young men to older men (1 Pet 5:5). But it is also used of the church to Christ (Eph 5:24), of Christians to one another (Eph 5:21), of Christ to God, and of all things to Christ (15:27-28).

14:33 *disorder.* Gr., *akatastasias* [TG181, ZG189]. Used only here in 1 Corinthians, it is the opposite of order. It is onomatopoetic in that the word itself sounds like chaos.

as in all the meetings of God's holy people. The NLT continues the decision of TLB, NASB, and Phillips to place this phrase as an addendum to the preceding phrase rather than as the preface to the phrase that follows (cf. NIV, ESV, RSV, NRSV, NEB, TEV, so also NLT mg), as can be seen in the paragraphing. In favor of this is the awkwardness of repeating the word "church" (*ekklēsia* [TG1577, ZG1711]), creating a redundancy (Bruce 1971:135; Clarke 2001:146), which would then be rendered as follows: "As in all the churches of the saints, let the women in all the churches keep silent." Against the NLT's placement is the awkwardness of saying "God is the God of peace" followed by the saying that "this is the practice of all the churches" (Blomberg 1994:281; Garland 2003:670), unless Paul means that the principle of order is a rule he instructed all the churches to follow and he had simply skipped a step in his logic (something he did from time to time). The evidence needed to make a decision on this is more balanced than the preponderance of versions suggests, but on the whole it goes against the NLT decision. Those who favor the NLT decision also tend to support the view that 14:34-35 was not originally part of 1 Corinthians (Fee 1987:697-698; Hays 1997:243).

14:34-35 The inclusion of these two verses at this point in 1 Corinthians is supported by very strong manuscript evidence: 𝔓46 ℵ A B Ψ 0243 33 1739 𝔐 Coptic Syriac. A few manuscripts (D F G) place it following 14:40. Though it has been argued that this movement of these restrictive words regarding women suggests that they were originally a marginal gloss carelessly or purposely inserted into the text (Conzelmann 1975:246; Fee 1987:699-703; Hays 1997:248; Horsley 1998:188), the fact that every known manuscript includes them (no matter in what order) presents an obstacle that cannot be overcome by internal arguments (Collins 1999:515; Garland 2003:675-676; Thiselton 2000:1148-1150). Excellent, detailed studies have been done, both against inclusion (Payne 1995:240-262) and in support of inclusion (Bryce 1997:31-39; Niccum 1997:242-255; Odell-Scott 2000:68-74). Original placement of these verses after 14:40 has minor support (Schulz 1998:128-131) since this was most likely a copyist's attempt to cope with the awkwardness of these verses being after 14:33.

14:34 proper. Gr., *epitrepetai* [TG2010, ZG2205]. Used here and in 16:7 in 1 Corinthians, this word means to entrust someone with a responsibility and can even refer to bequeathing items to others after death. It is translated "allowed" in the NIV and "permitted" in the ESV. It is used of Paul being permitted to speak to the crowd in Jerusalem (Acts 21:39-40) and to Agrippa (Acts 26:1). It is also used in 1 Tim 2:12, where women are encouraged to learn quietly. As here, such unobtrusive learning is viewed as appropriate public decorum that signals respect for their husbands. There, however, women bear the further restriction of not teaching men. This principle appears to extend from the idea that quiet submission in public is a sign of respect women show their husbands. The matter of propriety is not so easily accommodated to a contemporary, Western setting as 1 Corinthians 14:34. Although women who teach and speak publicly are not perceived as disrespectful to husbands today, further theological argumentation in 1 Tim 2:11-15 tags women as being too easily deceived as demonstrated by Satan's deception of Eve. Some would argue, though, that the naivete of most women in the first century has been overturned by the equal opportunity for education of women today that was not available then. This would make women as able as men to identify theological error and thus make them able and ready to be excellent teachers in the church today.

14:35 improper. Gr., *aischron* [TG150, ZG156]. Used earlier in reference to the shame a woman would experience to have her head shorn, as in the punishment for a prostitute (see note on 11:6), this word depicts the public scorn people are subjected to when they have broken with cultural norms. In this case the norm is that wives act with a decorum in public that honors their husbands, which is the same issue that causes Paul to require women to cover their heads when they participate in prayer and prophesy in the meetings.

14:38 you yourself will not be recognized. Gr., *agnoeitai* [TG50, ZG51], which is lit., "he himself is ignored." This has the support of ℵ A D 048 0243 33 1739. Some other significant manuscripts (𝔓46 B) support the reading, "If you are ignorant of this, stay in your ignorance" (cf. NLT mg), based on a third-person imperative form of the verb (*agnoeitō*). But the third-person passive form has adequate support and is the more likely of the two to have been changed by a scribe wanting to parallel the third-person imperative following the indicative directly above in 14:38. The third-person passive fits Paul's style of following up the indicative with the passive, as in 8:3.

14:40 *properly.* Gr., *euschēmonōs* [TG2156, ZG2361]. The word refers to outward decorum that matches the highest expectations in social propriety.

order. Gr., *taxin* [TG5010, ZG5423]. Only used here in 1 Corinthians, this word comes from military use referring to the line and position in which a soldier is placed—a reference point well-suited to the prominent number of retired military personnel and their descendants residing in Corinth.

COMMENTARY

In this section (14:26-40) Paul addresses another factor that was needed in the Corinthian gatherings: order. For the Corinthians, the priority that appears to have been given to unceasing tongues was part of an even bigger problem—a chaotic atmosphere of many speaking at once and some speaking too long. Such a noisy, circus atmosphere would even make intelligible speech unintelligible. In order to reestablish order over this detrimental situation, Paul laid down some general rules for improvement.

Paul begins in 14:26 by describing a sampling of the elements involved when the Corinthian believers gathered together. He mentions singing (referred to earlier in 14:15), teaching and revelation (cf. 14:6), speaking in tongues (cf. 14:2, 5, 6, 13), and interpreting tongues (cf. 14:5, 13). Surprisingly, he does not mention prophecy, which he advocated throughout chapter 14 as the supremely needed gift to be exercised in the gathered assembly. Teaching and revelation are probably presumed to include a range of intelligible communication that includes prophecy and knowledge (with which they are teamed in 14:6), as well as other gifts. Prophecy is also mentioned in chapter 11, as well as praying, consuming a meal, and celebrating the Lord's Supper, and it can safely be assumed that the meetings described both there and here are the same (Hays 1997:241), taking place in larger homes, at least weekly (Barrett 1968:325) in the evening. Paul reiterated his point from 14:4-6 and 14:12 that the purpose of these gatherings is edification, or strengthening and deepening the faith commitments of those present.

Strangely, given his dominant concern for order, he did not mention a moderator or presider over the assembly, though there must have been elders (since elders seem to have been appointed in every church) and those with the gift of leadership (12:28) among those assembled. He did, however, speak to issues requiring regulation, whether by the group or by people in the group assembled.

First, addressing tongue speaking in 14:27-28, he limited the number of tongue-speakers allowed to participate to two or three. It seems, though, that there were many more than this ready to speak in tongues and who had been doing so until then. The absence of able interpreters, as Paul notes, would also curtail the numbers involved now. The practical result of this situation is that the excess tongue-speakers, who cannot provide interpretation either through the gifts of others or through their own gift of interpretation, must be mute. Tongue speaking in the public setting of assembled believers absolutely requires interpretation. If any are speaking and there is not interpretation, they are to stop. If they have been speaking up to then with no interpretation, they are to quit doing so. The instruction for these to exercise their gift privately most likely means to do this at home (which will match the later instruction for women to unlock their silence at home) and not in the assembly, rather than that they are to somehow continue without vocalizing. Prayer and worship in the ancient world were always vocal, silent prayer being a relatively modern human invention.

Second, addressing prophecy in 14:29-33, Paul likewise limits their numbers to two or three participants. From Paul's earlier discussion, it sounds like this would be an increase from what had been happening so far in Corinth. However, the primary problem with the exercise of this gift seems to have been some individuals monopolizing the floor with overly lengthy comments. Paul enjoined such people to yield the floor to others with comments to share. He specifically mentions a "revelation." As before, this could be a separate gift or the necessary precursor to any non-tongue-speaking message, like a word of wisdom, knowledge, teaching, or prophecy. Though it appears that such revelations were spontaneous, it is possible that they could be the result of study or contemplation prior to the assembly (Thiselton 2000:1091-1092). The Spirit would prompt them to speak at this particular point, perhaps triggered by something said by the speaker who had the floor (not unlike normal human conversation).

These revelations that allow interruption of prophecy could perhaps also be tied to the evaluation of prophecy that Paul advances in 14:29 as an essential responsibility of all those assembled. This new twist, not mentioned anywhere before in Paul's discussion, takes the exact opposite position from the *Didache* (11:7), written only a generation later, that names questioning the word of a prophet as an unforgivable sin. Paul, however, as evidenced from his own letters (including 1 Corinthians), believed that speaking for God is not a matter of uttering commands that people must follow in lockstep.

Persuasion and lengthy dialogue are completely compatible with instructing God's people. Paul believed in the power of the Spirit to help people see the true word of God, especially among the assembled believers (5:1-5), but he did not think this meant they were barred from thoughtfully interacting with what they were hearing. The message could, in fact, be clarified in the course of evaluation, found unconvincing, or even be determined to be false. The early church and Paul, for good reasons, were concerned about false prophets damaging these fledgling churches. Eventually this became a big problem in Corinth as evidenced in 2 Corinthians 10–13.

So, prophets are to speak one at a time, be evaluated, and yield to others with messages that the assembled believers need to hear in order to be encouraged and grow. Lest they think they cannot stop their talking because they are being prompted by the Spirit, Paul addresses this in 14:32-33. Just like the tongue-speakers can silence their gift when no interpretation is possible, so also prophets can control their speech. People speaking can stop speaking, and people with urgent messages to share can wait their turn. This point applies to Paul's earlier principle addressed to tongue-speakers about having both their minds and their spirits engaged in the exercise of their gift (14:15). If the mind is engaged, as it is supposed to be, speech can and must be controlled.

God, whose character and presence is revealed in making order out of chaos, in creation and in humanity, trumps any attempt by the Corinthians to rebut Paul on this point. As God's new people, the church must endeavor to reflect God's character ("Be holy for I am holy") not only in principle but in the microcosm of the hours they spend together each week worshiping him. Order must prevail against all individualistic and egocentric cries of some claiming to be in the Spirit.

In 14:33b-35, Paul limits the participation of women in the public assemblies. This comes as a surprise, since this had not even been hinted at as any part of his concern so far. He had not qualified any of the spiritual gifts by gender, nor had he mentioned women at all since advocating they cover their head when they pray and prophesy in the assemblies (in 11:2-16). It must be assumed that in Paul's mind, his distress over the chaotic conditions of the Corinthians' gatherings went back to that point. So he was now resurrecting a piece of unfinished business on the matter of women. The formal connection to that section was his appeal at the conclusion of 11:16 and again here at the opening of 14:33 to universal practice in the churches. This connection would suggest that his underlying reasoning continued to be based upon the concern not to undermine the created differences between men and women, as well as to look to social norms of the day as the parameters of how to maintain this observance.

Women are the third category of persons who need to learn to discipline their speech in the assembly. All three (tongue-speakers, prophets, and women) are instructed with the same word, "be silent" (*sigaō* [TG4601, ZG4967]). All three must have been talking too much. Paul also reused the word "submissive" (*hupotassomai* [TG5293A, ZG5718]), first urging prophets to submit their spirits to their minds to stop speaking (14:32), then to women to submit to their husbands to stop speaking (14:34). Paul believed his goal of bringing the Corinthians' chaotic worship into order could be accomplished by limiting the formal participation of all three categories of people.

Paul's appeals to the women concurred with what was publicly acceptable behavior for married women both in Greek and Jewish culture. Cato, a Roman senator, asked a woman, "Could you not have asked your husband the same thing at home?" (Livy *History of Rome* 34:2.9). Plutarch urged a woman not to speak in public except through her husband (*Moralia* 142D). Philo wrote, "The husband seems competent to transmit knowledge of the law to his wife" (*Hypothetica* 8.7.14). Josephus wrote, "The woman, says the Law, is in all things inferior to the man. Let her accordingly be submissive" (*Against Apion* 2.201).

However much Paul's teaching coincided with these representative thoughts, Paul believed his support for women submitting to their husbands comes from the Old Testament. Though he did not say specifically what in the Old Testament verifies this position, suggestions include Genesis 3:16 (Mare 1976:276) or Numbers 12:1-15 (Liefield 1986:149-150). Even though Genesis 3:16 may be in view in 1 Timothy 2:14 (in reference to Eve's being deceived), it is less likely to be so here (Bruce 1971:136; Fee 1987:707; Garland 2003:672; Soards 1999:306; Thiselton 2000:1155) since the verse involves a prediction but not a law. It is more likely that Paul was thinking of the same creation passages of Genesis 1:26-27 and 2:21-23 that informed his discussion of head coverings in 11:2-16 (Blomberg 1994:282; Bruce 1971:136; Garland 2003:672; Oster 1995:341).

It is a mistake to read Paul's instruction for women to be silent in any fashion that expands beyond the type of situation he was concerned about in Corinth. He was not calling on all women everywhere not to talk or women to always defer to men in conversation. He defined the parameters of his concern very narrowly in 14:35 when he refers to asking questions. It would appear that while tongues-speakers were talking too much (without interpreters) and prophetic speeches were going on too long, the women were extending the questioning period too long, maybe even dominating the questioning. Paul acknowledges that asking questions is one of the best ways to learn, but he can also see that there was enough of a breach of public decorum occurring that this was another practical way to regain order.

Given that Paul presumes his own discussion regarding head coverings in 11:2-16 in the discussion of order here, it cannot be concluded that somehow Paul has countermanded his own teaching. Rather, in his limiting women speaking in the assembly in 14:33b-36, women who are prophesying or praying or singing or exercising any other spiritual gift among the assembled believers must be expected to continue doing so. All of that activity must be bracketed out from his concern over the problems with women that had arisen during the investigative period following prophetic words. Very similar to his advice to tongue-speakers who cannot present an interpretation, he invites the women to voice all the questions they have to their husbands outside of the public forum. Though Paul did not address women who are not married, his concern would be the same: that they find ways to learn at home, outside the public evaluation of the speakers.

The explanation just provided for resolving the difficulty between Paul's advocating women praying and prophesying in 11:2-16 and then preventing their speaking in 14:33b-35 is an increasingly well-endorsed position (Bruce 1971:175; Garland 2003:664-672; Thiselton 2000:1150-1162; Witherington 1995:287). However, at least two other approaches are current. The most prominent of these, though losing its earlier luster, suggests that 14:34-35 is an interpolation, or teaching interjected in the passage by someone other than Paul (Barrett 1968:330-333; Conzelmann 1975:246; Fee 1987:699-708; Hays 1997:247; Horsley 1998:188; Lockwood 1996:36-37). The common suggestion is that this was an insertion by someone else, perhaps influenced by what Paul says in 1 Timothy 2:11-15, who wrote something in the margin at some stage that was brought over in the passage. The major basis for this view is that some Greek manuscripts place these verses after 14:40. However, as discussed in the note on 14:34-35 (see above), every known manuscript includes these verses. In addition to the manuscript situation, some observe that the passage uses some unfamiliar Pauline language (Collins 1999:516), like his use of "law" as a general proof without a specific quotation (Hollander 1998:130). However, the counterargument is that plenty of words are carried over from the context, in addition to "be silent" and "be submissive," including "learn" (Gr., *mathein* [TG3129, ZG3443], translated "have . . . questions" in NLT; 4:6; 14:31), "their own husbands" (7:2), "shameful" (11:6), and even "the law says" (9:8). This more than suffices to consider the verses to have been original to the context.

An approach growing in prominence suggests that 14:33b-35 is not intended to be taken as Paul's own beliefs, but rather the views of some in Corinth with whom he disagrees. This type of person would be a theological conservative with the mind-set of the person who wrote 1 Timothy, presumed not to be Paul (Allison 1988:43-52; Arichea 1995:107-111; Collins 1999:514-517; Odell-Scott 1983:90-93; 1987:100-103; Vander Stichele 1995:246-248; Talbert 1987:92-93). When Paul blurts out, "Or do you think God's word originated with you?" (14:36), this is taken as a rebuttal of their view that endorses women to speak. The key to this argument is the particle (ē [TG2228, ZG2445]; NLT, "Or") indicating an exclamation, but this certainly is not a required understanding of this word, which normally means "or." Paul employs this technique of rebuttal elsewhere in 1 Corinthians, such as in 6:12; 7:1; 8:1, 4, 8; 11:2; 15:12.

That Paul occasionally employed this form of diatribe is not disputed. However, there are problems with claiming that this is another example of such use—namely, the so-called quote from those Paul opposed is (1) overly long, (2) not introduced in any formal way that would help readers recognize it as such, and (3) is not patterned like others found in 1 Corinthians (Garland 2003:667). In the end, without the apparent conflict with 11:2-16, nothing in this passage compels viewing it as an opponent's interjection (Jervis 1995:59). It seems far better to understand 14:33b-35 within the scope of 11:2-16.

Paul's limit on women speaking in the public assemblies of believers, then, must be said to be under the umbrella of advancing order in public worship. Being grounded on the wife's submission to her husband makes it no more a universal dictate for all churches for all time than a woman covering her head to pray and prophesy, as some contend (Maier 1991:91). Like 11:2-16, the concern is about honoring God's created distinction between genders by demonstrating a wife's respect for her husband publicly in conventional fashion (Isaak 1995:59-61). To do this in Paul's day, when participating in worship with other believers, she covered her head. Women in contemporary Western culture could show this respect in other ways.

Regarding women asking questions, the concern remains for wives to honor their husbands and God's created distinction. However, in Western culture, it would no longer dishonor her husband for a woman to ask a discerning question in a public setting or learn in a mixed classroom with her male and female peers. It certainly would not effect any concern about maintaining order. As with covering the head, though, Western culture should not be assumed to be the norm everywhere. Christians need to be sensitive to varying cultures around the globe regarding how women go about participating in public assemblies of Christians.

Paul's final approach to secure order in the Corinthian worship gatherings appeals to his own apostolic position (14:36-38). That he does this so rarely in his letters, including 1 Corinthians, evidences his deep concern about these matters. The hint of sarcasm in his two opening questions in 14:36 was his attempt to counter the arrogance displayed by some of the Corinthians who believed their gift of tongues set them higher than others.

Paul wanted to remind them who was speaking to them through this letter. It should not be forgotten that an apostle sits on top of the list of those with gifts to edify the body of Christ, most notably a rung above prophets (12:28-29). Fully confident that the Spirit would not be contradictory or add confusion, Paul invited those with special spiritual insight, even prophets in their midst, to consider his teaching and weigh its validity (14:37). He had no doubt that his instructions about the need for order, alongside the proper use of gifts, would align with what Christ himself desires. His challenge in 14:38 suggests that any prophet whose teaching contradicts his own on this matter must be a false prophet, who will be judged by Christ when he returns.

Though it may appear so, Paul was not being arrogant or simply authoritarian. He had, in fact, already done a large amount of teaching in the last four chapters to persuade the Corinthians about changes needed in their worship and exercise of gifts. This capstone appeal is based on his confidence about who he was in the exercise of his own call. True, Spirit-guided teaching simply would not undermine his own. Paul's position on this point also undergirds the deferential respect Paul's letters should be given in the church today.

Finally, in 14:39-40 Paul offers something of a postscript to everything he has said in chapters 12–14. He boiled down his corrections to two priorities: (1) prophecy over tongues speaking without devaluing tongues and (2) order and discretion in public gatherings without compromising spiritual vitality. Oddly, he did not mention the issue of women voicing their questions in this mix, which no doubt is why some manuscripts place 14:34-35 here after this summary. However, he probably considered this covered in the encouragement to do things "properly."

◆   ## E. Paul's Defense of the Resurrection (15:1-58)
1. Christ's resurrection witnessed by many (15:1-11)

Let me now remind you, dear brothers and sisters,* of the Good News I preached to you before. You welcomed it then, and you still stand firm in it. ²It is this Good News that saves you if you continue to believe the message I told you—unless, of course, you believed something that was never true in the first place.*

³I passed on to you what was most important and what had also been passed on to me. Christ died for our sins, just as the Scriptures said. ⁴He was buried, and he was raised from the dead on the third day, just as the Scriptures said. ⁵He was seen by Peter* and then by the Twelve. ⁶After that, he was seen by more than 500 of his followers* at one time, most of whom are still alive, though some have died. ⁷Then he was seen by James and later by all the apostles. ⁸Last of all, as though I had been born at the wrong time, I also saw him. ⁹For I am the least of all the apostles. In fact, I'm not even worthy to be called an apostle after the way I persecuted God's church.

¹⁰But whatever I am now, it is all because God poured out his special favor on me—and not without results. For I have worked harder than any of the other apostles; yet it was not I but God who was working through me by his grace. ¹¹So it makes no difference whether I preach or they preach, for we all preach the same message you have already believed.

15:1 Greek *brothers;* also in 15:31, 50, 58.   15:2 Or *unless you never believed it in the first place.*   15:5 Greek *Cephas.*   15:6 Greek *the brothers.*

NOTES

15:1 *remind.* Gr., *gnōrizō* [TG1107, ZG1192]. Though this verb is only used here and in 12:3 in 1 Corinthians, its noun cognate, "knowledge" (*gnōsis* [TG1108, ZG1194]), is used 10 times, beginning as early as 1:5 (see note), and is considered a major theme of the book. Some in Corinth seem to have claimed they had alternative or superior knowledge to others. The verbal form of this word normally refers to informing someone of previously unknown information, but the NLT (like NIV and ESV) recognizes that the context here dictates that Paul was drawing attention to matters he had taught them previously.

Good News. Gr., *euangelion* [TG2098, ZG2295]. Normally translated "gospel," as in the NIV and ESV, the NLT rendering successfully employs the dominant nonbiblical sense of the word but shows the special NT sense with capitalization. This approach is consistently applied in all uses of the word in 1 Corinthians (4:15; 9:12, 14, 18, 23) and its verbal cognate (1:17; 9:16, 18; 15:2). For Paul and all NT writers, this word encapsulates the redeeming message of Christ to all people (see note on 1:17).

welcomed. Gr., *parelabete* [TG3880, ZG4161]. Used twice in this context, here and in 15:3, and otherwise only in 11:23 in 1 Corinthians, this word refers to accepting or taking possession of something someone gives to another, whether it be land or even a political appointment. Paul used it here and elsewhere (Col 2:6; 1 Thess 2:13; 2 Thess 3:6) to refer to people, like the Corinthians, accepting the message of the gospel. Though Paul denied receiving the essence of the gospel from anyone but Christ himself (Gal 1:16), he did acknowledge that certain traditions surrounding the gospel, like the Lord's Supper and the witness roster of the resurrection, he received from others.

then. The NLT adds this to clarify that the past tense of the verb (aorist) indicates the historical point in time when Paul first came to Corinth and remained 18 months, described in Acts 18:1-17.

still stand firm. Gr., *hestēkate* [TG2476, ZG2705], a very common word in Greek, literally referring to causing something to stand. Paul used it consistently of continuing to remain loyal to the claims of the gospel (2 Cor 1:24; Eph 6:13-14; Col 4:12). The NLT adds "still" to emphasize the completed and current sense (perfect tense) in which this remains true of the Corinthians since they accepted the gospel.

15:2 *saves*. Gr., *sōzesthe* [TG4982, ZG5392]. The last of nine uses in 1 Corinthians (1:18, 21; 3:15; 5:5; 7:16 [twice]; 9:22; 10:33; 15:2), this is Paul's standard word for what the gospel does for those who believe. The present passive form used here, lit., "you are being saved" (ESV), is significant to this context, in which Paul wants to emphasize that the gospel provides both a present and a future sense of salvation (Garland 2003:683; Thiselton 2000:1185), the latter in the form of a bodily resurrection. See 1:18, where a middle/passive participle is used.

15:3 *I passed on . . . been passed on*. Gr., *paredōka* [TG3860, ZG4140] . . . *parelabon* [TG3880, ZG4161]. Paul used the exact same combination of these two Greek words in 11:23 with regard to the Lord's Supper tradition. Other than here and in 11:23, *paredōka* is mostly used negatively by Paul and elsewhere in the NT of Jesus' betrayal by being handed over to his executioners (Mark 15:15; Eph 5:2). See note on 5:5. NLT renders *parelabon* [TG3880, ZG4161] in 11:23 as "received." While *parelabon* would normally be expected to be "received" here also (cf. NIV and ESV), the NLT rendering of "been passed on" is trying to emphasize that Paul accepted this traditional testimony about the resurrection and other matters in the same way the Corinthians did and has faithfully transmitted it to them. This language was also used by rabbis to speak of the passing on of traditional teaching (Collins 1999:426).

15:8 *at the wrong time*. Gr., *tō ektrōmati* [TG1626, ZG1765]. Only used here in the NT, this word refers to a fetus that has been born so early that it has miscarried or aborted, arriving either deformed or stillborn. What Paul meant by using this term is debated. He could mean that he was a freak among the apostles, using an epithet his enemies used against him, on the order of 2 Cor 10:10; 12:7-10; Gal 4:13-14 (Barrett 1968:344; Bruce 1971:142; Fee

1987:733; Hays 1997:258). While this could be the case, it is more likely that Paul used this term to represent a profound truth about the effect of Christ appearing to him. Unexpectedly jerked out of his violent life of seeking to destroy the church, Christ's appearance to him on the Damascus road began a completely new life for him in which he sought to enlarge the church (Collins 1999:537; Soards 1999:323). His birth as believer and apostle was completely unanticipated and a massive disruption to his old life. His role as an apostle did not develop naturally over the course of time as it did for most others. His conversion and apostolic call erupted in an about-face for which he was not prepared. From the use of the word in the LXX, some suggest that Paul used this word to conceptualize his life as miserable before meeting Christ (Hollander and van der Hout 1996:227-228; Munck 1959:180).

15:10 without results. Gr., *kenē* [TG2756, ZG3031]. This is one of four uses of this word in this chapter (15:14 [twice], 58). Paul later used it for rhetorical effect, to prove the irrevocable damage to Christian faith if certain aspects of the gospel message are untrue. He repeats this concern in 2 Cor 6:1. See note on 1:17, where the verbal form of this word is used.

I have worked. Gr., *ekopiasa* [TG2872, ZG3159]. Used two other times in 1 Corinthians (4:12 [see note]; 16:16), this word refers to physical labor that is extended to the point of making someone weary. Paul referred to his apostolic work in this way regularly (Gal 4:11; Phil 2:16; Col 1:29).

through me. Gr., *sun emoi*, meaning "together with me." The preposition *sun* [TG4862, ZG5250] normally speaks of cooperation between partners. The NLT attempts to show that Paul is the subservient partner with God's grace. The NIV and ESV have "with me." The awkwardness of this preposition explains the replacement of *sun* in some manuscripts with *eis* [TG1519, ZG1650] (so 𝔓46) as found earlier in the verse. However, the more difficult reading, found in B and others, is most likely correct.

15:11 preach the same message. Gr., *kērussomen* [TG2784, ZG3062]. In this context (also in 15:12 and earlier in 1:23 and 9:27), this word refers to proclaiming or announcing a message as a herald going through the streets. It was commonly used by Paul to refer to preaching the gospel, though the word used in 15:1, "the Good News I preached" (*euangelizomai* [TG2097A, ZG2294]), is used slightly more often. Paul may have used it here to emphasize the wider central teachings of Christian belief like resurrection, rather than more strictly the missionary message of the gospel.

COMMENTARY

Completion of his response to the Corinthians' question about spiritual gifts and their appropriation in worship in chapters 12–14 frees Paul to address his last major concern in this epistle, very possibly *the* major problem Paul had been itching to get to from the beginning of the letter—namely, the Corinthians' confusion over the resurrection. Such confusion was not novel to the Corinthians. Notably, the Thessalonians needed holes in their understanding filled, too (1 Thess 4:13-18; 2 Thess 2:1-12). It may be true that teaching on the resurrection, particularly in the details, was not a priority of Paul's teaching to converts (Fee 1987:716). Further, it does not seem to be just a matter of how long he might spend initially with a start-up community of believers. He was with the Thessalonians perhaps only a month (Acts 17:2) but with the Corinthians 18 months (Acts 18:11). Paul probably taught the Corinthians in rudimentary form the basics of the resurrection of Christ as it relates to the gospel, but probably not in the detail as it relates to the resurrection of believers, as he will elaborate on in this chapter.

If this is the case, then it is not surprising that Paul did not speak harshly toward the Corinthians as a whole, toward any particular individual, or toward any faction as he moved through his argument on this subject. He also did not refer in any way to how he knew about this fundamental flaw in their understanding of Christian beliefs. As in the other chapters that do not arise from the Corinthians' official letter to him, Paul's information almost certainly came either from those associated with Chloe (1:11), the bearers of the letter (16:17), or from Apollos (16:12), who had recently returned to Paul from Corinth with strong reservations about returning. Given Apollos's reputation for theological acumen (Acts 18:24-28), he would be the more likely one to convey the subtleties of the Corinthians' errant positions on the complicated topic of the resurrection.

Eschatological assumptions have arisen from time to time before in the letter (3:13-15; 4:5; 5:5; 6:2, 3, 9, 14; 7:29-31; 9:24-25; 10:11-12; 11:26; 13:9-12), but it may well be that Paul's decision to address this crucial theological issue last signals his belief that proper understanding on this point is essential grounding for all the pragmatic issues he had addressed for the Corinthian believers (Barth 1933:11; Conzelmann 1975:249; Thiselton 1977–1978:510-526; 2000:1169). Certainly, understanding of the future will affect actions in the present.

Paul's approach in this chapter, like always, was first to establish common ground, then argue for his position (Keener 2005:123). This time common ground was established by his adaptation of an early creedal formula about Christ's resurrection and his autobiographical comment on it (15:3-11). This is followed by his careful responses to two questions he posed on behalf of those in Corinth who misunderstood the resurrection. The first, posed and responded to in 15:12-34, questions the "resurrection of the dead." The second, posed and responded to in 15:35-58, questions how dead bodies can be raised.

Beginning in 15:1, Paul announces that he needed to teach them once again the basic tenets of the gospel he taught them when he was first with them. This gospel knowledge they held in common with all believers, both then and with us today. It encompasses more than the crucifixion and resurrection of Christ, which Paul will highlight in 15:3-7, but it cannot be reduced smaller than this. He reminded them not only that he taught them this before but that they, for their part, accepted it. He applauded them for this and for sticking with it. He underscored that they impressed him by remaining firmly planted in the gospel generally. He did not question their commitment one iota. This should provide them good footing for the parts of the gospel he needed to reiterate and indeed to supplement in what follows regarding the resurrection of believers from the dead.

With 15:2, Paul reminds the Corinthians that the fundamental message of the gospel is salvation, deliverance from God's condemnation for sin. It is certainly true that the saving act of Christ on the cross occurred in the past. However, Paul speaks of the Corinthians' salvation in the present to bring out a subtle nuance that looks toward his later discussion. Salvation from the perspective of believers is a process that begins in the past when people confess the gospel and are baptized into Christ, continues in the present in development and maturity enabled by the Spirit, and culminates in a future resurrection to live with God for eternity. This future salvation is conditioned on remaining faithful to the gospel, both in word and in deed, and is jeopardized when people do not.

Paul fully expects the Corinthians to be true but suggests that failure to do so may imply that they signed on to the Christian faith without fully understanding what it encompasses. Perhaps such people became incorporated into the Christian community too hastily or without in-depth consideration of what the Christian community stands for. Such a situation would show up in the present lives of believers who do not manifest the principles of Christ, and thus could dangerously impact their future salvation. Paul will demonstrate in the verses that follow that he believes a comprehensive understanding of resurrection is one such crucial principle that should make a huge difference in a believer's life.

With 15:3, Paul prefaces his recitation of the resurrection creed by emphasizing its origin. Based on legitimate sources, he received it from others about three years after Jesus' crucifixion, most likely during his visit to Jerusalem immediately following his conversion (Acts 9:20-30). Using the traditional language of students passing on the teachings of their rabbinic tutors verbatim (Collins 1999:534), Paul recalls that one of the first and most important instructions he gave the Corinthians involved the carefully crafted traditional formula regarding the resurrection, which he was about to rehearse for them once again. Paul distinguished his receiving and passing on of this traditional instruction from his direct revelation of the gospel from Christ himself, which emphasized the radical inclusion of the Gentiles as underlined in Galatians 1:11-12, 15-16 (Bruce 1971:138; Garland 2003:684).

Although opinion varies, it is generally agreed that the creedal formula extends at least through the end of 15:5 (Collins 1999:831; Conzelmann 1975:251), and the key elements in its formulation are not original with Paul, particularly the words "buried," "raised," "third day," "the Twelve," "just as the Scriptures said," and the plural "sins" (Collins 1999:534; Horsley 1998:198). Notably absent is any mention of the cross (Collins 1999:530). By 15:6, although basic information about Christ's appearances is still traditional, Paul seems to adapt it freely in speaking of Christ's appearance to him (15:8). The creed may have functioned in various ways for the earliest Christian communities, as proclamation in preaching and worship or perhaps as confession for baptism and the Lord's Supper (Thiselton 2000:1188). In any case, Paul assumes the Corinthians, as all Christians, are fully invested in its meaning.

Four verbs form the structure of the formula (Talbert 1987:96), with two verbs being primary and two supportive. "Died" and "was raised" are primary faith affirmations, with "buried" buttressing "died" and "was seen" supporting "was raised" (Hays 1997:255). The repeated reference to Old Testament Scriptures grounds the two primary facts of Christ's death and resurrection in God's grand-scale plan to redeem the world. Although the creed begins with the purpose of Christ's death to replace the punishment we deserve because of our sins, the cursory nature of this point indicates that the focus is intended to dwell on Christ's resurrection in the lines that follow. Even the expression "was buried," confirming that Jesus really died, looks toward the resurrection in a way.

General reference to Scripture in the formula is fully intentional, indicating that

Christ fulfilled the whole plan of God (Garland 2003:685; Thiselton 2000:1195). That Christ's purpose can best be understood by studying Scripture is demonstrated by his own instruction to his disciples after his resurrection, as described in Luke 24:44-49. Yet, it is likely that passages like Psalms 16:8-11, 22:1-31, 110:1, and Isaiah 52:13–53:12 lie in the background of the early church's recognition of Christ's crucifixion and his ultimate resurrection. It is less likely that the details of Christ's "being buried" or his resurrection "on the third day" were thought to be fulfilling Scripture, but, if so, Hosea 6:2 and Jonah 1:17 could support the latter, and the language of Luke 24:46 likely reflects the same tradition. Affirmation of Christ's burial could also counter the earliest defamation of Christ's resurrection, reflected in Matthew 28:13, that his disciples stole the body (Thiselton 2000:1193).

Voicing the resurrection of Christ in the passive in 15:4 coincides with the vital theological perspective, reflected in all New Testament references to the resurrection, that God himself exerted his power to raise the lifeless body of Jesus (Barrett 1968:341; Dahl 1962:96-100; Garland 2003:686; Thiselton 2000:1193). Christ gave himself over to death for our sins and in doing so also relinquished all his divine power. He died helpless, at the mercy of God's judgment, until God breathed new life into his body and transformed it for eternity. Emphasis on the third day relates to the day the tomb was discovered empty (Bruce 1971:139; Garland 2003:686; Thiselton 2000:1196) based on computing both partial days of Friday and Sunday as whole days.

The listing of resurrection appearances begins in 15:5 with Peter, followed by "the Twelve." The listing is presented as chronological, yet it does exclude the very first appearance of the risen Jesus to Mary Magdalene and the other women depicted in the Gospels (Matt 28:1-10; Mark 16:1-8; Luke 24:1-8; John 20:1-2, 10-18). Peter, however, has esteemed standing as leader of the Twelve in the Gospels, and his mention separate from and preceding the reference to them reflects this.

Peter is referred to as Cephas here (as noted in the NLT footnote), which is what Paul usually calls him, not only in 1 Corinthians (1:12; 3:22; 9:5) but elsewhere (Gal 1:18; 2:9, 11, 14), and at this point Paul may have been injecting his own language into the formula. However, referring to the special disciples Jesus chose to follow him and who accompanied him throughout his three-year ministry as simply "the Twelve" is typical of the Gospels and Acts (see literal translations of Mark 14:43; John 6:67; Acts 6:2), but it is never used other than here by Paul. He, in fact, preferred to call them "the apostles."

The word is symbolic and not literal in this creedal formula. Strictly, Jesus never appeared to the original Twelve, since Judas was no longer one of them by the time of the appearances. In fact, Matthew 28:16 and Luke 24:33 refer to them as the eleven disciples after the exit of Judas. The resurrection appearance to the "Twelve" could be referring to his appearance to the eleven outdoors in Galilee, mentioned in Matthew and Luke, or to the second appearance to the ten plus Thomas (who was absent the first time) described by John 20:26-29 as occurring in a house probably in Jerusalem or Bethany. It could also refer to the general description in Acts 1:3 that "after his crucifixion, he appeared to the apostles from time to time, and he proved to them in many ways that he was actually alive."

From this point, Paul drops off the creedal structure he employed in 15:3b-5 (Conzelmann 1975:257) and simply attaches more instances of resurrection appearances to the verb "was seen," one in 15:6, two more in 15:7, and culminating in the appearance to Paul himself in 15:8. In this way he links the appearance to himself to the appearances to Peter and the Twelve (Fee 1987:730; Garland 2003:689), signifying that he saw exactly the same thing as they did, the risen Jesus. There is no certainty that any of these appearances Paul notes coincide with appearances recorded in the Gospels, and, therefore, Paul's publication of them very likely preserves tradition independent of the Gospels, but tradition he assumes the Corinthians already knew (Barrett 1968:342; Collins 1999:536; Fee 1987:730).

Interpreters attempt to connect Jesus' appearance to "500 of his followers at one time" to the gathering of the Twelve and other disciples immediately prior to his ascension, noted in Matthew 28:16-20, possibly paralleled in Acts 1:6-11 (Robertson and Plummer 1911:337) or with Pentecost (Lüdemann and Özen 1995:94-102), but neither of these make a compelling case. So, the exact historical occasion of this appearance to 500 is best understood as unknown. The emphasis that this very large group witnessed Jesus alive assures skeptics that Jesus' resurrection was no hoax perpetuated by a few individuals or the Twelve. Noting that some of the 500 had died since seeing the risen Jesus emphasizes that most were still alive at the time Paul wrote 1 Corinthians (AD 56) and that they could recount the event if asked.

The "James" listed by Paul in 15:7 is James the brother of Jesus, who is mentioned by name in Matthew 13:55 along with Jesus' other brothers and his sisters as a group. Although one might expect this to be James, the brother of John, who was in Jesus' innermost circle of disciples (Mark 9:2; 13:3; 14:33), that James was the first of the Twelve to be martyred (Acts 12:2) and he would be included among the Twelve mentioned earlier. Jesus' brother, who was not one of the Twelve, in fact a vocal skeptic along with the rest of his brothers according to John 7:3-5, would likely have required a personal appearance of the risen Lord as described here in order to believe. That James rose to be one of the pillars of the Christian movement (Gal 2:9) along with Peter, plus the leader of the Jerusalem church, probably before Paul's conversion (given that Peter directs that a report be made to James regarding his miraculous escape from prison—Acts 12:17), and even authored the Letter of James in the New Testament (Jas 1:1) solidifies him as the one referred to here. Paul also calls him an apostle in Galatians 1:19, and Acts 1:14 mentions Jesus' brothers, which surely included James, with the Twelve in Jerusalem following Jesus' ascension and previous to Pentecost, implying they were among the first believers.

Paul's reference to "all the apostles" might be confusing if one thinks the Twelve are the only apostles. In fact, though, Paul understands the word "apostles" to be wider than the Twelve (Collins 1999:537; Hays 1997:257), including at least James and himself, but he also refers to Andronicus and Junia, a husband and wife, as "apostles" in Romans 16:7. Acts 1:26 also refers to the replacement of Judas with Matthias, but in the process of choosing Matthias the principle is voiced that anyone who had been with Jesus and witnessed the resurrection could have been qualified (Acts 1:21-22). This assumes a substantial pool of individuals with potential in serving Christ in special ways, as Paul did, well beyond those specifically designated as official apostles. Acts 14:14 also calls Barnabas an apostle.

With 15:8, Paul arrives where he has been aiming all along: Christ's appearance to him on the Damascus road, recounted in Acts 9:1-19 and also by Paul in Galatians 1:13-17. Last on the list, Paul was apparently also literally the last to see Christ, with Christ appearing to him not only after his resurrection but even after his ascension, at least three years later than all the other appearances, which occurred during the 40 days between his resurrection and ascension. Paul called special attention to his tardiness by describing himself shockingly as an aborted fetus or one who had arrived prematurely, possibly dead. By this he probably meant that his life was heading the exact opposite direction from where God would place him (like a latter-day Jonah). From his life of violence against Christ and his church, to which he refers in 15:9, Christ grabbed him and jerked him through the Christian birth canal to arrive full-grown not only as a believer in Christ but one who was called to serve Christ as an apostle, so as to bring the gospel to the Gentiles. Indeed, he was late compared to Peter, James, and many others, but he caught up almost instantly. Because of this, no one was more aware of God's grace in the name of Jesus Christ (Thiselton 2000:1210) or more suited to develop its fullest implications for both Jews and Gentiles, indeed, for all people for all time in the form of his New Testament epistles.

In 15:9, Paul continues to expand on his feelings of unworthiness to be an apostle, rather surprisingly characterizing himself as "the least of all the apostles." Here, he references the raft of people he has just listed as eyewitnesses of the risen Jesus, not just the big two names of Peter and James. Paul would never have spoken of himself this way in Galatians, where he defends his apostolic status to the hilt because it was under attack, nor even later in 2 Corinthians, where some Corinthians seemed to find him an embarrassment, too weak to be a real apostle. He willingly used the term here because he was confident that his apostolic status was not in question. He did feel like the least apostle because he genuinely felt the most undeserving of that role because of the atrocities he committed against the church. No other apostle persecuted the church, precipitated the execution of Christians for blasphemy, ransacked their homes, and torturously dragged them back to Jerusalem in chains for sentencing (Acts 9:1-9; 22:3-11; 26:9-18; 1 Tim 1:13). His past haunted him even then.

In contrast to his former life, when he was filled with rage against the church, Paul depicts his life now as one filled with God's grace (15:10). Paul was not thinking so much of the grace of salvation as he was of the grace of his apostolic calling to share the Good News of salvation (Fee 1987:735). Though it might sound like bragging, he considered it his humble joy to know that God had accomplished a great deal through him (M. Mitchell 1993:285). Paul had brought the gospel to countless Jews and Gentiles and had established churches in cities throughout Asia Minor, Macedonia, and Greece, not the least of which was Corinth itself. The Corinthians were firsthand witnesses and fortunate beneficiaries of God's considerable investment in his reclamation project of Paul. Having once worked as vehemently against God's project as a person possibly could, through strength only God could provide, he redoubled his effort to advance the gospel of Christ to the world. Thus, unlike any other apostle, he had to do more to even equal their own efforts.

With 15:10, Paul states the point of his argument in 15:3-10—namely, not only was he an apostle of equal status to any other apostle, since he had seen the risen Christ, but he was an apostle who conveyed the very same message of the gospel that includes the oral traditions of the death and resurrection of Christ voiced in the creedal statements he just transcribed. The Corinthians themselves knew this to be true, but they knew because he gave these traditions to them when he came to Corinth to establish their church—and they believed them. Establishing that the Corinthians already embraced this apostolic teaching, particularly on the resurrection of Christ, was essential in order for Paul to move on to deal with the question he will posit in 15:12 and which will occupy his thoughts through 15:34.

◆   ## 2. No resurrection poses dire ramifications (15:12-19)

¹²But tell me this—since we preach that Christ rose from the dead, why are some of you saying there will be no resurrection of the dead? ¹³For if there is no resurrection of the dead, then Christ has not been raised either. ¹⁴And if Christ has not been raised, then all our preaching is useless, and your faith is useless. ¹⁵And we apostles would all be lying about God—for we have said that God raised Christ from the grave. But that can't be true if there is no resurrection of the dead. ¹⁶And if there is no resurrection of the dead, then Christ has not been raised. ¹⁷And if Christ has not been raised, then your faith is useless and you are still guilty of your sins. ¹⁸In that case, all who have died believing in Christ are lost! ¹⁹And if our hope in Christ is only for this life, we are more to be pitied than anyone in the world.

NOTES

15:12 *resurrection.* Gr., *anastasis* [TG386, ZG414]. The first of only four uses of this word in 1 Corinthians, all of which occur in this immediate context (15:13, 21, 42), it could refer to the common daily occurrence of simply waking up from sleep or standing up after sitting. Within Christianity, it refers to believers being brought into an afterlife following bodily death. Other than the Sadducees, most Jews of Paul's day, influenced by the teaching of the Pharisees, believed in the future resurrection of the body (Dan 12:2) that would take place on the Last Day. Paul's views expressed in 1 Corinthians 15 would run counter to many Jewish teachers of his day, who believed bodies would be raised in exactly the same form as they were buried, including any physical deformities (Keener 1993:487-488).

dead. Gr., *nekrōn* [TG3498A, ZG3738]. The first of 13 uses of this word in this chapter, this word in the singular refers to a dead body or corpse. In the plural, it can refer to multiple people who have died or to the realm of the dead where individuals who have died reside. This place is generally viewed neutrally, not necessarily indicating a place of punishment or reward.

15:14 *faith is useless.* Gr., *kenē* [TG2756, ZG3031]. This is the same Greek word translated "without results" in 15:10.

15:15 *lying.* Gr., *pseudomartures* [TG5575, ZG6020]. Used elsewhere only in Matt 26:60 during Jesus' trial before the Sanhedrin, this word technically refers to lying under oath in court or knowingly providing perjured testimony, a very serious offense named in the Ten Commandments (Deut 5:20).

COMMENTARY

With 15:12, Paul raises a question that bothered him so much he will spend the next 22 verses responding to its adverse implications for the gospel. His question juxtaposes the traditional gospel teaching of the apostles concerning the resurrection—exemplified by the creed rehearsed and expanded in 15:3-8 that he taught when he was among them—with the position held by "some" of the Corinthians. He quotes their position as being "there will be no resurrection of the dead."

Paul seems amazed that anyone, much less a group, could consider such a statement at all compatible with the gospel traditions they professed, which includes belief in the resurrection of Jesus Christ from the dead. The number of Corinthians who held these contradictory beliefs is unknown. Obviously, it was enough for Paul to believe it needed to be addressed. But even if it was only one influential person, Paul would still probably want to nip this in the bud because of its dire consequences for the truth of the gospel. Since he did not characterize those who didn't believe the resurrection of the dead in any negative way, he seems to consider their position more naive than sinister, with little doubt that his addressing the matter thoroughly will clear things up.

A few interpreters think these misinformed believers flat out denied that Christians will be raised from the dead (Bultmann 1951:169; Lambrecht 2000:143-145; 2001:35; Schmithals 1971:156). Some have suggested that these Corinthians believed the resurrection had somehow already occurred, which is like the opinion of those addressed in 2 Thessalonians 2:1-4 and 2 Timothy 2:16-18, and probably involved a form of super spirituality in the Christian life now (Bruce 1971:144; Talbert 1987:98). Usually called "realized eschatology," this view involves some unproven ways of interpreting other passages in 1 Corinthians, principally 4:8, 6:2-4, 9:24, and 10:1-13, that lead up to understanding the statement here in that way (Thiselton 1977–1978:510-526). Paul, then, misunderstood their position as a denial of the resurrection, and his arguments that follow were thus misaligned to the real problem. But it must be observed that Paul nowhere in 1 Corinthians states that anyone in Corinth or elsewhere advocated that the resurrection had already taken place (Hays 1997:259; D. Martin 1995:105).

The more convincing suggestion is that Paul does not explicitly voice the errant position of these people in Corinth until he articulates his second question in 15:35, representing them as questioning the means and mode of a bodily resurrection of believers (Dunn 2002:9; D. Martin 1995:106). Thus, here in 15:12, Paul begins with the general tenet of their queries, which he thought was a question of how a corporeal body, decomposed in the ground, tomb, or burial box, can be reconstituted for heaven—and for that matter, why anyone would think this was a necessary or good idea (Collins 1999:541; Garland 2003:699; Hays 1997:259; Horsley 1998:202; Thiselton 2000:1216).

Such a position resonated perfectly well with the vast majority of those in the Greco-Roman world. For them, any form of life after death was continued life of a person's soul, which thankfully had been freed from the drudgery and harmful effects of being encased in a fleshly body (Keener 2005:122; D. Martin 1995:108-117). Flesh was carnal and damaging to people, needing to be controlled in this earthly life in order for the purity of the soul to flourish. Salvation was deliverance from the bondage of this body right now. A person holding this position could very happily profess the resurrection of Christ (even in bodily form) while denying a like resurrection for believers.

So Paul begins by taking on the larger question of belief in the resurrection of the dead before taking on the real, specific problem of bodily resurrection. If he could get them to acknowledge that denial of resurrection is incompatible with belief in the resurrection of Christ, this would get them more than halfway to accepting his more narrow point about a bodily resurrection.

He proceeds, beginning in 15:13-19, to unpack the downward theological spiral that denying the resurrection of the dead creates for a believer. He does this in two sets of logically interconnected conditional sentences, one focusing on the apostles (15:13-15) and a second focusing on believers (15:16-19). In the first conditional set, he indicates that if one denies that the dead are raised, that person also denies that Jesus Christ has been raised—the bedrock of Christian faith, which Paul had just rehearsed as the incontrovertible traditional eyewitness testimony. Second, to deny the resurrection of Christ empties the apostolic teaching of its content and its purpose. What are people being converted to without Christ's resurrection? The faith Christians profess also becomes emptied. Third, invalidating the message of apostolic preaching puts the character and credibility of the apostles into question because they have pronounced repeatedly, as a matter of public record, that they personally saw and touched the risen body of Christ, watched him eat, and viewed that body ascend into heaven.

At 15:16, Paul resets his original premise in order to work through the downward spiral of logic in terms of its impact on the lives of believers. This follows with stating three logical consequences, again in terms of conditions.

In the first, in 15:17, Paul picks up on an undeveloped point made in 15:14, that denial of Christ's resurrection makes the faith of believers meaningless, but he adds to this a new consequence: Denial of Christ's resurrection means that believers remain in the clutches of God's condemnation because of sin. Though atonement for sin is usually developed by Paul in relation to the cross (Rom 3:23-25; 4:24-25; Gal 3:13), here, in effect, he is saying that any benefits accrued to humanity by Christ's death are negated without his resurrection from the dead. He cannot conquer sin for us without also conquering death (Rom 5:12-21; 6:22-23), a point Paul will celebrate later in this chapter (15:54-56).

Second, in 15:18, retention of sin now unatoned means that all those Christians who have died believing they were redeemed by Christ have in fact died to stand condemned by God's judgment for their sin. Most pointedly, this includes loved ones of the Corinthians. Third, and finally, since our buried loved ones have died with misplaced hope, then we must come to the realization that we have no hope beyond the grave either (15:19). Christian principles of living, then, are really just smart moral guidelines that will make our lives better now and help us succeed. If we adhere to the Christian faith, this makes us the biggest suckers in human history. To sacrifice and suffer to live a life pleasing to Christ for merely earthly reward—which may or may not come—validates all human mockery of believers who attempt to uphold the Christian way of life with dignity.

◆   ## 3. Christ's resurrection will make all things subject to him
        ## (15:20-28)

²⁰But in fact, Christ has been raised from the dead. He is the first of a great harvest of all who have died.

²¹So you see, just as death came into the world through a man, now the resurrection from the dead has begun through another man. ²²Just as everyone dies because we all belong to Adam, everyone who belongs to Christ will be given new life. ²³But there is an order to this resurrection: Christ was raised as the first of the harvest; then all who belong to Christ will be raised when he comes back.

²⁴After that the end will come, when he will turn the Kingdom over to God the Father, having destroyed every ruler and authority and power. ²⁵For Christ must reign until he humbles all his enemies beneath his feet. ²⁶And the last enemy to be destroyed is death. ²⁷For the Scriptures say, "God has put all things under his authority."* (Of course, when it says "all things are under his authority," that does not include God himself, who gave Christ his authority.) ²⁸Then, when all things are under his authority, the Son will put himself under God's authority, so that God, who gave his Son authority over all things, will be utterly supreme over everything everywhere.

15:27 Ps 8:6.

NOTES

15:20 *first of a great harvest.* Gr., *aparchē* [TG536, ZG569]. Just one word in Greek, lit., "firstfruits." It refers to the first sheaf of the first grain of the harvest, which Jews were told to bring to God in the temple on the 16th day of Nisan (Lev 23:10-11). In principle it was also applied to all crops (Exod 23:16) and other offerings (Exod 25:2-3). It was offered to God in thanks and as a harbinger and representative for the whole (Garland 2003:705-706; Holleman 1996:49-57; Thiselton 2000:1223-1224). It also has implications of not only being the first but the best of the whole (Collins 1999:548). Elsewhere Paul uses "firstfruits" to refer to (1) the Holy Spirit (Rom 8:23), (2) Gentile Christians as precursors to a mass of Jews converting to Christianity before Christ returns (Rom 11:13-16), (3) Epenetus, the first individual to become a Christian in Asia (Rom 16:5), and (4) to the household of Stephanas as the first Christian converts in Corinth (16:15).

15:23 *order.* Gr., *tagmati* [TG5001, ZG5413]. This word (used only here in the NT) refers to a body of soldiers lined up in their proper rank; Paul applied it here to God's providential sequencing of the resurrection events. The warfare texture remains in the context as the various enemies, including death, are defeated (A. Johnson 1996:462).

comes back. In Greek this is a noun (*parousia* [TG3952, ZG4242]) that means "coming." It is employed regularly by Paul (1 Thess 2:19; 3:13; 4:15; 5:23; 2 Thess 2:1, 8) and throughout the NT (Matt 24:27-39; Jas 5:7-8; 2 Pet 1:16; 3:4, 12; 1 John 2:28), as here, to refer to the specific occasion of Christ's return as the central, awaited eschatological event when God will draw this era to a close.

15:24 *the end will come.* Gr., *to telos* [TG5056A, ZG5465]. This word marks the completion or fulfillment of a task or goal. In the NT, it often is employed in a technical, eschatological sense (Matt 10:22; Mark 13:7; Heb 6:11; 1 Pet 4:7) as it is here. It supplants in the NT what rabbinic literature continually refers to as "the end of the age." In this passage, the Greek includes no verb, simply reading, "Then, the end." Following the sequencing of resurrection stages immediately above in 15:23, this led some older interpreters to conjecture that the "end" refers to a third stage of those resurrected, "the rest" who remain after believers have been resurrected (Lietzmann 1949:80-81; Weiss 1910:358). Following this view, the implication would be that this passage endorses a general resurrection of all humanity as the last stage of resurrection events, and perhaps then even to a sense of universal salvation. The fact that the word "end" (*telos*) cannot be found ever to have the sense of "the rest" militates against this interpretation (Barrett 1968:355; Collins 1999:593; Conzelmann 1975:271; Garland 2003:709). Rather, what this refers to is the completion of God's entire plan to save those who believe in Jesus Christ.

Kingdom. See notes on 4:20 and 6:9.

having destroyed. Gr., *katargēsē* [TG2673, ZG2934]. See notes on 2:6 and 6:13. A detailed word study by Dahl (1962:117-119) emphasizes that this word refers to rendering something inoperative, which in some form continues to exist. This has persuaded some interpreters (Garland 2003:709) to see that sense here. However, most contend that here and in 15:26, both death and the ruling powers are annihilated by Christ and cease to exist thereafter (Collins 1999:554; Conzelmann 1975:271; Soards 1999:336; Thiselton 2000:1231), thereby bringing this era to a close.

15:25 Christ must reign. Lit., "It is necessary for him to reign." Despite some who believe that "God," the authority in the original Psalm (Ps 8:6), should be retained, an option left open by the NIV's and ESV's "he" (Barrett 1968:358), Paul's third-person singular pronoun must refer to "Christ," as translated in the NLT (Fee 1987:755; Garland 2003:711; Oster 1995:369; Thiselton 2000:1234).

15:27 put . . . under his authority. Lit., "subjected . . . under his feet," repeating the prepositional phrase at the end of 15:24 but adding the verb "subjected" (*hupotassō* [TG5293, ZG5718]), which also appears in the quotation from Ps 8:6 [7]. From here on, Paul continues to use only the verb "subjected" (dropping the prepositional phrase), which the NLT renders "are under," "put," or "gave . . . authority" in the five uses that follow in 15:27-28. (See note on 14:32.)

15:28 the Son. Gr., *ho huios* [TG5207, ZG5626]. This is the only unmodified use of the word "son" with a definite article. Paul does refer to Christ as Son but usually as "his Son" (Rom 1:3, 9), "the Son of God" (Rom 1:4), or even as "his Son, Jesus Christ our Lord," as in the only other use of the word in 1 Corinthians (1:9). The concept of Jesus' sonship is the most common NT way to emphasize Christ's divine nature while also specifying his incarnational role to perform his voluntary work on behalf of God's providential strategy to save humanity. This subordination of the Son to the Father, after heavy debate in the third through fifth centuries, was finally concluded to be temporary and voluntary but not permanent (Thiselton 2000:1238).

COMMENTARY

Having reasoned that a premise of no resurrection leads to dishonoring the apostles and making the lives of believers pitiable (15:12-19), Paul offers the counter premise for analysis beginning in 15:20-29. What if Christ did rise from the dead? What value would there be in that?

Paul begins immediately in 15:20 to state the most important result of Christ's resurrection: the hope it offers those who have died. Those believers who have died, mentioned in 15:18 as abandoned without Christ's resurrection, now have the hope of being raised as well. The event of Christ's resurrection is not confined to an isolated historical moment. It is the harbinger of a mass, collective resurrection of all believers who have died. He was first, but he will be followed by many. Paul draws on the customary Jewish practice pertaining to firstfruits, which is the giving of the first ripened sheaf of grain to God as an offering. Giving him the first and the best foreshadowed a bountiful harvest; so also with the resurrection of Christ and those who will follow him.

In 15:21-22, Paul explains how Christ's resurrection can have this implication. Not unlike his more elaborate argumentation in Romans 5:12-21, Paul pictures the first created man, Adam, and Christ to be the head of two races of people. Thus, each person generated from them is, in a fashion, within their gene pool from the beginning and inherits their key traits (Bruce 1971:146; Thiselton 2000:1225). Thus, for Paul, when Adam sinned, all the human race sinned within him and inherited the death penalty for sin that he received. However, when Jesus Christ was raised from the dead, all of the Christian race was raised with him to begin a new life. They were also given an inheritance of eternal life, which includes a ticket for resurrection after death. Being in Christ does not remove them from being in Adam and inheriting his death penalty for sin. It does, however, reverse the consequences of being in him because in Christ they are guaranteed nullification of death's permanence through resurrection.

In 15:23, Paul first thinks of ordered military ranks to explain how resurrection works. There are two waves, first the captain leading the charge, followed by his troops. The captain, in this case Jesus Christ, has already charged, and the rest are just behind him, heading in the same direction toward the enemy in full confidence that they will be victorious because just ahead they have seen him break through the enemy line. This enemy will be identified in 15:26 as death, and his enemy troops in 15:24 as "every ruler and authority and power."

Paul also repeats the image of firstfruits from 15:20. Christ is the first harvested offering to God, guaranteeing the rest to come. At this point Paul identifies when the rest will come, when the troops will break the enemy line. He says this will happen at Christ's coming, meaning his return from heaven after his resurrection, having conquered death. He also stresses that the second wave of resurrection will occur only to those who are under his ownership. They must belong to him in order for him to take them back with him. Those outside of Christ, who do not believe in him, are not contemplated at all here (Barrett 1968:355; Garland 2003:709; Hays 1997:264). Presumably, they have no promise of resurrection, no promise of life beyond death, and thus no hope in this life, either. Elsewhere, Paul speaks of the resurrection of believers in two waves: those who have already died and those who are alive at Christ's coming (1 Thess 4:16-17).

In 15:24, Paul announces that after this mass resurrection of believers, the end of all things as we know them will come. God will have completed his massive plan to save fallen humanity, a plan conceived before the beginning and unfolding through Abraham, Moses, David, Isaiah, John the Baptist, Jesus Christ, the apostles, and the church. In a ceremony of Christ's willing service to the Father in coming to earth as a man and completing his mission through the cross, this resurrected, victorious king will present his realm to God himself (Lambrecht 1982:511), like a conquering hero presenting his prize to his Lord. This king will have conquered all other kings, all other rivals to power that have emerged throughout the course of human history, including the imperial power of mighty Rome (Horsley 1998:205; Witherington 1995:305).

As elsewhere in Paul's writings (Rom 8:38; Eph 1:21; 3:10; Col 1:16), these powers include not only those human in this earthly part of his realm but those spiritual, supernatural, and demonic forces who have opposed God's gracious plan (Conzelmann 1975:272; Forbes 2001:68-69; Garland 2003:708; Hays 1997:265). These authorities were the true power behind all tyrants and rulers who erected military and social structures to oppress the helpless (Thiselton 2000:1232). All of these in heaven and on earth are pictured as being pinned facedown to the ground by Christ's boot heel. Having mocked God in their blasphemous lust for power and their self-aggrandizement, they will be humiliated before God by Christ. As Proverbs 3:34 says, "The LORD mocks the mockers but is gracious to the humble."

Some contend that 15:24-25 implies a period in which Christ reigns over a temporary messianic kingdom on earth, a period between the general resurrection of believers and the humiliation of every rival power under his rule (Kreitzer 1987:142-145). However, this importation of a particular theological interpretation from Revelation 20:4-6 is unwarranted and unsustained by Paul's language (Barrett 1968:357; Collins 1999:552; Garland 2003:710). His reign currently is from heaven. His destruction of all opposition proceeds from there (Lewis 1998:55) until the resurrection of believers. Then he will crush all rivals finally and completely before presenting his kingdom to God.

Paul's touchstone verse to warrant his belief in Christ's victorious assault on all God's enemies is Psalm 110:1, to which he connects when he says, "He humbles all his enemies beneath his feet" (15:25). Although the verse originally was voiced as God speaking to David in the second-person singular ("your feet"), Christ dramatically applied this verse to himself as God's rightful Son (as seen in the Gospels: Matt 22:44; Mark 12:36; Luke 20:42-43). It fortified Peter's Pentecost sermon, as conveyed in Acts 2:34-35, and also anchors Hebrews 1:13. Paul's dependence on it here stands in solid company in considering this passage the bedrock for developing an authoritative understanding of Christ's work in relationship to the Father.

In 15:26, Paul highlights death as the final foe to be vanquished by Christ. Though personified here, this foe is not like the other foes who bring death by their wars and oppression. This is the penultimate evil result of all sin. This enemy is within the human encampment, brought in by the treachery of Adam when he sinned against God. This is a foe no human might nor human goodness can eradicate. Christ weakened the power of sin over believers when he was raised. He provided hope for the release of death's grip over humanity. But in his final, mighty act, he will eliminate death. He can do this because he already defeated death in the personal battle that resulted in his resurrection. Now, he will administer the crushing, fatal blow. Death itself will be dead.

Paul justifies this understanding of Christ striking down death as his destined resurrection act by citing Psalm 8:6. Originally a psalm addressed to God to celebrate the awesome responsibility he gave his human creation over the other aspects of his creation, it employs the term "son of man" to refer to humanity (Ps 8:4, NLT mg). The author of Hebrews (Heb 2:6-8) also picks up this designation as a messianic reference to Christ, no doubt because Christ favors the term Son of Man as his own self-reference as seen in the Gospels (Mark 10:33). Thus, God's subjection of all things to Christ is established in Psalm 8:6 when it says God has put "all things under their [lit., his] authority," even though "their" originally referred to humanity. Since both Psalm 8:6 (in literal translation) and Psalm 110:1 share the phrase "under his/your feet," Paul believed they can be interpreted in tandem. Thus, the "all things" from Psalm 8:6 appears in Paul's rendering of Psalm 110:1 in 15:25 as "all" enemies, though "all" does not literally appear in 110:1.

In the latter part of 15:27 Paul himself clarifies that "all things" does not include God and that the authority Christ has over all things comes from God himself. By implication, though, this means that because of his resurrection, Christ has authority over everything in the universe, except God. This, then, includes all other authorities like human rulers or demonic influences, and of course, the all-mystical superpower of death. But it also means he has authority over all life on this planet, all laws that govern this planet, the sun, the moon, the stars, and beyond. From this perspective, it is not at all difficult to picture Christ as the primary operative, even now, of all the forces that sustain life—as we know it and even beyond what we know (Eph 1:19-23; Col 1:15-20).

The last stage of this cosmic supremacy of Christ Paul announces in 15:28. Having subjected everything to himself, Christ in turn presents himself—and all things—to God. He has been working for God all along. In the divine plan, the grace is God's; the mission, the enacting of God's grace, the means of salvation, the humbling of all authorities, and the banishment of death come from Christ. Yet, in kind with his humility to enter into the human race to complete all this (as Paul articulates in Phil 2:6-11), Christ's final act is done with utter humility. All, including himself, is given over to God. The ultimate honor for victory in this cosmic drama belongs to God alone. Closure comes when God reigns gloriously over all. This picture of submission is with respect to Christ completing his messianic mission but does not pertain to his eternal relationship to God the Father, which is equal and complete (A. F. Johnson 2004:294-295).

◆   ### 4. Disbelief in the resurrection is an affront to God (15:29-34)

29 If the dead will not be raised, what point is there in people being baptized for those who are dead? Why do it unless the dead will someday rise again?

30 And why should we ourselves risk our lives hour by hour? 31 For I swear, dear brothers and sisters, that I face death daily. This is as certain as my pride in what Christ Jesus our Lord has done in you. 32 And what value was there in fighting wild beasts—those people of Ephesus*—if there will be no resurrection from the dead? And if there is no resurrection, "Let's feast and drink, for tomorrow we die!"* 33 Don't be fooled by those who say such things, for "bad company corrupts good character." 34 Think carefully about what is right, and stop sinning. For to your shame I say that some of you don't know God at all.

15:32a Greek fighting wild beasts in Ephesus.   15:32b Isa 22:13.

NOTES

15:29 *baptized for those who are dead.* What exactly Paul was referring to is one of the biggest puzzles of the NT. Most interpreters adopt some form of vicarious baptism as the solution, but sometimes with very creative twists. The earlier proposals of proxy baptism based on mystery religions (Schmithals 1971:257) or Gnostic views incorporated into the early church (Weiss 1910:363) have largely been abandoned. Some, however, suggest Christians may have been baptized for those of faith in the OT who have died (Soards 1999:338), unbaptized Christians who have died (Wedderburn 1987:288; Witherington 1995:305), or deceased family members or friends (Horsley 1998:206). More recent efforts stress believers themselves being baptized but with a spiritual identification specifically connecting to a deceased Christian friend or family member they revere (Bruce 1971:149; Jeremias 1955–1956:155-156; Reaume 1995:475; Thiselton 2000:1248) or to an apostle they revere or who has baptized them, taking up the matter of those baptizing Corinthians being a source of division (J. White 1997:493-494). See Thiselton 2000:1242-1248 for a complete perspective. My own view, as explained in the commentary below, is that Paul refers to normal Christian baptism, though in an odd way that has misled many interpreters.

15:30 *we ourselves risk our lives.* Gr., *kinduneuō* [TG2793, ZG3073]. The only use in 1 Corinthians, it refers to venturing into dangerous situations.

15:31 *dear brothers and sisters.* Gr., *adelphoi* [TG80, ZG81]. The inclusion of this word as original is questionable (Garland 2003:724; Thiselton 2000:1249). Supported in ℵ and B but unsupported in 𝔓46, its addition is more easily explained as an accommodation to Pauline style than any attempt to explain why a copyist would have omitted it if original.

I face death daily. Gr., *kath' hēmeran apothnēskō* [TG599, ZG633] (I die daily). The verb is present tense, implying that not only does Paul face the possibility of death every day, as the NLT conveys (Thiselton 2000:1250), but that he also dies every day—some days a little, some days a lot—as he carries on his apostolic ministry (2 Cor 1:3-7; 4:8-10; 6:1-10; 11:23-29).

15:32 *fighting wild beasts.* Taken literally, this would refer to doing battle with wild animals as a form of criminal punishment as documented in Diodorus Siculus *Bibiotheca historica* 3.43.7. As a Roman citizen, it is unlikely that Paul would ever have received this type of sentence (Fee 1987:770; Thiselton 2000:1252). Thus, the reference is surely metaphorical. Besides, he speaks of it as something he has survived, which would not be the case if it were literal. The obvious referent of this phrase would seem to be the dangerous riot in the Ephesian amphitheater instigated by the craftsmen who manufactured silver statuettes of Artemis (Acts 19:28-41). However, Paul probably wrote 1 Corinthians the year previous to the riot, staying on at Ephesus a year longer than what he anticipated in 16:8, but leaving shortly after the riot (Acts 20:1). In that case, he may have in mind other, unrecorded events in Ephesus that led up to the riot.

15:33 *bad company corrupts good character.* This quote is from Menander's largely lost play called *Thais.* He was a prolific fourth-century BC Greek writer who produced over 100 comedic plays. His continued popularity is evidenced by over 900 one-line adages like this one that appear in many other classical Greek authors after him (Sandbach 1970:669). Because his sayings infiltrated Greek culture like Shakespeare's have in English cultures, it is entirely unnecessary for Paul to have read Menander in order to quote this well-worn saying (Barrett 1968:367; Garland 2003:722; Thiselton 2000:1254).

15:34 *shame.* Gr., *entropē* [TG1791, ZG1959]. Only used here and in 6:5 in all the NT, this word literally means to turn toward someone in an attitude of respect and honor. It can also, as here, refer to feelings of unworthiness in facing someone who is respected.

COMMENTARY

Having extolled the glorious, cosmic value of Christ's resurrection and its implications for the future of believers within God's salvation plan in 15:20-28, Paul had more to say against the skeptical view in 15:29-34. He repeats nearly verbatim the motto of the skeptics, "there will be no resurrection of the dead," both in 15:29 and later in 15:32 to make this connection, with two additional arguments against this position. In both cases he creates conditional reasoning with "if," but in 15:29 he also adds (lit.) "actually" (*holōs* [TG3654, ZG3914]) to indicate he is picking up the earlier statement. In the first argument, occupying only two statements in 15:29, he throws in their faces a treasured practice of the skeptics that contradicts their skepticism about resurrection. In the second argument, occupying 15:30-34, Paul reflects on his life of sacrifice for the Christian cause and its emptiness apart from the reality of the resurrection.

Paul raises two questions in 15:29 intended to force the skeptics to recognize their predicament. To be consistent with their skepticism about the resurrection, they must abandon this treasured practice of theirs. Paul hoped they would see that their practice assumes resurrection and thus they should embrace it. But what is the practice? This is one of the great unsolved mysteries of New Testament studies. The trail of discovery is littered with inadequate suggestions. None has commanded the field. Most think there is little hope of finding a fully satisfactory explanation (Fee 1987:765-767; Thiselton 2000:1242-1248), the latest even abandoning long-held belief that Paul wrote this passage (Walker 2007:84).

The first question contains all the information we have to go on. Paul says that people are being baptized for the dead. What is this practice? There are scores of suggestions, with small sub-views within many of them. Essentially, though, they boil down to two. The view that is far and away most popular, despite almost everyone who holds it hoping it isn't so (Hays 1997:267), is that at least these skeptics, or perhaps others in Corinth, were administering some kind of vicarious baptism, people being baptized for the salvation of other people. If this is the case, Paul was using their practice of something he could not possibly condone as evidence against their position for the sake of winning his argument (Blomberg 1994:305; Conzelmann 1975:275; Garland 2003:717; Horsley 1998:207; Soards 1999:337; Witherington 1995:305). We have seen that he did use their own commonsense practices against them on occasion, for instance, in the arguing for a head covering from the customary practice of women wearing their hair long (11:15). But in that scenario he seems to agree with the assumption rather than disagree with it, as one would expect him to here.

Although Paul's odd phrasing does lend itself to vicarious baptism, there is absolutely no evidence of any practice among New Testament Christians or in the ancient world remotely paralleling this (J. White 1997:489-490). Some Christians, following Marcion and others, seem to have practiced this later (Talbert 1987:99), and these were opposed by the church fathers (Epiphanius *Heresies* 28; Philaster *Heresies* 49; Tertullian *Against Marcion* 5.10), but it is most likely that they based their practice on this text, as the Mormons do today. Because of this, interpreters have experimented with various scenarios in which the Corinthians might have done this for some theologically rooted yet misguided reason (see notes on 15:29). Yet all of these are no more than guesses, speculations based on no more than Paul's language here. Not only do all these proposed forms of vicarious baptism contradict everything Paul conveys about baptism being for one's own salvation, but it makes absolutely no sense for the skeptics to have practiced any of them given their skepticism about resurrection (Campbell 1999:45).

This leads to the second suggestion, one that is as old as Chrysostom (*Homilies on 1 Corinthians* 40:2), but recently receiving renewed attention (Campbell 1999:50-51; Garland 2003:717-719; O'Neill 1980:310-311; Talbert 1987:99; Thompson 1964:647-659): namely, that Paul here is referring to normal, Christian baptism, the universal rite of entrance into salvation through faith in Jesus Christ. Under this view, Paul draws on the believers' identification with Christ's death and resurrection that takes place at baptism, something he lays out in Romans 6:1-14. In fact, Romans 6:4-5 explicitly says: "For we died and were buried with Christ by baptism. . . . Since we have been united with him in his death, we will also be raised to life as he was." This theme of unification fills chapter 15. Death through identification with Christ even underlies Paul's pronouncement about himself in 15:31, the next immediate context.

Yet if Paul means to refer to normal Christian baptism, why have interpreters continually been dissatisfied with this view over the centuries? The reason is that if Paul intended to refer to Christian baptism, he has done so very oddly. Literally, he refers to "those who are being baptized for the dead ones." Normally, he would talk about being baptized for sin, and it sounds like the dead ones and those baptized are separate people. However, they are probably references to the same individual. His clumsy insertion of "the dead ones" could just be Paul's attempt to insert irony into his argument that has in the end thrown interpreters onto a wild-goose chase to understand it.

He already used the word "dead ones" or "dead" seven times since 15:12 and will use it five more times through 15:52. Since the skeptics, and certainly their Greek and Roman neighbors, doubted that corpses can be resuscitated and thus did not believe in a resurrection of the dead, Paul wanted to insist that baptism of one's body makes no sense for someone who holds this view. Though the body of a person who has died is just a corpse in their view, in Paul's view it is the seed of a new body, as he will explain shortly in great elaboration in 15:35-58. Baptism evidences belief that the natural body, once dead, will be raised a supernatural body.

Thus, Paul assumed that all the Corinthians had been baptized, as he voiced in 1:13-17. This includes those whom he pinpoints now as having an unacceptable understanding of resurrection. Their own baptism is an irrevocable sign against their position that corpses cannot rise. Their corpses *will* rise whether they believe it or not. Because of their identification with Christ in baptism, their body will rise as he did. This view could be demonstrated by putting "the dead" in quotation marks, indicating this is the view of the skeptics, not Paul. They may think their baptism was not for "the dead," but it was. Because Christ's once-dead body rose and they have been baptized into Christ, their dead bodies will rise too.

At 15:30, Paul begins the formulation of a new tactic that focuses on his personal sacrifices on behalf of the gospel but will move toward a confrontational challenge to the Corinthian believers. Expanding on what he said in 15:10, 14, and 19, in essence he says the daily risks that were a continual drain on his body would be wasted if there is no resurrection of the dead, if his body—which is moving daily toward death—will not be raised. With rhetorical drama he asks why he should endanger himself with each passing hour.

With 15:31, he increases the dramatic impact by saying he dies daily, underscored by an oath. For Paul, this is not simply a matter of the potential danger he experiences. Rather, he views his body as slowly wearing down as he expends himself for his apostolic ministry. After giving an overview of his terrorized life in 2 Corinthians 4:8-9, he will say: "Through suffering, our bodies continue to share in the death of Jesus so that the life of Jesus may also be seen in our bodies" (2 Cor 4:10). He details the damage to his body over the course of his ministry in 2 Corinthians 11:21-29.

Yet, as he describes it in 15:31, his gradual descent into death is worth it when it results in people like the Corinthians accepting the gospel of Christ. Despite all the things he had criticized the Corinthians for, Paul was genuinely proud of how far they had come in their development. However, they themselves were the outcome of the resurrection, because if it were not true, Paul would not have expended himself to bring them the gospel.

In 15:32, he brings up a specific, current aspect of his torturous life. Picturing himself being torn to shreds by wild beasts—a common form of death for entertainment purposes in ancient urban arenas—Paul employed the image to picture problems he was having even as he wrote this letter to the Corinthians. Referring to the same situation in Ephesus where he currently resided (clarified by the NLT's addition of "those people"), in 16:9 he says "many oppose me." His suffering for the cause of Christ was not only physical but emotional and spiritual. It was a drain on all aspects of his life. If the resurrection were not true, Paul further enjoins, it would make his life a ridiculous waste. Why not live a life partying and drinking, pursuing no purpose, no hope, no afterlife, like the oracle of doom Isaiah 22:13 expresses, which was also a crude popular caricature of the Epicurean philosophy of Paul's day (Fee 1987:770; Thiselton 2000:1253)?

Paul shifts his perspective in 15:33 to address the Corinthians directly through the end of 15:34. He cajoles them to see that they would be ignorantly deceived if they were to follow such a life philosophy as the depressing one he just mentioned. To get through to them, he issues a warning in the words of a popular adage that originated in an old Greek play by Menander (see note on 15:33): "Bad company corrupts good character." The idea that the crowd people associate with will affect their own conduct is well-known to every parent of teens today. The effort parents make to steer their children away from friends of bad influence to friends of good influence demonstrates belief in the truth of this saying.

Why Paul cites Menander here is not easy to understand, however. Did he think that the Corinthians who were skeptical about the resurrection had been adversely influenced by pagan culture or pagan friends (Hays 1997:268; Thiselton 2000:1254)? Was he warning Corinthian believers to separate themselves from fellow believers who were skeptical about resurrection (Barrett 1968:367; D. Martin

1995:107)? The second idea is unlikely, given the tenor of the passage so far. The first is very possible, but perhaps more in the sense of putting the two philosophies together (Fee 1987:775). In other words, associating skepticism about resurrection with the Christian faith spoils the Christian faith. It is a bad influence.

Using a word that normally is used to tell someone to wake up from a drunken stupor (15:34), which plays off the image of drunkenness in 11:21 (Conzelmann 1975:279), Paul rhetorically shouts at the Corinthians to snap out of it (NLT, "Think carefully"). Those holding on to their skepticism about the resurrection were sinning, presumably because of the way this view misrepresents Christ. Paul even ups the ante to question their so-called knowledge of God. In truth, given the nature of God, who created everything and who raised Christ from the dead, how could anyone think that he cannot bring a corpse back to life in a form prepared for eternity? He will elaborate on this in what follows in 15:35-58.

◆   ### 5. The resurrection bodies of believers are spiritual (15:35-49)

³⁵But someone may ask, "How will the dead be raised? What kind of bodies will they have?" ³⁶What a foolish question! When you put a seed into the ground, it doesn't grow into a plant unless it dies first. ³⁷And what you put in the ground is not the plant that will grow, but only a bare seed of wheat or whatever you are planting. ³⁸Then God gives it the new body he wants it to have. A different plant grows from each kind of seed. ³⁹Similarly there are different kinds of flesh—one kind for humans, another for animals, another for birds, and another for fish.

⁴⁰There are also bodies in the heavens and bodies on the earth. The glory of the heavenly bodies is different from the glory of the earthly bodies. ⁴¹The sun has one kind of glory, while the moon and stars each have another kind. And even the stars differ from each other in their glory.

⁴²It is the same way with the resurrec-tion of the dead. Our earthly bodies are planted in the ground when we die, but they will be raised to live forever. ⁴³Our bodies are buried in brokenness, but they will be raised in glory. They are buried in weakness, but they will be raised in strength. ⁴⁴They are buried as natural human bodies, but they will be raised as spiritual bodies. For just as there are natural bodies, there are also spiritual bodies.

⁴⁵The Scriptures tell us, "The first man, Adam, became a living person."* But the last Adam—that is, Christ—is a life-giving Spirit. ⁴⁶What comes first is the natural body, then the spiritual body comes later. ⁴⁷Adam, the first man, was made from the dust of the earth, while Christ, the second man, came from heaven. ⁴⁸Earthly people are like the earthly man, and heavenly people are like the heavenly man. ⁴⁹Just as we are now like the earthly man, we will someday be like* the heavenly man.

15:45 Gen 2:7.   15:49 Some manuscripts read *let us be like.*

NOTES

15:35 bodies. Gr., *sōmati* [TG4983, ZG5393]. Used 46 times in 1 Corinthians alone, this word usually refers to the physical form in which humans exist, as seen even in multiple uses in chapter 12. But it can also refer to the form of other things, like the product of seeds (15:37). Paul expands on the variety of things that have "bodies" throughout chapter 15. For people, though, he does not want to limit their bodies to the physical. Dunn (1998:55-61; 2002:9) says Paul conceives of a body as a "medium of existence" conducive for, among other things, communication with others.

15:40 *bodies in the heavens and bodies on the earth.* Lit., "heavenly bodies and earthly bodies." The NLT highlights location, but the reference may also include nature, origin, or substance, as the NIV and ESV translations allow (Collins 1999:567; Thiselton 2000:1287).

glory. Gr., *doxa* [TG1391, ZG1518]. See note on 2:8.

15:43 *buried in brokenness.* Gr., *speiretai en atimia* [TG819, ZG871]. Lit., "sown in dishonor," as in NIV and ESV. The NLT focuses on the human corpse rather than living human bodies.

15:44 *natural.* Gr., *psuchikon* [TG5591, ZG6035]. See notes on 2:8 and 2:13-14.

spiritual bodies. Gr., *sōma pneumatikon* [TG4983/4152, ZG5393/4461]. See note on 2:13.

15:47 *dust.* Gr., *choïkos* [TG5517, ZG5954]. Only used by Paul in the NT, all four times in this context, Paul seems to have coined this adjective from the noun form used in the LXX translation of Gen 2:7 (Collins 1999:571; Thiselton 2000:1286). It means dust, dirt, or clay.

the second man. Gr., *ho deuteros anthropos* [TG444, ZG476]. Marcion changed *anthropos* to *kurios* [TG2962, ZG3261] (Lord) to accommodate his own peculiar theology (so also ℵ² A D¹ Y 075 1739ᵐᵍ 𝔐), and 𝔓46 adds *pneumatikos* [TG4152, ZG4461] (spiritual) to coincide with the double use of this word in 15:46. However, manuscript evidence for *anthropos* alone, consisting of ℵ* B C D* 0243 33 1739, is overwhelmingly convincing.

15:49 *we will someday be like.* Gr., *phoresomen kai tēn eikona* [TG5409/1504, ZG5841/1635]. Lit., to "wear the image"—the ESV rendering it "we shall also bear the image" and the NIV "so shall we bear the likeness." This future indicative of the verb, supported by B, fits the context of providing assurance, unlike the subjunctive (*phoresōmen*) found in 𝔓46 and ℵ, which could be the result of a scribal error.

COMMENTARY

Paul's thorough response to the general issue of resurrection was preliminary to his overall concern about the views of some of the Corinthians. Having demonstrated in 15:12-34 that belief in the resurrection is not only compatible with Christian teaching and preaching but in fact a necessary truth in relation to Christ's resurrection, with 15:35 he initiates his response to what appears to be the chief problem the Corinthian skeptics have with resurrection. He does this by posing two successive questions as if they were being shouted by an anonymous objector in a crowd. This could actually happen in the ancient world as traveling philosophers shared their wares from city to city in the marketplaces, but it was also a very common speech tactic called diatribe.

The two questions are intertwined, with the second being a more specific version of the first (Fee 1987:780; Hays 1997:270). In order to address how bodies can be raised, Paul must first convince the Corinthians that their natural bodies are not conducive to a non-earthly plane of existence; that is, Christian belief in resurrection does not mean resuscitation or recomposition of a decomposed corpse. The common assumption still held today among believers that resurrection means the recomposition of their dead, physical bodies (a view which causes some to prefer burial to cremation) is contrary to the laws of creation and God's way of doing things, as Paul will demonstrate in his following argument.

Paul will first answer the second question ("What kind of bodies will they have?"), from 15:35-49, before commenting on the larger question ("How will the dead be raised?") in 15:50-58. Since he was responding to an imaginary person, Paul felt free to start off in 15:36 with a rhetorical assault on the person's judgment, calling the person a fool. This is a rhetorical attention getter as much as anything else, but Paul believed the answer was available by analogy with nature and should not need to be spelled out. Death and resurrection are inherent to the world God created, as can be observed in the cycle of life for plants. Since the vast majority of the population were farmers of some sort, this cycle was well-known. Farmers place seeds in the ground that spring to new life. But the seeds must be planted, a symbol of death, perhaps intended to conjure up images of dead human bodies that are interred or entombed. At any rate, Paul calls the planting of the seed death. In truth, any seed is as good as dead without being planted, and its being planted is absolutely necessary for it to come alive out of the ground.

In 15:37, Paul calls the seed a "bare seed" because he wants to contrast it with "new body" in 15:38 (Thiselton 2000:1264). Literally, this is a "naked" (*gumnos* [TG1131, ZG1218]) seed, or seed that is unclothed because it has not taken on its living form yet. However, its form or "new body" will eventually emerge from the ground in all its glory, as Paul points out in 15:38.

In terms of horticulture, the seed and the plant are organically the same despite being different in form; there is no loss in this process, just transformation. Neither the seed nor any part of it has been lost, just dramatically changed (Dahl 1962:27). The continuity and discontinuity in this natural process of a seed's transformation to a plant will be crucial in Paul's larger argument in 15:42-49 (Harrisville 1955:69-79; Hays 1997:270; Thiselton 2000:1264). Also crucial is Paul's identification of how this new body is achieved (Horsley 1998:209). God is the author of this transformation from seed to death to new, resurrected body. True to the nature of God's own creativity, Paul notes in 15:38 that God has created all manner of seeds and that continuity between the seed and its body, the plant, is always maintained. The variety of seeds and plants—and we could also say of "individual" seeds and plants—never gets confused. Wheat seeds grow into wheat plants; each wheat seed becomes its own plant. Before making any application to people, however, Paul wanted to draw attention to the wide application of this principle in God's creation.

Skipping over how the seeds' bodies are formed, in 15:39 Paul observes the same principle in more of God's creation as listed in Genesis 1. Naming them in the reverse order of their creation, he lists humans, then animals, birds, and fish. The common link between them is that their bodies are composed of "flesh." The point is that God has enabled them naturally to reproduce according to their own kind to have bodies that are perfectly suited to their function and place in God's world. There is no confusion between species any more than there is between varieties of plants. It's all natural, and it is under God's control.

That people, animals, birds, fish, and plants have bodies conducive to their nature and setting leads Paul to contemplate in 15:40-41 yet a third grouping of "bodies" God has created, far more distinctive in their form and substance than living creatures are from plants (Robertson and Plummer 1911:371). These he created even before the others, as recounted in Genesis 1: the sun, moon, and stars. Even though their *extra*terrestrial "bodies" are completely different from terrestrial bodies on earth of either animals or plants, they have their own "glory" in that the manifestation of their substance perfectly befits their "kind," function, and purpose in God's universe.

Aristotle speculated that their substance was a fifth element called "ether," beyond the common four of earth, air, fire, and water (D. Martin 1995:119; Padgett 2002:158). Regardless, Paul observed from their varying brilliance that each of these lights in the sky has its own "body," distinct from the others, just as God has determined. In this sense, the "glory" of the sun, moon, and stars is their "bodies," akin to the "flesh" of animals and the "bodies" of living plants.

Thus, there are bodies fit for heaven and bodies fit for earth. Up to this point Paul's rhetorical debating partner and the Corinthian skeptics would agree. In fact, this would be *their* point. Such bodies are *so* different that a terrestrial body could never become an extraterrestrial, or celestial body, hence their lack of enthusiasm for resurrection if it means the terrestrial body of any human is to become an extra-terrestrial body (Asher 2001:103). They are of such different kinds in God's creation that the gap cannot be bridged, and would not be bridged, even by God. Yet Paul begs to differ, and he will explain his position in 15:42-44 before demonstrating its theological justification in 15:45-49.

In 15:42-44, Paul develops his seed-plant analogy from 15:36-37 now in relation to humans and resurrection. He makes the common practice of placing dead bodies in the ground (or in caves), truly naked in a physical sense like seeds, a metaphor for actually describing the nakedness of human beings *before* their death and burial, the point at which even the seeds were naked in 15:37. The planting of seeds, then, is a metaphor for human burial, and human burial then becomes a metaphor for human life. The word "sown" (*speirō* [TG4687, ZG5062]), translated by the NLT as "planted in the ground" in 15:42, and then "buried" the three times thereafter, holds a series of four contrasts together. It could refer to people being sown on the earth rather than in the earth, as many interpreters advocate (Asher 2001:102; Garland 2003:734; Hays 1997:271; Soards 1999:344). The point is that live human bodies bear the characteristics Paul names (15:42-43), in some ways more than dead ones do.

The first characteristic, lost in the NLT's rendering of 15:42, is often translated "corruptible" or "perishable," referring to the decaying process of a corpse; but this process of decay begins from the inception of life and becomes apparent before most people die. The second characteristic, translated "brokenness" by the NLT in 15:43, is usually translated "dishonor." This could apply to an essentially "naked" human corpse, but it applies equally to the shame and disrespect people experience many times over in their lives. The third characteristic, translated "weakness" by the NLT in 15:43 along with most translations, would apply in an absolute sense to a lifeless corpse, but would seem to be a more fitting characteristic of living human bodies with their vulnerabilities and limitations.

But Paul's characterization of the human body in these ways goes beyond even a living human body as such. Corruption, dishonor, and weakness apply to human beings in their essence with respect to their immorality and sin. Their sinful natures are incorporated into their bodies as Paul puts it in Romans 5. They are corrupt (Rom 8:21; Gal 6:8; Col 2:22), dishonorable (4:11-13; 2 Cor 6:8), and weak (2 Cor 4:16; 12:9-10) because of immorality and sin (Barrett 1968:373; Garland 2003:733-734).

Thus, it is not just the physicality of their terrestrial existence in life or in death that makes the gap to an extraterrestrial body uncrossable; it is also a nature through and through that is sinful. Paul, in fact, sees the gap as a gorge, even more impossible to cross than his debate partner believes.

With such an impossible expanse to overcome, Paul's characterization of the risen human seed seems even more magnified. Repeating the image four times as the positive mirror of a sown body, without using the word "body" until the fourth and last time, Paul describes a human body that reverses the three characteristics of the sown body. This raised body is no longer corrupt, dishonored, or weak, but rather imperishable (NLT, "to live forever"), glorified and powerful. This raises the question of how these human seeds could possibly transform into such awesome bodies fit for extraterrestrial life. The yet-unspoken implication is that God alone can do this because he is the one who fits all species for their purposes in his creation.

Yet Paul makes a fourth point in 15:44 about these dichotomous bodies that launches him into how the necessary eradication of human sinfulness is to be accomplished. He describes the sown bodies as "natural," using the adjective form of the word often translated as "soul" (*psuchikos* [TG5591, ZG6035]). Yet the raised bodies are "spiritual" (*pneumatikos* [TG4152, ZG4461]; perhaps better translated "supernatural" to highlight the reversal). Immediately, he observes that this positive opposite follows logically as the climax to the three previous opposites. However, he knew this was not sufficient to carry his point. So, in 15:45-49 he follows up to show how certain it must be that such supernatural bodies will come from natural ones.

Paul bases his proof on the theological dichotomy that exists between Adam, the first created human, and Christ, whom he terms as the last Adam. In doing this, he was developing the point he made earlier in 15:21-22 (developed extensively in Rom 5) that Christ's resurrection reverses Adam's sin in humanity so that it is possible for those in Christ to overcome death.

In 15:45, Paul first quotes Genesis 2:7 (from the Septuagint), which describes Adam as becoming a "living person" after God breathed into his nostrils the breath of life. The word "person" (*psuchē* [TG5590, ZG6034]) is the noun form of the word "natural" (*psuchikos* [TG5591, ZG6035]) in 15:44, which explains why Paul used that distinguishing terminology to begin with. This quotation about Adam is followed by Paul's poignant application to his argument that Christ as the last Adam is "a life-giving Spirit." This description of Christ is jolting. After depicting raised human bodies as supernatural or "spiritual," we expect Paul to say that Christ is spiritual or has a spiritual body. But instead—echoing God's breathing life into Adam—he says that Christ in effect can breathe his spirit into people in such a way that they are transformed from corpses (dead in their sin) to new, living beings, with new bodies to match (B. Schneider 1967:462). *These* bodies Paul calls "spiritual" in 15:44. All people, since all are descendant from Adam, have natural or "soulish" bodies. Only those in Christ will receive this "spiritual body" after Christ comes; so Paul says it "comes later."

In 15:47, Paul explains why this is so. Again relying on Genesis 2:7, Paul says that Adam was formed from earth, from its dust. Human bodies *are* terrestrial. However, Christ and only Christ can release the power to transform them because he is the only man who has come from heaven, the extraterrestrial place, beyond the stars. He brought with him in his person this extraterrestrial power to transform dead human bodies into resurrected spiritual bodies (Padgett 2002:161). Not only did he bring it with him, he now gives it away to those who believe the gospel that tells of his own resurrection from the grave to new life. When this happens—upon their death, burial, and resurrection in the form of confession of faith and baptism—they, too, become "heavenly," as 15:48 says. Those who do not receive Christ as life-giving Spirit will return to the earth untransformed.

So, what does Christ breathe into bodies now equipped for heavenly existence? Though he does not say directly, Paul must mean the Holy Spirit (Abernathy 2002:9; Dunn 1973:133-134, 141). Translations are divided about whether to capitalize "spirit," as the NLT has done. In effect, what Christ gives surely is the Holy Spirit, but in Paul's depiction in 15:45, it is Christ's Spirit which is capable of imparting life to dead men, like the famous Old Testament depiction of God's doing so in Ezekiel 37 (B. Schneider 1967:157-159).

The result of receiving Christ's breath is the imparting of the Holy Spirit and eventual transformation into the likeness of Christ. In 15:49, Paul says that "we" (meaning believers in Christ like Paul and the Corinthians), though currently bearing the likeness of Adam—meaning in our natural bodies dead in our sin—have the sure promise of becoming like Christ, meaning that our natural bodies will be transformed into supernatural, spiritual bodies perfect for residing in heaven with him. In making this climactic point, Paul deftly employs the word "image" (*eikōn* [TG1504, ZG1635]), drawing once again from Genesis, which says that Adam's descendants bore his image (Gen 5:3) and that humans were created in the "image" of God (Gen 1:27; Collins 1999:572). And thus, in Christ, we realize the complete potential of our original creation by God.

◆   6. The resurrection of believers is natural because of Jesus' resurrection (15:50-58)

[50]What I am saying, dear brothers and sisters, is that our physical bodies cannot inherit the Kingdom of God. These dying bodies cannot inherit what will last forever.

[51]But let me reveal to you a wonderful secret. We will not all die, but we will all be transformed! [52]It will happen in a moment, in the blink of an eye, when the last trumpet is blown. For when the trumpet sounds, those who have died will be raised to live forever. And we who are living will also be transformed. [53]For our dying bodies must be transformed into bodies that will never die; our mortal bodies must be transformed into immortal bodies.

[54]Then, when our dying bodies have been transformed into bodies that will never die,* this Scripture will be fulfilled:

"Death is swallowed up in victory.*
[55] O death, where is your victory?
    O death, where is your sting?*"

[56]For sin is the sting that results in death, and the law gives sin its power. [57]But thank God! He gives us victory over sin and death through our Lord Jesus Christ.

[58]So, my dear brothers and sisters, be strong and immovable. Always work enthusiastically for the Lord, for you know that nothing you do for the Lord is ever useless.

15:54a Some manuscripts add *and our mortal bodies have been transformed into immortal bodies.*   15:54b Isa 25:8.   15:55 Hos 13:14 (Greek version).

NOTES

15:50 *our physical bodies.* Lit., "flesh and blood." This is a Jewish expression for what is merely human in its vulnerability and weakness (Collins 1999:579; Thiselton 2000:1291). The NLT attempts to make clear that Paul intended to refer to the natural, terrestrial bodies in his comments in 15:45-49.

dying bodies. Gr., *phthora* [TG5356, ZG5785]. Used earlier ("earthly bodies," 15:42), this word is a synonym of "mortal bodies" (*thnēton* [TG2349, ZG2570]; 15:53) that accentuates the ultimate decomposition of human bodies. The case made by Jeremias (1955–1956:153-154) that this word refers to people who have died, while "flesh and blood" refers to people living at the time of Christ's return (paralleling 1 Thess 4:13-18), though popular at one time, persuades few today (Collins 1999:579; Garland 2003:740; Witherington 1995:310).

inherit. Gr., *klēronomeō* [TG2816, ZG3099]. Only used here (twice) and in 6:9 and 6:10 in 1 Corinthians, it refers to receiving one's due portion from a kinsman's estate. Paul depicts those who are saved as sharing in the sonship of Christ and thus sharing in the inheritance from the Father as a way of understanding the eternal reward of salvation, with the Holy Spirit being an advance on the inheritance (Gal 3:26–4:7; Eph 1:11-14, 18; 5:5; Col 3:24).

15:51 *secret.* Gr., *mustērion* [TG3466, ZG3696]. See notes on 2:7 and 4:1.

We will not all die, but we will all be transformed! Gr., *ou koimēthēsometha* [TG2837, ZG3121], *pantes de allagēsometha* [TG236, ZG248]. This reading, supported by B and other manuscripts, is correct, but copyists made various attempts to amend this in light of the fact that all believers of Paul's generation did die. For example, A* replaces the *ou* [TG3756, ZG4024] (not) in the first clause with the article *hoi* [TG3588, ZG3836], yielding, "we will all die yet we will all be transformed"; ℵ C F G transfer the *ou* (not) to the second clause to make this a statement distinguishing between all humanity who will die and believers (only) who will be transformed ("we will all die, but we all will not be transformed"); and 𝔓46 Aᶜ negate both clauses ("we will not all die, and we all will not be transformed").

15:53 *never die.* Gr., *aphtharsian* [TG861, ZG914]. This word is used four times in this context (15:42, 50, 54); its cognate is used in 15:52. It refers to the transcendence of mortality— that which distinguishes gods from humans.

mortal bodies. Gr., *thnēton* [TG2349A, ZG2570]. Used only here and in 15:54 in 1 Corinthians and elsewhere only in Pauline texts (Rom 6:12; 8:11; 2 Cor 4:11; 5:4), this word refers to beings that are subject to death.

15:54 *Then, when our dying bodies have been transformed into bodies that will never die.* Cf. NLT mg. Gr., *hotan de to phtharton* [TG5349A, ZG5778] *touto endusētai aphtharsian* [TG861, ZG914] *kai to thnēton* [TG2349A, ZG2570] *touto endusētai athanasian* [TG110, ZG114]. Lit., "When this perishable has been clothed with the imperishable, and this mortal with immortality." This longer reading, supported by B and ℵ², is preferred over two shorter readings, both of which were likely created by a copyist's eye skipping over some words. In 𝔓46 and ℵ*, the eye likely skipped from *athanasian* ("immortality"; NLT mg, "immortal bodies"), the last word in 15:53, to *aphtharsian* (imperishable) in 15:54, thus omitting the first clause of 15:54. Some scribes (F G) even skipped from *athanasian* at the end of 15:53 to *athanasian* at the end of both clauses, thus omitting them entirely. The NLT follows the shorter reading of 𝔓46, but it includes a second phrase corresponding to that of the longer reading in its text note.

swallowed up. Used only here in 1 Corinthians, it is used elsewhere in the NT of swallowing a camel (Matt 23:24), the Red Sea swallowing the Egyptians (Heb 11:29), a lion swallowing people (1 Pet 5:8), and of the earth swallowing a river (Rev 12:16). In every case, it pictures something being swallowed completely. Paul also uses it metaphorically in the similar context of 2 Cor 5:4 of life swallowing what is mortal.

15:55 *victory? O death, where is your sting?* Gr., *nikos? pou sou, thanate, to kentron?* This reading has strong support from 𝔓46 ℵ* B 088 C 1739* it cop and is most likely correct. However, variations occur in order to accommodate the LXX reading of Hos 13:14. One, found in F and G, reverses the sequence of *kentron* (sting) and *nikos* (victory); another, found in ℵ² 0121 0243 33 𝔐 (so TR and KJV), replaces *thanate* [TG2288, ZG2505] (death) with *hadēs* [TG86, ZG87] (Hades).

sting. Gr., *kentron* [TG2759, ZG3034]. Used only here and in 15:56 by Paul, but used also in Rev 9:10 of scorpions' stings. In Acts 26:14 (RSV, "goads"; cf. NLT, "my will") it denotes a stick used to prod oxen. In Koine Greek in general, it can be used of any point or object that pricks or stings, including instruments of torture.

15:57 *victory.* Gr., *nikos* [TG3534, ZG3777]. Used only the three times in this context and one other time in the NT (Matt 12:20), this word refers not only to vanquishing another in military victory but winning a judgment against someone in a court contest. The verbal cognate of this word is common in Revelation, being used 17 times.

COMMENTARY

Paul begins this section in 15:50 by first restating the problem addressed in 15:42-49, that the terrestrial composition of human bodies should make it impossible for them to become extraterrestrial, superhuman, spiritual bodies capable of life in the hereafter in heaven. This will catapult Paul to answer the question of "when?" in 15:51-53, followed by a stirring doxology to God for his magnificent work (15:54-58).

Paul signals that 15:50 is a summary with his rhetorical opening "What I am saying," followed by calling his readers to attention again with "brothers and sisters." Using synonymous parallelism, he says the same thing two different ways. First, using fresh language to describe mere human bodies (literally, "flesh and blood"), he couches the problem in Jesus' eschatological language of inheritance. In the Gospels, Jesus speaks mostly of inheriting "eternal life" (Matt 19:29; Mark 10:17; Luke 10:25; 18:18), implying (Matt 25:34) but never stating this in terms of inheriting the Kingdom of God, as Paul does here and elsewhere (Gal 5:21; Eph 5:5). Second, he restates the problem by repeating the dichotomous language with which he began in 15:42, noting that "dying bodies" cannot "last forever." Literally, "perishable" cannot be "imperishable." Once again, he stipulates that this is true. *Those* bodies cannot enter heaven. They are completely incompatible and not built to last forever or to exist anywhere but on earth. They are terrestrial.

However, having already stated that such bodies can be entirely reconstituted by Christ through his breath of the Holy Spirit in 15:45-47, Paul now comes at the answer in another way. In case they did not catch this in the subtleties of his earlier argument, he says it bluntly, like a teacher writing the key point on the blackboard, "WE WILL ALL BE TRANSFORMED!" We will be changed from one thing into another. This is the ultimate Christian secret to the fountain of everlasting youth. It is not explainable, or reasonable, despite his earlier helpful explanations. It's just true. It will happen because God will make it happen. It will also happen at some point in human history, for not all will have died, but both the dead and living ("all" who are in Christ) will be transformed.

As if to put an exclamation mark on that point, in 15:52 Paul moves immediately into describing how instantaneous it will be (Thiselton 2000:1295). There will be no process of transformation, like a seed. When God's universe reaches its time, it will just happen, "in the blink of an eye," Paul says. The moment in human history when this happens will be signaled, Paul says, by a trumpet blast, the very last trumpet blast. In doing so, he takes up an eschatological image found elsewhere also in the Old Testament (Joel 2:1; Zeph 1:14-16; Zech 9:14) and in Revelation (Rev 8:2; 11:15), which is also embedded in his own teaching elsewhere (1 Thess 4:16). This trumpet sound is not depicted as a warning but as an end when human history and life as we know it stops. Like a battlefield trumpet, it signals the end of the battle, so that all can hear that the victory is won, a theme Paul will take to close his remarks in 15:54-55. This will be no normal trumpet because both those alive and dead, at the time, will hear its call—and be instantly changed.

Now that *is* a mystery—how the dead, whose natural, terrestrial bodies have utterly decomposed into dust, can be summoned (and where they are summoned from). But Paul pays this no mind; it does not matter. Paul is focused on the sameness of this utterly miraculous change that God performs for both the living and the dead. Both are raised exactly the same to immortality in bodies appropriate for their new purpose and setting in the presence of God.

His language about this transformation shifts from changing or exchanging one body for another (15:51) to that of changing clothes or putting on new clothes (15:53). Though the NLT does not show it, a change of verbs has taken place. Paul will continue to use the new verb (*enduō* [TG1746, ZG1907]) consistently through 15:54, a total of four times. This word pictures a change of clothes, or more likely putting new clothes over old (Garland 2003:744; Gillman 1988:444). Paul often uses this word in terms of putting something new over old in spiritual terms (Rom 13:14; Gal 3:27; Eph 4:24; 6:11, 14; Col 3:10, 12; 1 Thess 5:8), but he also uses this same word in 2 Corinthians 5:3, where he is also trying to explain what kind of resurrection body Christians will have. In this sense, the natural, mortal body will be cloaked with a supernatural one, which will transform it. It may sound like a magician's trick, but it will really happen, and it must happen for people to be fit for eternity.

One might ask what happens to a Christian's body at death and after death. I think if Paul were to answer that question, he would say it does not matter (and this is the counsel we must give to people who are mourning the death of a loved one). Who we are will be re-created into a form that is non-terrestrial, whether our bodies are buried, burnt into ashes, or annihilated by an atomic bomb. All becomes mixed into the earth to become nutrients in the soil, and all is destroyed when the heavens and earth are destroyed (2 Pet 3:10), after which a new heaven and earth are created (2 Pet 3:13). Paul does not explicitly tell us *when* the transformation will occur. However, the import of 2 Corinthians 5:1-4 (when Paul says that believers will not be naked after death—i.e., naked, bodiless spirits) suggests that this transformation may take place immediately at death. How that relates to eschatology and Christ's return is not easily answered. But it seems there has to be a sense in which eternity and life as we know it on earth are coexistent, even if the earth and universe will at some specific point be no more. So in the end, the transfiguration is a miracle that only God can do—only he can make a universe, make a human being, remake a universe that has continuity with the old one but be different, remake a human being that is totally without physicality yet be the same person in an eternal, nonphysical form.

In 15:54-55, Paul sings a victory song (Hays 1997:276) that exudes the emotional climax of all he has been talking about in this chapter. He constructs his lyric from two Old Testament passages, the first line from Isaiah 25:8 and the second and third lines from Hosea 13:14. His construction from Isaiah 25:8 surprisingly shows closer affinity to the Hebrew text than to the Septuagint (where it is numbered Isa 25:7), which speaks of the nations being swallowed up because of death's strength (Garland 2003:745; Hays 1997:275). The direct address to death comes from Hosea 13:14, but the reference to victory is added by Paul both here and at the end of the line from Isaiah 25:8. He also tinkers a bit with the word "plagues" in Hosea 13:14 to come up with "sting," likely taking up the Septuagint rendering.

At any rate, Paul certainly gets the sentiment of these passages right and adapts them superbly as predictive, underscoring God's amazing accomplishment on our behalf. Victory completely gulps down death till all the oceans are dry. It is gone. Death, the specter that haunts everyone with its pain and torture of execution, has been rendered harmless; it is a mere stingless scorpion, no longer to be feared—certainly not for those in Christ.

In 15:56, Paul applies his song of triumph and joy directly to the predicament of humanity in their sin. That the law leads to sin and that sin leads to death is something Paul extrapolates at length in Romans 5:12-14 and 7:7-11 and elsewhere (e.g., Gal 3:19). His mention of such things seems to come out of the blue, but for Paul these things are inextricably tied up together (Vlachos 2004:279). Humanity's guilt from breaking the law that leads to our death penalty must be remedied, too, not just the limitations of our natural bodies. This he tried to deal with earlier in 15:46-47 when he contrasted Christ and Adam. Also, the word "victory" plays into this because it is very often used of winning courtroom cases. Victory over death also means victory over the death penalty inflicted by the law.

Finally, in 15:57 Paul addresses (with exuberant thankfulness on behalf of all humanity) the one who made this victory possible. The plan, the grace, and the will to make it possible for people to live in the presence of God for eternity comes from God himself. The agent who accomplished this on God's behalf for us is Christ. His death was our death to sin and our death to death. However, mention of this triumphant life of victory with God being made possible only through Christ is Paul's staunch reminder that every word he has been talking about in this chapter concerns the transformation of the bodies of *believers* in Christ, not humanity in general.

It seems odd that Paul completed this chapter with an exhortation for the Corinthians to be firm in their faith and to keep working hard (15:58). However, it is not unusual for Paul to turn highly involved theological discussion into encouragement for moral and spiritual steadfastness. Indeed, he does the same thing in 1 Thessalonians 4:18 after an eschatological passage. He wanted to turn this supreme eschatological hope into something that has practical, everyday value. In this case, he notes that they should not, therefore, view anything in their life as having no meaning or purpose. Their lives, each minute, are full of purpose as they serve Christ in preparation for his coming. In making this point, he purposely bookends his concern noted at the beginning of this chapter in 15:2—namely, that if they do not hold to the truth of the gospel, they will have lived in vain.

◆   F. Matters Related to the Collection and to Apollos (16:1-12)
        1. Completion of the collection before Paul's arrival (16:1-4)

Now regarding your question about the money being collected for God's people in Jerusalem. You should follow the same procedure I gave to the churches in Galatia. ²On the first day of each week, you should each put aside a portion of the money you have earned. Don't wait until I get there and then try to collect it all at once. ³When I come, I will write letters of recommendation for the messengers you choose to deliver your gift to Jerusalem. ⁴And if it seems appropriate for me to go along, they can travel with me.

NOTES

16:1 *money being collected.* Gr., *logeias* [TG3048, ZG3356]. Only used here and in 16:2 in all the NT, this word is related to one of the meanings of *logizomai* [TG3049A, ZG3357] that involves counting or calculating and here refers to collection of money. It was the practice of Jews living outside Jerusalem to send money regularly to aid the poor of Jerusalem, at least partly to help support the role the Jerusalem inhabitants played in hosting pilgrims at the numerous Jewish festivals throughout the year (Robertson and Plummer 1911:382; Thiselton 2000:1320). By this time, Christian Jews in Jerusalem may have no longer qualified for sharing in this help. Since Paul elsewhere uses other words to refer to this collection effort (when he talks about it in Rom 15:25 and 2 Cor 8-9), very likely the particular word used here derives from the Corinthians' letter to him.

Galatia. This term in Paul's day could refer to the ethnic Galatians, who migrated from what is now France to the north central area of Asia Minor (modern-day Turkey) in 278 BC, or it could refer to the entire Roman political region that included the Gauls' home but extended south almost to the Mediterranean Sea. This would include the churches Paul and Barnabas established on their first missionary tour, including the cities of Iconium, Lystra, and Derbe. This is all part of the debate about whether the original recipients of Paul's letter to the Galatians were "North" or "South" Galatians. However, the excavated Roman road system that included the southern cities but not the northern, "ethnic" Galatian region favors the view that Paul wrote to the southern cites named in Acts. See fuller discussions in Bruce 1982:3-18.

16:2 *the money you have earned.* Gr., *euodōtai* [TG2137, ZG2338] (prosper, succeed). Used only here in 1 Corinthians, this word is normally used in the context of travel, as in Rom 1:10. Since travel in the ancient world was inherently dangerous, this word was used to speak of things going well on a journey. It could also be used generally of prosperity and good fortune, as in 3 John 1:2. The ESV has "as he may prosper," and the NIV has "in keeping with his income." The idea implied is that the believers are to save their money in correspondence to how God has blessed their lives. Note that a tithe is not commanded here or anywhere in the NT.

COMMENTARY

Before Paul ended this already lengthy letter to the Corinthians, he needed to respond to two more questions raised in their letter to him. Neither of these is theologically weighty nor involves any correction of unwise behavior or opinion, as in the first five questions the Corinthians asked, regarding marriage (ch 7), eating food sacrificed to idols (chs 8–10), believer gatherings (ch 11), and spiritual gifts (chs 12–14). As with those, Paul introduces his two remaining topics with "now regarding" (*peri de* [ᵀᴳ4012/1161, ᶻᴳ4309/1254]). The questions are about the collection of money Paul had authorized and about whether Apollos would return to Corinth in the near future. The first is addressed in 16:1-4, and the second is addressed in 16:12 as the final comment on travel plans involving Paul and his associates, including how Corinth fit into their itineraries (addressed in 16:5-11).

Paul's minimalist comments about the collection, beginning in 16:1, suggest that the Corinthians already understood its purpose and why they should be involved. His comments are entirely procedural and imply that their question asked for directions on how to go about it since they were ready to get started. Most likely they heard about it from Paul on his initial visit or perhaps from Apollos, who had recently returned to Ephesus from Corinth. The comment about Galatian churches shows that the efforts to collect this money were well under way elsewhere, even though the Corinthians were just beginning. It also indicates that this was a project Paul expected all the churches he had planted to sign on to.

Paul refers to this collection specifically in other letters, notably in 2 Corinthians 8–9, where he indicates that the Macedonian churches (Philippi, Thessalonica, and Berea) were setting the pace in terms of the generous self-sacrifice needed to complete this financial project successfully. Paul's purpose was entirely motivational because by that point, following his painful visit and severe letter, the Corinthians' initial enthusiasm for the project had waned.

In Romans 15:26-28 (written after both 1 and 2 Corinthians in AD 57), Paul informs the Romans about the plans to deliver the collection to Jerusalem but does not enlist them since he intended the project to be completed before he traveled there. It was seemingly the final item on his list before he felt free to come their direction. Written from Corinth just before sailing with the collection to Jerusalem (Acts 20:1-3), the letter to the Romans mentions both the Macedonians and, happily, the Achaians (Corinthians) as making contributions. Noting, as here, that it was for "God's people in Jerusalem," he added that the purpose of the collection was for "the poor" among them. He also explained the collection theologically as balancing the ledger between Jews and Gentiles—Jerusalem exporting the incalculable spiritual blessing of Christ while Gentiles bless the Jewish Christians in Jerusalem materially.

The impetus to launch this massive, widespread financial drive lies in Paul's eagerness to "remember the poor," as Galatians 2:10 indicates that the earliest pillars of the church (James, Peter, and John) asked him to do, supposedly to pacify those conservative Jewish Christians who thought Gentiles had to be circumcised before they could become part of the Christian church. He saw it as an opportunity to solidify the unity of the Gentile and Jewish portions of the growing church (Garland 2003:762). If he viewed it as fulfilling the Old Testament promise that Gentiles would bring gifts to Zion (Isa 2:2-4; 60:6-7, 11; Mic 4:13), then he would also have seen it as accelerating the return of Christ (Nickle 1966:129-142; McKnight 1991:47-48). This agreement may have been part of the formal Acts 15 concords of the Jerusalem council, though it is not mentioned there. It did, however, see its first enactment when Paul and Barnabas brought financial gifts from Antioch to the Jerusalem church, described in Acts 11:27-30. Paul's decision to widen the effort may have stemmed from the prophetic word from Agabus, mentioned in Acts 11:28, that the entire Roman world would experience a crippling famine.

In 16:2, Paul outlines the approach the Galatians (and presumably the other churches involved in the project) were using. How the Galatians received these instructions from Paul is unknown, perhaps in a letter subsequent to Galatians or orally from one of his traveling associates (Bruce 1971:158). Regardless, his recommendation to the Corinthians answers five questions: how often, who, how much, where, and by when. The best approach is to do something every week toward this project. He advocates the first day of the week, Sunday, almost certainly because by this time Christians were already gathering on this day to honor Christ's resurrection, worship, teach, and share in the Lord's Supper in various homes (Blomberg 1994:324; Fee 1987:814; Horsley 1998:221; Soards 1999:360).

Acts 20:7 implies a regular gathering on the first day, as well. However, despite the traditional interpretation of this passage (Collins 1999:587; Garland 2003:753), Paul says nothing about taking up this collection when they gathered, as congregations do today. His focus was on individual believers (the "who") appropriating part of their earnings for the week (how much) on Sunday and safeguarding this portion themselves, presumably in their own homes (Bruce 1971:158; Fee 1987:813; Hays 1997:286; Thiselton 2000:1324). The idea of weekly collection is not documented until Justin Martyr (1 Apology 67).

Planning ahead and acting with regularity would make this something the whole church can achieve together. This would make it unnecessary for a few wealthy patrons to make hefty donations at the end to bail out everyone else (Hays 1997:285; Witherington 1995:315). Paul wanted each one to participate as the Lord enabled through his abundance (Thiselton 2000:1319). In fact, Paul wanted each believer to do this regularly so that all would be completed before he came to receive everyone's portion as a whole. Exactly when everyone's portion would be gathered was uncertain. Since there were no banks in the ancient world, this would need to be as close as possible to when he arrived. His emphasis was not on its being collected by the congregation but on each individual setting it aside weekly and safeguarding it so each one was ready when he arrived (Blomberg 1994:324; Horsley 1998:222).

In 16:3, Paul explains the procedure after he would arrive to pick up the collection to take it to Jerusalem. First, they would select from among themselves official delegates to accompany the money on its movement toward Jerusalem. This was to ensure both that their money was guarded along the way and that Corinth would have its own people to represent them when the money was officially presented to the believers in Jerusalem. Paul wanted those in Jerusalem to see the multiethnic Gentile faces of their providers (Horsley 1998:222). He would provide official letters for them, a common practice to authorize representatives of another, mostly in case he himself did not end up going along.

Though Paul was as yet unsure if he would make the trip to Jerusalem with the delegates and the money, as indicated by 16:4, Acts 20 narrates that he did end up going. This, in fact, set in motion the events for him to be arrested and then eventually sent to Rome for trial. His equivocating probably had something to do with his anxiety about the dangers of going back to Jerusalem, mentioned both in Romans 15:31 and Acts 20:22-23 and 21:10-14, the latter of which includes a personal prophecy of warning from Agabus. Unfortunately, Acts never says anything more about the delegates and does not mention the collection. However, Acts 21:17-19 does document that the day after arriving in Jerusalem, Paul and the others with him met officially with James and other leaders to tell them about the great things God had done in bringing the gospel among the Gentiles. Presumably the delegates' presentation of the money occurred then.

◆   ## 2. Travel plans (16:5-12)

⁵I am coming to visit you after I have been to Macedonia,* for I am planning to travel through Macedonia. ⁶Perhaps I will stay awhile with you, possibly all winter, and then you can send me on my way to my next destination. ⁷This time I don't want to make just a short visit and then go right on. I want to come and stay awhile, if the Lord will let me. ⁸In the meantime, I will be staying here at Ephesus until the Festival of Pentecost. ⁹There is a wide-open door for a great work here, although many oppose me.

¹⁰When Timothy comes, don't intimidate him. He is doing the Lord's work, just as I am. ¹¹Don't let anyone treat him with contempt. Send him on his way with your blessing when he returns to me. I expect him to come with the other believers.*

¹²Now about our brother Apollos—I urged him to visit you with the other believers, but he was not willing to go right now. He will see you later when he has the opportunity.

16:5 *Macedonia* was in the northern region of Greece.   16:11 Greek *with the brothers;* also in 16:12.

NOTES

16:7 *if the Lord will let me.* This is a phrase found earlier in 4:19 and also in Acts 18:21, Heb 6:3, and Jas 4:15. It appears to have become a conventional formula among early Christians to acknowledge God's sovereignty over the future and their roles in it. Paul was also aware that God could redirect his plans as he did when he intervened to send Paul to Macedonia for the first time (Acts 16:6-10), and he wanted to be open to this (Rom 1:10; 15:32).

16:8 *Ephesus.* Paul established a church in this major city of over 200,000 inhabitants, the capital of the Roman province of Asia on the west coast of Asia Minor during his third missionary tour, immediately after starting the church in Corinth. Acts 19 recounts his time there, with Acts 19:10 saying he stayed there two years.

Festival of Pentecost. Gr., *pentēcostēs* [TG4005, ZG4300]. Only mentioned here and in Acts 2:1 and 20:16, it is the Hellenistic word for what in the OT is called the Feast of Weeks, celebrated on the 50th day from the beginning of harvest (Lev 23:15-16; Deut 16:9; 2 Macc 12:31-32). By the time of Paul, it was celebrated 50 days after Passover (Collins 1999:593). This became a significant day for Christians because of the initiating events recorded in

Acts 2, which included the dramatic arrival of the Holy Spirit and the conversion of the first 3,000 people to the Christian church.

16:10 When. Gr., *ean* [TG1437, ZG1569]. This conditional conjunction is used for the subjunctive case, when the potential for something not occurring exists. Thiselton (2000:1330) suggests "whenever" to indicate the uncertainty is about the timing, not the planning. Given that Paul also uses this same conditional conjunction in 16:7 to refer to his own planned travel as being conditioned on the Lord's will, this could be simply a shortened version of the same concern to respect God's will in whatever plans are made.

Timothy. See note on 4:17.

don't intimidate him. Lit., "Watch that he might be without fear (Gr., *aphobōs* [TG870, ZG925]) toward you." This word is the negated adverb form of the word for "fear" (*phobos* [TG5401, ZG5832]); thus, Paul wanted Timothy to come, lit., "*without* fear." Interpreters used to latch on to this comment by Paul as indication, in combination with 1 Tim 4:12; 2 Tim 1:7; 2:1-3, that Timothy was not a forceful personality. Hutson (1997:58-59) has been persuasive in challenging this traditional approach, suggesting that the word here could even mean that Timothy had a personality of being "fearless." Most suggest that the comment pertained to people who were indisposed toward Paul and would take this out on Timothy (Garland 2003:759).

16:12 Apollos. See note on 1:12.

COMMENTARY

Mention of his possible travel with the Corinthians' collection delegates naturally segues Paul into his travel itinerary, especially how Corinth fit into his plans (16:5-9). His tentative plan was to remain in Ephesus until Pentecost (50 days after Jewish Passover or Resurrection Sunday) in early June before he headed overland to Macedonia. He would stop briefly in Macedonia to check in on the congregations there in Philippi, Thessalonica, and Berea before coming down their way into Corinth, where he expected to spend the winter.

The point of this trip, as Acts 20:1-4 tells it, was to consolidate all the delegates before traveling together to Jerusalem, presumably with the collection (not mentioned there), whether he went with them or not. Perhaps he was eyeing the idea of going the opposite direction to Spain with a stop in Rome at that point, a wish he articulates in Romans 15:24. Since travel in the winter was particularly treacherous due to weather, Paul seemed to have made it a habit to put himself in places during this season that would be as productive for the gospel as possible (Thiselton 2000:1329), as was currently the case in Ephesus.

An open door as a metaphor for evangelistic opportunity (16:9) occurs also in 2 Corinthians 2:12 and in Colossians 4:3. For Paul this had little to do with whether opposition to the gospel was present, as was the case in Ephesus. Acts 19:23-41 narrates what must have been a terrifying riot occurring against Paul and the Christian church in Ephesus, but Acts 19:1-22 also narrates amazing success for the gospel there. The riot occurred at the end of Paul's time in Ephesus, after he wrote 1 Corinthians, but the difficulties leading up to this probably were already in mind when he depicted the opposition as "wild beasts" in 15:32.

Events did not unfold as Paul expected at the time he wrote 1 Corinthians. Despite what he says in 16:7 about not wanting to make a short trip to visit the Corinthians, this is precisely what he did. His comments in 2 Corinthians 1:15-16 and 2:1-4 indicate that not only did he make a short boat trip directly to Corinth when he left Ephesus, but he revised his plan to stop at Corinth first, then head up to the Macedonian churches before coming back down a second time to Corinth to arrive before the delegation went off to Jerusalem. But even this plan changed when the short trip to Corinth went horribly, so horribly that he went back to Ephesus, wrote them a stinging letter of rebuke (the severe letter) before adopting the original itinerary set out here: to go through Macedonia on the way to Corinth (Garland 2003:757). At that point he was not even sure he was going to proceed to Corinth, until he met up with Titus (the bearer of the severe letter) who told him that Corinth was again on board. At that point Paul wrote 2 Corinthians, partially to get the Corinthians back on track with the collection before he arrived.

While Corinth was a crucial component in Paul's personal travel plans, in 16:10-12 he informs them about two of his key associates, Timothy and Apollos, both of whom they knew. Apollos had just come from Corinth, and Timothy was there during part of the time when Paul was there but also spent time elsewhere, probably Macedonia, per Acts 19:22 (Barrett 1968:392; Thiselton 2000:1330).

Regarding Timothy, Paul knew that Corinth was the last scheduled stop on Timothy's current itinerary, but since he gave no timetable (like he did for himself), he must not have known exactly when Timothy would leave where he was currently, when he would arrive, or how long he would stay. Timothy was free to determine the best scenarios for his movements as he went along, and Paul always wanted to remain open to the Lord's shift in plans, as he notes regarding himself in 16:7. But Paul's expression of deep concern for how Timothy would be received and his earlier comment in 4:17 that he was sending Timothy their way indicate that he fully expected Timothy to arrive there at some point, sometime after they received this letter.

Paul instructed the Corinthians to treat Timothy with all the respect he was due as one who had given his life to serving Christ, as Paul had done. Timothy may in some respects have been under Paul's administrative authority, but Paul had also trusted him with significant responsibility and seems to have trusted him thoroughly. In this sense, Timothy was really Paul's coworker, like Apollos (3:9; 16:10).

Though Paul's warning to the Corinthians is sometimes taken along with references in 1 Timothy 4:12 and 2 Timothy 1:7 and 2:1-3 to imply that Timothy lacked confidence in situations like this because of his youth and inexperience, this need not be the case at all (Hutson 1997:58-59). Since Paul's warning was to the Corinthians themselves, if anything, Paul may have been concerned that some of them might treat Timothy badly because of their antipathy toward Paul (Hays 1997:287) or maybe aversion to the collection. However, that is mere speculation, since Paul's comments here seem friendly. He could well be only reminding them to show him the kind of hospitality Timothy deserved, including sending him on his way with "your blessing," meaning provisions for the last leg of his trip. Mention of "other believers" probably gives the Corinthians advance warning that others will be traveling with Timothy, whom the Corinthians will also need to accommodate with housing and provision.

Some assume Paul's comments about Timothy imply that he was carrying the letter of 1 Corinthians with him (Talbert 1987:106) and that the Corinthians were being warned to listen to it being read aloud by Timothy with the respect they would give to Paul himself. However, more likely the three men mentioned in 16:17 are the letter bearers, who, because they will go directly back to Corinth with 1 Corinthians, will arrive before Timothy gets there from Macedonia (Garland 2003:760).

Regarding Apollos, Paul did not expect him to come anytime soon (16:12). He seemed to sense that this would be disappointing to the Corinthians, underscoring that Apollos was a real favorite among them, as 1:12 and 3:4 indicate. Paul certainly had high regard for him, too, as 3:6-9 suggests, and felt close to him, as calling him "brother" here implies. However, it is likely that Paul's defensive comments about his own lack of eloquence (2:1) were due to the rhetorical skill Apollos displayed to the Corinthians. Apollos's unwillingness to go back to Corinth may be simply a matter of timing or scheduling, as Paul says. However, that Paul says he put pressure on Apollos to go—and yet he was unwilling—suggests bigger problems. Perhaps Apollos left to begin with because he was becoming uncomfortable with the way some of the Corinthians put him on a pedestal and used him to create a rivalry with Paul (Thiselton 2000:1332). Perhaps Paul viewed his unwillingness as God's will counteracting Paul's design for Apollos in his missionary strategy (Witherington 1995:317).

◆ V. Conclusion (16:13-24)
A. Final Admonitions (16:13-18)

13Be on guard. Stand firm in the faith. Be courageous.* Be strong. 14And do everything with love.

15You know that Stephanas and his household were the first of the harvest of believers in Greece,* and they are spending their lives in service to God's people. I urge you, dear brothers and sisters,* 16to submit to them and others like them who serve with such devotion. 17I am very glad that Stephanas, Fortunatus, and Achaicus have come here. They have been providing the help you weren't here to give me. 18They have been a wonderful encouragement to me, as they have been to you. You must show your appreciation to all who serve so well.

16:13 Greek *Be men.*   16:15a Greek *in Achaia,* the southern region of the Greek peninsula.   16:15b Greek *brothers;* also in 16:20.

NOTES

16:17 *Stephanas, Fortunatus, and Achaicus.* These three were not only authorized to bring the official letter from the Corinthian church to Paul, but they are also named here because Paul was commending them as the authorized bearers of his letter to the Corinthians, just as he did at the end of other letters (Rom 16:1-2; 2 Cor 8:16-24; Phil 2:25-30; Col 4:7-9). These appointees were charged to read the document aloud to the church and respond to questions on Paul's behalf (Garland 2003:768).

COMMENTARY

Toward the end of his letters, Paul characteristically wrote a series of short admonitions (technically called "paranesis"), which buffer the body of the letter from the formalities that compose the last details (cf. Rom 16:17-19; 2 Cor 13:11;

Phil 4:8-9; 1 Thess 5:12-22). These admonitions usually remind recipients of behavioral instruction mentioned earlier in the letter or well known to the recipients from traditional instruction. Thus, they can be stated with little or no explanation. This type of material comprises 16:13-18.

Paul's first five admonitions come rapid fire in 16:13-14 in a series of imperatives, followed by the much more meandering sixth admonition of 16:15-18. The first imperative, to "be on guard," replicates Jesus' admonition to "watch" (Matt 24:42-43; 25:13; Mark 13:33-35; Luke 12:37), most likely to underscore being prepared for Christ's coming, which has been a recurrent theme of the letter (Garland 2003:766). With "stand firm" following, it could also have moral or doctrinal motivation, implying they were to hold on to the traditions Paul passed on to them (11:23; 15:1-3). Urging courage and strength probably relates to the conviction required to withstand pressures of the pagan society around them to cannibalize their faith and practice through syncretism. Love, no doubt, is intended to remind them of chapter 8, regarding eating food sacrificed to idols; chapter 11, regarding the Lord's Supper; and chapter 13, regarding use of spiritual gifts.

Mention of Stephanas and his household in 16:15 intends to lead up to the admonition for the Corinthian believers to respect the leadership of people like him among them, noted in 16:16. Paul highlighted this household in 1:16 as a group of people he had baptized. Noting they were his first converts in Greece (NLT mg, "Achaia") means they certainly were his first converts in Corinth, the region of which Corinth was the capital, which explains in part why he would have baptized them. Technically, Acts 17:34 names Dionysius and Damaris of Athens (also in the Roman province of Achaia) as converts prior to Paul's arriving in Corinth, but Paul either did not remember them or considered Achaia informally to be only Corinth and the immediately surrounding area (Garland 2003:767).

Regardless, Paul's comments about the Corinthians submitting to them suggest that heads of households probably served as leaders (elders) of their households and other believers who met in their house. Mention of "others like them" suggests that others, like Gaius (1:14), maybe even Chloe (1:11), had positions of responsibility and leadership over those who met in their homes.

Complementing Stephanas's high commitment to serve the believers in Corinth prompted Paul to recognize him for a specific act of service—that of traveling to see Paul. Most people did not travel much. It was costly and dangerous. However, Stephanas, with two others, had come, almost certainly bearing the official letter from the church that Paul had been responding to since chapter 7 (Garland 2003:768; Hays 1997:290). Likely, Stephanas, named first (and also the first convert in Corinth), was delegated by the other leaders to head this entourage. The other two could be members of his household, traveling with him for safety, or other previously unnamed household leaders in Corinth. The "-us" at the end of Fortunatus and Achaicus signals that they were Romans, perhaps freedmen whose families had immigrated to Corinth (Collins 1999:603). Paul's exuberance over their having come seems sincere. This extra effort—not only to bring the letter and fill Paul in on other matters about the Corinthian believers, but just their personal presence—seems to have really given Paul an emotional lift.

Paul also mentions them at this point because this is when he often mentions the names of those who were carrying his letters to churches. His encouragement to the Corinthian believers to show their appreciation to them anticipates their return. No other church on record in the New Testament took the initiative both to send Paul a letter and to return with his letter via a delegation like this.

◆   ## B. Greetings, Invocations, and Benediction (16:19–24)

19The churches here in the province of Asia* send greetings in the Lord, as do Aquila and Priscilla* and all the others who gather in their home for church meetings. 20All the brothers and sisters here send greetings to you. Greet each other with Christian love.*

21HERE IS MY GREETING IN MY OWN HAND-WRITING—PAUL.

22If anyone does not love the Lord, that person is cursed. Our Lord, come!*

23May the grace of the Lord Jesus be with you.

24My love to all of you in Christ Jesus.*

16:19a *Asia* was a Roman province in what is now western Turkey.   16:19b Greek *Prisca*.   16:20 Greek *with a sacred kiss*.   16:22 From Aramaic, *Marana tha*. Some manuscripts read *Maran atha*, "Our Lord has come."   16:24 Some manuscripts add *Amen*.

NOTES

16:19 *Aquila and Priscilla*. This Christian couple was originally from Pontus, a coastal region in northern Asia Minor along the southern coast of the Black Sea. They were probably among the founders of the church at Rome (maybe even among those from Pontus or Rome mentioned in Acts 2:9-11 as present at Pentecost and among the first 3,000 converts to the Christian church). Acts 18:1-2 says they left Rome for Corinth because of Claudius's edict in AD 49 that expelled Jews from Rome. They met Paul in Corinth because they were also tentmakers, and they worked with Paul in the church. From this point on, they seem to have become senior members of Paul's missionary team, leaving with him when he moved on from Corinth to Ephesus (Acts 18:19), where they appear to have remained behind when Paul traveled back to Jerusalem. While there, they recruited Apollos onto Paul's missionary team and helped pave the way for him to go to Corinth (Acts 18:24-28). They appear to have still been in Ephesus when Paul wrote 1 Corinthians (AD 54–55), as this verse indicates; they were leading a house group in their home. However, by the time Paul wrote Romans (AD 57), they were back in Rome, the first ones to whom he sent greetings (Rom 16:3), whom he warmly describes as risking their lives for his (probably when they were together in Ephesus—Acts 19). They appear to have moved yet again to Ephesus by the time they were greeted by Paul in 2 Tim 4:19. It is noted that their business must have made it possible for them to move around whenever they wanted and that either their business was highly successful or that one of them, probably Priscilla (since she is mentioned first everywhere but here), may have been from a family of some means (Collins 1999:609). The appearance of her name before her husband's would have been highly unusual and suggests she was a highly respected woman of considerable influence. She is called "Priscilla" in Acts but "Prisca" by Paul, as the NLT footnote states.

16:22 *love the Lord*. The presence of the verb *phileō* [TG5368, ZG5797] for "love" rather than Paul's favorite word for "love" (*agapaō* [TG25, ZG26]) provides strong support for the entire formula originating outside of Paul (see next note; Barrett 1968:396).

***cursed*.** Gr., *anathema* [TG331, ZG353]. Found elsewhere only in 12:3, Acts 23:14 ("bound . . . with an oath"), Rom 9:3, and Gal 1:8-9, this word refers to something or someone who is to be set aside for God, mostly expecting his just condemnation. Some have considered this to be the first half of a liturgical formula believers were to utter upon participating in the Lord's Supper (Bornkamm 1969:169-179). Uttering the parallel sounds (*anathema / marana tha*) of these opposites would be striking in any congregational setting (see next note).

Our Lord, come! Gr., *marana tha* [TG3134, ZG3448]. Only here in the NT, this formulaic phrase originated as an Aramaic expression carried over into Greek. It was almost certainly a formulaic prayer inviting Christ's return born out of the expectation that he would return for his followers very soon. Some entertain the notion that it could intend to confess the presence of Christ in the church or in the Lord's Supper. It had this function and was part of the Lord's Supper liturgy by the time of the *Didache,* since the phrase in *Didache* 10:6 and in some manuscripts is divided as *maran atha* [TG3134A, ZG3448], meaning "Our Lord has come," as noted in NLT mg. However, this was most likely not as early as Paul's time (Moule 1959–1960:310; Witherington 1995:323). A similar (Greek) expression occurs in Rev 22:20.

16:24 *Christ Jesus.* Some manuscripts, including א A C D, include an "Amen" at the very end, but this was almost certainly added by an early scribe reflecting liturgical expressions. The word is absent in B F 0121 0243 33 1739*.

COMMENTARY

It was customary for Paul to close out his letters with greetings from himself and others with him to people he knew in the communities he was writing to, sometimes followed by his authentication of the letter with his own writing and final words, as seen here in 16:19-24. Unusual here are the invocations in 16:22.

Greetings in Paul's letters can take up nearly an entire chapter, as in Romans, or just a few verses, as here in 16:19-20. It is not unusual to communicate greetings from believers where he was. To do so on behalf of an entire continent seems overly exuberant, even if Paul only meant the western part of Asia Minor (modern-day Turkey), which the Romans designated as "Asia" (Acts 19:10, 26; Rom 16:5; 2 Cor 1:8; 2 Tim 1:15). Really, he was sending greetings from the churches in the regions extending from Ephesus, where he currently resided, which was the most influential city in the area.

Paul mentioned Aquila and Priscilla by name in 16:19 because they had been coworkers with him among the Corinthians from the earliest days (Acts 18:1-2; see note on 16:19). This extraordinary Christian couple appears to have followed Paul to Ephesus (Acts 18:18), leading a house church in their home. Paul generalized a greeting in 16:20 from the other believers who were in Ephesus.

His encouragement for Christians to show their love for one another with a conventional social custom is found at the end of 16:20. It literally refers to a "sacred kiss" (as noted in NLT mg) and was widely practiced in the early New Testament period (Rom 16:16; 2 Cor 13:12; 1 Thess 5:26; 1 Pet 5:14) as a formal sign of social acceptance (Garland 2003:772; Klassen 1993:132). It became part of the liturgy associated with the Lord's Supper by the time of Justin (*1 Apology* 65) but was not likely so this early (Collins 1999:610; Garland 2003:772; Thiselton 2000:1345).

Paul's addition of his own personal greeting in the form of an authentication (in 16:21) is not a signature exactly but it would have functioned similarly, adding a personal touch to the letter. It indicates that at this point Paul had picked up the writing instrument from Sosthenes, the secretary inscribing the letter, and began to write, and he would continue writing until the end of the epistle (Thiselton 2000:1347). The change in appearance would be distinctive, and some of the Corinthians would probably have recognized it as Paul's own writing. The NLT's small caps are a good way to signal this change. Paul did this at the end of Galatians (Gal 6:11), Colossians (Col 4:18), 2 Thessalonians (2 Thess 3:17), and Philemon (Phlm 1:19).

Paul's invocation in 16:22, combining an anathema warning, a "malediction" (Garland 2003:773; cf. NLT, "cursed"), with an invitation for the Lord to come is unique in the New Testament and adds a stern perspective to the close of the letter (Horsley 1998:227). Elsewhere he does invoke an anathema regarding those who reject the gospel (Gal 1:8-9) and warns against rejecting his teaching (2 Thess 3:14; Titus 3:10-11). Although the formula inviting the Lord to come appears elsewhere only in Revelation 22:20, Paul regularly offers expectant language regarding Christ's return throughout his letters, as he does in 1 Corinthians. The pairing of the malediction with the invitation may be simply a traditional invocation that comes out of a worship context that Paul repeated. The expression "Our Lord, come" comes from the Aramaic *marana tha*. Both are "Lord" warnings, in a sense, with eschatological assumptions that Christ will come to gather the faithful and execute judgment upon those hostile to his cause, especially those who professed to be believers at one time (Barrett 1968:398).

The benediction of Christ's grace is standard for Paul (Rom 16:24 [see 16:23, NLT mg]; Gal 6:18; Phil 4:23; 1 Thess 5:28; 2 Thess 3:18; Phlm 1:25). Unusual is the combination of "Lord Jesus" without "Christ." But this is rectified because he employs "Christ Jesus" in the line that follows. The personal expression of love to the Corinthians after the benediction in a postscript is unique in Paul's letters (Garland 2003:774). Whatever they may think of his instruction in this letter, he wanted them to be assured that they are and will remain dear to him.

BIBLIOGRAPHY

Abernathy, David
2002 Christ as Life-giving Spirit in 1 Corinthians 15:45. *Irish Biblical Studies* 24:2-13.

Allison, Robert W.
1988 Let Women Be Silent in the Churches (1 Cor. 14:33b-36): What Did Paul Really Say, and What Did It Mean? *Journal for the Study of the New Testament* 32:27-60.

Arichea, Daniel C.
1995 The Silence of Women in the Church: Theology and Translation in 1 Corinthians 14.33b-36. *Bible Translator* 46:101-112.

Asher, Jeffrey R.
2001 Σπείρεται: Paul's Anthropogenic Metaphor in 1 Corinthians 15:42-44. *Journal of Biblical Literature* 120:101-122.

Baker, William R.
1999 *2 Corinthians.* Joplin, MO: College Press.

Barré, M. L.
1974 To Marry or to Burn: *Purousthai* in 1 Cor. 7:9. *Catholic Biblical Quarterly* 36:193-202.

Barrett, C. K.
1968 *The First Epistle to the Corinthians.* New York: Harper & Row.
1971 Paul's Opponents in 2 Corinthians. *New Testament Studies* 17:233-254.

Bartchy, S. Scott
1973 *First-century Slavery and 1 Corinthians 7:21.* Society of Biblical Literature Dissertation Series 11. Missoula, MT: Society of Biblical Literature.

Barth, Karl
1933 *The Resurrection of the Dead.* London: Hodder & Stoughton.

Bauckham, Richard
1998 *God Crucified: Monotheism and Christology in the New Testament.* Grand Rapids: Eerdmans.
2001 James and Jesus. Pp. 100-137 in *The Brother of Jesus: James the Just and His Mission.* Editors, Bruce Chilton and Jacob Neusner. Louisville: Westminster John Knox.

Baur, F. C.
1831 Die Christuspartei in der korinthischen Gemeinde. *Tübinger Zeitschrift für Theologie* 4:61-206.
1876 *Paul the Apostle of Jesus Christ.* London: Williams & Norgate.

Beardsley, William
1994 *First Corinthians.* St. Louis: Chalice.

Beasley-Murray, G. R.
1962 *Baptism in the New Testament.* Grand Rapids: Eerdmans.

BeDuhn, Jason David
1999 Because of the Angels: Unveiling Paul's Anthropology in 1 Corinthians 11. *Journal of Biblical Literature* 118:295-320.

Blomberg, Craig
1994 *1 Corinthians.* NIV Application Commentary. Grand Rapids: Zondervan.

Blue, Brad
1991 The House Church at Corinth and the Lord's Supper: Famine, Food Supply, and the Present Distress. *Criswell Theological Review* 5:221-239.

Borchert, Gerald L.
1999 1 Corinthians 7:15 and the Church's Historic Misunderstanding of Divorce and Remarriage. *Review and Expositor* 96:125-129.

Bornkamm, Günther
1969 *Early Christian Experience.* Translator, P. L. Hammer. New York: Harper & Row.

Boswell, John
1980 *Christianity, Social Tolerance, and Homosexuality.* Chicago: University of Chicago Press.

Brewer, D. I.
1992 1 Corinthians 9:9-11: A Literal Interpretation of "Do Not Muzzle the Ox." *New Testament Studies*
38:554-565.

2001a 1 Corinthians 7 in the Light of the Graeco-Roman Marriage and Divorce Papyri. *Tyndale Bulletin*
52:101-116.

2001b 1 Corinthians 7 in the Light of the Jewish Greek and Aramaic Marriage and Divorce Papyri.
Tyndale Bulletin 52:225-243.

Bruce, F. F.
1971 *I and II Corinthians.* New Century Bible. Grand Rapids: Eerdmans.

1982 *The Epistle to the Galatians.* New International Greek Testament Commentary. Grand Rapids:
Eerdmans.

Bryce, D. W.
1997 As in All the Churches of the Saints: A Text Critical Study of 1 Corinthians 14:34-35. *Lutheran
Theological Journal* 31:31-39.

Bultmann, Rudolf
1951 *Theology of the New Testament,* vol. 1. New York: Charles Scribner.

Byrne, Brendan
1983 Sinning against One's Own Body: Paul's Understanding of the Sexual Relationship in 1 Corinthians
6:18. *Catholic Biblical Quarterly* 45:608-616.

Calvin, John
1960 *The First Epistle of Paul the Apostle to the Corinthians.* Calvin's New Testament Commentaries, vol. 9.
Editors, D. W. Torrance and T. F. Torrance. Translator, J. W. Fraser. Grand Rapids: Eerdmans.

Campbell, R. Alistair
1999 Baptism and Resurrection. *Australian Biblical Review* 47:43-52.

Caragounis, C.
1995 To "Boast" or to "Be Burned"? The Crux of 1 Cor 13.3. *Svensk exegetisk arsbok* 60:115-127.

Carson, D. A., Douglas Moo, and Leon Morris
1992 *An Introduction to the New Testament.* Grand Rapids: Zondervan.

Castelli, Elizabeth A.
1991 *Imitating Paul: A Discourse of Power.* Literary Currents in Biblical Interpretation. Louisville:
Westminster John Knox.

Cha, Jung-Sik
1998 The Ascetic Virgins in 1 Corinthians 7:25-38. *Asia Journal of Theology* 12:89-117.

Cheung, Alex T.
1999 *Idol Food in Corinth: Jewish Background and Pauline Legacy.* Journal for the Study of the
New Testament Supplement Series 176. Sheffield: Sheffield Academic Press.

Clarke, Graham
2001 As in All the Churches of the Saints (1 Corinthians 14.33). *Bible Translator* 52:144-147.

Collier, Gary D.
1994 That We Might Not Crave Evil: The Structure and Argument of 1 Corinthians 10.1-13.
Journal for the Study of the New Testament 55:55-75.

Collins, Raymond
1999 *First Corinthians.* Sacra Pagina. Collegeville, MN: Liturgical Press.

Comfort, Philip
2005 *Encountering the Manuscripts: An Introduction to New Testament Paleography and Textual Criticism.*
Nashville: Broadman & Holman.

2008 *New Testament Text and Translation Commentary.* Carol Stream, IL: Tyndale.

Conzelmann, Hans
1975 *1 Corinthians.* Hermeneia. Philadelphia: Fortress.

Corrington, Gail Patterson
1991 The "Headless Woman": Paul and the Language of the Body in 1 Cor 11:2-16. *Perspectives in Religious
Studies* 18:223-231.

Corry, Norma
1999 Questions of Authority, Status, and Power. *Scriptura* 70:181-194.

Dahl, M. E.

1962 *The Resurrection of the Body: A Study of 1 Corinthians 15.* Studies in Biblical Theology 36. Naperville, IL: Allenson.

Das, A. Andrew

1998 1 Corinthians 11:17-34 Revisited. *Concordia Theological Quarterly* 62:187-208.

Daube, David

1949 Κερδαίνω as a Missionary Term. *Harvard Theological Review* 40:109-120.

Dawes, Gregory W.

1996 The Danger of Idolatry: First Corinthians 8:7-13. *Catholic Biblical Quarterly* 58:82-98.

De Boer, Martinus C.

1994 The Composition of 1 Corinthians. *New Testament Studies* 40:229-245.

Deming, Will

1995 A Diatribe Pattern in 1 Cor. 7:21-22: A New Perspective on Paul's Directions to Slaves. *Novum Testamentum* 37:130-137.

1996 The Unity of 1 Corinthians 5-6. *Journal of Biblical Literature* 115:289-312.

Derrett, J. Duncan M.

1997a Paul as Master-builder. *Evangelical Quarterly* 69:129-137.

1997b Right and Wrong Sticking? *Estudios Biblicos* 55:89-106.

De Vos, Craig S.

1998 Stepmothers, Concubines, and the Case of Πορνεια in 1 Corinthians 5. *New Testament Studies* 44:104-114.

De Young, James B.

1995 The Source and Meaning of the Translation "Homosexuals" in Biblical Studies. *Evangelical Review of Theology* 19:54-63.

Dodd, Brian J.

1995 Paul's Paradigmatic "I" and 1 Corinthians 6:12. *Journal for the Study of the New Testament* 59:39-58.

Dunn, James D. G.

1970 *Baptism in the Holy Spirit.* London: SCM.

1973 1 Corinthians 15:45—Last Adam, Life-giving Spirit. Pp. 127-141 in *Christ and Spirit in the New Testament.* Editors, Barnabas Lindars, Stephen Smalley, and C. F. D. Moule. Cambridge: Cambridge University Press.

1975 *Jesus and the Spirit.* Philadelphia: Westminster.

1995 In Search of Wisdom. *Epworth Review* 22:48-53.

1998 *The Theology of Paul the Apostle.* Grand Rapids: Eerdmans.

2002 How Are the Dead Raised? With What Body Do They Come? Reflections on 1 Corinthians 15. *Southwestern Journal of Theology* 45:4-18.

Ebner, Martin

1991 *Leidenlisten und Apostelbrief.* Forschung zur Bibel 66. Wuerzburg, Germany: Echter.

Eckstein, H.-J.

1983 *Der Begriff Syneidesis bei Paulus.* Wissenschaftliche Untersuchungen zum Neuen Testament. Series 2, vol. 10. Tübingen: J. C. B. Mohr (Paul Siebeck).

Elliott, John H.

2004 No Kingdom of God for Softies? Or What Was Paul Really Saying? 1 Corinthians 6:9-10 in Context. *Biblical Theological Bulletin* 34:17-40.

Ellis, E. E.

1957 *Paul's Use of the Old Testament.* Grand Rapids: Eerdmans.

Ellis, J. Edward

2001 Controlled Burn: The Romantic Note in 1 Corinthians 7:1-9. *Perspectives in Religious Studies* 29:89-98.

Engberg-Pedersen, Troels

1991 1 Corinthians 11:16 and the Character of Pauline Exhortation. *Journal of Biblical Literature* 110:679-689.

1993 Proclaiming the Lord's Death: 1 Corinthians 11:17-34 and the Forms of Paul's Theological Argument. Pp. 103-132 in *Pauline Theology, vol. 2: 1 & 2 Corinthians.* Editor, David Hay. Minneapolis: Fortress.

Engelbrecht, Edward A.
1996 To Speak in a Tongue: The Old Testament and Early Rabbinic Background of a Pauline Expression. *Concordia Journal* 22:295-302.

Engels, Donald
1990 *Roman Corinth*. Chicago: University of Chicago Press.

Enns, P. E.
1996 The "Moveable Well" in 1 Cor 10:4: An Extrabiblical Tradition in an Apostolic Text. *Bulletin for Biblical Research* 6:23-38.

Farmer, William
1993 Peter and Paul, and the Tradition concerning "The Lord's Supper" in 1 Corinthians 11:23-26. Pp. 35-55 in *One Loaf, One Cup: Ecumenical Studies of 1 Cor 11 and Eucharistic Texts*. Editor, Ben Meyers. New Gospel Studies 6. Macon, GA: Mercer University Press.

Fee, Gordon
1980 1 Corinthians 7:1 in the NIV. *Journal of the Evangelical Theological Society* 23:307-314.

1987 *The First Epistle to the Corinthians*. New International Commentary on the New Testament. Grand Rapids: Eerdmans.

1995 Toward a Pauline Theology of Glossolalia. *Crux* 31:22-23, 26-31.

Fiorenza, Elizabeth
1992 *In Memory of Her: A Feminist Theological Reconstruction of Christian Origins*. New York: Crossroad.

Fisk, Bruce N.
1989 Eating Meat Offered to Idols: Corinthian Behavior and Pauline Response in 1 Corinthians 8-10 (A Response to Gordon Fee). *Trinity Journal* 10:49-70.

Fitzgerald, John T.
1988 *Cracks in an Earthen Vessel: An Examination of the Catalogues of Hardships in the Corinthian Correspondence*. Society of Biblical Literature Dissertation Series 99. Atlanta: Scholars Press.

Fitzmyer, J. A.
1993 *Kephale* in 1 Corinthians 11:3. *Interpretation* 47:52-59.

Forbes, Christopher
1995 *Prophecy and Inspired Speech in Early Christianity and Its Hellenistic Environment*. Wissenshaftliche Untersuchungen zum Neuen Testament 2/75. Tübingen: J. C. B. Mohr (Paul Siebeck).

2001 Paul's Principalities and Powers: Demythologizing Apocalyptic? *Journal for the Study of the New Testament* 82:61-88.

Ford, J. Massyngberde
1966 The Meaning of "Virgin." *New Testament Studies* 12:293-299.

Francis, J.
1980 As Babes in Christ: Some Proposals Regarding 1 Corinthians 3:1-3. *Journal for the Study of the New Testament* 7:41-60.

Furnish, Victor Paul
1999 *The Theology of the First Letter to the Corinthians*. New Testament Theology. Cambridge: Cambridge University Press.

Gaffin, Richard B.
1979 *Perspectives on Pentecost: New Testament Teaching on the Gifts of the Holy Spirit*. Phillipsburg, NJ: Presbyterian & Reformed.

1995 Some Epistemological Reflections on 1 Cor 2:6-16. *Westminster Theological Journal* 57:103-124.

Gardner, P. D.
1994 *The Gifts of God and the Authentication of a Christian: An Exegetical Study of 1 Corinthians 8:1–11:1*. Lanham, MD: University Press of America.

Garland, David
2001 The Dispute over Food Sacrificed to Idols (1 Cor 8:1–11:1). *Perspectives in Religious Studies* 30:173-197.

2003 *1 Corinthians*. Exegetical Commentary on the New Testament. Grand Rapids: Baker.

Garrison, Roman
1993 Paul's Use of the Athlete Metaphor in 1 Corinthians 9. *Studies in Religion/Sciences Religieuses* 22:209-217.

Gaventa, Beverly

1983 You Proclaim the Lord's Death: 1 Corinthians 11:26 and Paul's Understanding of Worship. *Review and Expositor* 80:377-387.

1996 Mother's Milk and Ministry in 1 Corinthians 3. Pp. 101-113 in *Theology and Ethics in Paul and His Interpreters: Essays in Honor of Victor Paul Furnish.* Editors, E. H. Lovering, Jr. and J. L. Sumney. Nashville: Abingdon.

Gentry, Lonnie

1999 Beyond Remembering: Proclaiming the Death in the Supper. *Restoration Quarterly* 41:241-243.

Giles, Kevin

2002 *The Trinity and Subordinationism: The Doctrine of God and the Contemporary Gender Debate.* Downers Grove, IL: InterVarsity.

Gill, D. W. J.

1990 The Importance of Roman Portraiture for Head Coverings in 1 Corinthians 11:2-16. *Tyndale Bulletin* 41.2:244-260.

1992 The Meat-market at Corinth. *Tyndale Bulletin* 43:389-393.

Gillihan, Y. M.

2002 Jewish Laws on Illicit Marriage, the Defilement of Offspring, and the Holiness of the Temple: A New Halakic Interpretation of 1 Corinthians 7:14. *Journal of Biblical Literature* 121:711-744.

Gillman, J.

1988 A Thematic Comparison: 1 Cor 15:50-57 and 2 Cor 5:1-5. *Journal of Biblical Literature* 107:439-454.

Glancy, J. A.

1998 Obstacles to Slaves' Participation in the Corinthian Church. *Journal of Biblical Literature* 117:481-501.

Gooch, P. W.

1987 "Conscience" in 1 Corinthians 8 and 10. *New Testament Studies* 33:244-254.

Goulder, Michael

2001 *Paul and the Competing Mission in Corinth.* Peabody, MA: Hendrickson.

Green, Gene L.

2001 As for Prophecies, They Will Come to an End: 2 Peter, Paul, and Plutarch on "The Obsolescence of Oracles." *Journal for the Study of the New Testament* 82:107-122.

Grindheim, Sigurd

2002 Wisdom for the Perfect: Paul's Challenge to the Corinthian Church (1 Corinthians 2:6-16). *Journal of Biblical Literature* 121:689-709.

Grudem, Wayne

1985 Does κεφαλη ("Head") Mean "Source" or "Authority over" in Greek Literature? A Survey of 2,335 Examples. *Trinity Journal* 6:38-59.

1990 The Meaning of κεφαλη: A Response to Recent Studies. *Trinity Journal* 11:3-72.

2001 The Meaning of κεφαλη ("Head"): An Evaluation of New Evidence, Real and Alleged. *Journal of the Evangelical Theological Society* 44:25-65.

Gundry, Robert H.

1966 "Ecstatic Utterance" (N.E.B.)? *Journal for Theological Studies* 17:299-307.

Gundry-Volf, Judith M.

1990 *Paul and Perseverance.* Wissenshaftliche Untersuchungen zum Neuen Testament 2/37. Tübingen: J. C. B. Mohr (Paul Siebeck).

1994 Celibate Pneumatics and Social Power: On the Motivations for Sexual Asceticism in Corinth. *Union Seminary Quarterly Review* 48:105-126.

1996 Controlling the Bodies: A Theological Profile of the Corinthian Sexual Ascetics (1 Cor 7). Pp. 519-541 in *The Corinthian Correspondence.* Editor, R. Bieringer. Bibliotheca ephemeridum theologicarum lovaniensium 125. Leuven, Belgium: Peeters.

1997 Gender and Creation in 1 Corinthians 11:2-6: A Study in Paul's Theological Method. Pp. 151-171 in *Evangelium Schriftauslegung Kirche.* Editors, J. Adna, S. J. Hafemann, and O. Hofius. Göttingen: Vandenhoeck & Ruprecht.

Hall, David R.

1994 A Disguise for the Wise: μετασχηματισμός in 1 Corinthians 4.6. *New Testament Studies* 40:143-149.

Hanges, James C.
1998 1 Corinthians 4:6 and the Possibility of the Written Bylaws in the Corinthian Church. *Journal of Biblical Literature* 117:275-298.

Hanson, A. T.
1987 *The Paradox of the Cross in the Thought of St. Paul.* Journal for the Study of the New Testament Supplement Series 17. Sheffield: Journal for the Study of the Old Testament Press.

Harrill, J. A.
1994 Paul and Slavery: The Problem of 1 Corinthians 7:21. *Biblical Research* 39:5-28.

Harris, G.
1991 The Beginnings of Church Discipline: 1 Corinthians 5. *New Testament Studies* 37:1-21.

Harris, W.
1982 "Sounding Brass" and Hellenistic Terminology. *Biblical Archaeology Review* 8:38-41.

Harrisville, Roy A.
1955 The Concept of Newness in the New Testament. *Journal of Biblical Literature* 74:69-79.

1976 Speaking in Tongues: A Lexicographical Study. *Catholic Biblical Quarterly* 38:35-48.

Hays, Richard
1989 *Echoes of Scripture in the Letters of Paul.* New Haven, CT: Yale University Press.

1997 *First Corinthians.* Interpretation. Louisville: John Knox.

1999 The Conversion of Imagination: Scripture and Eschatology in 1 Corinthians. *New Testament Studies* 45:391-412.

Henderson, Suzanne Watts
2002 If Anyone Hungers . . .: An Integrated Reading of 1 Cor 11.17-34. *New Testament Studies* 48:195-208.

Hengel, Martin
1977 *Crucifixion.* Philadelphia: Fortress.

Hjort, Birgitte G.
1979 The Workshop as a Social Setting for Paul's Missionary Preaching. *Catholic Biblical Quarterly* 41:438-450.

2001 Gender Hierarchy or Religious Androgyny? Male-female Interaction in the Corinthian Community—A Reading of 1 Cor. 11.2-16. *Studia Theologica* 55:58-80.

Hodge, Charles
1958 *First Epistle to the Corinthians.* 5th ed. London: Banner of Truth.

Hofius, Otfried
1993 The Lord's Supper and the Lord's Supper Tradition: Reflections on 1 Corinthians 11:23b-25. Pp. 75-115 in *One Loaf, One Cup: Ecumenical Studies of 1 Cor 11 and Eucharistic Texts.* Editor, Ben Meyers. New Gospel Studies 6. Macon, GA: Mercer University Press.

Holladay, Carl R.
1990 1 Corinthians 13: Paul as Apostolic Paradigm. Pp. 80-98 in *Greeks, Romans, and Christians: Essays in Honor of Abraham J. Malherbe.* Editors, D. L. Balch, E. Ferguson, and W. A. Meeks. Philadelphia: Fortress.

Hollander, Harm W.
1994 The Testing by Fire of the Builders' Works: 1 Corinthians 3.10-15. *New Testament Studies* 40:89-104.

1998 The Meaning of the Term "Law" in 1 Corinthians. *Novum Testamentum* 40:117-135.

Hollander, Harm W., and G. van der Hout
1996 The Apostle Paul Calling Himself an Abortion: 1 Cor. 15:8 within the Context of 1 Cor. 15:8-10. *Novum Testamentum* 38:224-236.

Holleman, Joost
1996 *Resurrection and Parousia: A Traditio-historical Study of Paul's Eschatology in 1 Cor 15.* Novum Testamentum Supplement 84. Leiden: Brill.

Hooker, Morna
1963-1964 Beyond the Things Which Are Written? An Examination of 1 Corinthians 4:6. *New Testament Studies* 10:127-132.

Horrell, David
1995 The Lord's Supper at Corinth and in the Church Today. *Theology* 98:196-202.

1997a The Lord Commanded . . . but I Have Not Used . . .: Exegetical Hermeneutical Reflections on 1 Cor 9.14-15. *New Testament Studies* 43:587-603.

1997b Theological Principle or Christological Praxis? Pauline Ethics in 1 Corinthians 8.1–11.1. *Journal for the Study of the New Testament* 67:83-114.

Horsley, Richard

1977 Wisdom of Word and Words in Corinth. *Catholic Biblical Quarterly* 39:224-239.

1978 Conscience and Freedom among the Corinthians. *Catholic Biblical Quarterly* 40:574-589.

1998 *1 Corinthians.* Nashville: Abingdon.

Hoskins, Paul M.

2001 The Use of Biblical and Extrabiblical Parallels in the Interpretation of First Corinthians 6:2-3. *Catholic Biblical Quarterly* 63:287-297.

Houghton, Myron J.

1996 A Reexamination of 1 Corinthians 13:8-13. *Bibliotheca Sacra* 153:344-356.

Hurd, John C., Jr.

1965 *The Origin of 1 Corinthians.* New York: Seabury.

Hurley, James B.

1981 *Man and Woman in Biblical Perspective.* Grand Rapids: Zondervan.

Hutson, C. R.

1997 Was Timothy Timid? On the Rhetoric of Fearlessness and Cowardice. *Biblical Research* 42:58-73.

Hyldahl, N.

1991 The Corinthian "Parties" and the Corinthian Crisis. *Studia Theologica* 45:19-32.

Ince, Gwen

2000 Judge for Yourselves: Teasing Out Some Knots in 1 Corinthians 11:2-16. *Australian Biblical Review* 48:59-71.

Isaak, Jon M.

1995 Hearing God's Word in the Silence: A Canonical Approach to 1 Corinthians 14.34-35. *Direction* 24:55-64.

Isenburg, M.

1975 The Sale of Sacrificial Meat. *Classical Philosophy* 70:271-273.

Jeremias, Joachim

1955–1956 Flesh and Blood Cannot Inherit the Kingdom of God. *New Testament Studies* 2:151-159.

Jervis, L. Ann

1993 But I Want You to Know . . .: Paul's Midrashic Intertextual Response to the Corinthian Worshipers. *Journal of Biblical Literature* 112:231-246.

1995 1 Corinthians 14.34-35: A Reconsideration of Paul's Limitation of the Free Speech of Some Corinthian Women. *Journal for the Study of the New Testament* 58:51-74.

Johnson, Alan F.

2004 *1 Corinthians.* IVP New Testament Commentary 7. Downers Grove, IL: InterVarsity Press.

Johnson, Andy

1996 Firstfruits and Death's Defeat: Metaphor in Paul's Rhetorical Strategy in 1 Cor 15:20-28. *Word and World* 16:456-464.

Judge, E. A.

1960 *The Social Pattern of Christian Groups in the First Century.* London: Tyndale.

Kaiser, Walter C., Jr.

1978 The Current Crisis in Exegesis and the Apostolic Use of Deuteronomy 25:4 in 1 Corinthians 9:8-10. *Journal of the Evangelical Theological Society* 21:3-18.

1981 A Neglected Text in Bibliology Discussion: 1 Corinthians 2:6-16. *Westminster Theological Journal* 43:301-318.

Keener, Craig

1993 *Bible Background Commentary.* Downers Grove, IL: InterVarsity.

2005 *1–2 Corinthians.* New Cambridge Bible Commentary. New York: Cambridge University Press.

Ker, Donald P.

2000 Paul and Apollos—Colleagues or Rivals? *Journal for the Study of the New Testament* 77:75-97.

Khiok-khng, Yeo
1998 Differentiation and Mutuality of Male-female Relations in 1 Corinthians 11:2-16. *Biblical Research*
     43:7-21.

Kierkegaard, Søren
1958 *Johannes Climacus.* Translator, T. H. Corxall. London: A. & C. Black. (Orig. pub. 1844.)

Kim, Chan-Hie
1972 *Form and Structure of the Familiar Greek Letters of Recommendation.* Society of Biblical Literature
     Dissertation Series 4. Missoula, MT: Society of Biblical Literature.

Kinman, Brent
1997 Appoint the Despised as Judges! (1 Corinthians 6:4). *Tyndale Bulletin* 48:345-354.

Kistemaker, Simon J.
1992 Deliver This Man to Satan: A Case Study in Church Discipline. *The Master's Seminary Journal* 3:33-46.

Klassen, W.
1993 The Sacred Kiss in the NT: An Example of Social Boundary Lines. *New Testament Studies* 39:122-135.

Klauck, Hans-Josef
1993 Presence in the Lord's Supper: 1 Corinthians 11:23-26 in the Context of Hellenistic Religious History.
     Pp. 57-74 in *One Loaf, One Cup: Ecumenical Studies of 1 Cor 11 and Eucharistic Texts.* Editor,
     Ben Meyers. New Gospel Studies 6. Macon, GA: Mercer University Press.

Klein, W. W.
1986 Noisy Gong or Acoustic Vase? A Note on 1 Corinthians 13:1. *New Testament Studies* 32:286-289.

Koester, Craig R.
1997 Promise and Warning: The Lord's Supper in 1 Corinthians. *Word and World* 17:45-53.

Kreitzer, Larry J.
1987 *Jesus and God in Paul's Eschatology.* Journal for the Study of the New Testament Supplement Series
     19. Sheffield: Journal for the Study of the Old Testament Press.

1993 1 Corinthians 10:4 and Philo's Flinty Rock. *Communio Viatorum* 35:109-126.

Kroeger, Catherine
1987 The Classical Concept of Head as "Source." Pp. 267-283 in *Equal to Serve.* Editor, C. G. Hull.
     Old Tappan, NJ: Revell.

Kuck, David
1992a *Judgment and Community Conflict: Paul's Use of Apocalyptic Judgment Language in 1 Cor. 3:5–4:5.*
      Novum Testamentum Supplement 66. Leiden: Brill.

1992b Paul and Pastoral Ambition: A Reflection on 1 Corinthians 3-4. *Currents in Theology and Mission*
      19:174-183.

Kümmel, Werner Georg
1975 *Introduction to the New Testament.* Translator, Howard Clark Kee. Nashville: Abingdon.

Küng, Hans
1978 *Does God Exist?* Translator, Edward Quinn. Garden City, NY: Doubleday.

Lambrecht, Jan
1982 Paul's Christological Use of Scripture in 1 Cor. 15.20-28. *New Testament Studies* 28:502-507.

2000 Just a Possibility? A Reply to Johan S. Vos on 1 Cor 15.12-20. *Zeitschrift für die neutestamentliche
     Wissenschaft* 91:143-145.

2001 Three Brief Notes on 1 Corinthians 15. *Bijdragen* 62:28-41.

Lampe, Peter
1994 The Eucharist: Identifying with Christ on the Cross. *Interpretation* 48:36-49.

Lanier, David E.
1991 With Stammering Lips and Another Tongue: 1 Cor 14:20-22 and Isa 28:11-12. *Criswell Theological
     Review* 5:259-285.

Lassen, Eva Maria
1991 The Use of the Father Image in Imperial Propaganda and 1 Corinthians 4:14-21. *Tyndale Bulletin*
     42:127-136.

Laughery, G. J.
1997 Paul: Anti-marriage? Anti-sex? Ascetic? A Dialogue with 1 Corinthians 7:1-40. *Evangelical Quarterly*
     69:109-128.

Lewis, S.
1998 *So That God May Be All in All: 1 Corinthians 15:12-34.* Tesi Gregoriana Serie Teologia 42. Rome: Pontifical Gregorian University Press.

Liefield, Walter L.
1986 Women, Submission and Ministry in 1 Corinthians. Pp. 134-154 in *Women, Authority, and the Bible.* Editor, A. Mickelsen. Downers Grove, IL: InterVarsity.

Lietzmann, H.
1949 *Die Briefe des Apostels Paulus: An die Korinther I, II.* Editor, W. G. Kümmell. Tübingen: J. C. B. Mohr.

Lim, Timothy
1987 Not in Persuasive Words of Wisdom, but in the Demonstration of the Spirit and Power. *Novum Testamentum* 29:137-149.

Litfin, Duane
1994 *St. Paul's Theology of Proclamation: 1 Corinthians 1–4 and Greco-Roman Rhetoric.* New York: Cambridge University Press.

Lockwood, Peter F.
1996 Does 1 Corinthians 14:34-35 Exclude Women from the Pastoral Office? *Lutheran Theological Journal* 30:30-38.

Lofthouse, W. F.
1955 "I" and "We" in the Pauline Epistles. *Bible Translator* 6:72-80.

Lüdemann, Gerd, and Alf Özen
1995 *What Really Happened to Jesus: A Historical Approach to the Resurrection.* London: SCM.

Macchia, F. D.
1998 Groans Too Deep for Words: Towards a Theology of Tongues as Initial Evidence. *Asian Journal of Pentecostal Studies* 1:149-173.

Maier, Walter A.
1991 An Exegetical Study of 1 Corinthians 14:33b-38. *Concordia Theological Quarterly* 55:81-104.

Malick, David E.
1993 The Condemnation of Homosexuality in 1 Corinthians 6:9. *Bibliotheca Sacra* 150:479-492.

Malina, Bruce
1993 *The New Testament World.* Louisville: Westminster John Knox.

Mare, W. Harold
1976 1 Corinthians. Pp. 173-297 in *The Expositor's Bible Commentary,* vol. 10. Grand Rapids: Zondervan.

Marshall, Peter
1987 *Enmity in Corinth: Social Conventions in Paul's Relations with the Corinthians.* Wissenshaftliche Untersuchungen zum Neuen Testament 2/23. Tübingen: J. C. B. Mohr (Paul Siebeck).

Martens, Michael P.
1996a First Corinthians 7:14: "Sanctified" by the Believing Spouse. *Notes on Translation* 10:31-35.
1996b First Corinthians 13:10: When That Which Is Perfect Comes. *Notes on Translation* 10:36-40.

Martin, Dale B.
1991 Tongues of Angels and Other Status Indicators. *Journal of the American Academy of Religion* 59:547-589.
1995 *The Corinthian Body.* New Haven, CT: Yale University Press.
1996 *Arsenokoitēs* and *Malakos:* Meaning and Consequences. Pp. 117-136 in *Biblical Ethics and Homosexuality.* Editor, Robert L. Brawley. Louisville: Westminster John Knox.

Martin, Ralph
1987 The Opponents of Paul in 2 Corinthians: An Old Issue Revisited. Pp. 279-287 in *Tradition and Interpretation in the New Testament.* Editors, Gerald F. Hawthorne and Otto Betz. Grand Rapids: Eerdmans.

Mauser, Ulrich W.
1996 Creation and Human Sexuality in the New Testament. Pp. 3-16 in *Biblical Ethics and Homosexuality.* Editor, Robert Brawly. Louisville: Westminster John Knox.

McElhanon, K. A.
1997 1 Corinthians 13:8-12: Neglected Meanings of ἐκ μέρους and τὸ τέλειον. *Notes on Translation* 11:45-53.

McKnight, Scot
1991 *A Light among the Gentiles: Jewish Missionary Activity in the Second Temple Period.* Minneapolis: Fortress.

Meeks, Wayne
1982 And Rose Up to Play: Midrash and Paranaesis in 1 Corinthians 10:1-22. *Journal for the Study of the New Testament* 16:64-78.

Meggitt, Justin J.
1994 Meat Consumption and Social Conflict in Corinth. *Journal of Theological Studies* 45:137-141.

Metzger, Bruce
1971 *A Textual Commentary on the Greek New Testament.* New York: United Bible Societies.

Mitchell, A. C.
1993 Rich and Poor in the Courts of Corinth: Litigiousness and Status in 1 Corinthians 6:1-11. *New Testament Studies* 39:562-586.

Mitchell, Margaret M.
1989 Concerning περι δε in 1 Corinthians. *Novum Testamentum* 31:229-256.

1993 *Paul and the Rhetoric of Reconciliation.* Louisville: Westminster John Knox.

1997 Reconciliation: Biblical Reflections. III. Paul's 1 Corinthians on Reconciliation in the Church: Promise and Pitfalls. *New Theology Review* 10:39-48.

Mitton, C. Leslie
1973 New Wine in Old Wineskins. *Expository Times* 84:339-343.

Moffatt, James
1938 *The First Epistle of Paul to the Corinthians.* London: Hodder & Stoughton.

Moule, C. F. D.
1959-1960 A Reconsideration of the Context of Maranatha. *New Testament Studies* 6:307-310.

Munck, Johannes
1959 Paulus Tanquam Abortivus (1 Cor. 15:6). Pp. 180-193 in *New Testament Essays: Studies in Memory of Thomas Walter Manson, 1893-1958.* Editor, A. J. B. Higgins. Manchester: Manchester University Press.

Murphy-O'Connor, Jerome
1980 Sex and Logic. *Catholic Biblical Quarterly* 42:482-499.

1984 The Corinth That Saint Paul Saw. *Biblical Archaeologist* 47:147-159.

1993 Co-authorship in the Corinthian Correspondence. *Revue Biblique* 100:562-579.

1996 *Paul, A Critical Life.* New York: Oxford University Press.

2002 *St. Paul's Corinth: Texts and Archaeology.* 3rd ed. Good News Studies 6. Collegeville, MN: Liturgical Press.

Newman, Carey
1992 *Paul's Glory-Christology: Tradition and Rhetoric.* Novum Testamentum Supplement 69. Leiden: Brill.

Niccum, Curt
1997 The Voice of the Manuscripts on the Silence of Women: The External Evidence for 1 Cor 14.34-35. *New Testament Studies* 43:242-255.

Nickle, K. F.
1966 *The Collection: A Study in Paul's Strategy.* Studies in Biblical Theology 48. London: SCM Press.

Odell-Scott, David W.
1983 Let the Women Speak in the Church: An Egalitarian Interpretation of 1 Cor 14:33b-36. *Biblical Theology Bulletin* 13:90-93.

1987 In Defense of an Egalitarian Interpretation of 1 Cor 14:34-36: A Reply to Murphy-O'Connor's Critique. *Biblical Theological Bulletin* 17:100-103.

2000 Editorial Dilemma: The Interpolation of 1 Cor 14:34-35 in the Western Manuscripts of D, G, and 88. *Biblical Theology Bulletin* 30:68-74.

Olender, Robert G.
1998 The Pauline Privilege: Inference or Exegesis? *Faith and Mission* 16:94-117.

2001 Paul's Source for 1 Corinthians 6:10-7:11. *Faith and Mission* 18:60-73.

O'Mahony, Kieran
1997 Roman Corinth and Corinthian Christians. *Scripture in Church* 27:15-124.

Omanson, R. L.
1992 Acknowledging Paul's Quotations. *The Bible Translator* 43:201-212.

O'Neill, J. C.
1980 This is My Body. . . . *Irish Biblical Studies* 24:32-43.

Oropeza, B. J.
1998 Laying to Rest the Midrash: Paul's Message on Meat Sacrificed to Idols in Light of the Deuteronomic Tradition. *Biblica* 79:57-68.

1999 Apostasy in the Wilderness: Paul's Message to the Corinthians in a State of Eschatological Liminality. *Journal for the Study of the New Testament* 75:69-86.

Orr, William, and J. Walther
1976 *1 Corinthians.* Anchor Bible. Garden City, NY: Doubleday.

Oster, Richard E.
1988 When Men Wore Veils to Worship: The Historical Context of 1 Corinthians 11:4. *New Testament Studies* 34:481-505.

1992 Use, Misuse and Neglect of Archaeological Evidence in Some Modern Works on 1 Corinthians. *Zeitschrift für die neutestamentliche Wissenschaft* 83:52-73.

1995 *1 Corinthians.* College Press NIV Commentary. Joplin, MO: College Press.

Padgett, Alan G.
1994 The Significance of *anti* in 1 Corinthians 11:15. *Tyndale Bulletin* 45:181-187.

2002 The Body in Resurrection: Science and Scripture on the "Spiritual Body." *Word and World* 22:155-163.

2003 Beginning with the End in 1 Cor. 11:2-16. *Priscilla Papers* 17:17-23.

Paige, Terence
1991 1 Corinthians 12:2: A Pagan Pompe? *Journal for the Study of the New Testament* 44:57-65.

Painter, John
1997 *Just James: The Brother of Jesus in History and Tradition.* Columbia: University of South Carolina Press.

Pascal, Blaise
1966 *Pensées.* Translator, A. J. Krailsheimer. Baltimore: Penguin. (Orig. pub. 1670.)

Payne, Philip B.
1995 Fuldensis, Sigla for Variants in Vaticanus, and 1 Cor. 14:34-35. *New Testament Studies* 41:240-262.

1998 MS. 88 as Evidence for a Text with 1 Cor 14.34-5. *New Testament Studies* 44:152-158.

Pearson, Birger A.
1973 *The Pneumatikos-Psychikos Terminology in 1 Corinthians 12.* Society of Biblical Literature Dissertation Series 12. Missoula, MT: Scholars Press.

Perriman, A. C.
1994 The Head of a Woman: The Meaning of κεφαλη in 1 Cor. 11:3. *Journal of Theological Studies* 45:602-622.

Peters, Greg
2002 Spiritual Marriage in Early Christianity: 1 Cor 7:25-38 in Modern Exegesis and the Earliest Church. *Trinity Journal* 23:211-224.

Petzer, J. H.
1989 Contextual Evidence in Favor of καυχήσωμαι in 1 Corinthians 13.3. *New Testament Studies* 35:229-253.

1993 Reconsidering the Silent Women of Corinth: A Note on 1 Corinthians 14:34-35. *Theologia Evangelica* 26:132-138.

Pierce, C. A.
1955 *Conscience in the New Testament.* Journal for the Study of the New Testament Supplement Series 143. Sheffield: Sheffield Academic Press.

Pogoloff, Stephen
1992 *Logos and Sophia: The Rhetorical Situation of 1 Corinthians.* Atlanta: Scholars Press.

Poirier, John C., and J. Frankovic
1996 Celibacy and Charism in 1 Cor 7:5-7. *Harvard Theological Review* 89:1-18.

Porter, Stanley E.
1991 How Should κολλώμενος in 1 Cor 6,16.17 Be Translated? *Ephemerides Theologicae Lovanienses* 67:105-106.

Ramsaran, Rollin A.
1995 More Than an Opinion: Paul's Rhetorical Maxim in First Corinthians 7:25-26. *Catholic Biblical Quarterly* 57:531-541.

Reaume, J. D.
1995 Another Look at 1 Corinthians 15:29, "Baptized for the Dead." *Bibliotheca Sacra* 152:457-475.

Roberts, P.
1997 Seers or Overseers? *Expository Times* 108:301-305.

Robertson, Archibald, and A. Plummer
1911 *First Epistle of St. Paul to the Corinthians.* International Critical Commentary. Edinburgh: T&T Clark.

Roetzel, Calvin J.
1999 *Paul: The Man and the Myth.* Edinburgh: T&T Clark.

Rosner, Brian S.
1991a Moses Appointing Judges. An Antecedent in 1 Cor 6.1-6? *Zeitschrift für die neutestamentliche Wissenschaft* 82:275-278.
1991b Temple and Holiness in 1 Corinthians 5. *Tyndale Bulletin* 42:137-145.
1992a Ουχι μαλλον επενθησατε: Corporate Responsibility in 1 Corinthians 5. *New Testament Studies* 3:470-473.
1992b A Possible Quotation of Test. Reuben 5:5 in 1 Corinthians 6:18a. *Journal of Theological Studies* 43:123-127.
1992c Stronger than He? The Strength of 1 Corinthians 10:22b. *Tyndale Bulletin* 43:171-179.
1994 *Paul, Scripture, and Ethics: A Study of 1 Corinthians 5-7.* Grand Rapids: Eerdmans.
1998 Temple Prostitution in 1 Corinthians 6:12-20. *Novum Testamentum* 40:336-351.

Rousselle, Aline
1992 Body Politics in Ancient Rome. Pp. 229-337 in *A History of Women in the West,* vol. 1. Editors, G. Duby and M. Perot. Cambridge, MA: Harvard University Press.

Ruthven, Jon
1993 *On the Cessation of the Charismata.* Journal of Pentecostal Theology Supplementary Series. Sheffield: Sheffield Academic Press.

Sandbach, Francis H.
1970 Menander. Pp. 669-670 in *Oxford Classical Dictionary.* Editors, N. G. L. Hammond and H. H. Scullard. Oxford: Clarendon.

Sandnes, Karl O.
1991 *Paul—One of the Prophets?* Wissenshaftliche Untersuchungen zum Neuen Testament 2/43. Tübingen: J. C. B. Mohr (Paul Siebeck).
1996 Prophecy—A Sign for Believers. *Biblica* 77:1-15.

Schmithals, Walther
1971 *Gnosticism in Corinth.* Nashville: Abingdon.
1973 Die Korintherbriefe als Briefsammlung. *Zeitshcrift für die neutestamentliche Wissenschaft* 64:263-288.
1993 The Pre-Pauline Tradition in 1 Corinthians 15:20-28. *Perspectives in Religious Studies* 20:357-380.

Schnackenburg, Rudolf
1962 *Baptism in the Thought of St. Paul.* Oxford: Blackwell.

Schneider, Bernadin
1967 The Corporate Meaning and Background of 1 Cor 15,45b—O Eschatos Adam Eis Pneuma Zoiopoioun. *Catholic Biblical Quarterly* 29:450-467.

Schneider, Walter
1979 Judgment. Pp. 361-367 in *New International Dictionary of New Testament Theology,* vol. 2. Editor, Colin Brown. Grand Rapids: Eerdmans.

Schottroff, Luise
2000 Holiness and Justice: Exegetical Comments on 1 Corinthians 11.17-34. *Journal for the Study of the New Testament* 79:51-60.

Schulz, R. R.
1998 Another Look at the Text of 1 Corinthians 14:33-35. *Lutheran Theological Journal* 32:128-131.

Schweitzer, Albert
1931 *The Mysticism of Paul the Apostle.* London: Black.

Scroggs, Robin
1983 *The New Testament and Homosexuality.* Philadelphia: Fortress.

Shanor, Jay
1988 Paul as Master Builder: Construction Terms in 1 Cor. *New Testament Studies* 34:461–471.

Shillington, V. George
1998 Atonement Texture in 1 Corinthians 5:5. *Journal for the Study of the New Testament* 71:29–50.

Shogren, Gary
1999 How Did They Suppose "the Perfect" Would Come? 1 Corinthians 13.8–12 in Patristic Exegesis. *Journal of Pentecostal Theology* 15:99–121.

Sigountos, J. G.
1994 The Genre of 1 Corinthians 13. *New Testament Studies* 40:246–260.

Smit, Joop F. M.
1993 Two Puzzles: 1 Corinthians 12:31 and 13:3. A Rhetorical Solution. *New Testament Studies* 39:246–264.

1994 Tongues and Prophecy: Deciphering 1 Cor 14.22. *Biblica* 75:175–190.

1997a Do Not Be Idolaters: Paul's Rhetoric in First Corinthians 10:1–22. *Novum Testamentum* 39:40–53.

1997b The Function of First Corinthians 10.23–30: A Rhetorical Anticipation. *Biblica* 78:377–388.

2000 You Shall Not Muzzle a Threshing Ox: Paul's Use of the Law of Moses in 1 Cor 9.8–12. *Estudios Biblicos* 58:239–263.

2002 What Is Apollos? What Is Paul? In Search for the Coherence of First Corinthians 1:10–4:21. *Novum Testamentum* 44:231–251.

Soards, Marion
1999 *1 Corinthians.* New International Biblical Commentary. Peabody, MA: Hendrickson.

South, James T.
1993 A Critique of the "Curse/Death" Interpretation of 1 Corinthians 5.1–8. *New Testament Studies* 39:539–561.

Stendahl, Krister
1977 *Paul among Jews and Gentiles.* London: SCM.

Still, E. Coye, III
2002 Paul's Aims Regarding Εἰδωλόθυτα: A New Proposal for Interpreting 1 Corinthians 8:1–11:1. *Novum Testamentum* 44:333–343.

2004 Divisions over Leaders and Food Offered to Idols: The Parallel Thematic Structures of 1 Corinthians 4:6–21 and 8:1–11:1. *Tyndale Bulletin* 55:17–41.

Stuckenbruck, Loren T.
2001 Why Should Women Cover Their Heads Because of the Angels? *Stone-Campbell Journal* 4:205–234.

Sumney, Jerry L.
2000 The Place of 1 Corinthians 9:24–27 in Paul's Argument. *Journal of Biblical Literature* 119:329–333.

Surburg, Mark P.
2000 Structural and Lexical Features in 1 Corinthians 11:27–32. *Concordia Journal* 26:200–217.

Talbert, Charles
1987 *Reading Corinthians: A Literary and Theological Commentary on 1 and 2 Corinthians.* New York: Crossroad.

Theissen, Gerd
1982 *The Social Setting of Pauline Christianity.* Philadelphia: Fortress.

1987 *The Psychological Aspects of Pauline Theology.* Translator, John Galvin. Philadelphia: Fortress.

2003 Social Conflicts in the Corinthian Community: Further Remarks on J. J. Meggitt, *Paul, Poverty, and Survival. Journal for the Study of the New Testament* 25:371–391.

Thiselton, Anthony C.
1973 The Meaning of Σαρξ in 1 Cor. 5:5: A Fresh Approach in the Light of Logical and Semantic Factors. *Scottish Journal of Theology* 26:204–228.

1977–1978 Realized Eschatology at Corinth. *New Testament Studies* 24:510–526.

2000 *The First Epistle to the Corinthians.* New International Greek Testament Commentary. Grand Rapids: Eerdmans.

Thomas, Robert L.
1993 1 Cor 13:11 Revisited. An Exegetical Update. *Master's Seminary Journal* 4:187-201.

Thompson, K. C.
1964 1 Corinthians 15,29 and Baptism for the Dead. Pp. 649-657 in *Studia Evangelica,* vol. 2. Editor, F. L. Cross. Texte und Untersuchungen 87. Berlin: Akademie Verlag.

Thrall, Margaret
1967 The Pauline Use of Συνειδησις. *New Testament Studies* 14:118-125.

Tyler, Ronald L.
2001 The History of the Interpretation of το μη υπερ α γεγραπται in 1 Corinthians 4:6. *Restoration Quarterly* 43:243-252.

Unnik, William C. van
1993 The Meaning of 1 Corinthians 12:31. *Novum Testamentum* 35:142-159.

Vander Broek, Lyle
1994 Discipline and Community: Another Look at 1 Corinthians 5. *Reformed Review* 48:5-13.

Vander Stichele, Caroline
1995 Is Silence Golden? Paul and Women's Speech in Corinth. *Louvain Studies* 20:241-253.

Vielhauer, Philipp
1994 Paul and the Cephas Party in Corinth. *Journal of Higher Criticism* 1:129-142.

Vlachos, Chris A.
2004 Law, Sin, and Death: An Edenic Triad? An Examination with Reference to 1 Corinthians 15:56. *Journal of the Evangelical Theological Society* 47:277-298.

Vogelstein, Hermann, and Paul Rieger
1895-1896 *Geschichte der Juden in Rom.* 2 vols. Berlin: Mayer & Müller.

Wagner, J. Ross
1998 Not Beyond the Things Which Are Written: A Call to Boast Only in the Lord. *New Testament Studies* 44:279-287.

Walker, William O.
2007 1 Corinthians 15:29-34 as a Non-Pauline Interpolation. *Catholic Biblical Quarterly* 69:84-103.

Watson, D. F.
1989 1 Cor 10:23–11:1 in the Light of Graeco-Roman Rhetoric: The Role of Rhetorical Questions. *Journal of Biblical Literature* 108:301-318.

Watson, Francis
1992 Christ, Community, and the Critique of Ideology: A Theological Reading of 1 Corinthians 1.18-31. *Nederlands Theologisch Tijdschrift* 46:132-149.

2000 The Authority of the Voice: A Theological Reading of 1 Cor 11.2-16. *New Testament Studies* 46:520-536.

Wedderburn, A. J. M.
1987 *Baptism and Resurrection: Studies in Pauline Theology against Its Graeco-Roman Background.* Wissenschaftliche Untersuchungen zum Neuen Testament 2/44. Tübingen: J. C. B. Mohr (Paul Siebeck).

Weiss, Johannes
1910 *Der erste Korintherbrief.* Göttingen: Vandenhoeck & Ruprecht.

1937 *History of Primitive Christianity,* vol. 1. Translator, editor, Frederick Grant. New York: Wilson-Erickson.

1959 *Earliest Christianity.* 2 vols. New York: Harper.

Welborn, Lawrence L.
1997 *Politics and Rhetoric in the Corinthian Epistles.* Macon, GA: Mercer University Press.

2002 Μωρὸς γένεσθω: Paul's Appropriation of the Role of the Fool in 1 Corinthians 1–4. *Biblical Interpretation* 10:420-435.

Wenham, David
1997 Whatever Went Wrong in Corinth? *Expository Times* 108:137-141.

White, Joel R.
1997 Baptized on account of the Dead: The Meaning of 1 Corinthians 15:29 in Its Context. *Journal of Biblical Literature* 116:487-499.

White, R. Fowler
1992 Richard Gaffin and Wayne Grudem on 1 Cor 13:10: A Comparison of Cessationist and Noncessationist Argumentation. *Journal of the Evangelical Theological Society* 35:171-181.

Williams, H. H. Drake, III
2003 Living as Christ Crucified: The Cross as a Foundation for Christian Ethics in 1 Corinthians. *Evangelical Quarterly* 75:117-131.

Williams, Ritva
1997 Lifting the Veil: A Social-science Interpretation of 1 Corinthians 11:2-16. *Consensus* 23:53-60.

Willis, Wendell
1985 *Idol Meat in Corinth: The Pauline Argument in 1 Corinthians 8 and 10.* Society of Biblical Literature Dissertation Series 68. Chico, CA: Scholars Press.

1989 The "Mind of Christ" in 1 Corinthians 2,16. *Biblica* 70:110-121.

Wilson, Kenneth T.
1991 Should Women Wear Headcoverings? *Bibliotheca Sacra* 148:442-462.

Wilson, R.
1972-1973 How Gnostic Were the Corinthians? *New Testament Studies* 19:65-74.

Wimbush, Vincent L.
1987 *Paul the Worldly Ascetic: Response to the World and Self-understanding according to 1 Corinthians 7.* Macon, GA: Mercer University Press.

Winter, Bruce
1978 The Lord's Supper at Corinth: An Alternative Reconstruction. *Reformed Theological Review* 37:73-82.

1989 Secular and Christian Responses to Corinthian Famines. *Tyndale Bulletin* 40:86-106.

1991 Civil Litigation in Secular Corinth and the Church. The Forensic Background to 1 Corinthians 6.1-8. *New Testament Studies* 37:559-572.

1994 *Seek the Welfare of the City: Christians as Benefactors and Citizens.* Grand Rapids: Eerdmans.

1997 Gluttony and Immorality at Elitist Banquets. The Background to 1 Corinthians 6:12-20. *Jian Dao* 7:77-90.

1998 Puberty or Passion? The Referent of υπερακμος in 1 Corinthians 7:36. *Tyndale Bulletin* 49:71-89.

2001 *After Paul Left Corinth: The Influence of Secular Ethics and Social Change.* Grand Rapids: Eerdmans.

Wire, Antoinette C.
1990 *The Corinthian Women Prophets: A Reconstruction through Paul's Rhetoric.* Minneapolis: Fortress.

Wiseman, James
1979 Corinth and Rome I: 228 B.C.–A.D. 267. *Aufstieg und Niedergang der römischen Welt,* part 2: *Principat,* vol. 7.1: *Politische Geschichte.* Editors, H. Temporini and W. Haase. Berlin: de Gruyter.

Witherington, Ben, III
1993 Not So Idle Thoughts about *eidolothuton. Tyndale Bulletin* 44:237-254.

1995 *Conflict and Community in Corinth: A Socio-rhetorical Commentary on 1 and 2 Corinthians.* Grand Rapids: Eerdmans.

Wong, Eric
2002 The Deradicalization of Jesus' Ethical Saying in 1 Corinthians. *New Testament Studies* 48:181-194.

Wright, N. T.
1992 *The Climax of the Covenant: Christ and Law in Pauline Theology.* Minneapolis: Fortress.

Wuellner, W. H.
1973 The Sociological Implications of 1 Corinthians 1:26-28 Reconsidered. Pp. 666-673 in *Studia Evangelica 6.* Editor, E. A. Livingstone. Text und Untersuchungen 112. Berlin: Akademie Verlag.

Yarborough, O. Larry
1985 *Not Like the Gentiles: Marriage Rules in the Letters of Paul.* Society of Biblical Literature Dissertation Series 80. Atlanta: Scholars Press.

Zerhusen, Bob
1997 The Problem of Tongues in 1 Cor 14: A Reexamination. *Biblical Theology Bulletin* 27:139-152.

Zuntz, G.
1953 *The Text of the Epistles: A Disquisition upon the Corpus Paulinum.* London: Oxford University Press.

2 Corinthians

RALPH P. MARTIN
WITH
CARL N. TONEY

INTRODUCTION TO
2 Corinthians

SECOND CORINTHIANS is one of the most autobiographical books of the Bible (Hengel 1983:69). In this epistle, Paul's emotions are displayed before the reader: both his depression and his elation. Paul's personal feelings and thoughts are time and again revealed unguardedly. Because he was speaking as a father to his beloved children in the faith, he forwent formality and even politeness. Here we see Paul as Paul, in his heights and in his depths. Because certain interlopers at Corinth were undermining his apostolic authority, Paul was forced to present his apostolic biography—with intimations of supernatural revelations and details about his sufferings. Acting as the Corinthians' spiritual father, he reproved them, encouraged them, disciplined them, and loved them. As a father jealously protective of his daughter, Paul wanted to preserve the Corinthians' spiritual purity and thereby present them as a chaste virgin to Christ (11:2).

AUTHORSHIP
The apostle Paul is the acknowledged author of 2 Corinthians, and the genuineness of his authorship remains unchallenged today. The only place where serious doubt is cast pertains to the authorship of 6:14–7:1, which is sometimes taken to be a non-Pauline insertion into the text on account of the unusual language and the way 6:13 links with 7:2 with no apparent break. But this is not certain. (See the commentary on this section for further discussion.)

The first possible allusion to the letter (9:12) is found in *1 Clement* 38:2, followed by later echoes in Polycarp (*To the Philippians* 6:2) and the letter to Diognetus (*Diognetus* 5:8-16; 6:8) and the explicit attribution of the letter to Paul in Tertullian (*Against Marcion* 5). (See the discussion in Becker 2004:140-166.)

The author of Acts tells us that "Saul, [was] also known as Paul" (Acts 13:9). "Saul" (Gr., *Saulos*) was Paul's Jewish birth name (*signum*). As a Benjamite (Rom 11:1; Phil 3:5), Saul was named after Israel's first king, who was from the same tribe. However, in his letters, Paul greets his audiences using the Greek *Paulos* (Paul), which is his Roman family name (*cognomen*) and means "small." Roman names consisted of three parts—personal (*praenomen*), clan (*nomen*), and family (*cognomen*). See Fitzmyer 1992:230-231.

While there is no physical description of Paul in the New Testament, we have some interesting extracanonical speculation. For example, the *Acts of Paul and Thecla* 3.1 (from the late second century AD) describes Paul as "a man small of stature, with a bald head and crooked legs, in a good state of body, with eyebrows meeting and a nose somewhat hooked, full of friendliness, for now he appeared like a man, and now he had the face of an angel" (Hennecke and Schneemelcher 1965:2.354). Such a portrait offers a lesson in the value of historical backgrounds. Although this portrait does not match modern ideals of beauty, it is still probably an idealized image of Paul. Short people were thought to be quick. Baldness was a distinctly human trait (animals do not go bald). Crooked legs showed a person to be realistic (i.e., firmly planted). Meeting eyebrows portrayed beauty. A hooked nose indicated a royal or magnanimous person (Murphy-O'Connor 1996:44-45; also see Malherbe 1986:173).

Within the New Testament, our portrait of Paul is a hybrid derived from his own letters and a cautionary use of Acts. According to Acts, Paul was born a Roman citizen (Acts 16:37-38; 22:27-28; 25:10-12) and was a citizen of Tarsus (Acts 9:11; 21:39; 22:3). At some point, he moved to Jerusalem and was educated under Gamaliel I (Acts 22:3; cf. Gal 1:14; Phil 3:5). Paul's letters reflect a basic familiarity with Greek literacy and rhetoric, presenting the possibility that in addition to his Jewish education, Paul also received some elementary and possibly secondary Greco-Roman education either in Jerusalem or Tarsus.

From Paul's letters we discover that he was a Benjamite (Rom 11:1; Phil 3:5). As a former Pharisee who zealously practiced the law, he considered himself a "Hebrew of Hebrews" and blameless by the law's standards (11:22; Phil 3:6; cf. Acts 23:6; 26:4-6). Paul's crisis on the Damascus road (Acts 9) involved his discovery not of the insufficiency of the law but rather of the abundant sufficiency of Christ, who came to fulfill the law. While Paul did not describe his vocation, he was boastful in his ability to be self-sustaining in his ministry (11:9; 1 Cor 9:14-15; 1 Thess 2:9), and Acts informs us that he was a tentmaker (Acts 18:3), who probably made linen tents and awnings (used in the marketplace, beaches, atriums of homes, etc.) rather than leather tents (which were mainly restricted to the military, which had its own tentmakers). Acts gives the impression that Paul made several missionary journeys, traveling to and from Jerusalem and Antioch (Acts 12:25-13:3; 14:26-15:6; 18:22-23; 21:15-17), while Paul's letters give a general impression of his movement from east to west.

Turning to 2 Corinthians, Paul revealed many autobiographical and personal details of his life, because in Corinth, Paul's defense of his gospel was equally a defense of his apostleship (4:5, 10; 13:3). A rejection of Paul was tantamount to rejecting his gospel and vice versa, so it became important for him to defend both. In the midst of such a defense, Paul painfully recounted his general troubles as an itinerant preacher, including his opposition in Corinth (2:5), his troubles in Asia, likely alluding to an Ephesian imprisonment (1:8-11; cf. 1 Cor 15:32; Thrall 1994:117), and his recent afflictions in Macedonia (7:5-6). He highlighted social and political dangers like receiving lashes five times (11:24), being beaten with rods three times (11:25), being stoned once (11:25), and escaping Damascus (11:32-33). He reminded the Corinthians that his missionary activities involved the dangers of travel (11:26), being shipwrecked three times (11:25), and experiencing hunger and loss of sleep (11:27). Paul's anchor in the midst of these troubles was his hope of God's continual deliverance. Paul placed himself in positions of weakness to identify with the sufferings of Christ, so that God could vindicate him as he did Christ. We overhear Paul's joy in sharing the gospel in Troas (2:12-13), his hurt in being rejected in Corinth (1:23; 2:1), and his elation at hearing of the hope of reconciliation with the Corinthians (ch 7). We also learn of Paul's mystical visionary experience (12:1-10) as well as his mysterious thorn (12:7).

As we listen in on Paul's half of his conversation with the Corinthians, modern readers are challenged on several fronts, especially as Christian leaders.

> We should be ready to forgive (2:10), grateful for uplifting news (2:13-14; 7:6), and courageous and hopeful in trying circumstances (4:8-10), recognizing that affliction is the church's true glory (4:8-10, 16-18; 6:3-10). There should be true ambition to please God (5:9). We should see that life contains paradoxes (6:10). There should be a concern to aid poor church members (chs 8–9). We should not be eager to defend ourselves against the attacks of others, but there are times when it is right and necessary to do so, especially when the integrity of the gospel is at risk (chs 10–11). We should be glad to suffer as God wills (12:8-10). We should be strictly honest (8:16-22; 12:17-18). The call of the Gospel is "come . . . and die" with Christ (4:10-12) in expectation of God's future, which, at present veiled from our eyes, is grasped by faith (5:7) and awaited with confidence. (R. Martin 1986:lxiii)

DATE AND OCCASION OF WRITING

Scholars are aware of at least five letters written to the Corinthians (or four, if 2 Corinthians is a unity). Prior to the writing of what is known as 2 Corinthians, Paul wrote three of those letters to the Corinthians: (1) a lost letter referred to in 1 Corinthians 5:9 (called a "previous letter"); (2) the letter known as 1 Corinthians, which may be dated in the spring of AD 54 or 55 (see commentary on 1 Corinthians); and (3) another lost, "severe letter" referred to in 2 Corinthians 2:4 and 7:8, which may be dated in the summer of AD 55. The last two letters have likely been combined into the canonical 2 Corinthians: (4) 2 Corinthians 1–9 was probably written in Macedonia during the fall of AD 55 after Paul left Ephesus and proceeded to northern Greece via Troas (2:12; 7:5); then (5) after Paul received word concerning a new crisis, Paul wrote 2 Corinthians 10–13 in AD 56 (on the compositional integrity of 2 Corinthians, see the discussion under "Canonicity and Textual History").

In 1 Corinthians 16:1-2 Paul implies that the collection for the poor Jewish Christians in Jerusalem had not been started at Corinth. But in 2 Corinthians 8:10 and 9:2 he writes that the Corinthians began the collection "a year ago." The relationship between the two canonical letters to the Corinthians turns on this time reference. Another clue is the role played by Titus. After Paul's "intermediate" visit, rather than returning to Corinth as promised (1:15-16), Paul had sent Titus to Corinth. After his stay in Ephesus (Acts 20:1), Paul first went to Troas (7:6; 12:18). Titus went to Corinth to deal with a crisis that had been provoked by a serious challenge to Paul's authority as an apostle (2:4-5; 7:8-13). Titus went there to enforce the apostle's views and bring back word to Paul concerning the effect produced by a previous letter, which Paul had written in view of a crisis in the Corinthian church. This letter (the third written by Paul to the Corinthians) is known as the "severe letter," concerning which Paul wrote, "I am not sorry that I sent that severe letter to you, though I was sorry at first, for I know it was painful to you for a little while" (7:8; cf. 2:4).

Paul came to Macedonia to seek Titus about AD 56. When he learned from Titus that the crisis was over—at least for the time being—he wrote and sent chapters

1–7, followed by an encouragement to Titus to take up the collection for Jerusalem (chs 8 and 9). So there was a year's interval between the sending of 1 Corinthians and the dispatch of 2 Corinthians (8:10). This places chapters 1–9 in the fall of AD 55 or 56 (probably the latter). The arrival of certain teachers, however, reopened the problems Titus thought he had solved (11:4, 13-15), thereby prompting Paul sometime later to write chapters 10–13, also from Macedonia. Therefore, the letter we know as 2 Corinthians most likely contains Paul's fourth letter (chs 1–9) and fifth letter (chs 10–13) to the church at Corinth.

This period of Paul's relationship with the church at Corinth was filled with days of anxious strain (2:13; 7:5). Paul failed to find Titus at Troas, which was where the two men had agreed to meet. So Paul left Troas to cross over to Macedonia (2:13). There Titus met him and brought good news. He reported that Paul's severe letter, written at great cost to the apostle (2:4), had done its work well, though Paul feared earlier that he might have written too severely (7:8). He now rejoiced, however, that the crisis was apparently over, and the estrangement between him and the church, occasioned by one prominent individual's opposition to him at Corinth (2:5-11), had passed, and the church had disciplined this person. The occasion of 2 Corinthians is to be found at this point. The major part of the letter (chs 1–7) is devoted to the theme of joy, expressing Paul's relief and thanksgiving to God.

Yet it is clear that the troubles at Corinth were not over. Beginning at 10:1 we learn that Paul was facing a new threat to his apostolic standing, following the arrival of a party of teachers who came to Corinth with what he regarded as false ideas (11:4, 13-15). The last four chapters (chs 10–13) are Paul's rebuttal of these teachers, expressed in vitriolic and ironical tones, unparalleled in his other letters. How this part of the canonical letter was received is unknown, but we may infer from the fact that it was preserved that it succeeded in answering these charges against him.

But perhaps not finally: By the time of a letter called 1 Clement, written in AD 96 from Rome, the church in Corinth was still racked by dissensions, infighting, and contending with false teachers (1 Clement 1:1; 47:5-6: "Consider who they are who have perverted you"). The lesson for the modern reader of 2 Corinthians is clear. There is no lasting reconciliation between antagonistic groups, even Christian groups, in this age. Every generation of believers needs to heed the apostle's call to live in peace and unity (13:11). And we can only respond by a continued reliance on those forces that moved and motivated Paul in his role as a reconciling agent to bring together alienated parties at Corinth, namely, "the grace of the Lord Jesus Christ, the love of God, and the fellowship of the Holy Spirit" (13:14).

In the midst of Paul's conflict with the Corinthians, one of the major points of contention was his shifting travel plans. Between 1 Corinthians and 2 Corinthians, we can see at least three itineraries, listed as follows:

1. Plan A: Ephesus—Macedonia—Corinth (second)—Jerusalem
2. Plan B: Ephesus—Corinth (intermediate)—Macedonia—Corinth (second)—Judea
3. Actual: Ephesus—Corinth (intermediate)—Macedonia—Ephesus—Troas—Macedonia

Future promised visits: Corinth (third)—Judea

Paul's first two plans never quite materialized. According to 1 Corinthians 16:2-8, after leaving Corinth the first time, Paul promised a lengthy second visit in Corinth *after* his ministry in Macedonia (Plan A). However, in 2 Corinthians 1:15-16, Paul presented a modified plan, intending to give the Corinthians the pleasure of a double visit before (intermediate) *and* after (second) going to Macedonia (Plan B).

In actuality, Paul left Ephesus and visited Corinth for an "intermediate" visit before going to Macedonia. Paul then left for Macedonia, but because he met such severe opposition in Corinth, he canceled his promised return for a second visit to Corinth (1:23; 2:1-11). Instead, he returned to Ephesus, opting to write a "severe letter," which he sent to Corinth with Titus, rather than make his promised second trip to Corinth (7:8, 12). Because Paul was anxious for the results of his letter and about news of the collection, and because he also saw an opportunity for evangelism, he went to Troas to meet Titus returning from Corinth (2:12-13a). Not willing to wait for Titus, Paul pushed on for Macedonia, where he found him (2:13b; 7:5-6). After hearing from Titus of the Corinthians' change of heart (7:7-16), Paul composed 2 Corinthians 1–9 and had to explain why they had now received two letters rather than the promised second visit. Finally, in response to the new crisis brought by outside opponents, Paul composed chapters 10–13 and promised to make his "third" visit to sort out the Corinthian situation (12:14; 13:1). The situation was resolved enough for Paul finally to visit Corinth, where he wrote Romans and sent it with a delegate from Cenchrea (Rom 16:1) and where he successfully gathered his Jerusalem collection (Rom 15:26). (For more on Paul's travel itinerary, see Barrett 1973:7 and the notes on 1:15-16, 23; 2:1; 12:14; 13:1.)

In light of the above discussion, the chronology of Paul's visits and letters to Corinth may be charted as follows:

CORINTH AD 50–51	First visit where Paul established the church but leaves for Ephesus after a judgment before Gallio (Acts 18:1-17).
EPHESUS AD 51–54 AD 54	**First Letter** (lost) mentioned in 1 Corinthians 5:9. **Second Letter** (1 Corinthians) written in response to problems (1 Cor 1:11) and questions (1 Cor 7:1).
CORINTH AD 55 (spring)	Emergency, "intermediate" visit (2 Cor 1:16; 2:1) prompted by Timothy's failed mission (1 Cor 4:17; 16:10), where Paul is confronted and leaves quickly with plans to return for a longer second visit for a "double blessing" (2 Cor 1:15-16, 23).
EPHESUS AD 55 (summer)	**Third Letter** (lost) is mentioned in 2 Corinthians 2:4; 7:8 as the "severe" letter.
MACEDONIA AD 55 (fall) AD 56 AD 56–57 (winter)	**Fourth Letter** (2 Cor 1–9) written in confidence because of Titus's report that the Corinthians had a change of heart. **Fifth Letter** (2 Cor 10–13) written in response to outsiders who turned the Corinthians against Paul. "Third" visit (2 Cor 12:14; 13:1) where Paul achieves reconciliation (Acts 20:2-3) and writes Romans (Rom 16:1-16).

All of these shifting promises created fertile ground for the accusation that Paul was fickle (1:17). In chapters 1–9, Paul answers this charge of fickleness with the image of Christ leading him in a triumphant procession. While Paul appeared to be a defeated prisoner being led in humiliation, in actuality Paul's weakness was what identified him with the sufferings of Christ, and this weakness was intended to display the strength of God (P. B. Duff 1994:20).

AUDIENCE

Second Corinthians is addressed not only to the congregation in Corinth but to "all of his holy people [believers] throughout Greece [Achaia]" (1:1; see NLT mg). Acts indicates that Paul visited Corinth on his second missionary journey (for about 18 months) and third missionary journey (for about 3 months). It was here that Paul met his fellow tentmakers Aquila and Priscilla (Acts 18:18-19). Paul's appearance before Gallio (Acts 18:12-17), who was in office as proconsul in AD 51–52, provides an anchor for Pauline chronology. Gallio's verdict allowed Christianity to operate legally in the city. Another anchor, which is mentioned in 11:32, is Paul's escape from Damascus when it was under the control of King Aretas IV between AD 37 and 39/40. In Paul's day, Corinth's population would have been anywhere from 70,000 to 100,000 people, with the Corinthian congregation consisting of a few house churches of up to around 30 members meeting in various wealthier members' homes.

While originally a prominent Greek city-state, Corinth was destroyed by Roman forces in 146 BC and left to ruin. However, in 44 BC it was refounded as a Roman colony by Julius Caesar with the formal name "Colony of Corinth in Honor of Julius" (*Colonia Laus Julia Corinthiensis*). Corinth was the capital of the senatorial province of Achaia, which was located in southern Greece (9:2; 11:10). As a Roman colony, the city was considered to be an extension of Rome operating under Roman law, governed by Roman citizens, and with Latin as the official language (although Greek was also spoken in the city, especially by locals and travelers from the eastern part of the Roman Empire). Both citizenship and, usually, the possession of property were required to be part of the local government, which consisted of an assembly of citizen voters, a city council, and annual magistrates (*duovir*), who were assisted by two business managers (*aedile*). Corinthian citizens (*cives*) were typically Romans who were the descendants of former soldiers and freed slaves, while the Greek Corinthians would have been resident aliens (*incolae*).

Corinth was a metropolitan city where opportunity existed for the ambitious entrepreneur (Apuleius *Metamorphoses* 10.19.25). There was a spirit of self-promotion and pride as the numerous public inscriptions throughout the city indicate. This spirit would have penetrated the Corinthian congregation, and it is no wonder that the Corinthians were attracted to Paul's boastful opponents while being suspicious of the apostle of weakness. In fact, there is an inscription crediting the *aedile* Erastus for paving the street near the Corinthian theater; he is very likely the same Corinthian Christian Erastus mentioned by Paul in Romans 16:23. The Corinthian Christians consisted of a mixture of the wealthy and poor, from all strati of society.

Corinth maintained a diverse economy with a focus on service and goods for those visiting the city. It was a natural center for trade because it controlled the narrow isthmus between the Aegean Sea and the Ionian Sea, as well as the land bridge between northern and southern Greece (Strabo *Geography* 8.6.20). Taking advantage of this narrow isthmus, merchants could have their cargo or small ships hauled across land on the Diolkos road rather than making the more perilous six-day sea voyage around southern Greece (cf. Acts 27). Among its manufacturing enterprises, Corinth produced high-tin bronze, pottery, and marble sculptures. Religious pilgrims visited the famous temple of Aphrodite (goddess of seafaring, love, beauty, fertility, and prostitutes), located on the Acrocorinth. Other temples included those of Asclepius (god of healing), Hera Argaea (goddess of marriage and women), Apollo (god of prophecy), Tyche (fate or luck), Demeter and Kore (chthonic deities related to fertility), and the imperial cult (which promoted loyalty to the emperor and empire). There were the quadrennial Imperial and Caesarean Games as well as the biennial Isthmian Games (which were nearly as famous as the Olympian Games). These games included athletic, oratory, and musical contests. Paul was likely in the city during at least one of the Isthmian Games, which were probably held in AD 49 and 51, and as a tentmaker, he would have had opportunity to ply his trade.

For more on the city and congregation's background, see the Introduction to 1 Corinthians. For more detail on the social setting of the Corinthian congregation, see the past studies of G. Theissen 1982 and W. A. Meeks 1983 and more recently B. W. Winter 2001. For even more detail on the city, see the classic studies including D. Engels 1990 and Jerome Murphy-O'Connor 2002, which is summarized in Murphy-O'Connor's 1984 article in *Biblical Archaeologist*. For a virtual tour of Corinth, see Dr. Carl Rasmussen's Web site, www.holylandphotos.org.

OPPONENTS

There are various rivals who appear on the pages of 2 Corinthians. In chapters 1–9, these rivals occasionally appear in the background of Paul's discussions. They were typically mentioned for the purpose of promoting reconciliation between Paul and the Corinthians. To "clear the air," Paul addressed some of the charges brought against him by the Corinthians, such as fickleness (1:17), lack of references (3:1), and his exposure to risk (4:7-12). Paul called for the forgiveness of a single Corinthian opponent who had caused him grief during his previous visit (2:5-11). Paul also contrasted himself with rival teachers (2:17; 3:1) in order to further endear himself to his Corinthian audience. We know little about these rivals' identities. They are likely outsiders since they seem to bear letters of recommendation (3:1). In light of Titus's good report (7:6-16), Paul was not primarily concerned about these various opponents in chapters 1–9 because he felt his relationship with the Corinthians was on the mend. However, shortly after composing these chapters, Paul received word that the situation had turned for the worse and a new group of outside opponents had infiltrated the community and stirred up trouble, which Paul needed to address.

Thus, in chapters 10–13, Paul turned to address directly this opposition and to defend vigorously his apostleship and gospel against outsiders who had invaded the community. Paul wrote *about* his opponents (11:4) in the third person (rather than writing *to* them), indicating that they were not part of the church. He distinguished these intruders from the church members, even if some of the members were influenced by these interlopers (10:10, 12; 11:4, 12, 18, 20, 22-23). These opponents were severely condemned (11:13-15) and were most likely different from those rival teachers mentioned in chapters 1–9 (2:17; 3:1).

The nature of the opposition had shifted between 1 Corinthians and 2 Corinthians. While Paul's opponents in 1 Corinthians were *insiders* within the congregation, the opponents found especially in 2 Corinthians 10–13, as noted above, were *outsiders*. First Corinthians dealt with factionalism aggravated by an over-realized eschatology with problems manifesting in the Corinthians' enthusiastic practices and libertine morality. These problems paved the way for the problems in chapters 10–13 because these rival teachers provided a new faction for Corinthians to join, and these opponents' promise of a gospel of power appealed to the Corinthians' enthusiastic leanings.

Scholars have variously identified these opponents as Judaizers (advocates of following the law; F. C. Baur 1876), Gnostics (promoting the spiritual as good over the earthly as evil; W. Schmithals 1971), divine men (seeking models in powerful men such as Moses and Abraham who participate in God's power; D. Georgi 1986), or pneumatics (those who demonstrate their authority through acts of the Spirit, such as miracles; E. Käsemann 1942:33-71). For an evaluation of each of these categories, see J. L. Sumney 1990.

In chapters 10–13, the issue for Paul was the nature of his apostleship and gospel message authenticated by lifestyle. In accordance with C. K. Barrett's (1982:80) suggestion, there were, in fact, two types of opponents mentioned in chapters 10–13—the "exalted apostles" (*hoi huperlian apostoloi* [TG652, ZG693]), who represented the leaders of the Jerusalem church (11:5; 12:11), and the "bogus apostles" (*hoi pseudapostoloi* [TG5570, ZG6013]), who were present at Corinth acting as emissaries either sent by or claiming to be sent from the first group (11:13), and they threatened Paul's mission (10:12-18). Paul used a more mild tone with the first group and a vitriolic tone with the second.

As P. Marshall (1987b) points out, Paul did not specifically name his opponents. This was part of his rhetorical strategy of comparison, which helped to create a caricature and to shame them. However, one clue to the identity of his opponents involves the label "Hebrews" (11:22) given to the opponents, indicating they were likely Jewish. This has led to the theory that they were Judaizers, but issues of circumcision, food laws, and Sabbath are missing from the letter. Instead, Paul made his comparisons using Greco-Roman idioms and arguments (e.g., the "fool" versus "wise" was patterned on Sophists' arguments). The work of Martin Hengel (1974) has helped scholars to see that Hellenistic thought and Palestinian Judaism are not as distinct as we often think, and the work of John M. G. Barclay (1996) has further eased this dichotomy for Hellenistic Judaism. The most likely solution is that Paul's opponents were Hellenistic Jews preaching a gospel of power focused on the "wonder-working" Jesus as a second Moses. G. Friedrich (1963:156-208) proposes that Stephen and Philip (Acts 6–8) offer such models of enthusiastic leaders in early Christianity. Paul's opponents emphasized power and strength, proposing a "theology of glory," *theologia gloriae*, but Paul presented a gospel of weakness, a "theology of the cross," *theologia crucis*.

CANONICITY AND TEXTUAL HISTORY

The early witnesses to the Canon included 2 Corinthians in their lists of authoritative books of the New Testament. These are Marcion, about AD 150; the Muratorian Canon in the late second century; Eusebius's *Ecclesiastical History*; the Festal Letter of Athanasius of Alexandria (367), and the Council of Carthage (397).

The earliest manuscript to include 2 Corinthians includes it as part of a Pauline codex (Romans—2 Thessalonians); this manuscript, known as 𝔓46, is dated to the late second century (Comfort 2005:131-139). Three other very early manuscripts to include 2 Corinthians are Codices Vaticanus and Sinaiticus (both fourth century), and Codex Washingtonianus (Pauline Epistles) of the fifth century.

The literary integrity of the letter—i.e., whether it is a unity in all 13 chapters or a collection of separate Pauline letters—has been much debated. As noted above under "Date and Occasion of Writing," our canonical letter of 2 Corinthians was most likely a composite of two letters (chs 1–9 and chs 10–13). There are several good studies examining the physical process of composing and collecting letters. E. R. Richards (2006) highlights the amount of time it would take to write 2 Corinthians, which would allow for some changes in the course of composition. A. Stewart-Sykes (1996) looks at the physical process of ancient copying and editing to caution against radical partition theories.

When examining the integrity of 2 Corinthians, the main points of discussion are: (1) the apparent break between chapters 1–9 and 10–13, suggesting that the change of style and tone is explained by a new situation that arose later (10:4, 13-15); (2) the apparent interruption in Paul's flow of thought by section 2:14–7:4, in which Paul defends his ministry; (3) the seemingly separate compositions of chapters 8 and 9; and (4) the appeal in 6:14–7:1, which is couched in language and theology that gives the appearance of being an independent piece of writing, especially as 6:13 connects smoothly with Paul's writing in 7:2 and following.

These features divide 2 Corinthians into five distinct sections—a narrative framework of Paul's ministry (1:1–2:13 + 7:5-16), the core of Paul's apostolic defense (2:14–6:13 + 7:2-4), an appeal to separate from "unbelievers" (6:14–7:1), the collection (chs 8–9), and a refutation of Paul's opponents (chs 10–13). For more detailed discussions on the compositional issues, see the commentary on 2:14–3:6, 6:14–7:1, 8:1-7, and 10:1-18, as well as the notes on 2:14 and 7:5.

Furthermore, the mention of the "severe letter" of tears in 2:4 has produced a number of theories. The chief ones are: (1) It refers to what is now known as 1 Corinthians; (2) it is contained in chapters 10–13, which is then out of place as our letter stands; or (3) it is now lost or was destroyed once it had done its work. The last is the most likely.

LITERARY STYLE

This letter, which is one of the "chief letters" (as Luther first called them) of Paul's correspondence (along with Galatians, Romans, and 1 Corinthians), contains all the typical stylistic traits of Paul's writing. The main examples are his encouragement to various people, especially Titus (ch 7), his appeal to the reader to embrace his teaching on reconciliation and virtue (5:18–6:1), and, in light of the new situation referred to in 11:4, his rebuke of intruders who came to Corinth with an alien gospel. He wrote as a father to his children (6:13) in tones both tender and yet on occasion severe (12:20-21). Yet the emphatic style is that of an apostle (1:1) and God's emissary (5:20), charged with authority (13:10) to build up the church and consolidate their faith (1:24). (For details of the literary style of the letter, see R. Martin 2000:63-82; good studies introducing the components of ancient letter writing include M. L. Stirewalt 1993 and E. R. Richards 2006.)

Recently, more attention has been given to the rhetorical structure and tone of the letter (see C. N. Toney 2010c). Several good studies examining 2 Corinthians as a whole letter include F. M. Young and D. F. Ford 1988, Ben Witherington III 1995, and Fredrick Long 2004. Other studies following partition theories that give attention to rhetoric include deSilva 1998 (chs 1-7), K. J. O'Mahony 2000 (chs 8-9), M. M. DiCicco 1995, and B. K. Peterson 1998 (chs 10-13). Burton Mack (1990) offers a good general introduction to rhetorical criticism and the New Testament. R. D. Anderson (1996) applies ancient rhetorical theory to Paul.

Some of the major ancient authors and texts are the following: Aristotle's *Ars Rhetorica* is a good starting point for those interested in exploring ancient rhetorical theory, since it is a foundational text on Greek rhetoric and introduces the basic categories of rhetorical theory and practice (although it must be kept in mind that it was typically unavailable during the New Testament period). Two of the major Latin authors are Cicero, whose *De Inventione Rhetorica* explores Hellenistic rhetorical theory, and Quintilian, whose *Institutio Oratoria* offers a full treatment of Roman rhetoric. Also useful for discussion are two epistolary handbooks of Demetrius and Pseudo-Libanius (found in A. Malherbe 1988). Demetrius's *De Elocutione* helpfully discusses the connection between rhetoric and letters as well as classifying 21 letter types. Scholars sometimes also appeal to Pseudo-Libanius's *Epistolimaioi Charaktēres* with its 41 letter types (however, its late-fourth to fifth-century date makes it of little use).

Formal rhetorical education was the crown of the three stages of Greco-Roman education, which few students entered. The first stage, primary education, began around age seven and typically involved learning to read, write, and add. Secondary education began around ten or eleven (involving fewer students) with students learning grammar and literature. Tertiary education (very few students made it this far and were primarily aristocratic youth) began around fifteen, with formal rhetorical training under a philosopher or, typically, an orator. (Prior to his conversion, Augustine was a teacher of rhetoric.) For more on education, see Ronald Hock 2003:198-227.

Although rhetorical training formally occurred at the tertiary level, students engaged in informal rhetorical education at the primary and secondary levels because they would copy speeches as part of school exercises. While there is debate concerning Paul's use of ancient rhetoric, he at least appears to be trained through the secondary level of education, and his letters do contain rhetorical touches, which could be picked up from his copying exercises.

Scholars using Greco-Roman rhetorical categories will sometimes classify letters according to one of the three species (*genera*) of ancient speech—judicial (which accuses or defends past actions in court settings), deliberative (which persuades or dissuades future actions in debates), and epideictic (which offers praise or blame in public settings, often at funerals). According to these categories, 2 Corinthians best fits as an apologetic letter adapting the form of a judicial speech because Paul is defending his apostleship and gospel (see Long 2004).

Further insights can be gained by noting the five stages for producing a speech, which are invention, disposition, elocution, memory, and delivery. While the last two stages focus on the oral delivery (which would involve hypothetical reconstructions of those settings), the first three provide a more concrete grid for examining 2 Corinthians using rhetorical categories (K. J. O'Mahony 2000:41).

Invention determines the core issues and form of argumentation. In 2 Corinthians, the core issues concern the legitimacy of Paul's apostleship, his gospel, and his Christology. These issues are most noticeable with the charges concerning his questionable travel plans and the collection, as well as his weakness (e.g., 10:10).

Disposition concerns the optimal arrangement of arguments. Here, attention is given to persuasive power. After noting the epistolary opening (1:1-2) and closing (13:11-14), scholars outline the body of the letter(s) according to the parts of a speech. Looking at the canonical form of 2 Corinthians as a whole, and based on the work of F. Long (2004), we can give the following rhetorical outline (the Latin names for the rhetorical units are given in the parentheses):

   I. The epistolary greeting (1:1-2).
   II. The opening (*exordium*) begins the speech (1:3-7).
   III. The narration (*narratio*) gives a brief statement of the disputed facts.
       In the case of 2 Corinthians, there are several (1:8-16; 2:12-13; 7:2-16).
   IV. The proposition (*propositio*) is like a thesis (1:17-24).
   V. The proofs (*probatio*) are the arguments in the main body (2:1–9:15).
   VI. The refutation (*refutatio*) turns the argument directly against the
       opponents (10:1–11:15).
   VII. The digression (*digressio*) comes in the form of a self-adulation
       (11:16–12:10).
   VIII. The conclusion (*peroratio*) finishes the argument, often with a summary
       (12:11–13:10).
   IX. The epistolary conclusion (13:11-14).

Elocution gives attention to the style of embellishing and fortifying a speech. It concerns things such as the selection of words, images, and syntax. Giving attention to the speech patterns can offer clues to the identity of subunits within a speech, which can help determine the overall outline of a speech.

At the end of the day, not all are convinced that we can outline Paul's letters according to categories of ancient speeches. In fact, some, like Fredrick Long (2004), will outline the entire letter, while others, like Hans D. Betz (1985), will outline only portions. However, rhetorical criticism benefits the reader because it draws attention to the persuasive power of the letters using ancient categories.

MAJOR THEMES

Paul's Apostolic Ministry. Outstanding in this letter is Paul's role as an apostle. He was God's special messenger for the establishing and growth of the churches.

At Corinth his ministry was under fire in several ways, so he was called upon to defend himself. In fact, the entire letter is really a spirited defense of the apostolic ministry.

One of the charges brought against him was insincerity and fickleness (1:17), which purportedly arose from his change of travel plans. So he repeatedly addressed the theme of his integrity and honesty as a preacher (2:17; 4:2) and a church builder (10:12-18). A special accusation brought against him had to do with his handling of money, especially in connection with the raising of gifts for the Jerusalem church (chs 8–9). In a later part of the letter, which is his rebuttal of false teachers who had arrived on the scene (11:4), he defends himself against the insinuation that he was untrustworthy in dealing with money matters (12:18-19).

Again, yet another fault his opponents found with him was his exposure to risk (graphically portrayed in 4:7-12; 11:21-33) and his obvious weakness (12:1-10). While freely admitting these limitations (12:11-13), in a moving piece of descriptive self-confession he showed how Christian service is patterned on the suffering Jesus (4:11-12). To those who demanded proof of his credentials (13:3) and faulted him for his lack of "signs," which they said would accredit him (12:12), he replied by pointing to the cross of Christ (4:10; 13:4). True apostolic ministry, he responded, is established on human weakness yet reinforced by divine strength (13:4). The aim is to build up the churches (13:10), not dominate them (1:24).

The Gospel and Resurrection. As an apostle, it was Paul's responsibility to present the gospel message of Jesus Christ's cross and resurrection. After his encounter with the philosophers at Athens, Paul's first visit to Corinth was marked by the preaching of the cross (1 Cor 2:2)—with a lifestyle that complemented that preaching (1 Cor 2:3). These twin ideas are closely related in 2 Corinthians.

Earlier Paul built his message on the centrality of the cross (1 Cor 2:1-5), but his first letter says little about the deep meaning of that event. In this second letter he gives the fullest exposition of what the death and resurrection of Jesus meant (5:18-21). The way God dealt with human sin is spelled out. God became one with humanity's need through the incarnation of Jesus Christ and assumed the burden of sin so that men and women might be restored to a relationship with God as his family. The word Paul used for this restored relationship is reconciliation, which means changing enemies into friends (Rom 5:1-11). The price paid for this new relationship is stated as follows: "For God made Christ, who never sinned, to become sin itself, so that we could be made right with God through Christ" (5:21, NLT mg). This relationship needs to be maintained throughout the believer's whole life. So Paul urged the Corinthians, "Come back to God!" (5:20; lit., "Be reconciled to God"). This call implies a renewed commitment to the message of reconciliation and a separation from moral evils (6:14; 7:1; 12:20-21).

For the apostle Paul, the message of Christ's cross was closely linked with that of Christ's resurrection. Two terms frequently used for resurrection are the noun "rising up/resurrection" (*anastasis* [TG414, ZG386]) and the verb "to raise/awaken" (*egeirō* [TG1453, ZG1586], which bears a connection to the metaphor of sleeping for death). In the opening ascription of praise, Paul writes of God as the one "who raises the dead" (1:9). The resurrection of Jesus is the foundational event of history, as we see from what Paul wrote in 4:14 and 5:17. With Jesus' triumph over death, a new eon was born, and the eschatological turning point of the ages occurred.

Evidently some of the Corinthians seemed to have misinterpreted the significance of this resurrection event. They imagined that, as they were raised with Christ in his resurrection, this new life gave them exemption from suffering and release from temptation. These were ideas Paul refuted in 1 Corinthians, with the predominant discussion in chapter 15.

In 2 Corinthians, the baneful effects of the Corinthians' wrongheaded notions of the resurrection (a life free from suffering and release from temptation) are seen in their criticism of Paul as an apostle of weakness whose life and service were beset by continual danger and exposure to sufferings and hardships. The Corinthians were attracted to the outsiders' gospel because of its emphasis on power, which lined up with their notions that the resurrection gave them power in the here and now. Paul took on these problems and was forced to defend himself in some very dramatic passages (4:7-18; 11:23-33).

Another particular slant on the Corinthian idea of resurrection is that, when Christ was raised, his people rose with him when they were baptized (Rom 6:3-10), and so (they wrongly inferred) they achieved a new resurrection life that set them free from all moral constraints. This interpretation led them to deny a future resurrection (2 Tim 2:18). Paul challenged this error (5:1-10) by pointing to the new resurrection that will happen only after death; then and only then the believers will be "away from these earthly bodies . . . [and] at home with the Lord" (5:8). In the meantime, the believers are called to live lives that are pleasing to God, after which they will stand before Christ to be judged and held accountable for the good or evil they did in their earthly bodies (5:10).

There is debate whether Paul's views regarding the resurrection are consistent between 1 and 2 Corinthians. In 1 Corinthians 15, Paul clearly centered the resurrection event during Christ's return (the Parousia). However, in 2 Corinthians 5, Paul may be centering the resurrection in the present, at death, or at the Parousia. For a fuller discussion, see C. N. Toney 2010b.

In 1 Corinthians 15, Paul told the Corinthians that they would receive a "spiritual body" (*sōma pneumatikon*) only at the Parousia (1 Cor 15:44). In calling this new body "spiritual," Paul was not trying to contrast the flesh as bad versus the spirit or soul as good. Nor was he describing the soul as being stripped of its flesh so that it could enter into the spiritual realm of God. Rather, Paul was affirming that this new body (*sōma* [TG4983, ZG5393]) would be under the direction and control of the Spirit (*pneuma* [TG4151, ZG4460]) of God (Barrett 1968:372; Thiselton 2000:1278). Both the living and dead must wait until the Parousia to receive this body, and Paul believed that he would be alive at the Parousia (1 Cor 15:51; cf. 1 Thess 4:15).

In 2 Corinthians 5, Paul grappled with the state of a person at the moment of death—the Parousia was never explicitly mentioned. Apparently Paul now considered the possibility of his own death before the Parousia either in light of his struggles in Asia (1:8-11) or, more likely, as an answer to the charges from his opponents as being an apostle of weakness—God would remain faithful to Paul, even if he should die (cf. 4:7-18).

Debate arises about *when* Paul thought a believer will receive his or her new body in 2 Corinthians 5. Some argue that the present tense of the verb in the phrase "we have a building from God" (5:1, NIV) indicates that a believer already receives a new body before death (understanding this to mean that believers are already part of the body of Christ). However, the present tense most likely generalizes the statement rather than giving any temporal force. Others argue that Paul believed he would receive his body at death, noting his fear in 5:3 of being found "naked" (*gumnos* [TG1131, ZG1218]). Unfortunately, either of these two views would be radical departures from Paul's views in 1 Corinthians 15, and we would expect Paul to elaborate further if he was attempting to present new ideas.

A third option sees Paul remaining consistent and building upon his views from 1 Corinthians 15 in 2 Corinthians 5. In 1 Corinthians 15:35-38, 42-44, Paul explained that the dead would exist in a temporary, bodiless state, and in 2 Corinthians 5:1-4 Paul's language of a tent being dismantled and being "naked" versus being "clothed" reflects this same view of a temporary, bodiless state. Paul's longing to be clothed with his permanent, heavenly dwelling in 2 Corinthians 5:2 reflected his hope of receiving a spiritual body at the Parousia in 1 Corinthians 15:22. In 1 Corinthians 15, Paul explained that he ultimately hoped to bypass death via the Parousia and receive his new body. In 2 Corinthians 5, Paul explained his second hope, that if he should die, he would still be in the presence of Christ (5:8) until he received his permanent body (which would be at the Parousia). Unfortunately, Paul did not elaborate on what this intermediate, bodiless state looks like.

Between 1 Corinthians 15 and 2 Corinthians 5 we discover a more robust theology of death and hope than is often taught in churches today. Paul expresses hope of his spirit being with Christ (for many, the equivalent of going to heaven), and he expresses his hope that one day he will be re-embodied when Christ returns to the earth at the Parousia (the equivalent to language of resurrection and a new heaven and earth). Tom Wright (2003b) calls this twofold hope "life after life after death."

Names and Metaphors for the Church. In 2 Corinthians Paul used several names and metaphors to depict the church. Those who form "God's church in Corinth" (1:1) are called "his holy people." As such, they are summoned to live in a special way as men and women both separated from the moral evils of their surrounding society and consecrated to God, whose character is holy. The call is stated very clearly: "Let us cleanse ourselves from everything that can defile our body or spirit. And let us work toward complete holiness because we fear God" (7:1).

Paul spoke of the church as being the bride of Christ. He viewed himself as being the one who leads the believers to her husband, Christ (11:2-3). The imagery is taken from Jewish premarriage customs wherein a groomsman (Heb., *shoshbin;* cf. Jastrow 1996:1543) acted as an intermediary in escorting the future bride to her intended spouse.

This thought leads on to that of the church being the family of God, wherein God is the father of his people (1:3; 6:18; 11:31). In a quotation of 2 Samuel 7:14, Paul adds "and daughters" to the citation so as to underline the inclusive nature of God's parenthood. The apostle himself also speaks of himself as being a parent to his spiritual children (6:13; 12:14).

Finally, the church is depicted as a temple (6:14–7:1). Building on his earlier teaching in 1 Corinthians 3:16-17, Paul viewed the church as a holy shrine for God. As such, it must be kept sacred and undefiled (7:1).

Christology. As noted above, 2 Corinthians is one of the four epistles the Reformers dubbed "the chief letters" (Luther's word is *Hauptbriefe,* lit., "capital letters"), which were considered to be Romans, 1 and 2 Corinthians, and Galatians. One of the primary functions of 2 Corinthians, with respect to Christology, is that the letter functions to lead readers to Christ (Luther's words are *Christum treiben,* lit., "to urge [us] to Christ"). So it is fitting that we express this distinctive as the letter's *Christology,* containing Paul's teaching on the person and place of Jesus Christ. (For a good survey of Paul's Christology, see G. Fee 2007.) Central to the Good News Paul brought to Corinth was the person of "Jesus Christ, the Son of God. . . . He is the one whom Silas, Timothy, and I preached to you" (1:19).

Some recent studies (see Kim 1982; Newman 1997) have argued that Paul's conversion on the Damascus road should be understood in terms of his receiving a revelation of the divine glory in the person of the risen Lord Jesus (Acts 9, 21, 26). The glory enjoyed by the eternal Christ is compared to wealth in 8:9 ("he was rich"). However, Christ gave up his enjoyment of the divine splendor with the Father in return for accepting a life of poverty at his incarnation. This means he identified himself with our human condition and then became sin for us (5:21). In this act of condescension Paul found the epitome of divine grace.

God reversed the judgment on the one who took the sinner's place and died the sinner's death (5:18-21) by raising him from the dead and giving him the title of Lord (*kurios* [TG2962, ZG3261]), a title that implies his authority of rule over people's lives and destiny and, on a vaster scale, to rule over the universe as rightful Lord. It is the lordship of Christ that Paul proclaimed (4:5) with the corollary that the apostle was Christ's servant (*doulos* [TG1401, ZG1528], a title not so much of bondage as of dignity and privilege in service, corresponding to the Heb. *'ebed* [TH5650, ZH6269], "the servant [of Yahweh]").

The lordship of Christ is seen (in 3:15-18) as the fulfillment of Old Testament Scripture with his glory eclipsing and replacing that of Moses, the great Jewish lawgiver. Moses's face was illumined by divine glory in communion with Yahweh (Exod 34:34), but it was a glory that faded. By contrast, the glory that is Christ's as the mediator of a new covenant endured. This glory is that which transforms God's people through the Spirit (3:18). So, when Paul writes of his colleagues who worked at Corinth on his behalf, he can describe them as "the glory of the Lord" (8:23; NLT, "They bring honor to Christ"), a phrase that seems to mean that they reflect in their lives the character of the incarnate Lord, whose traits are "gentleness and kindness" (10:1).

OUTLINE

2 Corinthians

◆ I. Opening Greetings (1:1–2)

This letter is from Paul, chosen by the will of God to be an apostle of Christ Jesus, and from our brother Timothy.

I am writing to God's church in Corinth and to all of his holy people throughout Greece.*

²May God our Father and the Lord Jesus Christ give you grace and peace.

1:1 Greek *Achaia*, the southern region of the Greek peninsula.

NOTES

1:1 *Paul, chosen by the will of God to be an apostle of Christ Jesus.* Paul greets his audience with his Roman family name (*cognomen*), which means "small" (see Acts 13:9; also see the Introduction on "Authorship"). Paul's name stands first, following the custom of how letters were written in the ancient world. The author's name is followed by that of the person(s) addressed. What is unusual in Paul's letter writing is (1) his appeal to his own authority, conveyed in the title "apostle of Christ Jesus" backed by his claim that his role as God's messenger is endorsed by the divine will, and (2) his inclusion of "brother Timothy" along with his own name. See the Introduction for more on Paul's biographical details.

The note of apostolic authority is sounded throughout 2 Corinthians (1:21; 2:17; 4:5; 5:20; 10:8; 13:10). These references pay tribute to Paul's self-conscious claim to be God's servant uniquely set apart and commissioned for the task of ministry in the "new covenant" (3:6). In this letter Paul has to defend his apostleship in opposition to those who made the same claim (which he denies by labeling them "false apostles," 11:13) and who denied his apostolic calling (implied in 2:17). More significantly, this epistle contains the real meaning of what Paul meant by apostleship (Barnett 1993:45-51; Barnett 1997:35-46).

C. K. Barrett considers 2 Corinthians to be Paul's fullest and most passionate account concerning his understanding of apostleship (1970:35-46; 1973:53). On the term "apostle" (lit., "one sent"; *apostolos* [TG652, ZG693]) there is much recent discussion, especially as Paul's claim to apostleship was questioned at Corinth, and there is a full discussion of the term in Barnett 1993:45-51. In Corinth there were those who claimed to be apostles and challenged Paul's authority. They are the occasion for his writing chs 10–13. The issue is not merely personal apostolic authority, but also the geographic territory belonging to Paul (see notes on 10:12-18).

Prior to the NT, "apostle" was used rarely—in classical Greek it is found in seafaring contexts, and the LXX uses it only once for "messenger" (1 Kgs 14:6, LXX), but it is found 80 times in the NT and 34 times in Paul's letters. The term is usually used either in a technical sense for someone bearing divine authority (1 Cor 1:1) or in a nontechnical sense for a messenger (8:23; Phil 2:25).

There is no doubt Paul claimed to be a genuine apostle by virtue of his having seen the Lord and receiving a commission to be a missionary to the Gentiles (cf. 1 Cor 9:1; 15:8; Gal 1:11-17). Further, Paul claimed his initially successful ministry in Corinth to be a metaphorical letter of his apostolic authority (on this letter metaphor, see the note on 3:3). Although Paul considers himself an apostle, that is, "one sent" from Christ, he does not group himself among the Twelve nor does he consider James the brother of Jesus to be among the Twelve, but he does consider himself among a wider collection of apostles (cf. 1 Cor 9:1; 15:5-9). It is possible that Paul understands himself to be the least of the apostles (1 Cor 15:9) because he considers himself to be the last of the apostles, having received a distinct vision and calling on the Damascus road. (For more on how the Damascus road experience shaped Paul's self-understanding, see S. Kim 1982.) It is also debated whether Paul's Damascus road encounter with Christ is modeled after a prophetic calling (often highlighting Christianity as the fulfillment or continuation of Judaism) or a conversion (often highlighting Christianity as a distinct movement from Judaism).

and from our brother Timothy. Timothy is designated "the brother" (so in Greek), the same wording found in Col 1:1; 1 Thess 3:2. In other places (1 Cor 4:17; Phil 2:22) it speaks of the intimate relationship between Paul and his "child in the faith," as in the letters to Timothy. Here it suggests a more formal relationship, since Timothy was Paul's envoy to Corinth (1 Cor 4:17), and the term "brother" suggests a title of one of Paul's authorized messengers to the churches (as in 8:22). The use of the definite article (*the* brother) supports this idea (Thrall 1994:84-85). This portrayal of Timothy and the portrayal of Titus as an envoy are helpful reminders of the authority that these men bore as coworkers of Paul, which is sometimes forgotten when reading the Pastoral Epistles.

God's church in Corinth. The "church" (*ekklēsia* [TG1577, ZG1711]) means the assembly of believers as the people of the new covenant (a theme developed in ch 3), the new Israel of God.

his holy people. Christians are the "holy ones" (*hagioi* [TG40A, ZG41]), a title with roots in the OT, deriving from the Hebrew word meaning "to separate," which LXX renders by the term *hagios* in its various forms. The "holy ones" (traditionally rendered as "saints") are separated in a twofold way: Negatively, there is separation from moral evil, and positively, there is dedication to God and his service as his "holy nation" (Exod 19:5-6; Lev 11:44-45; 19:1-2; Deut 7:6). Outward signs of this separation included the physical separation created by circumcision, Sabbath observance, and food laws. Allegiance to these customs became marks of a covenantal loyalty during the intertestamental period (1 Macc 1:62-63; cf. 2 Macc 5:27; 4 Macc 4-18; Josephus *Antiquities* 11.346). Paul vigorously argues against Gentiles taking up these practices for purposes of salvation (Gal 2:3, 11-14; 4:10; 5:1-12; 6:12-15) while allowing Jews to maintain them so long as they are done in service to Christ (Rom 14-15; 1 Cor 7:18-20). For Paul, these marks no longer define covenantal loyalty or the people of God; rather, it is belonging to Christ (Gal 3:28-29) and having the Holy Spirit that now mark off the people of God (Rom 15:13; Gal 5:18). See C. N. Toney 2008 for Paul's stance on the law and his inclusive ethic.

throughout Greece. Lit., "the whole of Achaia" (so NLT mg). After 27 BC "Achaia" became the name of the whole of Greece, but in earlier times it denoted a smaller territory on the northern coast of the Peloponnese, i.e., southern Greece (so NLT footnote). Paul's usage here (as in 1 Cor 16:15; cf. Rom 15:26; 1 Thess 1:7-8) probably reflects the earlier designation, with Corinth as the chief city and the important trading center of the province.

1:2 *grace and peace.* Paul modified the standardized greeting in Hellenistic letters (*chairein* [TG5463, ZG5897], "greetings") by using the Christian terms "grace" (*charis* [TG5485, ZG5921]), which sounds like *chairein*) and "peace" (*eirēnē* [TG1515, ZG1645]), which is virtually the Greek equivalent of the Heb. *shalom* [TH7965, ZH8934], meaning the blessing of God's salvation (Num 6:26). In this way he turned the colorless contemporary greeting into a wish-prayer for his readers, calling down God's gracious favor to the undeserving and his gift of well-being. A strikingly similar expression occurs in Jewish literature in *2 Baruch* 78:2: "Thus speaks Baruch, the son of Neriah, to the brothers who were carried away captive: Grace and peace be with you" (A. F. J. Klijn 1983).

COMMENTARY

Paul's opening address and greeting focus attention on a number of issues that will be developed and enlarged in the rest of the letter. Foremost among these is the question of his authority as an apostle. From what we know of Paul's dealings with the congregations that had their central meeting place in the city of Corinth, this authority was under fire and was a matter of heated debate. Throughout the letter Paul is on the defensive (albeit with a new set of opponents in chapters 10–13).

How Paul offers his defense will be addressed throughout this commentary. It is simply noted here that he was engaged in an extended debate with those who made two claims. On the one hand, they asserted that they were the true apostles of Christ since they alone represented the original apostles in the mother church at Jerusalem. And, on the other side, these persons took exception to Paul's claim to be Christ's apostle to the Gentiles (as in Rom 15:16) and even doubted his Christian standing (a criticism implied in 10:7).

For these two reasons Paul began his letter with a robust assertion of his calling as "chosen by the will of God to be an apostle of Christ Jesus." The expanded description of his calling "by the will of God" recalls his account of his conversion in Galatians 1:15-16, and this allusion is well brought out by the NLT's rendering, "chosen by the will of God," to underline Paul's sense of conviction that his vocation was not his own choice. Rather, he was responding to the divine summons for his life (1 Cor 9:16).

We should not fail to notice how Paul thought of his apostolic service. He claimed to have received his authority from the Lord himself (13:10), yet it was not an authority that was overbearing and dictatorial, imposing itself on others in a rough and insensitive manner. So he was clear to qualify his authority in two ways. First, he denied any coercive attitude when he wrote, "That does not mean we want to dominate you. . . . We want to work together with you" (1:24). Second, he saw such God-given authority as serving to build up the church, not tear it down (10:8; 13:10). He viewed his authority as modeled on the figure of the suffering Lord Jesus, whose weakness became the power of compelling love (13:4). The Lord's word spoken to him, "My power works best in weakness" (12:9), is a true reminder to all who aspire to leadership in the church that our stewardship is best exercised when we follow this road.

The character and calling of the church is the other prominent feature highlighted in this prefatory address. By using the title "holy people," Paul described the intention and design of the church's Lord that they should be like him in holiness. This is the call to consecrated living and service in the world, even when the setting is the unpromising moral atmosphere of such a city as Corinth. Moral problems plagued

Corinth. In several places in the following letter (e.g., 6:14–7:1; chs 10–13) Paul would have to deal severely with various issues of idolatry and immorality. So it is appropriate at the beginning of the letter that the character of the church as God's "sanctified" people, set apart for him and his service as Israel of old, should be displayed and held up before this congregation as its calling in the world.

◆ II. Thanksgiving for God's Comfort (1:3-11)

[3]All praise to God, the Father of our Lord Jesus Christ. God is our merciful Father and the source of all comfort. [4]He comforts us in all our troubles so that we can comfort others. When they are troubled, we will be able to give them the same comfort God has given us. [5]For the more we suffer for Christ, the more God will shower us with his comfort through Christ. [6]Even when we are weighed down with troubles, it is for your comfort and salvation! For when we ourselves are comforted, we will certainly comfort you. Then you can patiently endure the same things we suffer. [7]We are confident that as you share in our sufferings, you will also share in the comfort God gives us.

[8]We think you ought to know, dear brothers and sisters,* about the trouble we went through in the province of Asia. We were crushed and overwhelmed beyond our ability to endure, and we thought we would never live through it. [9]In fact, we expected to die. But as a result, we stopped relying on ourselves and learned to rely only on God, who raises the dead. [10]And he did rescue us from mortal danger, and he will rescue us again. We have placed our confidence in him, and he will continue to rescue us. [11]And you are helping us by praying for us. Then many people will give thanks because God has graciously answered so many prayers for our safety.

1:8 Greek *brothers.*

NOTES

1:3 *All praise to God.* Lit., "Blessed [be] God." Paul's use of this formulaic statement is taken from the worship of the Jewish synagogue, in particular the prayers known as the Eighteen Benedictions, which are intercessions framed by the call to praise the Lord. In Jewish prayers God is "blessed," that is, praised for his kindness and grace to Israel. There are parallels, too, in the Dead Sea Scrolls; one scroll is actually called "Thanksgivings" or "Praises."

the Father of our Lord Jesus Christ . . . our merciful Father. Also taken from Paul's Jewish worship heritage is the character of God as "the Father of mercies." It forms a praise of God in the daily prayer known as the Shema ("Hear, O Israel") based on Deut 6:4. For Paul as a Jewish believer in Jesus, the fatherhood of God is patterned on the sonship of the Lord Jesus Christ, in whom God's mercy (favor-in-grace) is clearly known as he redeems his people. However, it should be noted that God is neither male nor female and the Bible does, in fact, also use female images for God—a mother (Jer 31:15-22; Isa 66:7-14; Job 38:28-29), a pregnant woman (Isa 42:14), a midwife (Ps 22:9), a mistress (Ps 123:2), a woman (Luke 15:8-10; Matt 13:33//Luke 13:20-21).

comfort. The connection of God's mercy to "comfort" (*paraklēsis* [TG3874, ZG4155]) may imply Paul's sharing in the messianic deliverance promised in the OT (Isa 40:1; 51:3, 12, 19). The Messiah is described in Jewish literature as Israel's "comforter."

1:4 *He comforts us . . . same comfort God has given us.* The alternative rendering to "comfort" is "encouragement" (*paraklēsis* [TG3874, ZG4155]), since it is linked with Paul's affliction (*thlipsis* [TG2347, ZG2568]; NLT, "troubles"). Then the term refers primarily to Paul's experience of deliverance from some specific trial and God's strengthening of his servant in such a time. *Paraklēsis* and its cognate verb (*parakaleō* [TG3870, ZG4151]) are found 10 times in five verses here (1:3-7).

1:5 *we suffer for Christ.* Lit., "the sufferings (or woes) of Christ." Two ideas are implied here: (1) Christ's own sufferings that, in some way, are extended to others and experienced by them—a difficult notion, since Paul was emphatic that Christ's atoning death is unique (Rom 5:17). (2) Christ's suffering as he identifies with his people when they undergo persecution and specifically with Paul in his apostolic ministry (Eph 3:13; Phil 3:10; Col 1:24). It is not said that the Corinthians were being persecuted, but the pain they caused Paul in doubting his true apostleship may well have been in his mind.

1:6 *it is for your comfort and salvation!* Paul had to remind the Corinthians that his sufferings (i.e., Christ's sufferings in him) had been for their encouragement "and salvation." "Salvation" in this context does not mean eschatological deliverance or receiving eternal life; rather, it means their spiritual health and preservation in wholeness (as in Phil 1:19, 28, and especially Phil 2:12).

1:7 *We are confident.* "Confident" (*bebaios* [TG949, ZG1010]) is a commercial term for security or a guarantee and is related to God's promises (cf. Rom 4:16). The readers are assured of Paul's confidence in them. Paul often adopted a congratulatory tone in the opening of his letters. The entire benediction (1:3-7) has been regarded by some as praise directed to the Corinthians as much as to God (so McCant 1999:29-30). But this seems unlikely. What is clear is the partnership (*koinōnia* [TG2842, ZG3126], "sharing" or "fellowship") that unites apostle and congregation (see next note).

you share in our sufferings. There is a play on the words "sufferings" (*pathēma* [TG3804, ZG4077]) and "encouragement" (*paraklēsis* [TG3874, ZG4155]). Paul gives a reason for the Corinthians to share in his sufferings, which is to share in his encouragements. This language points toward vindication by God—God will vindicate the sufferer, just as he vindicated Christ (connecting the suffering of Paul with the suffering of Christ; cf. 1:5). Encouragement comes via God's deliverance from these sufferings. While the Corinthians share in Paul's suffering of Christ, they do not share exactly in the same sort of trials as Paul (see O'Brien 1977:247-248).

1:8 *We think you ought to know.* This sentence opens a new section of the letter since it is couched as a disclosure and the style is different from 1:3-7. However, there are links between 1:3-7 and what follows, including the connecting *gar* [TG1063, ZG1142] ("then"; not reflected in NLT) in v. 8. In addition, the "sufferings" and "encouragement" of v. 7 point forward to the specific situation mentioned in 1:8-11.

crushed and overwhelmed. The affliction that came to Paul in the province of Asia put Paul under intense pressure like a heavy burden almost beyond his power to bear.

1:9 *we expected to die.* In vv. 9-10 Paul appears to be alluding to an imprisonment in Ephesus (Thrall 1994:115-117; see commentary on 1:3-11 below for other options and further discussion). It seemed to be a death sentence, which suggests that the courts at Ephesus served him a death warrant. The alternative is to deny any juridical sense in the word and see it as Paul's awareness that he would not escape death before the Parousia (cf. 5:1-10). But that idea lifts the verse out of its context in ch 1, since Paul did not die in Asia. The conclusion Paul reached that he should not trust in himself but in God who raises the dead suggests that Paul might have extricated himself by personal effort (such as an appeal to Caesar in Rome), but chose not to do so. Prevailing social disturbances at Ephesus in the period of Acts 19:23-41 and its aftermath probably made it impossible to exercise this right as a citizen (as in Duncan 1929:100-107). The issue turns on the assassination of the procurator Junius Silanus and the social anarchy that followed this event in AD 54, that is, during the period of Paul's ministry in Ephesus during AD 52–55. Luke omits a mention of this imprisonment probably because he wishes to make Paul's attitude to Roman power appear in a good light (R. Martin 1976:48-51).

1:10 *he did rescue us from mortal danger, and he will rescue us.* God did deliver his servant from "mortal danger" (lit., "so awful a death") when all human hope was gone. To take the expression to mean "danger of death" links with what Paul writes in 11:23. The expression "he rescued us and he will rescue" has the best textual support: 𝔓46 ℵ B C P 0209vid 33 cop. Inferior manuscript support (D² F G 1739 𝔐) is behind the reading "He rescued us and he rescues" and "He rescued us" (A D* Ψ itᵃ, ᵇ syrᵖ). The reading behind the NLT indicates that Paul was thinking of a specific time or times in which he was rescued from death and of the ultimate deliverance from final death—through resurrection. The first variant conveys the idea of God's ongoing ability to rescue the believers from death. The second variant is limited to a specific, past occurrence. "As the shortest reading, it could be original, but it is more likely that at one point the text was purposely pruned" (Comfort 2008:533).

1:11 *you are helping us by praying for us.* At the same time Paul "remembers that God acts through the prayers of his people" (Barrett 1973:67) in a train of thought similar to Phil 1:19. The participle rendered "you are helping us by praying for us" is picturesque, meaning support that both cooperates with and undergirds the person in need, as in Rom 15:30. The Greek word (*sunupourgountōn* [TG4943, ZG5348]) is a monstrous verb of 15 letters, a composite word with three ideas: (1) work (*ergon* [TG2041, ZG2240]); (2) cooperation with God—or rather here, with others who share our burden—(*sun* [TG4862, ZG5250]); and (3) prayer as undergirding support (*hupo* [TG5259, ZG5679]) by which our needy fellow believers are sustained and upheld. Paul frequently solicited prayer and expected his congregations to stand by him (Rom 15:30-32; Phil 1:19; 1 Thess 5:25; Phlm 1:22). Again, Paul's language is calculated to establish good relations with the Corinthian readers.

COMMENTARY

Human suffering is a mystery, especially undeserved suffering that believers endure for the sake of the gospel. Yet one reason for such painful experiences is given here. Those who receive encouragement from God are well able to enter sympathetically into the experience of others who share their suffering (1:4-7). Just as the Lord Jesus both suffered as their Savior and suffers in his people (see Acts 9:4, 13), so the apostle was united with his converts. His example would serve to encourage them in their share of suffering that comes to Christ's faithful people in a hostile world (see Acts 14:22, which has the same word, *thlipsis* [TG2347, ZG2568]; NLT, "hardships"; lit., "affliction"). While these sufferings may be cause for criticism of Paul as an apostle of weakness, Paul attempts to counter any criticism by orienting his suffering as works of comfort on behalf of the Corinthians. Just as Christ's suffering brought comfort to others, so Paul's suffering brings comfort to the Corinthians. Paul's suffering is not propitiatory in itself; rather, his suffering identifies Paul with the ministry and work of Christ (see note on v. 5).

In retelling his account of his ordeal in Asia Minor (including his stay in Ephesus), Paul made it plain that he underwent a harrowing trial and a life-threatening experience. He was in mortal danger and nearly lost his life. What that "trial" was is interpreted in a number of different ways. The options are: (1) his recent experience in the amphitheater at Ephesus (Acts 19:23-41); (2) severe illness that seemed to be fatal at the time, sometimes linked with Paul's thorn in the flesh (12:7); (3) the onset of depression and stress caused by the opposition of the Corinthians; and (4) a more virulent attack than that in Acts 19, which landed Paul in conflict with the Ephesian civil authorities and threatened his life with a death sentence. (See 1 Cor 15:32 for a possible allusion to this life-threatening event.) Thrall (1994:115-117) discusses these possibilities and chooses the fourth interpretation, namely, "violent persecution, perhaps in the form of incarceration."

In spite of the many trials that weighed upon Paul—in particular, facing the criticism of the readers that his sufferings belied and contradicted his claim to be Christ's representative at Corinth—Paul was glad he had received the strength God had given him (1:4). Paul told the Corinthians he had been "rescued" by God's favor in answer to prayer (1:10). The Corinthians were his partners in prayer (see note on 1:11). The value Paul set on these prayers of supplication is seen in the consequence: Many people will have occasion to give thanks to God for the favor (*charisma* [TG5486, ZG5922]; which here must mean his deliverance from death) freely bestowed (NLT, "graciously answered") by God in response to the many who prayed. The identity of these many believers is not clear. Probably Paul was reflecting on the Jewish belief that the more people who pray, the more effectual prayer becomes (Barrett 1973:67). Prayer is a work involving strenuous, corporate enterprise (as Col 4:12-13 recalls); it involves the privilege of partnership with those for whom we pray and those on whose prayers we rely.

◆ III. Paul's Defense of His Travel Plans and Severe Letter (1:12–2:13)
   A. Paul's Change of Travel Plans (1:12–22)

¹²We can say with confidence and a clear conscience that we have lived with a God-given holiness* and sincerity in all our dealings. We have depended on God's grace, not on our own human wisdom. That is how we have conducted ourselves before the world, and especially toward you. ¹³Our letters have been straightforward, and there is nothing written between the lines and nothing you can't understand. I hope someday you will fully understand us, ¹⁴even if you don't understand us now. Then on the day when the Lord Jesus* returns, you will be proud of us in the same way we are proud of you.

¹⁵Since I was so sure of your understanding and trust, I wanted to give you a double blessing by visiting you twice—¹⁶first on my way to Macedonia and again when I returned from Macedonia.* Then you could send me on my way to Judea.

¹⁷You may be asking why I changed my plan. Do you think I make my plans carelessly? Do you think I am like people of the world who say "Yes" when they really mean "No"? ¹⁸As surely as God is faithful, our word to you does not waver between "Yes" and "No." ¹⁹For Jesus Christ, the Son of God, does not waver between "Yes" and "No." He is the one whom Silas,* Timothy, and I preached to you, and as God's ultimate "Yes," he always does what he says. ²⁰For all of God's promises have been fulfilled in Christ with a resounding "Yes!" And through Christ, our "Amen" (which means "Yes") ascends to God for his glory.

²¹It is God who enables us, along with you, to stand firm for Christ. He has commissioned us, ²²and he has identified us as his own by placing the Holy Spirit in our hearts as the first installment that guarantees everything he has promised us.

1:12 Some manuscripts read *honesty.*   1:14 Some manuscripts read *our Lord Jesus.*   1:16 *Macedonia* was in the northern region of Greece.   1:19 Greek *Silvanus.*

NOTES

1:12 *confidence*. Paul continues with his theme of confidence (1:7, 10). "Confidence" here refers to Paul's assurance that his ministry at Corinth was commissioned by God, a conviction to which his conscience bears witness.

***holiness*.** The Greek term behind this is *hagiotēs* [TG41, ZG42]; it has the strong textual support of 𝔓46 ℵ* A B C 33 1739. A variant reading is *haplotēs* [TG572, ZG605] (simplicity, honesty), with the weaker support of ℵ² D F G 𝔐. Either word could have been confused for the other in the copying process because the two words differ in only two letters. Thrall argues for the first reading (1994:132-133), but grants the evidence is only marginally stronger. I have argued for the second reading, found in the NLT mg (R. Martin 1986:18). A translation such as "probity" would cover both ideas and fits in with Paul's appeal to a clear conscience.

1:13 *straightforward*. Paul's letters were not intended to deceive. Rather he had striven to say exactly what was on his mind. This is against the accusation of double-dealing that he will shortly take up (1:17) as he reviewed his travel plans and travel promises. By the use of a wordplay Paul can insist that his readers don't have to read "between the lines," but what they read (*anaginōskō* [TG314, ZG336]) they can readily understand (*epiginōskō* [TG1921, ZG2105]). Paul's letter writing will be referred to later (in 10:10).

1:14 *even if you don't understand us now*. It is not easy to disentangle Paul's thought here. Yet the thrust is clear. At that time, the Corinthians knew only part of Paul's story, as his earlier letter (1 Cor 16:2-8) had told it concerning his plans to visit Corinth. He hoped they would bear with him as he retold it in greater detail. Then they would see why he acted as he did. The outcome would be a restored relationship of mutual trust, based on a reciprocal confidence.

***on the day when the Lord Jesus returns, you will be proud of us in the same way we are proud of you*.** He had confidence in them, almost a pride in them (NLT); at the final day of the Lord's return, they will be as confident in his true apostleship. Then his work will be vindicated—a common theme in Paul (Phil 2:16; 1 Thess 2:19). Paul appealed to the day when the Lord Jesus returns because that is the time when all human motives will be judged (1 Cor 4:4-5).

1:15-16 *I wanted to give you a double blessing*. This "blessing" or "benefaction" (*charis* [TG5485, ZG5921]) may be the anticipation of Paul's presence in Corinth (most translations). Paul was probably referring to his quick "intermediate" visit to Corinth prior to traveling to Macedonia and his promised "second" visit to Corinth after his mission in Macedonia (see Introduction for an explanation of Paul's visits to Corinth; see also notes on 1:23; 2:1; 12:14; 13:1). This also may mean "grace," "favor," or "gift." This "gift" (i.e., "grace") was both experienced by the Corinthians and proved by their "gift" of the Jerusalem collection (e.g., Gordon Fee 1977-1978:533-538). Paul may have intended to visit Corinth twice to ensure the success of the collection. Most often, Christians think of the "grace" of God (8:9; cf. Rom 6:23). It also means "thanks" or "gratitude" in response to beneficence (2:14; 8:16; 9:15).

***Then you could send me on my way to Judea*.** Paul had originally planned for some Corinthian delegates to join him to bring the collection to Jerusalem after his second visit to Corinth.

1:17 *Do you think I make my plans carelessly?* One possible itinerary reconstruction is that Paul did not return to Corinth (for his "second" visit) from Macedonia as he had originally promised but returned to Ephesus because of the severe opposition he had met during his intermediate visit (Barrett 1973:7, 75). With Paul's intention and change of travel arrangement (namely, his failure to come for a promised second visit to Corinth), it is not surprising that he was charged with "fickleness," "vacillation," "duplicity" (*elaphria* [TG1644, ZG1786]; NLT, "carelessly").

like people of the world. Paul's vacillation seemed to his Corinthian opponents to be the mark of a "worldly" person (NIV), literally a person marked by self-interest (*kata sarka*, "according to the flesh"); *sarx* [TG4561, ZG4922] (flesh), which is part of the worldly realm, is opposite of the realm of God and the Spirit, who, Paul claimed, guarded and controlled his actions (1:22; cf. Gal 5:16-26). For more, see J. D. G. Dunn 1998:62-73.

who say "Yes" when they really mean "No." Promises are made in words spoken. Paul's Corinthian opponents had accused him of saying "Yes" (I will visit you) when he really meant "No" (he reneged on that promise). The NLT takes this view of the Greek, which is complicated (see Thrall 1994:142-143). What is clear is that the charge was one of inconsistency, or maybe confused speaking as a sign of making decisions according to the flesh (*kata sarka*, i.e., being worldly), a trait he had already denied in 1:12.

1:18 *As surely as God is faithful.* In appealing to the trustworthiness of God, Paul indicated that more was at stake than simply a defense of his character. It was bad enough that his reputation and care for the Corinthians should be assailed; it was worse when it was insinuated that his message was unreliable and unsure.

1:19 *whom Silas, Timothy, and I preached to you.* In presenting his case, Paul reminds the Corinthians who first proclaimed the gospel to them (cf. Acts 18:5). This also may reflect the need to establish a case with two or three witnesses (Deut 19:15).

1:20 *For all of God's promises have been fulfilled in Christ with a resounding "Yes!"* Paul reverses this yes/no charge of worldly fickleness by rooting his decisions (and ultimately his character and gospel) in God's faithfulness (v. 18) and the person of Christ.

our "Amen" (which means "Yes") ascends to God for his glory. This "Amen" (Heb., *'amen* [TH543, ZH589]; "so be it," "confirmed") is probably intended to be the community's affirmative response to God's "Yes!" (cf. Rev 22:20), or it may be the conclusion of a prayer expressing agreement.

1:21 *enables.* Gr. *bebaioō* [TG950, ZG1011] (lit., "confirm, establish") is a common juristic term, expressing that God legally guarantees the security of believers.

1:22 *he has identified us as his own.* Lit., "He has sealed us." "Seal" (*sphragizō* [TG4972, ZG5381]) is not used in the eschatological sense (see Rev 7:2-8; 10:4). Rather, in ancient times, items such as documents and vessels were marked by a seal making an impression in clay so as to indicate personal identification. Many people had their own individualized seals. God's seal on Christians indicates his personal ownership of them. Sealing became a description of the Spirit's actions in baptism (Eph 1:13; 4:30; Shepherd of Hermas *Similitude* 8:6; *2 Clement* 7:6; 8:6), although J. D. G. Dunn (1970:131-134) does not see any connection to baptism in water.

the first installment that guarantees. Gr., *arrabōn* [TG728, ZG775]. The word was used as a secular, commercial term for a down payment or payment that obligates the contracting party to make further payments. Thus, the presence of the Spirit in the hearts of the believers is the guarantee that God's promises will be fulfilled.

COMMENTARY

The opening paragraph (1:12-14) begins Paul's defense to the Corinthians for his past actions. Paul was leading up to a frank statement of his change of mind by declaring his motives in his dealings with the audience at Corinth. These motives are seen in a network of relationships, especially in three such areas: his pastoral dealings that have been marked by his probity and sincerity as his conscience attests; his words that are a true index of his character; and his letter-writing habits in which the chief feature is his frankness or plain speaking (another meaning of the Greek term in 1:12, *haplotēs* [TG572, ZG605]; see note).

Since Paul's motives were under suspicion, it was imperative that he should clarify that his actions had been honorable and beneficial. (For a parallel statement by Aristotle, see *Rhetoric* 3.15.12, cited by McCant 1999:33.) In many pieces of Greek rhetorical writing, a person whose motives had been doubted sought to set the record straight. This is what Paul wanted to do.

Yet more was at stake than Paul's personal reputation. If his word about travel plans had been double-tongued, what about the message he brought when he first came to Corinth as a pioneer evangelist (Acts 18)? That probing question haunted Paul, who felt he had to defend his own ministry and that of his colleagues, Silas (= Silvanus; Acts 15:22, 27, 32; 1 Pet 5:12) and Timothy (2 Cor 1:1).

Paul had thought it wise to alter his originally promised plan to visit Corinth. He had learned of some disaffection with his ministry while at Ephesus. He paid a hurried visit to see the situation firsthand. This trip is not mentioned in the Acts story line, but that it happened is clear from 2:1, 12:14, and 13:1-2, which speak of a painful visit, followed up by a severe letter and a proposed additional visit. In these circumstances it seemed right to postpone the promised visit en route to Macedonia (1 Cor 16:5-7). And for that change of plan Paul was being criticized as indecisive and shifty. When Paul wrote that he "wanted to . . . [visit] you twice" and then goes on to speak of "a double blessing," it is clear what his original travel plan was. He proposed to visit Corinth, then go on to Macedonia in northern Greece, and afterward come back to Corinth for a second visit. It is this second visit that was the occasion of dispute between the apostle and his readers: He chose not to make it for the reason given in 2:1: "So I decided that I would not bring you grief with another painful visit." This last verse implies that the first visit (in 1:15-16) caused pain both to them and especially to him—and more so since it was followed by a letter written with tears (2:3-4). It should be noted that one of the purposes of the first visit was that Paul intended to enlist the help of the Corinthians to accompany him on his journey with the money collection for the church in Jerusalem. Paul exhorts the Romans to contribute to the collection in light of the examples of the churches in Achaia and Macedonia (Rom 15:26), indicating a degree of success at the time of writing Romans. Yet we learn from Acts 20:2-4 that the group which set out from Greece did not include the Corinthians. The probable reason for this was that the disaffection at Corinth was not fully settled. (See also the comments at 9:6-15.)

Paul had felt obliged to give reasons for his altered itinerary. When he did so (as in 1:23–2:13; 7:5-16), much about his plans is left in obscurity. Yet what is clear is that Paul appealed to his message as authenticated by God's own faithful character, by Christ's person as Son of God and the fulfiller of Old Testament prophecies, and by Christian experience as life in the Spirit. Paul was certain of these realities; they formed the basis of his defense, which was threefold. First, he appealed to God's character, which is trustworthy. God is the guarantor of his promises (Deut 7:9; cf. Ps 89:33-37; Isa 49:7). Underlying these references is the thought of Israel's God as dependable and true to his covenant promises (Heb., *'amen* [TH543, ZH589], "so be it," "confirmed"; quoted in 1:20). Second, Paul linked divine trustworthiness with the person of his Lord, who is the great affirmation of God's truth and promises (1:20). Third, Paul appealed to the experience of the Christians at Corinth when they heard his message. The starting point is in 1:18, which speaks of "our message" (NLT translates literally as "word," *logos* [TG3056, ZG3364]). Denney (1900:38) indicates that the term *logos* carries a double weight: It covers what Paul said regarding his travel plans and also the substance of his preaching at Corinth.

The appeal then shifts to what happened in the lives of the people when they responded to the apostle's message. The first verb is "confirm," meaning that the believers were initiated into the Christian life and experience brought about by God's endorsement of the apostle's witness, which led to the believers' incorporation into Christ. God "anointed" them, he says, with an obvious wordplay on "Christ," the Anointed One. God also "sealed" the believers (that is, identified them as his own), and he has given all Christians the earnest of the Spirit. What we are reading here, as Barrett (1973:81) remarks, is a comprehensive statement of the entire reception of believers into their new life in Christ, involving conversion, faith, and baptism (pictured as a "sealing"; see Eph 1:13-14; 4:30), as well as the reception of the Holy Spirit, who guarantees both our present salvation and our future hope of resurrection (5:5).

◆   ## B. Paul's Justification of His Severe Letter (1:23–2:13)

23Now I call upon God as my witness that I am telling the truth. The reason I didn't return to Corinth was to spare you from a severe rebuke. 24But that does not mean we want to dominate you by telling you how to put your faith into practice. We want to work together with you so you will be full of joy, for it is by your own faith that you stand firm.

CHAPTER 2

So I decided that I would not bring you grief with another painful visit. 2For if I cause you grief, who will make me glad? Certainly not someone I have grieved. 3That is why I wrote to you as I did, so that when I do come, I won't be grieved by the very ones who ought to give me the greatest joy. Surely you all know that my joy comes from your being joyful. 4I wrote that letter in great anguish, with a troubled heart and many tears. I didn't want to grieve you, but I wanted to let you know how much love I have for you.

5I am not overstating it when I say that the man who caused all the trouble hurt all of you more than he hurt me. 6Most of you opposed him, and that was punishment enough. 7Now, however, it is time to forgive and comfort him. Otherwise he may be overcome by discouragement. 8So I urge you now to reaffirm your love for him.

9I wrote to you as I did to test you and see if you would fully comply with my instructions. 10When you forgive this man, I forgive him, too. And when I forgive whatever needs to be forgiven, I do so with Christ's authority for your benefit, 11so that Satan will not outsmart us. For we are familiar with his evil schemes.

12When I came to the city of Troas to preach the Good News of Christ, the Lord opened a door of opportunity for me. 13But I had no peace of mind because my dear brother Titus hadn't yet arrived with a report from you. So I said good-bye and went on to Macedonia to find him.

NOTES

1:23 *I call upon God as my witness.* This is an example of mild oath taking, often used by Paul (Rom 1:9; Phil 1:8; 1 Thess 2:5, 10). In this context, the point is that Paul was anxious to clear the air by calling on God to attest to his intentions.

The reason I didn't return to Corinth. The reason he changed his travel plans is made plain: It was to spare the Corinthians that he chose not to revisit Corinth as he had promised. That he would have come to judge them is clear from what he said in 1 Cor 4:21. For more on Paul's travel plans, see Introduction and the notes on 1:15-16; 2:1; 12:14; 13:1.

1:24 *But that does not mean we want to dominate you.* Paul decided to spare the church more pain (in addition to the "sorrow" mentioned in 7:8, 11) since he was no dictator seeking to "dominate" them (a strong verb, *kurieuō* [TG2961, ZG3259], which is the verbal form of the noun *kurios* [TG2962, ZG3261], "lord"). Paul considered himself a fellow worker (as in 1 Cor 3:5-9) whose hallmark of service to the community of believers was one of sustaining them in joy and of assuring them of their Christian standing.

by your own faith that you stand firm. This is one way of understanding Paul's language. Probably better, it means they should be firm in their loyalty (*pistis* [TG4102, ZG4411], otherwise meaning "faith") to the apostolic gospel.

2:1 *So I decided that I would not bring you grief with another painful visit.* At last Paul set down the contrast arising from his recent plans and proposals. He wished only for the Corinthians' joy. But if he had paid them "another painful visit" (as his intermediate visit had been), the result would have been the direct opposite, namely, "grief." Moreover, his own joy would have been sacrificed when he wanted only to share in their joy as faithful believers. So he determined not to make his "second" promised visit (1:15-16) to Corinth until the problem between him and them was settled. For more on Paul's travel plans, see Introduction and notes on 1:15-16, 23; 12:14; 13:1.

2:2 *if I cause you grief.* This looks forward to 2:4; the letter he wrote caused sorrow to the recipients as it did to the writer (see 7:8).

someone I have grieved. This phrase identifies Paul's individual opponent in Corinth (cf. 2:6). The NLT translates this Greek participle (*ho lupoumenos* [TG3076A, ZG3382]) to reinforce the pain that Paul has caused the Corinthians. However, it is possible to take this participle in a different way to mean "the one who caused me sorrow" in order to indicate that this opposition caused Paul pain.

2:3 *when I do come.* Paul was looking ahead to a future visit that he calls his third visit (12:14; 13:1), which he expected would be an occasion of rejoicing. He prefaces this hope with one reason why he wrote a painful letter, mentioned in 2:4, 9. This is the plain sense, but Paul's writing here is difficult to sort out (see Thrall 1994:167-169 for some textual and interpretive issues).

2:4 *many tears.* Because Paul wrote with "many tears," this previous letter cannot be 1 Corinthians but rather was a letter that has not survived (see Introduction). Paul delineated his emotions and motivations clearly to counter any false assumptions such as seeking vindication or retaliation (Harris 2005:221).

2:5 *I am not overstating it when I say.* This verse opens a new section. At last we have "some indication of the root cause of the unhappy situation" (Héring 1967:15) that prevailed in the background of Paul's dealings with the church. At the center of the scene was an individual (2:6-7) who caused the pain Paul frequently alludes to. And in 2:10 it is clear that Paul himself was the object and target of this person's outburst. Yet more than a personal insult was involved: The offending person's attitude and action brought grief to the whole congregation, who rose up to punish him.

2:6 *Most of you opposed him.* The censure imposed on the offender by the majority of the congregation had resulted in the individual's being distressed, perhaps by the severity of the reprimand, or perhaps by its duration if it involved a permanent exclusion from the fellowship or (possibly) the church's love feast.

2:7 *Now, however, it is time to forgive and comfort him.* Paul was now ready to suggest a different attitude, presumably because the severe rebuke had done its remedial work. "Now, however" (*hōste tounantion mallon* [TG5620/3588/3123, ZG6063/3836/3437]) creates a contrast to the previous course of punishment; Paul desired the Corinthians to pursue the opposite course from punishment. They were now to "forgive" (*charizomai* [TG5483, ZG5919], which also means to "be gracious or generous towards" [cf. Rom 8:32; Phil 2:9] and when connected to wrongdoing or sin means to "forgive or pardon" [cf. 12:13; Col 2:13]), and this verb is related to the noun *charis* [TG5485, ZG5921] ("grace" or "gift") and to the verb *parakaleō* [TG3870, ZG4151] ("comfort" or "encourage"). Paul did not want this person to experience further pain or sorrow, that is, beyond the punishment. In this passage Paul had a deep interest in the offender's welfare in contrast to the stern measures of 1 Cor 5:5 (which indicates that these were separate incidents).

Otherwise he may be overcome by discouragement. Paul sought to avoid this person's discouragement if the church dealt too harshly with him.

2:8 *reaffirm your love for him.* The Corinthians may have expected Paul to "reaffirm" (*kuroō* [TG2964, ZG3263], which is a legal term meaning to "ratify") their punishment of this person; instead, Paul called them to reaffirm their love (*agapē* [TG26, ZG27]) for this person. The exhortation indicates that this person was someone who was part of the Corinthians' community and not an outsider. The call is to forgive, and Paul's verb changes to one of a directive.

2:9 *to test you and see if you would fully comply with my instructions.* The Corinthians' attitude to the offending person would be a "test" (*dokimē* [TG1382, ZG1509]) to see if they were "obedient" (*hupēkoos* [TG5255, ZG5675]) not simply to the apostle's words but also to the gospel he proclaimed and lived by. There is some question regarding to whom or what Paul expects obedience. However, as an ambassador of God bearing the gospel, Paul would not make a distinction between obedience to God, to the message of God (the gospel), or to the person bearing the message (himself). As M. J. Harris notes (2005:231), *dokimē* can refer to a "test" as well as "proven character" from testing (cf. 9:13; Phil 2:22). This test of obedience was the third reason for this painful letter. The first was to avoid the painful visit (2:3); the second was to reassure his love (2:4).

2:10 *When you forgive this man, I forgive him, too.* On "forgive" (*charizomai* [TG5483, ZG5919]), see the note on 2:7. While Paul commanded the Corinthians to forgive this person in 2:7, we discover in 2:10 that Paul already assumed that the Corinthians would forgive this person. The responsibility to forgive lay with the Corinthians, but through Paul's already-present support, he trusted they would make the right decision. The summons to forgive is backed by Paul's taking the lead: "When you forgive this man, I forgive him, too." The need for Paul's personal forgiveness gives good evidence that the nature of this person's sin was a personal offense to either Paul or one of his delegates (cf. 2:5). Granted, Paul framed this act of forgiveness as a "test" of their loyalty (2:9) to Paul and his gospel, but Paul was not being egocentric. If he was concerned merely about his own personal reputation, he could have withstood (1 Cor 6:7). Instead, Paul was concerned about the welfare of the Corinthians. Loyalty to Paul meant loyalty to his gospel, which meant loyalty to God. In Paul's mind, if there was any break in this chain, the end result of loyalty to God could not be achieved. Paul was concerned that this one person's sin could have infected the whole church (1 Cor 5:6).

2:11 *so that Satan will not outsmart us. For we are familiar with his evil schemes.*
"Satan" (*satanas* [TG4566, ZG4927], from Heb. *satan* [TH7854, ZH8477], means "adversary"
or "accuser"; cf. Job 1:6-12) also is found in 11:14; 12:7. As Harris notes (2005:233),
Paul used three other designations for Satan in 2 Corinthians—"the god of this age" in
4:4 (the NLT adds "Satan"), Beliar in 6:15 (NLT, "the devil"), and the serpent in 11:3.
(For more on Satan in 2 Corinthians, see the notes on 4:4; 6:15; and 11:3. See also Reid
1993a:862-867 and Uddin 1999:265-280.) If the Corinthians were too tolerant and lax
or too unforgiving, Satan would gain a victory. To fail on either count would be to play
into Satan's hands. The enemy "knows" what can and does divide Christians, but we may
take refuge and assurance in that "we know" (2:11) what he knows and can circumvent
his ploys. The Corinthians would either through forgiveness be on the side of Christ
(2:10), or they would be unforgiving, siding with Satan and bringing turmoil to the
community (2:11).

2:12 *Troas.* Alexandrian Troas, the port of embarkation for sea travelers from Asia to
Macedonia (Acts 16:8, 11; 20:5-6; cf. 2 Tim 4:13). It was here that Paul received his vision
to evangelize Macedonia (Acts 16:9). Paul, anxious about the collection and about news
from Corinth, set out from Ephesus and went to Troas in order to meet Titus, who was
returning from Corinth.

the Lord opened a door of opportunity. As to the historical circumstance of this evangelistic ministry, we can only guess. The metaphor of an open door occurs throughout the
NT (1 Cor 16:9; Col 4:3; Rev 3:8), indicating the presence of opportunity. Some scholars
(Windisch 1924:94) think it implies provision of a house for Paul's lodging and so a base
of operations to launch a mission to an important town.

2:13 *But I had no peace of mind.* Paul was restless because of Titus's absence, which
meant he did not have a report about the situation in Corinth. Paul recalled his anxious-
ness about Titus's absence and lack of report in order to illustrate his affection for the
Corinthians (cf. 2:4, 9). This short section of vv. 12-13 rounds off Paul's recital of his
travel plans. The paragraph links with 7:5, where the arrangement to meet Titus at Troas
on his return from Corinth is picked up in the narrative. As it happened, on not finding
Titus, Paul moved across to Macedonia, where the story is resumed at 7:5-16. Although
there is continuity between 2:13 and 7:5, there are also some differences as seen by the
parallel lines *ouk eschēka anesin tō pneumati mou* (lit., "I did not have relief in my spirit")
and *oudemian eschēken anesin hē sarx hēmōn* (lit., "Our flesh did not have relief"). There is
a shift from the singular to the plural and a synonymous use of "my spirit" (*tō pneumati
mou*) in 2:5 with "our flesh" (*hē sarx hēmōn*) in 7:5. Paul was not using "spirit" (*pneuma*
[TG4151, ZG4460]) and "flesh" (*sarx* [TG4561, ZG4922]) in his usual antithetical manner; rather,
each term refers to Paul's whole person (possibly with "spirit" highlighting his inward
turmoil and "flesh" highlighting his outward turmoil). Paul seemed to intentionally
recapitulate 2:13 in 7:5 in order to bookend his apostolic defense with the travel narrative.
In doing so, Paul rooted his apostolic events in the past, possibly as an appeal to memory.
Also, 2:12-13 deals with divine power overcoming human weakness in the context of
evangelism, while 7:5-16 focuses on the context of affliction and suffering (Belleville
1996:25). For more detail regarding how 2:13 and 7:5 relate to the composition of
2 Corinthians, see C. N. Toney 2010a.

So I said good-bye and went on to Macedonia to find him. This trip to Macedonia is
often equated with the events of Acts 20:1, dated near the end of AD 55. The thought of
Macedonia evokes the following thanksgiving in 2:14-17. The Macedonians were active
in sharing the gospel.

COMMENTARY

Paul's pastoral attitudes are much on display in this passage. He found it needful to explain why he acted as he did, presumably because this apparent going back on his promise was a bone of contention at Corinth. He was under fire, and his apostolic character was assailed because he did not visit Corinth as he had originally planned. Doubtless, this course of action was held against him by someone at Corinth who used it as grounds for an attack on him personally. Paul saw this affront not so much as a personal insult to be borne, but as a denigration of his apostolic work and an obstacle to be removed (see note on 2:10).

His counter-reply was to unfold the reasons for his nonappearance and to paint it in the background of the sending of a sorrowful letter (2:4). Evidently it cost him a lot to put his emotional thoughts into writing: "I wrote that letter in great anguish, with a troubled heart and many tears" (2:4). This sentence opens a window into the writer's inner life at the time the letter was composed (see comments on 7:8). We know that this sorrowful letter cannot be our 1 Corinthians, as Denney, P. E. Hughes, and earlier commentators thought, because 1 Corinthians could not be described as a letter of anguish. It must be the letter sent directly following Paul's "painful visit" (2:1; see 7:8) and committed to Titus to carry to Corinth (7:6-8). Nor is it likely that this letter has survived as chapters 10–13, as others believe (J. H. Kennedy 1900; C. H. Talbert 2002), since that part of our 2 Corinthians is written more in indignation than sorrow. Further, the "painful letter" was intended to replace Paul's visit (1:15, 23; 2:1), yet chapters 10–13 indicate that Paul intended to visit (12:14; 13:1). We conclude then that the letter had done its work but has not survived.

Grief and joy mingle in the opening paragraph (2:1-4), as Paul rehearsed the pain and the relief that came once the offender had relented in his opposition. The group in the church that had sided with the offender was also won back. It was now a time for making amends. Paul's skillful comments pointed the way forward. The severe reprimand had worked; it was time to forgive and reinstate the errant brother. To do otherwise would have disastrous consequences; namely, it would lead to Satan's victory over the church. Two measures would bring about this result. If, on the one hand, the offender were to be lost to the church, then Satan's work would be achieved. If, on the other hand, Paul and the church were to withhold their love and acceptance, the church's enemy would be just as pleased. As it is, neither extreme would come about, and Satan (a Hebrew word for the archenemy of God and humans) would not win the day. Paul said, "We are familiar with his evil schemes" (noēmata [TG3540, ZG3784], lit., "thoughts," a word that has bad associations in this letter—see 3:14; 4:4; 10:5; 11:3). Satan's role to trip up unwary Christians is found elsewhere (1 Pet 5:8; Rev 2:24; 12:10).

To avoid Satan's trap, the loyal Corinthians must affirm their love for the offender and set about restoring the church's unity of spirit—a concern always present in Paul's pastoral handling of all congregational disputes. Wisely, Paul steered a course between the Scylla of indifference and dissension on the one hand, and the Charybdis of rigorism and an unforgiving spirit on the other. The strains of Paul's "concern for all the churches" (11:28) did not blind him to what must be done at

Corinth: A firm stand and a severe letter with its reproof were needful. But then the sternness needed to be replaced by a warm, generous, appealing gesture of pardon and restitution to the church's fellowship. To fail here was to play exactly into Satan's hands. The enemy "knows" what can and does divide Christians, but we take refuge in that "we know" (2:11; NLT, "we are familiar with") what he knows and can circumvent his ploys.

The last two verses of this section (2:12-13) make it clear that the agitation that troubled Paul's spirit diminished his evangelistic ministry at Troas. When pastoral concerns weighed heavily on him, he could not put his heart into missionary opportunity. Therefore, it seemed better for him to leave Troas and press on to meet his colleague Titus on his return from Corinth. So Paul left the people of Troas and went on to Macedonia on the other side of the Thracian sea, presumably by boat, as Ignatius, bishop of Antioch, was later to do (*Polycarp* 8: "because of my sudden sailing from Troas to Neapolis"). Or Paul could have gone by land, hoping to meet Titus en route. Barrett (1969:8) conjectures that the two men missed each other. This may explain Paul's distress when he did reach Macedonia (see 7:5, which has the same wording: "When we arrived in Macedonia, there was no rest for us"). Alternatively, Titus's nonappearance to greet Paul in Macedonia may be accounted for by his tardiness in reaching Macedonia from Corinth.

◆ IV. Paul's Apostolic Ministry (2:14–7:1)
A. Paul's Qualifications for Ministry (2:14–3:6)

[14]But thank God! He has made us his captives and continues to lead us along in Christ's triumphal procession. Now he uses us to spread the knowledge of Christ everywhere, like a sweet perfume. [15]Our lives are a Christ-like fragrance rising up to God. But this fragrance is perceived differently by those who are being saved and by those who are perishing. [16]To those who are perishing, we are a dreadful smell of death and doom. But to those who are being saved, we are a life-giving perfume. And who is adequate for such a task as this?

[17]You see, we are not like the many hucksters* who preach for personal profit. We preach the word of God with sincerity and with Christ's authority, knowing that God is watching us.

CHAPTER 3

Are we beginning to praise ourselves again? Are we like others, who need to bring you letters of recommendation, or who ask you to write such letters on their behalf? Surely not! [2]The only letter of recommendation we need is you yourselves. Your lives are a letter written in our* hearts; everyone can read it and recognize our good work among you. [3]Clearly, you are a letter from Christ showing the result of our ministry among you. This "letter" is written not with pen and ink, but with the Spirit of the living God. It is carved not on tablets of stone, but on human hearts.

[4]We are confident of all this because of our great trust in God through Christ. [5]It is not that we think we are qualified to do anything on our own. Our qualification comes from God. [6]He has enabled us to be ministers of his new covenant. This is a covenant not of written laws, but of the Spirit. The old written covenant ends in death; but under the new covenant, the Spirit gives life.

2:17 Some manuscripts read *the rest of the hucksters.*   3:2 Some manuscripts read *your.*

NOTES

2:14-15 *But thank God!* This verse marks the beginning of Paul's apostolic defense of 2:14–7:4, which is bracketed by his travel narrative in order to defend his apparent apostolic wanderings. While Paul appears "to be paraded by God as a humiliated prisoner of war to his death (2:14) . . . his suffering [in reality] results not from the vengeance of God for his alleged inappropriate activities [e.g., the collection] . . . but his sufferings are the reiteration of the sufferings of Christ" (Duff 1994:20).

made us his captives and continues to lead us along in Christ's triumphal procession. The meaning of this expression (which is much more terse in the Greek) is much debated, with a recent agreement among scholars (see Savage 1996:103-104) that it does not imply Paul's triumph as much as it implies his role as a slave in Christ's triumphal procession being exposed to public shame (1 Cor 4:9-10, 13) while, in a paradox, he shared in Christ's victory. The emphasis falls on Paul's teaching on "strength-in-weakness" (see 4:10; 12:9).

Traditionally, the Roman triumph involved Roman generals whose return to Rome was marked with a victory procession, but during the Empire this privilege was reserved for the emperor. Leading the procession to the Capitoline Hill were the magistrates and senate, followed by trumpeters, spoils of war, flute players, white oxen to be sacrificed, captives (in which select representatives were executed, i.e., "perishing" or led "to death," *eis thanaton* [TG2288, ZG2505] as in 2:16), and finally, the chariot of the triumphant general with his victorious army (i.e., those "being saved" or led "to life," *eis zōēn* [TG2222, ZG2437] as in 2:16) shouting, "Hail, triumphant one!" For more on the Roman triumph (with a good bibliography), see D. G. Reid 1993b:948.

sweet perfume . . . fragrance. The more neutral term, "sweet perfume" (*osmē* [TG3744, ZG4011], "odor"), may be a pleasant or unpleasant odor, but "fragrance" (*euōdias* [TG2175, ZG2380]) is always pleasant and in the LXX usually refers to the sweet smell of the burnt offerings (e.g., Gen 8:21; Exod 29:18; Lev 1:9). This "sweet perfume" metaphor may allude to the incense scattered along the victor's route or may involve an appropriation of Jewish thought regarding the Torah as being a "medicine" (Mishnaic Heb., *sam*; Aramaic, *samma'*; Jastrow 1996:998) that can bring harm or hurt according to use. Now Paul applies this metaphor to Christ. With these two terms, Paul transitions from a metaphor regarding the Roman triumph to OT sacrifice.

2:16 *And who is adequate for such a task as this?* This is a natural question. The answer will come in 3:5: "Our qualification [i.e., adequacy to fulfill the gospel ministry] comes from God."

2:17 *we are not like the many hucksters.* Paul's work as an apostle is set in contrast to the many rival preachers at Corinth. We know little about their identity, except that they were evidently different from the opponents later mentioned in chs 10–13, who were intruders who brought a different gospel (11:4) and are severely condemned (11:13-15). The opponents here are branded as "hucksters," lit., "those many who adulterate God's message" (*kapēleuontes* [TG2585, ZG2836]), just as wine merchants in contemporary society diluted their product to make a greater profit (cf. Isa 1:22, LXX, where the traders mingle water with wine). On the contrary, Paul's task was to proclaim faithfully the message with sincerity (see 1:12) and with Christ's authority (lit., "in Christ") and as in God's sight.

3:1 *letters of recommendation.* These kinds of letters are mentioned elsewhere in the NT (Acts 9:2; 18:27; 22:5). Romans 16:1 shows how Christian letters were used to establish credibility among believers. Paul had little regard for such documents. What interested him was the Christian character of his converts. So the Corinthians' standing in Christ is the test of what he regarded as valid ministry (see 3:3).

3:2 *Your lives are a letter written in our hearts.* This reading is supported by several important manuscripts (𝔓46 A B C D 1739 𝔐). A few other manuscripts (א 33 1881) read, "your lives are a letter written in your hearts." The reading with "your hearts" is preferred because the letter in question was Paul's letter written on the transformed lives of his readers. And this ministry was evident to all, just as the letter can be "read" and "recognized" (a pun in the Greek, as earlier in 1:13; see note). Thrall (1994:223-224) notes that the first reading, though strongly attested, may be due to assimilation with the wording of 7:3.

3:3 *you are a letter from Christ.* Paul's role as agent is explicated in the letter-writing metaphor—Christ is the author, and Paul is the scribe (amanuensis). Paul's opponents rooted their authority in letters of recommendation, possibly from the Jerusalem church. In contrast to his opponents' letter, which was written by humans with pen and ink, Paul claimed that his previous ministry in Corinth *is* his letter of recommendation, which was authored by Christ, who transformed the Corinthians' lives. Paul's letter was superior because it was written first, and it was not written by humans, even those as notable as leaders of the Jerusalem church.

pen and ink. Tools of writing were black ink (a mixture of carbon and gum), a reed pen, and papyrus or parchment (animal skin). Black ink was erasable, but the Spirit's marks are permanent.

It is carved not on tablets of stone, but on human hearts. Using "stone" (*lithinos* [TG3035, ZG3343]) as a link word, Paul's imagery connected the "tablets of stone" (*plaxin lithinais* [TG4109, ZG4419]) of the old covenant found in Exod 31:18, LXX, with the unresponsive "hearts of stone" (*tēn kardian tēn lithinēn* [TG2840, ZG2588]) found in Ezekiel (Ezek 11:19; 36:26-27, LXX). Paul's image of the "letter" being written on the human heart recalled the OT promise of God's law being written on human hearts in Jer 31:33. The effect of these combined images was that the old covenant was associated with Ezekiel's unresponsive heart and the new covenant was associated with the responsive heart created by God's Spirit. The validation of Paul's ministry involved the fulfillment of the promises in Ezekiel and Jeremiah.

3:4 *We are confident of all this.* The theme is that of confidence, which in turn focuses on Paul's claim to be competent (3:5; NLT, "qualified") to fulfill his ministry. "Confidence" (*pepoithēsis* [TG4006, ZG4301]) is used four times (1:15; 3:4; 8:22; 10:2), and this phrase harks back to 2:17. He is confident in his role as minister of the new covenant because he knows that he is suitably qualified because he acts as one whom Christ is working through (*dia tou Christou*).

3:5 *not that we think we are qualified . . . on our own. Our qualification comes from God.* With "not that," *ouch hoti* [TG3756/3754, ZG4024/4022] (as in 1:24), Paul was correcting a possible misinterpretation of his claims. This also answers Paul's rhetorical question in 2:16. Paul considered it inappropriate to take credit for his own ministry, just as he indicated in a similar statement in 1 Cor 15:9-10. There may also be an allusion to the frailty of humans in relation to the divine as found in Joel 2:11.

3:6 *ministers of his new covenant.* This ministry was one based on the "new covenant." There is evidence that Jewish teachers thought of themselves as "ministers" (*diakonoi* [TG1249, ZG1356], 11:23), but the expression "new covenant" (*kainē diathēkē*) is Paul's assertion, based on Jer 31:31-34. Paul used the word "new" (*kainos* [TG2537, ZG2785]) to stress that his gospel is not a renovated Judaism but speaks of a new chapter in God's dealings with humankind (see 5:17; cf. Rom 7:6; 1 Cor 5:7; Gal 4:24; Eph 4:22-24; Col 3:9-10).

The old written covenant ends in death; but under the new covenant, the Spirit gives life. This is an expanded rendering of Paul's more cryptic original: "The letter (*gramma* [TG1121, ᶻᴳ1207]) kills, but the Spirit (*pneuma* [ᵀᴳ4151, ᶻᴳ4460]) imparts life" (see similar statements in Rom 2:29; 7:6). Paul will unpack this dense statement concerning the two covenants linked with Moses and Christ through a series of contrasts in 3:7-18. Paul's choice of "letter" (*gramma*) is a reference to the Torah and may also be intended to refute his opponents' letters (*epistolē* [ᵀᴳ1992, ᶻᴳ2186]) of recommendation (3:1) versus his own ministry through the Spirit (Jervell 1960:178). With such strong language as "the letter kills," it is tempting to read Paul's views on the law only negatively. However, Paul does not fault the law itself (Rom 7:12, 14). The law gives the best description of God's moral expectations (Rom 7:7); however, it fails to empower people to meet those expectations (Rom 8:3). Thus, the weakness of the law is its failure to empower people, who have been marred by sin, to live righteous lives. It simply points out people's faults and condemns them, hence being a ministry of death. In contrast, the "Spirit gives life" by empowering people to *live* righteous lives (Rom 8:1). These lives of righteousness will ultimately end with God granting eternal life (not because of human works, but because of the work of Christ). It is important to see, for Paul, that grace involves a Spirit-empowered, righteous life in the here and now as well as the hope of eternal life in the future.

COMMENTARY

It should first be noted that the narrative breaks off at 2:13 to be completed in 7:5, leaving 2:14–7:4 as a lengthy excursus devoted to the theme of the apostolic ministry. The first portion of this excursus is 2:14–3:6. Paul wanted to demonstrate the validity of his apostolic ministry in a context where it was under suspicion. His Corinthian opponents evidently were challenging his competence, but the issue was deeper than merely personal. Underlying the debate over ministry is the theological tension of what kind of ministry has divine approval.

The section begins with an image unfamiliar to modern readers. In Hellenistic times, the people in Rome could often see Roman generals leading a victory parade in which captives taken in war were led in chains, while the Roman soldiers were greeted with acclaim. As part of his strength-in-weakness theme, Paul is portrayed as one of the captives being led in Christ's victory procession! Paradoxically, Paul the prisoner is sharing in Christ's victory (see notes on 2:14-15). Scattering fragrance along the route was part of the celebration, with a double effect. To the prisoners it led to their death in the arena; to the victorious army it was a token of joy and life. So Paul's gospel had this twofold effect: To the lost it was a deadly fume, but to those who responded to Paul's ministry it was "a life-giving perfume."

Paul's rivals (2:17) regarded themselves as accredited "servants of Christ" (11:23). They had come to Corinth armed with letters of authority that gave evidence of their prowess and exploits in Christian service. By contrast, Paul's ministry looked feeble and ineffectual. So he made his defense. He charged that these so-called ministers were hucksters who adulterated God's message (see note on 2:17). By contrast, he proclaimed the word with sincerity and Christ's authority. He did not need letters of recommendation. Rather, he appealed to his own character and regarded the Corinthian converts as his testimonial letters of recommendation (see note on 3:2).

This letter, Paul claimed, was not written with ink but by the Spirit—or, to make the contrast clearer, not on "stone tablets, written with the finger of God" (Exod 31:18, LXX). Texts in Exodus 31:18, 32:19, and Deuteronomy 9:17 refer to the covenant given by God to Moses, yet Jeremiah 31:33 mentions the "new" covenant to which Paul alluded in 3:6. Also in the apostle's mind was Ezekiel (Ezek 11:19; 36:26), where tablets of flesh will replace tablets of stone. For Paul it is what is engraved on "human hearts" that really matters. The inner working of God's Spirit in a person's life shows itself in their newness of life. Based on the promise of Jeremiah 31, God had inaugurated a new chapter in dealing with his people. And Paul was a minister of this new way.

◆ ## B. Life under the Two Covenants (3:7-18)

7The old way,* with laws etched in stone, led to death, though it began with such glory that the people of Israel could not bear to look at Moses' face. For his face shone with the glory of God, even though the brightness was already fading away. 8Shouldn't we expect far greater glory under the new way, now that the Holy Spirit is giving life? 9If the old way, which brings condemnation, was glorious, how much more glorious is the new way, which makes us right with God! 10In fact, that first glory was not glorious at all compared with the overwhelming glory of the new way. 11So if the old way, which has been replaced, was glorious, how much more glorious is the new, which remains forever!

12Since this new way gives us such confidence, we can be very bold. 13We are not like Moses, who put a veil over his face so the people of Israel would not see the glory, even though it was destined to fade away. 14But the people's minds were hardened, and to this day whenever the old covenant is being read, the same veil covers their minds so they cannot understand the truth. And this veil can be removed only by believing in Christ. 15Yes, even today when they read Moses' writings, their hearts are covered with that veil, and they do not understand.

16But whenever someone turns to the Lord, the veil is taken away. 17For the Lord is the Spirit, and wherever the Spirit of the Lord is, there is freedom. 18So all of us who have had that veil removed can see and reflect the glory of the Lord. And the Lord—who is the Spirit—makes us more and more like him as we are changed into his glorious image.

3:7 Or ministry; also in 3:8, 9, 10, 11, 12.

NOTES

3:7 *The old way.* The NLT translates *diakonia* [TG1248, ZG1355] as "way" (it can also mean "ministry" or "dispensation"). Of Paul's 23 uses, this term is used 12 times in 2 Corinthians (3:7, 8, 9 [2x]; 4:1; 5:18; 6:3; 8:4; 9:1, 12, 13; 11:8). Here it refers to the whole system of the Mosaic law, which Paul considered leading to death, in contrast to the Jewish perspective that it was life-giving. (For more on Paul's view on the law, see note on 3:6.)

his face shone with the glory of God. An important feature of law giving in Moses's time was that it came with glory. This is a key term in the section (3:7-18), occurring 19 times in chs 1–8, of which 15 references are in chs 3 and 4. It refers to the manifest splendor of God's radiance, the Shekinah, the light that followed Israel in the desert, and the brilliance that lit up the face of the lawgiver, Moses (Exod 34:29). So both the law (3:7, 11) and the human lawgiver Moses (3:7) were glorious. The Jewish background to this is interesting. For example, in the Targum to Pseudo-Jonathan it is said: "And Moses did not know that the splendor of his features was made glorious, which (happened) to him from the splendor of the glory of the Shekinah of the Lord." Philo (*Life of Moses* II.70) says, "[Moses] descended [from the mount] with a face far more beautiful than when he ascended, so that those who saw him were filled with awe and amazement; nor even could their eyes continue to stand the dazzling brightness that flashed from him like the rays of the sun." The allusion to "rays" picks up the Hebrew text of Exod 34:29, which reads, lit., "The skin of his face sent forth beams [or horns]" that struck terror into the people (Exod 34:30, "they were afraid to come near him").

3:8 *under the new way, now that the Holy Spirit is giving life.* The future eschatological age has begun to be experienced in the here and now through the Spirit (cf. 1:22; 5:5). Paul contrasts the ministry of death with the ministry of the Spirit. The NLT reinforces this contrast by adding that the Spirit "is giving life" based upon 3:6. For more on the life-giving Spirit, see the note on 3:6.

3:9 *the old way . . . condemnation . . . the new way . . . makes us right with God.* The old covenant fell short by only pointing out and condemning humanity's sinful condition without offering relief (Rom 8:3); however, through the Spirit, people of the new covenant are empowered to overcome sin!

3:10 *first glory . . . glorious.* The NLT's "first glory" and "glorious" are passive uses of the verb *doxazō* [TG1392, ZG1519], "to be glorified." These verbs are an allusion to the three times the passive is used to describe Moses's face shining in Exod 34:29-35, LXX, which Paul expands as a reference to the entire law. With this paradoxical statement Paul acknowledged that the Mosaic law at one time reflected God's glory. Just as the glow of Moses's face was temporal, so is the old covenant. This one-time "good" has been replaced by the "best." A lightbulb may light a room, but the sun lights up the universe.

3:12 *such confidence.* Gr. *elpida* [TG1680, ZG1828] also means "hope."

we can be very bold. Unlike the boldness and radiant presence of Moses, after whom Paul's opponents modeled their ministry, Paul had appeared weak and only had a feeble presence (4:7-12, 17; 5:12-13; 6:4-10; 10:1, 10; 11:6; 12:5-10; 13:4). Here Paul boldly claimed to have the last word over Moses in God's plan of salvation.

3:13 *Moses, who put a veil over his face so the people of Israel would not see the glory.* When Moses descended from Sinai the second time, he spoke with the Israelites and veiled his face (Exod 34:33). After this, a pattern emerged where Moses would enter the Tent of Meeting and remove the veil to speak with God, then exit to speak with the people to convey God's commands, and finally replace the veil (Exod 34:34-35). Paul adapted this story to his present circumstances (see comments below). He cast Moses in a neutral light. Paul did not fault him for putting a "veil" (*kalumma* [TG2571, ZG2820] = Heb., *masweh* [TH4533, ZH5003]) over his face, keeping in mind the positive purpose of the veil noted in Exod 34:30: The veil covered his radiant face, which struck fear in the Israelites. (Moses apparently thought this fear or awe to be an appropriate response when he was God's spokesperson; however, he covered his face in his day-to-day activities.) Rather, Paul faulted the Israelites who otherwise could "gaze at intensely" (*atenizō* [TG816, ZG867]; NLT, "see") a face whose glory continued to fade. The fading glory indicated, for Paul, the temporary nature of the old covenant. The veil merely contributed to the problem, at times hiding the fading glory. The Israelites failed by their persistence of looking at a face of fading radiance that symbolized a "way" or "ministry" that was temporal.

3:14-15 These verses are Paul's commentary on Exod 34:34-35. Verse 15 restates verse 14. Paul turns to address the unbelief of Israel as an apology concerning his gospel (see also Romans 9–11). The fault lies not with God's word but with those who read it.

the old covenant. Gr., *hē palaia diathēkē* [TG1242, ZG1347], a phrase Paul appears to have coined as a derivative from Jeremiah's "new covenant" (*diathēkēn kainēn*; cf. Jer 31:31 [38:31], LXX). When choosing a word for "old," Paul chose *palaios* [TG3820, ZG4094], which carries the more negative sense of "antiquated" or "dated" rather than *archaios* [TG744, ZG792], which carries a positive meaning of "ancient" or "venerable."

their minds . . . their hearts. Both the "mind" (*noēma* [TG3540, ZG3784]; also "thought") and the "heart" (*kardia* [TG2840, ZG2588]) refer not only to the faculty of understanding, but to the inner life of a person. "Thought" (*noēma* [TG3540, ZG3784]) is the resulting activity of the "mind" (*nous* [TG3563, ZG3808]). According to J. D. G. Dunn (1998:73-75), "mind" is used 21 times, while "heart" (*kardia*) occurs 52 times in Pauline letters. The mind, primarily a Greek concept, stood for reason, the highest human faculty, which distinguished people from plants and animals and was often connected to the divine. The heart, as conceived by both Jews and Greeks, stood for the innermost person, which was the seat of emotions, thoughts, and the will. For Paul, the mind was the rational, thinking person, while the heart was the experiencing, motivating person.

And this veil can be removed only by believing in Christ. Lit, "for in Christ it is removed." The NLT emphasizes the faith of the Christian that trusts in the work of Christ by adding "believing" to the translation.

3:16 *whenever someone turns to the Lord, the veil is taken away.* Paul cites Exod 34:34, LXX. While his opponents saw the veil as a sign of authority, Paul highlights the veil's removal in the presence of the Lord.

3:17 *the Lord is the Spirit . . . the Spirit of the Lord.* This verse acts as a commentary on the previous verse. The way believers experience the Lord Jesus Christ is by the Spirit because the Spirit is Jesus Christ's invisible presence indwelling the spirits of believers.

3:18 *reflect the glory of the Lord.* This is a reflection as in a mirror (so NRSV); the verb translated "reflect" (*katoptrizomai* [TG2734, ZG3002]) can have an alternate meaning of "gazing" (NLT mg [first edition] renders "so that we can see in a mirror"; so Thrall 1994:238, 290-295). This rendering is preferred by many scholars.

COMMENTARY

In this section Paul proceeds to unpack the statement "the letter kills, but the Spirit imparts life" (3:6, lit. rendering) in an elaborately drawn set of contrasts. Letter and Spirit stand for the two covenants, linked with the lawgiving Moses and Christ as the life-giving Spirit (3:18). Maybe the mention of "letter" looked back to the "letters of recommendation" carried by his rivals, and this led Paul to connect them with the Jewish religion.

There are three lines of Paul's argument: In 3:7-11 two of them are discussed. First, while Paul found no fault with the law itself (Rom 7:12, 14), he knew that the law set a standard but offered no power to reach it. For that reason Paul did not mince his words: The law "kills" (3:6; NLT, "ends in death"); it is called "the old way, with laws etched in stone [that] led to death" (3:7; lit., "a ministry of death"), and one that "brings condemnation" (3:9). These strong terms can mean only that the law set the target of a perfect standard requiring complete obedience. Yet human beings, who are sinfully weak by reason of what Paul calls their "flesh" (i.e., their self-life), are unable to attain it. So what God intended as good turned into a death-dealing instrument (Rom 7:13) because of human frailty (Rom 8:3).

Paul discovered that the law mocked him and taunted him by calling him to an impossibly high level and offering no help. So what God intended as good either condemned him to failure and frustration or to pride if he boasted that he could keep it (Phil 3:6). Under law, it was a no-win situation.

Second, the law had an honorable place, but it was only temporary. The illustration of the law's "parenthetic character" (being both preceded and followed by faith, as Paul illustrates in Gal 3:16-19) is seen in the way in which the glory of the law (3:7, 11) and the lawgiver Moses (3:7) was a passing one. The background is clearly Exodus 34:29-35, which pictures the splendor shining from Moses's face when he returned from communing with God. That radiance, however, faded in time and at length disappeared. In Paul's perspective, the lawgiver Moses represents Judaism, whose glory, once a reality, was now fading away. Indeed, its day was over, and its impermanence had given way to that which had come to stay, namely, the gospel of the Messiah Jesus (3:10-11)—a conclusion elaborated in Hebrews 8:1-13.

In the next section (3:12-18), the chief issue turns on the meaning of the veil. For Moses the veil acted as a barrier between him and the people because that glory was too much for them to see (Exod 34:33). Paul applied this to the veil (or covering) that was spread over the minds of the Jewish readers of the Old Testament. They imagined that the latter was the final revelation of God, whereas Paul maintained it was a preparatory agent to make God's people ready to receive the Messiah (Gal 3:24). So tragically they remain hardened and blinded (4:3-4; Rom 11:25) in spite of their inestimable privileges as God's ancient people to whom the law was entrusted (Rom 3:1-2; 9:4-5; see Savage 1996:133-144).

Having taken his Corinthian readers so far, Paul was now ready for a third part of his discussion of the contrasts between the two covenants. The law betokened a barrier between Yahweh and the people of Israel, both in Moses's day and in Paul's.

Why did Moses place a veil over his radiant face (3:13; Exod 34:33)? Part of the reason was to prevent the people's disappointment when they saw the glory fading. But Exodus 34:30 speaks of another reason: That glory caused fear as Moses's face gave off rays (lit., "horns") of effulgence like radiation. (In medieval statues of Moses, he is shown as having protuberances on his forehead.) Paul saw in this a profound meaning for the veil Moses wore. It spoke of a barrier hiding the truth from the reader and hearer of the old covenant, i.e., the Torah of Moses, in the synagogue worship (3:15). Yet, just as Moses took off the veil when he went into Yahweh's presence, so it is with readers who turn to the Lord (Jesus). They see Scripture fulfilled in him, like the disciples did on the road to Emmaus (Luke 24:27, 32, 44-45).

Now we come to the last two verses of the chapter (3:17-18). The key sentence is "the Lord is the Spirit." Once we recall that the previous verses were drawn from Exodus 34:34, we are on the right track. Paul's statement in 3:17 ("for the Lord is the Spirit") is his comment on the reference to Moses's turning to God's presence. It is as though Paul was saying, "Now as to my last statement ('whenever someone turns to the Lord, the veil is taken away'), the Lord whom Moses experienced is now the Spirit who leads believers to turn their hearts to the Messiah and confess his lordship" (1 Cor 12:3).

The work of the Spirit is further described in 3:17b-18. The Spirit brings the Jewish believers out of bondage into liberty, and the Spirit transforms all believers, Gentiles as well as Jews, into God's ideal for living. That is seen in the perfect model, Christ Jesus. This is a progressive experience based on communion with God, such as Moses enjoyed face-to-face. So "we have the veil removed" and "every Christian has become a Moses" (Héring 1967:27). Such a progressive transformation (lit., from "glory to glory") is God's plan for his church, until our transformation is complete in sharing his final glory at Christ's Parousia (Rom 8:29; Gal 4:19; Phil 3:20-21).

◆   ## C. The Setting for Paul's Ministry (4:1-7)

Therefore, since God in his mercy has given us this new way,* we never give up. ²We reject all shameful deeds and underhanded methods. We don't try to trick anyone or distort the word of God. We tell the truth before God, and all who are honest know this.

³If the Good News we preach is hidden behind a veil, it is hidden only from people who are perishing. ⁴Satan, who is the god of this world, has blinded the minds of those who don't believe. They are unable to see the glorious light of the Good News. They don't understand this message about the glory of Christ, who is the exact likeness of God.

⁵You see, we don't go around preaching about ourselves. We preach that Jesus Christ is Lord, and we ourselves are your servants for Jesus' sake. ⁶For God, who said, "Let there be light in the darkness," has made this light shine in our hearts so we could know the glory of God that is seen in the face of Jesus Christ.

⁷We now have this light shining in our hearts, but we ourselves are like fragile clay jars containing this great treasure.* This makes it clear that our great power is from God, not from ourselves.

4:1 Or ministry.   4:7 Greek We now have this treasure in clay jars.

NOTES

4:1 *God in his mercy has given us this new way.* "This new way" is lit., "this ministry" (*diakonia* [TG1248, ZG1355]; NLT mg). This kind of statement refers to Paul's sense of privilege in serving God, as seen in verses such as 1 Cor 15:9-10; Gal 1:13; 1 Tim 1:15 (cf. Acts 9:3; 22:6; 26:13)—texts all going back to Paul's conversion (so most commentators) or call. It could also refer to God's strengthening Paul in his trials (so Barrett 1973:127).

4:2 *underhanded methods.* Lit., "hidden things of shame," that is, practices of evangelism that would cause shame.

We don't try to trick anyone. Lit., "We do not walk with cunning" (*mē peripatountes en panourgia*). "Cunning" (*panourgia* [TG3834, ZG4111]) literally means "ready or able to do anything," which is a pretentious claim based on an impossible feat, so it is linked with cunning, craftiness, and trickery (BDAG 754). This is to use cunning in order to gain favor. This accusation against Paul will surface again in 12:16.

distort the word of God. This means to tamper with God's message, to falsify it, like the false teachers did (2:17).

We tell the truth before God, and all who are honest know this. More literally, "We make an open declaration of the truth in God's sight, and appeal to the human conscience of all our hearers."

4:3 *the Good News . . . is hidden behind a veil.* This verse looks back to 3:15 and to the veil that covered Moses's face. This time it is a sad comment on the lack of response to Paul's preaching his Good News (*euangelion* [TG2098, ZG2295], lit., "gospel").

4:4 *Satan . . . the god of this world, has blinded the minds.* Paul attributed the failure of belief to the schemes of Satan, not to the inadequacy of his gospel or apostolic calling. The

NLT correctly identifies "the god of this world" as Satan. (There are three other references
to the devil [2:11; 6:15; 11:3]; for more on Satan, see the notes for these verses.) "World" or,
lit., "age" (*aiōn* [TG165, ZG172]) reflects the Jewish apocalyptic dualistic belief that history is
divided into two ages, this one and the coming messianic era (1QS 3:13–4:26). Satan controls this present evil age under God's decree, and people either belong to the old age under
Satan's dominion, or they belong to the new age under Christ's reign (Gal 1:4; 4:8-9). For
Paul that "new age" had arrived with the coming of Jesus, yet the two ages overlap (1 Cor
10:11). This present age will ultimately end with the coming of Christ (1:14; 1 Cor 1:8;
2 Thess 2:1; Phil 1:6) and the final establishment of the Kingdom of God (1 Cor 15:23-28;
1 Thess 2:12; cf. Eph 5:5; 2 Tim 4:1).

glory . . . exact likeness. Although the new age had come, Satan kept his control by blinding unbelievers' minds, thereby preventing them from seeing "the glory of Christ, who is
the exact likeness of God" (lit., "image," as in Col 1:15; cf. Phil 2:6). This glory appeared to
Paul in his encounter on the Damascus road (Acts 9:3; 22:6; 26:13; cf. 1 Cor 15:9-10; Gal
1:13; 1 Tim 1:15). Subsequently his missionary call was to rescue people from Satan's grip,
according to Acts 26:18, by opening their eyes as God enabled him. Paul gave a theological
view of this task in 5:17 and Col 1:13-14. For more on Satan, see the note on 2:11.

4:5 *Jesus Christ is Lord.* This succinct statement is the earliest Christian creedal confession
(Rom 10:9-10; 1 Cor 12:3; Col 2:6). Paul appeals to the orthodoxy of his preaching by citing this common tradition. By confessing Jesus as "Lord" (*kurios* [TG2962, ZG3261]), Paul may
be asserting his role as a "slave" (*doulos* [TG1401, ZG1528]; see Rom 1:1; Phil 1:1; Gal 1:10) of
Jesus. There is only room for one lord, which is why Paul does not "rule" over the Corinthians (1:24), unlike his opponents who are making grabs for power. As "Lord," the risen
Christ controls all forces, good and evil (Phil 2:6-11) and delivers creation from its bondage
and darkness so as to enter into the freedom and light of restored fellowship with its Creator and Redeemer (Rom 8:18-25; Col 1:12-14). Understanding Jesus as "Lord" may also
have high Christological implications by connecting with the understanding of Yahweh
as "Lord" (Bauckham 1999:34, 56-61; see note on 10:17). This confession may also have
some political overtones by standing in contrast to the lordship of the Roman emperor
(e.g., Virgil *Georgica* 1.24-42). Both the Christian and Jewish refusal to confess "Caesar as
Lord" led to the martyrdom of some (Josephus *War* 7.10.1; Tacitus *Annales* 5.5; *Martyrdom
of Polycarp* 8).

servants for Jesus' sake. Part of Paul's arguments defending his missionary activities and
weakness are that they are all done as a servant of his Lord Jesus (1:19-22), that is, as the
agent of the gospel. Paul's overriding concern was that by rejecting him, Christ's agent, the
Corinthians rejected his Lord, the one who sent him, and his gospel, the message from his
Lord—all three were bound together for Paul.

4:6 Now the meaning of how new life comes to blinded sinners is explained. The first part
of the verse is a quotation from Gen 1:3, LXX. The chaos of the world's darkness (Gen 1:2;
Jer 4:23) is changed by God's light.

**4:7 *We now have this light shining in our hearts, but we ourselves are like fragile clay
jars containing this great treasure.*** Lit., "We now have this treasure in clay jars" (NLT mg).
Paul did not define the treasure, which may be the gospel message of Christ (4:5) thought
of as a light carried in clay lamps. These cheap, fragile clay lamps were well-known and easily bought in the shops in Corinth. While believers may have frail mortal bodies (like clay
jars), they still bear the light of Jesus. Their frailty (being easily broken) underlies the idea
of the weakness of God's servants to "[make] it clear that our great power is from God, not
from ourselves."

COMMENTARY

"This new way" is Paul's ministry (see note on 4:1), which looks back to the previous section concerning the contrast with the Old Testament covenant and Christ, who now supersedes the covenant given through Moses. Such service of the gospel was committed to the apostle in the amazing mercy of God. The reference to mercy is either an allusion to Paul's conversion (cf. 1 Tim 1:12-14), as some commentators take it (Savage 1996:152), or his call (Kim 1982:11, 26, 288). As a consequence, he could exercise his work for God with confidence and "never give up"—lit., "not lose heart."

If we inquire why Paul would be tempted to grow discouraged, the following verses give some reasons. If he relied on human resources, or if he was foolish enough to practice "shameful deeds and underhanded methods" in order to gain some quick success (4:2), or if he considered the hardness of the human heart that remains obdurate to the message of divine love, he might well have given up. On the contrary, his confidence rested on several grounds: (1) his own sincerity, which should be obvious to all (4:2); (2) the gospel itself, which is God's truth and shines in its own light; and (3) the fact that failure of many to respond was not due to any lack of adequacy or relevance of the message (4:3-4). Rather, the reason lies in the satanic grip on the human heart and mind (4:4). Above all, Paul believed that his message was that of Jesus Christ the Lord (see note on 4:5). "Lord" (*kurios* [TG2962, ZG3261]) as a title speaks of authority given to the risen Christ to control all forces, good and evil (Phil 2:6-11), and to deliver the creation, held formerly under Satan's thrall, from its bondage and darkness so as to enter into the freedom and light of restored fellowship with its Creator and Redeemer (Rom 8:18-25; Col 1:12-14).

Paul himself was part of unredeemed creation, shrouded in darkness, until he was illumined by the radiance of God's glory in the face or person of Jesus Christ—a vision that is illustrated by Stephen's experience (Acts 7:55) and came to Saul on the way to Damascus. He later was able to give deep insight into that transforming encounter in terms of God's revealing his Son in him (Gal 1:15-16, NLT mg) and Christ's living in him as a new creation (5:17; Gal 2:20).

Such a message may well be described (as in 4:5-7) without exaggeration as a "treasure" (*thēsauros* [TG2344, ZG2565]). Treasure, whether of gold or precious stones, has a value in no way diminished by the cheap and disposable pots that carry it. The exact phrase "fragile clay jars" (*ostrakinois skeuesin* [TG3749/4632, ZG4017/5007]) may refer to pottery lamps such as those that have been found at the site of ancient Corinth and throughout the Roman world. Though Kim (1982:93-99) sees the term as linked with honorable service more than fragility or humility, the following section (4:8-12) emphasizes the weakness of the messengers, whose dignity is only that they are carriers of the divine treasure (that is, the gospel). Paul's ministry is so designated in Acts 9:15, where he is called a chosen instrument (*skeuos* [TG4632, ZG5007]).

The purpose of this arrangement in which the truth of God is deposited in frail receptacles is then made plain (4:7b). It displays the preeminent power of God, a "great power [that] is from God, not from ourselves." Far from being protected and preserved from harm—as Greek popular religion believed that the human messengers of the gods would be specially favored—the servants of Christ are consigned to a life of humiliation and danger. This thought is a lead-in to what follows, namely, a recital of Paul's sufferings (4:8-18).

◆   **D. Paul's Life of Hardship (4:8-18)**

⁸We are pressed on every side by troubles, but we are not crushed. We are perplexed, but not driven to despair. ⁹We are hunted down, but never abandoned by God. We get knocked down, but we are not destroyed. ¹⁰Through suffering, our bodies continue to share in the death of Jesus so that the life of Jesus may also be seen in our bodies.

¹¹Yes, we live under constant danger of death because we serve Jesus, so that the life of Jesus will be evident in our dying bodies. ¹²So we live in the face of death, but this has resulted in eternal life for you.

¹³But we continue to preach because we have the same kind of faith the psalmist had when he said, "I believed in God, so I spoke."* ¹⁴We know that God, who raised the Lord Jesus,* will also raise us with Jesus and present us to himself together with you. ¹⁵All of this is for your benefit. And as God's grace reaches more and more people, there will be great thanksgiving, and God will receive more and more glory.

¹⁶That is why we never give up. Though our bodies are dying, our spirits are* being renewed every day. ¹⁷For our present troubles are small and won't last very long. Yet they produce for us a glory that vastly outweighs them and will last forever! ¹⁸So we don't look at the troubles we can see now; rather, we fix our gaze on things that cannot be seen. For the things we see now will soon be gone, but the things we cannot see will last forever.

4:13 Ps 116:10.   4:14 Some manuscripts read *who raised Jesus.*   4:16 Greek *our inner being is.*

NOTES

4:8 *pressed on every side by troubles.* This is the first of four lists of Paul's sufferings in 2 Corinthians (4:8-9; 6:4b-5, 8-10; 11:23-28; 12:10; see Rom 8:35-39; 1 Cor 4:9-13; Phil 4:11-12). Paul was not his own source of power in his ministry (4:7). Rather, he was weak (13:4)—a condition described in memorable, poetic, and moving language. "Pressed on every side by troubles" recalls the psalmists in their hardships (Pss 3:2; 12:5; 22:5; 34:19) in their loyalty to Yahweh. Just as they felt harassed and persecuted, so was Paul. Yet like them, Paul was not "crushed" (*stenochōreō* [TG4729, ZG5102]) and left to "despair" (*exaporeō* [TG1820, ZG1989]; cf. Ps 88:15 [87:16, LXX]). One such trying experience is mentioned in 1:8, where Paul spoke of his recent troubles in Asia.

4:9 *We get knocked down, but we are not destroyed.* In Greek the expression is poetically vivid: *kataballomenoi all' ouk apollumenoi* [TG2598/622, ZG2850/660]. The idea is that though he can be "knocked down," the hard trials can never "knock him out."

4:10 *Through suffering, our bodies continue to share in the death of Jesus.* "To share in the death of Jesus" may refer to the Christian's baptismal identification with Christ's death (Rom 6:3-5) or to daily dying to sin (Gal 5:24), but in this context, it refers to Paul's ongoing suffering. Paul recognized that any of his daily trials could result in his death. Unlike in 1 Corinthians, Paul was now unsure whether he would survive until the Parousia. Paul's life as an apostle offered a strange paradox, signified by his close union with the suffering Jesus (cf. 13:3-4). Schlatter puts it well: "As Jesus' herald he told the story of the passion; but he not only told it, he experienced it as well" (1934:553).

so that the life of Jesus may also be seen in our bodies. Paul's share in the death of Jesus is a prelude to the (risen) life of Jesus—a thought repeated in the next verse. A major point of contention between Paul and the Corinthians, which was exacerbated by the opponents of chs 10-13, was his apparent weakness. The Corinthians were looking for "manifestations" (NLT, "seen"; Gr., *phanerōthē* [TG5319, ZG5746]) of God's power through charismatic manifestations of the Spirit as seen in OT figures like Moses (see Introduction). Paul contended that God's power was actually "manifested" (*phanerōthē*) in the suffering of his body. God's power was manifested every time that Paul was delivered from the brink of death, just as God's power was manifested through the resurrection after the death of Christ.

4:11 *constant danger of death.* This echoes the experience described in 1:8-10. The purpose of the arrangement by which the treasure of God is deposited in frail vessels (4:7) is now made plain. So far from being protected and preserved unharmed from "the slings and arrows of outrageous fortune"—as the Greek cults believed their "divine men" to be favored—Christ's messengers were consigned to a life of humiliation and danger. The literal translation is "I die every day" (cf. 1 Cor 15:31). At first glance, this may be dismissed as an exaggerated remark, but rather it points out the hardships he endured often with mortal risk.

4:12 *we live in the face of death.* This may be dismissed, at first glance, as a piece of Paul's rhetoric. Yet the evidence in Acts suggests otherwise. Paul's life as an apostle was always at risk. He will come back to this in 11:23-29.

but this has resulted in eternal life for you. This is a surprising conclusion, says Collange (1972:159), since we are not prepared for it. The Corinthians became the direct beneficiaries of Paul's sufferings (see Eph 3:1; Col 1:24; 2 Tim 2:10, which make the benefits real for many churches). Paul's apostolic suffering turns the Greco-Roman value of benefaction on its head. The wealthy and strong normally would offer benefits to the weak, which resulted in gratitude. The wealthy Corinthians had attempted to be Paul's patron through financial support (cf. 1 Cor 9). Instead, in these verses Paul claims to be their benefactor through his weak and shameful behavior, not his strength. Paul does this because he knows that only God provides true benefits, and people make room for those benefits by stepping aside in their weakness. (For more on Paul as benefactor, see S. J. Joubert 2000 and D. Downs 2008.)

4:13-14 *I believed in God, so I spoke.* Citing Ps 116:10, Paul appealed to the OT to buttress the claims of his ministry. The God of the psalmist was, for Paul, the God of resurrection (see 1:8-10), the proof of which is evidenced in his raising Jesus from the dead. Note the repetition of the name "Jesus"—some nine times in this chapter (4:5 [2x], 6, 10 [2x], 11 [2x], 14 [2x]).

4:15 *All of this is for your benefit. And as God's grace reaches more and more people.* Note the emphasis on "all" and "more and more." Paul's work as the apostle to the non-Jewish people (especially the Corinthians) was a cause for praise. So "God's grace reaches more and more people," leading to "great thanksgiving," and "more and more glory [= praise]" to God. There are two ways of explaining this: (1) God will be praised by more people coming to know him, or (2) it is the "majority of the church at Corinth [that] had grasped their dependence on the grace of God" (Barrett 1973:145)—looking back to 2:6, where the person who insulted Paul was disciplined by "the majority" (*pleinonōn* [TG4119A, ZG4498], "the more"). The former view is preferred, as in the NLT.

4:16 *we never give up.* This verb picks up what was said in 4:1. The "outward person" (literal rendering, which NLT translates with the colorless "our bodies") and the "inward person" (NLT mg "our inner being") are apparently contrasted with the obvious truth that our human bodies are "dying" (lit., "wasting away"), while for believers our real self is being renewed daily. This dichotomy seems to be Platonic, but it is not. For Paul "the person is one, indivisible whole" (Fallon 1980:47). On Paul's anthropology, see Dunn 1998. Paul's ultimate hope is re-embodiment (5:1-10; 1 Cor 15). His teaching on two Adams (e.g., Rom 5:12-21) was clearly in his sights.

4:17 *present troubles.* Gr., *thlipsis* [TG2347, ZG2568] (affliction), reverting to 1:8-10, where the same word appears.

small and won't last . . . a glory that vastly outweighs them. These troubles are dubbed "small" and momentary, yet they yield an impressive "weight of glory"—a fine contrast, and a play on the Hebrew word for "glory" (*kabod* [TH3519, ZH3883]), which means "heaviness," "weight." So the NLT helpfully has the wording "a glory that vastly outweighs them."

4:18 *So we don't look at.* This verse begins with an implicit proviso. The Greek participle *skopountōn* [TG4648, ZG5023] means to have something in your sights as an aim, not merely to look at (Phil 2:4). Paul says we do not focus on what is visible (i.e., our troubles) but on what cannot be seen.

the things we see now will soon be gone, but the things we cannot see will last forever. Visible objects are transient. What cannot be seen with the eye is eternal, so it "will last forever." This observation about our faith resting in the invisible God (see Heb 11:27) paves the way for ch 5 (especially 5:7); it is an observation founded on Paul's doctrine of the new creation in Christ (5:17).

COMMENTARY

"Our bodies continue to share in the death of Jesus" (4:10). "We live under constant danger of death" (4:11). At first glance, these somber sentiments look like a piece of Pauline rhetoric, even as he said in 1 Corinthians 15:31: "I face death daily." But this was not rhetoric, it was reality for Paul. Put in simple language, his work as an apostle required that he shared in his Lord's humiliation in the confidence that he would also share in his triumphant life (4:14).

His writing in this solemn mood came out of a distressful period of his life when he knew himself to be bereft of human support. And he saw the prospect of his life's mission evaporate before his eyes as the congregation at Corinth was in danger of sliding away from his fatherly control. Yet the hope of final vindication, when death will lead through resurrection to the last home gathering of the church, was not Paul's vision exclusively. Those who are with him in Christ will share the victory, too. That was his eager longing (Phil 1:21-23; 3:10).

Meanwhile, no other proof of the finiteness and frailty of Paul's physical frame is needed than the reminder he gives in 4:16. His body, with weakness and exposure to hazard, was constantly in the process of decay both in the normal course of "growing old" and (more so) in pursuit of his apostolic mission. "Our present troubles are small" (4:17) must be one of his understatements. Yet the phrase serves to highlight where his hope was set: His real life in his spirit was being renewed and revitalized by the power of God (4:16). So he said, "We never give up."

The outcome is not in doubt because Paul's horizon was bound by an eternal prospect (4:18). With the eye of faith he was able to see beyond the visible and tangible to the eternal realities of that world where God's glory shines in the person of Jesus Christ (4:6). Moving to the fulfillment of that hope would involve both death and the Parousia of Jesus Christ—themes that Paul addresses in chapter 5.

◆ **E. The Heavenly House (5:1-10)**

For we know that when this earthly tent we live in is taken down (that is, when we die and leave this earthly body), we will have a house in heaven, an eternal body made for us by God himself and not by human hands. ²We grow weary in our present bodies, and we long to put on our heavenly bodies like new clothing. ³For we will put on heavenly bodies; we will not be spirits without bodies.* ⁴While we live in these earthly bodies, we groan and sigh, but it's not that we want to die and get rid of these bodies that clothe us. Rather, we want to put on our new bodies so that these dying bodies will be swallowed up by life. ⁵God himself has pre-pared us for this, and as a guarantee he has given us his Holy Spirit.

⁶So we are always confident, even though we know that as long as we live in these bodies we are not at home with the Lord. ⁷For we live by believing and not by seeing. ⁸Yes, we are fully confident, and we would rather be away from these earthly bodies, for then we will be at home with the Lord. ⁹So whether we are here in this body or away from this body, our goal is to please him. ¹⁰For we must all stand before Christ to be judged. We will each receive whatever we deserve for the good or evil we have done in this earthly body.

5:3 Greek *we will not be naked.*

NOTES

5:1 *this earthly tent.* This "tent" (*skēnos* [TG4636, ZG5011]) refers to human bodies that are subject to decay and ultimately death. As a tentmaker and a traveler, Paul was personally familiar with the differences between the temporary shelter of a tent and a permanent home. This may also conjure the image of the tents erected in the city during the Imperial, Caesarean, and Isthmian Games. It may also make an allusion to the Tabernacle (Exod 26; cf. Lev 23:42) in contrast to the Temple as the permanent dwelling place of God. We need to be careful not to conceive of Paul as a Greco-Roman dualist who considered the human body as evil, a corrupting influence, or at least a hindrance that must be removed, while the spirit was good and must be liberated or preserved. Rather, he maintains a Jewish holistic perspective, envisioning God restoring and redeeming a person's body and spirit.

we will have a house. This future, permanent "house" (*oikia* [TG3614, ZG3864]) stands in contrast to the present, temporary "tent" (*skēnos* [TG4636, ZG5011]). Paul's metaphor will shift from "house" to "clothing" in the next verse. This house is "made without human hands" and "eternal in the heavens," and the language here is reminiscent of the "spiritual body" (*sōma pneumatikon* [TG4983/4152, ZG5393/4461]) of 1 Cor 15:44, indicating that Paul's metaphor refers to the new body given to the believers at the Parousia. Paul was aware that his hardships were wearing out his body and might lead to his death. Such actions were in accordance with the temporary nature of this body, and he believed that one day he would receive a new, permanent body. Paul was aware that the risk of such actions was that he might die before the Parousia, in which case he would be in the presence of Christ (but bodiless). So, Paul had two hopes—his immediate hope when facing death was that if he died, he would be in Christ's presence, but his ultimate hope was that Christ would return before his death. (See 5:3 and Introduction for a discussion of Paul's views on the resurrection.) In light of the Moses and Exodus imagery in 2 Corinthians, Paul may also be alluding to the Tabernacle (i.e., "tent") versus Temple (i.e., "house"), although the exact Greek words do not correspond. God is sojourning with people in this present life of wanderings and will one day permanently dwell with believers.

5:2 *We grow weary.* Lit., "We groan" (see Rom 8:23). This suggests anxious anticipation of what is to come more so than distress at what is now. Paul longed to receive his new body, which would be given to him at the Lord's return (1 Cor 15:51-54; Phil 3:20-21).

5:3 *For we will put on heavenly bodies; we will not be spirits without bodies.* Lit., "If indeed having been unclothed, we will not be naked" (see NLT mg). The "unclothing" is death; the image of not being found naked suggests that Paul did not look forward to being left bodiless after his death—that is, to enter this intermediate state as spirit. As previously expressed in 1 Cor 15, Paul had said the new body was not given until the Parousia—the time of Christ's return and the believer's resurrection. However, here, Paul did not talk about the Parousia; rather, he talked about the point of death. In discussing his potential death occurring before the Parousia, Paul gave the hope that at least this spirit would be in the presence of Christ (unfortunately, Paul did not give any further details regarding this state).

It should be noted that some scholars think that Paul, as a result of his trying experience in Asia (1:8-10), changed his thinking about when a Christian gets a new body. In 1 Cor 15, the new body is given at the Parousia, but in 2 Cor 5, Paul thought he would receive his new body at the moment of death (see Harris 2005). For an argument against Paul presenting a new hope in receiving a body at death, see J. Osei-Bonsu 1986:81-101. Other scholars consider Paul expressing his confident hope that the Lord would return while Paul was still alive, and he would be given a new body and therefore not have to enter the intermediate state as a spirit. My view is that Paul continued to believe that he would only receive a new body at the Parousia as in 1 Cor 15, but now he kept two hopes alive: His primary hope was to survive until the Lord's return (and receive the new body)—this is expressed in 1 Cor 15. His second hope was that if he died before the Parousia, he would be in the presence of his Lord at his death (where he would remain until he received the new body at the Parousia)—this is expressed in 2 Cor 5.

5:4 *it's not that we want to die and get rid of these bodies that clothe us. Rather, we want to put on our new bodies.* This is an expansion of the metaphor Paul was using in 5:2-4—"we do not want to be unclothed but over-clothed" (see commentary below).

5:5 *God himself has prepared us for this, and as a guarantee he has given us his Holy Spirit.* The pledge (Gr., *arrabōn* [TG728, ZG775]; NLT, "guarantee") guaranteeing the eventuality of the resurrection is the Holy Spirit. A "pledge" was a down payment (see note on 1:22).

5:6 *as long as we live in these bodies we are not at home with the Lord.* In 5:6, 8, and 9, Paul contrasted being "at home" with being "away." For Paul, "at home" (*endēmeō* [TG1736, ZG1897]) means living among one's own people (*dēmos* [TG1218, ZG1322]), and being "away" (*ekdēmeō* [TG1553, ZG1685]) means living abroad or in exile. Thus, he recognized a tension in his present existence since it is like being in exile while his true place is with Christ.

5:7 *For we live by believing and not by seeing.* "We walk" (*peripatoumen* [TG4043, ZG4344]; NLT, "we live") carries, for Paul, an ethical sense of one's entire lifestyle with the Hebrew equivalent being *halak* [TH1980, ZH2143] (e.g., Prov 15:21; Isa 30:21; Mal 2:6; for more on the background of the term, see the note on 12:18). Paul contrasted a lifestyle of "seeing" (*eidos* [TG1491, ZG1626]) with "believing" (*pistis* [TG4102, ZG4411]), which may be like the "seeing" and "believing" contrasts found in John 20:29 and 1 Pet 1:8. However, the terms for "seeing" are not quite the same. In 5:7 Paul used *eidos* (cf. Num 12:8, LXX) to contrast with *pistis*, rather than *oraō* [TG3708, ZG3972] as in John 20:29 and 1 Pet 1:8. While Christ was not seen, he was still present with the believer through faith. This notion of Christ's presence with believers today reflects the already/not-yet tension often seen in Paul's writing concerning the Christian hope. Experiencing Christ's presence through faith is the "already," but the ultimate goal of the believer is to see Christ and to consummate fellowship with him, the "not yet."

5:8 *we would rather be away from these earthly bodies, for then we will be at home with the Lord.* Paul emphasizes the clearly better choice of being with Christ by using the word "rather" (*mallon* [TG3123, ZG3437]) and the verb "be pleased" (*eudokeō* [TG2106, ZG2305]) plus an infinitive ("be away from," *ekdēmēsai* [TG1553, ZG1685]), indicating a definite choice. On the "away" versus "home" contrast, see 5:6.

5:9 *So whether we are here in this body or away from this body.* The thought of the apostle is eminently practical. His theology was rooted in experience; he never forgot that our doctrine is meant to influence behavior. So, "our goal (lit., "ambition, aspiration") is to please him"—a typically Pauline application as we see from Rom 12:1-2; 14:18; Eph 5:10; Phil 4:18; Col 1:10; 3:20. So also in the apostolic fathers, such as in *1 Clement* 35:5 ("if we seek out these things which are pleasing and acceptable to him") and 62:2 ("you must fervently please almighty God").

5:10 *we must all stand before Christ to be judged.* Lit., "before the judgment seat of Christ." The "judgment seat" in Greek is *bēma* [TG968, ZG1037]; the Corinthians would be familiar with the word as the place where the Roman proconsul sat to administer justice (see Acts 18:12, which has the same Greek word, rendered as "before the governor for judgment"). Paul had, of course, previously stood before the judgment seat of Gallio due to his mission in Corinth (Acts 18:1-17).

We will each receive whatever we deserve for the good or evil we have done in this earthly body. The "earthly body" will be called to account, meaning what we have done here in our service or lack of it. God's approval (or its opposite) is a powerful incentive (Barrett 1973:88-89).

COMMENTARY

This section (5:1-10) concludes Paul's defense of his credentials for ministry, in spite of his sufferings. Against those who placed confidence in visible tokens of success, Paul posited his view of reality on the basis of believing in what is not seen but what is expected to come. Paul put his faith in the Lord's return, with the expectation that he would receive a new body. Paul attempts to explain this expectation using images of dwelling places.

Paul began by using an image of "the earthly tent." Taking a metaphor from Leviticus 23:42, Paul alludes to the tents or tabernacles the Israelites built each fall (during the Festival of Shelters) as reminders of their pilgrim life en route to Canaan. A temporary structure (see Heb 11:9-10), a tent is quickly "taken down." The opposite is "a house in heaven," a building with the association of permanence and security. (Something like a Tabernacle versus Temple image may also be in the background, although the exact Greek words do not correspond.) The earthly body, like a tent, is temporary—it is wasting away. Yet because it is the home of the Holy Spirit, it will one day be replaced by a permanent dwelling—the new body awaiting the return of Christ. Paul considered the indwelling Spirit to provide the guarantee that God has a future for him and all believers, whether they will have already died or will be alive at the time of Christ's Parousia (1 Cor 15:51-58; 1 Thess 4:13-18).

In a complex use of the same verb ("clothe") with a change of prefix (over-clothed, unclothed—see notes on 5:2-4), Paul seems to be saying that his hope was not to be "unclothed" but "over-clothed" (like putting on a topcoat to cover his present body). The fear is one of nakedness which for Paul the Jew was something to be abhorred. For example, according to the rabbis (*m. Berakhot* 3:5), only a person who is clothed (i.e., possessing a body) should recite the creed of "one God," the Shema (Deut 6:4), since without a body a person "ceases to be truly and properly man [human]" (P. E. Hughes 1962:171). By contrast, the Greeks looked for achieving immortality by shedding the body, since the body is an encumbrance. Not so Paul, who according to 1 Corinthians 15, looked forward to surviving until the Parousia as his chief desire. Then his present body in all its weakness would "be swallowed up by life." Various scholars (see R. Martin 1984:ch 8) see this statement as a polemic against some of the Corinthians who had the wrong idea that there was no prospect of a future resurrection (1 Cor 4:8; 15:12).

In 2 Corinthians, Paul developed his views in a slightly different direction by orienting his hope not upon receiving a new body at the Parousia but upon being in the presence of Christ. The deficiency of being without a body was overwhelmed by the hope of being in Christ's presence. Paul spoke of this present life as being, unfortunately, a time when "we are not at home with the Lord" (5:6). Since the present life is likened to an exile, Paul's hope is spelled out in terms of wanting to return home to God (Webb 1993). In an important statement, Paul defines the way Christians live out their present life as exiles and pilgrims: "We live by believing and not by seeing" (5:7). While the Lord is not one we see now, we are assured of his presence (Barrett 1973:158), just as Israel was accompanied on the long journey to the Promised Land by Yahweh's presence (similar to the thought in 1 Pet 1:8-9). Paul's confidence develops what he said in 3:18. Thus, when putting together the thoughts of 1 Corinthians 15 and 2 Corinthians 5, we get a more complete picture of Paul's theology of the afterlife. In 1 Corinthians 15, Paul's primary hope was to be alive at the Parousia and receive his new body (circumventing death); however, in 2 Corinthians 5, the reality of death was upon Paul, so he offered his second hope that, even if he died, he would be in the presence of Christ, which is far better than being embodied in this life. (For more on the resurrection, see Introduction, "Major Themes: The Gospel and Resurrection.")

Again, some scholars treat this section as Paul's defense of the nature of faith. The Corinthian enthusiasts evidently placed their trust in tangible tokens such as ecstatic visions and miraculous proofs. Thus, they stressed the importance of external manifestations in the types of leaders they admired, manifestations in the form of human wisdom, rhetoric, and powerful presence (see later on 5:12). On the contrary, Paul asserted, "We live by believing and not by seeing." Verse 7 is a parenthesis, a break in Paul's thought, as we see from the way he opens the next verse. "Yes (meaning, "I repeat," from 5:6), we are fully confident." Christians can be assured, whether in the body or not, that death will usher them into the Lord's presence, where they will be "at home with the Lord" (5:8).

Paul's closing thought applies this eschatology to practical living. Until death, or the Parousia, occurs, all Christians must seek a life pleasing to the Lord, since what we have done with our earthly bodies will be called to account (Rom 14:10-12).

◆   F. Motives for Paul's Preaching and Living (5:11-15)

¹¹Because we understand our fearful responsibility to the Lord, we work hard to persuade others. God knows we are sincere, and I hope you know this, too. ¹²Are we commending ourselves to you again? No, we are giving you a reason to be proud of us,* so you can answer those who brag about having a spectacular ministry rather than having a sincere heart. ¹³If it seems we are crazy, it is to bring glory to God. And if we are in our right minds, it is for your benefit. ¹⁴Either way, Christ's love controls us.* Since we believe that Christ died for all, we also believe that we have all died to our old life.* ¹⁵He died for everyone so that those who receive his new life will no longer live for themselves. Instead, they will live for Christ, who died and was raised for them.

5:12 Some manuscripts read *proud of yourselves.*   5:14a Or *urges us on.*   5:14b Greek *Since one died for all, then all died.*

NOTES

5:11 *to persuade others.* This most likely speaks of the sincerity of the preachers' motives. Some scholars, remarking on the missionary motive expressed by the verb "persuade," think it speaks more of Paul's desire to convince his hearers to accept God's salvation. What follows, however, makes the first view more likely.

5:12 *Are we commending ourselves to you again?* This is a refusal to resort to self-commendation, a practice much valued by Paul's opponents.

brag about having a spectacular ministry. This is an amplification of Paul's verb "to boast," which was used of the opponents' appeal to what they thought of their credentials. Of the 55 references to boasting in the letters of Paul, over one-half (29) are in 2 Corinthians, showing how this was a leading issue of contention between the apostle and his detractors at Corinth.

5:13 *If it seems we are crazy.* This is one understanding of Paul's verb (*existēmi* [TG1839, ZG2014]). More probably this should be rendered by an expression of elation, akin to ecstasy (Tasker 1958:84) rather than insanity (for which Greek has another verb, *mainomai* [TG3105, ZG3419]).

5:14 *Either way, Christ's love controls us.* Whether Paul was in an ecstatic or in a rational frame of mind, he was motivated on the Corinthians' behalf by "Christ's love" that "controls us." This strong verb means to hold a person in one's grip, more than just to sustain a person (Furnish 1968:167-168). It is probably better to translate it as "exert domination" (Lietzmann 1949:124). It is Christ's love, meaning his love for his people, that impelled Paul to proclaim the gospel (1 Cor 9:16).

Since we believe that Christ died for all, we also believe that we have all died to our old life. The substance of the gospel ("We believe"; lit., "We conclude") is stated in clear terms: "Christ died for all" and in him "we have all died to our old life." Paul spoke of Christ's act of representation, as he (lit., "one" as in NLT mg, but clearly it means Christ) died for all. The pronoun "all" signifies all those who embrace Christ's salvation; the same term "all" applies to those who have been renewed by him in dying to their former sinful life (as in Rom 6:1-11). The idea of representation includes substitution, inasmuch as Christ did for believers what they could never do for themselves.

5:15 *He died for everyone.* Lit., "all," in the sense just indicated (see previous note). Paul here refers to those who no longer live under the power of the life of "self" (lit., "flesh," *sarx* [TG4561, ZG4922]; see Rom 8:1-9; Gal 5:16-21), but live the new life of Christ, "who died and was raised for them" on their behalf. For more on uses of *sarx*, see the notes on 1:17; 11:18.

COMMENTARY

What Paul presents in this section is the paradigm that pervades the New Testament. God's love, demonstrated in Christ's death and resurrection, compels believers to live a life dedicated to God. This is the essence of Paul's apostolic ministry and message.

Unfortunately, Paul had not been accepted by the Corinthians as a model leader. Because he exemplified divine power in weakness, his credentials as a minister of the gospel were in doubt. Desiring a "powerful" leader and preacher, some in the church at Corinth had attacked Paul as inferior. Reminding the Corinthians that Jesus died for all his people, Paul insisted that the same people are summoned to die with and in him. This is not a physical death, but a spiritual one in the sense of denying one's selfish interests and desires.

Whatever other people may have said of Paul and his ministry, he wanted his critics to see that his "life-in-weakness" was the result of his living united to Jesus Christ. "Fear of the Lord" and "living for Jesus" go hand in hand. This charge of being "weak" was a major contention between Paul and the opponents of chapters 10–13 (as he will elaborate in 12:9; 13:1-4). But in a startling paradox, he declared this weakness as his true strength. Only in that self-confessed weakness does God's power come to true realization, and so Paul could claim, "I am strong" (12:10). (On this Pauline paradox of "death to self and life for God," see Black 1984.)

Paul's life is a model for all those who want to live the Christ life. To live this life is to share in Jesus Christ's death and resurrection. Manson says it poignantly: "The death of Christ is something in which all his followers have a share; and equally they share in his risen life, which means that they can no longer live their old selfish life but must live for him who inaugurated the new life for them by dying and rising again" (1953:156).

◆   G. Living in the New Creation (5:16-6:2)

¹⁶So we have stopped evaluating others from a human point of view. At one time we thought of Christ merely from a human point of view. How differently we know him now! ¹⁷This means that anyone who belongs to Christ has become a new person. The old life is gone; a new life has begun!

¹⁸And all of this is a gift from God, who brought us back to himself through Christ. And God has given us this task of reconciling people to him. ¹⁹For God was in Christ, reconciling the world to himself, no longer counting people's sins against them. And he gave us this wonderful message of reconciliation. ²⁰So we are Christ's ambassadors; God is making his appeal through us. We speak for Christ when we plead, "Come back to God!" ²¹For God made Christ, who never sinned, to be the offering for our sin,* so that we could be made right with God through Christ.

CHAPTER 6

As God's partners,* we beg you not to accept this marvelous gift of God's kindness and then ignore it. ²For God says,

"At just the right time, I heard you.
   On the day of salvation, I helped
   you."*

Indeed, the "right time" is now. Today is the day of salvation.

5:21 Or *to become sin itself.*   6:1 Or *As we work together.*   6:2 Isa 49:8 (Greek version).

NOTES

5:16 *So we have stopped evaluating others.* The link with the foregoing is obvious. Paul has entered on a new worldview as a person who has died to self and is alive to Christ (5:14-15).

from a human point of view. Lit., "according to the flesh," (*kata sarka*) that is, human life organized without reference to God and his purposes (see notes on 1:17; 11:18). Now, in the new creation brought about by Christ and the Spirit (3:6), Paul sees others differently— that is, as persons in Christ. And the same reevaluation applies to the Lord himself. Formerly, as a Pharisee, Paul saw Jesus as a messianic pretender or false Messiah. Now he views him as King of creation and Redeemer from sin.

5:17 *This means.* This transition from "then" to "now" marks the newness of the new life.

anyone who belongs to Christ has become a new person. Lit., "Anyone in Christ is a new creation" (cf. Gal 6:14-15). The new creation is the new order of existence brought about by Christ's work of reconciliation. The term "new creation" is often thought of in exclusively personal terms, especially when the word *ktisis* [TG2937, ZG3232] is rendered "creature." It is taken to refer to a person's conversion to Christ when the old life is exchanged for a new relationship to the Lord. This is undoubtedly part of Paul's meaning, but there is more. Recent scholars see here a cosmic setting; hence "new creation," recalling the old created world marred by human sin (e.g., Hubbard 2002). In Christ a new order of existence is called into being, and believers enter by faith into that new world with a fresh orientation and outlook on life with the promise of resurrection to God's final world. This is called an eschatological hope and entails the dawn of a new age, promised by God in the OT prophetic hope (e.g., Isa 65:17-25). That hope, says Paul in this phrase, is now realized in the coming of Christ.

The old life is gone. *Archaia* [TG744, ZG792] (NLT, "the old life") means "former, ancient," that is, the old order of things in reference to the old world of sin and death. This old regime has been broken although its power remains (Gal 5:16-21, 24) to be neutralized in Christ. This is because of the turning point in world history that the coming of Jesus effected.

5:18 *all of this is a gift from God.* Paul attributed the new transformation solely to God as his "gift." The essence of this gift lies in the deed of reconciliation achieved on the cross. The initiative throughout the NT is always ascribed to God. Yet it is an event that led to the Good News, which in turn must be proclaimed by humans. It is called here "the task" (lit., "ministry") of reconciliation.

5:19 *For God was in Christ, reconciling the world to himself.* Here is the sum total of Paul's message of how God restored broken relationships with sinners by Christ's coming, death, and offer of righteousness to believers. "Reconciliation" may be the key word in Paul's gospel, as I have argued elsewhere (see R. Martin 1989:3-6, 235-242). Paul used the term "reconciliation" (*katallassō* [TG2644, ZG2904]) to sum up the message he declared. This is essentially a term of relationships. It denotes the repairing of the broken relationship between God and humankind caused by human sin. Separation between God and humanity forms Paul's backdrop against which his Good News shines brightly, since God has in Christ taken steps to restore the fractured relationship. This event is centered in the death of his Son, who took the sinner's place and died to bring men and women back to God (see Rom 5:1-11). Yet there is more than just the personal restoration to God, vital as that is for Paul. There is a cosmic dimension in which the entire universe is affected (see Col 1:15-20). And there is a horizontal application, since Christ's death led to the breaking down of ethnic and religious barriers that divided the world of Paul's day (see Eph 2:11-22).

this wonderful message of reconciliation. This is the Good News, that God has turned enemies into friends in a restored relationship (see Rom 5:1-11; the wider implications of reconciliation are seen in Eph 2:11-22; Col 1:15-20).

5:20 *we are Christ's ambassadors; God is making his appeal through us.* Paul was appealing to the Corinthians both to embrace the fruits of divine reconciliation—since some of them have moved away from his gospel—and to heed and accept his offered gesture of friendship (a theme to be elaborated in 6:1-2, 11-13; 7:2-4).

Come back to God! Lit., "Be reconciled to God," spoken here to Christians, though Paul is using the language of evangelism. The thrust is for them "to accept the true gospel [which] means also to accept Paul as an authentic apostle of it" (Fallon 1980:52).

5:21 *Christ, who never sinned.* Lit., "Christ did not know sin." The NLT reflects the Heb. *yada'* [TH3045, ZH3359] (to have personal acquaintance or experience with) behind the Gr. *ginōskō* [TG1097, ZG1182] (to know). Paul affirms that Christ was aware of sin but did not have any personal involvement with it.

to be the offering for our sin. Lit., "to be sin" (*hamartia* [TG266, ZG281]). Paul is probably following a use of "sin" similar to Isa 53:10, LXX, or Lev 4:24, LXX.

so that we could be made right with God through Christ. This expression may be understood as participation in the righteousness of God—people do what God considers right—but the most common meaning of *ginomai* [TG1096, ZG1181] (NLT, "be made") indicates a change in status. This verse presents a juxtaposition—while God reckoned Christ as "sin," he reckoned believers as "righteous."

6:1 *As God's partners.* This is one way to translate Paul's Greek word (*sunergountes* [TG4903, ZG5300]; lit., "working with," leaving open the required complement). Three options are possible: (1) the complement is the Corinthians themselves, "because we are fellow workers" (NET)—an unlikely view, given the hostility Paul encountered at Corinth; (2) Paul's fellow workers (NLT mg); (3) God himself (so NLT in company with many translators and commentaries from Calvin to Barrett). Confirming the third option is 1 Thess 3:2, where Timothy is a worker-with-God or God's coworker, as well as 1 Cor 3:9. Thus, the third choice is preferred. Taken with what follows ("we beg you not to accept this marvelous gift of God's kindness and then ignore it"), there is an unbroken logic.

6:2 *At just the right time, I heard you.* To buttress his appeal, Paul cited Scripture (Isa 49:8, LXX). The force of this quotation is to underline the urgency of their response, an enforcement that is made more powerful by the double use of *idou* [TG2400, ZG2627] ("look"; not in NLT) and *nun* [TG3568, ZG3814] (NLT, "now . . . today"). Paul had a vivid sense of the immediacy of the end time (Rom 13:11; 1 Cor 7:29-31).

COMMENTARY

This weighty section has many facets but one master theme. In it Paul was setting down the Christian conviction that in the coming of Christ a new world has been born and a new age has supervened on world history. Phrases like (lit.) "a new creation" (NLT, "new person"), "reconciliation," and "[believers] might become the righteousness of God" (NLT, "we could be made right with God") speak of this new eon that has radically affected both God's dealings with humankind and all earthly relationships.

The images are drawn from the Old Testament, most likely the suffering servant of Isaiah 53, who bore the sin of many and became an offering for sin. Yet the language baffles close analysis and contains several expressions not found elsewhere in Paul (e.g., believers becoming the righteousness of God in 5:21). This suggests that Paul was using creedal material that was known in the churches (akin to 1 Cor 15:3-5) but adapted by him to serve his purposes. The modern reader, however, is left to puzzle over these profound teachings. For instance, how did the crucified Christ become sin for us? And, from the standpoint of exegesis, why does Paul use the appeal, "Come back to God" (more accurately, "Be reconciled to God"), to believers at Corinth, who presumably have already been reconciled as forgiven sinners?

The first question finds its answer in the spiritual reality that Christ became a substitutionary offering through his death on the cross. The leading thought is of Christ's sacrifice as the sin offering mentioned in Isaiah 53:10 (or less likely as the animal of Leviticus 16). Christ's death became the death of all in the sense that he died the death they should have died. The penalty of their sins was borne by him, so he died in their place. This is why his love has such a compelling power over believers and engenders in them such undying gratitude (Tasker 1958:86).

The answer to the second question may be that some of the Corinthians had deserted Paul's gospel and needed to be restored. Having learned that Jesus died for them, they chose not to die to themselves (see 5:15). The failure to do so is seen in their unwillingness to support Paul when he was attacked at Corinth. Though he had forgiven the offender (2:8-11), they either punished him too harshly (2:7) or failed to join him in sorrow for his opposition to Paul.

The final verses (6:1-2) tell us that Paul cooperated with God (see note on 6:1) in bringing the message of reconciliation to the Corinthians. He also cooperated with God in exhorting the readers not to receive this message in vain. Paul's teaching on reconciliation was made intensely personal, so what looks like an original statement of cosmic recovery (God reconciled the world) was applied in Paul's inspired reworking as a pastoral admonition and call for his readers to live as reconciled children and no longer as rebels. This application will be ever clearer in chapters 10–13.

The teaching in 5:18-21 has been often overlooked in the debate on penal substitution, meaning that God in Christ took the penalty for human sin, bore its consequences, and in Christ's death opened the way to forgiveness and a new life. Critics of penal substitution have fastened on some unguarded statements, for example, by W. Grudem (1994:575), who writes: "God . . . poured out on Jesus the fury of his wrath: Jesus became the object of the intense hatred of sin and vengeance against sin which God had patiently stored up since the beginning of the world." It is not surprising that such a view of the cross leads to the accusation that it presents a caricature of God as a "cosmic child abuser" (S. Chalke and A. Mann 2003:182): "The cross isn't a form of cosmic child abuse—a vengeful Father punishing his Son for an offence he has not committed."

Admittedly, the historical events of Good Friday were marked by violence, but the apostle Paul is careful never to say or imply that God was angry with his Son. Rather, as this text states, God was in Christ reconciling the world to himself. As I. H. Marshall (2007:62) writes, "God . . . initiated the cross and . . . he . . . bore the sin of the world."

So in 5:18-21, we have the center of Paul's teaching on the Atonement, with its stress on human estrangement from God by reason of sin and the accomplishment of God "when in the death of Christ He put away everything that on His side meant estrangement, so that He might come and preach peace" to guilty sinners (Denney 1900). Or, as A. M. Hunter (1954:91-92) puts it in remarking on 5:21, the Cross was "a divine deed wherein, by God's appointing, our condemnation came upon the sinless Christ, that for us there might be condemnation no more." The same writer adds a further elucidation: "Christ's suffering was 'penal' in the sense that He had to realize to the full the divine reaction against sin in the human race in which He was incorporated."

Nor should we overlook the application of this teaching. What God has done in Christ needs to be brought home to sinners. It is important to grasp the sense of these verses. It is not so much that God calls on us to lay aside our hostility to him and be at peace. Rather the accent falls on objective atonement. He invites us to enter into the peace with himself that he has made possible by the sacrifice of his Son (Rom 5:1). The reconciliation on his side is complete, for Christ's work on the cross is accomplished (John 19:30). Paul's gospel call, therefore, is "Receive the reconciliation. Believe that God has at tremendous cost, through the death of his sinless son, who took the sinner's place and died under sin's curse (Gal 3:13), put away all that on his part stood between you and peace (Rom 5:6-11)."

◆   H. Paul's Defense of His Ministry (6:3-10)

³We live in such a way that no one will stumble because of us, and no one will find fault with our ministry. ⁴In everything we do, we show that we are true ministers of God. We patiently endure troubles and hardships and calamities of every kind. ⁵We have been beaten, been put in prison, faced angry mobs, worked to exhaustion, endured sleepless nights, and gone without food. ⁶We prove ourselves by our purity, our understanding, our patience, our kindness, by the Holy Spirit within us,* and by our sincere love. ⁷We faithfully preach the truth. God's power is working in us. We use the weapons of righteousness in the right hand for attack and the left hand for defense. ⁸We serve God whether people honor us or despise us, whether they slander us or praise us. We are honest, but they call us impostors. ⁹We are ignored, even though we are well known. We live close to death, but we are still alive. We have been beaten, but we have not been killed. ¹⁰Our hearts ache, but we always have joy. We are poor, but we give spiritual riches to others. We own nothing, and yet we have everything.

6:6 Or *by our holiness of spirit.*

NOTES

6:3 *We live in such a way that no one will stumble because of us.* At this point Paul's line of thought takes a new turn. The new task is his stance of commending his ministry to the Corinthians as one worthy of their trust. This is because it is approved by God. This self-commendation is arranged in a set of contrasts, beginning with 6:4.

6:4a *In everything we do, we show that we are true ministers of God.* Lit., "Rather, in everything, we commend ourselves as servants of God." Paul takes up again the theme of "commendation" (*sunistēmi* [TG4921, ZG5319]; 3:1; 4:2). Although others may need letters of commendation, Paul has previously noted that his work in Corinth is his letter of commendation (3:1). Now, he cites his ministry of weakness as another commendation (i.e., validation) of his apostleship and gospel. Paul is taking the very point of contention—his apparent weakness—and highlighting it as a mark of his apostolic office.

6:4b-5 *We patiently endure.* This is the second of four lists of Paul's sufferings in 2 Corinthians (4:8-9; 6:4b-5, 8-10; 11:23-28; 12:10; see Rom 8:35-39; 1 Cor 4:9-13; Phil 4:11-12). In the first of four stanzas (6:4b-5, 6-7a, 7b-8a, 8b-10), Paul gives nine forms of suffering he has endured (*hupomonē* [TG5281, ZG5705]). This term, one of Paul's favorite expressions, is a dogged determination not to quit in the face of "troubles and hardships and calamities of every kind." What such trials are is spelled out in two ways. First, they include external hardships: beatings, time in prison, and facing "angry mobs" (lit., "disorders") in social disturbances caused by his preaching a revolutionary gospel, which some enemies took to be anti-Roman and therefore politically subversive—a charge Paul rebuts. There are numerous examples in Acts (Acts 13:50; 14:5, 19; 16:22; 17:5; 18:12; 19:23-41; 21:27-36). Second, there are trials of a voluntary nature: "worked to exhaustion, endured sleepless nights," and going "without food." Paul's life as an apostle was no soft pillow or sinecure.

sleepless nights. Some translators (P. E. Hughes 1962:225) render these times of insomnia as "watchings"—that is, vigils, staying awake to pray (Eph 6:18 and echoes in the Gospels, e.g., Mark 14:37-38). If this is seen as paralleling 11:27, then it is probably associated with Paul's exposure to risk in order to share the gospel (cf. Acts 16:25).

6:6-7a *We prove ourselves.* In the second stanza (6:6-7a), Paul now turns to his own motives for ministry. This shift of thought is "a breathing place in the outburst of the apostle's feeling" (Denney 1900:231). His appeal is to his "purity" (better, "innocence"; see Barrett 1973:186). It means the integrity of his service and his sincere intentions (3:13; 4:2). Other virtues follow from this: (1) "understanding" (lit., "knowledge," Gr., *gnōsis* [TG1108, ZG1194]—a key word in his debate with the Corinthian "Gnostics"); (2) "patience" (lit., "being far from anger," *makrothumia* [TG3115, ZG3429]); (3) "kindness" (a quality of Christian *agapē* [TG26, ZG27]—1 Cor 13:4) that seeks the best interests of other people, unlike that of the false apostles to be denounced in 11:13-15, 20; 12:14-17; (4) "the Holy Spirit within us," which is a surprising mention of the Spirit of God in this context—therefore, some prefer to make the phrase adjectival, so NLT mg, "by our holiness of spirit"; and (5) "sincere love" (Rom 12:9).

We faithfully preach the truth. Throughout 2 Corinthians, Paul continues to affirm the correctness of his gospel (1:12, 13; 2:17; 4:2; 10:11). He turns to consider the substance of his message. It is "the truth," made effectual by "God's power . . . working in us" (as he discussed in 1 Cor 2:3-5).

6:7b-8a *weapons of righteousness.* In the third stanza (6:7b-8a) Paul describes his ministry in military metaphors (10:3-4; Rom 13:12; Eph 6:13-18). Whether the message was offensive or defensive, i.e., likened to a sword or a shield, Paul was thoroughly equipped (Barrett 1973:188).

6:8b-10 In this fourth stanza (6:8b-10), Paul spoke of his service in a style of writing rightly called "his paradoxical rhetoric" (Barrett 1973:189).

6:8b *We are honest, but they call us impostors.* The NLT has reversed the order in the Greek ("as deceivers, yet true"). In the Greek of 6:8b-10, Paul presents a series of negatives paired with a positive. Some accused Paul of being a deceiver (cf. 1:12–2:4; 12:16-18), which Paul refutes, promoting his honesty.

6:9 *We are ignored, even though we are well known.* Lit "as unknown, yet well known." Both verbs are present passives indicating the action was done by others. Being "unknown" (NLT, "ignored") probably refers to the charge presented by his opponents that Paul lacks the credentials of apostleship (cf. 5:12). Yet Paul has been arguing that his apostleship is well known by the one being who matters, God (cf. 1 Cor 13:12). Paul's hope is that the Corinthians will likewise know his apostleship (1:13-14).

close to death, but . . . alive. With Paul's paradoxical rhetoric, sometimes it is hard to know if he intended his words to be taken literally ("we live close to death" is more exactly "as dying"; Paul had been exposed to the perils of death—1:8-9; 11:23-26; see Acts 14:19) or figuratively (as in 1 Cor 15:31—"I face death daily").

beaten . . . killed. "We have been beaten" is more precisely "we are chastened" by suffering, a possible allusion to the righteous person's afflictions in Ps 118 (Ps 117, LXX), which has the wording, lit., "The Lord has severely chastened me, but he did not give me over to death" (Ps 118:17-18 [117:17-18, LXX]).

6:10 *we always have joy.* In all of his trials Paul declared he had joy, an "inalienable feature of his life" (Barrett 1973:190), as Phil 4:4 evidences.

we give spiritual riches to others. Lit., "enriching many." The NLT interprets Paul's idea of wealth in a way that avoids the impression that being a believer is a passport to luxury. Quite the opposite, as Paul's other teachings make plain.

COMMENTARY

This section is an "apology" in the sense of a religious teacher's defense of his convictions and lifestyle, somewhat like Plato's *Apology* written to defend Socrates' teaching. In offering such a defense, Paul gives us a window into the nature of his service for Christ.

The text is set in the form of four stanzas (6:4b-5; 6-7a; 7b-8a; 8b-10) in which a rich and unusual vocabulary is found. Some scholars find a parallel in *2 Enoch* 66:6: "Walk, my children, in long-suffering, in meekness, in affliction, in distress, in faithfulness, in truth, in hope, in weakness, in derision, in assaults, in temptation, in deprivation, in nakedness, having love for one another, until you go out from this age of suffering, so that you may become inheritors of the never-ending age" (Windisch 1924:206; see Harris 2005:466 n. 5). But a closer analogy may be the way Greek moral philosophers, such as the Stoics, used such contrasts in praise of noble persons. The best parallels, however, are found in Jewish literature in which God's righteous servants are faced with trials and obstacles (see Pss 22, 73).

No accusing finger could be justly pointed at Paul, charging him with insincerity or wrong motives (6:3-4a). He began the defense by rehearsing his life of hardships in a litany of trials, familiar in contemporary moral teachers. There are nine such trials enumerated in three groups: (1) The first group are tribulations of a general character (called "troubles and hardships and calamities of every kind"). He met these with endurance—a resolute determination not to give up. (2) Specific sufferings are next described. He had been "beaten," had been thrown in jail, and had been the victim of riots (NRSV; NLT, "faced angry mobs"). (3) Next follows a list of self-imposed experiences, all in the cause of the gospel: "worked to exhaustion" (NEB has "overworked"—a problem in the modern church, where too few often attempt to do too much); "endured sleepless nights," caused by overwork or voluntary denial of sleep; "gone without food," which may be fasting or an experience of hunger (NEB, "starving").

Paul then described the spirit or disposition in which he faced these bitter experiences (6:6-8a). His character was often attacked, and he was even branded as an impostor (6:8). Yet he insisted that everything about his character was beyond reproach in spite of the inevitable dishonor and ill repute that his opponents raked up as evidence to discredit him. Whatever the reaction of others, especially his detractors, Paul declared, "We serve God" (6:8).

From this section in 6:9-10 we may learn what they thought of Paul: (1) He was a nobody and could be safely ignored (6:6-9); (2) he was a foolhardy person who ran unnecessary risks that made him as good as dead already and so of little esteem in the eyes of his detractors (6:9b); (3) his sufferings were a mark of God's displeasure (6:9c); (4) he was of melancholy disposition (6:10, "Our hearts ache" is lit., "We are sorrowful"); and (5) above all, he had no influence in the world where money is power and possessions count (6:10, "We own nothing, and yet we have everything"—a proverbial tag with a rhyme in the Greek). Indeed, Paul was "poor" (in the sense of not having material possessions), but he gave spiritual riches to others. The supreme model for this life is the incarnate Lord, who became poor to enrich his people with salvation (stated clearly in 8:9; Phil 2:6-11).

◆   I. The Temple of the Living God (6:11–7:1)

¹¹Oh, dear Corinthian friends! We have spoken honestly with you, and our hearts are open to you. ¹²There is no lack of love on our part, but you have withheld your love from us. ¹³I am asking you to respond as if you were my own children. Open your hearts to us!

¹⁴Don't team up with those who are unbelievers. How can righteousness be a partner with wickedness? How can light live with darkness? ¹⁵What harmony can there be between Christ and the devil*? How can a believer be a partner with an unbeliever? ¹⁶And what union can there be between God's temple and idols? For we are the temple of the living God. As God said:

"I will live in them
and walk among them.
I will be their God,
and they will be my people.*
¹⁷ Therefore, come out from among
unbelievers,
and separate yourselves from them,
says the LORD.
Don't touch their filthy things,
and I will welcome you.*
¹⁸ And I will be your Father,
and you will be my sons and
daughters,
says the LORD Almighty.*"

CHAPTER 7

Because we have these promises, dear friends, let us cleanse ourselves from everything that can defile our body or spirit. And let us work toward complete holiness because we fear God.

6:15 Greek *Beliar;* various other manuscripts render this proper name of the devil as *Belian, Beliab,* or *Belial.*   6:16 Lev 26:12; Ezek 37:27.   6:17 Isa 52:11; Ezek 20:34 (Greek version).   6:18 2 Sam 7:14.

NOTES

6:11 *We have spoken honestly with you.* Lit., "Our mouth is open toward you"—a vivid expression of Paul's tender affection for the Corinthians. The sense of the verb is "to speak freely." Paul considers the Corinthians his friends despite the ways that some of the Corinthians have treated him.

our hearts are open to you. This echoes Ps 119:32 [118:32, LXX], "since you have enlarged my heart" as a prayer to Yahweh. The theme of open hearts in 6:11-13 will be taken up again in 7:2-3, bookending the material of 6:14–7:1, which focuses on exclusivism and purity. Paul intends for the Corinthians to follow his appeals of separation in 6:14–7:1 as a sign of their open hearts.

6:12 *no lack of love on our part.* The Greek is expressive, lit., "We are not restricted" (*stenochōreisthe* [TG4729, ZG5102]; the same verb translated "crushed" in 4:8). In 6:11 Paul declared he was enlarging his heart; here he states a similar idea with a metaphor like "we are not squeezing you out of our affections," and he hoped that the Corinthians would not continue to restrict theirs.

but you have withheld your love. Paul repeats the verb, again using a strong metaphor, lit., "But you are restricted in your affections." Affections (NLT, "love") is the more elegant expression for the Greek thought *splanchnon* [TG4698, ZG5073] ("bowels"; cf. Heb., *rakhamim* [TH7356, ZH8171]) as the seat of the emotions. Gossip and slander had filled their hearts, so that there was no room for affection toward Paul.

6:13 *I am asking you to respond.* "In return" (NRSV), as a sort of quid pro quo, Paul was asking them to respond to his love as his children. He had opened up his heart in love. Now he pleads that his "children" (1 Cor 4:14, 17; Gal 4:19; Phlm 1:10 of his converts) would do the same.

6:14 *Don't team up with those who are unbelievers.* This begins the self-contained unit of 6:14–7:1. Paul's exhortation to not "team up" or be mismatched/unevenly yoked recalls the OT prohibitions of Lev 19:19 and Deut 22:10, highlighting purity as a prohibition against siding with unbelievers. The opening statement's call for separation is reinforced by five antithetical questions (6:14b, c, 15a, b, 16a). All begin with the interrogative pronoun "what" (*tis* [TG5101, ZG5515]). On the one side are ethical living, light, Christ, believers, and God's temple, and on the other are lawlessness, darkness, Satan, unbelievers, and idols. These "unbelievers" (*a*, "not" + *pistos*, "believer" = *apistos*, "unbeliever") may be non-Christians (traditional view), false apostles/opponents (Dahl 1977:62-69), or immoral Christians (Goulder 2003:47-57). Paul appropriated this traditional material, which called for separation from "unbelievers" (*apistoi* [TG571, ZG603]), by applying it to his present situation. Paul was equating his opponents with these unbelievers. A mark of reconciliation between Paul and the Corinthians was separation from the unbelieving world, of which his opponents, by preaching a false gospel, were a part.

How can righteousness be a partner with wickedness? "Wickedness" (*anomia* [TG458, ZG490]) is contrasted with "righteousness" (*dikaiosunē* [TG1343, ZG1466]), indicating that righteousness is used here ethically, as in right living (cf. 6:7; 11:15; Rom 6:13-19; 14:17; Phil 1:11), not as in acquittal.

How can light live with darkness? The second question contrasts "light" and "darkness." The metaphorical antithesis between light and darkness also occurs in 4:4-6 and 11:14 with Satan's schemes involving blinding unbelievers in darkness and masquerading as light. Believers are associated with the true light, and unbelievers are associated with darkness. This metaphor also occurs elsewhere in Pauline literature (Rom 13:12; Eph 5:11-14; 1 Thess 5:5), elsewhere in the NT (Luke 16:8; John 1:4-9; 12:36; 1 Pet 2:9), and in Qumran literature (e.g., 1QS 1:9-11; 1QM 1:1; 1QH 12:6; 4QFlor 1:9).

6:15 *What harmony can there be between Christ and the devil?* The third question literally asks the difference "between Christ and Beliar?" Beliar (or Belial, Belian, Beliab; see

NLT mg) is not found in the OT as a name for the devil, but means "worthlessness" (see literal rendering of 1 Sam 2:12). In later Jewish literature (*Jubilees* 1:20; *Testament of Reuben* 4:11; *Testament of Simeon* 5:3; *Testament of Levi* 19:1; *Testament of Dan* 4:7; 5:1; *Testament of Naphtali* 2:6; 3:1; *Ascension of Isaiah* 3:11), especially at Qumran (e.g., 1QS 1:18, 24; 2:19; ch 5; 1QM 1:1, 5; 11:8; 13:1-4, 1QH 6:21; 4QFlor 1:8; 2:2), it stands for God's adversary, not the Messiah's. Here, reflecting Christian thinking, Belial is not simply the adversary of God but of Christ. For more on Satan, see the notes on 2:11, 4:4, and 11:3.

How can a believer be a partner with an unbeliever? Paul was not demanding isolation from non-Christians; rather, this was a warning against shared commitments and values. Believers must be committed to the will of God. Paul's opponents have aligned themselves with Satan, so he places them into the category of nonbelievers. With this question, Paul encourages the Corinthians to separate themselves to avoid destructive influences.

6:16 And what union can there be between God's temple and idols? This fifth question reminds the Corinthians of the incompatibility of monotheism with pagan idols. Idolatry was sinful because it involved worshiping false gods, as well as licentious and immoral behavior (1 Cor 5:10-11; 6:8-9; 10:7, 14, 19; 12:2; Gal 5:19-20; Col 3:5; 1 Thess 1:9; cf. Wis 14:12). In 1 Cor 10, Paul corrected idolatrous behavior by reminding his readers of God's punishment of Israel (Toney 2008:182-188). God's temple is a reference to the church, as the second half of this verse notes (cf. 1 Cor 3:16-17; 6:19). Just as the Jerusalem Temple would be defiled with the introduction of an idol (e.g., Antiochus Epiphanies' abomination of desolation), so the spiritual temple of believers would be defiled by idolatry.

For we are the temple of the living God. God's temple (his holy place) and idols form the stark contrast between devotion to God and idolatry, which was prevalent at Corinth (1 Cor 3:16-17; 6:12-20).

I will live in them and walk among them. This citation of Lev 26:11-12, LXX, is influenced by Ezek 37:27, LXX, and acts as a promise. God's presence was now in his people, not merely within the Temple. The second half of this citation, "I will be their God, and they will be my people," applies the covenant formula (cf. Ezek 11:20; 36:28) between God and Israel to the church (Bruce 1978:215). With this covenantal privilege comes the expectation of holy living (cf. 5:10; 6:1).

6:17 come out . . . separate yourselves. . . . Don't touch their filthy things. This command draws upon Isa 52:11, LXX (depart . . . touch nothing unclean . . . go out). Just as exiled Israel, as a priestly community, was ordered to leave Babylon, so Paul expected an immediate and decisive withdrawal. Contact with unbelievers threatened the purity of this temple of God's people.

and I will welcome you. This promise of "welcome" is based on Ezek 20:34, LXX, in which God is promising rescue from exile. The result of this welcome is given in the next quotation—people become God's family.

6:18 Father . . . sons and daughters. This is an allusion to 2 Sam 7:14, where God promised David a special father-child relationship, which was ultimately extended to the whole nation (Jer 31:9). Now this relationship is extended to believers. Paul's addition of daughters could be due to influence from Isa 43:6, LXX. Paul has moved from the image of temple to family.

7:1 promises. This is a term that Paul usually used as referring to messianic prophecies, but here it has to do with the holiness of the church. Three promises were given—God's presence (6:16b; Lev 26:11-12), God's welcome (6:17b; Ezek 20:34, LXX), and God's fatherhood (6:18; 2 Sam 7:14, LXX).

let us cleanse ourselves. Paul has reminded the Corinthians that their identity is rooted in holiness. He has warned them that their current mixture with the "unbelievers" (cf. 6:14) endangers their core identity, so he calls them to excise the unbelievers from their midst.

COMMENTARY

From an impassioned statement of the apostolic ministry in 6:3-10, Paul's appeal continues with an intense expression of his yearning over the Corinthian congregation. Second Corinthians 6:11-13 provides readers with an impressive revelation of Paul's inner feelings, which, as we saw, is continued in the same vein in 7:2. "We have spoken honestly with you" means simply, "We've let ourselves go" by speaking without reserve or restraint. This is then matched by 7:2, "Open your hearts to us," that is, don't be reserved, but express how you feel because of the mutual trust and regard we have for one another.

The next section (6:14–7:1) is puzzling to scholars. Either (1) it is penned by Paul as a digression or as an integral part of his argument, or (2) it is interpolated material (either non-Pauline material or a fragment from another Pauline letter) inserted by Paul or a later redactor. Paul is most likely modifying preexistent material influenced by similar ideas found in Qumran (Furnish 1984; Fitzmyer 1961:271-280; Gnilka 1968:48-68) in order to develop his appeal to accept his gospel of reconciliation and to break with Paul's opponents.

In support of this being preexisting material, notice how the common wording of open hearts in 6:11-13 is continued in 7:2, suggesting that 6:14–7:1 is a detached section with a theme of its own. In addition the section contains a number of terms (eight in all) found only here in Paul's letters, including a lengthy quotation of Old Testament proof texts. The call not to "team up with those who are unbelievers" suggests that some Corinthian believers were going over to the opponents' side (on the term "unbeliever," see the note on 6:14). The reference to Christians proposing to take non-Christian spouses is secondary. Paul was warning, in both cases, against compromising the integrity of faith (P. E. Hughes 1962:246). Paul was affirming the need for God's people to be a holy community, free from the contamination of their surrounding culture.

Paul's appeal enforces a single point: The call to reconciliation should involve wholehearted commitment to him as God's apostle and loyalty to his gospel. The tone is strident and severe, but evidently such was needed. Paul then moves deftly into a short resumption (7:2-3) to moderate what he may have regarded as too impersonal and rigorous.

◆ V. The Good Report of Titus (7:2-16)

²Please open your hearts to us. We have not done wrong to anyone, nor led anyone astray, nor taken advantage of anyone. ³I'm not saying this to condemn you. I said before that you are in our hearts, and we live or die together with you. ⁴I have the highest confidence in you, and I take great pride in you. You have greatly encouraged me and made me happy despite all our troubles.

⁵When we arrived in Macedonia, there was no rest for us. We faced conflict from every direction, with battles on the outside and fear on the inside. ⁶But God, who

encourages those who are discouraged, encouraged us by the arrival of Titus. ⁷His presence was a joy, but so was the news he brought of the encouragement he received from you. When he told us how much you long to see me, and how sorry you are for what happened, and how loyal you are to me, I was filled with joy!

⁸I am not sorry that I sent that severe letter to you, though I was sorry at first, for I know it was painful to you for a little while. ⁹Now I am glad I sent it, not because it hurt you, but because the pain caused you to repent and change your ways. It was the kind of sorrow God wants his people to have, so you were not harmed by us in any way. ¹⁰For the kind of sorrow God wants us to experience leads us away from sin and results in salvation. There's no regret for that kind of sorrow. But worldly sorrow, which lacks repentance, results in spiritual death.

¹¹Just see what this godly sorrow produced in you! Such earnestness, such concern to clear yourselves, such indigna-

tion, such alarm, such longing to see me, such zeal, and such a readiness to punish wrong. You showed that you have done everything necessary to make things right. ¹²My purpose, then, was not to write about who did the wrong or who was wronged. I wrote to you so that in the sight of God you could see for yourselves how loyal you are to us. ¹³We have been greatly encouraged by this.

In addition to our own encouragement, we were especially delighted to see how happy Titus was about the way all of you welcomed him and set his mind* at ease. ¹⁴I had told him how proud I was of you— and you didn't disappoint me. I have always told you the truth, and now my boasting to Titus has also proved true! ¹⁵Now he cares for you more than ever when he remembers the way all of you obeyed him and welcomed him with such fear and deep respect. ¹⁶I am very happy now because I have complete confidence in you.

7:13 Greek *his spirit.*

NOTES

7:2 *Please open your hearts to us.* This resumes the appeal of 6:12-13. The Greek text does not include the phrase "your hearts to us," but the context demands it.

We have not done wrong to anyone. This contains the key verb *adikeō* [TG91, ZG92] (to treat someone unjustly) for this chapter (see especially 7:12). The background is that someone at Corinth had done wrong to Paul, causing him pain (2:4-5). Now Paul introduces the topic by denying that the fault was on his side. He had not "led anyone astray" (lit., "ruined") by taking their money (a charge in 12:16-18), nor was he "taking advantage of anyone," as Satan would do of the Corinthians (2:11).

7:3 *I'm not saying this to condemn you.* Paul heard from Titus (7:7-16) of the Corinthians' concern for him and did not want to jeopardize this step in a positive direction. Paul's aim was to clear his name, not to condemn the Corinthians.

we live or die together with you. Such expressions of affection are found in various works in ancient literature. For example, the poet Horace penned "with you [Lydia] I shall choose to die and live" (*Odes* 3.9.24); the character Electra in Euripides' *Orestes* 307f declares "with you I shall choose to die and live"; and in 2 Sam 15:21, LXX, Ittai protests to David, "wherever my lord the king shall be, whether for death or life, there your servant will be." Paul also may be alluding to his recent ministry experience, where he apparently had a near-death experience.

7:4 *I have the highest confidence in you.* This looks forward to what this chapter will contain, namely, Titus's arrival and report. It will engender Paul's encouragement and joy in the midst of his trials (going back to 1:8-10 and looking forward to 11:23-33).

7:5 *When we arrived in Macedonia . . . We faced conflict from every direction, with battles on the outside and fear on the inside.* This verse connects with the situation described in 2:13. Paul's time in Macedonia may correspond with Acts 20:1-2, which Luke spoke of positively. However, Paul was evidently in low spirits at that time: "Conflict . . . battles . . . and fear" are all telling terms (see 1:8-10; 4:8-12). With this verse, Paul returned to his travel narrative left off in 2:13. Paul, anxious about news from Corinth, continued westward to meet Titus, who was returning from the city. The continuity of 2:12-13 and 7:5-16 (see note on 2:13) has caused some scholars to posit that 2:14–7:4 was inserted from a distinct letter (L. L. Welborn 1996:559-583). However, arguments for unity include connections between 7:5-16 and previous material such as the words "encourage" (7:4, 6), "happy/joy" (7:4, 7), and "troubles/conflict" (7:4, 5), as well as statements about boasting (7:4, 14) and abundant joy (7:4, 13)—see Thrall 1994:21. For more on the relationship of these verses and the composition of 2 Corinthians, see C. N. Toney 2010b.

7:6 *But God, who encourages those who are discouraged, encouraged us by the arrival of Titus.* While *tous tapeinous* may mean "humble" (Bruce 1978:218), here it means "discouraged" or "depressed" in reference to the weighty pressures that had been exerted upon Paul during his Macedonian ministry. Titus brought good news to lift Paul's spirits. Portraying God as his comforter may allude to Isa 49:13 (LXX), and in 6:2 Paul already quoted from this same chapter in Isaiah. The theme of divine comfort can also be found in Isa 40:1; 51:3; 52:9; 61:2; 66:13.

7:7 *the news he brought of the encouragement.* According to Titus, Paul's painful letter to Corinth (2:4-5) had done its work; it had been favorably regarded and acted on (see 7:12). This is the chief cause of Titus's joy and so of Paul's joy as well. The letter had led to the Corinthians' sorrow for their opposition to Paul. Unfortunately, the situation was not as resolved as Titus had believed, since after he left, a new set of outsiders were able to step in and turn the Corinthians against Paul again (which would prompt the writing and dispatching of chs 10–13).

7:8 *I am not sorry that I sent that severe letter.* It was Paul's turn to feel regret, though his language is guarded. He was not sorry he sent the severe letter, which inflicted pain on the readers, but glad that it was worth it. It led the Corinthians to true repentance.

7:9 *Now I am glad.* Lit., "Now I rejoice" (*nun chairō*). Paul is not rejoicing over the pain of the Corinthians (1:24; see 1 Thess 2:19-20). Instead, Paul rejoices that their pain and sorrow led to repenting of past opposition.

the pain caused you to repent and change your ways. The noun *metanoia* [TG3341, ZG3567] ("repentance" or "turning away") is rarely used in Pauline literature (7:9-10; Rom 2:4; 2 Tim 2:25), and the verb *metanoeō* [TG3340, ZG3566] ("repent" or "turn away") is only used in 12:21. Elsewhere, Paul's focus was on the change of relationship between people and God; here, Paul's focus was on the Corinthians' change of attitude toward him (as the minister of God's gospel).

7:10 *sorrow.* Two kinds of "sorrow" are indicated. One is "worldly sorrow, which lacks repentance"; the other is expressed in the words *kata theon* [TG2596/2316, ZG2848/2536] (lit., "according to God," that is, as God intended). These two types of sorrow recall examples of Esau and David (P. E. Hughes 1962:273; Windisch 1924:231; see Gen 27:38; Heb 12:16-17). In contrast to Esau, David acknowledged his sin (Ps 51:1-11) and was restored to God's favor (Ps 51:12-19).

7:11 *Just see what this godly sorrow produced in you!* "Godly sorrow" led to beneficial consequences: "earnestness" ("concern to clear yourselves"), "indignation" (at the person who caused the trouble [Barrett 1973:211] or possibly at themselves for being misled [Strachan

1935:129; Tasker 1958:106]), "alarm" (lit., "fear" at having offended Paul), "longing to see me" (as in 7:7), "zeal" (in acknowledging Paul's authority), and "a readiness to punish wrong" (not so much to punish a wrong against himself as to right a wrong).

7:12 *My purpose, then, was not to write about who did the wrong or who was wronged. I wrote to you so that in the sight of God you could see for yourselves how loyal you are to us.* This is a difficult verse. On the face of it, it means that Paul wrote the severe letter not in order to deal with the offender or to recall the Corinthians to obedience but to elicit their "zeal" (*spoudē* [TG4710, ZG5082]; NLT, "how loyal you are to us"). The difficulty is cleared up if the clause, "although I wrote to you" (NLT, "My purpose, then, was not to write") is completed in the main verb in 7:13 ("We have been greatly encouraged by this"). The rest of 7:12 is a parenthesis with the sense that Paul was reassured by the revelation of the Corinthians' zeal for him "in the sight of God" (a phrase which comes last in Paul's writing, for emphasis).

7:13 *how happy Titus was . . . set his mind at ease.* Titus, too, was encouraged in that his favorable reception set his mind (NLT mg has the more accurate "his spirit," *pneuma* [TG4151, ZG4460]) at ease.

7:14 *my boasting to Titus has also proved true!* Although the Corinthian situation seemed bleak, Paul's confidence in reconciliation was illustrated by his boasting (a key word in this letter—words from this root are used almost 30 times) to Titus prior to sending the severe letter that the situation would improve. In an honor-shame culture, Paul was not ashamed, and he challenged the Corinthians' honor to maintain hospitable relations. Rhetorically, Paul was providing a positive characteristic of the Corinthians in the hope that they would feel obligated to continue exhibiting good relations.

7:15 *welcomed him.* The wording of Titus's welcome and joy recalls the way Epaphroditus was received at Philippi (Phil 2:25-30).

7:16 *I am very happy now because I have complete confidence in you.* "I rejoice" (*chairō* [TG5463, ZG5897]; NLT, "I am very happy") echoes the noun "joy" (*chara* [TG5479, ZG5915]) in 7:4 from the same root, forming an *inclusio* for this section. Because of Paul's confidence in his improved relationship with the Corinthians, he now could turn to the collection (chs 8–9). This tone of confidence is sharply different from the defensive and combative tone of chs 10–13, indicating a change for the worse between the writing of chs 1–9 and 10–13.

COMMENTARY

Though Paul knew the outcome of Titus's visit to Corinth, his welcome, and his meeting with his colleague in Macedonia, he rehearsed the circumstances of this happy event. He did this to spell out the way he was encouraged (a key thought, as in 1:3-7) by the way the Corinthians acted on receiving both the messenger and the letter (referred to in 2:4) he carried.

He reminded the Corinthians that he had done nothing to hurt them, even if the "severe letter" of 2:4 caused grief to him and a momentary shock to them. We have a remarkable insight into Paul's letter-writing habits in this section. It cost him a lot to put his thoughts down in writing, even to the point of wishing he had never written this "letter with tears." Yet on reflection he was glad he did so. In short, Paul was so relieved and refreshed by the results that he reviewed the past events to show how much had taken place since he entrusted the letter to Titus's keeping and sent him on his way. At Troas he was impatient (see 2:12-13) to meet Titus and hear the outcome of the letter. In his anxiety he crossed over to Macedonia, where Titus was awaiting him with good news: The church had disciplined the offender and was reinstated to Paul's side. This note of reconciliation was the main reason for Paul's encouragement and joy (in which Titus shared, too).

At a time when Paul was facing great distress (7:5), this interlude must have come as uplifting news to him and reassured him that his mission to southern Greece was not a failure. The restored relationship with the church there meant a new beginning. Though an individual had opposed him, the situation at Corinth had now brightened considerably. With this in mind, Paul was ready to continue his mission in Macedonia. He could count on the church's loyalty, which was due to be tested further when new troubles broke out (attested in chs 10–13). For the moment, he could proceed toward the completion of the collection that was started a year before (8:10-12) but was on hold while the disaffection at Corinth was brewing. The collection for the believers in Jerusalem (Rom 15:25-26; 1 Cor 16:1) was then reactivated by Titus (8:6).

◆ VI. The Collection for the Jerusalem Church (8:1–9:15)
   A. The Macedonians' Example (8:1-7)

Now I want you to know, dear brothers and sisters,* what God in his kindness has done through the churches in Macedonia. ²They are being tested by many troubles, and they are very poor. But they are also filled with abundant joy, which has overflowed in rich generosity.

³For I can testify that they gave not only what they could afford, but far more. And they did it of their own free will. ⁴They begged us again and again for the privilege of sharing in the gift for the believers* in Jerusalem. ⁵They even did more than we had hoped, for their first action was to give themselves to the Lord and to us, just as God wanted them to do.

⁶So we have urged Titus, who encouraged your giving in the first place, to return to you and encourage you to finish this ministry of giving. ⁷Since you excel in so many ways—in your faith, your gifted speakers, your knowledge, your enthusiasm, and your love from us*—I want you to excel also in this gracious act of giving.

8:1 Greek brothers.   8:4 Greek for God's holy people.   8:7 Some manuscripts read your love for us.

NOTES

8:1 **kindness.** Gr., charis [TG5485, ZG5921], whose most familiar meaning is "grace" (e.g., Eph 2:8). In chs 8–9, charis is found 10 times with a wide range of meanings: (1) generosity (8:9; 9:14), (2) privilege, favor (8:4), (3) act of giving (8:7), (4) the collection of gifts for the poor (8:6, 19), and (5) thanks (8:16; 9:15). See also the note on 9:14.

the churches in Macedonia. These include especially the believers at Philippi as part of the Roman province in northern Greece, extending from Apollonia in the west to Philippi in the east. Their place in Paul's mission strategy is important, as Phil 4:15 makes clear.

8:2 **They are being tested by many troubles.** The poverty and trials of the Macedonians are well illustrated in Paul's letter to the Philippians, as well as their generosity.

8:3 **they did it of their own free will.** Their giving was marked by sacrifice made of "their own free will" (authairetoi [TG830, ZG882]; a rare word, but found again in 8:17). Note that Paul did not plead with the Macedonians to give; they begged him to be allowed to give.

8:4 **privilege of sharing in the gift.** This spirit is one of koinōnia [TG2842, ZG3126], sharing in the fellowship of support of believers in need.

8:5 give themselves to the Lord. This was done in response to Paul's preaching.

and to us. Though the Corinthians gave themselves to Paul and his coworkers, Paul denied that he domineered over their faith (1:24).

8:6 So we have urged Titus. Now the scene changes. Paul was instructing Titus to return to Corinth to restart the collection and "finish this ministry of giving" (*charis* [TG5485, ZG5921]) they had started a year ago (8:10). The collection was in abeyance until the troubles at Corinth cleared.

8:7 this gracious act of giving. This refers to the collection that was supposed to be taken at Corinth.

COMMENTARY

In chapters 8–9, we have come to the second major part of the letter. Paul has turned his thoughts to consider the collection he was taking in the Gentile churches (Philippi and Galatia, as well as Corinth) for the impoverished Jewish Christians in the mother church at Jerusalem.

Some scholars posit one or both chapters to be separate compositions because of the topic shifts to the collection, with repeated content potentially directed at two different audiences—chapter 8 (Corinth) and chapter 9 (Achaia). H. D. Betz (1985) is one of the strongest advocates for two separate compositions. While noticeably abrupt, the transition between chapter 7 and chapter 8 is understandable in light of the change of topic from Paul's apostleship to the collection. In regards to the break between chapter 8 and chapter 9 and repeated material, S. K. Stowers (1986) has demonstrated that the Greek clause *peri men gar* (for now concerning) does not signal a new topic but indicates that chapter 9 expands upon chapter 8, specifically, the topic of boasting in 8:24 (cf. J. Lambrecht 1999).

It is important to see the significance of this collection in the life of Paul's missionary work (see Nickle 1966; Georgi 1992). This enterprise was (1) a fulfillment of his promise made to Peter and James to "[help] the poor" (Gal 2:10) and (2) a testimony to the believers in Israel of the love of the Gentile churches expressed in a realistic way. There was no more compelling way of demonstrating the unity of both Jewish and Gentile members of the one church than this. At the same time, there was no more powerful refutation of the Judaizers (Jewish-Christian legalists) who tried to insinuate that Paul was out of sympathy with the Jewish-Christians and their leaders (Rom 15:25-27).

The noble example of the Macedonian churches should become an incentive to the Corinthians (8:7). They were called to "excel also in this gracious act of giving" (*charis* [TG5485, ZG5921]). Paul had previously praised them for their rich endowment of spiritual gifts-in-grace (1 Cor 1:7; 12:7-11; 14:12); now they were being summoned to excel in this raising of the offering as well. In sounding this call, Paul did not want the Corinthians to think he was finding fault with them (Plummer 1915:238); nevertheless, he clearly was calling the Corinthians to action.

The Macedonians, of whom the Philippians are the best known, were renowned for their "rich generosity" in the way they supported Paul's ministry, as well as the fund for Jerusalem (Phil 4:10-19). Furthermore, the Philippians' generous giving came at a time when they were in the grip of a financial squeeze. (On the poverty of the Macedonians, see D. J. Downs 2008, 2010.) Yet this state of their economy did not stint their sacrificial giving (8:3), even to the point of their imploring Paul to take the money.

Paul had appointed Titus as his agent for the collection (8:6). But with the trouble at Corinth, the matter was put on hold. Now that the air had cleared and good relations were restored, Titus was encouraged to complete the matter.

◆   ## B. Appeal to the Corinthians (8:8-15)

8I am not commanding you to do this. But I am testing how genuine your love is by comparing it with the eagerness of the other churches.

9You know the generous grace of our Lord Jesus Christ. Though he was rich, yet for your sakes he became poor, so that by his poverty he could make you rich.

10Here is my advice: It would be good for you to finish what you started a year ago. Last year you were the first who wanted to give, and you were the first to begin doing it. 11Now you should finish what you started. Let the eagerness you showed in the beginning be matched now by your giving. Give in proportion to what you have. 12Whatever you give is acceptable if you give it eagerly. And give according to what you have, not what you don't have. 13Of course, I don't mean your giving should make life easy for others and hard for yourselves. I only mean that there should be some equality. 14Right now you have plenty and can help those who are in need. Later, they will have plenty and can share with you when you need it. In this way, things will be equal. 15As the Scriptures say,

"Those who gathered a lot had
    nothing left over,
    and those who gathered only a little
    had enough."*

8:15 Exod 16:18.

NOTES

8:8 *I am not commanding you to do this.* Paul was not issuing an order (*epitagē* [TG2003, ZG2198]), because he needed to handle the situation delicately and with tact. Rather, he was using the Macedonians and their generosity as a benchmark to test the reality of the Corinthians' love.

eagerness. This concept will be used later (8:11) as an encouragement to the Corinthians to emulate the Macedonians.

8:9 *the generous grace of our Lord Jesus Christ.* Possibly the mention of love in the preceding verse prompted Paul to appeal to the highest illustration of love in action. Note the parallel "kindness of God" (*tēn charin tou theou*) in v. 1 and the "generous grace of our Lord Jesus Christ" (*tēn charin tou kuriou hēmōn Iēsou Christou*) in v. 9. God's grace is demonstrated through the Macedonians' generous giving (v. 2), and Christ's grace is demonstrated in his generous self-giving (v. 9). Paul presents both these models to challenge the Corinthians to be generous.

he was rich . . . he became poor. With this phrase, Paul's appeal references the Incarnation for the sake of believers' *spiritual* (not economic) enrichment ("make you rich"). See commentary below.

8:10 *finish what you started.* This looks back to the Corinthians' eagerness a year earlier to have a part in the collection. With the disaffection cleared up, they were called to finish what they started.

8:11 *Give in proportion to what you have.* This is a lower standard than the Macedonians' heroic example (8:3).

8:12 *Whatever you give is acceptable if you give it eagerly.* This verse reinforces and expands on the previous injunction to give "in proportion to what you have." Paul recognizes that it is not the size of the gift, but God's acceptance of the gift that is of primary importance (Gen 4:3-5; 8:20-21; Lev 9:22-24; Phil 4:18; Heb 13:16). The right attitude goes hand in hand with the right gift. Paul's advice cautions Christians about making the mistake of giving greatly without a generous attitude, and Christians must also be cautious of abstractly having a generous attitude while being miserly with gifts. This verse is reinforced in 9:7.

8:13 *there should be some equality.* The basis of giving to the fund was "equality," a principle backed by Paul's citation of Exod 16:18 (see 8:15). Paul did not intend that the Jerusalem believers should be relieved by causing the Corinthians to be burdened. The golden rule is "fair shares for all." Let those who have share with those who do not have, so that both may be provided for.

8:14 *Right now you have plenty and can help those who are in need.* As noted in the Introduction, the Corinthian church possessed wealthy members. While Paul did not place himself under their patronage by seeking personal monetary aid, he did appeal to them as their spiritual benefactor to help other churches in need. It is not likely that the "need" of the Jerusalem church was related to the famine in AD 54 or a sabbatical year, since Paul's collection took around five years, AD 53–57. Rather, Paul was addressing a longstanding need. The famine collection of Acts 11 was probably the prototype for this collection (Harris 2005:591). Paul was responding to the apostles' request to remember the needs of the poor (Gal 2:10) as well as seeking to improve his relationship with the Jerusalem church.

8:15 *Those who gathered a lot had nothing left over, and those who gathered only a little had enough.* Paul was sure to equal the playing field so that the Corinthians did not feel as though the Jerusalem church owed them anything. He recalled the Exodus story of God's provision of manna and quail (Exod 16:18). Regardless of how much one gathered— either too much or too little—when it was measured, everyone miraculously had the same amount. Thus, Paul reminded the Corinthians that God acts with equity in order to eliminate inequalities and expects his people to likewise eliminate inequality.

COMMENTARY

By following the Macedonian believers' splendid example of giving out of their poverty (8:3), Paul's readers would prove the authentic quality of their love (8:8). Yet an even higher and more compelling example of giving out of poverty is invoked by the next verse (8:9), tacked on almost as an aside, yet arresting in the picture of ultimate love that it gives: "You know the generous grace of our Lord Jesus Christ. Though he was rich, yet for your sakes he became poor, so that by his poverty he could make you rich."

Paul's appeal is the incarnation of the Son of God based on "the generous grace of our Lord Jesus Christ." The expression "he was rich" takes us back to his preexistent life as being in the form of God (Phil 2:6; see Hengel 1977). The expression "he became poor" speaks on two levels. First, he became poor by his coming to earth and identifying with the economically poor (Luke 4:18; 6:20; 7:22). Second, at a deeper level, the phrase "for your sakes" implies that the incarnate Lord embraced the human condition of sinners by his death on the cross for his people's sake (as

Paul elaborated in 5:18-21; see also Mark 10:45). Therefore, his poverty was not so much his social deprivation as his forsaking his heavenly glory and his obedience to death. It was by that death that believers become rich, not materially, but by receiving the abundant gift of salvation (see 6:10).

Paul's teaching on Christian stewardship is highlighted in this section. True giving springs from both promising to help and then following through with it (8:11). This was the Corinthians' responsibility—not only to begin a good work, but to finish it. Furthermore, giving is governed by opportunity, as expressed in the phrase, "Give according to what you have, not what you don't have." This is a determining factor in the matter of the amount we give. It is not to be measured by the quantity of the gift, but by the extent of the sacrifice involved (Mark 12:43-44).

The quotation from Exodus 16:18 in 8:15 brings to light what may be called the law of reciprocity, that is, giver and receiver should be equally involved, with fair shares all around. Paul did not intend that the Jerusalem church should be relieved in its need by causing the Corinthians to be burdened with debt (8:13). Let those who have money share with those who are in distress so that both will have their needs met.

Yet there is probably a deeper and more theological note sounded in Paul's writing. The Gentile Christians' support of the Jewish Christians in Jerusalem would enhance God's plan in history and move his purposes to their appointed goal. One day, the blessings would go the other way. Paul saw the future Israel (as opposed to Israel according to the flesh; see Rom 2:28; 9:6-8) as becoming a fountainhead of blessings to the Gentile nations (*ethnē* [TG1484, ZG1620]). This was clearly his hope, as stated in Romans 11:12. (See my fuller explanation in R. Martin 1986:268-270; see also C. N. Toney 2008:127-166 for how Paul envisioned using his Gentile mission to promote the salvation of Israel.)

◆   ## C. The Forthcoming Visit of Titus and His Associates (8:16-24)

¹⁶But thank God! He has given Titus the same enthusiasm for you that I have. ¹⁷Titus welcomed our request that he visit you again. In fact, he himself was very eager to go and see you. ¹⁸We are also sending another brother with Titus. All the churches praise him as a preacher of the Good News. ¹⁹He was appointed by the churches to accompany us as we take the offering to Jerusalem*—a service that glorifies the Lord and shows our eagerness to help.

²⁰We are traveling together to guard against any criticism for the way we are handling this generous gift. ²¹We are careful to be honorable before the Lord, but we also want everyone else to see that we are honorable.

²²We are also sending with them another of our brothers who has proven himself many times and has shown on many occasions how eager he is. He is now even more enthusiastic because of his great confidence in you. ²³If anyone asks about Titus, say that he is my partner who works with me to help you. And the brothers with him have been sent by the churches,* and they bring honor to Christ. ²⁴So show them your love, and prove to all the churches that our boasting about you is justified.

8:19 See 1 Cor 16:3-4. 8:23 Greek *are apostles of the churches.*

NOTES

8:16-17 *But thank God! He has given Titus the same enthusiasm.* In these verses Paul commended his envoys, beginning with Titus. The Corinthians' eagerness to cooperate in the offering (8:11) was matched by Titus's "enthusiasm" or "zeal" (*spoudē* [TG4710, ZG5082], the most important requirement of a Hellenistic administrator), also shared by Paul himself. This same "zeal" given by inspiration was given to the Corinthians (8:7) and the Macedonians (8:8). In a typically Pauline way of thinking, he ascribed this impulse to God's working in Titus's heart. According to 8:17 the two evidences of Titus's zeal were (1) welcoming the appointment by Paul ("request," *paraklēsis* [TG3874, ZG4155], is the noun form of the verb, which refers to accepting a legal mandate) and (2) his own personal decision to return to Corinth. On the collection, see D. J. Downs 2010.

8:18 *another brother.* The first companion of Titus is a "brother," that is, a Christian colleague and Paul's fellow worker; his description is tantalizingly vague. In order to ensure the integrity of the collection, Paul sent two unnamed brothers (8:18, 22) with Titus. This models the importance of acting with integrity as well as avoiding the appearance of evil in matters of money.

All the churches praise him as a preacher of the Good News. This means he was probably an evangelist (Eph 4:11; 2 Tim 4:5), though not a Gospel writer such as Luke as some (like Origen and Jerome) have thought. The term "gospel" in Paul's day always refers to the spoken message, not the written record. No one can say who is meant, yet the Corinthians must have known because Paul would not introduce an unknown person (Lietzmann 1949:136-137). Of all guesses, Apollos is the most plausible (see Acts 18:24-28 for a similar commendation of this person). In this context, if Apollos is intended, Paul praised him more for his assistance in carrying the collection than for his preaching. So this brother was a person of probity and honesty with respect to money. This is the first qualification of this unknown person.

8:19 *appointed by the churches.* This is the second qualification of this unknown person. "To appoint" (*cheirotoneō* [TG5500, ZG5936]) originally included with its meaning the mode of raising one's hands to appoint. In NT times, it had a broader sense of appointment with the means not being closely tied, and after NT times it gained the sense of laying on hands as the means of appointment. We do not know the number or identity of the churches appointing this brother. It is unlikely that they were from Judea, since the collection was serving to improve Paul's relationship with Jerusalem. However, they could have been Asian, reflecting Paul's wider missionary activity (P. E. Hughes 1962:316), or Macedonian, since he had been ministering in the area and lifted these churches up as model believers (Harris 2005:603).

a service that glorifies the Lord and shows our eagerness to help. Paul's twofold motivation for the Jerusalem collection is now stated. First, it is "for the glory of the Lord"—the "Lord" probably referred to God rather than to Christ (cf. 3:18; 8:21). Paul hoped a successful collection would result in praising God. Second, Paul wanted all to see his "eagerness" or "goodwill" (*prothumia* [TG4288, ZG4608]) toward the Jerusalem church (cf. 9:12). Paul was hoping to secure better relations with this church, an issue important in light of Paul's opponents' claiming their authority from this church.

8:20 *We are traveling together to guard against any criticism for the way we are handling this generous gift.* Money has been a sensitive issue between Paul and the Corinthians. In the past, Paul had argued for his financial independence from Corinth (11:9-12; 1 Cor 9:12, 15, 18). Paul was being sure to avoid the charge of embezzlement by traveling together. Paul offers a good lesson for modern church leaders to avoid any appearance of evil in regards to donated money.

8:21 *We are careful to be honorable before the Lord, but we also want everyone else to see that we are honorable.* This verse is a positive restatement of 8:20 with Paul adapting Prov 3:4, LXX: "And you should provide honor before the Lord and people" (Gr., *kai pronoou kala enōpion kuriou kai anthrōpōn*).

8:22 *We are also sending with them another of our brothers.* The other fellow Christian also had been "proven," that is, tested as to his trustworthiness. He is also unnamed.

8:23 *he is my partner who works with me.* Titus, the leader of the trio, was especially commended in the tribute as "my partner" (*koinōnos* [TG2844, ZG3128]; a personal relationship is denoted).

sent by the churches. The second and third persons were "sent by the churches." The NLT mg reading is better, "are apostles of the churches," since it preserves the semitechnical term *apostoloi* [TG652, ZG693]. In this context it denotes delegates authorized by the congregations. This was patterned on the synagogue practice of appointing delegates to carry the half-shekel tax to the Temple.

they bring honor to Christ. Gr., *doxa Christou* [TG1391/5547, ZG1518/5986] (glory of Christ). This may be understood in different ways: (1) "they reflect Christ" (NEB mg); (2) "these men are the representatives of the heavenly splendor of Christ" (Georgi 1992:75), perhaps in contrast to Moses's glory in ch 3.

8:24 *So show them your love, and prove to all the churches that our boasting about you is justified.* The "so" (*oun* [TG3767, ZG4036]) connects this verse with the previous verse and indicates that this appeal is based on 8:16-23. This appeal includes a play on words: "demonstrate the demonstration" (*endeixin . . . endeiknumenoi;* NLT, "show . . . prove") with a slight nuance between the noun (*endeixis* [TG1732, ZG1893]), which refers to the act of making something known, and the verb (*endeiknumi* [TG1731, ZG1892]), which emphasizes the public nature or clarity of the demonstration (Harris 2005:612). Thus, by showing these representatives love, the Corinthians gave public or clear proof to the delegates' home churches (most likely in Macedonia). This "love" (*agapē* [TG26, ZG27]) demonstrated Christian hospitality and community (see the Epistles of John for another example of an early Christian community where insiders and outsiders are marked by "love").

COMMENTARY

This section forms an introduction to the three individuals who were sent to Corinth to attend to the matter of the collection. The reason Paul was careful in arranging these visits and commending certain persons to accompany Titus in carrying the gifts to Jerusalem is stated in 8:21: "We are careful to be honorable before the Lord, but we also want everyone else to see that we are honorable." The apostolic messengers (see note on 8:23) were persons of proven worth. Titus's character was appreciated by Paul as a tested and trusted colleague (8:17, 22-23). The other two unnamed coworkers were persons of similar integrity (8:19, 23).

The reason they are mentioned is that these delegates of the churches, along with Titus, were to be sent to Corinth for the administration of the relief fund and the care of the money raised. Therefore, they had to be people of sterling reputation and probity (8:22). They had the highest accreditation possible, as stated in 8:23: "They are the delegates of our congregations [presumably in Macedonia]; they reflect Christ" (NEB mg).

◆   ## D. The Delegation Commended to the Corinthians (9:1-5)

I really don't need to write to you about this ministry of giving for the believers in Jerusalem.* ² For I know how eager you are to help, and I have been boasting to the churches in Macedonia that you in Greece* were ready to send an offering a year ago. In fact, it was your enthusiasm that stirred up many of the Macedonian believers to begin giving.

³ But I am sending these brothers to be sure you really are ready, as I have been telling them, and that your money is all collected. I don't want to be wrong in my boasting about you. ⁴ We would be embarrassed—not to mention your own embarrassment—if some Macedonian believers came with me and found that you weren't ready after all I had told them! ⁵ So I thought I should send these brothers ahead of me to make sure the gift you promised is ready. But I want it to be a willing gift, not one given grudgingly.

9:1 Greek *about the offering for God's holy people.*   9:2 Greek *in Achaia,* the southern region of the Greek peninsula. *Macedonia* was in the northern region of Greece.

NOTES

9:1 *I really don't need to write to you about this ministry.* While Paul continued the discussion of "this ministry of giving" to Jerusalem, his focus changed. In ch 8 he used the example of the Macedonians to influence the readers; here he recommended the delegates to the churches of southern Greece and praised what had been achieved at Corinth (9:3).

9:2 *were ready to send an offering a year ago.* The Corinthians' "enthusiasm" (*zēlos* [TG2205, ZG2419], "zeal") had encouraged the Macedonians to start the collection in their churches. The Corinthians' start to the collection (see 8:2, 6) was part of the report of the delegation sent to Corinth, about which Paul boasted. He did not want to be embarrassed by their refusal to reactivate the collection.

9:3-4 Paul gave three reasons for sending the brothers to Corinth: (1) to make sure the Corinthians were ready when Paul arrived (v. 3a), (2) to make sure his boasting (8:24) is justified (v. 3b), and (3) to avoid shame if the Macedonians came (v. 4). Paul's language of boasting and embarrassment fits with his culture's desire to avoid shame and seek honor as well as with the competitive nature of Corinth (see Introduction).

9:5 *I thought I should send these brothers.* The "brothers" who were the delegates are the colleagues mentioned in 8:16-24.

a willing gift, not one given grudgingly. Lit., "a blessing (*eulogia* [TG2129, ZG2330]), not as an exaction" (*pleonexia* [TG4124, ZG4432])—i.e., money wrung out of them, like blackmail (Barrett 1973:235). Héring (1967:66) cites 2 Kgs 5:15, LXX, which spoke of Naaman's present to Elisha: "Take the bounty (*eulogia*) from your servant."

COMMENTARY

This paragraph sets two congregations—one in Macedonia and one in southern Greece including Corinth—in some kind of contrast. The Macedonians had already been praised for their offerings (8:1-5); it was the Corinthians' turn to make good on their promise to contribute, based on Paul's confidence in them (9:3).

Paul's reputation was at stake because he had already set forth the churches in southern Greece as a model of "enthusiasm" in giving. But their tardiness in completing the matter—for reasons not given—seemed to belie that confidence. Presumably it was the trouble at Corinth that suspended the collection a year earlier. So Paul prodded them to fulfill the task and, in so doing, to confirm the expectation he had of them. Above all, he wanted the gift to be both freely forthcoming and generous in its amount: "I want it to be forthcoming as a generous gift, not as money wrung out of you" (9:5, Moffatt 1954). Paul made his appeal in two ways: (1) emulation, with the Macedonians setting the standard and responding to the Corinthians' zeal in starting the collection a year previously, and (2) shame, lest the Corinthians' slackness to restart the offering should in any way reflect adversely on Paul's confidence in them or their own self-respect (9:4).

◆   E. The Collection for Christian Unity (9:6-15)

6 Remember this—a farmer who plants only a few seeds will get a small crop. But the one who plants generously will get a generous crop. 7 You must each decide in your heart how much to give. And don't give reluctantly or in response to pressure. "For God loves a person who gives cheerfully."* 8 And God will generously provide all you need. Then you will always have everything you need and plenty left over to share with others. 9 As the Scriptures say,

"They share freely and give generously
    to the poor.
Their good deeds will be
    remembered forever."*

10 For God is the one who provides seed for the farmer and then bread to eat. In the same way, he will provide and increase your resources and then produce a great harvest of generosity* in you.

11 Yes, you will be enriched in every way so that you can always be generous. And when we take your gifts to those who need them, they will thank God. 12 So two good things will result from this ministry of giving—the needs of the believers in Jerusalem* will be met, and they will joyfully express their thanks to God.

13 As a result of your ministry, they will give glory to God. For your generosity to them and to all believers will prove that you are obedient to the Good News of Christ. 14 And they will pray for you with deep affection because of the overflowing grace God has given to you. 15 Thank God for this gift* too wonderful for words!

9:7 See footnote on Prov 22:8.   9:9 Ps 112:9.   9:10 Greek righteousness.   9:12 Greek of God's holy people.   9:15 Greek his gift.

NOTES

9:6 the one who plants generously will get a generous crop. Paul illustrated Christian giving from the world of agriculture. The keynote is generosity, and what is at stake is the spirit of giving.

9:7 don't give reluctantly. Gr., ek lupēs [TG1537/3077, ZG1666/3383] (lit., "out of grief").

or in response to pressure. Gr., ex anankēs [TG1537/318, ZG1666/340] (lit., "out of constraint"). Giving should be the result of a person's free volition.

For God loves a person who gives cheerfully. Paul reiterates 8:12. The first OT proof text (see note on 9:9) is drawn from Prov 22:8, LXX, which reads: "He who sows injustice will reap calamity; it is the cheerful giver God loves," matched on the positive side by Prov 11:25, LXX, "every generous soul receives blessing." Sirach 35:11 [35:8, LXX] reads "with every gift put on a cheerful face."

9:8 And God will generously provide all you need. Lit., "God is able to make all grace overflow to you." With this overflowing "grace" (charis [TG5485, ZG5921]), Paul emphasized God's favor, encouraging his audience to count on God to grant both their desire as well as ability to share. Paul had moved from encouraging gifts based on human limits (8:12) to giving gifts based on God's abundance.

9:9 The second OT proof text (see notes on 9:7) is Ps 112:9 [111:9, LXX], quoted in full by Paul. More literally, this verse reads, "He [the righteous person] has scattered widely; he has given to the poor; his righteousness endures forever." Righteous people in Israel were known for their almsgiving (Dan 4:27), and in the Psalms and Paul "righteousness" (NLT, "good deeds") tends to be equated with giving charitably (cf. Matt 6:1-4; see J. Reumann 1982:52-53, 234). But the word "righteousness" (*dikaiosunē* [TG1343, ZG1466]) may also be regarded as a forensic term in the sense that care for the poor is a token of a person's right relationship with God, as in Jas 1:27; 2:14-26; 1 John 3:17-18 (Barrett 1973:238). In this same way, "righteousness" comes to mean generosity (9:10, NLT mg).

9:10 *For God is the one who provides seed for the farmer and then bread to eat.* Again (cf. 9:6) Paul drew on an agricultural metaphor, this time reworking a partial quote from Isa 55:10, LXX. Paul affirmed that God himself bountifully provided these resources, and assurance of God's provisions should empower the Corinthians to give generously.

and then produce a great harvest of generosity in you. Lit., "And he will increase the harvest of your righteousness." The "harvest of righteousness" (*ta genēmata tēs dikaiosunēs* [TG1079.1/1343, ZG1163/1466]) alludes to Hos 10:12, LXX, which says, "Sow for yourselves in righteousness (*eis dikaiosunēn*) . . . seek Yahweh until the fruits (or harvest) of righteousness (*genēmata dikaiosunēs*) come to you." The Corinthians had the opportunity via the collection to participate in God's righteous harvest and to reap the benefits. Paul saw this financial contribution as a sign of the Gentiles' willingness to participate in the restoration of Israel and reconciliation of the world (Rom 11:12, 15).

9:11 *to those who need them.* This refers to the messianic believers in Jerusalem, led by James, the Lord's brother (Acts 11:27-30; 21:17-18; 24:17; Gal 2:9-10).

9:12 *they will joyfully express their thanks to God.* Lit., "This ministry of giving overflows through many thanksgivings to God." The Greek verb for "overflows" is *perisseuousa* [TG4052, ZG4355] (the same verb as in 8:7, translated there as "excel").

9:13 *obedient to the Good News of Christ.* Paul made it plain that the unity of the church, which bound together his mission churches and the mother church at Jerusalem, was an expression of the gospel (Rom 3:29-30; 10:9-13; 1 Cor 10:32; Gal 3:28-29).

9:14 *deep affection.* Verses 8:1 and 9:14 form a sort of *inclusio* to this section. Paul typically used the verb "to show deep affection, yearn for" (*epipotheō* [TG1971, ZG2160]) to express his tender desire to see others (cf. Rom 1:11; Phil 1:8; 2:26; 1 Thess 3:6).

grace. In these two chapters, several nuances of *charis* [TG5485, ZG5921] are used. In 9:14 it is used as "grace," a meaning most familiar to modern Christians. However, in chs 8 and 9 *charis* typically has been used according to its broader meaning of "gift" in reference to the collection. In 9:15, another shade of meaning appears with Paul giving "thanks" (*charis*) to God. Paul concludes by reminding his audience that God's grace enables Christians to be generous with their gifts. On all the various meanings of *charis* in chs 8-9, see the note on 8:1.

9:15 *this gift too wonderful for words!* In a chapter full of emphasis on the Gentiles' giving, it is fitting for Paul to recall that God is the great giver—with reference either to giving his Son (8:9) or giving the gospel, which unites the divided peoples of Hebrew and Greek origin into one church (Eph 2:11-22).

COMMENTARY

The ruling theme of this chapter, devoted to a continuation of the apostle's call to the Corinthians to restart the collection for the believers in Jerusalem, is one of generosity. Paul's honor was at stake, because he presented the Corinthian church as a model of charity. Their reluctance to complete the matter (caused, no doubt, by the upset in the church) seemed to contradict and deny that honor. So he called on them to fulfill their promise and, in so doing, confirm the confidence he had in them. Above all, he wanted the money to be given freely. So he chose a number of expressive ways of getting home this appeal (9:2, 5). He also resorted to an agricultural illustration (9:6) that would register with the Corinthians, who, for all their urban mentality, lived in a city that was a hub of agricultural trade, as farmers brought their produce to market in Corinth. On the several questions of farming at Corinth, see the article by Barry N. Danylak (2008:231-270).

The application of generous giving is described in 9:9-14. Paul promised that their giving would yield a rich harvest of thanksgiving to God (9:9-12), who is honored when they take their promises to give seriously and honor their commitment. Then, the generous giving of the Corinthians would bear spiritual fruit. Not only would it meet an obvious need and relieve poverty and distress, it would convincingly show the mother church in Jerusalem the true Christian standing of the Gentile believers (9:13) and thereby serve to unify the church—a passionate belief of Paul. The possible danger was that the churches would be polarized with two centers, one in Jerusalem, the other in places like Antioch (which stood behind the Pauline mission). This possible division would be based on ethnic grounds, which formed one of the toughest barriers in the ancient world. Paul's gospel came to reconcile and heal these divisions (Eph 2:11-22; Col 3:11). Paul saw the Gentiles' offering as substantiating his gospel of reconciliation (9:13).

Paul hoped that when the Corinthians provided a generous offering to the Jewish Christians in Jerusalem, this largesse would promote the spirit of intercessory prayer and a longing to be drawn to the Gentiles because of the grace of God so evidently resting on these fellow Christians (9:14). According to Romans 15:26, at the time of writing Paul considered his collection in Corinth to be met with success. However, as D. J. Downs (2008) notes, the final outcome with this collection's arrival in Jerusalem remains a mystery, with the last description from Paul being found in Romans 15:14-32. The absence of a Corinthian delegation with Paul upon his return to Jerusalem in Acts 20:2-4 may indicate some continued issues between Paul and the Corinthians, but this is also an argument from silence, which should not be taken as definitive proof against Paul's successful collection in Corinth. While the collection was a major concern of Paul's, it is not a major concern for Luke's presentation of Paul. Further, it is possible that the "alms" for Israel and offerings in Acts 24:17 are a reference to Paul's Jewish piety rather than the collection (Downs 2006:50-70; Bowen 1923:49-58; see also the comments on 1:12-22). "Grace" (*charis* [TG5485, ZG5921]), which is a term that has several shades of meaning in chapters 8 and 9 (e.g., "gift," "grace," "thanks"—see notes on 8:1 and 9:14), is the capstone of Paul's discussion on the collection for the believers. In the final verse he exclaims "thank God (*charis tō theō* [TG2316, ZG2536]; lit., "grace to God") for this gift." This gift is either (1) the gift of salvation through Christ (8:9), (2) the offering of the Gentile believers, or, more likely here, (3) the way both Jewish and non-Jewish believers came to express their mutual interdependence and oneness in the gospel.

◆ VII. Paul's Defense of Himself and His Apostleship (10:1–12:21)
A. Paul's Defense of His Authority (10:1-18)

Now I, Paul, appeal to you with the gentleness and kindness of Christ—though I realize you think I am timid in person and bold only when I write from far away. ²Well, I am begging you now so that when I come I won't have to be bold with those who think we act from human motives.

³We are human, but we don't wage war as humans do. ⁴*We use God's mighty weapons, not worldly weapons, to knock down the strongholds of human reasoning and to destroy false arguments. ⁵We destroy every proud obstacle that keeps people from knowing God. We capture their rebellious thoughts and teach them to obey Christ. ⁶And after you have become fully obedient, we will punish everyone who remains disobedient.

⁷Look at the obvious facts.* Those who say they belong to Christ must recognize that we belong to Christ as much as they do. ⁸I may seem to be boasting too much about the authority given to us by the Lord. But our authority builds you up; it doesn't tear you down. So I will not be ashamed of using my authority.

⁹I'm not trying to frighten you by my letters. ¹⁰For some say, "Paul's letters are demanding and forceful, but in person he is weak, and his speeches are worthless!" ¹¹Those people should realize that our actions when we arrive in person will be as forceful as what we say in our letters from far away.

¹²Oh, don't worry; we wouldn't dare say that we are as wonderful as these other men who tell you how important they are! But they are only comparing themselves with each other, using themselves as the standard of measurement. How ignorant!

¹³We will not boast about things done outside our area of authority. We will boast only about what has happened within the boundaries of the work God has given us, which includes our working with you. ¹⁴We are not reaching beyond these boundaries when we claim authority over you, as if we had never visited you. For we were the first to travel all the way to Corinth with the Good News of Christ.

¹⁵Nor do we boast and claim credit for the work someone else has done. Instead, we hope that your faith will grow so that the boundaries of our work among you will be extended. ¹⁶Then we will be able to go and preach the Good News in other places far beyond you, where no one else is working. Then there will be no question of our boasting about work done in someone else's territory. ¹⁷As the Scriptures say, "If you want to boast, boast only about the LORD."*

¹⁸When people commend themselves, it doesn't count for much. The important thing is for the Lord to commend them.

10:4 English translations divide verses 4 and 5 in various ways.   10:7 Or *You look at things only on the basis of appearance.*   10:17 Jer 9:24.

NOTES

10:1 *Now I, Paul*. A new section of the letter begins at this point, wherein Paul adopts a personal tone. Chapters 10–13 were originally written after Paul received news of outside opponents infiltrating the community (see Introduction).

though I realize you think. The NLT adds this to clarify the background. Paul was being ironic by reporting what his opponents at Corinth were thinking and saying: "I am timid in person (i.e., self-abasing) and bold only when I write from far away" (i.e., arrogant).

10:2 *those who think we act from human motives.* They accused Paul of being governed by worldly (lit., "fleshly," *sarx* [TG4561, ZG4922]) motives. These people were not the Corinthian readers but the false apostles who had arrived on the scene (11:4; Barrett 1973:249).

10:3-6 These verses form one sentence in Greek. Paul used a sustained military metaphor in these verses. Paul was not simply fighting against spiritual forces, but he singled out his human opponents in Corinth. Siege imagery was commonly used, especially among the Stoics (Malherbe 1983:143-156). The following words that Paul used *may* be technical military terms: in v. 4, "siege engines" (*hopla* [TG3696, ZG3960]; NLT, "mighty weapons"), "demolition" (*kathairesis* [TG2506, ZG2746]; NLT, "knock down"), "strongholds" (*ochurōmata* [TG3794, ZG4065]), and "bastions" (*logismoi* [TG3053, ZG3361]; NLT, "false arguments"); in v. 5, "raised rampart" (*hupsōma epairomenon* [TG5313/1869A, ZG5739/2048]; NLT, "proud obstacle"), "take prisoner" (*aichmalōtizō* [TG163, ZG170]; NLT, "capture"), "battle plan" (*noēma* [TG3540, ZG3784]; NLT, "rebellious thoughts"), and "subjection" (*hupakoē* [TG5218, ZG5633]; NLT, "teach . . . to obey"); and in v. 6, "be ready like a soldier on standby" (*en hetoimō echontes* [TG2092/2192, ZG2289/2400]; not reflected in the NLT) and "insubordination" (*parakoē* [TG3876, ZG4157]; NLT, "disobedient"). For more discussion, see Harris 2005:676-677.

10:3 *We are human, but we don't wage war as humans do.* This is a play on the word *sarx* [TG4561, ZG4922] (flesh), which the NLT renders "human." It is "human" nature under the control of sin that Paul was denying.

10:4 *weapons.* Other weapon imagery in the Pauline corpus includes Eph 6:11 and 1 Thess 5:8. The KJV marks this verse off as a parenthesis with the participles dependent upon the finite verb, "wage war" (*strateuometha* [TG4754, ZG5129], 10:3). However, the NLT favors translating the masc. participles *kathairountes* [TG2507, ZG2747] (destroy) and *aichmalōtizontes* [TG163, ZG170] (capture) in 4b-5 as nominative absolutes acting as finite verbs.

to knock down the strongholds of human reasoning and to destroy false arguments. The wording of the Greek may allude to Prov 21:22, LXX: "A wise man scales the strong cities and brings down the stronghold (*ochurōma* [TG3794, ZG4065]) in which the ungodly trust." Paul challenges his opponents' "sophist arguments" (*logismoi* [TG3053, ZG3361]) as being faulty reasoning (cf. Rom 1:21; 1 Cor 3:20; Phil 2:14).

10:5 *proud obstacle.* Gr. *hupsōma epairomenon* reflects a combination of the noun, *hupsōma* [TG5313, ZG5739], meaning "height" (Rom 8:39) or "exaltation" (Job 24:24, LXX), which metaphorically can mean "proud," and the participle *epairomenon* [TG1869A, ZG2048] (that rises up). Paul sets out to destroy this tall obstacle of rivalry that Paul's opponents have raised between himself and the Corinthians, since alienation from Paul and his gospel is a sign of alienation from God (4:2-4; 6:7; 13:8).

We capture their rebellious thoughts and teach them to obey Christ. The term "capture" (Gr., *aichmalōtizō* [TG163, ZG170]) refers to a prisoner of war bound hand and foot. "Thought" (*noēma* [TG3540, ZG3784]) is used negatively throughout 2 Corinthians (2:11; 3:14; 4:4; 11:3).

10:6 *punish everyone who remains disobedient.* This tells us that all was not well at Corinth, in spite of the glowing report Titus brought (ch 7). The reason lies in the arrival of false teachers (11:4).

10:7 *Look at the obvious facts.* This is one way to translate *ta kata prosōpon blepete* [TG991, ZG1063] (lit., "Look at what is in front of you"), which considers the verb, *blepete*, to be an imperative indicating a command. The verbal form also could be an indicative and be rendered either as a statement of the facts ("You look at things only on the basis of appearance," NLT mg) or as a question ("Do you look at things according to the outward appearance?" NKJV/KJV). The NLT text is preferred by several commentators, especially P. E. Hughes (1962:355). Paul was probably speaking in the imperative mood because he was confronting the Corinthians who were attracted to what gave a good appearance (5:12).

belong to Christ. Lit., "to be of Christ." The opponents doubted Paul was even a Christian, a description they claimed for themselves.

10:8 *authority.* Gr., *exousia* [TG1849, ZG2026], a leading topic in chs 10–13 (see 13:10), coupled with Paul's distaste of "boasting" (elaborated in 10:15-18; see note on 10:17). Paul does not possess his own apostolic authority; rather, it comes from the Lord (1 Cor 1:1; Gal 1:1, 15-16). This stands in contrast to his opponents, who root their authority in their own wonder-working power and the Jerusalem church (10:12, 18). For more on Paul's comparison with his opponents, see notes on 10:12-13, 18.

builds you up. "Upbuilding" (*oikodomē* [TG3619, ZG3869]) is a key term in Paul's practice of ministry, and it is a familiar theme in the Corinthian letters (10:8; 12:19; 13:10; 1 Cor 3:9; 8:1, 10; 10:23; 14:3-5, 12, 17, 26). Paul's commission as an apostle was to "build up" the church, which is likened to a house erected by the servants of Christ (1 Cor 3:9-15). Paul was committed to promoting unity (1 Cor 1:10-13; 3:4-9, 21-23; 11:17-22, 27-34), which contrasted the deconstructive divisions created by his opponents (11:2-4; 12:20). In light of Paul's present and past conflicts with the Corinthians, it was important to remind them of his overall good intentions.

10:9 *I'm not trying to frighten you by my letters.* Paul gave a report of how his letters were received. He wrote letters to compensate for his enforced absence from his congregations. This is substantiated by Polycarp: "When he (Paul) was with you, he taught you; when he was absent, he wrote letters" (*Polycarp to the Philippians* 3:2). Paul's enemies put a negative construction on this by insinuating that Paul chose the safety of distance rather than a personal encounter with his people.

10:10 *in person he is weak.* Paul's "weak" appearance was evidently unimpressive, and he may have been lacking in the charismatic gifts of a forceful personality (11:6, "unskilled as a speaker").

10:11 *Those people.* Paul is refuting the outside opponents mentioned in 10:12 who have been recommending themselves.

our actions when we arrive. Despite his opponent's charges of Paul's ineffective physical presence, Paul claims that he will translate his forceful words into forceful deeds when he arrives.

10:12-13 This is a difficult sentence in the Greek (vv. 12-13), which the NLT has done well to clarify. Nonetheless, the text is uncertain (see R. Martin 1986:315 for details). Paul adapted a stance of mock humility as his rhetorical strategy as he attacked his opponents' boasting, using a pun in the Greek: *enkrinō* [TG1469, ZG1605] (to pair)/*sunkrinō* [TG4793, ZG5173] (to compare). Paul was sarcastically saying that these people are *so* wonderful that he could not "pair" himself with them or "compare" himself with them. Later, Paul changed tactics by playing the fool in his boasting (12:11).

using themselves as the standard of measurement. This verse introduces one of the themes of vv. 12-18, which is the means to *measure* the validity of ministry, with a cluster of key words concerning measurement (*metreō* [TG3354, ZG3582], 10:12; *metron* [TG3358, ZG3586], 10:13; *ametros* [TG280, ZG296], 10:15; *kanon* [TG2583, ZG2834], 10:13, 15, 16). In v. 12 Paul attacked his opponents for using themselves as "their own standard of measurement" (lit., "to measure"; *metreō*) particularly in determining their own geographical territory of apostolic authority. Paul opposed his enemies' self-judgment, since by that standard they are naturally well qualified. In v. 13 Paul contrasted his opponents, who boast outside their "area of authority" (lit., "unmeasured," *ametra* [TG280, ZG296]), with his own self-control at boasting only about "what has happened," that is, the "work God had given" (lit., "measurement," *metron*). Paul appealed to the measuring judgment of God, as well as reminding the Corinthians that these opponents had stepped outside their proper sphere of influence. Finally, in v. 15 Paul claimed propriety by not boasting beyond his limits (*ametra*; NLT does not translate), that is, about what was not his, unlike his opponents, who were claiming the fruits of Paul's works in Corinth. Intertwined with these verses, Paul called attention to the fact that it was proper for God, not people (i.e., his opponents) to draw the "boundaries/territory" (*kanon*; 10:13, 15, 16) of apostolic service.

boundaries of the work God has given us. Such spheres of service that Paul accepted as part of his calling to be "apostle to the Gentiles" (Rom 15:16; Gal 2:1-10) included Corinth; in fact, he was a pioneer missionary and church planter there (1 Cor 3:10). His policy was not to enter a field of service already occupied by other Christian missionaries (Rom 15:20).

10:14 *not reaching beyond these boundaries.* It was possible that Paul's opponents had accused him of hubris by overreaching (*huperekteinō* [TG5239, ZG5657]) in the Corinthian mission. Moderation (Aristotle's principle of the mean) and the avoidance of overreaching were important values in the Greco-Roman world (often Greek tragedies dealt with issues of overreaching, e.g., Sophocles' *Oedipus Rex, Antigone,* etc.). Paul's response did not deny the value of this principle; rather, he turned this argument against his opponents by reminding the Corinthians that he made Corinth his territory by being there first.

10:15 *Nor do we boast and claim credit for the work someone else has done.* Paul reminded the Corinthians of his sensitivity to the work of others (cf. Rom 15:20). He tactfully avoided mentioning who this other person was.

10:16 *Then we will be able to go and preach the Good News in other places far beyond you, where no one else is working.* Paul believed he had already established Corinth as a home base (10:13) for future evangelism (cf. Rom 1:1-15; 15:23-24, 28). "[Paul] was a herald [of the gospel] both in the East and in the West, he gained the noble fame of his faith, he taught righteousness to all the world, and when he had reached the limits of the West he gave his testimony before the rulers" (*1 Clement* 5:6-7 [K. Lake, LCL]).

10:17 *If you want to boast, boast only about the LORD.* After arguing against improper boasting in 10:12-16, Paul offered the measuring principle for proper boasting, citing Jer 9:23-24 [22-23, LXX], which says, "But in this let the boaster (*ho kauchōmenos*) make his boast (*kauchasthō* [TG2744, ZG3016])." Paul had previously quoted this text in his Corinthian correspondence (cf. 1 Cor 1:31). Paul intended this quote from common tradition to secure his argument. Paul modified the OT text, clarifying it as a maxim by adding "in the Lord." Some scholars consider this phrase to be a reference to God because the noun is anarthrous. However, it is most likely a reference to Christ because for Paul the phrase "in the Lord" regularly referred to Christ (Rom 16:2, 8, 11-13, 22; 1 Cor 16:19; Gal 5:10; Phil 2:24; 3:1; 4:1, 2, 4, 10; Col 3:18, 20; 4:7; 1 Thess 3:8; 5:12; 2 Thess 3:4, 12; Phlm 1:16, 20), and the similar quote in 1 Cor 1:31 referred to Christ. Paul's high Christology is evident in his interpretation of OT references to Yahweh as applying to Jesus (e.g., Rom 9:33 [citing Isa 28:16]; 10:12-13 [citing Joel 2:32]; Phil 2:10-11 [citing Isa 45:23]; see Richard Bauckham 1999:34, 56-61). Boasting is valid only when it focuses upon who the Lord is and what the Lord has done, and when it remains within a person's divinely ordained sphere of activity (Harris 2005:724-726).

10:18 *commend.* This verse is an expansion upon v. 17. It also forms a ring composition via an *inclusio* with v. 12 using the hook word "to commend" (*sunistēmi* [TG4921B, ZG5319])— "those who commend themselves (a group of unnamed people) . . . the person who commends himself (an abstract self-praiser)." Paul was opposed to self-praise rooted in human accomplishments and authority, but he was not opposed to praise rooted in divine calling (cf. 4:2; 6:4). Between Paul and his opponents, only Paul was worthy of divine praise because only he had stayed within his divinely appointed boundaries.

COMMENTARY

To everyone who reads through 2 Corinthians as a continuous piece of writing—as distinct from those who take only a small portion at a time—it becomes immediately clear that 10:1 opens a new section altogether. There is a distinct break at this point, which has been explained in a number of ways. One opinion notes the break but considers the letter to be unified (e.g., Tasker 1958; Witherington 1995; Harris 2005). Thus, Paul turns now to deal with the still recalcitrant and factious minority within the church or possibly outside opponents who must now be dealt with directly. The whole section of four chapters may be called *a statement of his apostolic authority,* which was the point at issue between himself and his traducers who were upsetting the Corinthians. The great majority of believers in the church had been won back by his past visit and previous letter, but there was still a pocket of resistance; it is to them that these chapters are addressed.

However, while it is true that seeds of problems are mentioned in chapters 1–9, the overall tone is conciliatory; but the tone of chapters 10–13 is confrontational and combative. This change of tone strongly suggests two different letters in chapters 1–9 and 10–13. One view is that chapters 10–13 form a separate letter and are to be identified with the "severe letter" of 2:4 and 7:8, sent earlier to Corinth (e.g., Kennedy 1900; Talbert 2002). However, chapters 10–13 cannot be the "severe" letter because these chapters anticipate an upcoming visit (12:14–13:2), while the "severe" letter was written in place of a visit (1:23–2:4). Another view (that of this commentary) places the composition of chapters 1–9 prior to chapters 10–13, noting that the letters' assembly follows a similar precedent illustrated in other letter collections (e.g., Cicero's letter collections). Paul himself may very well have been the final redactor putting the two letters together (D. Trobisch 1994). E. R. Richards (2006) reminds us that letter writing in the ancient world was a lengthy process whereby a letter such as 2 Corinthians could take several days, which could allow for a new report in the midst of composition (although the question then arises why Paul would not start a fresh letter).

As noted in the Introduction, Paul wrote chapters 1–9 after receiving word from Titus that the situation in Corinth had improved. However, shortly after composing and possibly dispatching chapters 1–9, a new situation arose—the arrival of rival missionaries (mentioned in 11:4) creating fresh problems to which Paul responded in the last four chapters of our letter (e.g., Barrett 1973; Bruce 1978; Furnish 1984; R. Martin 1986). For a more detailed survey and discussion of compositional issues, see C. N. Toney 2010a.

Second Corinthians 10:1-6 is an impassioned appeal to the Corinthians themselves. Paul stated his own clear motives and sincerity by defending himself against the suspicion that he was acting "from human motives" (10:2). He rebutted this charge with a military metaphor (10:3-5). Though he was encumbered with human infirmities, he resolutely denied using any false methods, which he calls "weapons of the flesh" (NLT, "worldly weapons"). His chosen weapons were instilled with divine power, with which he could demolish all arguments and plans that are simply human fantasies (10:4-5; see NEB).

In 10:7 he told his critics to "look at the obvious facts" (see note). This was Paul's answer to his critics' charge, as implied in 10:1: "Though I realize you think I am timid in person." Paul's counterargument was directed against his opponents who claimed a special position as Christ's servants (10:7). Though the identity of these people is not clear, they evidently posed a serious threat to the church since their teachings (11:4) provoked Paul's condemnation (11:13-15). They did not hesitate to criticize the apostle on the ground that he was inferior to them (10:10). They made out that they enjoyed a special place in the church as authoritative teachers possessing a commanding presence. Moreover, they had one great advantage in their favor: Unlike Paul, they were at Corinth and able to influence the church firsthand.

It seems that they turned their presence at Corinth to their own designs, for implicit in Paul's paragraph is the thought that he was under fire because of his absence. The point on which they had fastened was that Paul preferred to stay at a safe distance and conduct his defense by correspondence (10:9-10). This policy, they were suggesting, was a coward's refuge, for it seemed to imply that Paul was a strong personality when he wrote his letters, but when he appeared on the scene, his personal presence was nowhere near as impressive. Perhaps his opponents were also harking back to his supposed indecisiveness of action (1:17) and failure to come to Corinth as he had promised (2:1). They told the Corinthians that he was afraid to come and that he could terrify people only by letters written from a comfortable distance (10:9).

Paul began his defense by taking the offensive—charging his enemies with a false set of values (10:12). At the same time, he made it clear that he had not trespassed on the limits that God had set for his missionary service. He was the apostle to the Gentiles par excellence, a vocation spelled out to him at his conversion (Acts 9:15; 22:21) and accepted by the major apostles as part of the missionary agreement at Jerusalem (Gal 2:9). Indeed, the mission to the Gentiles was his special province God had apportioned to him (10:13)—and Corinth was in that category as a non-Jewish community.

This reference was clearly intended as a side look at the Jewish Christian proselytizers who were molesting a Gentile church and endeavoring to impose a yoke of false ideas and certain extraneous beliefs upon them. Paul's gospel was prone to misunderstanding because he believed the gospel was free of any ethnic markers. Thus, a Jew did not need to become a Gentile (by giving up the law), nor did a Gentile need to become a Jew (by following the law and being under the authority of Jerusalem). For more on Paul's inclusive ethic, see C. N. Toney 2008.

Paul stated that if any preacher was "out of bounds" at Corinth, it was not him, but the Jewish teachers who had gone beyond the limit assigned to them. Paul probably rooted his understanding of his sphere of influence in light of the Jerusalem agreement mentioned in Galatians 2. Paul understood himself to be the apostle to the Gentiles, while Peter and James had been called to the Jews. Paul already had encountered difficulties with these boundary markers in Antioch, then in Galatia, and now here in Corinth. However, in the case of Corinth, it is not entirely clear whether these opponents had been officially sanctioned by Jerusalem.

Paul carefully justified his integrity (10:14), insisting that when he first came to Corinth, he did so with clear conscience and intended in no way to "poach" on the missionary territory of other Christians (10:15-16; cf. Rom 15:20). At Corinth he may justifiably claim to be the human founder of the church (1 Cor 3:6). What right did the opponents have to encroach on *his* work (3:2; 1 Cor 9:1)?

Yet the final arbiter in this matter of evangelistic "division of labor" and territorial comity is no human committee, nor does an agreement made between Christians mean much unless it is the Lord who directs it. True—and herein is the relevance for modern missionary service—the Lord expects his servants to honor their arrangements and not to act irresponsibly in defiance of agreements as to mission fields. Since it is the Lord's work, whatever success is achieved comes from him to whom alone the credit and glory belong (10:17, which cites Jer 9:24). The final verse of this section is the seal of Paul's apostolic ministry: He did not commend himself (which amounts to nothing); rather, he looked to the Lord for his approval (10:18).

◆   ## B. The Opponents Identified and Condemned (11:1-15)

I hope you will put up with a little more of my foolishness. Please bear with me. ²For I am jealous for you with the jealousy of God himself. I promised you as a pure bride* to one husband—Christ. ³But I fear that somehow your pure and undivided devotion to Christ will be corrupted, just as Eve was deceived by the cunning ways of the serpent. ⁴You happily put up with whatever anyone tells you, even if they preach a different Jesus than the one we preach, or a different kind of Spirit than the one you received, or a different kind of gospel than the one you believed.

⁵But I don't consider myself inferior in any way to these "super apostles" who teach such things. ⁶I may be unskilled as a speaker, but I'm not lacking in knowledge. We have made this clear to you in every possible way.

⁷Was I wrong when I humbled myself and honored you by preaching God's Good News to you without expecting anything in return? ⁸I "robbed" other churches by ac-cepting their contributions so I could serve you at no cost. ⁹And when I was with you and didn't have enough to live on, I did not become a financial burden to anyone. For the brothers who came from Macedonia brought me all that I needed. I have never been a burden to you, and I never will be. ¹⁰As surely as the truth of Christ is in me, no one in all of Greece* will ever stop me from boasting about this. ¹¹Why? Because I don't love you? God knows that I do.

¹²But I will continue doing what I have always done. This will undercut those who are looking for an opportunity to boast that their work is just like ours. ¹³These people are false apostles. They are deceitful workers who disguise themselves as apostles of Christ. ¹⁴But I am not surprised! Even Satan disguises himself as an angel of light. ¹⁵So it is no wonder that his servants also disguise themselves as servants of righteousness. In the end they will get the punishment their wicked deeds deserve.

11:2 Greek *a virgin.*   11:10 Greek *Achaia*, the southern region of the Greek peninsula.

N O T E S

11:1 *I hope you will put up with a little more of my foolishness.* Within his overall argument against his opponents, Paul digressed by playing the role of a "fool"—a part that will
recur in 11:16, 17, 19, 21; 12:6, 11. The tone is ironical, with mock humility and rhetorical
devices such as calling his opponents to make comparisons (an ancient rhetorical device
known as *synkrisis*) with himself. In Jewish Wisdom Literature, "fool/foolishness" (*aphrōn/
aphrosunē* [TG878/877, ZG933/932]) is contrasted with "wise/wisdom" (*sophos/sōphrosunē*
[TG4680, ZG5055]). Harris (2005:729-730) notes that this section functions much like Prov
26:4-5: "Don't answer the foolish arguments of fools, or you will become as foolish as they
are. Be sure to answer the foolish arguments of fools, or they will become wise in their own
estimation." Paul was not trying to answer his foolish opponents; rather, he hoped to keep
the Corinthians from stumbling in this foolishness. Paul hoped his reply would expose
the foolishness of his opponents. Paul's reply was "foolish" because of the self-praise and
comparisons focusing on outward appearances.

11:2 *I promised you as a pure bride to one husband.* God is "zealous" for the purity of the
church. This would conjure up images of Israel as God's faithless wife (Ezek 16; Isa 50:1-2;
54:1-8; 62:5; Hos 1-3). Like the prophets, Paul was calling the Corinthians to faithful living. This call to purity and separation is also reflected in 6:14-7:1. The church is the "pure
bride" of Christ, meant to be unsullied by false teaching and practice. The background for
this imagery is also Gen 3 and maybe some extracanonical writings, as well as rabbinic
legend (e.g., the rabbis told how the serpent in Eden sexually seduced Eve; also in *1 Enoch*
69:6; *2 Enoch* 31:6: "The devil entered paradise and corrupted Eve"). See also 1 Tim 2:14.

11:3 *the cunning ways of the serpent.* This recalls 4:2 and is based on Gen 3:13, LXX,
where Eve remarks, "The serpent beguiled me and I did eat." In some versions of Gen 3:1,
namely, Aquila and Symmachus, the same word is used as here for "cunning" (*panourgia*
[TG3834, ZG4111]). For more on Satan see the notes on 2:11, 4:4, and 6:15. There are some
textual problems in this verse—does "and (of) purity" follow "from devotion" as part of
the original text? D. A. Kurek-Chomyez (2007:54-84) argues for the longer text, which is
found in some of our earliest and most reliable manuscripts (e.g., 𝔓46 ℵ* B G, etc.) and
used by the NLT.

11:4 *You happily put up with whatever anyone tells you.* Or, "You bear with him quite
beautifully!" This statement is actually at the end of the verse in Greek, coming as the sarcastic climax at the end of the series of "if" statements.

different Jesus . . . different kind of Spirit . . . different kind of gospel. Although the Greek
terms for "different" vary (*allos* [TG243, ZG257] for the first and *heteros* [TG2087, ZG2283] for the
next two), the meaning is probably the same. It is different not as an alternative but as a rival
or substitute. A "different Jesus" could refer to seeing him as an earthly, political deliverer
(as in 5:16), but more likely it refers to the character of Jesus (as in 10:1) setting the standard
for Christian living and service. The opponents proclaimed Jesus as a lordly figure who was
a stranger to suffering. By contrast, Paul lived a life of hardship as he followed Jesus. This
suffering and hardship is a major theme in 2 Corinthians (especially chs 11–13). A "different Spirit" is not a spirit (*pneuma* [TG4151, ZG4460]) distinct from the Holy Spirit, but the way
Christians and especially leaders act in relation to others. (For this meaning of *pneuma*, see
1 Cor 4:21.) Paul's phrase "a different kind of gospel" is a misnomer, since what they offered
to the Corinthians was not really the gospel at all (cf. Gal 1:6-9).

11:5 *super apostles.* Who they were is a matter of debate. They claimed (maybe wrongly) the
authority of the leading apostles (Peter, James the Lord's brother) in Jerusalem. There is no
evidence they were "Judaizers" preaching circumcision (a word missing in 2 Corinthians).

Rather, they were preachers rejoicing in their powerful gifts, especially in oratory and persua-siveness. Paul's statement in the next verse ("I may be unskilled as a speaker") leads to this understanding.

11:6 *I may be unskilled as a speaker, but I'm not lacking in knowledge.* Paul acknowl-edged that he was "unskilled" (*idiōtēs* [TG2399, ZG2626]) in speech, that is, not formally trained in rhetoric. For a discussion of Paul's use of rhetoric in his letters, see the Introduc-tion. This may be an ironic statement, or it may be a concession for the sake of argument; however, the sentence turns on the "but" (*alla* [TG235, ZG247]) with the key qualification being "knowledge" (*gnōsis* [TG1108, ZG1194]) of God and the gospel.

11:7 *preaching God's Good News to you without expecting anything in return.* Paul addressed another issue of what these intruding preachers expected of the Corinthians, name-ly, financial reward. (This is developed in 12:16-18.) By contrast, Paul did not become a finan-cial burden to any church. Rather, he worked at his trade to make money (Acts 18:3; 1 Thess 2:9). From Paul's perspective, his opponents' receiving of payment marked them as false teach-ers. Issues of itinerant missionaries preying upon the hospitality of early Christian communi-ties is evident from other texts such as the *Didache* 11:7–12:5, which cautions against preachers who stay longer than one or two days. From the Corinthians' perspective, it was a mark of dis-honor that Paul would not allow himself to receive their benefaction. However, Paul knew that along with financial support would come indebtedness and a potentially corrupting influence on his gospel, so he offered it free of charge (1 Cor 9). As D. J. Downs argues (2008:85-89), Paul subverted the Corinthians' notion of patronage by metaphorically framing the collection as a cultic act of worship. The praise of the gift goes not to the human benefactor but to God, from whom all benefactions come. (For more on Paul as benefactor, see S. J. Joubert 2000.)

11:8 *I "robbed" other churches by accepting their contributions.* Paul did admit that he received funds from other churches (cf. Phil 4:15-17), which may have frustrated the Cor-inthians, since he would not take money from them. Paul used two military metaphors here. The verb *sulaō* [TG4813, ZG5195] ("rob" or "plunder") was for stripping a dead soldier of his armor in a battlefield (P. E. Hughes 1962:385). The noun *opsōnion* [TG3800, ZG4072] (con-tributions) refers to the soldier's payment for buying rations. Paul's language indebts the Corinthians not only to himself but also to other churches in his missionary sphere.

11:9 *I did not become a financial burden.* Paul acknowledged that his ideal aim of self-sustaining ministry could not always be achieved in Corinth. In such a close community, it would be easy enough to see when Paul was not working, and suspicion arose concern-ing from where his income was derived. The root of the verb "to be a financial burden" (*katanarkaō* [TG2655, ZG2915]) is *narkaō* (not used in NT), which means "to numb by applying pressure" and may indicate that Paul was charged with pressuring the Corinthians for his own financial gain. This accusation of being a burden is also found in 12:16 (see similar concerns in 1 Thess 2:9; 2 Thess 3:8; 1 Tim 5:16).

For the brothers who came from Macedonia brought me all that I needed. I have never been a burden to you, and I never will be. Paul explained that he did not underhandedly seek out money from the Corinthians; rather, his funding came from the Macedonian churches. However, this also raises an issue for the integrity of Paul's Jerusalem collection. How were the Corinthians to be sure that Paul would not go to another city and "receive" money from the Corinthians in order to live? The issue of the collection's integrity is addressed in chs 8–9.

11:10 *As surely as the truth of Christ is in me.* Paul's opening is an oath formula (11:31; cf. Rom 9:1). The subjective genitive, *Christou*, indicates that Christ is speaking through Paul rather than Christ being the content of Paul's preaching—in other words, "truth *given by* Christ" (subjective genitive), not "truth *about* Christ" (objective genitive).

no one in all of Greece will ever stop me. Again, the issue of missions boundaries arises—Paul counterclaimed that all of Greece was under his sphere. The verb for "stop" (*phrassō* [TG5420, ZG5853]) was also used as a military term meaning "to put up as a fence, to secure, to fortify (joining spear to spear or shield to shield)" (LSJ 1953); it also could refer to blocking a road or damming a river (Hos 2:6 [8], LXX; Lam 3:9, LXX).

boasting. Gr. *kauchēsis* [TG2746, ZG3018] is a catchword in the entire "Fool's Speech" (11:12, 16, 17, 18, 30; 12:1, 5, 9), which Paul used here ironically or indignantly, since he would only boast (like his opponents) under duress (11:21; 12:11).

11:11 Why? Because I don't love you? God knows that I do. Paul's questions and answers reflect elements of diatribe. His love for the Corinthians had been called into question either because his opponents had introduced the question or his refusal of support had provoked it. As in 12:15, he was sure to affirm his affection for the Corinthians. He did not want them to think his refusal of monetary support was a slight of their friendship marked by brotherly love. Ironically, Paul probably considered it a mark of his love and friendship that he refused their support. In reply, rather than present a proof or argument, he appealed to God as his witness (reflecting oath formulas as in 1:18, 23; 11:10, 31; 12:2-3). The brevity of his replies in 11:10-11 and the inclusion of multiple oaths strike the reader with the sense of Paul's agitated emotions when faced with these charges.

11:12 I will continue doing what I have always done. Paul was defending his initial evangelism at Corinth (Acts 18:1-17), as well as his ongoing work, against charges made by the Jewish representatives from Jerusalem.

11:13 These people are false apostles. This explains why their message was to be refused (11:4). Paul's apostleship was valid, but not that of those "who claim to be believers but are not" (11:26; NLT mg, "false brothers"). The parallel in Gal 1:7-9 should be compared.

disguise themselves. Gr., *metaschēmatizō* [TG3345, ZG3571] (to change appearance). The same verb is used in the next two verses (see notes).

11:14 Satan disguises himself as an angel of light. The verb in Greek means "to change appearance" (*metaschēmatizō* [TG3345, ZG3571]). Satan did this to deceive Eve (11:3; 1 Tim 2:14). There is no allusion to this transformation in Genesis; it seems to belong to a tradition that Paul knew and that later found a place in the Jewish writing called *The Life of Adam and Eve,* where Satan changed himself into the shining form of an angel and then spoke to Eve (*Life of Adam and Eve* 9:1). For more on Satan, see note on 2:11. For the rhetorical force of this concept, see L. A. Johnson 1999:145-155.

11:15 his servants also disguise themselves as servants of righteousness. This has the same verb (*metaschēmatizō* [TG3345, ZG3571]) as in 11:13 and 11:14. It is possible that the false apostles called themselves "servants of righteousness." If so, Paul would not accept these claims as valid (Thrall 2000:697). Paul's opponents had presented a false gospel (11:1-6). Reflecting his dualistic thought, Paul associated his opponents with Satan and himself with God (4:4; 1 Cor 7:5; Gal 1:4; 4:8-9; Col 1:13). In associating his opponents with Satan, Paul was undermining any of their claims to be working for the benefit of the Corinthian community. Such overtures were disguises rooted in satanic deception. A similar notion is found in Johannine thought: It is not enough to be filled with a spirit; rather, one should always ask *what kind* of spirit (1 John 4:1).

the punishment their wicked deeds deserve. Works are a common Jewish norm for divine reckoning (Ps 62; Prov 24:12; Acts 10:35; Jas 2:14-26; 1 John 3:7, 12, 18). Since they had done Satan's work, they would share Satan's fate (Matt 25:41, 46).

COMMENTARY

In terms of the overall flow of chapters 10–13, 11:1-15 may have a vague connection with 10:12-18 or may start a new topic with the previous verses being a digression. A more favorable choice is to consider 11:1-15 a slight digression between 10:12-18 and 11:16-33, which discuss the primary theme of the appropriate sphere of missionary service, while all sections have a common link of "boasting." In 11:1-15, Paul turned to discuss more directly the threat of rival missionaries. (See the Introduction's discussion on the identity of these opponents.)

One of the difficulties we face as we read Paul's correspondence with the churches of his day is that of not knowing precisely the background behind the language he employed. It is true that we have a good picture of the overall scene in Corinth at that time, but some smaller details remain—and perhaps must always remain—obscure to us. The present chapter, along with chapter 12, is a good illustration.

We the readers are able to sketch the character of the opponents, who are later severely reprimanded (11:13-15), by three descriptions of their work given in 11:1-6. First, we learn that their most dangerous work was that of enticing the believers away from single-hearted devotion to Christ (cf. Mark 13:22), and in attempting this they were doing the devil's work for him, as the serpent did in Eden (11:3, 14—both texts are based on Gen 3:4, 13). Second, we discover that Paul's antagonists were in error because they preached a different gospel, which centered on a different Jesus from the person of the apostolic message (11:4). It is true that Paul prefaced this statement with an "if" (not clear in NLT, but see NIV), but "he is not likely to cherish real fears on the ground of imaginary suppositions" (Strachan 1935:18); so "if" (11:4) really means "as is the case." It is difficult to be sure what this warning is intended to refer to. Was it a purely human Jesus whom the false teachers presented, or a heretical picture altogether, like the later Gnostics, who turned him into a sort of demigod? We cannot tell. More likely it is their failure to live out the servantlike character of Jesus (10:1) that was in view. Third, we learn that these men claimed the authority of the Jerusalem apostles, surnamed ironically "super apostles" (NLT) or "extra-special messengers" (Phillips). They bolstered their opposition to Paul by appealing (perhaps on their own initiative) to Peter, James, and John against him. But Paul knew of no such rivalry nor accepted any inferiority (11:5-6).

Paul found it necessary, even if distasteful, to justify himself and clarify his actions. It was needful because of the close link he claimed to have with the church (11:2), which he likened to the bride of Christ (see Eph 5:25-33). Because he cared so much for Christ's people, he was most solicitous lest they should be led astray (11:3). What agitated Paul's mind and caused him some reluctance was that he had to justify his missionary policy of refusing to accept money from the churches (11:7). The implication of this is that he had been taken to task on this score, with the innuendo that he did not claim his rightful due (see 1 Cor 9:12-14; 1 Tim 5:17; 2 Tim 2:6) because he knew in his heart that he had no apostolic standing and so no entitlement to it. So Paul took pains to go into the matter in some detail, although he had already made his position clear in 1 Corinthians 9. In effect, he reiterated the same disinterested concern to offer his service freely ("without expecting anything in return," 11:7). He did this, not because of any inferiority complex or unwillingness to receive financial help. Indeed, he had already received and grate-fully acknowledged help from the Macedonian churches (11:9), notably the Philip-pians, who had sent a gift regularly to relieve his need (Phil 4:15-19). The issue at Corinth—as at Thessalonica—turned on the significance that his enemies placed on his receiving or not receiving money. Both at Corinth and in other places (1 Thess 2:9; 2 Thess 3:8-9) Paul intentionally refrained from exercising his prerogative—and not always for the same reason (see Dodd 1953a:67-82; 1953b:83-128).

According to 11:11, Paul's refusal to accept money from the Corinthians was being used in another way by his enemies: They were accusing him of being spu-rious and therefore compelled to honestly refuse the support. Consequently, his friends at Corinth were professing to be grieved that he took this line of action, which they interpreted as a sign that he had no regard for them. This evoked Paul's heartfelt cry, "God knows that I do [love you]."

If Paul's enemies simply attacked him and sought to discredit his work, that would have been one thing; far more serious was their advocacy of a false gospel, by which they placed themselves under the judgment of Galatians 1:6-9. They pro-fessed to be able to draw upon apostolic authority for their credentials. Paul retort-ed, "'Apostles'? They are spurious apostles, false workmen—they are masquerading as 'apostles of Christ'" (11:13, Moffatt 1954). For in so doing they were emulating their leader, Satan, who himself masquerades as a messenger of God.

The lesson is clear: Appearances are deceptive. We should not be too readily impressed by the superficial attractiveness of teachers who claim to be heaven-sent messengers. The test is more rigorous and vital: What do they teach, and does their character conform to the message they bring—and do both doctrine and manner of life square with God's revelation? We recall Jesus' teaching here (Matt 7:15-23). The apostle's no less stringent criteria (2 Tim 3:10-17) are clear, as are the serious admonitions of John (1 John 4:1-5; 2 John 1:7-11).

◆ C. Paul's Many Trials (11:16-33)

[16]Again I say, don't think that I am a fool to talk like this. But even if you do, listen to me, as you would to a foolish person, while I also boast a little. [17]Such boasting is not from the Lord, but I am acting like a fool. [18]And since others boast about their human achievements, I will, too. [19]After all, you think you are so wise, but you enjoy putting up with fools! [20]You put up with it when someone enslaves you, takes every-thing you have, takes advantage of you, takes control of everything, and slaps you in the face. [21]I'm ashamed to say that we've been too "weak" to do that!

But whatever they dare to boast about—I'm talking like a fool again—I dare to boast about it, too. [22]Are they Hebrews? So am I. Are they Israelites? So am I. Are they de-scendants of Abraham? So am I. [23]Are they servants of Christ? I know I sound like a madman, but I have served him far more! I have worked harder, been put in prison more often, been whipped times without number, and faced death again and again. [24]Five different times the Jewish leaders gave me thirty-nine lashes. [25]Three times I was beaten with rods. Once I was stoned. Three times I was shipwrecked. Once I spent a whole night and a day adrift at sea. [26]I have traveled on many long journeys. I have faced danger from rivers and from robbers. I have faced danger from my own people, the Jews, as well as from the Gentiles. I have faced danger in the cities, in the deserts, and on the seas. And I have faced danger from men who claim to be believers but are not.* ²⁷I have worked hard and long, enduring many sleepless nights. I have been hungry and thirsty and have often gone without food. I have shivered in the cold, without enough clothing to keep me warm.

²⁸Then, besides all this, I have the daily burden of my concern for all the churches.

11:26 Greek *from false brothers.*

²⁹Who is weak without my feeling that weakness? Who is led astray, and I do not burn with anger?

³⁰If I must boast, I would rather boast about the things that show how weak I am. ³¹God, the Father of our Lord Jesus, who is worthy of eternal praise, knows I am not lying. ³²When I was in Damascus, the governor under King Aretas kept guards at the city gates to catch me. ³³I had to be lowered in a basket through a window in the city wall to escape from him.

NOTES

11:16 *Again I say.* This looks back to 11:1.

don't think that I am a fool. This is the opening of Paul's own "Fool's Story"—a form of rhetoric he used to ridicule his opponents' claims by adopting their stance and speaking as a "fool," whose trait is self-praise. It refers in Greek society to a person who has lost the correct measure of oneself and the world around them (Fallon 1980:92).

while I also boast a little. The tone is ironic, with Paul speaking tongue in cheek. Paul ironically rebukes his boastful opponents, who professed to be "so wise" (1 Cor 4:10), another parody of their pretensions to knowledge (*gnōsis* [TG1108, ZG1194]) and wisdom (*sophia* [TG4678, ZG5053]).

11:17 *Such boasting is not from the Lord, but I am acting like a fool.* Paul understood that it was necessary to compare his human achievements with those of his opponents in order to prevent the Corinthians from being misled. However, he was being careful not to offer a double standard. He was sure to note that such an argument was not speaking "on the Lord's authority" but in his own human foolishness. He would answer the fools, but his hope was to direct the Corinthians toward proper boasting in the Lord.

11:18 *about their human achievements.* Gr., *kata sarka* (lit., "according to the flesh"). For Paul, the "flesh" (*sarx* [TG4561, ZG4922]) is not the outward shell of a person housing the spirit, nor does it simply refer to being human or just human sinfulness. Rather, the "flesh" refers to human frailty, which causes humans to be subject to sin and, as such, is part of the world, which is the realm opposed to God (and to God's realm, i.e., that of the "spirit"). For Paul, the term "flesh" (*sarx*) tends to be negative, while the term "body" (*sōma* [TG4983, ZG5393]) is more neutral. For more, see J. D. G. Dunn 1998:62-73.

11:19 *After all, you think you are so wise, but you enjoy putting up with fools!* Paul's ironic invective continued to cut at the Corinthians' values—because the Corinthians were so adept at welcoming even the most foolish, they should be able to tolerate the fool Paul. His designation of them as "wise" (*phronimoi* [TG5429, ZG5861]) was intended in a derogatory manner (cf. 1 Cor 4:10). Paul's words caution us today in our own measurement of wisdom to be careful to distinguish between a generic tolerance and Christian inclusivity, which moves toward freedom as well as limits in light of the lordship of Christ. Paul laid the foundation for these principles in 1 Cor 8–10 (see C. N. Toney 2008).

11:20 *takes everything you have.* Lit., "eats you up." Paul's opponents were guilty of covetousness, a theme to be taken up in 12:16-18, unlike Paul, who waived the right to receive financial assistance (Barrett 1973:291).

takes advantage of you. This is a verb of violation often used with respect to sexual violation.

takes control of everything. Lit., "exalts himself." This speaks of insolence and haughtiness—unlike Paul's behavior (in 12:7, same verb).

slaps you in the face. This was a calculated insult meant to humiliate (Matt 5:39). The Mishnah (*Baba Qamma* 8:6) prescribes a heavy fine for this behavior.

11:21 *too "weak" to do that!* This is another deeply ironical remark, paving the way for Paul's self-confessed weakness in 13:3-4.

11:22 *Are they . . . ? So am I.* Paul appears to make point-by-point counterclaims to his opponents' pedigrees in 11:22-23a. Paul was not simply stating his ethnicity here—this would have been abundantly clear to both the Corinthians and his opponents—nor are these merely synonyms. Rather, this could be a dispute regarding his law-free gospel. Essentially, by not demanding nor always practicing the law, especially circumcision, food laws, or Sabbath observance (e.g., Rom 14:5-6, 14; 1 Cor 9:21; Gal 4:9-11; 5:6; 6:15), Paul did not seem like a Jew. Paul was not willing to enter into a debate regarding these identity markers, because he wanted to focus his identity on the fourth comparison of the series—being a servant (*diakanos* [TG1249, ZG1356]) of Christ (see 11:23). It is also interesting to note that the term "circumcision" does not appear in 2 Corinthians, which indicates that the issues his Jewish opponents brought are much different than in Galatians, where the Gentiles were expected to be circumcised (for more on the opponents, see the Introduction, "Opponents").

Hebrews. This term (cf. Acts 6:1; Phil 3:5) may refer to a speaker of Hebrew, a pure-blood Jew, or a Palestinian Jew. Paul's opponents may have discredited him for being a Hellenistic Jew from Tarsus or for not living in Palestine, thereby not having an earthly knowledge of Jesus and diminishing his apostolic authority.

Israelites. The designation refers to the social and religious distinction provided by a national identity (cf. John 1:47; Rom 9:4; 11:1; Gal 6:16). In salvation history, his opponents may be privileging Israel over the nations (i.e., Gentiles) in God's salvific plans (Isa 2:2-3; 56:6-8; Jer 3:17; Zech 8:20-22; 14:6-21; cf. Tob 14:6-7).

descendants of Abraham. Lit., "seed (*sperma* [TG4690, ZG5065]) of Abraham," which may be an honorific title that Paul's opponents used. It may recall an ongoing debate Paul had with Jewish Christians regarding the true heirs of Abraham. In Gal 3:16, Paul cited Gen 12:7, interpreting the "seed" of Abraham to be Christ, thus cutting out any claims for Jewish priority or law observance. In Rom 4:18, Paul cited Gen 15:5, interpreting the "seed" more broadly to be anyone having faith. In both cases, Paul placed priority on a person's identity in Christ as a mark of being a true heir of Abraham.

11:23 *Are they servants of Christ? . . . I have served him far more!* Paul broke the rhetorical pattern of "so am I" (*kagō* [TG2504, ZG2743]) found in 11:22 with "far more [am] I" (*huper egō* [TG5228 /1473, ZG5642/1609]), meaning, "I am a better servant." Paul was not willing to grant that his opponents were also servants (*diakanoi* [TG1249, ZG1356]) of Christ—Corinth was his missionary field, not theirs. If this was so, then these opponents were clearly not any of the Twelve. The title of servant was, for Paul, the paramount identity marker as indicated by his expansion on only this final title.

worked harder, been put in prison more often, been whipped times without number, and faced death again and again. This list parallels Paul's previous list of sufferings (6:4b-5, 8-10), which identify him as a "servant of God"; now, he is a "servant of Christ" (for other lists of sufferings see 4:8-9; 12:10; cf. Rom 8:35-39; 1 Cor 4:9-13; Phil 4:11-12). Overall, there are 26 catalogued items proving his superiority as Christ's servant—four acts of increasing exposure in v. 23, a list of five "times" in vv. 24-25, eight dangers in v. 26, six hardships in v. 27, and three acts of sympathy in vv. 28-29 (Harris 2005:789-815). This first group ("worked harder," "prison," "whipped," "faced death") is in ascending order of danger. Some, but not all, of Paul's prison (*phulakē* [TG5438, ZG5871]) experiences are recalled in 1:8-10; Acts 16:23-40; Rom 16:3-7; 1 Cor 15:32. *First Clement* 5:6 mentions Paul's being in chains seven times. For a consideration of the data, see R. Martin 1981:26-32. Paul hyperbolically described his *plēgai* [TG4127, ZG4435] (his "blows," "beatings," or "floggings") as beyond measure. In Gal 6:17 Paul asked his audience to remember the marks on his body. "Faced death again and again" suggests Paul was in constant exposure to threats, a theme throughout 2 Corinthians (1:9-10; 4:11; 6:9; cf. Rom 8:36; 1 Cor 15:32). While Paul was slighted as an apostle of weakness, he considered these hardships to be true marks of being a servant of Christ.

11:24 *thirty-nine lashes.* This was the Jewish punishment for breaking the Torah (*m. Makkot* 3:10, on the basis of Deut 25:2-3). The locations where Paul received these lashings are unknown, and none are mentioned in Acts. The reason for punishment may have been that Paul did not strictly observe the law (e.g., breaking the Sabbath, not following food laws, downplaying the role of Torah) or inclusion of Gentiles without prerequisites (e.g., not requiring circumcision), or it may have been for the blasphemy of declaring Jesus as Lord (since only Yahweh is Lord; cf. Acts 22:19; 26:11; *m. Makkot* 3:15). (For more on the implications of Jesus as Lord, see note on 4:5.) Paul's opponents valued battle scars of victory and the triumph of Christ, not those of beatings, and derided Paul's scars and his stress on the cross of Christ (Glancy 2004:99-135).

11:25 *beaten with rods.* This was a Roman penalty. In Philippi (Acts 16:22), Paul was beaten as a public warning. Usually, Roman citizens were exempt (Acts 16:37-38), but beatings did sometimes occur in the provinces (Cicero *In Verrem* 5.62-66; Josephus *War* 2.308). Lictors (Latin, *lictores;* lit., "rod-carriers," *rhabdouchoi* [TG4465, ZG4812]), who attended Roman magistrates, carried bundles with an axe and elm or birch rods to signify the ruler's right to inflict corporal or capital punishment (Harris 2005:803).

I was stoned. Paul experienced this in Lystra, which nearly cost him his life (Acts 14:5, 19). Stoning was a Jewish capital punishment for apostates, blasphemers, and adulterers (Deut 17:5; 22:22-24; *m. Sanhedrin* 7:56-60).

Three times I was shipwrecked. Here he speaks of incidents unknown to us, since what happened en route to Malta (Acts 27) was yet in the future at the time of writing. The dangers of sailing were well-known in the ancient world (e.g., Homer's *Odyssey;* Virgil's *Aeneid*). P. E. Hughes (1962:411) notes that Acts mentions at least nine voyages prior to this letter, and Harris (2005:804) adds the "painful visit" as a tenth (1:16; 2:1).

11:26 *men who claim to be believers but are not.* Lit., "false brothers" (*pseudadelphoi* [TG5569, ZG6012], as in Gal 2:4). Such persons were not only Paul's opponents but Satan's agents (11:13-15). Thrall (2000:722, 742-743) classifies Paul's list of eight dangers as two pairs (rivers-bandits, Jews-Gentiles), a triplet (city-desert-sea), and a climax (among pseudo-Christians).

11:27 *worked hard and long.* This marks the first pair in an A-B-A-B-A pattern in which A is a pair of Greek words (cf. NLT, "worked hard and long," "hungry and thirsty," and "cold . . . without enough clothing") and B is a phrase bookended by the words *en . . . pollakis* [TG4178, ZG4490] (cf. NLT, "many sleepless nights" and "often . . . without food"). As a whole, the pattern catalogues what Paul lacked in his missionary activities.

sleepless nights. Lit., "wakefulness" or "inability to sleep." These came either through voluntary vigils or, more likely, from necessity (Acts 16:25).

gone without food. This poses the same choice of voluntary fasting (Barrett 1973:300) or hunger (Windisch 1924:359).

shivered in the cold. This would befall Paul at Malta (Acts 28:2).

11:28 *the daily burden of my concern.* NLT renders *epistasis* [TG1987.1, ZG2180] ("attention" or "care") as the burden of oversight which lay upon the apostle; it is virtually synonymous with *merimna* [TG3308, ZG3533], an emotional word for "anxiety" (1 Cor 7:32-34; 12:25; Phil 2:20; 4:6; cf. 1 Pet 5:7), usually a human weakness but occasionally a rightful concern for others' needs, as here.

11:29 *Who is weak without my feeling that weakness?* The key words are "weak" and "weakness" (*astheneō* [TG770, ZG820]) in the "Fool's Speech" (11:21a, 30; 12:5, 9-10). It means either physical sickness or the religious sense of a sensitive conscience or an innate inability to lead within the congregation. In whatever sense, Paul shared it as part of his pastoral care.

led astray. Paul knew that the Corinthians had been led astray by the interlopers (11:2-3).

11:30 *If I must boast.* Now comes a sudden switch to a piece of Paul's history. To prove his weakness, he told of his unceremonious exit from Damascus in a fish basket down the city walls (Acts 9:23-25), probably in AD 39–40 (Barrett 1973:304; P. E. Hughes 1962:424-428). This event, which happened within two years of his conversion, was the first opposition Paul met, leaving an indelible impression on him.

11:31 *God, the Father of our Lord Jesus, who is worthy of eternal praise.* Paul added to his oath (lit., "The God and Father") a Christological confession ("of the Lord Jesus"; see 4:5) as well as a Jewish eulogy—God is forever "praised" or "blessed" (*eulogētos* [TG2128, ZG2329] = Heb., *baruk* [TH1288A, ZH1385]). This oath recalls Paul's blessing in 1:3 and connects back to Paul's previous oath formula in 11:10. Again, Paul invoked God as a witness that he was speaking the truth (an issue raised also in 13:3). Paul was validating his boasting in weakness and authenticating his ministry.

I am not lying. The *pseud*-verb, *ou pseudomai* (I am not lying), contrasts Paul, God's truthful servant, with the *pseud*-noun, *pseudapostoloi* [TG5570, ZG6013] (false apostles), Satan's deceptive servants, of 11:13-15.

11:32 *King Aretas.* R. Riesner (1998:75-89) concludes that Paul must have fled Damascus before the death of King Aretas IV in AD 40. He was the father-in-law of Herod Antipas (who divorced Aretas's daughter to marry Herodias [Mark 6:17-18]). In addition to Paul's appearance before Gallio (Acts 18:12-17), who was in office in AD 51–52 (see Introduction), this flight is one of the anchors of Pauline chronological reconstructions.

11:33 *I had to be lowered in a basket through a window.* A *sarganē* [TG4553, ZG4914] is "a net to catch fish" (K. Prümm 1960:657) or "a basket to conceal weapons under bran or wool" (F. J. A. Hort 1909:571). This is not the same word for "basket" used in Acts 9:25 (*spuris* [TG4711, ZG5083]) or Mark 6:43 (*kophinos* [TG2894, ZG3186]). E. A. Judge (1966:45) and S. H. Travis (1973:530) see Paul contrasting his own weakness with a Roman soldier's courage in scaling the walls of a city under siege, for which he would be rewarded an honor—it was called "the crown of the wall" (Latin, *corona muralis*; see Livy 23.18). A corresponding siege metaphor may be found in Prov 21:22, LXX, which says, "A wise man scales the cities of the mighty and brings down the stronghold in which the godless trust." Whichever background one sees, Paul deliberately contrasted his weakness with the exploits of the wise—they scale walls and conquer enemies, but Paul was assisted in escaping his enemies via a fish basket. This movement down the wall of the city in humility contrasted Paul's exaltation by being lifted up to the heavenly regions (12:1-4). Thus, in both humiliating defeat (11:32-33) and exaltation (12:1-4), Paul relied on Christ and boasted in the Lord (10:17-18).

COMMENTARY

More irony peeps through at 11:16, where Paul says, "Don't think that I am a fool to talk like this." As on previous occasions, the term "fool" was one which probably formed the substance of a charge brought against him. And when we remember that he includes the little term *also* ("while I also boast a little"), it seems that the pattern of boasting had already been set by the teachers themselves. Why shouldn't Paul have his turn? The statement in 11:17 is a qualification that the writer felt he must insert lest his readers should fail to catch the spirit in which he is writing. He was not boasting "after the Lord," but as a man who deliberately put himself in the place of those whose pretensions he wanted to expose.

The intruders had been conspicuously successful in the inroads they made into the Corinthian assembly. Verse 20 is a surprising statement of the way in which they had been welcomed in Corinth. The Corinthians had shown a singular lack of discernment, almost naiveté, in welcoming the false prophets with their grandiose claims and pretensions. Would they (Paul was asking) extend the same attitude to him as he played the role of a fool? They had tolerated these persons, allowing themselves to be ordered about, robbed of their money (cf. 2:17), and duped by these false teachers—even to the point of being insulted by them in a way which any Jew would regard as a most humiliating experience, a slap on the face (see Matt 5:39). Paul, in this tremendously sarcastic passage, simply asked for a hearing as he presented *his* case.

Having taken up his assumed position of foolishly boasting, Paul gave a record of his past life of service for Christ's sake and the gospel's. The true tests of apostleship, he avers, are not in loud claims and unsupported pretensions. The litmus test is found in the appellant's record of suffering, service, and sympathy with others for their good (so Rom 15:15-19; 2 Tim 2:10; 3:10-12). Paul had a notable record of his trials, and in retelling them, he reported many things that we never would have known otherwise.

Paul often used a list of trials to make it clear that he had true credentials as an apostle (already in 4:8-10; 6:4-10; see Rom 8:35-39; 1 Cor 4:10-13). He listed the ways in which his service for Jesus Christ surpassed those of his opponents: "Worked . . . put in prison . . . whipped . . . faced death" are in ascending order of severity. Paul's prison experience is often referred to in the New Testament (1:8-10; Acts 16:23-30; Rom 16:3-7; 1 Cor 15:32; and according to *1 Clement* 5:6, Paul was in chains seven times). Added to the physical strain of a life of hardship (11:23-27), there was a mental and spiritual liability he carried: "my concern [lit., "anxiety"] for all the churches" (11:28). And no church gave him more anxiety than Corinth! Finally, he added the ever-pressing and exacting responsibility of the care of souls, looking for the opportunity to help others in distress, entering sympathetically into their deep need and sharing something of their travail (11:29).

As a postscript, he added a personal account of the Damascus episode of Acts 9:23-25. We might ask why this event was put last, when it seems trivial in contrast with the hair-raising experiences and hazards of 11:23-27. One possible solution is that Paul's objectors had fastened on this incident, distorted it, and turned it into an accusation of a cowardly escape from Damascus. More likely, however, is the view that Paul singled out this experience because it was his first trial for the sake of Christ after his conversion and therefore left an ineffaceable impression on Paul's thinking.

◆   ## D. Paul's Vision and Weakness (12:1-10)

This boasting will do no good, but I must go on. I will reluctantly tell about visions and revelations from the Lord. ²I* was caught up to the third heaven fourteen years ago. Whether I was in my body or out of my body, I don't know—only God knows. ³Yes, only God knows whether I was in my body or outside my body. But I do know ⁴that I was caught up* to paradise and heard things so astounding that they cannot be expressed in words, things no human is allowed to tell.

⁵That experience is worth boasting about, but I'm not going to do it. I will boast only about my weaknesses. ⁶If I wanted to boast, I would be no fool in doing so, because I would be telling the truth. But I won't do it, because I don't want anyone to give me credit beyond what they can see in my life or hear in my message, ⁷even though I have received such wonderful revelations from God. So to keep me from becoming proud, I was given a thorn in my flesh, a messenger from Satan to torment me and keep me from becoming proud.

⁸Three different times I begged the Lord to take it away. ⁹Each time he said, "My grace is all you need. My power works best in weakness." So now I am glad to boast about my weaknesses, so that the power of Christ can work through me. ¹⁰That's why I take pleasure in my weaknesses, and in the insults, hardships, persecutions, and troubles that I suffer for Christ. For when I am weak, then I am strong.

12:2 Greek *I know a man in Christ who.*   12:3-4 Greek *But I know such a man,* ⁴*that he was caught up.*

NOTES

12:1 *This boasting will do no good.* Paul's "boasting" was a necessity, driven by his opponents' insistence that theirs was the true ministry and Paul's weakness was a deficit.

reluctantly. Lit., "though it is no advantage." Because Paul thought his boasting would not edify the church, he was reluctant to boast (cf. 1 Cor 6:12; 10:23; 12:7).

visions and revelations from the Lord. These experiences are not the same as those recorded in Acts 18:9-10; 22:17-21; 23:11; 27:23-24. They were experiences that could be dated "fourteen years ago" (12:2), which would have been around AD 40 (Barrett 1973:308). Others date it somewhere in the period AD 41–44 (Lincoln 1981:77).

12:2 *I was caught up.* The Greek is more ambiguous: "I know a man who was caught up." M. D. Goulder (2003:303-312) argues that this is not autobiographical. However, most scholars (as reflected in NLT) consider this to be autobiographical. Paul wrote as a narrator adopting the role of a protagonist in the third-person singular. For more on the "third heaven," see comments on 12:4.

in my body or out of my body. Paul viewed his experience at a distance, as though he were an onlooker. He was at a loss to describe its real nature.

12:3 *Yes, only God knows whether I was in my body or outside my body. But I do know.* This verse either repeats or parallels the event in the previous verse with only a few minor changes in the Greek order and words. "I know a man *in Christ* . . ." // "I know *this* man" and "whether in the body *I don't know* or *out of* (*ektos* [TG1622A, ZG1760]) the body, I don't know, but God knows" // "whether in the body or *apart from* (*chōris* [TG5565, ZG6006]) the body, I don't know, but God knows." The NLT has chosen to add the "Yes" to signify an emphatic parallel.

12:4 *caught up to paradise.* Gr. *paradeisos* [TG3857, ZG4137] is probably a Persian loan word originally referring to a park or garden (Neh 2:8; Eccl 2:5; Song 4:13). In the LXX, it is used for the Garden of Eden (e.g., Gen 2:8-10, 15-16, LXX). In Jewish literature, it became a resting place for the dead (*1 Enoch* 60:8; *2 Enoch* 8–9; *2 Baruch* 51:3). This paradise is "the third heaven" mentioned in 12:2. Jewish scholars taught that there are several heavens, with "paradise" (lit., "a park") being the equivalent of God's presence (so *2 Enoch* 8; *Apocalypse of Moses* 37:5; see TDNT 5.765-773). For more on paradise in Jewish thought, see J. F. Maile 1993:381-383. Paul evidently thought he had passed through two heavens to attain paradise. See Rev 2:7, which describes paradise as a garden, based on Eden (see Thrall 2000:792-793). P. E. Hughes (1962:432-434) considers the background of three-heaven division (atmospheric, stellar/firmament, and spiritual/limitless, where God is located) to be the OT (1 Kgs 8:27; 2 Chr 2:6; 6:18; Neh 9:6; Ps 148:4). A sevenfold division was also popular (*Testament of Levi* 3:1; *2 Enoch* 20:1; *Ascension of Isaiah* 9), but also five (*3 Baruch* 11:1) and ten (*2 Enoch* 20:3b). The NT sometimes uses the plural "heavens" (*ouranoi* [TG3772, ZG4041]), which is probably a result of the Heb. *shamayim* [TH8064, ZH9028], which is dual in form. For an alternative view, P. R. Gooder (2001:190-211) argues that this was a failed heavenly ascent by Paul, which parallels his defeat at Damascus (11:30-32)—he was opposed by King Aretas, a human agent, and a demonic agent (linked with Isa 14:12-15 and Ezek 28:13).

things so astounding. Lit., "unspeakable words." Though the idea of a secret revelation is a feature of later Gnostic religions, it is also found in the OT (Isa 8:16; Dan 12:4; cf. *2 Enoch* 17) and in the later NT (Rev 14:3).

12:5 *That experience is worth boasting about, but I'm not going to do it.* In spite of his giftedness with such a revelation, Paul would not boast of it.

I will boast only about my weaknesses. Now, Paul began to speak directly of himself. If he was to boast, it would be of his limitations as a human being. Here, we become aware that this "other man" in 12:1-10 is Paul.

12:6 *If I wanted to boast, I would be no fool in doing so, because I would be telling the truth. But I won't do it.* Speaking the truth is a polemic stance against his opponents, whom Paul considered to be liars. Paul acknowledged that he could keep telling visionary stories ("I could relate more experiences like that" [Bultmann 1976:225]) because they were true (although subjective and therefore unverifiable), but telling those stories was not beneficial. They resulted in self-promotion, which is foolishness. Rather, Paul's principle was to boast in the Lord, so he would talk about his tangible acts of ministry (open to the judgment of all).

give me credit. Gr., *logizomai* [TG3049A, ZG3357] (reckon, consider) is a slogan in 2 Corinthians (10:2, 7, 11; 11:5; 12:6) and may relate to commercial accounting (relevant for a commercial city like Corinth). Paul knew that some Corinthians would accept his word that he received a vision, but Paul urged his audience instead to focus on his ministry and gospel. Too much praise of visions interfered with the gospel, the very thing Paul accused his opponents of doing. In addition, Paul considered his mission and gospel to display his own weakness and the power of Christ.

12:7 *I was given.* Gr., *edothē moi* [TG1325, ZG1443] (there was given me [by God]). This construction is called a divine passive, where the action is attributed to God.

a thorn in my flesh. Two questions are raised: What does "my flesh" mean? What was the "thorn"? The Greek behind "flesh" is *sarx* [TG4561, ZG4922], which has several meanings in

Paul's writings. It can stand for his bodily existence, or it is Paul's way of expressing his sinful self. Most commentators see the first meaning here. Paul endured some physical liability, such as illness. Yet the second sense may be in mind (so Tasker 1958:174), implying that the limitation was intended to prick the bubble of pride and keep him humble. The term "thorn" (*skolops* [TG4647, ZG5022]), found in the OT (Num 33:55; Ezek 28:24; Hos 2:6, LXX), means something causing pain, like a splinter in the flesh (Bruce 1978:248). See commentary below for further discussion as well as G. H. Twelftree 1993:379 and J. C. Thomas 1996:39-52.

12:8 Three different times I begged the Lord. "The Lord" is Christ, since it was Christ's power that came to him. Prayers to the risen Lord are remarkable for a former Pharisee who confessed the unity of God (Deut 6:4). The number "three" may denote an urgency and persistence in prayer.

12:9 My grace is all you need. "This divine gift is perpetually sufficient, good for his whole life" (Plummer 1915:354).

My power works best in weakness. NLT renders the verb *teleō* [TG5055, ZG5464] (to fulfill, to perfect) as "works best."

the power of Christ can work through me. Lit., "The power of Christ may shelter over me." The Greek verb *episkēnoō* [TG1981, ZG2172] denotes "sheltering" or "resting," as when the presence of God rested on the Tabernacle and then the first Temple. Christ is here likened to the glory of God coming to indwell human lives as he lives in them (John 1:14; Rev 7:14; 12:12; 13:6; 21:3).

12:10 That's why I take pleasure in my weaknesses. This is the last list of Paul's sufferings in 2 Corinthians (4:8-9; 6:4b-5, 8-10; 11:23-28; 12:10; cf. Rom 8:35-39; 1 Cor 4:9-13; Phil 4:11-12). All his hardships and pains suffered as an apostle had a noble purpose, so that he could say, "I take pleasure" in them, not in a macho sense but in the sense that only as he recognized his weakness could he appreciate the strength Christ gives.

For when I am weak, then I am strong. Paul climaxed this section with a paradoxical saying. The best illustration of this is in 4:7: "We ourselves are like fragile clay jars. . . . This makes it clear that our great power is from God, not from ourselves." In light of Paul's power struggle in Corinth, Paul understood that human weakness, not strength, was the necessary prerequisite for God's vastly superior strength to flow through a person. Ironically, a person depending upon his or her own strength was "weak" because they lacked God's power. Whenever Paul claims to have strength, it is God's, not his own. For more on Paul's understanding of strength and weakness, see C. N. Toney 2008:74-89.

COMMENTARY
There was one more charge Paul's accusers at Corinth had to level against his right to be called an apostle, and correspondingly Paul had one further need to boast (12:1) by way of self-justification. Paul's defamers, no doubt, taxed him with deficient spiritual experience, insinuating that he was lacking in experiences of a mystical nature, "visions and revelations from the Lord" (12:1). By contrast, he was a plain, prosaic man, they would assert (see 11:6).

Paul, therefore, felt compelled to reveal his inner heart, speaking of himself as "a man in Christ" (12:2, NLT mg). He related a datable experience in which he was transported in an ecstasy to the presence of God. There he "heard" indescribable words in the sense that no human language can adequately convey the experience of the divine presence. Such an elation of spiritual experience may very well have proved an invaluable and unanswerable debating point, giving evidence that his apostleship carried a credential which none of his rivals could challenge. But strangely Paul goes on straightaway to renounce any confidence he may have placed in this type of authorization (12:5-6). He never made mystical experience a ground of claiming apostolic authority. To his opponents such experiences would have been remarkable accomplishments, giving to their status and teaching an added authority and impressive kudos. Paul placed no such value on ecstatic experience, nor did he imply that he was nearer to God then—when caught up into paradise—than at other times under normal conditions. This is an important observation, which should set us on our guard against all forms of mysticism and exceptional experiences that are made the basis for some claim in any matter of Christian doctrine or practice. We do not deny that God may visit us or other believers in special ways; but all subjective experience must be tested by fixed objective standards.

Paul would not boast of his rapturous fellowship with the Eternal; rather, he would speak freely of his weaknesses (12:5), telling his readers how he suffered a "thorn in my flesh" (12:7). This is a curious phrase admitting of at least two meanings. It is clear that (1) it was inherently evil as coming from Satan's emissary; and (2) it came to him as an affliction. But just what was this thorn? There are a plethora of different interpretations (a history of the different views is provided in P. E. Hughes 1962:443-446), ranging from a pain in the ear or head, or weak eyesight (Gal 4:13; 6:11), or an attack of epilepsy (Lightfoot 1880), or malaria (Alexander 1904:469-473, 545-548; a theory used in W. M. Ramsay 1908:94-97). More recently it has been proposed that the thorn was the rejection of Paul's gospel by his own compatriots, the Jews who caused him distress (Menoud 1953:169; cf. Rom 9-11), or the person at Corinth who insulted him (2:5-11; 7:12), or his opponents (as in 11:13-15) at Corinth who mocked his speech (10:10; Bieder 1961:319-333). The truth is, we cannot tell. We may take this to be providential concealment, so that all who suffer for Christ may find Paul as their companion. Whatever the affliction was, we know it was allowed by God and inspired as a "messenger of Satan."

Some definite handicap which restricted Paul's missionary service is evidently in view, so much so that he prayed repeatedly for its removal. The answer that came was a paradoxical one: The thorn remained, but its sting was drawn, and its limiting purpose (so designed by Satan) was turned to good effect. The bane became a blessing; and we may say that through God's "No," Paul learned God's "Yes."

The positive value of the thorn remaining in Paul's life was threefold: (1) By this satanically inspired attack (cf. 2:11), God's purpose was achieved in keeping his servant in humble dependence on him. "To keep me from becoming proud" (12:7) is perhaps the key phrase. Paul learned humility by enduring a crippling weakness that reminded him always of his frailty and finitude. (2) Because God denied Paul's request to remove the thorn (12:9), Paul came to experience Christ's presence and power in a new way. In a hard school of discipline and suffering Paul learned lessons of trust and dependence on God's strength, which presumably he could never have known without the restricting presence of some weakness. As only the self-confessed ignorant can really be taught, so only those who know their need find Christ to be the fullness of God. (3) Many scholars, led by Sir William Ramsay, have found in this reference an indication that Paul was a sick man, attacked often by malarial fever. They say this explains his short stay in the lowlands and unhealthy climate of Pamphylia (Acts 13:13) and his swift journey, beyond the Taurus Mountains, to the more bracing regions of Galatia. Galatians 4:13-14 would confirm this view and illustrate the truth that illness, instead of closing a door on service for Christ, actually prompted Paul to venture forth and claim the Galatian towns for the gospel.

◆   ## E. Paul's Defense of His Apostleship (12:11-21)

[11]You have made me act like a fool— boasting like this.* You ought to be writing commendations for me, for I am not at all inferior to these "super apostles," even though I am nothing at all. [12]When I was with you, I certainly gave you proof that I am an apostle. For I patiently did many signs and wonders and miracles among you. [13]The only thing I failed to do, which I do in the other churches, was to become a financial burden to you. Please forgive me for this wrong!

[14]Now I am coming to you for the third time, and I will not be a burden to you. I don't want what you have—I want you. After all, children don't provide for their parents. Rather, parents provide for their children. [15]I will gladly spend myself and all I have for you, even though it seems that the more I love you, the less you love me.

[16]Some of you admit I was not a burden to you. But others still think I was sneaky and took advantage of you by trickery.

[17]But how? Did any of the men I sent to you take advantage of you? [18]When I urged Titus to visit you and sent our other brother with him, did Titus take advantage of you? No! For we have the same spirit and walk in each other's steps, doing things the same way.

[19]Perhaps you think we're saying these things just to defend ourselves. No, we tell you this as Christ's servants, and with God as our witness. Everything we do, dear friends, is to strengthen you. [20]For I am afraid that when I come I won't like what I find, and you won't like my response. I am afraid that I will find quarreling, jealousy, anger, selfishness, slander, gossip, arrogance, and disorderly behavior. [21]Yes, I am afraid that when I come again, God will humble me in your presence. And I will be grieved because many of you have not given up your old sins. You have not repented of your impurity, sexual immorality, and eagerness for lustful pleasure.

12:11 Some manuscripts do not include *boasting like this.*

NOTES

12:11 *You ought to be writing commendations for me.* Letters of recommendation (see Acts 18:27) were valued in the early church, and the Corinthians set great importance on them (3:1-3). Here Paul turns the tables and, comically, seeks the approval of the Corinthians.

super apostles. See 11:5. This designation evidently refers to Peter, James (the brother of Jesus), and John, the "pillar" apostles (Gal 2:9) whose authority the false apostles (11:13) were claiming to have received. See "Opponents" in the Introduction.

12:12 *I patiently did many signs and wonders and miracles among you.* This remark interprets Paul's statement about the "signs" (*sēmeia* [TG4592, ZG4956]) of true apostleship, though the term is evidently being used in two different ways in this verse ("proof" and "signs"). The issue is one of having valid proof or the marks of one called and commissioned by God. The Corinthians were impressed by what they regarded as true credentials:

"signs and wonders and miracles among you." Paul added that he had these (see Rom 15:19), but above all they needed to be aware of the spirit in which such a ministry was exercised, namely, "patiently," lit., "with persistence" (*hupomonē* [TG5281, ZG5705]). This relates to his refusal to give up on the wayward Corinthians.

12:13 *financial burden.* This was a touchy matter at Corinth, not the least because the intruders made a point of insisting on their right to be paid by the congregation (see 11:20), and Paul did not (1 Cor 9).

Please forgive me for this wrong! Paul was speaking ironically.

12:14 *coming to you for the third time.* As Paul announces a forthcoming visit, it is clear that he had already visited the church since his first mission recorded in Acts 18. This phrase is clear evidence of an intermediate visit. In 1 Cor 16:5-7, we see Paul promising a "second" visit after going to Macedonia, which Paul decided to "double" (according to 1:15-16) by adding an "intermediate" visit before going to Macedonia. Unfortunately, this "intermediate" visit was "painful" (2:1), so Paul canceled his "second" visit and wrote chs 1-9. However, with a new crisis in Corinth, Paul now intended to make a "third" visit (on this counting, the "intermediate" visit is number two) after writing chs 10-13. For more on the chronology of Paul's visits, see the Introduction.

I don't want what you have—I want you. His return to Corinth was to reclaim the only prize he desired, namely, the Corinthians and their loyalty—"not yours, but you" (Denney 1900:365). Paul had "not sought after their goods, but themselves, that is their good" (Héring 1967:96). Rather than expecting support from them, he, their spiritual father (1 Cor 4:15), would provide for them, as parents do for their children. Philo calls this "a natural law" (*Life of Moses* 2.245), though it says nothing about care of parents in their old age (Windisch 1924:399-400).

12:15 *I will gladly spend myself and all I have for you.* While the surrounding context concerned money, Paul sprang beyond money to also include himself, declaring what he would spend. The NLT merges the two verbs for spending (*dapanēsō* [TG1159, ZG1251] and *ekdapanēthēsomai* [TG1550, ZG1682]) into one English verb, "will spend," which helpfully smoothes the sentence out for an English reader. Each verb has a slightly different force. Paul "will spend all I have" (*dapanēsō*), that is, any resource he had (his money, time, energy, and love for the church), and he "will be spent" (NLT, "will spend myself"; Gr., *ekadapanēthēsomai*)—a future passive indicating that he would utterly sacrifice himself (his energy, health, reputation, affections—anything!).

even though it seems that the more I love you, the less you love me. This answers the charge of being loveless in 11:11. Paul's fear was that he would come to Corinth a third time, expend his resources, and not be well received, but he was willing to take the risk. The NLT makes this clause a statement (as in KJV), while others favor this clause as a question (NIV, NRSV, NASB, NEB, ESV), making the force of the clause a bit less blunt. We must remember that Greek writing did not have the convenience of punctuation, and either construction is permissible in the Greek.

12:16 *others still think I was sneaky.* Continuing in an ironical tone, Paul denied that he deceived the Corinthians. The Greek for "sneaky" is *panourgos* [TG3835, ZG4112], used previously in 4:2. Titus's mission (8:20-21) and that of "another brother" (8:18, 22) were under suspicion as the Corinthians reflected on it.

took advantage of you by trickery. Paul defended both his colleagues against this allegation. There is an element of circularity in Paul's writing. He appealed to Titus to prove his own integrity, then defended Titus's integrity by linking it with his own. Both men share "the same spirit" of honesty in their dealings (12:17-18).

12:17 But how? Did any of the men I sent to you take advantage of you? In Greek, all of 12:17 is the first of a series of four rhetorical questions in two sets in 12:17-18, of which the last two (12:18) are made into a statement by the NLT to reflect the positive conclusion that Paul expects from these questions. The first set looks to the example of others and expects a negative answer—(1) Did my emissaries defraud you? (2) Did Titus? The second set applies to Paul and expects a positive answer—(3) Do we have the same spirit? (4) The same walk? Key to these verses is a defense against fraud; Paul used the verb "take advantage" (*pleonekteō* [TG4122, ZG4430]) in 2:11; 7:2; 12:17, 18. In 2:11, it was Satan who must be guarded against defrauding the church. In 7:2, Paul urged the Corinthians to accept him as someone who had not defrauded anyone. In chs 8–9 Paul went to great lengths to guard against suspicion of his collection (cf. 8:20-21).

12:18 When I urged Titus to visit you and sent our other brother with him, did Titus take advantage of you? Paul raises Titus as an example because his multiple visits made him familiar and his integrity was apparently undisputed, so Paul becomes innocent by association. Titus's visits are documented in 2:12-13; 7:7-15 (Titus delivered the severe letter), 8:6a (Titus started the collection [which may be the same trip as the "severe letter"]), and 8:16-24 (Titus seeks to complete the collection). The start of the collection as mentioned in 8:6a is the most likely time when issues of being taken advantage of would arise. The collection is also mentioned in 8:16-24, but Titus is accompanied by multiple brothers, while this verse mentions one.

For we have the same spirit and walk in each other's steps. Lit., "Did we not walk in the same spirit? [Did we not walk] in the same footprints?" "Walking" (*peripateō* [TG4043, ZG4344] = Heb., *halak* [TH1980, ZH2143]) carries the encompassing ethical sense of one's entire lifestyle (e.g., Prov 15:21; Isa 30:21; Mal 2:6). Later rabbinic midrash ("interpretation") had two categories: (1) Halakhah (noun from the verb "to walk")—legal interpretation intended to flesh out laws by creating a lifestyle that avoided possible violation of law; (2) Haggadah (noun from the verb "to tell")—homiletical interpretation intended to fill in the gaps and answer discrepancies in Scripture. In a letter that recalls and defends so much of Paul's missionary travels as well as his emissaries, the travel imagery of "walking" and "footprints" (cf. Rom 4:12; 1 Pet 2:21) defending all of Paul's activities is quite appropriate! While *pneuma* [TG4151, ZG4460] could refer to the Holy Spirit (cf. Gal 5:16), making walking by the Spirit an ethical imperative (Fee 1994:357-359), the parallel with "footprints" points to understanding this "spirit" to mean having the same mind-set or attitude. See also Paul's statement of walking by faith in 5:7.

12:19 Perhaps you think we're saying these things just to defend ourselves. Paul's defense was not simply on personal grounds.

to strengthen you. Lit., "for your building up" (Gr., *oikodomē* [TG3619, ZG3869]). This term is also found in 10:8; 13:10 (cf. 1 Cor 3:9; 8:1, 10; 10:23; 14:3-5, 12, 17, 26). To build up the congregation was Paul's chief task as an apostle (Barrett 1973:328) for which he received authority from the Lord (13:10). In connection with 13:10, Paul had received authority from God to upbuild the Corinthian church. Unfortunately, sometimes this upbuilding may come in the form of harshness, or, more properly, stern love. The aim of Paul's self-defense was not personal justification; rather, it was to edify the Corinthians. Paul did not want them to reject his apostleship or gospel because he believed that in doing so they would reject God. The classic study on "upbuilding" is by I. R. Kitzberger (1986:117-138), who puts the thrust of this verse as "Not I, but you!" (1986:129).

12:20 For I am afraid that when I come I won't like what I find, and you won't like my response. In the past, Paul's physical presence had not been aggressive (10:1). While Paul previously chided the church through the "severe letter," he allowed them to discipline the offender (2:5-11; 7:8-12). With the intrusion of the false teachers (11:4, 19), the positive results of the severe letter were reversed, which necessitated the composition of chs 10–13. Paul's tactics were becoming increasingly forceful. (This slower progression toward force reveals a more tactful side of Paul, which is not always seen; compare Galatians, where Paul immediately opens with a more aggressive response [especially Gal 5:12].) The "for" (*gar* [TG1063, ZG1142]) connects this verse with 12:19, indicating that the purpose of this potential discipline is the building up of the Corinthians. The subjunctive verb, "I might find" (*heurō* [TG2147, ZG2351]), indicates that Paul was hopeful that the matter would be settled before his arrival and this discipline would not be necessary. This option of self-correction is an underlying theme of 12:19–13:10. Paul hoped for the best but expected the worst.

I am afraid that I will find. There is no explicit verb in this clause, but the words *mē pōs* [TG3361/4458, ZG3590/4803] (lit., "not somehow") calls for an extension of what Paul was afraid to find in Corinth, which the NLT smoothes out for the English reader. The following vice list of sins reflects a divided church; those sins in 12:21b reflect immoral sexual behavior. While Paul would tailor vice lists to fit new occasions (e.g., Rom 1:29-32; 13:13; Gal 5:19-21; Col 3:8), we should remember that vice lists function more stereotypically to illustrate generally bad morals.

quarreling. That is, "strife" or "discord," (*eris* [TG2054, ZG2251]), which is the opposite of "peace" (*eirēnē* [TG1515, ZG1645]) and is found in vice lists (Rom 1:29; 13:13; Gal 5:20). Part of this discord could have been created by Paul's opponents. This may be paired with the next vice of "jealousy" (cf. 1 Cor 3:3).

jealousy. The Greek word (*zēlos* [TG2205, ZG2419]) can be positive, meaning "zealous" (7:7; 11:2), or negative, as in "envy" (cf. 1 Cor 3:3). Paul uses it in other vice lists (Rom 1:29; 13:13; Gal 5:20).

anger. Gr. *thumos* [TG2372, ZG2596] can also be rendered "rage" or "wrath," and the plural form in this text renders it "outbursts of anger." This term is found in other vice lists (Gal 5:20; Eph 4:31; Col 3:8).

selfishness. "Selfish ambition" (*eritheia* [TG2052, ZG2249]) originally referred to seeking political office for selfish reasons (Aristotle *Politics* 5, 3, 1302b, 1303a, 14). It can denote a factious or party spirit. See the vice lists (Gal 5:20; cf. Phil 1:17; 2:3). As noted in the Introduction, the Corinthians sought self-promotion, and apparently this vice crept into the church.

slander. This sin of the tongue may be paired with the next sin of "gossip." Gr. *katalalia* [TG2636, ZG2896] can mean "evil speech." And the word family is used in Rom 1:30; Jas 4:11; 1 Pet 2:1.

gossip. Gr. *psithurismos* [TG5587, ZG6030] means "whisperer" or "tale-bearer," which conveys the idea of gossip.

arrogance. Gr. *phusiōsis* [TG5450, ZG5883] means "inflated" and conveys the idea of arrogance or conceit. This sin is found throughout 1 Corinthians (1 Cor 4:6, 18, 19; 5:2; 8:1; 13:4), indicating an ingrained problem for the church.

disorderly behavior. The word *akatastasiai* [TG181, ZG189] is a composite noun suggesting social disturbances or anarchy. This self-seeking behavior could be a result of some of the previous vices and would be a result of the disturbances caused by Paul's opponents.

12:21 *I am afraid that when I come again, God will humble me in your presence.* The adverb "again" may go with the verb to "come" (so NLT) or with "humble," suggesting that Paul had previously experienced being humiliated on his second visit (2:1, 5; 7:7).

impurity. In this context *akatharsia* [TG167, ZG174] refers to sexual impurity (cf. Rom 1:24; Eph 4:19). This vice leads a triplet of vices (impurity, sexual immorality, lustful pleasure) bound together by a single article giving an overall connection to sexual misconduct. These terms also could have a connection with idolatry as well as a Jewish stereotype of immoral pagan behavior. The same triplet is found among the vice list of Gal 5:19. See also the vice list of Col 3:5.

sexual immorality. Gr. *porneia* [TG4202, ZG4518] refers to fornication or prostitution and can more broadly refer to illicit sexual activity, a problem that plagued the Corinthian congregation (1 Cor 5:1; 6:13, 18; 7:2). See this occurrence in the vice lists of Gal 5:19; Col 3:5.

lustful pleasure. Finally, Gr. *aselgeia* [TG766, ZG816] connotes lacking any moral restraint; this excessive sexual activity can be unbridled, shameless, and comparable to animals. It is included in other vice lists (Mark 7:22; Rom 13:13; 1 Pet 4:3).

COMMENTARY

In 12:11-13 Paul again reminds his readers that his writing had a distinct purpose in view—and the mood he was adopting as much as the contents of the letter were both dictated by the immediate situation at Corinth. *They* had compelled him to play the part of a braggadocio and to parade himself as though he were out of his mind with conceit and self-importance (12:11). He bragged without restraint—and all to show that the accusations leveled at him by those who were undermining the Corinthian community were without substance.

The first three verses (12:11-13) give a résumé of his case against the intruding teachers: (1) "He is nobody," they say. "Very well," Paul replies, "but I am not, on any showing, a bit inferior to the so-called 'super apostles' whose authority my enemies are laying claim to" (12:11). (2) "He is a plain, ordinary man, ungifted and undistinguished." But Paul had a ready answer: "I have the signs to accredit me as an apostle—miracles, wonders, and deeds of power, and even something more convincing still, the patience to cope with fractious people" (12:12). (3) "He doesn't really care for you Corinthians. He has neglected the church." Paul could say that this insult is without foundation and cannot be substantiated. Yet, ironically, only in one matter is it true—"The only thing I failed to do, which I do in the other churches, was to become a financial burden to you" (12:13; cf. 11:20). "Please forgive me for failing to sponge off you!" (12:13).

In 12:14-18 Paul turns to consider his future relations with the Corinthian church (12:14), holding out the promise of a third visit. This implies, as we saw earlier, an intermediate visit, referred to in 2:1 (see also Introduction). Now, as he contemplates the visit ahead, he makes it clear that what he wants is not money but the wholehearted acceptance by the church of his authority, a submission to Christ and a confidence in him (Paul), with a clearing of the air of all suspicions and mutual recriminations.

It is possible that the Corinthians still believed that Paul had deceived them with clever tricks (12:16). This insinuation maintains that Paul was astute enough not to take any money directly from them, but he shared in the proceeds for the collection that they gave to his agents, notably Titus. The answer to this is a reminder of the facts that relate to the mission of Titus and the unnamed brother of 12:18 (the same man as in 8:22?). This latter person would be a man well-known to the Corinthians who would be able to testify to Titus's honesty—and incidentally to Paul's, too. His presence would guarantee the integrity of the other Christians involved in the collection (cf. 8:6).

Earlier we took our guide from what Paul wrote at 8:21: "We are careful to be honorable before the Lord, but we also want everyone else to see that we are honorable." Both elements in this statement are important, but it came to a question of priority. Paul made it clear that his main concern was that his motives were pure in the sight of God (2 Tim 2:15). In the end it is God's approval that counts, even if others misconstrue and misrepresent (12:19). After all, the apostle had nothing personally to gain as he sought, above all, the well-being of the Corinthians.

This thought of the church's growth in grace led him to express his fear of its sorry condition at the time he wrote his earlier letter (2:3-4; 7:8, 12). In 12:20-21, as Strachan comments (1935:36), we have the fullest description of the state of affairs that called for the "tearful letter." Yet this is unlikely if chapters 10–13 were written later than chapters 1–7, as seems more probable. (See discussion on this in the Introduction.) We have here a picture of a Christian congregation that contained men and women who retained worldly ambition and who had not been purged from motives of self-seeking and moral laxity. Indeed, the word pictures conjured up by these verses make us think of professed Christians who practiced a sub-Christian morality, as sins of a bad spirit (12:20) and sins of the flesh (12:21) regrettably joined to form a composite whole.

It is small wonder, therefore, that Paul had to write so severely to them, castigating such unchristian moods and practices as are listed. A large part of his concern for the "upbuilding" (12:19; cf. 13:10) of the church required the elimination of these malpractices and the rooting out of every wrong spirit that prompted them. His great fear (12:21) was that his stern words would be misunderstood, and his authority further defied, so that again he would be humiliated before them. In place of a legitimate pride in his converts' growth in holy living, he would have only a cause for deep sorrow.

◆VIII. Warnings and a Promised Third Visit (13:1-10)

This is the third time I am coming to visit you (and as the Scriptures say, "The facts of every case must be established by the testimony of two or three witnesses"*). 2I have already warned those who had been sinning when I was there on my second visit. Now I again warn them and all others, just as I did before, that next time I will not spare them.

3I will give you all the proof you want that Christ speaks through me. Christ is not weak when he deals with you; he is powerful among you. 4Although he was crucified in weakness, he now lives by the power of God. We, too, are weak, just as Christ was, but when we deal with you we will be alive with him and will have God's power.

5Examine yourselves to see if your faith is genuine. Test yourselves. Surely you know that Jesus Christ is among you*; if not, you have failed the test of genuine faith. 6As you test yourselves, I hope you will recognize that we have not failed the test of apostolic authority.

7We pray to God that you will not do what is wrong by refusing our correction. I hope we won't need to demonstrate our authority when we arrive. Do the right thing before we come—even if that makes it look like we have failed to demonstrate our authority. ⁸For we cannot oppose the truth, but must always stand for the truth. ⁹We are glad to seem weak if it helps show that you are actually strong. We pray that you will become mature.

¹⁰I am writing this to you before I come, hoping that I won't need to deal severely with you when I do come. For I want to use the authority the Lord has given me to strengthen you, not to tear you down.

13:1 Deut 19:15.   13:5 Or *in you.*

NOTES

13:1 *third time.* This refers to the promised visit to the Corinthians (cf. 12:14), presupposing two previous visits (one described in Acts 18, the other the "painful" visit mentioned in 2:1). The third visit is that of Acts 20:2. (For more on Paul's travel plans, see Introduction and notes on 1:15-16, 23; 2:1; 12:14.)

The facts of every case must be established by the testimony of two or three witnesses. This closely follows Deut 19:15, LXX, which is similar to Matt 18:16 (see Hafemann 1998:246-257). While this idea of needing multiple witnesses is rooted in Jewish thought, there is disagreement as to Paul's meaning here. (1) Paul may be suggesting that upon his next visit, he will judge the Corinthian situation, seeking out two or three witnesses (P. E. Hughes 1962:475). However, this would be unnecessary because the sins mentioned in 12:20-21 were a matter of public record. (2) Paul's three visits may be the witnesses (Plummer 1915:372; Bruce 1978:253). Yet, it is hard to see how his first visit would indict the Corinthians. (3) Paul's previous visit and the letter of chs 10–13 may be the two witnesses (Bultmann 1976:243). (4) More likely, Paul is making a general warning (so we cannot make a specific, literal numerical connection) that when he comes, he will judge the church if necessary (Barrett 1973:333).

13:2 *Now I again warn them and all others.* There is uncertainty as to what Paul intended to do on this third visit. Some think he planned to set up a formal investigation to identify his rebellious opponents (P. E. Hughes 1962:475; Tasker 1958:188). Others note that the sins were openly known, so there was no need for an "inquisition" (Plummer 1915:372). The three visits are, therefore, the witnesses against the Corinthians (Bruce 1978:253), but the initial visit when the church was formed is hardly a witness *against* them. Probably, then, the numbers are general (Barrett 1973:333).

13:3 *proof.* Gr., *dokimē* [^{TG}1382, ^{ZG}1509], the key word in this section. Paul's apostleship had been questioned and doubted. Now he defends himself again, in spite of his weakness. The pattern is that of the crucified Jesus, who was "weak" as he died, but now "lives by the power of God" in his resurrection (13:4). The theme of power in weakness sets the model for Paul's ministry (see Savage 1996).

13:4 The first half of this verse parallels the second half to identify Paul with his Lord; this parallel is furthered with the phrases "in Christ" and "with Christ." In this section, Paul oscillates between the singular (I) and plural (we) in reference to himself.

A. Christ crucified (aorist tense) in weakness (*astheneias* [^{TG}769, ^{ZG}819]),
   B. yet (*alla* [^{TG}235, ^{ZG}247]) he is living (*zē* [^{TG}2198, ^{ZG}2409], present tense) from (*ek* [^{TG}1537, ^{ZG}1666], marking the source) God's power.
A'. Paul was weak (*astheneoumen* [^{TG}770, ^{ZG}820], present tense) *in* Christ,
   B'. yet (*alla* [^{TG}235, ^{ZG}247]) he will live (*zēsomen* [^{TG}2198, ^{ZG}2409], future tense) *with* Christ from (*ek* [^{TG}1537, ^{ZG}1666]) God's power for you.

To be weak united Paul in fellowship with Christ. Paul's past dealings as an apostle of weakness reflected Christ's coming in weakness. Paul's future dealings with the Corinthians would reflect Christ's vindication by God's power (not his own).

13:5 *Examine yourselves to see if your faith is genuine.* The NLT gives the sense of Paul's Greek, lit., "to see if you are in the faith." "In the faith" (1 Cor 16:13) means obedience to Paul's gospel (Furnish 1984:577); "genuine" is implied in the next verb, "test yourselves" (*heautous dokimazete* [TG1381, ZG1507], like *dokimē* [TG1382, ZG1509], "proof," in the previous verse). Rather than expending energy on testing Paul, the Corinthians should be testing themselves. In Paul's dualistic thought, people are either on the side of God or on the side of Satan. In rejecting Paul's apostleship and gospel, the Corinthians were rejecting God, acting in essence as unbelievers (see 6:14). For a balanced discussion of whether Paul thought some Corinthians were true believers or not, see Brown 1997:175-188 (he argues for the former).

Surely you know that Jesus Christ is among you. Other versions (see NRSV) pose this as a test question: "Do you not realize that Jesus Christ is in you" (cf. NLT mg "in you," which is better than "among you").

13:6 *As you test yourselves.* This phrase is not in the Greek, but NLT adds it to make explicit the connection of the tests in 13:5 and 13:6.

we have not failed the test of apostolic authority. If Paul were to fail this apostolic test, so would the Corinthians, the community he founded, bringing into question their Christian standing. The Corinthians had tested and accepted Paul on his first visit as well as when they received his "severe letter," and he invited them to recapitulate that test when he came again (with the same results). In proving his own apostolic authority, Paul also had disproven the authority of his opponents (see notes on 10:12-13, 18) and condemned them with associations to Satan (see notes on 11:13-15).

13:7 *not do what is wrong by refusing our correction.* Lit., "not that we appear as having passed the test." The NLT is a good paraphrase of Paul's difficult Greek. Paul was evidently regarded as having failed at Corinth because he was weak and so "non-approved" (*adokimoi* [TG96, ZG99]) in 13:5.

Do the right thing. They will do this by their repentance and adherence to Paul's message embodied in the messenger, Paul.

13:8 *For we cannot oppose the truth, but must always stand for the truth.* The "for" (*gar* [TG1063, ZG1142]) continues the thought of 13:7, and this general maxim anticipates 13:10. Whether coming in "weakness" or in God's "power," Paul demonstrated God's truth, i.e., the gospel. Again, this emphasis on truth is part of Paul's polemic against his opponents.

13:9 *that you will become mature.* Lit., "be restored," echoed in 13:11. Gr. *katartisin* [TG2676, ZG2937] means "completion" or "putting something in its proper condition" (as in Matt 4:21; Mark 1:19; NLT, "repairing").

13:10 *I want to use the authority the Lord has given me to strengthen you, not to tear you down.* Paul's authority (as in 12:19) is here claimed as a commission to be exercised "to strengthen (lit., "upbuilding"; Gr., *oikodomē* [TG3619, ZG3869]) you, not to tear you down" (see Jer 1:10). This hope of their restoration was evidently made good, given that the letter was preserved (Harris 2005:54), but the church at Corinth reverted to its old ways, as the evidence of 1 *Clement* (dated AD 96) sadly shows.

COMMENTARY

The promise and prospect of a third impending visit (12:14) are renewed in 13:1. Paul had already issued a direct and strong warning as an authoritative spokesperson of Christ about the ethical laxity of the members that had sinned. He reiterated that warning (13:2) and told them plainly that he would deal firmly with any repeated lapse of Christian moral standards.

In the opening verses there was a veiled threat of some discipline (in 13:2-3), which Paul would exercise, not in his own right or name, but simply and solely because he was the genuine messenger of Christ, who sought, as an overriding consideration, the highest welfare of the church (13:9).

Yet Paul's threat of a severe reprimand was tempered by some paradoxical thoughts (13:3b). While he was weak in himself and seemingly powerless to remedy the menacing situation at Corinth, he was endued with an authority that derived from his status as Christ's apostle—almost his personal representative. Because of this, Paul had the ability to cope with the ugly problem and to bring to bear upon it Christ's own power as head of his people. "The church is subject to Christ" (Eph 5:24, RSV) and to the apostle who represents Christ to the congregation. Yet (if we recall 1:24) this authority was exercised in no dictatorial or authoritarian fashion, as though Paul were simply imposing his own personal whims and wishes on the church. It was an authority exercised in the spirit of the crucified Christ (13:4), which will bring the Corinthians to see the folly of their ways. In other words, it is love that subdues—by turning disobedience and hostility into a glad acceptance of God's will and a willing alignment of their selfish ends to his nobler purposes for their lives. It is the message of the cross applied to a difficult and delicate situation, created by a rebellious minority at Corinth.

We are left in no doubt that Paul cherished the church's highest good—their correction (13:9), their building up (13:10), and their stability as a Christian community with the Lord at the center (13:5). The ways to achieve these exemplary ends are as follows: (1) *Self-examination* (13:5), which *may* be a painful process of self-analysis. Self-examination meant that they had to deal ruthlessly with the present condition and not refuse to face the unpleasant sight of their own sins and failures. (2) This leads to *repentance,* i.e., a confession of our past evil ways as deserving of God's judgment and a turning from them (12:21). Paul had no room for cheap grace or any easy way back to favor. Penitence—and all that is involved in a forsaking of sinful practices and tempers—is an indispensable condition to restoration and renewed fellowship. (3) The apostle's *prayers* were also a powerful force (13:7-8). Paul prayed earnestly for the Corinthians because he carried the burden of the church's good on his pastoral heart and yearned to see them in right relationship with the Lord and himself. (4) Paul was also not afraid to use *threat* (13:10)—reminding the readers that he may have to deal severely with the offenders if they do not, in his absence, set matters right. And he would have no compunction in claiming the God-given authority that he possessed as apostle to the Gentiles to ensure the church's highest well-being. (5) *Optimism* is a final factor, for Paul was irrepressibly hopeful for his churches. He had confidence that the truth is mighty and that it prevails (13:8). So, once the Corinthians perceived the truth of the appeal he made, they would accept it and act upon it. So he expected that all will be put right in the end (13:9).

◆ IX. Final Greetings (13:11-14)

¹¹Dear brothers and sisters,* I close my letter with these last words: Be joyful. Grow to maturity. Encourage each other. Live in harmony and peace. Then the God of love and peace will be with you.

¹²Greet each other with Christian love.*

¹³All of God's people here send you their greetings.

¹⁴*May the grace of the Lord Jesus Christ, the love of God, and the fellowship of the Holy Spirit be with you all.

13:11 Greek *Brothers.*   13:12 Greek *with a sacred kiss.*   13:14 Some English translations include verse 13 as part of verse 12, and then verse 14 becomes verse 13.

NOTES

13:11 *brothers and sisters.* The NLT's addition of "sisters" is permissible, since the term "brothers" (*adelphoi* [TG80, ZG81]) includes male and female church members (BDAG 18-19).

I close my letter with these last words. This is added by the NLT as a clarifying expansion of the term "farewell" (*chairete* [TG5463, ZG5897], the Greek for a closing greeting) to signal the conclusion of the letter.

Grow to maturity. This is one way to translate the verb *katartizesthe* [TG2675, ZG2936] (as in 13:9). Otherwise, it means "aim at restoration," which fits nicely with Paul's urgings for harmony as well as his wider aims of dealing with his new opponents and achieving reconciliation with the Corinthians.

Live in harmony. Lit., "Be of the same mind" (*phroneite* [TG5426, ZG5858]), a common Pauline exhortation (see Rom 12:16; 15:5; Phil 2:2, 5; 4:2). It implies a summons to adopt an attitude and an exhortation to carry that attitude into practice.

13:12 *with Christian love.* Lit., "with a sacred kiss" (NLT mg). The kiss was a common form of salutation (Rom 16:16; 1 Cor 16:20; 1 Thess 5:26; 1 Pet 5:14), especially in the worship life of the congregation (Tasker 1958:191), and later it played a role in the bishop's consecration (Hippolytus *Apostolic Tradition* 4) or the rite of baptism (*Apostolic Tradition* 21).

13:13 *God's people.* Lit., "the holy ones" or "saints," a title for all believers.

13:14 *the grace of the Lord Jesus Christ, the love of God, and the fellowship of the Holy Spirit.* Grace, love, and fellowship are ascribed respectively to the three members of the Christian Godhead: the Lord Jesus Christ, the Father, and the Holy Spirit. Christ's grace leads the believers into knowing God's love and experiencing the fellowship of the Holy Spirit. The term "fellowship" (*koinōnia* [TG2842, ZG3126]) can denote the fellowship inspired by the Spirit or fellowship with the Spirit—i.e., a common life shared with and in the Spirit (see NRSV mg). The latter is preferable (George 1953:175-177). For more on the Spirit, see R. Martin 1988:113-128.

COMMENTARY

The final section concludes Paul's appeal and contains his *adieu* (i.e., his "farewell"). Perhaps we should also add, in view of 12:14 and 13:1-2, 10, the note of *au revoir* (i.e., "until we meet again"). These final words assure the Corinthian believers of his continuing interest, and they give a call for harmony within a divided congregation. The statements "agree with one another" and "live in peace" confirm the view taken earlier that chapters 10–13 were written to a minority group within the church that had been influenced by the arrival of false teachers (11:4, 15). This prompted a final appeal for coming together in mutual consent and for unity within their ranks.

The divine blessing is promised (13:11b) to a church whose reconciliation Paul fervently anticipated. The outward token of this is expressed in the practice of the "holy kiss." Associated with early Christian worship as a mark of true unity (Rom 16:16; 1 Cor 16:20; 1 Thess 5:26; 1 Pet 5:14), this practice persisted into the later liturgical life of the church. The references to it at the close of various New Testament epistles give extra support to the belief that these epistles were intended to be read out loud in public worship services (clearly in Col 4:16; 1 Thess 5:27; and probably Rev 1:3). The reading was to be followed by the Lord's Supper. The practice of the kiss would be an act of mutual affection and confidence, implying a putting away of all disagreements between the church members in anticipation of a fresh realization of unity as they shared in a common loaf and cup (so Matt 5:23-24; 1 Cor 10:16-17).

The closing verse, a familiar apostolic benediction, provides a clear statement of New Testament Trinitarianism (cf. Matt 28:19-20), which would be called "economic Trinitarianism"—i.e., the relationships of the three persons of the Godhead are described in connection with the reception of the believers. Hence, the order is that of Christian experience. "The grace of the Lord Jesus Christ" stands first because it is by him, incarnate, crucified, and triumphant, that we come to know the Father's love (John 1:14-18; Rom 5:8-11; Heb 9:14) and to rejoice in the fellowship of the divine Spirit. The "fellowship of the Holy Spirit" may mean either the fellowship that he promotes between believers (Eph 4:3) or the individual Christian's fellowship with him as a person (John 14:17). Probably both ideas are included, with a preference for the latter.

BIBLIOGRAPHY

Alexander, W. M.
1904 St. Paul's Infirmity. *Expository Times* 15:469-473, 545-548.

Anderson, R. D.
1996 *Ancient Rhetorical Theory and Paul.* Kampen: Kok Pharos.

Barclay, J. M. G.
1992 Thessalonica and Corinth: Social Contrasts in Pauline Christianity. *Journal for the Study of the New Testament* 47:49-74.

1996 Jews in the Mediterranean Diaspora: From Alexander to Trajan (323 BCE–117 CE). Edinburgh: T&T Clark.

Barnett, Paul W.
1993 Apostle. Pp. 45-51 in *Dictionary of Paul and His Letters.* Editors, Gerald F. Hawthorne, Ralph P. Martin, and Daniel G. Reid. Downers Grove, IL: InterVarsity.

1997 *The Second Epistle to the Corinthians.* The New International Commentary on the New Testament. Grand Rapids: Eerdmans.

Barrett, C. K.
1968 *A Commentary on the First Epistle to the Corinthians.* Harper's New Testament Commentaries. New York: Harper & Row.

1969 Titus. Pp. 1-14 in *Neotestamentica et Semitica: Studies in Honor of Matthew Black.* Editors, E. Earle Ellis and Max Wilcox. Edinburgh: T&T Clark.

1970 *The Signs of an Apostle: The Cato Lecture 1969.* London: Epworth.

1973 *The Second Epistle to the Corinthians.* Harper's New Testament Commentaries. New York: Harper & Row.

1982 Paul's Opponents in 2 Corinthians. Pp. 60-86 in *Essays on Paul.* London: SPCK. Repr. from *New Testament Studies* 17 (1970–1971): 233-254.

Bauckham, Richard
1999 *Christ Crucified: Monotheism and Christology in the New Testament.* Grand Rapids: Eerdmans.

Baur, F. C.
1876 *Paul, the Apostle of Jesus Christ, His Life and Work, His Epistles and Doctrine.* 2 vols. London: Williams & Norgate.

Becker, E.
2004 *Letter Hermeneutics in 2 Corinthians.* London: T&T Clark.

Belleville, L. L.
1996 *2 Corinthians.* InterVarsity Press New Testament Commentary Series 8. Downers Grove, IL: InterVarsity.

Best, E.
1987 *Second Corinthians.* Interpretation. Atlanta: John Knox.

Betz, H. D.
1985 *2 Corinthians 8 and 9: A Commentary on Two Administrative Letters of the Apostle Paul.* Hermeneia. Philadelphia: Fortress.

Bieder, W.
1961 Paulus und seine Gegner in Korinth. *Theologische Literaturzeitung* 17:319-333.

Black, David A.
1984 *Paul, Apostle of Weakness: Astheneia and Its Cognates in the Pauline Literature.* American University Studies, Series VII, Theology and Religion, vol. 3. New York: Peter Lang.

Bowen, C. R.
1923 Paul's Collection and the Book of Acts. *Journal of Biblical Literature* 42:49-58.

Bray, G., editor
1999 *1–2 Corinthians.* Ancient Christian Commentary on Scripture 7. Downers Grove, IL: InterVarsity.

Brown, Perry C.
1997 What is the Meaning of "Examine Yourselves" in 2 Corinthians 13:5? *Bibliotheca Sacra* 154:175-188.

Bruce, F. F.
1978 *1 & 2 Corinthians*. New Century Bible Commentary. London: Marshall, Morgan & Scott.

Bultmann, Rudolf
1976 *Der zweite Brief an die Korinther*. MeyerK 6. Göttingen: Vandenhoeck & Ruprecht. Translated by
      Roy A. Harrisville as *The Second Letter to the Corinthians*. Editor, Erich Dinkler. Minneapolis: Augsburg,
      1985.

Calvin, John
1996 *The Second Epistle of Paul the Apostle to the Corinthians and the Epistles to Timothy, Titus, and
      Philemon*. Translator, T. A. Smail. Calvin's New Testament Commentaries 10. Grand Rapids: Eerdmans.

Chalke, S., and A. Mann
2003 *The Lost Message of Jesus*. Grand Rapids: Zondervan.

Collange, J. F.
1972 *Énigmes de deuxième Épître de Paul aux Corinthiens*. Cambridge: Cambridge University Press.

Comfort, P. W.
2005 *Encountering the Manuscripts: An Introduction to New Testament Paleography and Textual Criticism*.
      Nashville: Broadman & Holman.

2008 *New Testament Text and Translation Commentary*. Carol Stream, IL: Tyndale House.

Dahl, N. A.
1977 A Fragment and Its Context: 2 Cor. 6:14–7:1. Pp 62–69 in *Studies in Paul: Theology for the Early
      Christian Mission*. Editor, Nils Alstrup Dahl. Minneapolis: Augsburg.

Danker, F. W.
1989 *II Corinthians*. Augsburg Commentary on the New Testament. Minneapolis: Augsburg.

Danylak, Barry N.
2008 Tiberius Claudius Dinippus and the Food Shortages in Corinth. *Tyndale Bulletin* 59.2:231–270.

Denney, James
1900 *The Second Epistle to the Corinthians*. The Expositor's Bible. 2nd ed. New York: A. C. Armstrong & Son.

deSilva, D. A.
1998 *Credentials of an Apostle: Paul's Gospel in 2 Corinthians 1–7*. BIBAL Monograph Series 4.
      N. Richmond Hills, TX: Bibal.

DiCicco, M. M.
1995 *Paul's Use of Ethos, Pathos, and Logos in 2 Corinthians 10–13*. Mellen Biblical Press 31. Lewiston, NY:
      Mellen Biblical Press.

Dodd, C. H.
1953a The Mind of Paul: I. Pp. 67–82 in *New Testament Studies*. Manchester: The University Press.

1953b The Mind of Paul: II. Pp. 83–128 in *New Testament Studies*. Manchester: The University Press.

Downs, David J.
2006 Paul's Collection and the Book of Acts Revisited. *New Testament Studies* 52:50–70.

2008 *The Offering of the Gentiles: Paul's Collection for Jerusalem in Its Chronological, Cultural, and Cultic
      Contexts*. Wissenschaftliche Untersuchungen zum Neuen Testament 2/248. Tübingen: Mohr Siebeck.

2010 The Collection in 2 Corinthians (1985–2008). In Ralph P. Martin, *2 Corinthians*. Rev. ed. Word Biblical
      Commentary. Nashville: Thomas Nelson.

Duff, P. B.
1994 2 Corinthians 1–7: Sidestepping the Division Hypothesis Dilemma. *Biblical Theology Bulletin*
      24:16–26.

Duncan, G. S.
1929 *St. Paul's Ephesian Ministry: A Reconstruction with Special Reference to the Ephesian Origin of the
      Imprisonment Epistles*. New York: Charles Scribner's Sons.

Dunn, James D. G.
1970 *Baptism in the Holy Spirit*. London: SCM Press.

1998 *The Theology of Paul the Apostle*. Grand Rapids: Eerdmans.

Engels, D.
1990 *Roman Corinth: An Alternative Model for the Classical City*. Chicago: University of Chicago Press.

Fallon, Francis T.
1980 *2 Corinthians*. New Testament Message 11. Wilmington, DE: Michael Glazier.

Fee, Gordon D.
1977–1978 ΧΑΡΙΣ in II Corinthians 1:15: Apostolic Parousia and Paul-Corinth Chronology. *New Testament Studies* 24:533-538.

1994 *God's Empowering Presence: The Holy Spirit in the Letters of Paul.* Peabody, MA: Hendrickson.

2007 *Pauline Christology: An Exegetical-theological Study.* Peabody, MA: Hendrickson.

Fitzmyer, Joseph A.
1961 Qumrân and the Interpolated Paragraph in 2 Cor 6:14–7:1. *Catholic Biblical Quarterly* 23:271-280.

1992 *Romans.* Anchor Bible 33. New York: Doubleday.

Friedrich, G.
1963 Die Gegner des Paulus im 2 Korintherbrief. Pp. 181-221 in *Abraham unser Vater: Juden und Christen im Gespräch über die Bibel.* Festschrift for O. Michel. Editors, O. Betz, M. Hengel, and P. Schmidt. Leiden: Brill.

Furnish, Victor Paul
1968 *Theology and Ethics in Paul.* Nashville: Abingdon.

1984 *2 Corinthians.* Anchor Bible 32A. Garden City, NY: Doubleday & Company.

George, A. R.
1953 *Communion with God in the New Testament.* London: Epworth.

Georgi, D.
1986 *The Opponents of Paul in Second Corinthians: A Study of Religious Propaganda in Late Antiquity.* Philadelphia: Fortress.

1992 *Remembering the Poor: The History of Paul's Collection for Jerusalem.* Nashville: Abingdon.

Glancy, J. A.
2004 Boasting of Beatings (2 Corinthians 11:23-25). *Journal of Biblical Literature* 123:99-135.

Gnilka, J.
1968 2 Cor 6:14–7:1 in the Light of the Qumran Texts and the Testament of the Twelve Patriarchs. Pp. 48-68 in *Paul and Qumran: Studies in New Testament Exegesis.* Editor, J. Murphy-O'Connor. London: Chapman.

Gooder, P. R.
2001 *Only the Third Heaven? 2 Corinthians 12:1-10 and the Heavenly Ascent.* Library of New Testament Studies 213. London: T&T Clark.

Goulder, M. D.
2003 Visions and Revelations of the Lord [2 Corinthians 12:1-10]. Pp. 303-312 in *Paul and the Corinthians: Studies on a Community in Conflict.* Festschrift for M. E. Thrall. Editors, T. J. Burke and J. K. Elliott. Novum Testamentum Supplements 109. Leiden: Brill.

Grudem, W.
1994 *Systematic Theology.* Leicester: Inter-Varsity.

Hafemann, S. J.
1990 *Suffering and Ministry in the Spirit: Paul's Defense of His Ministry in II Corinthians 2:14–3:3.* Grand Rapids: Eerdmans.

1995 *Paul, Moses, and the History of Israel: The Letter/Spirit Contrast and the Argument from Scripture in 2 Corinthians 3.* Wissenschaftliche Untersuchungen zum Neuen Testament 2/81. Tübingen: J. C. B. Mohr (Paul Siebeck).

1998 Paul's Use of the Old Testament in 2 Corinthians. *Interpretation* 52:246-257.

2000 *2 Corinthians.* NIV Application Commentary. Grand Rapids: Zondervan.

Hall, D. R.
2003 *The Unity of the Corinthian Correspondence.* Journal for the Study of the New Testament Supplement Series 251. London: T&T Clark.

Harris, Murray J.
1983 *Raised Immortal.* London: Marshall, Morgan & Scott.

2005 *The Second Epistle to the Corinthians.* The New International Greek Testament Commentary. Grand Rapids: Eerdmans.

Hengel, Martin
1974 *Judaism and Hellenism: Studies in Their Encounter in Palestine during the Early Hellenistic Period.* Translator, John Bowden. Philadelphia: Fortress.

1977 *The Son of God: The Origin of Christology and the History of Jewish-Hellenistic Religion.*
Philadelphia: Fortress.

1983 *Between Jesus and Paul.* Translator, J. Bowden. Philadelphia: Fortress.

Hennecke, E., and W. Schneemelcher
1965 *The New Testament Apocrypha.* London: Lutterworth.

Héring, Jean
1967 *The Second Epistle of Saint Paul to the Corinthians.* Translators, A. W. Heathcote and P. J. Allcock.
London: Epworth.

Hock, Ronald F.
1980 *The Social Context of Paul's Ministry: Tentmaking and Apostleship.* Philadelphia: Fortress.

2003 Paul and Greco-Roman Education. Pp 198-227 in *Paul in the Greco-Roman World: A Handbook.*
Editor, J. Paul Sampley. Harrisburg, PA: Trinity Press International.

Hort, F. J. A.
1909 A Note on κόφινος, σπυρίς, σαργάνη. *Journal of Theological Studies* 10:567-571.

Hubbard, M. V.
2002 *New Creation in Paul's Letters and Thought.* Society for New Testament Studies 119. New York:
Cambridge University Press.

Hughes, Philip Edgcumbe
1962 *Paul's Second Epistle to the Corinthians.* New International Commentary on the New Testament.
Grand Rapids: Eerdmans.

Hughes, R. K.
2006 *2 Corinthians: Power in Weakness.* Wheaton, IL: Crossway.

Hunter, A. M.
1954 *Interpreting Paul's Gospel.* Philadelphia: Westminster.

Jastrow, M.
1996 *A Dictionary of the Targumim, the Talmud Babli and Yerushalmi, and the Midrashic Literature.*
New York: Judaica Press. (Orig. pub. 1926.)

Jervell, J.
1960 *Imago Dei. Gen 1,26f. im Spätjudentum in der Gnosis und in den paulinschen Briefen.* Forschungen zur
Religion und Literatur des Alten und Neuen Testaments 76. Göttingen: Vandenhoeck & Ruprecht.

Johnson, L. A.
1999 Satan Talk at Corinth: The Rhetoric of Conflict. *Biblical Theology Bulletin* 29:145-155.

Joubert, S. J.
2000 *Paul as Benefactor: Reciprocity, Strategy and Theological Reflection in Paul's Collection.*
Wissenschaftliche Untersuchungen zum Neuen Testament 2/124. Tübingen: Mohr Siebeck.

Judge, E. A.
1966 The Conflict of Educational Aims in New Testament Thought. *Journal of Christian Education* 9:32-45.

Käsemann, Ernst
1942 Die Legitimität des Apostels; Eine Untersuchung zu 2 Korinther 10–13. *Zeitschrift für die
neutestamentliche Wissenschaft* 41.33-71.

Keener, C. S.
2005 *1–2 Corinthians.* New Cambridge Biblical Commentary. New York: Cambridge University Press.

Kennedy, J. H.
1900 *The Second and Third Epistles of St. Paul to the Corinthians.* London: Methuen & Co.

Kim, S.
1982 *The Origin of Paul's Gospel.* Grand Rapids: Eerdmans.

Kitzberger, Ingrid R.
1986 *Bau der Gemeinde: Das paulinsche Wortfeld oikodome/(ep)oikodomein.* Würzburg: Echter Verlag.

Klijn, A. F. J., translator
1983 *2 (Syriac Apocalypse of) Baruch.* Pp. 615-652 in *The Old Testament Pseudepigrapha,* vol. 1. Editor,
James H. Charlesworth. New York: Doubleday.

Kurek-Chomyez, D. A.
2007 Sincerity and Chastity for Christ: A Textual Problem in 2 Cor. 11:3 Reconsidered. *Novum Testamentum*
49:54-84.

Lambrecht, J.
1999 *Second Corinthians.* Sacra Pagina 8. Collegeville, MN: Liturgical Press.

Lietzmann, Hans
1949 *An Die Korinther I/II.* Handbuch zum Neuen Testament 9. Tübingen: J. C. B. Mohr.

Lightfoot, Joseph B.
1880 *Saint Paul's Epistle to the Galatians: A Revised Text with Introduction, Notes, and Dissertations.* London: Macmillian.

Lincoln, A. T.
1981 *Paradise Now and Not Yet: Studies in the Role of the Heavenly Dimension in Paul's Thought with Special Reference to his Eschatology.* Society for New Testament Studies 43. New York: Cambridge University Press.

Lindgård, F.
2005 *Paul's Line of Thought in 2 Corinthians 4:16–5:10.* Wissenschaftliche Untersuchungen zum Neuen Testament 2/189. Tübingen: Mohr Siebeck.

Long, Fredrick
2004 *Ancient Rhetoric and Paul's Apology.* Society for New Testament Studies Monograph Series 131. Cambridge: Cambridge University Press.

Mack, Burton
1990 *Rhetoric and the New Testament.* Minneapolis: Fortress.

Maile, J. F.
1993 Heaven, Heavenlies, Paradise. Pp. 381-383 in *Dictionary of Paul and His Letters.* Editors, Gerald F. Hawthorne, Ralph P. Martin, and Daniel G. Reid. Downers Grove, IL: InterVarsity.

Malherbe, Abraham J.
1983 Antisthenes and Odysseus and Paul at War. *Harvard Theological Review* 76:143-173.

1986 A Physical Description of Paul. Pp. 170-175 in *Christians among Jews and Gentiles.* Festschrift for K. Stendahl. Editors, G. W. E. Nickelsburg and G. W. MacRea. Philadelphia: Fortress.

1988 *Ancient Epistolary Theorists.* Sources for Biblical Study 19. Atlanta: Scholars Press.

Manson, T. W.
1953 2 Cor 2:14-17: Suggestions towards an Exegesis. Pp. 155-162 in *Studia Paulina in honorem Johannis de Zwaan septuagenarii.* Editors, W. C. van Unnik, J. N. Sevenster, and C. K. Barrett. Haarlem: de Erven F. Bohn N. V.

Marshall, I. Howard
2007 *Aspects of the Atonement.* London: Paternoster.

Marshall, P.
1987a *Enmity in Corinth: Social Conventions in Paul's Relations with the Corinthians.* Tübingen: J. C. B. Mohr.

1987b Invective: Paul's Enemies in Corinth. Pp. 359-373 in *Perspectives on Language and Text.* Festschrift for F. I. Andersen. Editors, E. W. Conrad and E. G. Newing. Winona Lake, IN: Eisenbrauns.

Martin, Dale
1995 *The Corinthian Body.* New Haven, CT: Yale University Press.

Martin, R. P.
1976 *The Epistle of Paul to the Philippians: An Introduction and Commentary.* New Century Bible. London: Oliphants.

1981 *Colossians and Philemon.* New Century Bible Commentary. Grand Rapids: Eerdmans.

1984 *The Spirit and the Congregation.* Grand Rapids: Eerdmans.

1986 *2 Corinthians.* Word Biblical Commentary 40. Waco: Word. (2010 rev. and expanded ed. forthcoming.)

1988 The Spirit in 2 Corinthians in Light of the "Fellowship of the Holy Spirit" in 2 Corinthians 13:14. Pp. 113-128 in *Eschatology and the New Testament.* Festschrift for G. R. Beasley-Murray. Editor, W. H. Gloer. Peabody, MA: Hendrickson. Repr. in Ralph P. Martin, *2 Corinthians.* Rev. ed. Word Biblical Commentary. Nashville: Thomas Nelson, 2010.

1989 *Reconciliation: A Study of Paul's Theology.* Rev. ed. with a new appendix. Eugene, OR: Wipf & Stock.

2000 Theology and Mission in 2 Corinthians. Pp. 63-82 in *The Gospel to the Nations.* Editors, Peter Bolt and Mark Thompson. Leicester: Inter-Varsity. Repr. in Ralph P. Martin, *2 Corinthians.* Rev. ed. Word Biblical Commentary. Nashville: Thomas Nelson. 2010.

McCant, Jerry W.
1999 *2 Corinthians*. Readings: A New Biblical Commentary. Sheffield: Sheffield Academic.

Meeks, Wayne A.
1983 *First Urban Christians: The Social World of the Apostle Paul*. New Haven, CT: Yale University Press.

Menoud, P. H.
1953 L'écharde et l'ange satanique [2 Cor 12.7]. Pp. 163-171 in *Studia Paulina in honorem Johannis de Zwaan septuagenarii*. Editors, W. C. van Unnik, J. N. Sevenster, and C. K. Barrett. Haarlem: de Erven F. Bohn N. V.

Moffatt, James
1954 *A New Translation of the Bible Containing the Old and New Testaments*. New York: Harper & Row.

Murphy-O'Connor, Jerome
1984 The Corinth that Saint Paul Saw. *Biblical Archaeologist* 47.3:147-159.

1996 *Paul: A Critical Life*. Oxford: Clarendon.

2002 *St. Paul's Corinth: Texts and Archaeology*. 3rd ed. Collegeville, MN: Liturgical Press.

Newman, C. C.
1997 *Paul's Christology: Tradition and Rhetoric*. Leiden: Brill.

Nickle, K. F.
1966 *The Collection: A Study in Paul's Strategy*. Studies in Biblical Theology 48. Naperville, IL: A. R. Allenson.

O'Brien, P. T.
1977 *Introductory Thanksgivings in the Letters of Paul*. Novum Testamentum Supplements 48. Leiden: Brill.

O'Mahony, K. J.
2000 *Pauline Persuasion: A Sounding of 2 Corinthians 8-9*. Sheffield: Sheffield Academic.

Osei-Bonsu, J.
1986 Does 2 Cor 5:1-10 Teach the Reception of the Resurrection Body at the Moment of Death? *Journal for the Study of the New Testament* 28:81-101.

Peterson, B. K.
1998 *Eloquence and the Proclamation of the Gospel in Corinth*. Society of Biblical Literature Dissertation Series 163. Atlanta: Scholars Press.

Pickett, R.
1997. *The Cross at Corinth: The Social Significance of the Death of Jesus*. Journal for the Study of the New Testament Supplement Series 143. Sheffield: Sheffield Academic.

Plummer, A.
1915 *A Critical and Exegetical Commentary on the Second Epistle of St. Paul to the Corinthians*. The International Critical Commentary. Edinburgh: T&T Clark.

Porter, S. E., editor
2005 *Paul and His Opponents*. Pauline Studies 2. Leiden: Brill.

Prümm, Karl
1960 *Diakonia Pneumatos: Der 2. Korintherbrief als Zugang zur apostolischen Botschaft,* vol. 1. Rome: Herder.

Ramsay, W. M.
1908 *St. Paul the Traveller and Roman Citizen*. London: Hodder & Stoughton.

Reid, Daniel G.
1993a Satan, Devil. Pp. 862-867 in *Dictionary of Paul and His Letters*. Editors, Gerald F. Hawthorne, Ralph P. Martin, and Daniel G. Reid. Downers Grove, IL: InterVarsity.

1993b Triumph. Pp. 946-953 in *Dictionary of Paul and His Letters*. Editors, Gerald F. Hawthorne, Ralph P. Martin, and Daniel G. Reid. Downers Grove, IL: InterVarsity.

Reumann, J.
1982 *Righteousness in the New Testament*. Philadelphia / New York: Fortress / Paulist Press.

Richards, E. R.
2006 *Paul and First-century Letter Writing. Secretaries, Composition and Collection*. Downers Grove, IL: InterVarsity.

Riesner, R.
1998 *Paul's Early Period: Chronology, Mission, Strategy, Theology*. Grand Rapids: Eerdmans.

Sampley, J. P.
2000 The Second Letter to the Corinthians. Pp. 3-180 in *The New Interpreter's Bible*, vol. 11. Nashville: Abingdon.

Savage, T. B.
1996 *Power Through Weakness: Paul's Understanding of the Christian Ministry in 2 Corinthians.* Society for New Testament Studies 86. New York: Cambridge University Press.

Schlatter, A.
1934 *Paulus, der Bote Jesu: Eine Deutung seiner Briefe an die Korinther.* Stuttgart: Calwer Vereinsbuchhandlung.

Schmithals, Walter
1971 *Gnosticism in Corinth.* Translator, John E. Steely. Nashville: Abingdon.

Scott, J. M.
1998 *2 Corinthians.* New International Biblical Commentary on the New Testament 8. Peabody, MA / Carlisle: Hendrickson / Paternoster.

Stewart-Sykes, A.
1996 Ancient Editors and Copyists and Modern Partition Theories: The Case of the Corinthian Correspondence. *Journal for the Study of the New Testament* 61:53-64.

Stirewalt, M. L., Jr.
1993 *Studies in Ancient Greek Epistolography.* Resources for Biblical Study 27. Atlanta: Scholars Press.

Stowers, S. K.
1986 *Letter Writing in Greco-Roman Antiquity.* Library of Early Christianity 5. Philadelphia: Westminster.

Strachan, R. H.
1935 *The Second Epistle of Paul to the Corinthians.* Moffatt New Testament Commentary. New York: Harper & Brothers.

Sumney, J. L.
1990 *Identifying Paul's Opponents: The Question of Method in 2 Corinthians.* Journal for the Study of the New Testament Supplement Series 40. Sheffield: Sheffield Academic.

Talbert, C. H.
2002 *Reading Corinthians: A Literary and Theological Commentary on 1 and 2 Corinthians.* Rev. ed. Macon, GA: Smyth & Helwys.

Tasker, R. V. G.
1958 *The Second Epistle of Paul to the Corinthians.* Tyndale New Testament Commentaries. Grand Rapids: Eerdmans.

Theissen, G.
1982 *The Social Setting of Pauline Christianity: Essays on Corinth.* Philadelphia: Fortress.

Thiselton, Anthony C.
2000 *The First Epistle to the Corinthians.* New International Greek Testament Commentary. Grand Rapids: Eerdmans.

Thomas, J. C.
1996 "An Angel from Satan": Paul's Thorn in the Flesh (2 Cor 12:7-10). *Journal of Pentecostal Theology* 9:39-52.

Thrall, M. E.
1994 *The Second Epistle to the Corinthians,* vol. 1. The International Critical Commentary. Edinburgh: T&T Clark.
2000 *The Second Epistle to the Corinthians,* vol. 2. The International Critical Commentary. Edinburgh: T&T Clark.

Toney, Carl N.
2008 *Paul's Inclusive Ethic: Resolving Conflicts and Promoting Mission in Romans 14-15.* Wissenschaftliche Untersuchungen zum Neuen Testament 2/252. Tübingen: Mohr Siebeck.
2010a The Composition of 2 Corinthians (1985-2008). In Ralph P. Martin, *2 Corinthians.* Rev. ed. Word Biblical Commentary. Nashville: Thomas Nelson.
2010b Resurrection in 2 Corinthians. In Ralph P. Martin, *2 Corinthians.* Rev. ed. Word Biblical Commentary. Nashville: Thomas Nelson.
2010c Rhetorical Studies in 2 Corinthians. In Ralph P. Martin, *2 Corinthians.* Rev. ed. Word Biblical Commentary. Nashville: Thomas Nelson.

Travis, S. H.

1973 Paul's Boasting in 2 Corinthians 10–12. *Studia Evangelica* 6:527-532.

Trobisch, D.

1994 *Paul's Letter Collection: Tracing the Origins.* Minneapolis: Fortress.

Twelftree, G. H.

1993 Healing, Illness. Pp. 378-381 in *Dictionary of Paul and His Letters.* Editors, Gerald F. Hawthorne, Ralph P. Martin, and Daniel G. Reid. Downers Grove, IL: InterVarsity.

Uddin, M.

1999 Paul, the Devil and "Unbelief" in Israel (With Particular Reference to 2 Corinthians 3–4 and Romans 9–11). *Tyndale Bulletin* 50:265-280.

Verbrugge, V. D.

1992 *Paul's Style of Church Leadership Illustrated by His Instructions to the Corinthians on the Collection.* San Francisco: Mellen Research University Press.

Walker, D. D.

2002 *Paul's Offer of Leniency (2 Cor 10:1): Populist Ideology and Rhetoric in a Pauline Letter Fragment.* Wissenschaftliche Untersuchungen zum Neuen Testament 2/153. Tübingen: Mohr Siebeck.

Walker, W. O.

2001 *Interpolations in the Pauline Letters.* Journal for the Study of the New Testament Supplement Series 213. Sheffield: Sheffield Academic.

Wan, S. K.

2000 *Power in Weakness: Conflict and Rhetoric in Paul's Second Letter to the Corinthians.* New Testament in Context. Harrisburg, PA: Trinity Press International.

Watson, N.

1993 *The Second Epistle to the Corinthians.* Epworth Commentaries. London: Epworth.

Webb, William J.

1993 *Returning Home: New Covenant and Second Exodus as the Context for 2 Corinthians 6:14–7:1.* Journal for the Study of the New Testament Supplement Series 85. Sheffield: Journal for the Study of the Old Testament Press.

Welborn, L. L.

1995 The Identification of 2 Corinthians 10–13 with the "Letter of Tears." *Novum Testamentum* 37:138-153.

1996 Like Broken Pieces of a Ring: 2 Cor 1:1–2:13, 7:5-6 and Ancient Theories of Literary Unity. *New Testament Studies* 42:559-583.

1997 *Politics and Rhetoric in the Corinthian Epistles.* Macon, GA: Mercer.

Windisch, Hans

1924 *Der zweite Korintherbrief: für die 9. Auflage bearbeitet.* Göttingen: Vandenhoeck & Ruprecht.

Winter, B. W.

2001 *After Paul Left Corinth: The Influence of Secular Ethics and Social Change.* Grand Rapids: Eerdmans.

Witherington, Ben, III

1995 *Conflict and Community in Corinth: A Socio-rhetorical Commentary on 1 and 2 Corinthians.* Grand Rapids: Eerdmans.

Wright, N. T.

2003a *Paul for Everyone: 2 Corinthians.* London: SPCK.

2003b *The Resurrection of the Son of God.* Minneapolis: Fortress.

Young, F. M., and D. F. Ford

1988 *Meaning and Truth in 2 Corinthians.* Grand Rapids: Eerdmans.